Telephone : 01 - 340 3343

HIGHGATE LITERARY & SCIENTIFIC INSTITUTION

937 GRA

II, SOUTH GROVE, N.6

13618

Time allowed FOURTEEN Days

Date Issued	Date Issued	Date Issued
2 JAN 1971		
2 FEB 1971		
2 9		
3 NOV 1976		
8 NOV 1982		
17 JAN 1987		
12 MAR 1990		
8 JAN 1992		
20 JAN 1994		
6 MAR 1996		
1 JUN 1997		
3 JUN 1998		

THE ANCIENT HISTORIANS

THE ANCIENT HISTORIANS

Michael Grant

WEIDENFELD AND NICOLSON
5 WINSLEY STREET LONDON W1

Printed in Great Britain by
The Garden City Press Limited
Letchworth, Hertfordshire

Contents

List of Illustrations   vii
Acknowledgements   xi
Foreword   xiii

INTRODUCTION   BEFORE HERODOTUS
(a) The Near Eastern Background   3
(b) The Greek Beginnings   15

PART 1   HERODOTUS
1   The Life and Work of Herodotus   23
2   The Background and Beliefs of Herodotus   38
3   The Methods of Herodotus   57

PART 2   THUCYDIDES
4   Thucydides and the Peloponnesian War   69
5   Speeches and Personalities in Thucydides   88
6   Power and Politics in Thucydides   102
7   The Methods of Thucydides   114

PART 3   THE LATER GREEKS
8   Xenophon   125
9   The Dramatic Historians   136
10   Polybius   144

PART 4   LATIN WRITERS OF THE REPUBLIC
11   Cato the Censor and after   167
12   Caesar   181
13   Sallust   195

PART 5   THE TWO FACES OF EMPIRE
14   Livy   217
15   Josephus   243

Contents

PART 6   TACITUS

16   *Tacitus and the Empire*   271
17   *Tacitus and the Emperors*   283
18   *Anarchy and Humanity in Tacitus*   300

PART 7   GREEK AND LATIN BIOGRAPHERS

19   *Plutarch*   309
20   *Suetonius*   329

PART 8   CHRISTIAN AND PAGAN

21   *Eusebius*   343
22   *Ammianus*   358

Epilogue. The Survival of the Ancient Historians   387
Chronological Table   411
Notes   415
Some Books on the Ancient Historians   467
Index   473

vi

List of Illustrations

[*Between pages 206 and 207*]

1 Relief of King Ahmosis
2 Hittite official history
3 Relief of King Mesha of Moab
4 Cylinder of King Cyrus of Babylon
5 Double bust of Herodotus and Thucydides
6 Bust of King Leonidas
7 Red-figure amphora illustrating story from Herodotus
8 Coin of Syracuse
9 Coin of Cyzicus
10 Bust of Socrates
11 Coin of Alexander the Great
12 Mask of Ptolemy I Soter
13 Megalopolis in Arcadia, birthplace of Polybius
14 Relief with figure of Polybius
15 Bust of Posidonius
16 Coin issued by Julius Caesar commemorating his Gallic War
17 Masada near the Dead Sea
18 Coin showing Lucius Brutus and Ahala, portrayed by Marcus Brutus
19 Relief showing Triumphal celebration after fall of Jerusalem
20 Water-pipe from Deva (Chester)
21 Bronze head of Tiberius
22 The Lion of Chaeronea in Boeotia, central Greece
23 Part of statue of Hadrian
24 Coin of Nero

List of Illustrations

25 Silver missorium showing Theodosius I
26 Sallust recalled on a bronze fourth century piece
27 First page of manuscript of Caesar's *Gallic War*
28 Title page of manuscript of Sallust, *Catiline* and *Jugurtha*
29 Page from Aldine edition of Herodotus
30 Title page of North's Plutarch
31 Theodor Mommsen

Maps

1	The Middle East	6
2	Asia Minor	8
3	Central Greece	26
4	Western Asia Minor	32
5	Southern Greece	70
6	Southern Italy and Sicily	73
7	Northern Greece, Macedonia and Thrace	75
8	Gaul and Northern Spain	183
9	Northern Africa	210
10	Central Italy	219
11	Northern Italy	234
12	Syria and Palestine	249
13	Northern Europe	277
14	The Roman Empire: Second Century AD	313

Acknowledgements

The author and publishers would like to thank the following for supplying photographs for this book: Lehnert & Landrock, plate 1; Staatliche Museum, Berlin, plate 2; Mansell Collection, plates 5 (which also appears on the jacket), 6, 7, 9, 11, 14, 15, 19, 22; British Museum, plates 4, 28, 29, 30; Ny Carlsberg Glyptothek, Copenhagen, plate 12; National Tourist Organization, Greece, plate 13; Grosvenor Museum, Chester and the Chester Archaeological Society, plate 20; Max Hirmer, plate 25; Bibliotheque Nationale, Paris, plate 27.

The author and publishers also wish to acknowledge the following for granting permission to quote from copyright sources: Simon & Schuster Inc. for Polybius, *The Histories* (tr. M. Chambers); Routledge & Kegan Paul Ltd and Basic Books Inc. for *Latin Biography* (ed. T. A. Dorey); Mr Robert Graves and Collins-Knowlton-Wing Inc. for *The Twelve Caesars* (tr. R. Graves); Routledge & Kegan Paul Ltd and Quadrangle Books Inc. for S. Moscati, *The Face of the Ancient Orient;* Penguin Books Ltd for Plutarch, *Fall of the Roman Republic* (tr. R. Warner), Xenophon, *The Persian Expedition* and *A History of My Times* (both tr. R. Warner,) Julius Caesar, *The Conquest of Gaul* (tr. S. A. Handford) and *The Civil War* (tr. J. F. Mitchell), Livy, *The Early History of Rome* and *The War with Hannibal* (both tr. by A. de Selincourt), Josephus, *The Jewish War* (tr. G. A. Williamson), Tacitus, *The Histories* (tr. K. Wellesley) and *The Annals of Imperial Rome* (tr. M. Grant), Plutarch, *The Rise and Fall of Athens* (tr. I. Scott-Kilvert), Eusebius, *The History of the Church* (tr. G. A. Williamson), Herodotus, *The Histories* (tr. A. de Selincourt); Chatto &

Windus Ltd and Indiana University Press for R. H. Barrow, *Plutarch and His Times*; The Bodley Head Ltd and Penguin Books Ltd for Thucydides, *The Peloponnesian War* (tr. R. Warner); William Heinemann Ltd and Harvard University Press for Cicero, *De Oratore* (tr. E. W. Sutton) and *Brutus* (tr. G. L. Hendrickson), *Sallust* (tr. J. C. Rolfe), *Livy* (tr. A. C. Schlesinger), *Ammianus Marcellinus* (tr. J. C. Rolfe), *Suetonius* (tr. J. C. Rolfe), *Tacitus, Dialogus, Agricola, Germania* (tr. Peterson, Hulton), Josephus (tr. Thackeray and Marcus); L. P. Wilkinson for *Letters of Cicero* (ed. L. P. Wilkinson); the Clarendon Press for Pindar (tr. C. M. Bowra); Cambridge University Press for F. E. Adcock, *Thucydides and His History* and A. D. Momigliano in *Cambridge Ancient History*, Vol. X; Harper & Row for A. D. Momigliano, *Studies in Historiography*; Methuen & Co. Ltd for Adolf Erman, *The Literature of the Ancient Egyptians* (tr. A. M. Blackman); Collins Publishers for *Jerusalem and Rome: The Writings of Josephus* (tr. N. N. Glatzer); Faber & Faber Ltd for *The Agamemnon of Aeschylus* (tr. L. MacNeice); the New English Library for *Sallust, Jugurtha and Catoline* (tr. I. Scott-Kilvert); the New American Library for *The Essential Eusebius* (tr. Colm Luibheid); Mr M. B. Yeats and Macmillan & Co. Ltd for W. B. Yeats, *Sophocles Oedipus Colonus*.

Foreword

THIS book is about the ancient Greek and Latin historians. That is to say, it is about the men who virtually invented the writing of history, by what seems at first sight to be a sort of miracle. On further investigation, it does turn out that they had predecessors of a kind. Yet it still remains true that history, as we understand the term, is a Greek invention. The outstanding Greek historians, Herodotus and Thucydides, are writers of the same gigantic stature as their contemporaries the tragic poets; and they raised history at once to one of the supreme literary arts. It is advisedly described as an 'art', because the ancients maintained that history, to be worth the name, must not only be written as truthfully as human frailty permits, but must also be written well. The Romans, above all Tacitus, carried on the tradition with that curious blend of extreme originality and adherence to the Greek tradition which is the mark of the Latin genius.

It is unusual to attempt the story of the Greek and Latin historians in a single volume. But I believe the attempt is justified. Certainly, the civilisations and languages are very distinct. But the panorama is consecutive and continuous, and the two sets of historians, too, are inextricably interwoven. This immediately becomes clear when we consider two writers of very great stature indeed – Polybius and Ammianus. Both were Greeks, or perhaps the latter was Greco-Syrian, yet both wrote about the affairs of Rome, one in Greek and the other in Latin. The study of the ancient historians breaks down parochialisms and chauvinisms, for the historians broke them down themselves. Herodotus, Thucydides, Xenophon and Polybius were all exiled from their native countries. Moreover, the first two of them are unlikely to have been completely Greek; and the same applies to Ammianus, who originated from Antioch. Livy and Tacitus were Roman patriots, yet came from beyond the Italian peninsula. The historians of the Jews and Christians, Josephus and Eusebius, were Palestinians who wrote in Greek; the first edition of the *Jewish War* was in Aramaic. Suetonius, who wrote in Latin, probably came from north Africa.

He and Plutarch in their own day were not included among historians because they were biographers. The two arts, as will be seen, were considered distinct, since biographies had started as mere works of praise, and the tendency to regard them in this light persisted. The question whether biography is history is arguable; indeed it has been argued at very great length. But here the view will be taken that the biographers (and autobiographers, in so far as their efforts have survived) should be included in an account of ancient historiography. For one thing, this is a matter of practical convenience, because they provide vital historical evidence. But it also seems right on principle to classify biography not as an outcast from history, but as one of its branches. It is history applied to individuals and not groups, but it is history all the same – as our ancestors appreciated, since the separate word 'biography' did not appear until the 1660s.

Latin history did not die with Ammianus, for there were other writers in the language, spread over hundreds of years to come.[1] At Byzantium, there continued to be Greek historians for longer still. One of them, Procopius (*c.* 550), nearly equalled the very greatest of his predecessors. Indeed, the story of these Greek writers could be continued until the fifteenth century.[2] But I have stopped at about 400, accepting the convention that this was a watershed between antiquity and the Middle Ages. For the subject of historians for five hundred years had been the unity of the Mediterranean area; and now the divisions which this unity had superseded were in existence once again. A whole epoch had drawn to its close. It is true that written Greek and Latin still prevailed, for it was still inconceivable that there should be vernacular literary languages. But such was the ultimate consequence of the political fragmentation. Yet, even when that stage came, the effects of the classical world long remained paramount, and the influence of the Greek and Roman historians continued to be overwhelming. I have provided some details in the Appendix at the end of this book.

The effects of these writers still persist; no modern historian could possibly write as he does unless these models had given him conscious or unconscious inspiration. For many of the principal ways of looking at history were worked out by the Greeks and Romans, and what followed has often been repetition or variation within their themes.

There have, of course, been more recent innovations, such as economic history. Writers such as Thucydides or Sallust or Tacitus were fully aware of the economic element; but they did not possess the statistical apparatus to consider it deeply. And in any case they did not want to, because they did not regard it as a dominant factor in the epochs they were considering. Besides, ancient historians were not interested in statistics. They were more concerned to offer guidance. A feature which sometimes seems strange to us is their determined conviction that history is able to provide lessons which can help us act sensibly ourselves. We, on the other hand, are very conscious that history does not repeat itself exactly – though its best ancient practitioners never thought it did – and we have therefore, perhaps, gone too far in rejecting its instructive role. Was Churchill really so wrong to declare, in the antique tradition, that it is only from a knowledge of the past that one can gain some idea of how the future will turn out?

Another thing that may strike us as peculiar about the ancient writers is that the guidance they propose to give is inclined to be moral. They were more determined than ourselves to estimate history and public affairs by a moral yard-stick. Lord Acton, who died in 1902, seems to us to have been asking rather too much when, following this attitude, he demanded the application of the strictest rules of private morality to the actions of public men. What he was suggesting, in fact, is something already inherent in the natural structure of many languages – including our own – which makes it difficult to speak or write at any length without expressing or implying some ethical point of view. It is true that the private lives of public men are only of limited interest, except when they affect a wider sphere. But, if we refuse altogether to take a moral view of *public* affairs, we are forced back to ludicrous pie-faced utterances reminiscent of the historian whose desire for detachment made him write: 'The enemy sawed the Commandant and his wife in halves, and committed other grave breaches of international law.'

In our own century, Hitler has brought us up against this problem. In discussing him, would it not be actually misleading (as well as outrageous) to refrain from pointing out that he was a monster – an explicable monster, perhaps, but a monster all the same? If so, then the attitude of the ancient historians, even if, being human, they sometimes applied it wrongly, was fundamentally right.

This brings us to the question of bias. It is easy to detect this in even the most objective of the ancient historians. In saying Hitler was a monster, it might be said that we, too, are displaying a bias. As Mark Twain observed, 'the Recording Angel doubtless had convictions which to Satan would seem prejudices'. In other words, biases are quite unavoidable. If there are disorders at Londonderry (or Corcyra), the facts, as reported by extremists of either side, will turn out to be strangely different. One version, certainly, may be *nearer* the truth than the other. But neither can possibly *be* the truth. Both sides, in varying degrees, are affected by conscious or unconscious biases; there is no other possibility. So we, in approaching history, had better make sure, as far as we can, that our biases are conscious, since then we shall at least know where we are going. If not, this will not stop us from being biased all the same. The very process of selecting facts, which is inevitable if we are going to write or think about history at all, cannot help being subjective – indeed, doubly so, because we can only select from what we have been given. And so Ranke's idea that one could write history 'as it actually happened' is a fallacy. He himself was a Prussian conservative of 1824, and he wrote with the prejudices of that time and condition – as the ancient historians had written with theirs.

The same applies to ourselves. Does our difference in time, place and outlook give today's historical writers any justification for regarding themselves as better than their ancient counterparts? In one way, yes. The best moderns are in a position to write a more exact sort of history than the ancients, because they have been given the opportunity to become better scholars. This might already have happened in Greek and Roman times if their authors had not decided to divorce antiquarian research from history. It was only the Göttingen Historical Institute (1766) and Edward Gibbon (1776–88) who put them together again. The result was more expert scholarship; but not less bias. In regard to that, we have no special reason to feel superior to the ancients.

Since, therefore, we too are subject to this inevitable factor, there is nothing very damaging or sensational about the discovery of how often the Greeks and Romans aired their prejudices. To say that they neglected truthfulness in so doing would be to do far less than justice to their achievement in extracting so much of the truth from almost inconceivably fragmentary and unsatisfactory sources. It is true enough that, being without benefit of Sigmund Freud, they often believed, or at least asserted, that everyone else (especially their immediate predecessor) was wrong, whereas they themselves were not. However, they also tended to show an engaging modesty. This emerges from their willingness to admit that they do not know all the answers. For that is why they have so much to say about the part played by chance, or the supernatural, or destiny, in bringing about events. Much anxious research has been devoted to the uses of these and similar words by the ancient historians. But the words are little more than the terminology of literary convention. What lies behind them is a genuine, humble agnosticism about matters on which the writers regarded it as a mistake to feel too certain.

The greatest of these historians, and some of the less great as well, were by no means the sort of people to accept unprovable theories too easily. They were not readily taken in. They did not need Freud to make them feel an intensely, indeed savagely, keen appreciation of the gap between people's proclamations of intention and what they actually do. And this appreciation gave them a sceptical attitude to World Progress (in any sense other than a purely material one) which was more realistic than the mechanical optimism bequeathed to us by the nineteenth century. The thinkers of antiquity may sometimes have erred in the opposite direction. They recognised that progress was possible; as Xenophanes said, 'The gods did not reveal to men all things from the beginning, but men through their own search find in the course of time that which is better'. But the ancients knew very well, as that passage shows, that there is nothing automatic about this. There will be no progress unless human beings get to work and produce it. This is one more illustration of the capacity of some Greeks, and some Romans, to see things clearly. Given differences of conventional expression, they were no more blinkered than any of their successors.

Indeed, there was one reason why they were less likely than most of us to be hampered by any such subjective limitations. This is because certain of them possessed talents of a portentous order. These are the qualities that I shall attempt to describe in the present book. In order to bring them before the eye as vividly as I can, I have interspersed my comments with many quotations from translations of their works.

My debts to modern authors who have written studies of the ancient historians are of course enormous. There are great masters in this very active field. But all I have been able to do by way of acknowledgment is to offer at the end of the book a list of some of the works which I have found particularly useful and valuable.

My wife's assistance with this book, as with my others, has been completely indispensable. I also want to thank Mr Julian Shuckburgh and Mr Peter Hames of Messrs George Weidenfeld & Nicolson Ltd for a great deal of editorial assistance, and Miss Suzanne Harsanyi for collecting the illustrations. I am grateful to Mr Edward Leeson for helpful suggestions and to Mr Arthur Banks for the maps.
GATTAIOLA, 1970   MICHAEL GRANT

Introduction
Before Herodotus

(a) The Near Eastern Background

IT is natural for people to want to know about their forbears and forerunners. But the periods of time in which mankind has satisfied this desire by religion and myth are far longer than those in which history has been the medium. The great civilisations of the most ancient near and middle east, for example, offered official interpretations of the past based on the assumption that their rulers enjoyed the goodwill of the gods. These interpretations gave the monarchs an opportunity to glorify themselves, and at the same time enabled the worshipping public to avoid divine wrath.

'The Egyptians who live in the cultivated part of the country,' said Herodotus, 'by their practice of keeping records of the past, have made themselves much the best historians of any nation of which I have had experience.'[1] In the very earliest times of a united Egypt, or even just before (c. 3200 BC), the deeds of kings were already sculptured upon reliefs.[2] Cheops (Khufu) and Chephren (Khafre) of the Fourth Dynasty are shown by inscriptions of the twenty-sixth century to have possessed libraries,[3] and at least as early as the Fifth Dynasty (c. 2500–2350) there were written records, comprising annals and king-lists going back to the fourth millennium BC. The next line of kings (c. 2350–2180) displays the earliest of a long series of triumph-songs describing victories,[4] and another landmark was reached when a military event, the punishment of rebels, was described not by an official spokesman but by a patriotic private individual, Mery-Re, an officer of King Pepi I. In the twentieth

3

century BC the tale attributed to the exiled court-official Sinuhe (framed as his obituary) is an early example of autobiography and travel literature, with a happy ending back home in favour with the pharaoh Senusert I. 'Years were made to pass away from my body. I was plucked, and my hair was combed. A load [of dirt] was given to the desert and my clothes to the Crossers of the Sands. I was clad in fine linen and anointed with prime oil. I slept upon a bed. . . . I was under the favour of the king's presence until the day of death came[5].' As time went on abundant official descriptions of battles[6] came to include a fresh infusion of picturesque detail, as in this account of the campaign of Thothmes III in Phoenicia during the fifteenth century BC.

Their orchards were filled with their fruit. Their wines were found lying in their vats, as water flows, and their grain was on the threshing floors being ground. They were more plentiful than the sands of the shore. The army overflowed with its possessions. . . . Why, His Majesty's army was as drunk and as anointed with oil every day as if at feasts in Egypt.[7]

Ostensible autobiography also attained a more elaborate form in the life story of the magnate Inni, which was, in fact, a document prepared for his funeral ceremony. Then, in *c.* 1000, the genre represented by Sinuhe's wanderings was expanded in a much more imaginative way by Wen-Amon, who described his journey to Byblos on the Phoenician coast, an account founded on fact or implying a skit on current travellers' tales.

However, it is questionable whether any literary production of the ancient Egyptians can be properly described as history. Their language had no known word to express the idea. The nearest is probably *gn wt*, a plural term that seems to refer to historical documents as physical objects. Although outside influences were stronger than has been supposed, the world of the Egyptians, with its peculiar geographical situation and prolonged immunity from interference, was static. It seemed that the conditions of their existence as a people had always been, and always would be, controlled by the gods, whose purpose was inscrutable. Everything depended on their earthly representative the pharaoh. Apart from that, there was little conception of the processes of cause and effect which make history.

Sumerians and their Semitic (Akkadian or Babylonian) neighbours and fellow-inhabitants of southern Mesopotamia were equally pre-occupied with the divine will. But they were rather less passive and more anxious, since the very perilous and unpredictable floods of the Euphrates and Tigris meant that the research needed to pacify heaven had to be all the more meticulous. So the Sumerians were forever noting theological signs from bygone times, and extracting their lessons. From the later third millennium BC onwards there is a spate of such records, recounting political, military and economic incidents spread over several generations.

The Sumerians believed that their country had always been more or less the same, since the gods had planned and decreed that this should be so. And yet they knew all too well that catastrophes could occur. Reflecting a country where inundation threatened every year, the Epic of Gilgamesh profoundly stressed this restless, insecure impermanence. A king of the town of Nippur (where 20,000 clay tablets have been discovered) tells a story foreshadowing classical beliefs in an avenging Nemesis.[8]

Round about 2000 BC a group of writers at Lagash, presumably palace and temple archivists, gave varied and explicit descriptions of events. Under King Entemena, for example, a scribe narrates the restoration of the boundary ditch between Lagash and Umma. The leading role is attributed to Enlil, the principal deity of the Sumerian pantheon; yet considerable historical background is included.

Enlil, the king of all the lands, the father of all the gods, marked off the boundary for Ningirsu [the patron deity of Lagash], and Shara [the patron deity of Umma] by his steadfast word, and Mesilim, the king of Kish, measured it off . . . and erected a stele there. But Ush, the ruler of Umma, violated both the decree of the gods and the word given by man, ripped out the boundary stele, and entered the plain of Lagash. Then did Ningirsu, Enlil's foremost warrior, do battle with the men of Umma in accordance with Enlil's straightforward word; by the word of Enlil he hurled the great net upon them, and heaped up their skeleton[?] piles in the plain in their various places.[9]

The gods ruled history, but history also to some extent ruled the gods; divine patronage was not an insuperable barrier to historical narra-tive. Particular attention was devoted to the legendary times of Sargon the Great and Naramsin of Akkad. They were the subject of epics and poetic folk-tales, and a fragmentary text of *c.* 1700 seems to comprise a chronicle, unique in the present state of our knowledge,

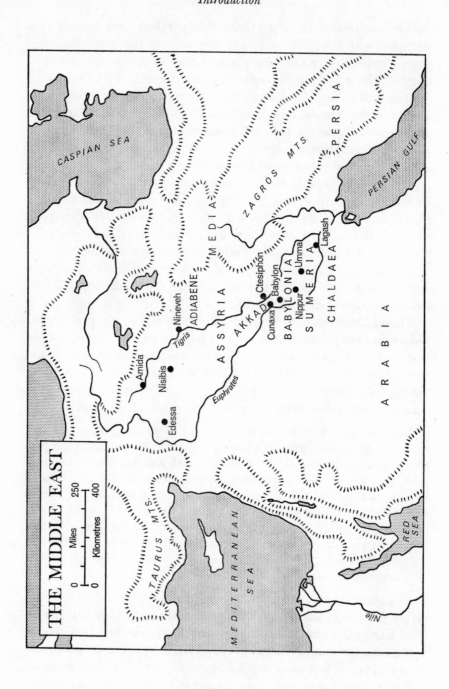

which purports to describe the events which had led up to Sargon's rise to power.[10] These sagas of the past display an increasingly artistic talent for integrations of episodes. The chronicles of Babylonia and Assyria, inscribed on tablets in the national cuneiform (wedge-shaped) characters, include royal annals, succession-lists of kings, geographical itineraries and building-inscriptions. These documents are not quite history. But they are developed catalogues of events and personages which could have become the raw material of history – if they had not been so heavily impregnated with official bias. By the time of Ashurbanipal of Assyria (668–631 BC), two large rooms at Nineveh were filled with archives; and these monarchs were accustomed to conduct a widespread search for old inscriptions.

A closer approach to historical writing is found among the Hittites who, soon after 1800 BC, started to extend their control over the greater part of Asia Minor. At the beginning of the second millennium, the Assyrians had established trading-posts on the eastern confines of the peninsula, and an eighteenth-century text, written in Old Hittite though perhaps going back to an earlier people, shows that initial Assyrian influences were strong.[11]

At the Hittite capital of Hattushash (Bogazköy) the 15,000 tablets and fragments that have been found during the past sixty-five years include documents which show an advance on the historical attitudes of Mesopotamia or Egypt. One of the discoveries of 1957 was the testament of King Hattusilis I (*c*. 1600), written in Akkadian.[12] After describing a military operation against Aleppo, the monarch explains in detail why he had to change his mind about who the designated successor to his throne should be: 'I fell sick. I had presented to you the young Labarnas as him who should sit upon the throne. I, the king, called him my son, I embraced him, I exalted him, I cared for him without cease. But he proved himself a young man not worth looking upon: he did not shed tears, he did not sympathise, he is cold and heartless.'[13] This record of insubordination strikes a fresh note by its frank admission of a royal setback. The novel literary manner reveals a capacity to think and write in the sort of terms we expect of a historian, granted, of course, that it is a royal historian justifying his own policy.

Next, King Telepinus (*c*. 1500), inspired by the precedent of Hattusilis I, prefaces one of his decrees with a long historical preamble

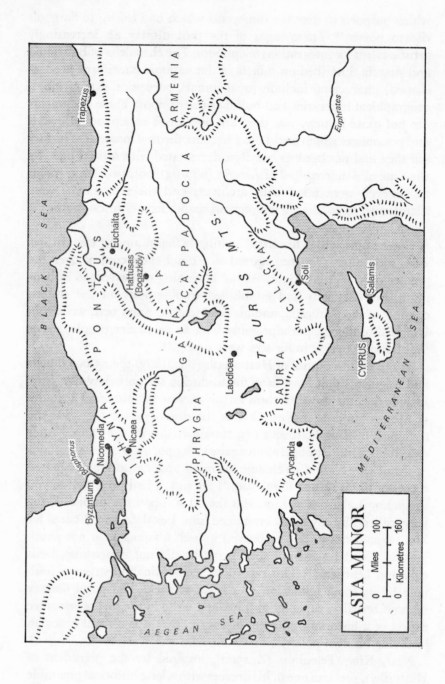

ARMENIA

Euphrates

BLACK SEA

Trapezus

Euchaita

P O N T U S

Hattusas
(Bogazköy)

G A L A T I A

C A P P A D O C I A

T A U R U S   M T S.

C I L I C I A

Soli

CYPRUS

Salamis

MEDITERRANEAN SEA

Laodicea

I S A U R I A

P H R Y G I A

Nicomedia
Nicaea

Bosphorus

Byzantium

B I T H Y N I A

Arycanda

ASIA MINOR

Miles	100
0	
Kilometres	160
0	

AEGEAN   SEA

illustrating the evil results of discord by a survey of the seven previous reigns. This is an example of the Hittite practice of diversifying state documents by the insertion of lively, admonitory, historical narratives. From *c.* 1400 the political treaties of the country strike a similar note, unfamiliar elsewhere in the near east, by including reports on the previous relations between the parties concerned, with due attention to the workings of cause and effect on the material plane. A hundred years later Mursilis II achieved an even wider range of semi-historical analysis, recording previous kingships, composing Hittite versions of earlier documents in other languages (such as the testament of Hattusilis I) and producing comprehensive annals of his own reign as well. As elsewhere, the underlying theme is generally religious and propagandist, recording the king's successes as a thank-offering to the gods. Yet these manifestations of the Hittite capacity to reflect on motives, results and thoughts show greater sophistication than anything known to us from earlier times. A thirteenth-century usurper, Hattusilis III, produced a complex autobiographical document which displays a blatant talent for the adjustment of history. In the course of a survey of his life from childhood onwards he explains his supersession of a royal nephew by a reasoned, legalistic defence of his own 'just cause', which is proved by the results of war (an early success story) and guaranteed by the favour of the goddess Ishtar.

The Hittites were very keen to get the record straight, or make it seem straight. None of these various chronicles, it is true, achieves an artistic fusion into a single comprehensive whole. Yet they attain an organic view of the nexus of events, with due attention to the aims of the people behind them. History no doubt began with Herodotus, but there was something not altogether unlike it more than a thousand years before his time – though it was still officially prompted.

When the Hittite Empire broke up in the twelfth century BC, many of its traditions merged with indigenous elements in a series of small 'neo-Hittite' states on the borders of Asia Minor, Mesopotamia and Syria. These states in their turn, together with influences from Babylonia and Assyria, helped to mould the way of life of the Phoenicians, who from their ports of Tyre and Sidon became a major maritime power. Neighbouring Byblos was a very ancient harbour-town, and a little to the north lay Ugarit (Ras Shamra), where archaeological discoveries have revealed a huge and diverse literature of the fourteenth century BC, including an elaborate mythology and epic.

Thereafter, according to the Jewish historian Josephus, it was the Phoenicians who 'made the largest use of writing, both for the ordinary affairs of life and for the commemoration of public events'.[14] Not only was it from these people that Greece learnt to write, but they may also provide a record of the earliest identifiable historian. His name was Hellenised as Sanchuniathon. We owe the reference to Herennius Philo of Byblos (AD 64–161), who, in publishing a nine-book *Phoenician History*, now lost, claimed that he had translated it from a work by this man, allegedly a priest of the eleventh century BC at Berytus (Beirut). Herennius Philo's accounts of cults, rites and customs evidently made use of Greek collections purporting to reproduce old Phoenician writings. Some have doubted whether Sanchuniathon ever existed. However, recent Ugaritic discoveries leave less grounds for scepticism, because they indicate that this is just the sort of material which the Phoenicians were likely to have produced, employing Ugarit and other centres as the transmitters of older near-eastern traditions about the gods and the origins of civilisation. Phoenician literature has not survived, but there is no reason to doubt that such writers existed; and probably they exhibited a closer approach to historical writing than had ever appeared before.

On the southern borders of Phoenicia, at the turn of the millennium, the Jewish state was taking shape. The extent to which Phoenician literature had been god-centred cannot now be measured. But the writings of the Jews were wholly bound up with the purposes of Jehovah – interpreted as the sole god of their country, for, whereas government and Temple were often controlled by men prepared to worship other divinities in addition to Jehovah, the Old Testament writers belonged to the rival school of thought which rejected this course. Their examination and assessment of the divine aim as displayed in past epochs endowed history with immense importance, far greater importance than it had ever assumed in any previous culture. The God of Israel has made a pact, a covenant, with Israel; the working-out of this covenant year after year is history.

To an unprecedented extent, therefore, the sacred literature of the Hebrews is a record and interpretation of bygone ages. Moreover, it tells of the relationship of God not only with a ruler as hitherto, but with an entire people. And nationalism turns into universality, because he is regarded as the God of all nations. He is working his purpose out first for his chosen race and through them for mankind. He is therefore responsible for all past happenings; and so the existence and purpose of man also becomes didactic and instructive about the future, with which the past is inseparably linked. The writing of history, then, became the driving-force of action, and it was therefore imperative to draw up a single narrative showing how God has guided the fates of one generation after another thoughout time.

Consequently, as G. R. Elton remarks, 'no other primitive sacred writings are so grimly chronological and historical as the Old Testament'. It selects from the course of events those facts and signs which seem relevant to the interpretation of God's Order, advancing from myth and legend to factual annals which selectively compile and edit earlier literary documents. Passing through the semi-fabulous biographical tales of earlier personages, we come in the eleventh and tenth centuries BC to Saul, David and Solomon. The accounts of their reigns far outdo, in literary eloquence, anything which has survived from earlier peoples or times. Most striking of all is the group of stories collected around the popular national hero David. This material includes a mass of detail from varied sources. In particular, the anonymous and composite work known as the Second Book of Samuel, written in admirable Hebrew prose, provides a full, frank and not wholly unobjective historical narrative, based on information from an eyewitness or at least a contemporary. Perhaps it was drawn up in the reign of David's successor Solomon.[15] The principal compiler of the Book of Kings, which carries on the story, refers to the existence and availability of earlier royal chronicles.

The revolt of Absalom, who conspired against his father David and was slain and wept over, is a tragedy comparable to the dramas narrated by Herodotus, and as in Herodotus there is also room for entertaining episodes which foreshadow the historical novels of the future.

So David and all the house of Israel brought up the ark of the Lord with shouting, and with the sound of the trumpet. And as the ark of the Lord came into the city of David, Michal, Saul's daughter, looked through a window, and saw king David leaping and dancing before the Lord; and she despised him in her heart. . . . And Michal the daughter of Saul came out to meet David, and said, How glorious was the king of Israel today, who uncovered himself today in the eyes of the handmaids of his servants, as one of the vain fellows shamelessly uncovereth himself.[16]

David does not show up very brilliantly there. Indeed, in more serious matters too, he is subjected, for all his heroism, to a critical, un-idealising gaze. This is the man whose descriptions in the Old Testament suggested to Thomas Carlyle 'the inner secret, the re-morse, temptations, the often baffled, never ended struggle'. Cer-tainly, the tradition employed by the final compiler sees him as fore-ordained and chosen by Jehovah. But the account, as we have it, seems to draw upon two types of sources, one royalist and the other anti-royalist. The favourable tradition was supported by the priestly Levites, whom David established, but the unfavourable version measures him critically by the supposed degree of his fidelity to the Covenant. The operation of this criterion, which is applied to many others also, has the disadvantage, from a secular historian's point of view, of linking history very closely with theological standards. But it also has the advantage of detaching it from purely royal and official attitudes.

When the great kingdom of David and Solomon split in two, it was only a question of time before these little states of Judah and Israel would succumb to their powerful eastern neighbours. And so writers of the eighth and seventh centuries BC become more and more urgent in their reminders of the utter dependence of the Jews upon Jehovah. Even more emphatically than hitherto they dwell on the lessons of past history, lessons which show that salvation had come from him alone.

And when we cried unto the Lord God of our fathers, the Lord heard our voice, and looked on our affliction, and our labour, and our oppression: and the Lord brought us forth out of Egypt with a mighty hand, and with an outstretched arm, and with great terribleness, and with signs, and with wonders.[17]

Those sentiments in Deuteronomy (?eighth–seventh century BC) represent the essence of the Jewish historical view. In such efforts to instil piety into the nation by stressing its spiritual foundations, history is narrowed down to this single theme of the necessity of obedience to Jehovah. Even Israel's enemies, punishing its faults, are seen as instruments of the divine will: the chroniclers and prophets ram home the point that disasters were a divine judgment for unrighteousness. These writers are unconcerned with other aspects of history, and have little or no interest in natural causes. Later, an apocalyptic end to the world's troubles became an article of belief, but the early prophets were more historically minded since they rejected a mechanistic solution in which man will have no say. Thus Amos, for example, rejects any such facile optimistic view of the historical denouement, since he warns grimly that the eventual Day of the Lord may not be a happy ending at all.[18] It is up to mankind: it depends on how we behave.

Even a powerful Israelite ruler like Omri in the ninth century, who founded a dynasty the Assyrians thought worth mentioning in an inscription, only rates a few verses in the Hebrew record[19] – because his religion was regarded as incorrect. And yet this belief that the kings did not necessarily do right, that the human party to the covenant was not the ruler but the people, proved the salvation of the Jewish religion. For when the states of Israel and Judah succumbed to Assyria and Babylon respectively (772, 586 BC) the detachment of Judaism from royal houses enabled it to survive in exile and Dispersion. And the same detached attitude continued to perpetuate the valuable point of view that history was not just the mouthpiece of princes.

Subsequently, the Jews lost interest in history. The story of their kings, prophets and priests no longer needed to be told. The people's fate no longer depended on the mediation of such men, but instead the lot of each individual Jew was mediated by the eternal scriptures. And so the Hebrews, formerly the most historically minded of ancient eastern nations, became for a time as indifferent to history as any other people in the world.[20] But some centuries before the gradual compilation of the Written and Oral Law which produced this effect, there had been a vigorous, momentary resuscitation of Hebrew history. This occurred in the later sixth and fifth centuries BC, when the Persians, succeeding to the dominions of Assyria and Babylonia, allowed groups of Jews to filter back to their homes. One of the ablest of them was Nehemiah, cup-bearer of the Persian king Artaxerxes I (*c.* 444). His account of a surreptitious reconnaissance of the walls of Jerusalem strikes a vivid autobiographical note.

And I arose in the night, I and some few men with me; neither told I any man what my God had put in my heart to do at Jerusalem: neither was there any beast with me, save the beast that I rode upon. And I went out by night by the gate of the valley, even before the dragon well, and to the dung port, and viewed the walls of Jerusalem, which were broken down, and the gates thereof were consumed with fire. . . . And the rulers knew not whither I went, or what I did.[21]

Nehemiah and his fellow-writer Ezra, who apparently came to Jerusalem a little earlier (*c.* 458), could have used and translated many Babylonian, Egyptian and Persian models. Cyrus I (559–529), founder of the Persian monarchy, had inherited the historical traditions and the records of his Mesopotamian forerunners. He also added distinctive features of his own. Stressing the moral principle, he was at pains to present himself as the legitimate successor to the dynasties of the past; and when he adopted their institutions he took over their archives as well.

Elements hostile to the Jews, and eager to demonstrate their rebellious past, urged Artaxerxes I 'that search may be made in the book of the records of thy fathers'.[22] Again, when Darius II (424–405 BC) ruled in favour of a Jewish claim to be allowed to rebuild the Temple, 'a search was made in the house of the rolls, where the treasures were laid up in Babylon';[23] and a hundred-and-fifty-year-old tablet of Cyrus I was duly found. But, if anyone in those eastern monarchies ever wrote anything private or unofficial or subversive, it did not get on to those files. The historical records were there, but their character was official. There was nothing comparable to the Jewish literature, which had taken such an aloof view, not indeed about the divine purposes, but at least about the rulers who were failing to carry it out. Nor was there anything so interesting and introspective as the official Hittite pronouncements of a thousand years before.

(b) The Greek Beginnings

In the eighth and subsequent centuries BC some of these near-eastern influences greatly affected the Greeks. From the Phoenicians they learnt how to write. But there was no prose literature yet, and the time was not ripe for history. Nor had the work yet taken on its later meaning: in the *Iliad* the *histor* is a man of skill before whom legal disputes are brought. He enquires into the facts and decides what they are.[1]

Homeric poetry is not ancient history (as subsequent Greeks usually believed it was), for its personages are half-gods or heroes. Their stories, whatever factual core they may or may not possess, are framed in terms of myth and legend. However, there were historical implications in the Homeric young noble's training, for he was educated to be a speaker of words as well as a doer of great actions;[2] and Achilles with his lyre sang of the glorious deeds of warriors.[3] The travellers' tales of the *Odyssey* are pseudo-history like Egyptian stories on similar themes (p. 4). The *Theogony* attributed to Hesiod displays the early story of the world in terms of warring gods. But the *Works and Days* of the same school, with its Five Ages of the World, reveals some conception of the history of civilisation. Unlike the apocalyptic hopes gradually formed by the Jews, it is a pessimistic conception, because each successive Age had been worse than the last:[4] and this pessimism was taken over, with variations, by the majority of ancient historians.

The bards who recited at festivals and in private houses told of the past. Greeks on the coasts of Asia Minor – Ionians and the others – revered these epic poets as the preservers of historical memory.

15

Continually revising the old stories in a spirit of local pride, the poets stimulated Ionian patriotism against the menace of a hostile hinterland. Like their counterparts in mainland Greece, they recalled the foundation of their city and the establishment of its ancient cults. They also celebrated the pedigree of their lords and leading families,[5] though, among this individualistic people, such expressions of respect fell short of the praise or self-praise of an Egyptian or Assyrian inscription.

In the seventh century BC, at least a few people were becoming more critical. Archilochus of Paros (*c.* 648) sang his views about society with a new frankness, and gods and heroes were looked at with a colder eye. Already the *Iliad* and the *Odyssey* had shown a certain flippancy about gods and goddesses,[6] and soon Stesichorus, from Mataurus in south Italy, was writing with scepticism about the story of Helen of Troy (?*c.* 600). Yet it remained customary to see a core of fact in the epic poems.

The intellectual revolution which now took place in Ionia, the part of Greece in closest touch with the near east, represented the triumph of a spirit of enquiry. That is what *historie* came to mean, a search for the rational explanation and understanding of phenomena. The results of this search, for the first time, were expressed in prose as well as verse. When the alphabet was adopted from the Phoenicians, it had not only been employed to write down poetry. Like the scripts of earlier peoples, it had also be utilised, no doubt, for unpoetical records and archives and inventories. Before long its use was extended to narrative as well. Prose meant a break with the old view that the past was something variable with each poet, and in any case only recoverable by inspiration from the Muse. It was also a less restricted medium. 'The teller of stories in prose', points out H.C.Baldry, 'could not claim the lofty inspiration of Demodocus [the minstrel of the *Odyssey*],[7] with his lyre and his language specially adapted to his art. Prose tales were the pastimes of the market-place, not the servant's hall.'

And so, in the mid-sixth century, Anaximander of Miletus used prose to set out his views about the universe. He concluded that nature consists of fundamental opposites, which give place to one another in different seasons, thus causing the cyclical changes of the year.[8] It is uncertain whether this hypothesis was prompted by ancient and persistent ideas of Nemesis and divine jealousy or by observable facts. Probably it was a mixture of both; and in any case it had implications which were followed up later on by historians (p. 48). At the same time, making use of geographical lists and itineraries and outline charts from Assyria and Babylonia,[9] Anaximander drew up a map of the known world. Although it was schematic, and the earth was surrounded by an encompassing ocean, he had moved on from the travel tales of the *Odyssey* to the observational geography which was now to form the kernel of early historical writing.

When the Ionians started asking critical questions, their investigations were primarily concerned with the nature of the cosmos and the world. But the attitude which such enquiries implied was bound, sooner or later, to make them turn to man, and to start asking questions about him too. Ionia became dependent on Lydian overlords who ruled the interior of Asia Minor from Sardis. The next suzerains were the Persians. The Greek subjects of the one people and then the other, being inquisitive, wanted to know what these foreigners, so important but so remote, were like. There were no myths to help or get in the way, so that descriptions of such eastern nations were able to concentrate on the facts. The next step was for the technique thus evolved to be used to study institutions nearer home, among the Greeks and Ionians themselves. And the Ionians also wanted to know something about the many other peoples with whom their adventurous seafarers brought them into contact.

This sort of study involved tentative essays in ethnology and anthropology. Furthermore, when blended with up-to-date, less credulously mythological versions of current sagas, it made something like history. The works of these first prose recorders (*logographoi*) are lost. No doubt they incorporated myths, fables, legends and folktales. But the change of medium was significant, for it marked a stage towards the use of prose for factual enquiries. And indeed the old fictional material was soon combined, in somewhat naïve fashion, with chronicles, dynastic lists, genealogies (more or less tampered with), and accounts of journeys and places. It was stated later that there had been city and family archives upon which these early prose writers could draw.[10] That is uncertain, but politically the city-states were already advanced, and it is therefore possible that they had acquired from the Persians and other easterners the habit of forming such collections.

This whole activity, conducted in a clear, simple prose employing the Ionic dialect of Greek, was probably well under way by the end of the sixth century BC. Spoken story was nearly as old as speech itself. But, now that it was written down, and written down in prose, with attention focused on particular topics and places and periods, history was not far off.

Round about 500 BC a decisive turn was given by Hecataeus of Miletus. In spare but elegant and vigorous Ionic, he wrote two prose works, *Journey round the World* and *Genealogies*. Hecataeus played a leading part, though perhaps not quite such a leading part as subsequent accounts claimed, in the Ionian revolt against the Persians (500–494). His *Journey round the World* came in for criticism later on, but enjoyed long-lived popularity.[11] Constructed in two parts, the work consisted of itineraries and notes, describing first Europe and then Asia, which was held to include north Africa as well.

Such 'Journeys', of which this is the first known to us though evidently not the first to have been written,[12] represented one special aspect of the quasi-scientific studies which were now throwing off their versified framework. A survey like that of Hecataeus was also very much in demand as a practical mariner's handbook, because many early colonising expeditions – of which Miletus was the out-standing promoter – are known to have come to grief owing to topographical ignorance. And topography figures largely in surviving fragments of the book, as befitted a writer who himself drew up an improved map.[13] Hecataeus made the whole subject of geography into a much more serious study than it had been before. He also inserted patient observations on peoples and fauna and flora, as well as on local religious and historical peculiarities, adding comments on place-names and inserting passages of narrative. Aided by these varied researches, people could now study man in his physical environment, and ponder upon shafts of brilliance such as the perception of the con-temporary philosopher Xenophanes that every different race credits the gods with its own particular characteristics.

But Hecataeus determined that human development should be seen in its temporal, chronological perspective also. Written, perhaps, some years later that the *Journey*, his *Genealogies* did not reject the myths, but modified them here and there on commonsense, rationalistic grounds,

18

examining them on their supposed merits in the light of his own judgment so as to make them more sane and credible[14] – a misleading procedure which fell short of the freethinking of Xenophanes but continued to possess many adherents throughout antiquity. Hecataeus adopted a similar blend of acceptance and criticism in regard to the genealogical boasts of aristocratic families. Their privileges were being challenged and claimed by outsiders. He did not join in the attack, but his aim was to cut out the dead wood;[15] within the limits he set himself, he was keen to assert truth and individual opinion. He also struck out in a new direction by dealing not only with mythical times but with more recent epochs as well. Although systematic chronology still belonged to the future, it seems probable that Hecataeus used the Spartan king-list to construct for historical times some sort of chronological scheme founded on a framework of forty-year generations. His *Genealogies* included his own, which he proudly traced back through sixteen generations to the settlement of Miletus by colonists from the Greek mainland (*c.* 1000 BC) – the founder of the line being a god. But when Hecataeus went to Thebes in Egypt, Herodotus later said, the priests expressed surprise, indicating that their own lists of kings went back 341 generations without the appearance of any god.[16] Nothing could illustrate better than this slightly malicious story the widening of parochial Greek outlooks which had been brought about by contacts with the ancient civilisations of the east.

Hecataeus' personal inspection of these wonders caused him to preface his book by a statement which shows that, even if myths were not discarded, novel, unheard-of, critical attitudes were rapidly developing. 'What I write here', he said, 'is the account I believe to be true. For the stories that the Greeks tell are many, and in my opinion ridiculous.' Here was a new scientific ideal of emancipation from passive acceptance – an equivalent, in the historical field, of Xenophanes' assertion that we must do the best we can with probability, since the truth can only be found by laborious searching.[17] Although too much reliance on this 'probability' could become dangerous in the wrong hands, Greek thought was rapidly reaching the point of liberation at which masterpieces of historical interpretation would become possible. If Herodotus was history's father, Hecataeus might be called its grandfather. What Anaximander, two or three generations earlier, had done for natural science, he achieved for history.

Such a pioneer performance was sure to breed smaller works, and quite early in the fifth century BC there sprang up a new type of more or less historical literature. This took the form of separate monographs, including a number dealing with contemporary history.[18] People had already become interested in learning about the great eastern powers (p. 17), and the Persian Wars meant that Persia was likely to be a favourite subject, and one, moreover, which permitted narrative to be accompanied by patriotic reflections.[19] In the years following Hecataeus, Lydia, too, continued to be the subject of at least one special study;[20] though the dates of these shadowy works are uncertain.

Evidently, however, an original figure in this development of historical science was Ion. Born of a rich family at Chios in *c.* 490 BC, from his forties onwards he gained distinction at Athens as a tragic dramatist. He also wrote travel books and a *Foundation* of his city which converted this old type of composition into prose. Furthermore, Ion devised a novel kind of memoir[21] in which the personal touch, an individual's notable act or witty saying or idiosyncrasy or physical peculiarity, attains a new prominence. These reminiscences, which are regrettably lost, dealt with other people more than with himself, and included references to Aeschylus, and to a visit he received at Chios from Sophocles. Shortly before Ion was born, the philosopher Heraclitus had stressed that character plays a part in man's destiny – it *is* his destiny, he says.[22] Since then the first attempts at biographical writing may have been launched,[23] but Ion is one of the first people whom we can identify as playing an important part in its gradual evolution.

I

Herodotus

I

The Life and Work of Herodotus

HERODOTUS of Halicarnassus (*c.* 490/480–429/5 BC) tells the story of the Persian Wars in which a coalition of Greek city-states, achieving momentary co-operation, defeated a first Persian invasion at Marathon in Attica (490), and then repelled a second invasion at sea off the island of Salamis (480) and then again in the following year on land at Plataea (Boeotia) and Mycale (western Asia Minor). Herodotus wrote more than a generation after these events.

To introduce the theme, he goes back to the first political and military contacts of the Greeks with the east, that is to say with Lydia which reduced the Ionian cities on the coast of Asia Minor and its offshore islands. After an account of earlier clashes between east and west, largely of a mythical or legendary character, the main part of the story begins with the Lydian king Croesus (*c.* 560–546), who completed the subjugation of the Ionian cities. However, Croesus was defeated and overthrown by the Persian king Cyrus I, who had supplanted the Medes and founded an empire extending throughout the middle east. Cyrus reduced the Asiatic Greeks, and his son and successor Cambyses (529–521) invaded Egypt (525). The second book of Herodotus' Histories provides a description of the geography, history and ethnography of that country, and the third tells of its conquest by Cambyses. He was helped by the powerful ruler of the Ionian island of Samos, Polycrates (*c.* 540–522), whose régime is described. Cambyses was succeeded, after a revolt, by Darius I (521–486), who intervened at Samos and took Babylon. Book IV is devoted to his first, largely abortive, expedition into Europe (512), when he crossed the Danube and marched into Scythia (south Russia).

At the same time a Persian expedition was launched against the Greek settlements in Cyrenaica, of which a description is given as part of a general survey of north Africa. The fifth book tells how Megabyzus, whom Darius on his return from Scythia had left in Europe, reduced a large part of Thrace.

A revolt against Persian rule that broke out among the Ionian and other Asiatic Greeks received help from Athens (which was of Ionian origin) and from the town of Eretria on the island of Euboea. An account is next given of the recent history of Athens and the raid it now launched on Sardis, the headquarters of the Persians in Asia Minor. But the rebellion collapsed, and the sixth book tells of the naval defeat of the Greeks off Lade (495) and the fall of the principal Ionian city of Miletus in the following year.

As the Persians, having reconquered Ionia, strengthened their hold over Thrace and Macedonia, the Athenian political exile Miltiades, who had established himself as an independent ruler on the Hellespont (Dardanelles), moved back to Athens. While Darius' envoys proceeded round Greece demanding homage, the Athenians appealed to Sparta. Herodotus describes the constitutional system of the Spartans and the accession and downfall of their king Cleomenes I. In 490 the Persians, under Datis and Artaphernes, conducted a punitive expedition against Athens and Eretria, and after overwhelming the latter town were defeated at Marathon by the Athenians and Plataeans, under the leadership of Miltiades. The Persian expedition withdrew to Asia. A Spartan contingent, which had arrived too late for the battle, visited the battlefield. Then Herodotus appends a note on the great Athenian family of the Alcmaeonidae, which was suspected of flashing a signal to the Persians. Miltiades died in disgrace after an abortive expedition against the island of Paros.

The seventh book begins with the death of Darius and succession of his son Xerxes I (485–465). In 480 Xerxes launched a huge co-ordinated invasion of Greece by sea and land. The Greeks, uniting (in spite of exceptions) to a degree unprecedented in their history, prepared to resist. The allied forces were under the supreme command of a Spartan, but Themistocles the Athenian was the guiding spirit. Leonidas, king of Sparta, fell heroically at Thermopylae, and central Greece was lost. The eighth book tells of three delaying actions fought by the Greek fleet off Artemisium (on the east coast), followed by the retirement of the Greek naval force, the occupation of Athens by the Persians, and the shattering defeat of their navy between the island of Salamis and the mainland.

Xerxes returned to Asia, but left an army in Greece. The ninth book describes how its commander Mardonius was defeated and killed at Plataea by Peloponnesians and Athenians under the Spartan regent Pausanias (479). The remnants of the Persian army evacuated Greece, and meanwhile across the Aegean another Persian force was destroyed at Mycale by a Greek force under the Spartan king Leotychidas. Now the cities of Ionia again revolted from the Persians; and this time they were successful. Leotychidas left for home, but the Athenian portion of the Greek fleet sailed north to liberate the cities on the Hellespont from Persian rule. The story ends with anecdotes illustrating Persian misconduct, cruelty and toughness.

The work of Herodotus falls into two halves.[1] The first deals with the origins of the quarrel between east and west, the rise of the Persian Empire, and the historical background at Athens and Sparta. The second half begins after the northern expedition of Darius has won Persia a land-frontier with Greek States in Macedonia. The historian then goes on to tell the story of the wars fought by the Persians, first Darius and then Xerxes, against the Greeks. The division into nine books was probably first made long after Herodotus' death, by a scholarly editor at Alexandria. The task was skilfully done, because each of the books has a leading theme: Cyrus, Egypt, dynastic revolution, Scythia, the Ionian rebellion, Marathon, Thermopylae, Salamis, Plataea-Mycale.[2]

Throughout two-thirds of the work the Persian Wars provide a connecting link. They seemed to Herodotus the outstanding feature of world history. They had compelled the Greeks, for once, to work together, almost as a single group. When Herodotus wrote, the moment had passed, but its afterglow was still vivid. The wars had opened vast horizons to the Greeks, and had stirred them to want

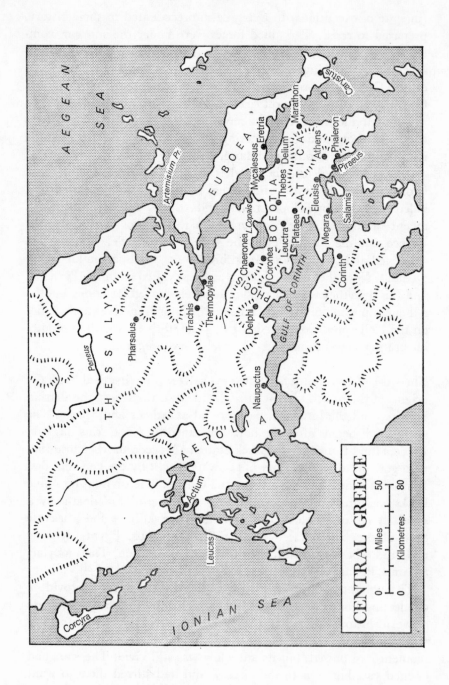

CENTRAL GREECE

these sensational events placed on record and to ask what manner of people the enemy had been. Indeed, the Persian Wars gave a decisive turn to the whole story of the Western world. 'The battle of Marathon,' said John Stuart Mill, 'even as an event in English history, is more important than the battle of Hastings.'

In making a great war, and its causes and events, the framework for his analysis of human behaviour, Herodotus turned warfare into the central theme of history. A vast number of his successors throughout all the ages have agreed that war deserves pre-eminent status. Moreover, this conviction has possessed a large measure of justification, because war, raging almost continuously throughout the centuries, has proved to be the greatest of all catalysts of emotions, customs and values. And yet it has owed its predominance in histories to something else also: to the incomparable, irresistible example of Herodotus.

Yet his work is loosely knit. He himself declares that his purpose is a double one – the Persian Wars only form one of his themes, for there is another as well.

In this book, the result of my enquiries into history, I hope to do two things: to preserve the memory of the past by putting on record the astonishing achievements both of our own and of the Asiatic [barbarian] peoples; secondly, and more particularly, to show how the two races came into conflict.[3]

This modest programme does not cover nearly all that Herodotus has to offer. But it points to his major aims. The first and more general of the two purposes is largely served by digressions, some short and some extremely long. The early part of the Histories includes an outline of the rise of Persia, and long descriptions of Lydia, Ionia, Egypt, Scythia and north Africa, with a shorter note on Thrace and Macedonia.[4] In the later books, as the story gains speed, the excursions are fewer, but room is still found to fill in, for example, the historical backgrounds of Athens and Sparta. In addition to such major digressions, the whole work is abundantly interspersed with those spicy anecdotes and parables for which Herodotus is famous.

He himself refers to these deviations from his main path as supplements and insertions, and professes at times to call himself back to the main stream of his narrative:[5] 'A remarkable fact occurs to me – I need not apologise for the digression; it has been my plan throughout this book to put down odd bits of information not directly connected with my main subject.'[6] And then he goes on to report – in the middle of discussing a country hundreds of miles away – that mules cannot be bred in Elis, though Elis is not a cold place. And he is, in fact, well aware that these digressions, long or short, form an integral part of his work; they are something he is not prepared to dispense with. For 'Herodotus will not deny himself', as Albin Lesky says, 'the pleasure of picking flowers at the roadside'. Some of these out-of-the-way pieces of information go far beyond the war theme and far back in date, and were added from the pure pleasure of telling a story. Conventions have changed, and this large view of what constitutes unity and relevance would scarcely be practicable for a modern historian. But the attitude of the Homeric poets had been the same; and all his readers had been brought up on the *Iliad* and *Odyssey*. It was right to call him the most Homeric of authors.[7] Even the deliberate digressions *within* digressions, anticipatory of the Arabian Nights, have epic precedents.

Besides, the whole feat of organisation is handled with extreme ingenuity. Sometimes, indeed, the skill merely consists of finding the most appropriate place to introduce a piece of loose material. Generally there is no great attempt to tie the links together firmly. But it will often be found that the digressions are located in such a way as to give the maximum effect both to themselves and to the portion of the narrative which they accompany.[8] Accounts of foreign peoples, for example, are supplied at the moment when these nations first came into contact with Persia. Descriptive notes on the vital early history of Athens and Sparta, all necessary and relevant, occur piecemeal in a series of apparently casual asides, usually at a critical juncture in the relations between east and west. Every moment of direct impact is thrown into relief so that the general pattern shall emerge more clearly. Frequently, too, digressions are sandwiched neatly between the preliminary statement of a theme and its subsequent working out in greater detail.

Although deeply interested in geography and prepared to enlarge on its ramifications at considerable length, Herodotus never lets the historical dimension out of sight: Egyptian customs merge into Egyptian history. His loose construction reflects a complete awareness of the complexity of history. The main line must be a unified orderly account. And yet, after all, the Persian Wars had resulted from the interplay of varied and disjointed factors; so that broad horizons are necessary. There seemed to be a general pervasive principle of interconnection between the expansive tendencies of the various oriental empires. Since eastern attacks on Greece had begun not with Persia but with Lydia, the work starts with the Lydian King Croesus (*c.* 560–546), who first 'within my knowledge inflicted injury on the Greeks'.[9] But Herodotus' concept of unity is wider and more subtle still. For when every incidental digression is over, we find that we have what is virtually a continuous story of Greece from the mid-sixth century onwards.

One reason for the episodic, apparently disjointed structure of the Histories is that they were written to be read aloud. Herodotus recited extracts of the work at Olympia and Athens, and he made his living by readings and lectures of this kind. The whole work could not be recited all at once, so that composition in well-defined parts was essential. In any case silent reading, if not totally unknown, was still infrequent. It is first attested in 405 BC,[10] and people could obviously read in silence minor compositions such as letters,[11] but the practice of dealing with literary works in this way continued to be rare throughout antiquity. The Greeks and Romans reacted more responsively and immediately to the eloquent spoken word than we do, and in the absence of numerous copies of books it was natural that history, like other compositions, should be read aloud, at public or private gatherings.

That is what Herodotus did[12] (and historians were still doing so eight hundred years later). The fact that the text of his work, as it has come down to us, comprises passages designed for recitation explains certain features of his style: 'squeeze-outs' in which strict grammatical sequence is lost sight of, minor corrections as he went along, connecting links and recapitulations that display an associative rather than a rational continuity.[13]

The practical requirements of recitation were also bound to modify the actual substance and contents of the history. Our knowledge of the sounds of Greek is too imperfect for us to understand the effects that were produced. Yet it is clear enough that they were all-important. Herodotus also had to keep his audience amused. We learn that at Olympia he once went on speaking for too long; though his fascinating material, displayed in that easy flowing style which looks so simple but is the product of consummate skill, makes that hard to believe.

Like many writers, Herodotus did not completely fulfil his plan. For example, he promised a digression on Assyria, to balance the long Egyptian survey.[14] If it was written, however, it was omitted; or else it was never written. Such indications, as well as the surprising design of the whole work, have inspired the view that the book was first intended to be quite different from what finally emerged. According to this opinion, Herodotus originally proposed to write a 'Journey', very much on the lines of the Journey of Hecataeus. Or perhaps he intended, again like previous writers, to offer a description of the Persian Empire (p. 17), into which these various disquisitions about foreign countries would be woven. But then, it is conjectured, he became caught up instead with the absorbing subject of the Persian Wars, and radically changed direction so as to make those his leading theme. Nevertheless, the argument continues, he decided to incorporate in the new plan the geographical, ethnological portions of his original project, and these are the major digressions that still appear.

Scholars who oppose this interpretation admit that the digressions represent the old, Hecataean type of approach, and that the second half of the work shows a more close-knit structure than the first. But they attribute this greater tightness to intensified emotional concentration rather than to a radical change of design, and see no reason why Herodotus should not have combined them with his narrative in a single creative act representing a single, once-and-for-all, unaltered plan. The controversy between these two contrary views, and the establishment of various intermediate points of view, comprises one of the main preoccupations, often *the* main preoccupation, of Herodotean scholars today.

Perhaps there were two main phases of composition. First, extending over a number of years, came the highlights, presented as recitations or lectures, but not published. Whether these recitations mostly consisted of geographical or historical passages we cannot tell; probably both, with the geographical parts (of the earlier books) composed first. Then, at a later stage, these already existing portions were supplemented by others, and welded together into what had now become a single and larger work.

But rewriting was a laborious business in the ancient world, when books were copied singly on to papyrus rolls or scrolls. These could easily get lost or transposed. They were also much harder to handle than the later parchment codex. There was no separation of words. Enlarged initials were not used. Accents were omitted – except occasionally in lyric poems. Inverted commas did not exist. Punctuation was at best highly arbitrary, and much more often wholly absent. Furthermore, until 403 BC Athens officially used an old and inaccurate alphabet. For all these reasons the task of trying to rewrite what had already been written was a formidable one, and it is unlikely that Herodotus undertook it on any extensive scale.

Certainly, he may have added some marginal corrections and deleted certain passages. But, if so, the job of welding was thoroughly done, for the literary texture of the early books (especially II) is particularly close-knit; this is a compensation for the loose unity of the subject. On the other hand, the later books possess an internal near-repetitive allusiveness which suggests production during a single, more or less uninterrupted, period of sustained composition. Perhaps, though we cannot be sure, this took place at the time when they were blended with the pre-existent portions and the whole work was thrown into the shape in which it has come down to us.

The two sections, on the whole, stood for two different types of literature, because Herodotus lived and wrote at precisely the transitional moment of historical writing when he was able to combine detailed geographical digressions of the type familiar from Hecataeus with a new sort of narrative history bent on reconstructing the past.

Details about the lives of ancient writers, as opposed to men of action, were not usually preserved with any care or accuracy; and we know far too little about who Herodotus was. He is the subject of no ancient Life except a short notice in a lexicon (Suidas), and he himself is modest and reserved about his own remarkable personality and travels. We do not know the names of any of his close friends; we are not even told if he was single or married. Although anecdotes about other people abound in his work, personal reminiscences are austerely ruled out. The reader is reduced to guessing; for example, when he remarks that no Egyptian would kiss a Greek on the lips, one wonders if he is speaking from personal frustration.

He was the son of Lyxes and Dryo. His father came of a good

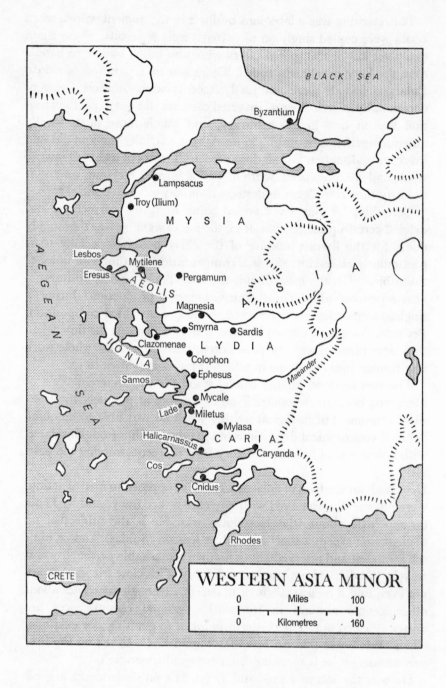

BLACK SEA

Byzantium

Lampsacus

Troy (Ilium)

M Y S I A

A S I A

Lesbos

Mytilene

Eresus

A E O L I S

Pergamum

A E G E A N   S E A

Magnesia

Smyrna

Sardis

I O N I A

Clazomenae

L Y D I A

Colophon

Ephesus

Samos

Maeander

Mycale

Lade

Miletus

Mylasa

Halicarnassus

C A R I A

Caryanda

Cos

Cnidus

Rhodes

CRETE

WESTERN ASIA MINOR

| 0 | Miles | 100 |

| 0 | Kilometres | 160 |

family at Halicarnassus (Bodrum) on the coast of south-western Asia Minor, a defensible wine-producing harbour-town that was traditionally the place of eternal spring and had once been called Zephyria. It was fitting that Herodotus should write about the clash between the western and eastern ways of life, because this was the fringe where Greeks and Asiatics met. Originally the place had belonged to Carians, but in the ninth century BC these 'barbarians' (that is to say, speakers of a language that was not Greek) had been subdued by Greek immigrants,[15] Dorians who then intermarried with the native population. The name of Herodotus' father, Lyxes, was Carian, and the historian is very unlikely to have been a pure Greek.

Just north of this Dorian zone of the coast was the more popular and prosperous Ionian region, with cities such as Miletus and Ephesus. The Ionian influence spread southwards, and by the fifth century the Dorian–Carian community of Halicarnassus had become sufficiently Ionicised to speak in the Ionic dialect. This appears on a Halicarnassian inscription of 454 BC,[16] and it is the language of Herodotus. Before the wars against the Persians the place had been controlled by them; the historian speaks proudly of the somewhat questionable exploits of its queen Artemisia on the Persian side at Salamis.[17] Then Halicarnassus was ruled by her son Lygdamis, who became engaged in a civil war that resulted in the death of Herodotus' uncle Panyassis, a distinguished epic poet (461). Herodotus withdrew to the island of Samos. By 454/3 Halicarnassus had got rid of its despot and was a member of the Delian League dependent on Athens.[18] Herodotus may possibly have returned home to take part in the expulsion of Lygdamis, but if so he did not stay. Instead, he remained an exile, thus widening his experience and sharpening his emotions.

He travelled. Perhaps he had made earlier journeys, since he was already well known in the early sixties.[19] At any rate he ranged widely now. He went to Athens. His visit to that city decisively influenced his life and outlook, and may well have been the happening which caused him to abandon his mainly geographical interests and write instead about the Persian Wars in which the Athenians had played so great a part. He enjoyed among them a large reputation as a man whose travels and experience of foreign lands had given him much unfamiliar knowledge. His pro-Athenian attitude was

33

likewise welcome; and it is recorded that he was paid an unprecedentedly large sum for reciting at Athens.

Later, however, he embarked on his travels again, joining a new Greek settlement that was being founded at Thurii or Thuria on the Gulf of Taras (Taranto), the instep of Italy, just across the Ionian Sea from Greece. Thurii was intended to replace Sybaris, which had been obliterated by its neighbour Croton in 510 and is today being sought for again by excavators. At first the coins of the new foundation bore the old name of Sybaris, but then the new one ('rusher') was adopted from a neighbouring spring, which was channelled in a bronze pipe. The town of Thurii, set in front of a series of semi-circular hill-terraces resembling a huge amphitheatre, stood in a small fertile plain built up by two rivers, one of which, the Crathis, pointed a short cut to the western (Tyrrhenian) sea. The new foundation had come into existence because the ageing survivors of Sybaris had asked Athens and Sparta to help them re-establish their city. Sparta refused, but when the group from Sybaris made a first attempt in 452, and were suppressed by Croton, the Athenians gave aid to the fugitives.

Soon afterwards Athens, instigated either by Pericles (as his first overseas venture) or by Thucydides the son of Melesias (not the historian) who preceded him as a leading figure in the Government, launched a remarkable pan-Hellenic migration to settle the place (444/3). By now the Athenians had become the leaders of maritime trade; and they were keen to offset the power of Sparta's daughter-state Taras near the new site. It was Athens, therefore, which provided the money, the naval escort, a democratic constitution and the founders. These included a famous expounder of sacred law, Lampon, and other notable intellectuals including the philosopher Protagoras of Abdera who drew up the civil law code, and Hippodamus of Miletus, a famous town-planner. In spite of all the building-projects requiring labour at home, Athens, in contrast to Sparta which still stood aside, was demonstrating its ability to lead a joint undertaking of the Greeks. For the membership of the community was impressively varied. The ten 'tribes' into which it was divided included not only four from the Athenians and other peoples of Ionian origin, but three from the Peloponnese (Arcadia, Elis, Achaea) and three from the eastern areas of central Greece.

One of the original colonists, or a very early recruit, was Herodotus.

It is not known why he went. Possibly he was disappointed by a law of 451/50 at Athens which prevented him from gaining full citizenship there. At any rate he became a citizen of Thurii, and good manuscripts of the Histories describe him as a man of Thurii, and no longer of Halicarnassus.[20] Presumably he went there in order to obtain franchise and land. He could, it would seem, have gone back to his original home instead. But the exciting breadth of the new project, a practical application of the new spirit of scientific experiment, must have appealed to a man whose mind was not limited by ordinary horizons.

Thurii became prosperous. Yet Pericles could not or did not prevent it from falling successively into civil strife, war and unfavourable peace with Taras; and the settlers became disillusioned with the alleged high-minded internationalism of imperial Athens.[21] We do not know whether Herodotus stayed on at Thurii until he died, or returned to mainland Greece for a short final period. But Thurii may have been uncomfortable for an Athenian sympathiser after the outbreak of the Peloponnesian War between Athens and Sparta (431). The Histories contain a few references to the years 432–429[22] which seem to suggest that he returned to Greece and perhaps to Athens for his last few years. But they do not prove it – and his tomb and epitaph were shown at Thurii. Later, Halicarnassus commissioned his statue and, in Roman imperial times, portrayed him on its coins.

The date when the historian collected his various categories of material can be deduced, at least conjecturally, from the little that we know of his career. Since so many of his travels belong to the years 454–443 a great deal of the geographical data must have been collected then. Facts about the western Mediterranean could naturally have been added while he was living in south Italy, though his occasional references to that area are not systematic.[23] As for the main part of the book and its treatment of the Persian War, this information is most likely to have been collected at Athens before 444/3, perhaps with some additions (if he ever revisited the city) at the end of his life.

The question when the work was completed and published is, of course, quite a different one. If the final version of his Histories came from something like a single act of composition (p. 30), this is likely to have been accomplished not earlier than the first years of the

Peloponnesian War, to which, as has been seen, there are references in the text. On the other hand the work was available by 425, for that was the year in which the comic dramatist Aristophanes seemed to be making fun of Herodotus' survey of the mythical 'origins' of the war (a little unfairly since Herodotus had written the passage with his tongue in his cheek).[24] That is to say the Histories, as we have them, date from the very end of his days, when he was probably in his mid-fifties. Under the lowering clouds of the Peloponnesian War, there was a strong impulse to write. At a time when Greece was falling apart, the victory over Persia seemed a particularly glorious triumph of co-operation between Greek and Greek.

There are indications that he died before he had quite finished (p. 30). Moreover, the last chapter provides an unexpected and enigmatic conclusion. This goes right back to Cyrus I, founder of the Persian Empire. Herodotus records the king's reactions to a suggestion that the Persians, now that they were powerful, should quit their small and barren country and find a better one. Cyrus, he says, disagreed with the proposal, pointing out (in accordance with a doctrine later enunciated by the medical school of Hippocrates of Cos)[25] that strength and courage thrive on a hard soil. And so the Histories end. It is possible to argue that they were *not* meant to end here, but would have gone on – perhaps the author himself never decided what his terminal point would be. Yet this does not seem a necessary deduction, especially as the date at which the work breaks off is dramatically satisfactory, coinciding with the final elimination of the Persian menace. Furthermore, from a formal point of view this sort of conclusion can be paralleled from earlier Greek compositions, which often began elaborately and wound up abruptly.

Let us assume, then, that this termination could have been intentional and deliberate. But, if so, what message did Herodotus intend it to convey? Perhaps he is harking back to the beginning of the work, in which he had very soon, and then again, praised healthy moderation. There had likewise been an early reference to Cyrus.[26] Yet, however good Herodotus' memory may have been, there was a limit to what readers (or audiences) could be expected to remember. And, in any case, his final words seem to carry an underlying allusion to Athens. Not that there was any plan for transferring its location, as the Persians were said to be considering the transference of theirs. But the empire of the Athenians had given them just the sort of tendency to luxury which is under discussion. Perhaps we are being told, with a tactful obliqueness, that luxury, in spite of Cyrus' warning, had caused his successors to fail, and the story must not be repeated by Athens. For Attica, too, was an austere country which had now tasted empire, and ancient moralists, among whom most oɩ the historians were numbered, always liked to advocate a return to simpler modes of life. Herodotus himself had migrated to a richer land, in southern Italy. Was he saying that he had made a mistake, and that the Athenians should note the lesson for themselves?

2

The Background
and Beliefs of
Herodotus

HERODOTUS had lived in Ionicised Halicarnassus, in Ionian Samos,
in Athens which was of Ionian origin, and in Thurii where Ionia
played a leading part with Athens. In very many ways, therefore,
he was an Ionian. His Histories are written in literary Ionic, less
simple than the language of Hecataeus or Heraclitus,[1] and not, it
appears, a version that was actually spoken in any part of Ionia,
but one combining the general features common to most of the
forms of speech to be found in that country.

Not unnaturally, the Histories give very detailed treatment to
Ionia. Herodotus was patriotic about his home-town Halicarnassus,
and he gratefully and rightly declared that the Ionian island of
Samos, where he took refuge, was a remarkable place which
deserved detailed description.[2] And yet, partly because Samos was
at variance with other Ionian towns that were readier to accept
Persian rule, he adopts a critical attitude to the qualities of the
Ionian people as a whole, who are unfavourably contrasted not only
with Dorians but with their own distant relatives the Athenians on
the mainland. A view, said to be current in Scythia, that the
Ionians made splendid slaves but were inadequate as free men, is

quoted with evident relish; and Aristagoras of Miletus, who led their rebellion against Persia and then abandoned them, is dismissed as a poor-spirited creature.[3] Indeed the whole Ionian revolt is condemned as a foolish enterprise which was doomed to failure. Herodotus declared that it started three generations of troubles for Greeks and Persians alike.

And yet what he owed to Ionia was enormous. Not only are his specific debts to lost Ionian writers (pp. 416f., nn 5, 18, 19) evidently greater than we can recapture, but the whole idea of writing history was directly derived from the enquiring, explaining spirit of the Ionian philosophers. 'His general beliefs', says W.G. Forrest, 'are basically those of a typical, if non-professional, product of the Ionian enlightenment.' The broad cosmopolitanism and tolerance of Herodotus are derived from the Ionian cities which were so accustomed to contacts with a variety of Asian lands, and from Ionia again comes the uncommitted detachment with which he studied foreign customs, recognised how one people differed from another, and desired to attain scientific explanations on the basis of systematic evidence.

Here is the Ionian determination to discover what is knowable. The scientist-philosophers of the country had primarily dealt with physics, and Herodotus adopted the doctrine that each regional variety of mankind possesses its own process of *physis*, growth, as well as special modes of behaviour (*nomoi*) conforming with its own habitat. There seems to be an echo here, though a cautious and fairly conservative one, of the thinking of the philosopher Protagoras, the contemporary of Herodotus and his companion at Thurii, whose saying that 'man is the measure of all things' implied that all customs are relative. There are also links, or at least analogies, with the school of the physician Hippocrates (469–399), which explained the connection of national characteristics with soils in terms suggestive of Herodotus (p. 36). The historian might have learnt of such views from Hippocrates himself; or perhaps this sort of idea was generally in the air.

The scientific writer, however, to whom Herodotus was obviously likely to owe most was the geographer Hecataeus, since so much of the Histories is geography. He repeats a great deal from the earlier writer, including some of his mistakes. Indeed, although the main purposes of their work were different, his geographical account may be described as pure Hecataeus, *plus* his own observations and enquiries. Yet Herodotus only names him once as a source, citing him for an alternative version of a story without passing judgment. He also twice speaks of Hecataeus as an actor in historical events, treating his part in the Ionian revolt sympathetically;[4] and he mentions him once as a traveller, with the implication that he took a shorter view than the Egyptians (p. 19). Very few ancient historians were exempt from the vice of criticising their immediate predecessors, and Herodotus makes it clear, by implication, that he found the geography and cartography of Hecataeus childishly schematic.[5] Yet, although he mocks his forerunner's symmetrical patterns of an equal-sized Europe and Asia, Herodotus himself is not wholly free from such ideas with reference to the north and south of Europe. But he does realise there may be an indefinite eastern extension of the continent, and he will not accept the circumambient Ocean River handed down by Hecataeus from Anaximander.[6]

One of the specific improvements introduced by Herodotus was to tie up all this geography much more closely with history. He could have said, with Michelet, that without a geographical basis the people who make history are walking on air. And, indeed, so inseparable did the two subjects seem to him that he freely applied the geographical, scientific methods of the Ionians to the entirely different field of human affairs.

But Herodotus was an Ionian not only in his adherence to these recently established standards, but above all in his debt to the Homeric *Iliad* and the *Odyssey*. Though he had advanced beyond the idea that myths explained wars, the poetic language and zest for digressions and catalogue which he derived from the Ionian epic made him the 'most Homeric' of writers (p. 28). Homeric, too, was his desire to ensure by his literary art that great deeds should be preserved from oblivion, so that fresh splendour might be spread over the glorious past. There was the same wide epic canvas, the same profound and sympathetic understanding of the human soul, and the same sense of divine interposition, however much at variance with the new scientific spirit this might be. Shared with the epic poets, again, was the theme of a struggle between west and east, Europe and Asia, and reminiscent of them, also, was his ambivalence towards this central subject of warfare. Homer had called war hateful and baleful, but he had spoken, nevertheless, about the joy and exaltation of the fight. Herodotus, too, profoundly felt the evil of war,[7] and yet none could have described with deeper feeling the glory of Leonidas at Thermopylae.

The speeches quoted in the Histories of Herodotus are another profoundly Homeric feature. The great majority of ancient historians regarded such speeches as an important feature of their work. But they are a considerable stumbling-block to the modern reader, who often reads them with a suspicion that no such speech was ever delivered, if, indeed, the occasion was accompanied by any speech-making at all; and, even if it was, the writer who provides the report possessed no means of knowing what had been said. The practice of every Greek and Roman historian in this respect has been analysed with care, and critics have frequently been kind enough to 'defend' them. But such defences are largely beside the point. The suspicions of the reader are often justified, but they are not entirely relevant. It was not for the sake of the exact accuracy of a first-class newspaper-report or Hansard record that the speeches were included. They were included to provide a background to situations, to explain the thoughts or feelings or points of view of the participants or of the author himself, to underline patterns of behaviour, to engage with the reader in that discourse or enquiry which is the essence of *historie*.

In the Homeric poems, similar orations had formed a superb and integral part of the whole. Like any of his compatriots – to whom talk was a way of life – Herodotus enjoyed discussion and made whatever literary use of it he could. His work is therefore studded with speeches. Most of them form a natural enough part of the story, counterbalancing the annalistic narrative with spicy diversity. But they also point the way to all the roles which such orations were destined to fulfil in the works of historians from now onwards, forging, as time went on, a close relation between history and rhetoric. Herodotus' speeches are often admonitory, coming from a warning friend, perhaps in the form of an illustrated parable.[8] His dialogues, likewise, are effective, ranging from a counterpoint of long speeches to a rapid fire of altercation. In one case, too, there is a set piece, a debate between Persian plotters on the rival merits of different constitutions.[9] Here was a fashionably modern theme (p. 44), and Herodotus was to some extent indebted to the forensic speeches of contemporary rhetoric and drama (p. 43). But, for all that, his oratory remains in the Homeric tradition.

He was also influenced by the epic and lyric poets who had come after Homer. In contrast to prose models, they are cited frequently by name, with snatches of quotations. This is because Herodotus was reciting, and the educated people who formed his audiences knew the poets but could not be expected to know prose authors. In particular, it may be surmised that Herodotus owed a great deal to a writer who had revised epic in his own day, Panyassis, who was his own kinsman, probably his father's brother. It was because of Panyasses' death at the hands of the local autocrat that Herodotus had been forced to leave Halicarnassus (p. 33). Interested, like his nephew, in oracles, Panyassis wrote an *Ionica* about the foundation of Ionian cities, and his epic poem about Heracles caused him to be ranked among the five greatest epic poets.[10]

Herodotus, reticent as always about matters relating to himself or his family, has nothing to say about his relative. But if the poems of Panyassis had survived we might well have found that they represented a major influence on the historian. For example, Panyassis had almost certainly echoed the Homeric desire to shed renown on the past, perhaps in terms similar to those in which his contemporary Pindar of Cynoscephalae in Boeotia gloriously reasserted the same ambition.

> Even high deeds of prowess
> Have a great darkness if they lack song;
> We can hold up a mirror to fine doings
> In one way only:
> If with the help of Memory in her glittering crown
> Recompense is found for labour
> In words' echoing melodies.[11]

The finest of fine deeds, Herodotus believed, was the contribution which Athens had made to the victory over the Persians. At Marathon in 490 the Athenians had behaved heroically.

> They came on, closed with the enemy all along the line, and fought in a way not to be forgotten. They were the first Greeks, so far as I know, to charge at a run, and the first who dared to look without flinching at Persian dress and the men who wore it.[12]

42

Eleven years later their spokesman was able to say;

'In that fight we stood alone against Persia – we dared a mighty enterprise and came out of it alive – we beat forty-six nations to their knees!'[13]

And by that time they had again, in Herodotus' view, been the saviours of Greece, for they had saved it in 480 as well. Writing in the full flood of Athenian imperialism (p. 71), he knows very well that such opinions will not please everyone, and admits as much. Yet he still feels obliged to maintain that the policy of the Athenians before Salamis, when they evacuated their city but insisted on fighting at sea instead of retreating behind the isthmus of Corinth, proved the salvation of the whole of Greece.[14] He also makes them the heroes of Plataea (479), although modern historians allot them a less pre-eminent role, and in the same year he declares that it was likewise the Athenians who were the bravest of the Greeks fighting at Mycale. And there was a particular reason why these tributes must be paid to them: because their deeds had been devoted to the defence of the pan-Hellenic ideal.

There is the Greek nation – the common blood, the common language; the temples and religious ritual; the whole way of life we understand and share together – indeed, if Athens were to betray all this, it would not be well done.[15]

It is not surprising that these magnificent eulogies helped to earn Herodotus the largest rewards any lecturer or reciter had ever received (p. 34). He did not write his final work exclusively *for* the Athenians – they are described as 'those' people, and their statesman Solon is twice introduced in words they would have found superfluous.[16] Yet other allusions presume an Athenian public, and the influence of the historian's residence at the city is detectable on many of his pages.

The new Athenian fashion of rhetoric, it is true, made little impression on his style. This novel and elaborate art from Sicily, which had just been described in the first known manuals,[17] was introduced to Athens by Gorgias from Leontini in that island. But Gorgias only came to Athens in 427, and at most it can be said that some of Herodotus' speeches, advancing beyond their Homeric models, show traces of the new formal structure,[18] and echo current

43

arguments from 'probability' which the rhetoricians were adapting from the philosophers (p. 92).[19]

Much more important, however, was the whole impact of Athens upon his historical thinking and feeling. For when he turned from his geographical interests to the chronicling of the Persian Wars there were recitations or writings by Athenian genealogists which could be of assistance (p. 417, n. 15), and he could listen to many other Athenians, too, as they welcomed and befriended him in their city. Indeed, perhaps he listened to them too much, since there are signs of the party politics of Athens in his work. The great family of the Alcmaeonidae, once radical and always rich and elegant, taught him much of his Athenian history, and he favours them against the upstart Themistocles, to whom Herodotus, growing up at the time of his decline, gives credit indeed, but slightly grudging credit all the same.[20] The widely held belief that the Alcmaeonids treasonably flashed a shield as a signal to the Persians in 480 is rejected – though Herodotus admits a shield *was* flashed.[21] And it was they, he said, who had been the true liberators of Athens from its tyrant Hippias (the son of Pisistratus), turned out of the city in 511.

As for Pericles (d. 429), the leader of Athens in his own day, he too, on his mother's side, was of Alcmaeonid blood, and Herodotus, in a single passage, displays sympathy with him and echoes one of his phrases.[22] Whether he was a whole-hearted admirer of Pericles we cannot say. But he was certainly alive to the glamour and glory of Athens. For one of his main basic themes is the frequently expressed contrast between the irrational despotism of the Persians and the rational freedom of the Greeks, which alone allowed the individual and the community to attain full spiritual development:[23] and the best example of that freedom seemed to him the democratic government of Athens.

When Herodotus made Persian plotters debate the best form of government (p. 41), he was probably not the very first to discuss this theme. For Hippodamus of Miletus, who was with him at Thurii, had also dealt with such matters.[24] Moreover, a surviving work by someone else, a rather rough, sarcastic *Constitution of Athens*, written by an anti-democratic author whom we know as the 'Old Oligarch', has now been dated to *c.* 443 instead of *c.* 428–425 (p. 112). Herodotus joins these writers in pointing the way to many a future Greek analysis of the rival merits of constitutions. In the

44

Persian discussion, which is a blend of traditional ideas and a more novel philosophical approach, a monarchist has to be made to win, because monarchy was the form of government which, in fact, continued to prevail among the Persians. But democracy gets the better of the argument. Herodotus knew that history was a pendulum perpetually alternating between authority and liberty, and he chose the latter. He saw its finest manifestation in the Athenian system, of which the principal elements had been established by Cleisthenes at the end of the sixth century. It was not for nothing that the ancients said 'the Athenians' where we would say 'Athens'.

However, he was by no means blind to the faults of democracy, as is shown by his remark that it is easier to deceive a multitude than one man.[25] He agreed, therefore, with the type of Athenian aristocrat who accepted democracy so long as it did not go too far. This was also the view of contemporary dramatists, Sophocles and Aristophanes. Aeschylus, too, had already offered commentaries on various aspects of the same theme. His *Persae* (472 BC) foreshadowed Herodotus' contrast between oriental despotism and Greek freedom. The *Oresteia* trilogy (*Agamemnon, Libation Bearers, Eumenides*; 458), culminating in the emphasis on a just régime over which it is the duty of a state to preside, had praised the enlightened workings of democracy. And the *Prometheus Bound* dwelt disturbingly on the brutalities of autocratic governments. The date of play is uncertain, but was the tragedian warning the Athenians that even in a new and vigorous democratic system relapses were still possible and must be guarded against?

For in the long period of guidance by Pericles, Athens, although democratically governed, had become a strongly guided democracy. Herodotus was prepared to put up with this arrangement and indeed to admire it, provided there was no infringement of the rule of law over free individuals. And yet, already when he was writing, there was a somewhat old-fashioned air about his identification of law with freedom. For 'law' was no longer regarded as such a simple concept. He himself recognised the regional variability of customs, and the modernist thinking of Athenian sophists had gone a good way further in its emphasis on the relative, subjective nature of legal codes (p. 39).

Old-fashioned, too, was Herodotus' straightforward contrast between Greek freedom and Persian despotism. The contrast was

45

not, it is true, very old. As Herodotus himself reports (using the word 'democracy' for the first time), the Persian Mardonius had himself chosen to give Greek cities puppet administrations of this very sort in 492. However, the antithesis between the Hellenic and Persian spirit had become established during the Persian Wars and is enshrined in Aeschylus' *Persae*. But by 425 the generation which heard Aristophanes making mild fun of Herodotus' remarks on the origins of the east–west struggle no longer thought of Persia in quite the same hostile way. Indeed the country had ceased to be in the forefront of their thought, because they had been plunged for the past six years in the Peloponnesian War between Greek and Greek. That is why Herodotus felt it so imperatively necessary to evoke those events of half a century earlier in which the Greeks had been united together in freedom's cause.

When he admitted the likelihood that his pro-Athenian attitude about those events would be unpopular, he was expressing awareness that times had changed since the Persian Wars because of the brutal imperialism and power-politics of Athens in recent years. In 446 Pindar had written:

> Force trips up at last
> Even the loud boaster.
> Cilician Typhos with a hundred heads did not escape her,
> No, nor the Giants' king.
> They went down before
> The thunderbolt and the arrows of Apollo.[26]

This was meant as a warning to Athens, the enemy of his native Boeotia.

Herodotus, on the other hand, even if he allowed himself an oblique reference to Athenian luxury (p. 37), steered clear of condemnations. He preferred to dwell instead on the glorious past. His attitude to the role of the Spartans in the Persian War is not unfavourable; for his home-town Halicarnassus was still predominantly Dorian, and Herodotus respected Sparta as the leading Dorian city. Consequently, King Demaratus is made to tell Xerxes that the Spartans, fighting together, are the best soldiers in the world, and that they too, like the Athenians, obey the rule of law.[27] The historian admired their political stability and rich land,[28] and by giving credit to Sparta as well as Athens for the victories over

Persia he reflected the pro-Spartan views of many Athenian nobles.

And yet on a further scrutiny he does not seem quite to do justice to Sparta after all. For, in fact, the Spartans had been the leaders of Greece in the Persian Wars, and Athens a member of their confederacy; retrospective Athenian claims to a hegemony at that time were a myth. Again, he stresses how right the Athenians were, and how wrong the Spartans, in their strategy that led up to the successful battle of Salamis. And on such occasions he treats the Spartans with an irony which, at times, tends to conceal their gallantry in the war.

These attitudes echo contemporary events. Herodotus could not fail to rally to his beloved Athens at a time when, from 431 onwards, Spartan armies were ravaging Attica every year (p. 71). Indeed the fact that he even achieved the measure of impartiality that he did argues almost miraculous objectivity. And already during the formative stages of his work he must have been deeply affected by a preliminary outbreak of hostilities between Athens and Sparta (457–451), which is sometimes known as the First Peloponnesian War.

But the influence of Athens upon Herodotus went much deeper than this. Ionian enlightenment had not yet fully made its appearance in the city. The great Athenian tragedies were preoccupied less with the democratic movement than with the whole divine background of cause and effect. And so was the historian. The tragic poets enunciated the view that prosperous men were bound to arouse the jealousy of the gods, who would bring them down in the end. Aeschylus in his *Agamemnon* declares the penalties of success:

> For Ruin is revealed the child
> Of not to be attempted actions,
> When men are puffed up unduly
> And their houses are stuffed with riches.
> Measure is the best. Let danger be distant:
> This should suffice a man
> With a proper part of wisdom.[29]

This view that all happiness and well-being are insecure forms a very large part of the philosophy of Herodotus as well. Artabanus is made to say as much to his master, King Xerxes:

> You know, my lord, that amongst living creatures it
> is the great ones that God smites with this thunder,

47

out of envy of their pride. The little ones do not
vex him. It is always the great buildings and the
tall trees which are struck by lightning. It is God's
way to bring the lofty low.[30]

And most conspicuous of all is the overthrow of King Croesus of
Lydia, even though he has served the gods with meticulous devotion.
He declares to his Persian conqueror, Cyrus: 'If you recognise the
fact that both you and the troops under your command are merely
human, then the first thing I would tell you is that human life is
like a revolving wheel and never allows the same man to continue
long in prosperity.'[31] For to the Greeks, as to the Jews and
Dostoievsky's Alyosha Karamazov, pride brought hideous delusion
or *ate*. Aeschylus sees this as a personal fiend in a world full of
demons, under an angry, Homeric, authoritarian Zeus of arbitrary
caprices, like the whims of 'archaic Greek nobles'. And so Herodotus, too, regards anything that threatens the norms as liable
to incur the ill-will of the gods. Only once, in relation to Croesus,
does he describe it as Nemesis. Elsewhere it is Jealousy. This was a
special characteristic of the divinity – though it was interpretable
also, when he was feeling more Ionian and scientific, as the restoration of a physical balance, reminiscent of Heraclitus' identification
of justice with strife (*c.* 500). For one of the leading ideas of Herodotus
is this compensation and balance in mortal actions and destinies. As
certain philosophers were saying, there is a cycle in the affairs of
men (p. 416), and well-being never stays in one place.[32] For retribution intervenes. Psychologists have called this the Polycrates Complex, after the king of Samos (*c.* 540–522) whose excessive power
Herodotus showed to be the cause of his ruin. We, too, are subject
to this complex when we note that there is good weather, and say,
'We shall have to pay for this'.

Herodotus allows his characters to be actuated by personal
motives; but they get carried away to disaster by *ate*. Though
human purposes seem to be directing events, the penetrating eye
can see Jealousy working secretly beneath. There is no consistent
divine plan at work, but suffering finds an occasion to seize upon a
man.[33] The way the gods choose to inflict suffering is amoral or
even downright immoral; it is evil, and evil is what comes of it.
This was a doctrine of the early poets which worried Aeschylus in his
Prometheus Bound, and shocked Plato in the following century. But

Herodotus did not see things in quite this way, because he noted that, however blind the stroke, at least it restored the balance. To him, as Forrest remarks, 'jealousy is the force that maintains justice; a god who is "fond of disturbing our lot" will hardly worry a man who takes it for granted that disturbance is part of the natural order of things'.

Alongside this attitude, at the time of Herodotus, there was a second point of view maintaining that what arouses divine jealousy is not so much prosperity as sin. This ethical approach was more recent; a product of the transition from Shame Culture to Guilt Culture. The Zeus of 'God's in his heaven, all's wrong with the world' had been transformed into an agent of morality. Indications of such an attitude had occurred in the Homeric poems, but they had been rare.[34] Thereafter, however, it was this view that tended to prevail. In the words of Solon, writing early in the sixth century B C,

> Zeus forever is watching the end, and
>   strikes of a sudden. . . .
> He does not, like a mortal, fall in a rage
>   over each particular thing. And yet
> it never escapes him all the way when a man has a
>   sinful spirit; and always, in the end,
> his judgment is plain.[35]

In the tragedies the theme is all-pervasive.

> The mortal who sacks fallen cities is a fool;
> Who gives the temples and the tombs, the hallowed places
> Of the dead to desolation. His own turn will come.[36]

Yet this doctrine that sin is what causes the overthrow of men is closely linked with the other belief that prosperity by itself is fatal, for the simple reason that the lofty are very easily led to commit wickedness. Success causes arrogance (*hubris*), and this, as Heraclitus warned, 'is more to be extinguished than a conflagration',[37] because it is bound to be followed by disaster. That is the spirit in which Aeschylus speaks of

> Those high hearts that drive to evil
> houses blossoming to pride and peril.[38]

Herodotus, too, emphasises this direct connection between prosperity and sin when he makes Themistocles say that 'the gods and heroes

49

were jealous that one man should be king at once of Europe and Asia – *more especially a man like this, unholy and presumptuous*'.[39]

He is speaking of Xerxes, who seemed to him the classic case of *hubris*. He had appeared in the same light to Aeschylus,[40] who told of the king's reversal of the elements, when he turned sea into land by a bridge which impiously cast the Hellespont into chains. Aeschylus had created the Persian legend in this mould, and anyone wishing to please the Athenians must now conform to it. Herodotus evidently felt a special sympathy with Aeschylus, who had actually taken part in these great events, fighting at Marathon and Salamis. And so the historian, too, emphasises the barbarity and presumption of Xerxes, who ordered the strait to be whipped and rebuked.[41] To him, then, as to Aeschylus, the downfall that followed was due not merely to grandeur but to wickedness. The ferocious autocracy of Xerxes is continually stressed, and so is his power of life and death, and a peculiarly horrible tale is told of the fate which befell a woman who attracted his roving eye.[42]

Croesus, too, did not fall entirely because of his success and the rhythmical rise and fall of human fortunes. For, although devout, he was also proud, considering himself the most fortunate of men. He did not listen to warnings; and he exacted tribute from the Greeks and then failed to defend them. Herodotus repeatedly asserts that wrong behaviour brings retribution, 'in which the hand of heaven is most plainly manifest'; and the worse the behaviour the graver the penalty.[43] The idea that evil falls arbitrarily is abandoned, at least to the extent that no unjust man shall fail to pay the penalty.[44] Perhaps he would not always have to do so in his own person, for there is such a thing as inherited guilt, which likewise pervades the tragedies of Aeschylus.[45] The unfairness was recognised, but such a sanction was effective at a time when family solidarity was strong. Thus Herodotus sees yet another cause of Croesus' downfall in the action of his ancestor Gyges, who had murdered his own predecessor and incurred punishment from Apollo.

He was in sympathy, then, with the attitudes of Aeschylus. But he was also a personal friend of Sophocles, whose *Antigone* (441 BC) pays him the compliment of a direct echo showing that the dramatist had heard one of his famous recitals.[46] We also have a considerable fragment of an ode which Sophocles wrote in honour of the historian, perhaps when the latter was leaving for Thurii. Sophocles, while interested in up-to-date sophistic attitudes and arguments – more interested than Herodotus – was also the last great exponent of the old view of human beings helpless before vindictive heaven. His *Women of Trachis* is a play which contains much magic, and there are many archaic features in the *Ajax* and *Antigone* as well. The attitudes revealed in these works show numerous correspondences with Herodotus. Ths historian does not emphasise the ordeal of suffering like Sophocles, but he resembles him closely in his employment of dramatic irony, the *double entenore* by which a character uses words to mean one thing to himself and another to the reader. Both writers persistently use this method to explain apparent failures of oracles which are nevertheless fulfilled, and men's vain planning to elude them. There are also various other analogies, for example between Herodotus' account of Darius' Scythian expedition and the *Philoctetes* of Sophocles. Like Neoptolemus, who was the hero of that play, Darius comes through after enduring the gravest peril.

The Lydian section of Herodotus' work demonstrates the same dramatic Athenian influences even more clearly. Not only is the whole downfall of Croesus a conception involving the tragic modes of thought, but it also exhibits, in a typical fashion, the dramatic reversal (*peripeteia*) of tragedy. Moreover, the same reversal is found again in smaller Lydian plots within a plot, such as the death of Croesus' son Atys. Herodotus' tale of the capture of Sardis,[47] too, is told in terms that must have been strongly reminiscent of a sensational play (now lost), *The Capture of Miletus*, which was produced in 494 BC by the tragic dramatist Phrynichus and caused such distress among the audience that it was banned and the playwright fined.

But, above all, the saga of Gyges, the forbear of Croesus, provides explicit evidence of Herodotus' links with Athenian tragedy, because fragments have now been found of a play actually telling the same stories and telling them in the same way.[48] Although a third-century BC date has been proposed for this work, it could also be contemporary with Herodotus and Aeschylus, in which case the historian and the unidentified tragic poet were drawing on a common source – or one may even have been drawing on the other. The analogy between the new history and the Athenian drama could not be clearer. Their subject-matter, over a wide range, was the same. Ancient writers compared their purposes, too, declaring that both aimed at stirring the emotions and both offered consolations and deterrents. That is why Aristotle called Herodotus a *mythologos*, a teller or weaver of plots, dramatically setting acts or incidents in relation to one another. Dramatic, again, are many of his literary devices: the care with which a digression about Athens is balanced against one about Sparta; the virtual abandonment of digressions, towards the end, in favour of direct narrative, just as the choral odes of plays are followed by a rapid sequence of tightly packed events; even the flow of Herodotean prose often falls for a time into the very rhythms of tragic poetry.

The spiritual life of Athens during Herodotus' formative years 460–400 BC is largely unknown to us. Yet it is clear enough that the religious attitudes which the tragedians had inherited and adopted from the past were gradually being overlaid by Ionian scientific ideas. The phenomenon is already visible in Aeschylus: and Herodotus follows him in attributing events to human agencies *as well as* to divine chains of causation. Thus Croesus fell not because of the wrath of the gods alone but also partly because his foreign policy failed. Xerxes, too, was not only driven to war by a dream sent by heaven: he was also prompted by the human motive of ambition, just as he was later misled at Salamis both by the jealousy of the gods and by a cunning Greek who deceived him. And so modern, rational explanations of cause and effect – explanations, moreover, in which immediate and permanent causes are carefully distinguished – blend into the divine pattern.[49] This had also, no doubt, been the procedure of Hecataeus. To us it looks like a rather disconcerting oscillation, inviting us, in effect, to look at each case on its merits and judge whether its motivation is natural or supernatural. But 'the Greeks', as P.A. Brunt observed, 'did not make the sharp distinction between the divine and the human which we have derived from Jewish thought'.

And so Herodotus neither accepts nor denies the Athenian belief that a great snake lived on the Acropolis. 'They present a honeycake every month as to a creature existing.' Again, writing of madness, he believes that there are both natural and heaven-inspired forms of these disturbances. Narratives of divine management are customarily given at second hand, or as antecedents rather than causes. Sometimes the conclusion tentatively comes down on the side of scepticism. 'The Chaldaeans say – though I do not believe them – that the god

Bel enters his shrine at Babylon in person and takes his rest upon the bed.'[50] A discussion of a geographical feature displays a similar suspension of belief.

> The natives of Thessaly have a tradition that the gorge which forms the outlet for the river Peneus was made by Poseidon. And the story is a reasonable one; for if one believes that it is Poseidon who shakes the earth and that chasms caused by earthquake are attributed to him, then the mere sight of this place would be enough to make one say that it is Poseidon's handiwork. It certainly appeared to me that the cleft in the mountains had been caused by an earthquake.[51]

And so this question, allegedly involving the supernatural, is handled with deliberate delicacy. For Herodotus, evidently aware of the incompatibility of the two attitudes, regards the whole subject as inflammable, and considers it best evaded whenever possible.

> Such animals as there are in Egypt – both wild and tame – are without exception held to be sacred. To explain the reason for this, I should have to enter into a discussion of religious principles, which is a subject I particularly wish to avoid – any slight mention I have already made of such matters having been forced upon me by the needs of my story.[52]

This attitude of caution is prompted by the feeling that such deviations into rationalism as he may permit himself could be interpreted as blasphemy – the offence for which the philosopher Anaxagoras was indicted at Athens, either in *c.* 450 or in *c.* 430.

> If Heracles was a mere man (as they say he was) and single-handed, how is it conceivable that he should have killed tens of thousands of people?
> And now I hope that both gods and heroes will forgive me for saying what I have said on these matters.[53]

And yet Herodotus, for all his tentative straying into rationalisation, remains a thoroughgoing believer in divine intervention. 'Many things prove to me', he says, 'that the gods take part in the affairs of man.' It was a special providence, for example, that caused the winds to blow the Samian explorer Colaeus all the way from the eastern Mediterranean to the Strait of Gibraltar and beyond. Again, various reasons were alleged for the death of the Spartan king Cleomenes I. But Herodotus accepts the version that it was a judgment upon him for doing wrong.[54]

In the last three books of the Histories, perhaps under the influence of Athens and its tragedians, the divine direction of affairs becomes strongly accentuated. After the battle of Plataea we are told that not a single Persian soldier was found dead in the holy precinct of Demeter. 'My own view is – if one may have a view at all about these Mysteries – that the Goddess herself would not let them in, because they had burnt her sanctuary at Eleusis.' Herodotus' diffidence about speaking of the Mysteries, that characteristic institution of archaic Greek religion, recalls that he himself had been initiated into secret sites of the same sort that were practised on the island of Samothrace.[55] In Egypt, too, he had received teaching of a comparable mystic character.

When the approach of the Persians to Delphi was heralded by alleged miracles, Herodotus found these less surprising than the natural accidents (falls of rock, thunderbolts) that also befell them on the way.[56] But this shows a degree of credulity that was unusual in him, representing a mark of deference towards the exceptional sanctity of the Delphic shrine, about which he never shows any scepticism whatever.[57] Elsewhere, on the other hand, dealing with other matters, he generally draws the line at the physically impossible, and does not claim it for the gods. About alleged *signs* from heaven, however, as opposed to actual miracles, he is far more credulous. Indeed, this is the most conspicuous element in the whole of his religion. His older relative, the poet Panyassis, had been an expert on the subject, and Herodotus believed most firmly that forthcoming events can be foretold by divine indications. There is nearly always, he says, a warning sign of some kind, when disaster is about to overtake a city or a nation.

This might take the form of a portent, or a dream.[58] But above all he believed in oracles; and that was why Delphi – though strongly suspected of a feeble surrender to the Persians – is treated with so much reverence. If he had not done more than to point out that oracles were history because they influenced people's conduct, he would have been right. But he also expressed himself strongly against incredulous attitudes towards divine warnings. After a seer, typical of an outgoing age of ecstatic religion, had supposedly prophesied the sea-battle at Salamis, he declared: 'With that utterance of Bacis in mind, absolutely clear as it is, I do not venture to say anything against prophecies, nor will I listen to criticism from others.'[59]

Oracles were a vital part of his conception of the world. He knew of existing collections of such pronouncements, and he quoted examples with great care. But he felt they could very easily be perverted.[60] Above all, they frequently *seemed* wrong – seemed to have failed. But that was because they had been misinterpreted; and then they came true after all. This theme gave Herodotus some of his best stories, and many opportunities to display dramatic irony in the manner of Sophocles, who makes this the theme of two of his plays, *The Women of Trachis* and *Oedipus the King*. And Sophoclean, again, is the ironic contrast between the ineluctable fulfilment of oracles and the useless scheming of people like Croesus to escape them.

In view of Herodotus' special devotion to oracles, the god whose name figures most prominently in his writings is Apollo, the patron of these manifestations. Yet the historian has risen somewhat beyond the Homeric belief in individual members of a Hellenic pantheon. To us it is a little tedious to read careful identifications, which have no historical basis, between this or that Greek and Egyptian deity. But a remark that no nation knows more about religion that any other[61] suggests that Herodotus pursued this line because he had a more advanced conception in mind. He believed, that is to say, in a heavenly power that is common to all humanity. And, like the Ionian scientist Anaximander before him, he describes such a power by a neuter adjective 'the divine' (*to theion*), without any personal differentiation. When this agency spoke in oracles, it was convenient to departmentalise its activity by the bestowal of a name. Yet what keeps the balance in the universe and the world is deity undefined.

The relation of this divinity and of human beings towards fate was a subject which engrossed contemporary tragedians, as it had also engaged the earlier poets who stressed the mighty, almost malevolent inscrutability of destiny. The problem exercised Herodotus, whose treatment of his theme illustrates the profound conviction that the course of events is ruled by fateful means. Men are doomed to meet their ends, and their disastrous decisions are predetermined.[62] Apollo may want to help Croesus, but he cannot do so except in minor respects, because, like the gods in Homer, he is unable to divert the destined course of events. The role of fate is in one passage of Herodotus played by Zeus, who repels a plea by Athena.

Sometimes men have a tragic foreknowledge of their future destiny. And yet all Herodotus' stories imply at least the illusion of free will, and much free will, too, that is not illusory but authentic. For it had now become clear that a historian's very subjects, the actions of men in communities, presuppose that human decisions have some power. But they are hampered by fate. What is more, they are hampered by accident, since Herodotus, like the tragedians, was very conscious that this is another factor which widens and deepens the gap between real and ideal. Accordingly, at the beginnings of his threads of causation, there is often an unresolved, irrational strand.[63] Greek nouns such as Chance (*Tyche*) can mean anything between an abstraction and a goddess receiving worship. Chance had appeared in Greek literature as early as the post-Homeric epics, and had gradually taken shape until it was represented and portrayed by sixth-century sculptors. It was also occasionally personified in tragedy.[64] Later Greeks would elevate it to a major deity, but its role in Herodotus, though vital, is not as great as that. The operations of Chance may be neutral, or catastrophic, or favourable. Its insertion into a story was a way of saying that some links in the course of events are not known. A complete understanding of causation is not claimed, and there is still room for the unique and decisive accident – a factor that is under-estimated by many modern historians.

3

The Methods of Herodotus

SUCH, then, was the background against which Herodotus told his story. The interaction of human and divine motives which he saw at work left him with a powerful conviction of the difference between right and wrong. His desire to instruct was, it is true, less urgent and pervasive than that of many successors. Yet it was he who initiated among the Greeks the moral and didactic view of events which was already so familiar in Hebrew literature, and which later persisted, often to an exaggerated extent, among almost all subsequent ancient historians.

Universal truth seemed to him only discoverable through this or that human being. It is true that he often attributed to them what he regarded as the typical motives of their type and class. All the same, he was convinced that the individual is the driving-force of history. He is up to date enough to talk about the fashionable subject of city constitutions, but the actions of persons are represented as much more important. Indeed, his stories about men such as Cyrus and Cambyses and Themistocles and a hundred others foreshadow the art of historical biography. It is foreshadowed, again, by his preference for private rather than public motives. Even when public affairs are discussed, political causes are not clearly defined, and personal motives still predominate. Granted that he does not take too seriously his mythical account of the origins of the Persian Wars, in which everything is seen to go back to personal wrongs concerned with women, Persian expansion is very much equated with the anger of Darius and Xerxes.

The Greeks were not greatly interested in the hidden conflicts of the human mind. Nevertheless, Herodotus, like the philosopher Democritus who was his younger contemporary, believes that the will matters as much as the execution.[1] The historian likes to explain both will and execution by recording what the doer said, or might have said, or would reasonably say, in order to justify his action. By these and many other means a few words are made to conjure up, with superb skill, a vast range of human portraits, Greek and Asiatic and Egyptian alike. Great men receive correspondingly great attention. But rather than blame Herodotus for what Nietzsche and Carlyle made a perilous approach, we should recall that in the ancient world decisive happenings were engineered by a minute proportion of the population, so that these potent personages deserved to receive very close attention.

This preoccupation with great men, a preoccupation tinged with strongly ethical ideas of man's destiny, gave depth to Herodotus' conviction that the Persians, represented by such dramatic and terrible figures as Darius and Xerxes, were wrong, and the Greeks were right. We are left in no doubt that the east–west struggle, which had been suggested by Homer and was to be crystallised by Virgil, is part of a divinely ordered plan. Unlike Homer, Herodotus underlines for the first time the utter difference in outlook between Greeks and non-Greeks or 'barbarians'. The contrast continually emerges, not only in the opposition between autocracy and democracy, but in profound differences of customs.[2] This theme, as J.B. Bury remarked, gives the work's external structure a deeper inner unity. It also had ominous repercussions on later peoples, who have erected such distinctions into chauvinisms and colour bars.

But it would be wrong to impute anything of the kind to Herodotus. It is true that, having been born inside the Persian Empire, his knowledge of foreigners had sharpened his Hellenic patriotism. Yet he based this concept, by a significant advance, on customs as well as blood.[3] It is also true that his decisive years 460–440 were a time in which the Greco-Persian clash was still on and had not become out of date: an Athenian fleet even attacked Persian-controlled Egypt, launching an invasion which lasted for five years (p. 71). However, Herodotus himself adopted an extraordinarily tolerant attitude towards the Persians. Their virtues are not allowed to disguise their faults;[4] but he specifically praises some of their customs, for example the habit of keeping their children with women until they are five years of age, and the rule that forbids even the king to condemn anyone to death for a single offence.[5] He had claimed it was one of his principal tasks to describe the achievements of eastern non-Greeks (p. 27), and the promise is amply fulfilled by a magnificent series of portraits of great Persians. All this was too advanced for many Greeks, with their local patriotisms, and more than five hundred years later Plutarch (who had other and more parochial reasons for his dislike) still saw him as *philobarbaros*, a pro-barbarian or lover of wogs.

Such tolerance was part of a widely ranging, cheerful broadmindedness. The object of all travelling was to learn,[6] and it was this spirit of enquiry, revealed in a hundred passages, which gave 'history' its modern meaning. It meant that parochial prejudices were impossible. The insertion of speeches is only one of a hundred devices employed to bring out viewpoints transcending purely regional considerations. And so the first comprehensive historical work ever produced was also a cultural history, a story of civilisation.

Herodotus' interest and curiosity were combined with an inexhaustible flair for good stories. Today we have few historical authors who rely so much on narrative, but in the right hands the method cannot be bettered. Herodotus is the most amusing of all historians; only Gibbon comes anywhere near him. A characteristic anecdote occurs when King Cleisthenes of Sicyon invites his daughter's suitors to dinner.

When dinner was over, the suitors began to compete with each other in music and in talking on a set theme to the assembled company. In both these accomplishments it was Hippocleides who proved by far the doughtiest champion, until at last, as more and more wine was drunk, he asked the flute-player to play him a tune and began to dance to it. Now it may well be that he danced to his own satisfaction; King Cleisthenes, however, who was watching the performance, began to have serious doubts about the whole business. Presently, after a brief pause,

Hippocleides sent for a table; the table was brought; and Hippocleides, climbing on to it, danced first some Laconian dances, next some Attic ones, and ended by standing on his head and beating time with his legs in the air.

The Laconian and Attic dances were bad enough; but Cleisthenes, though he already loathed the thought of having a son-in-law who could behave so disgracefully in public, nevertheless restrained himself and managed to avoid an outburst. However, when he saw Hippocleides beating time with his legs, he could bear it no longer. 'Son of Tisander,' he cried, 'you have danced away your wife!' 'I could hardly care less', was the cheerful reply.[7]

Whatever Herodotus may have done for the word *historie*, this is not history in the modern sense, because it is myth. The story has in fact been traced back to an Indian tale with a peacock as its hero. Such stories have a splendid good-humoured flippancy that owes some- thing to epic. But, most of all, it comes from Herodotus himself, and however careful he might be about religion it made Plutarch regard him as impious and immoral.[8]

But the technique is as valid for history as for myth, and it provides a unique succession of pictures of historical or quasi-historical events and episodes in a modernised Homeric manner. These pictures, which are the core of Herodotus' work, may be long and complex,[9] or they may be short and vivid.[10] Sometimes they are noble, some- times grotesque or tragic or horrible or murderous, and often, even in gloomy circumstances, they are funny. When, for example, the Greeks in Macedonia and Thrace complained how expensive it was to have to entertain Xerxes' army, 'a man of Abdera called Mega- creon spoke to the point when he advised all the people of the town to take their wives to the temples and pray heaven to continue to spare them one half of their troubles, with proper gratitude for the blessing already received, that King Xerxes was not in the habit of taking *two* dinners a day'.[11]

This taste for spicy points and tales provides a mass of piquant information about foreign parts. It is impossible for a reader or listener not to be intrigued by this tit-bit about the health service at Babylon: 'The Babylonians have no doctors, but bring their invalids out into the street, where anyone who comes along offers the sufferer advice on his complaint, either from personal experience or observation of a similar complaint in others. Anyone will stop by the sick man's side and suggest remedies. . . . Nobody is allowed to pass a sick person in silence.'[12] Herodotus remarks what a good system this is. And the Arabian method of collecting a spice likewise appeals to his sense of the ridiculous. 'Still more surprising is the way of getting ledanon – or ladanum as the Arabians call it. Sweet-smelling substance though it is, it is found in a most malodorous place: sticking, that is to say, like glue in the beards of he-goats who have been browsing among the bushes.'[13] Paradox, again, is what fascinates him about the Atarantes in the interior of Africa; people who deviated interestingly from two universal customs – the possession of personal names, and the worship of the sun. 'The Atarantes are the only people in the world, so far as our knowledge goes, to do without names. Atarantes is the collective name – but individually they have none. They curse the sun as it rises and call it by all sorts of opprobrious names, because it wastes and burns both themselves and their land.'[14] And then there are the Lydians, whose 'way of life, apart from the fact that they prostitute their daughters, is not unlike our own'. We are also invited, not altogether seriously, to believe a tall story about their inventive capacity, displayed at a time when the whole of the country was suffering from a severe famine.

They began to look for something to alleviate their misery. Various expedients were devised: for instance, the invention of dice, knuckle-bones, and ball-games. In fact, they claim to have invented all games of this sort except draughts. The way they used these inventions to help them endure their hunger was to eat and play on alternative days – one day playing so continuously that they had no time to think of food, and eating on the next without playing at all. They managed to live like this for eighteen years.[15]

Herodotus listened to such stories in an immense number of different places. The range of his travels, extending from Scythia and Persia to south Italy, is undeterminable in detail, but it cannot have been equalled for centuries to come. Probably he travelled as a trader or with traders; this makes him interested in ships and navigable waters, commercial goods and industries, the interpreting of foreign languages, the weights and measures of various lands. His determination to get at the truth is beyond all praise. Interested in an Egyptian god he identified with Heracles, 'to satisfy my wish to get the best information I possibly could on the subject, I made a visit to

Tyre in Phoenicia, because I heard that there was a temple there, of great sanctity, dedicated to him. I also saw another temple there, dedicated to the Thasian Heracles; so I went on to Thasos. . . .'[16] Two thousand miles, remarks Forrest, on a point of comparative religion! This was one of the many subjects which stimulated Herodotus' spirit of enquiry; and, even if his identifications between the gods of different nations were facile, he did notice real parallels between Greek and oriental religious customs.

He also knew, even better than Hecataeus, that human habits form an essential part of both geography and history. He was the pioneer not only of history but of anthropology and enthnology. His description of the Argippaei of Scythia is a model specimen of field observation which brings race, language, institutions, appearance and diet into play.[17] No sort of curious fact is beneath his attention.[18] He is as interested in geology and agriculture and methods of fighting as he is careful to note physique and dress. And, although breed counts for a lot, he knows that custom does too. Each people has customs of its own, but even they are by no means immutable.[19]

Why does the Nile flood? Why were the Dodona priestesses called doves? That is the sort of question Herodotus asks. And if we want to know how the pyramids were built, why no wine jars are found in Egypt, why Persians have thin skulls and Egyptians thick ones, why Scythians climb trees to wait for the animals they are hunting, he will tell us. And the view that all these tales can be dismissed as pure romance is now out of date. Indeed, it is clear that he actually erred on the side of over-scepticism in doubting land crossings of the Sahara, and questioning circumnavigations of Africa when 'the sun is on the right hand'.[20] His description of the embalming of corpses by the Scythians has been dramatically confirmed by the discovery of royal tombs in the Kuban. His ants 'smaller than dogs but larger than foxes' seem to be marmots on the Tibetan border. His Amazons were some Asiatic people or other which possessed matriarchal customs. His 'river beyond the Sahara' was the middle Niger, filled with crocodiles that are vividly if inaccurately described. His long account of Egypt, though occasionally mythical, displays at many points the results of an acute and conscientious survey.

His sources for all this material were very mixed – personal observation, oral hearsay and tradition, literary sources and documents. Of his personal observation it need only be repeated that this was the man who crossed the entire eastern Mediterranean to check a single fact. Yet he is characteristically modest about everything he was able to see. When enquiring into the sources of the Nile, he emphasises not so much that he journeyed nearly six hundred miles south of the Mediterranean, but that what happened farther on still is unknown to him except at secondhand. 'On this subject I could get no further information from anybody. I went as far as Elephantine to see what I could with my own eyes, but for the country still further south I had to be content with what I was told in answer to my questions.'[21] The conditions facing a traveller of the fifth century BC presented such almost inconceivable difficulties that the extent of Herodotus' journeyings and personal observations can scarcely be comprehended or credited. It is true that oral traditions were more extensive than we can easily appreciate since they continued to be handed down on a large scale even after writing had been introduced. Yet they were also incomplete, untrustworthy and contradictory. Herodotus cites verbal reports from forty Greek states and almost as many foreign countries. If he did not visit all these places himself, at least he deliberately questioned people from every one of them. It is hard to see how he managed to tackle this mass of oral material. We can only admire the stupendous achievement, and tentatively identify an occasional informant.[22]

Oral evidence was paramount, and it was best if it came from eyewitnesses; and the principle that their reports are the best substitute for personal observation remained a cardinal doctrine of historians. Literary sources were less important. They were not, probably, quite so sparse as our deficient knowledge leads us to suppose. Yet they were still extraordinarily meagre. 'The slender current of history', said F.M. Cornford, 'flashed only here and there a broken gleam through the tangled overgrowth of legend and gorgeous flowers of poetry'. Moreover, the consultation of any books at all, poetry or history, involved the most laborious unwindings and rewindings (p. 31). But eastern inscriptional records, archives and official chronicles and land surveys, are explicitly or implicitly referred to on a number of occasions.[23] It is because of all this material that the oriental sections of Herodotus' work are the richest in biography. These documents, in whatever form they became accessible to him, were also of assistance in helping to solve the appalling task of achieving a relative chronology,[24] the job which Hecataeus had begun to tackle. But they were only of limited use to a writer whose whole work was the very denial of the official history which was all that the Mesopotamian and Persian civilisations had provided. And not much of this archive material related to Greece, where history was still mainly transmitted by word of mouth.

In the light of this situation Herodotus' choice of the Persian Wars as his theme was exceptionally audacious. Hard facts about the subject were desperately few. A whole generation had passed; his problem has been compared, fairly enough, with that of a modern journalist chasing an unpublished story thirty years old. Never has any practitioner of history had a more difficult task than its father.

It is therefore scarcely surprising that Herodotus' accounts of battles scarcely enable the reader to reconstruct what really happened. Apart perhaps from a little street fighting in Halicarnassus, he had no personal experience of warfare, and he is demonstrably far astray on strategies and numbers. The strength of Xerxes' army, for instance, is magnified as much as tenfold. Besides, detailed technical descriptions of battles were unsuitable for oral delivery. But he does show us what the men in the ranks thought was happening. Besides, granted that his accounts of the engagements are confused, so were the engagements themselves. After discovering what he could about them, he felt like Pierre Bezukhov in Tolstoy's *War and Peace* who found the battle of Borodino no set piece but a haphazard collection of struggling individuals. Yet Tolstoy converted the result into unforgettable pictures; and so did Herodotus.

For his desire to tell a good story came before everything else. This invites further reflection about his critical method. He believes his friends too much, he makes mistakes,[25] he includes a good deal against his better judgment – very often because, in a world where information was scarce, it seemed important that the evidence should be preserved. Divine causation gets in the way, and the story of Hippocleides is only one among many myths scattered throughout his work,[26] following classical patterns of epic, tragedy, folklore and romance. Yet, even if he did believe, like most of his successors, that the epic sagas are garbled history that only needs to be tidied up, he knows well enough that fifty-century wars were not caused by myths. He is also thoroughly well aware that ancient traditions defy precise assessment.[27] After all, probability is often the best one can achieve (p. 44).

With few exceptions, he refuses to admit the physically impossible (p. 54).[28] And when presented with inadequate information he is fully conscious of its shortcomings. 'About the far west of Europe I have no definite information. . . . In spite of my efforts to do so, I have never found anyone who could give me first hand information about the existence of a sea beyond Europe to the north and west.'[29] Sometimes he has acquired several divergent accounts of an event or series of events. When that is the case, he makes a great effort to reach the truth: 'I could, if I wished, give three versions of Cyrus' history, all different from what follows. But I propose to base my account on those Persian authorities who seem to tell the simple truth about him without trying to exaggerate his exploits.'[30] Although the total dossier remains very sparse, alternative versions mount up in the later books.[31] But Herodotus remains just as careful. At a time when the historical approach had not been formulated, when it was still being formulated by himself, no one can read of his attitude to hearsay evidence without a feeling of exhilaration. No doubt such second-hand material was often the best that could be obtained, and 'My business is to record what people say. But I am by no means bound to believe it – and that may be taken to apply to this book as a whole.'[32] These are the words of good sense that went with a critical eye and ear.[33] There was no line of professional historians for Herodotus to draw upon. Yet his exceptionally intelligent and observant attitude to his material was what created the line of professionals which has continued from his day to ours.

Once this material had been acquired, his arrangement and presentation were very much his own. Employing a style of which the central features are speed and a comfortable expansive directness, he improved upon the writing of his forerunners and made prose into a fine art. The close connection he established between history and poetry stayed with historians throughout the ancient world. Modern historians are likely to find this relationship alien, or indeed incomprehensible. Nevertheless, the Histories of Herodotus are a work of subtle genius, displaying perfect control of the medium its author had selected. Some have seen him as an artist at perfect peace with the world. Others, more accurately, have detected beneath his cheerful humour a certain fundamental pessimism and sadness. He did not survive to endure more than a fraction of the horrors of the Peloponnesian War. But he had lived through troubles enough. Moreover, he still suffered from the anxieties about divine interposition which some other men of his day were beginning to throw off. He was not only an entertainer but a deep and powerful thinker, though like Mozart he does not always get the credit for this. Herodotus ranks with the giants of his century: and, since that was the fifth century BC, there could be no higher praise. He must also have been a very nice man, kind, sympathetic and understanding.

People giving an account of ancient historical writing are faced with a difficult artistic problem. When one reflects upon Herodotus, it is impossible to imagine how anything to follow can fail to be anticlimax. This does not, in fact, prove to be the case. But it was very soon clear that no one could ever excel him in his own sort of history. And so a new sort had to be invented.

2
Thucydides

4

Thucydides and the Peloponnesian War

THUCYDIDES the Athenian (*c.* 460/455–? *c.* 399/8 BC) wrote the history of the Peloponnesian War between Athens and the Spartan alliance. The war continued from 431 until 404, with a break of some years from 421, but Thucydides' work stops in mid-narrative during the winter of 411. It was subsequently divided into separate books, at first thirteen in number and now eight.

He begins by explaining that this was the greatest war which had ever been fought. This conclusion is then demonstrated by an account of the ancient past. Next the writer briefly analyses the causes of the Peloponnesian War. A description is given of the dispute between the maritime power Corinth and its independent settlement or 'colony' Corcyra (Corfu) regarding the control of their joint offshoot Epidamnus (Durazzo, Durres, on the Albanian coast). The Athenians sent a squadron to support Corcyra (433). Corinth and its ally Sparta, who were the rivals of the Athenians on sea and land respectively, next encouraged the Corinthian colony of Potidaea in Macedonia to free itself from Athens, to which it was subject (432). The situation is discussed by a Corinthian deputation visiting Sparta.

Thucydides then gives a sketch of the expansion of Athens during the fifty years that had passed since the Persian Wars. He describes

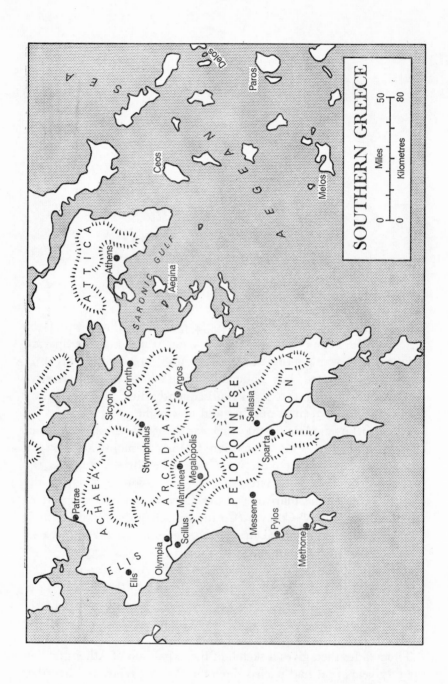

how Athens had founded the Confederacy of Delos, comprising the Greek cities on the Asian and Thracian shores and on most of the Aegean islands. One of these islands was Naxos, which was forcibly brought back to allegiance in *c.* 467. The continuing war with Persia ended at about the same time with Cimon's naval and military success at the River Eurymedon in southern Asia Minor. But Athens, aggressive on several fronts, was checked when it supported an Egyptian revolt against Persia (459–454). The Athenians also fought an inconclusive series of campaigns against Sparta, sometimes known as the First Peloponnesian War (457–451). Then, however, they signed a Five Years' Truce with the Spartans, and this was subsequently converted into a Thirty Years' Treaty (445). Meanwhile the Delian League had been gradually transformed into an Athenian empire, competing with Corinth on the seas. The national leader now was Pericles, who suppressed revolts on the islands of Euboea and Samos (446, 440–439).

Returning to 432, the historian tells how a further debate at Sparta led to the declaration of war between Athens and the Spartan confederation. The second book describes the initial military operations – an attack on Plataea by Thebes, Sparta's ally in central Greece, and the first Spartan invasion of the Attic countryside, the homeland of the Athenians. Pericles' funeral speech for the dead sought to justify the empire of Athens and its whole way of life. But plague then broke out – its ravages are described at length – and Pericles was obliged to speak again (430) in order to defend his policy of relying on maritime superiority and doing nothing to resist the annual Spartan devastations of Attica. On sea, however, the Athenian admiral Phormio won two victories over superior Corinthian naval forces off Naupactus in the Gulf of Corinth.

Book III tells of the unsuccessful revolt of Mytilene (Lesbos) from Athens (428). This was followed by a debate at Athens in which the new Athenian leader, Cleon, argued for ruthless punishment on grounds of imperialistic self-interest, but a political opponent named Diodotus prevailed with somewhat milder counsels. Civil war inside Corcyra gives the opportunity for an analysis of the horrors of this phenomenon that increasingly attacked Greek cities. The fourth book describes an Athenian success at Pylos on the west coast of the Peloponnese (425), counterbalanced by a defeat at Delium in Boeotia and by the victories of the Spartan Brasidas in Thrace.

These successes included the capture of the ship-building centre Amphipolis, as a result of which the historian Thucydides, himself the Athenian general in the area, was deprived of his command and went into exile. Book v records the deaths both of Cleon and Brasidas, and a subsequent treaty between Athens and Sparta, named the Peace of Nicias after one of the principal Athenian leaders of the day (421).

Nicias' young political opponent Alcibiades, however, soon stirred up a fresh anti-Spartan alliance in the Peloponnese. But the Spartans asserted themselves and dissolved the coalition by a victory at Mantinea in Arcadia (418). The small island of Melos refused to pay tribute to Athens (416), and its enslavement is made the occasion for a debate showing Athenian power-politics in their most naked light.

The sixth and seventh books tell the story of the Athenian expedition against Syracuse in Sicily (415–413). Alcibiades, one of the joint commanders, was recalled because of his alleged mutilation of sacred statues (the Hermae), and fled to Sparta. The expedition ended in the annihilation of the invaders by the Syracusans. The final book describes Ionian rebellions against Athenian rule, followed by a *coup d'état* at Athens which abolished democracy in favour of the tyrannical oligarchy of the Four Hundred (411). Alcibiades, recalled from exile after four years of service with the enemy, took charge of the Athenian democrats at Samos. Under the impulse of a Euboean revolt against the rule of Athens, the Four Hundred were replaced by Theramenes' compromise constitution of the Five Thousand, a moderate oligarchy. Athenian naval victories followed, and the work concludes with references to the role of the Persians. They were now proposing to join in the war on the Spartan side, and rebuild the Peloponnesian fleet. These developments, however, and the other events leading up to the total defeat of Athens (404), are not described in the work, which comes to an abrupt end at this point.

There are two very inadequate Lives of Thucydides. The more detailed account is a collection which goes under the name of the sixth-century-AD grammarian Marcellinus. This rather strange combination of biographical sketch and literary criticism, based on sources of various dates, probably started as a university class-lecture. We learn that the historian's father was called Olorus. This was

SOUTHERN ITALY
AND SICILY

0   Miles   100
0   Kilometres   160

Tiber

ADRIATIC

SEA

ROME

SAMNIUM

Capua
Caudine
Forks

CAMPANIA

Cannae

Neapolis

Capreae

CALABRIA

Taras (Tarentum)

Rudiae

TYRRHENIAN

SEA

Sybaris (Thurii)

Crathis

Croton

C. Lacinium

Calacte

Locri Epizephyrii

Agyrium

Tauromenium

SICILY

IONIAN SEA

Leontini

Syracuse

Assinarus

also the name of the grandfather of the statesman Cimon, to whom, therefore, Thucydides was probably related. Cimon, the son of Miltiades the victor of Marathon, was an aristocratic conservative who had been banished (ostracised) in 461 but subsequently arranged the Five Years' Truce with Sparta (p. 71). Although he had perhaps co-operated with his democratic opponent Pericles in arranging the Truce, Cimon the pro-Spartan was opposed to Pericles' imperialistic designs. From Cimon's death in 449 until his banishment in 443–442, the leader of this oligarchic, anti-imperialistic party was Thucydides the son of Melesias. He was related by marriage to Cimon and consequently also, it may be surmised, to Thucydides the son of Olorus – though the latter tells us nothing about such matters, nor about the banishment of the two leaders either.

Olorus was a Thracian name, so that the historian, like Herodotus, may well not have been of pure Greek blood. It was probably from his father (unless it was from his wife) that he obtained a Thracian estate at Scapte Hyle on the mainland opposite the island of Thasos. With this property went the right of working the adjacent gold mines which the Athenians, in the middle of the fifth century, had seized from the non-Greek monarch of Thrace, a large, populous, quasi-feudal and semi-barbarous kingdom of recent creation.

Where Thucydides spent his early life is uncertain, but when the Peloponnesian War came he was in Athens. There he caught the plague,[1] which is the subject of one of his vivid descriptions. In 424 he was given a military command in Macedonia, no doubt owing to his regional connections. His subsequent exile, due to failure to save Amphipolis from Brasidas (p. 72), was presumably by Athenian order rather than his own volition. If Sparta had given Amphipolis back, as was agreed in the Peace of Nicias,[2] he might have been recalled. But the agreement was never carried out, and he only returned to Athens twenty years afterwards, when the Peloponnesian War was over.[3] Where he spent the intervening years we do not know, but he says they enabled him to get better information, since he was in a position to draw on both sides. He shows a knowledge of the end of the war (404), but no awareness of anything later, except that a reference to King Archelaus of Macedonia (d. 399) could be thought to sound an obituary note.[4] Thucydides himself died either at Athens or in Thrace.[5]

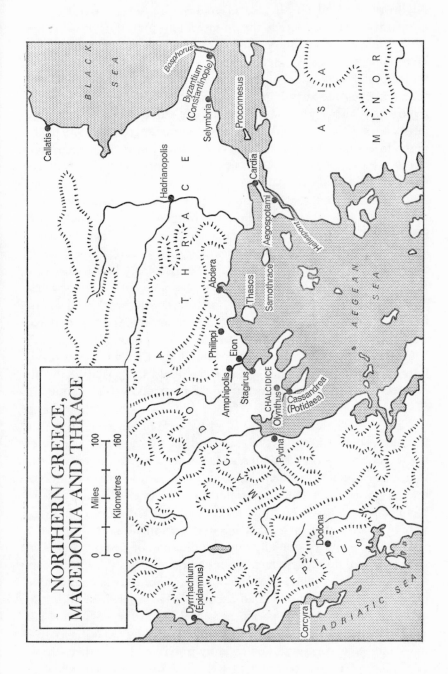

NORTHERN GREECE, MACEDONIA AND THRACE

His work is based on an idea of genius: the idea of writing contemporary history. During the immediately preceding period, the conception of *past* history had been defined and developed by Herodotus, who had written about a war that few people could still remember. Thucydides adapted this approach to his own times, and recorded events as they happened. He wrote of the present in all its nakedness. This had a vast effect on subsequent historians of the Greek and Roman world. Almost all contemporary history composed forever afterwards in the Western world originates from him.

Like Herodotus, he chose a war as his subject, accepting his forerunner's idea that wars are the main events in history. The consequence was that the Peloponnesian War has always been seen through the eyes of its historian. He justifies his choice of subject in very strong terms. Although conceding that there is a tendency for people to consider the war which they are actually experiencing as the most important that has ever taken place, he declares that the Peloponnesian War is, in fact, the greatest of all time. 'Thucydides, an Athenian . . . began his history at the very outbreak of the war, in the belief that it was going to be a great war and more worth writing about than any of those which had happened in the past.'[6] The subsequent course of events, he maintained, fully confirmed this forecast; and so the whole of the past should be looked at in this perspective, and reduced to an explanation of the Peloponnesian War.

The point is abundantly made in two important sections of the first book, one relating to the early and partly legendary history of the Greeks before the Persian Wars, and the other to the Fifty Years that had elapsed since then.[7] Indeed, these two preparatory studies are only inserted in order to demonstrate the unique significance of the Peloponnesian War. In the first period, 'For a long time the state of affairs everywhere in Hellas had been such that nothing very remarkable could be done by any combination of powers, and even the individual cities were lacking in enterprise'.[8] In the Fifty Years there was no need to demonstrate the absence of wars of comparable gravity, for obviously none had occurred'. However, in addition to assessing the role of this period as a prelude to the Peloponnesian War, Thucydides had a special reason for dealing with it, because he wanted to correct a version recently published by another writer, Hellanicus of Lesbos (*c.* 500–415 BC). 'The only historian who has touched upon this period [the Fifty Years] is Hellanicus, in his *Attic History*, but he has not given much space to the subject and he is inaccurate in his dates.'[9] The *Attic History* of Hellanicus, like his other local histories, is lost. But he inaugurated quite an important line of local Athenian historians (p. 428, n. 4), and the remark of Thucydides does not appear to do justice to his contribution to chronological method, which evidently represented a considerable improvement on his predecessors. But one trouble was that Hellanicus' writing, though a versatile last fling of the old story-telling tradition, was not built on observation or enquiry, but merely on other people's conclusions. Later authors criticised his style, and they also confirmed the charges of inaccuracy which Thucydides had felt it his duty to bring forward.[10]

In doing so, he exhibited the spirit of censure which animated most remarks made by ancient historians about their immediate predecessors, since such criticisms justified what they themselves had attempted and achieved. It was scarcely to be expected, therefore, that his elder contemporary Herodotus would wholly escape – especially as the largest potential obstacle to Thucydides' belief in the supremacy of the Peloponnesian War obviously consisted of the wars against Persia. The verdict of Thucydides about the relative significance of the two phenomena is predictable. 'The greatest war in the past was the Persian War; yet in that war the decision was reached quickly as a result of two naval battles and two battles on land. The Peloponnesian War, on the other hand, not only lasted for a long time, but throughout its course brought with it unprecedented suffering for Hellas.[11] The point, as far as it goes, is a just one. But it needed demonstrating, for it was not easy to see how this struggle between groups of Greek city-states could really be more significant than the epic struggle between entire nations in the Persian Wars. Just as Herodotus had belittled Hecataeus, so Thucydides is depreciating Herodotus. This is not done too crudely. The older historian is not specifically mentioned; and it is implied that the Persian Wars have received adequate historical treatment.[12] But Herodotus is censured by implication, in regard to a number of minor details.[13] It is doubtful whether, as some have supposed, Thucydides meant to minimise the importance of Marathon.[14] Yet his reference to chroniclers who please the ear rather than speak

77

the truth seems to imply a criticism of Herodotus.[15] He owes his predecessor far more stimulus and example than he admits; he even pays him the compliment of starting his review of the Fifty Years exactly where Herodotus left off. All the same, he claims to outbid him not only in greatness of subject but in soundness of method as well.

The relative importance of this or that war is, to some extent, a subjective matter. However, it is true that the Peloponnesian War was the fateful convulsion that heralded the downfall of the charac-teristic Hellenic political structure and civilisation. Greece had reached a bi-polar deadlock, which could only be resolved by force. The trial of force would decide whether any city-state was going to be strong enough to impose pan-Hellenic unity; the struggle that followed answered the question in the negative. Nevertheless, in spite of this momentous significance of the war, it owed its memorable nature more to Thucydides than to the actual events. For the special greatness of the war lay in the fact that it provided political experiences of a varied and profoundly suggestive character; and it is in the pages of Thucydides that these experiences have been dissected, by the scalpel of a master-surgeon, and are therefore available for us to study.

He was well aware of the value of what he was imparting.

If those who will wish to study the clear record of what happened in the past and what will, in due course, tend to be repeated with some degree of similarity (as is the way of human events) judge this work to be of help to them, it will content me.

It has been composed to be a possession for ever rather than a show piece for a moment's hearing.[16]

This statement has been subjected to intensive study in recent years. It presents the programme of the historian who, building a new structure upon the moral approach which Herodotus had blended with pure entertainment (p. 49), exploited the influential ancient belief (long held by the Jews) that history ought to teach. Satisfaction of the reader's curiosity, and the stimulation of his patriotic pride, are no longer regarded as primary motives. Thucydides' history is designed to be instructive because a knowledge of the past will be a useful guide to the future. It will enable men to act more sensibly, and to avoid mistakes. Exact situations will not recur; the historian is not trying to reveal what is bound or destined to happen. But analysis is able to point to timeless forces, and these will continue to apply. The eternal springs of human behaviour will continue to flow into comparable and identifiable channels, and it is therefore necessary to find out what these springs and channels are.

This declaration contains two lines of thought. First, there is an emphasis on the durability of historical knowledge, since it is applicable not only to a single occasion but to the whole of the future as well. This is not didactic history in the simplest sense, since it aims not so much to supply direct instructions as to provide study material – evidence which will assist future scientific observers in their task of interpreting the events of their day. But, although some think otherwise, it does seem that Thucydides also meant his history to be useful to statesmen and politicians. True, it is not supposed to serve them as a practical handbook, for he does not fully adopt the idea, which was beginning to be current among the sophists (p. 91), that statesmanship can be taught. Yet politicians, like other readers, are expected to find this presentation of the evidence useful, because of the likelihood of near-repetition. Untutored genius being rare (p. 95), rulers and ruled alike have a need for this kind of information. They will be able to profit by the study of past successes and failures, and they will learn from history how to avoid follies and perils, 'how to brace themselves against the unpredictable', as Kurt von Fritz put it, 'and also to predict the predictable'.

Thucydides resembles the school of the contemporary physician Hippocrates in his search below the surface for causes.[17] He had also learnt something about method from the Ionian philosopher Anaxagoras, said to have been his teacher, who observed: 'that which appears is an earnest of what does not'.[18] And so the historian, too, devotes all his great gifts to the search for underlying causes.

In view of the unique significance of the Peloponnesian War, he is naturally at pains to identify the processes which made it break out – a difficult enough question, as any student of the First World War will know. Consequently, those who want to assess Thucydides' position as a historical thinker have felt obliged to devote a great deal of attention to his analysis of this problem.

79

War began when the Athenians and the Peloponnesians broke the Thirty Years Treaty which had been made after the capture of Euboea. As to the reasons why they broke the treaty, I propose first to give an account of the causes of complaint which they had against each other and the specific instances where their interests clashed: this is in order that there should be no doubt in anyone's mind about what led to this great war falling upon the Hellenes. The truest cause – about which least was said in public – was, in my opinion, that the growing power of the Athenians frightened the Spartans and compelled them to make war.[19]

It will be seen that he divides the process into two parts, the causes of complaint (*aitiai*) and the real or 'truest' reason (*prophasis*).[20] The causes of complaint – the quarrels about the allegiance of Corcyra and Potidaea, leading to increasingly open Athenian interventions at both places – are grievances, chains of mutual grievances, such as were common precursors of Greek wars, many of which originated from an alleged injury or breach of sworn obligations.[21] Thucydides believes that in all wars it needs to be explained not only why the contestants go to war, but why they do so at that particular time, and his description of the grievances fulfils the latter task. He adopts what seems the rather strange procedure of drawing a *contrast* between the two types of motivation. To us they do not seem contradictory or incompatible, and indeed, from a Spartan viewpoint, the happenings at Corcyra and Potidaea were illustrations of the 'truest reason', Athens' rise to power. But under the influence of contemporary sophists, rhetorical antitheses were fashionable; and indeed they abound elsewhere in Thucydides' work (p. 92). A challenging expression of this kind was needed to warn historians that they must look behind outward appearances. And any discomfort at the peculiar turn of phrase is rapidly superseded by a feeling of admiration for this insidiously plausible account of how one thing leads to another, with ultimately fatal results.[22]

The *real* cause of the war, however, was Sparta's fear of Athenian expansion. The Thirty Years' Treaty between the two powers (each associated with its dependants or adherents), had reaffirmed the balance of power between the two groups (p. 71). The aggressor in the Peloponnesian War, which broke out fourteen years later, was clearly whichever side had broken that treaty. But the question which state committed the fatal act was and is, as so often, a highly complex problem, and we get from Thucydides a suitably complex answer, over which lawyers could pore indefinitely before giving a verdict one way or the other. All the same, in the end, he does come fairly close to saying that Athens was spoiling for a fight. At any rate, it was creating a situation in which Spartans believed they must make war if they did not want their allies to be detached from their control. In so far, then, as Sparta's feeling was justified – and there is no suggestion that the opposite might have been the case – Athens did not lack responsibility for what followed. The fears felt in Sparta are never directly analysed, but they are illustrated in passing and we understand them.[23]

By thus turning our attention from immediate grievances to the fundamental realities of power-politics, the historian made a major contribution to political thought. It has, however, been regarded as strange that he should describe this 'truest' reason as something which was 'least mentioned in public'. For the Spartans must have been talking about nothing else. But what Thucydides surely means is that the point played no part in current debates at Athens. It is not, for example, treated as a cause of the war in the speeches attributed to Pericles. Indeed few powers, when a war is about to break out or has broken out, are prepared to attribute it to fears arising out of their successful aggressions. They prefer to find some other reason farther afield, or, as in this case, to concentrate on immediate causes and pretexts instead.

But there may be another reason also for the seemingly too vigorous juxtaposition, or antithesis, of the immediate causes of the war and its real underlying cause. For Thucydides took a long time to write his history. He started it, as he tells us himself, 'at the very outbreak of the war' in 431 (p. 76). He also refers explicitly to the conclusion of hostilities in 404, when the Athenians were at last overthrown.[24] Now, the *immediate* causes were abundantly clear at the time of the outbreak: the enemy of Athens in both the relevant incidents was maritime Corinth and not Sparta. Corinth, at the time, warned the Spartans what was at stake for themselves, but it was only on the long-term view, and in retrospect, that it became possible to justify the theory that Sparta's fear of Athenian aggression was the background of the entire war.

Indeed, was it practicable to speak of a single war at all? After its first phase, the Ten Years' War which was brought to a conclusion by the Peace of Nicias (421), there were no hostilities between Athens and Sparta for several years. Then, when the war resumed, the direct connexion between its new stage and its old one seemed to Thucydides abundantly clear. To him this appeared to justify the hypothesis that both phases together could be regarded as a single phenomenon explicable by a single underlying reason. He is therefore at pains to treat the interlude as an entirely phoney peace.

It is true that for six years and ten months they refrained from invading each other's territory. Abroad, however, the truce was never properly in force, and each side did the other a great deal of harm, until finally they were forced to break the treaty made after the ten years, and once more declare war openly upon each other.

The history of this period also has been written by the same Thucydides, an Athenian, keeping to the order of events as they happened by summers and winters, down to the time when the Spartans and their allies put an end to the empire of Athens and occupied the long walls and Piraeus. By then the war had lasted altogether twenty-seven years, and it would certainly be an error of judgment to consider the interval of the agreement [the Peace of Nicias] as anything else except a period of war.[25]

And the argument is then elaborated in further detail. This needed doing, since the 'grievances' of 431 were, in fact, far removed from the causes of the war's resumption after the Peace of Nicias and the pause which followed it.

When the historian breaks off to make this point, and declares that he will next describe the events that followed the Peace of Nicias – that is to say, when he announces his intention of narrating the rest of the Peloponnesian War – he is evidently marking a pause, not only in the war, but in the history. In this 'Second Preface', as it has been called, he appears to be telling us that he has now written his account of the Ten Years' War from 431 to 421 and is going on to complete his full project of the Twenty-Seven Years' War. And he takes the opportunity of emphasising why he is right in regarding the events of the whole of these twenty-seven years as one single process.

When this new and wider conception dawned on Thucydides we cannot tell. Possibly, like others, he was conscious of the instability of the compromise Peace of Nicias as soon as it took place, and therefore continued to take notes on the assumption that the war would be resumed. At all events the battle of Mantinea (418), in which Athens helped a new coalition against Sparta, showed that further full-scale hostilities were not far off. Then, after the Athenians' attack on Melos (416) and the subsequent failure of their expedition to Sicily – a disaster of which Sparta and its allies would inevitably take advantage – the war was again in full swing. At some time during this period Thucydides concluded that it was the same war as the old one. And so he decided to enlarge his history to cover both phases together, treating them as a single, inseparable unit.

He tells us himself that the work was given its final form after the end of the whole war in 404. It was apparently not published until after his death. But had the portion relating to the Ten Years' War *already* been published immediately on the conclusion of that war in 421? Not, certainly, in its present shape, since this section, as we have it, contains passages relating to 404 (p. 81). Moreover, if such a work had come out, we should probably have had some record of its publication, and indeed a version – differing from our own, since it could not have included the end-of-war passages – would have been expected to survive.

But, in any case, what do we mean by 'publication'? The term is rather ambiguous in regard to ancient books. There was a sort of book trade in Greece from the middle of the century; the comic dramatist Eupolis referred to a section of the Athenian market where books could be bought, and Plato makes Socrates say that anyone can buy Anaxagoras for a drachma in the theatre.[26] But books might be copied by a single scribe before they were dictated to a group of them, so that there could be an intermediate stage of semi-publication in which one or more copies were shown to friends. The work on the Ten Years' War might have been brought to this stage in 421, or soon afterwards, by the revision and collation of the items that had hitherto been compiled year by year. Alternatively, this part of the work still existed by 421 only in the form of the original separate annual compilations, and perhaps, to some extent, in the more or less fragmentary form of notes.

These may have included drafts, rough or otherwise, of recitations and lectures Thucydides had delivered before leaving for his northern command in 424. At first sight such recitations may seem improbable owing to his pointed claim of his work's permanent value, which includes a specific criticism of those who produce show-pieces or prize compositions at public gatherings (p. 78). And yet in the same passage he apologises for the fact that the lack of romance in his work may make it less agreeable to the ear. Herodotus had recited, and Thucydides seems to be saying that he, too, recites, but that audiences must be prepared to find his material more austere.

Though the finished work was intended for a reading public, recitations of selected portions would surely have exercised a profound effect on the Athenians. Receptive as usual to the spoken word, they were now reacting excitedly to the fireworks of the rhetoricians with whose style Thucydides had so much in common.[27] For Gorgias of Sicilian Leontini arrived in Athens in 427. It was he more than anyone else who introduced the city to these new exploitations of verbal utterance – from which subsequent Greek literature never freed itself again. Gorgias made the very most of the emotional effects of oratory: and Athenians began to find orators as exciting as tragic dramatists. Historians, imitating Gorgias, were soon aiming at the same effects, and it is very likely that this process started with recitations by Thucydides. Indeed, there is ancient evidence to confirm his harrowing impact on people's emotions, although we are not told whether readers or audiences are meant.[28]

His History, then, was begun in 431, written in some sort of incomplete form up to 421, and completed after 404. From the very outbreak of the war he was writing, or at least taking notes. But, since a certain number of passages were demonstrably composed many years after the events to which they refer (p. 83), there remains the possibility that the same may be true of a substantial proportion of the work. If so, the results for students of history are formidable: for it will mean that the information he has given us – and all too often it is information that we cannot check from any other source – may be framed not as it originally reached him but in the light of retrospective views and afterthoughts developed at different stages a good many years later. Revising the first version of an ancient book was, admittedly, difficult (p. 31). But a man of Thucydides' determination could perhaps have conquered this technical problem, writing and rewriting as his historical consciousness deepened and changed.

Thucydidean studies, during the last century and a half, have paid a great deal of attention to this question, and many valuable advances have been made, though without reaching any final or incontrovertible results. Since later indications are more frequent and widely distributed than early references,[29] and since, moreover, there are interlockings, repetitions and internal reminiscences throughout, some prefer to attribute most of the work to the final stage – regarding it as a basic unity which dates from that point even though it contains survivals from earlier strata. Others disagree, thinking that Thucydides wrote most of his annals as the events described in them occurred, and that what has come down to us is fundamentally this material, constructed according to an early and contemporary design. Others again, while assuming a unity of (late) composition, postulate a distinct unity of (early) thought: they believe he planned the work early, and wrote it in its final form much later on.

One of the crucial points in this controversy is Pericles' Funeral Speech. Mourning the dead in the first year of the war, Pericles propounds a memorable defence of the whole Athenian way of life.[30] No doubt Pericles did deliver a funeral speech on the occasion in question (although the fallen in this year must have been few). Yet the eulogy of Periclean Athens which we are given does not sound like a contemporary oration. It seems, rather, to echo the retrospective idealistic nostalgia of the years after final defeat. There is also a distinct post-war ring about Pericles' third and last oration (430).[31] Purporting to be a renewed justification of his naval strategy after the lowering of Athenian morale by plague, the speech forms an apt illustration of Thucydides' final judgment on Pericles (p. 97) – taking cognisance of the leaders who had come after him, and indeed of all that had happened up to the end of the war. And it must be significant that this declaration is immediately succeeded by a specific reference to the ultimate disaster and the events that led up to it.[32]

Another serious problem is raised by Book VIII, the last book of the History. Although the writer himself stated that his work was to continue down to the termination of the war, it does not, in fact, do so. Instead it ends abruptly seven years earlier, in 411. Nor is it possible to suppose that a subsequent section was published but lost, since it is from 411, not 404, that other writers deliberately 'continue' Thucydides (p. 129). It is possible, at least theoretically, that more was written but lost, since the abrupt ending might coincide with the end of a papyrus roll, followed originally by others that have now vanished. But this conclusion seems unlikely, because there are reasons to suppose that the eighth book itself was left unfinished. For one thing, it contains certain contradictions.[33] That, however, would not in itself be conclusive, owing to the difficulties of correcting an ancient book (p. 31). But more significant is the fact that documents are quoted verbatim. This is not Thucydides' normal practice, and it is legitimate to suppose that he intended, as usual, to rewrite them in his own style.

Another important feature is the total absence of speeches in Book VIII.[34] These were such a vital and integral element in Thucydides' procedure that he does not seem likely to have proposed to leave a whole book without them (p. 88).[35] It has been suggested, against this, that the rapid, kaleidoscopic, diversified course of events in these years 414–411 did not lend itself to the speech technique any longer, making it preferable for the writer to offer his judgments in other ways instead. It has also been suggested that there were no important debates at the time. But this is implausible, since there were excellent occasions for debates: and, that being so, no doubt they took place, and impassioned speeches, as usual, were delivered. An obscure ancient tradition explained the peculiarities of Book VIII by guessing that it was written not by Thucydides but by his daughter. But it is much more probable that the book, as we have it, is unfinished. Admittedly it is a full account, going into considerable detail. And yet, because there are no speeches, we lack the sort of explanatory background to which Thucydides has accustomed us. Surely it was his intention to rectify this deficiency. But why, in that case, did he not do so? For he lived on at least until the end of the war, and probably for several years after that. Possibly, in view of the complicated, revolutionary events of 411, he was waiting for more information before he inserted the speeches that would make these happenings clear.

Since, on this assumption, Book VIII was left unfinished, it may be regarded as certain that subsequent books, if they were written at all – if they ever advanced beyond rough notes – were nothing like complete. Perhaps it was at this time that he went back to the earlier period and began to give a final form to its history – only concluding the process after the war was over. But by then his life was nearly finished, and he was left no time, after all, to compose or complete his account of the last nine years of the war.

5

Speeches and Personalities in Thucydides

THUCYDIDES' history would not have been at all the same without the speeches. This device, which seems so strange to us in a historical work, had been adapted by Herodotus from Homer, and Thucydides – who after all came from Athens, where talk was a fine art – carried its employment a good deal further. Twenty-four per cent of his whole work consists of such orations, which number no less than forty, and, like his other digressions, are carefully and ingeniously spaced.[1] Phoenix, in the *Iliad*, had instructed Achilles to be a speaker of words as well as a doer of deeds,[2] and Thucydides couples words and deeds together as the materials of history.

It is very clear to him that the two forms of activity are closely linked. Diodotus, offering moderate counsel about Mytilene (p. 71), is made to say that 'anyone who denies that words can be a guide to action must either be a fool or have some personal interest at stake'.[3] For one thing, speeches *create* action – good or evil, for Diodotus' opponent Cleon is chosen to show how disastrous the gift of the gab can be. Besides, Thucydides holds the very Greek opinion that no one will get anywhere at all unless he is articulate. 'Someone', Pericles is made to say, 'who has the knowledge, but lacks the power clearly to express it, is no better off than if he never had any ideas at all.'[4]

Man, that is to say, is a rational being whose actions are based on decisions, and these can only be the outcome of verbal formulations. Speech is the root of all political life, and the point had never been so evident as it was at this time. For professional rhetoricians were intensely active, and the practical fruit of their efforts, formal speech-making, also underwent far-reaching developments. Pericles, whose orations play such a leading role in Thucydides' work, was said to have been the first to deliver a written speech in court – and the fact that he had learnt philosophy from Anaxagoras (who was also Thucydides' teacher) inspired Plato to describe him as the greatest of orators. The earliest Greek speech which has come down to us – relating to the murder of a certain Herodes – likewise belongs to the period of the Peloponnesian War (*c.* 417). It was delivered by the rhetorician Antiphon of Rhamnus,[5] whose style has a good deal in common with Thucydides; and indeed it was from him that the historian was reported to have learnt his rhetorical skills.[6]

Apparently Thucydides recited parts of his work (p. 84); and surely these recitations included some of the speeches which were so appropriate to such a medium. Moreover, these orations form a perfect illustration of his view that the whole of history is based on articulateness – on words as well as deeds. A historian, therefore, must take pains to record what people said. The method he himself uses is a carefully calculated one.

In this history I have made use of set speeches, some of which were delivered just before and others during the war. I have found it difficult to remember the precise words used in the speeches which I listened to myself, and my various informants have experienced the same difficulty. So my method has been, while keeping as closely as possible to the general sense of the words that were actually used, to make the speakers say what, in my opinion, was called for by each situation.[7]

Perhaps Herodotus had been criticised for inventing speeches; and that may be why Thucydides felt it incumbent on himself to explain how he is going to proceed. He admits that his speeches do not set out to represent the exact words of the speakers, for this, as he reasonably says, would have been impossible. He aims, instead, at conveying a general impression – the essence rather than the substance.

The additional indication that he included 'what was called for' might be held to mean that he tells us what the speakers 'had to' say, and therefore what they *did* say. But the phrase seems more likely to signify 'what the various occasions demanded'. If that is so, he is admitting that scope has been given to his imagination. Such a criterion could clash with the requirement that the general sense of what had actually been said should always be reproduced. And indeed, just as Herodotus had included purely mythical orations, it is pretty clear that Thucydides very often pays more attention to what a situation seems to him to 'call for' than to any texts of actual discourses that could have been available to him.

His speeches make little attempt to reproduce speakers' individual characteristics or probable styles.[8] Like a simple nurse in Aeschylus, and a policeman in Sophocles, the speakers talk the language not of themselves but of their author. Their orations are closer in structure to rhetorical textbooks than to any genuine extant speech. They are also much shorter than the sort of harangues that were actually delivered on public occasions – as we can tell from those that have survived. Moreover, some of Thucydides' speeches are singularly out of place, indeed tactless, in relation to their occasion. For example the admiral Phormio's address to his sailors could not possibly have been delivered to any crowd of mariners in such a form, though it is apt enough as an explanation of Athenian policy for the benefit of the reader.[9] And the Assembly meeting to discuss Mytilene surely cannot have proceeded as Thucydides said it did. Moreover, Attic oratorical style had been moving rapidly during the war, but the style of Thucydides does nothing of the kind; quite apart from the question of whether their substance is authentic, the speeches in later books such as vi and vii must have been, stylistically, far removed from any possible originals. But some of the speeches quoted in Thucydides may never have been delivered at all.[10]

If they were delivered, the fact that he does not exactly reproduce them does not necessarily mean that he was ignorant of what had been said. He may sometimes, it is true, have written down a version while his memory was vivid. But even then, like other ancient historians, he felt free to select, add and elaborate before transcribing the oration for his history. The fact that a speech may have been known, so that any alternations he introduced could be detected, constituted no objection. For verbatim inclusion would have been artistically damaging.

He had quite other purposes in mind; and they were purposes which entirely overrode and overruled the criterion of mere fidelity to what had actually been said. In his view, the speakers are not just there in their own right. To a certain extent, they are mouthpieces of the historian, in that they provide the medium for a substantial part of his huge contribution to the development of abstract and rational thinking. But they are much more than merely his mouthpieces. They are there to reveal underlying causes; to display the characters and tempers and motives of individuals and nations; to penetrate to general truths which might not have emerged from the details of the narrative; to get the participants in events, political or military, to speak for themselves; and to bring out, by methods impossible for a mere chronicle, subjective elements that are indispensable to our understanding.

We shall win, and why, explain typical speakers.[11] And then subsequent developments show whether their calculations were good or bad – ostensibly without the historian intervening, so that the reader is given the illusion of independence. In this way, for example, we are introduced to the essence of Athenian power and to its gradual deterioration from the Periclean ideal. The clashes of opinion at Sparta before the war, and the reactions to these various views expressed by Pericles on the Athenian side, show an interlocking arrangement of one point answering another, often at a distance of time and place: and in reporting one oration the historian sometimes shows foreknowledge of a later one.

The influence of contemporary sophists – described by one of their number, Prodicus of Ceos, as men half-way between philosophers and political scientists* – is clearly detectable in the manner in which close concentration is focused upon a single argument. The method used is often that of 'ring' or 'loop' composition: statement, proof, restatement. By these means, unarguable truth being so elusive, the attempt is made to achieve the 'probability' stressed by the

* First used to indicate any skilled, wise man, the term gradually came to be applied to the itinerant professional lecturers who claimed to show how to make a success of life, teaching either 'virtue' (Protagoras) or oratory (Gorgias), also mnemonics, etc. (Hippias). Antiphon (the sophist) and Thrasymachus encouraged abandonment of moral restraints.

sophist-rhetorician Gorgias, like philosophers before him, as the best attainable ideal (p. 44). The potentialities and powers of the spoken and written word were now appreciated as never before.[12] And so colliding intellectual theses are stated, by Thucydides, in extreme forms – corresponding with the antithetical tastes of this age in which Protagoras of Abdera (an Ionian town in Thrace) (485–415) was admitting the possibility of opposite views on any and every question.[13] Consequently, Thucydides' speeches often occur in pairs. But sometimes, for example when Pericles is speaking, or the able Syracusan Hermocrates,[14] the cogency of what they say is implied by the omission of any riposte from another orator. The same expository technique, without reply or antitheses, is adopted for additional set-pieces of special significance, for which, although speeches are not involved, the technique of speeches is used: such as the plague at Athens, and civil strife in Corcyra, and the dispatch sent by the Athenian general Nicias from Sicily.

To identify the historian's speeches with the choral odes of tragedy would be going too far. Yet they do owe many features to the tragic dramatists. They, too, for several decades past, had been introducing imaginary forensic speeches into their plays. The whole procedure of Thucydides is theatrical, bringing the past vividly before the reader like a drama on the stage, with the intention of revealing character and not just recording events. The whole depiction of national and personal psychologies in these speeches is analogous to the practice of the tragedians. In particular, on a great many occasions, we are strongly reminded of Euripides (*c.* 485–406 BC), who was essentially the dramatist of the Peloponnesian War. Thoroughly Euripidean, for example, is Thucydides' debate on the doom of rebellious Melos, in which sophisticated arguments are put forward in a dramatic dialogue form. Reminiscent of tragedy, also, is the historian's un-modern tendency to generalise, to seek the eternal in every event, often coining abstract terms for the purpose, again in the manner of Euripides.[15] The reputation of Thucydides throughout the ages has scarcely fallen short of the tragedians, with whom he has so much in common; and this reputation has largely been due to the impact of his speeches.

Moreover, there is a strong poetic, tragic tinge about his actual language, and this feature, too, is particularly accentuated in the speeches; their precision and passion are those of poetry. Gorgias observed that the effects of orally delivered poetry upon audiences included 'fearful anxiety, tears and lamentation, and grief-stricken yearning'.[16] His own success owed a lot to poetical effects; and so did the emotional highlights of Thucydides' story.

And yet this style is archaic and harsh. Crammed with meaning and overtone, sentence after sentence possesses the astringent conciseness of a gnomic utterance. The order of words is unnatural, and diction is contorted almost to the breaking-point of the language – and the translator. These elaborate, twisted antithetical rhythms are very different from the loose and easy fluency of Herodotus. They breathe the spirit of an age of rhetoricians and sophists which had only dawned at Athens after Herodotus wrote. Gorgias was the first to speak of 'figures of speech', and Thucydides noted and adapted not only his methods of argument but his diction.[17] The historian's aim, says H. C. Baldry, 'was to master the new-fangled game of abstract thought'.

And yet his response was entirely his own. For example, he characteristically avoided the normal symmetry of the antithetical style, breaking up its formal balance. The whole effect is one of estrangement, individual and wilful. This surprising method has even inspired conjecture that Thucydides, whose father had a Thracian name, only learnt Greek as a second language. That is unlikely, but it does so happen that two antithetical and epigrammatic writers who influenced him, Protagoras and Democritus, were fellow-Thracians, both from the city of Abdera. And, without accusing Thucydides of writing pidgin Greek, it is possible to suppose that his insistence on a curiously old-fashioned idiom – the feature that particularly struck ancient critics[18] – reflects the geographical and spiritual isolation of his banishment from Athens. Exile had not affected Herodotus, or at least not in this way – it had broadened and not soured him. The experience has seldom failed to leave its stamp, in one way or another, on any writer; and it marked Thucydides with an alienation that is reflected in his peculiar, unnatural Greek.

His narrative style possesses the same characteristics as his speeches and set-pieces, but to a far less extreme degree. The language is still compact, but not so much contorted as succinct. His writing was also famous for its speed, a quality likewise attributed to

Democritus.[19] Severe, grave, and terrifyingly intense, Thucydides presses on with inexorable rapidity. Occasionally, if the dramatic requirements of the narrative demand it, there is instead a slow and halting march.[20] But when he has something terrible to write about, such as the final destruction of the Athenian expeditionary force in the Sicilian river Assinarus, the tale rushes ahead.

When day came Nicias led his army on, and the Syracusans and their allies pressed them hard in the same way as before, showering missiles and hurling javelins in upon them from every side. The Athenians hurried towards the river Assinarus.

Once they reached the river, they rushed down into it, and now all discipline was at an end. Every man wanted to be the first to get across, and, as the enemy persisted in his attacks, the crossing now became a difficult matter. Forced to crowd in close together, they fell upon each other, trampled each other underfoot. Some were killed immediately by their own spears, others got entangled among themselves and among the baggage and were swept away by the river.

Syracusan troops were stationed on the opposite bank, which was a steep one. They hurled down their weapons from above on the Athenians, most of whom, in a disordered mass, were greedily drinking in the deep river-bed. And the Peloponnesians came down and slaughtered them, especially those who were in the river. The water immediately became foul, but nevertheless they went on drinking it, all muddy as it was and stained with blood. Indeed, most of them were fighting among themselves to have it.[21]

In his account of the Sicilian expedition the historian deploys all his talents, because the Syracusans were the only people in whom Athens met its match.[22] Full of tragedies and dramatic ironies, this account of an utter catastrophe which wisdom could have avoided was the climax of Book VII. Macaulay described the book as the summit of human art.

Thucydides' way of telling the story is cerebral, the product of an exceptionally powerful mind. It conveys the intellectual effort which had given birth to the work.

For his history, throughout, is a glorification of intelligence. Its purpose is not only to enable people to know. That is not enough, being a mere meaningless accumulation. The aim is also to make readers understand. In keeping with Gorgias' teaching that full, total knowledge is beyond attainment, the task must be tackled in a humble spirit. When, therefore, Thucydides has general laws in mind, he does not lay them down dogmatically, but only suggests what is likely. Thucydides agreed with Democritus' assertion that to understand the cause of any one thing was worth more to him than the whole kingdom of the Persians[23] – and another contemporary, Socrates, was reported to have expressed similar sentiments.[24]

For these men lived in an epoch when the Ionian spirit of investigation had finally taken deep roots in the fertile soil of Athens. People were prepared to investigate everything; and the comparatively few years that had elapsed since Herodotus composed his work had established great gains in the efficiency of their techniques. And so, just as Thucydides probes incessantly to comprehend events, this capacity to understand is also the quality he admires most in the characters of his history. Protagoras was now asserting that man is the measure of all things,[25] but his fellow-townsman Democritus added that no one is likely to prevail by native qualities alone without training.[26] Thucydides, however, believed that even an untutored person could succeed if only his intellect was powerful enough. The career of Themistocles, for example, seemed to him to show how mind, granted perseverance and subtlety, is capable of rising even above the disadvantage of a deficient education.[27]

But it is far better to have the opportunity to learn, and Thucydides above all wants his readers, whether students or statesmen, to be given the greatest possible opportunities of comprehending what is going on (p. 79). For all attendant circumstances are merely subordinate, or should be made subordinate, to the minds of man. Thucydides, says Antony Andrewes, 'sees events as one great dialectical argument in which human intelligence is the final arbiter in the seat of judgment'. His insistence on reason as the ideal anticipates Aristotle's emphasis both on wisdom and on practical intelligence. The distinction was a refinement that came after Thucydides; he is content to stress the cerebral quality in general as the criterion by which people and causes must be judged.

All his important personages, therefore, are shrewd planners and calculators, and the word for 'understand' or 'judgment' (*gnomai, gnome*) occurs 305 times in his work. The Greeks admired the middle course so much because they found it hard to achieve; and similarly Thucydides appreciated intelligence because he knew that even in his own city, crammed with intelligent people, it did not by any means always prevail. Instead he felt, as Cornford says, that 'human affairs move along a narrow path lit by a few dim rays of foresight (*gnome*) or the false, wandering fires of hope'. Most of all was this true of politics, the sphere which Thucydides had chosen for his analysis of the applications of human reason.

To understand the successes and failures of this power, it was obviously necessary to study psychology. Earlier philosophers had concentrated on physics and metaphysics, but now Socrates and Democritus and the sophists had turned the eyes of the Greek world on to human behaviour. We have the former's views filtered through (or invented by) Plato, and Democritus' ethical and psychological works survive in fragments,[28] which, although numerous, are not numerous enough to enable us to reconstruct his system. As for Thucydides, this interest in the human personality is deficient in a certain necessary quality of variegated untidiness, because his pursuit of this aspect is subordinated to other aims. He likes biography; his delineations of famous men contributed to the formation of that literary genre. But everything judged to be irrelevant and trivial is rigorously excluded. For what the historian wants to do is to eluci-date, through his characters, the *types* of person who react to given sets of circumstances, who fix the characters of states, who decide the features which oppose Athens to Sparta. This is to say, we are far, deliberately far, from Herodotus' preference for more personal and private factors. Thucydides judges men not as individuals but as politicians.

That, for example, is how he sees Pericles. Only two years after he beginning of the Peloponnesian War, Pericles was already dead. Yet he is the central figure of the work, and in a sense its hero. There is no knowing what Thucydides thought of the earlier, pre-war Pericles, the young, demagogic, imperialist on the make; for he does not choose to tell us.[29] But about his conduct of the initial period of the war we are told a good deal; and the background of these events is described in the speeches attributed to him. Two of these orations, it seems, only reached their present form many years after his death (p. 85). Yet it is difficult to read the Funeral Speech without feeling that Thucydides had to some extent, later if not sooner, become infected with the glory of the imperial state. The ideal may not have been perfect, but it was magnificent; and, looked at in retrospect, it provided a dramatic foil to the disastrous present.

Admiration of the departed order implied respect for the man who had brought it into being. And indeed, when we come to the actual subject of the history, namely the war, its outbreak is not regarded as Pericles' fault. There is no suggestion that he could have avoided it, and the gossip that he started hostilities from private motives of his own is dismissed with contempt.[30] As regards the actual conduct of the military operations, the verdict of Thucydides, at whatever date or by whatever stages it was reached, again spoke unequivocally in favour of Pericles. 'During the whole period of time when Pericles was at the head of affairs the state was widely led and firmly guarded, and it was under him that Athens was at her greatest. And when the war broke out, here also he appears to have accurately estimated what the power of Athens was.'[31] In the end the Athenians lost the war, it is true. But they only lost it many years after Pericles' death. And, although his calculations had admittedly been turned awry by the plague, it was not because of him that they failed. On the contrary, if he had continued to be in charge, they would have won. They lost because his successors did everything he had told them not to do. He had counselled them to look after the navy, but to refrain from imperial expansion during the war (though perhaps he was less purely defensive than Thucydides made out). He also advised them to avoid taking any action which might risk the safety of Athens itself. But they did the exact opposite, in all respects. *They*, not Pericles, pursued private motives; and they fell fatally into civil strife. Pericles, with his 'position, intelligence and human integrity', had been able to respect their liberty and yet lead them at the same time. Those who followed him could not.[32]

Of these successors to Pericles we know very little. Except for some caricatures by the comic dramatist Aristophanes, there is scant information except from Thucydides himself – and his pictures merely consist of a few malevolent flashes. After Pericles' death, the leading politician for some years was Cleon.[33] Thucydides brings him to our notice in three episodes. He was the man who, in 427, proposed the decree to execute the rebellious Mytileneans, which was passed but rescinded the next day. In 425 it was he who won a considerable victory at Pylos on the western coast of the Peloponnese, when members of the Spartan military *élite* were (exceptionally) taken prisoner on the island of Sphacteria. And in 422–421 it was again Cleon who proceeded to Macedonia to win Amphipolis back from the Spartan Brasidas. But on this occasion he failed, and the enemy killed him.

Like the conservative Aristophanes, who treated Cleon as a lamentable and violent demagogue, Thucydides has the lowest possible opinion of the man, and says so in lethal asides. He is degraded to the status of a clown unworthy of the dignity of history – someone who throve in an atmosphere of disturbance, because 'in a time of peace and quiet, people would be more likely to notice his evil doings and less likely to believe his slander of others'.[34]

In regard to Mytilene, Cleon was unnecessarily brutal and revengeful – which was an unwise way of treating allies. He also proclaimed a deplorable desire to prevent his fellow Athenians from engaging in free discussion. At Pylos he was grasping and arrogant, and made a 'mad' promise (though it came off). And thereafter, when we learn of his sordid end in Macedonia, it is hard to forget that Amphipolis, which Cleon had failed to recover, was the very same place which Thucydides himself had lost. The recovery of the town might have meant his return from the exile his failure had earned him (p. 74). Moreover, the circumstances that had led to the city's loss and Thucydides' disgrace could reasonably be ascribed to Cleon's overbearing measures against the allies. These were all reasons for regarding Cleon acrimoniously.

Coarse fellow though he may have been, he was able, particularly as a financier – and he earned respect from orators in the following century. However, his merits were of no concern to the purpose of Thucydides. His point was that Cleon displayed a dramatic antithesis, a debased perversion, of Pericles: vulgarian contrasted with man of culture, second-rate with first-rate, inferior demagogue with enlightened guide. Cleon's savagery towards the allies was a typical example of how he did everything Pericles told his successors not to do.[35] The violence of his domestic and foreign policy over a period of years could, in the view of the historian, be partially blamed for the lapse into civil strife which was really what cost Athens the war. And the same sort of censure was merited by his successor Hyperbolus, another butt of comic poets, who was exiled (ostracised) in 417, 'not from any fear of his power and influence, but for his villainy, and because the city was ashamed of him'.[36]

Thucydides' characterisation of two other leading Athenian figures in the war is more subtle. One is Nicias, who was responsible for the Peace of 421 but met with utter disaster in the expedition to Sicily, and was executed by the Syracusans (413). The historian's verdict is an unexpected and cryptic one: 'Nicias was a man who, of all the Hellenes in my time, least deserved to come to so miserable an end, since the whole of his life had been devoted to the study and practice of virtue.'[37] Not a word, here, about the usual political and military subjects, or about his gifts in those spheres – gifts which were adequate but not brilliant, and earned him a reputation of respectable timidity from Aristophanes. The comment of Thucydides, as far as it goes, is accurate enough. But its omissions and implications are significant. First of all, there is a tragic contrast between his pious, conventional virtues and his appalling end. But, above all, it is implied, with a grim and ironical clearsightedness, that these qualities, excellent though they are in their way, will not guarantee the intelligent and effective conduct of affairs. The Sicilian catastrophe had proved as much, with terrifying finality. 'Thucydides' epitaph on Nicias', remarks C.M. Bowra, 'is the verdict of a man who knew that, in the destinies of peoples, goodness is not enough.'

All the same, even if not enough, it is a useful thing to have. For example, the absence of these standard, solid merits in Nicias' young opponent Alcibiades was a serious political handicap both to himself and to Athens. Before the Sicilian expedition, says the historian, Alcibiades had not been given important commands because of his debauched personal habits.[38] Obviously these were bound to intensify his estrangement from the very proper Nicias, and so they contributed to dangerous dissension in the State. And the radicals disliked his extravagances quite as much as Nicias did.

Unlike Herodotus, Thucydides does not usually go into a man's private life. But in this case he had to, since it affected Alcibiades' career and consequently exercised a direct influence on the war. For when, in 415, Alcibiades was withdrawn from the Sicilian expedition and took refuge with the enemies of Athens (p. 72), it was again suspicion of his lack of principles which had turned his fellow-citizens against him. Ostensibly, the charge was impiety, but what really inspired his opponents was the generally unreliable unsolidity of his character. However, after Alcibiades had come back to an Athenian command (411), he deserved well of his fellow-countrymen. For when the fleet at Samos wanted to attack their own city of Athens – temporarily under an oligarchic dictatorship – he refused to let them. Politically unprincipled though he was,[39] by this intervention, says Thucydides, 'he rendered as eminent a service to the state as any man ever did'.[40] This exceptionally high praise prepares us for the conclusion that, in spite of the flaws in his private life, his rejection and dismissal by his own people (repeated all over again in 406[41]) was ruinous to Athens. And the historian is probably thinking of Alcibiades (and deliberately speaking in warmer terms than Herodotus) when he praises Themistocles, that equally brilliant and unsound figure of the earlier war.[42] Here was another man whose unreliable, hazardous character and conduct had likewise helped to drive him into the arms of Athens' enemies. And yet, when not hampered by this defect, he too had performed splendid actions.

How had Themistocles managed to achieve these things? Not because of his background, because he had none, but because of his intellect, foresight and ability to make quick decisions (p. 95). This continual emphasis on brain-power sometimes makes Thucydides' verdicts rather disconcerting. The standard translation of *arete* is 'virtue'. But the term is applied not only to the devout Nicias, but also to Antiphon, who, whatever the merits of his prose style, was a sanguinary, treacherous plotter, the leading oligarchic extremist of 411. The surprising attribution of virtue to such a man is intended, as Bury pointed out, 'to express the intelligence, dexterity and will power of a competent statesman, in sharp contradistinction to the conventional *arete* of the popular conception'. This was not virtue as most people understood it, but something more closely comparable to the *virtù* which Machiavelli saw in tough, skilful Sforzas and Borgias of his own day. Thucydides liked men who concentrated their energy on the tasks at hand. There is not much talk of natural benevolence. Instead, speeches prefer to harp on action-enhancing qualities such as courage.

Courage operates in the mass as well as in individuals. The psychology of masses and groups is a field in which Thucydides achieved extraordinary pioneer advances. With the acutest perceptiveness he analysed and expressed the changing attitudes of states, factions, councils, assemblies, and above all armies. Generals' speeches are skilfully adapted to the thoughts and feelings of their various contingents – unless it suits his purpose to do otherwise (p. 90). The results of Greek battles depended on morale rather than tactics, and here we see the mentality of the soldiers, their excitements and exaltations and despairs. As the Sicilian expedition draws towards its calamitous close in a decisive sea-battle in Syracuse harbour, there is an unforgettable picture of the agonised Athenian troops looking on, their fears for the future like nothing they had ever experienced before, their bodies agonisedly swaying this way and that to match the vicissitudes of their ships, on which everything depended.[43]

6

Power and Politics
in Thucydides

THIS account of the Sicilian expedition is, metaphorically, the height of tragedy. How far ought it also to be regarded as reflecting the convictions of contemporary tragic dramatists about the universe? How much room, that is to say, does all this emphasis on the human will and intelligence leave for the tragic beliefs in Nemesis, divine jealousy and fate which had been so important to Herodotus? The answer appears to be that Thucydides framed his narrative in terms of such concepts, but that in doing so he was adopting a dramatic structure and convention and not intending to express a theological doctrine.

The expedition is described in the phrases and terms of high tragedy, with all the temptations and delusions and arrogances and ironies and disasters which abound on the tragic stage. But the catastrophe could have been avoided by human means – for example, if Alcibiades had not been dismissed. There was no question of any divine necessity. Similarly, two nations with the psychological characteristics of Athens and Sparta seem as certain to be involved in strife as any Creon or Medea of mythological tragedy: but here again the situation of the two states was not of heaven's making but of man's. Tragic, too, was the ultimate fall of Athens. Yet it was due not to Nemesis but to the unwise politics of Pericles' successors.

Thucydides needed no divine machinery to provide his tragic reversals and deceptions. The story was redolent with them without any such intervention. The contrasts of which he is so fond are embedded in events – they supply him with dramatic juxtapositions ready-made. Just after the splendour and optimism of the Funeral Speech comes the plague; and the downfall of the Athenians in Sicily immediately follows their imperialistic excesses against Melos. *Hubris*, infatuated arrogance, is very much in the air. So it had been when the Athenians were so conceited after Pylos that they refused the chance of a favourable peace.[1] However, there is nothing supernatural about this. On the contrary, it comes from an all too typical fault of human nature – the same sort of failure that brought Cleon down after he himself had been so brutal to others.

Thucydides is interested in religion as a historical phenomenon. For example, he notes the blood-guilt which was alleged to rest upon Pericles' family.[2] But this is because the allegation has become a factor in events, not because any such taint really could have existed. The same applies to the alleged mutilation of religious statues (Hermae) by Alcibiades. That, too, had a profound effect on history, since it was responsible for his recall from the Sicilian expedition. He was not guilty of the profanation. But, even if he had been, Thucydides would have seen his action not as blasphemy but as deplorable imprudence.

His contemporary Euripides stood on the threshold of the new world, nearly but not quite willing to cut adrift from the old. In his heart Thucydides had cut adrift. He still finds life a tragedy, but it is now a secular one. His style and structure retain the paraphernalia of the dramatists because he shares their artistic approach – not because he shares their beliefs, or is even worried by their problems.

Does this secular attitude mean that he wholly disbelieved in the gods? When he was writing of the Athenian success at Pylos, he declared that Chance played a great part. He also used the sort of language which suggested that this factor is of divine origin. He does not, however, attribute it to any particular god or goddess, but uses the impersonal neuter. Herodotus, too, had often employed this, but Thucydides is going farther than his predecessor, for the suggestion of divinity is again a literary convention: Chance had no divine meaning for him at all. From other passages it is quite evident that he does not accept the idea of providential government, the doctrine favoured, for example (in a non-theological way), by his teacher Anaxagoras who spoke of mind as a unitary animating principle. Thucydides is closer, as so often, to the Ionians from Thrace: Democritus who eliminated the gods from the government of the universe but thought of them as psychic factors which could bring good or bad fortune;[3] and Protagoras whose essay *About the Gods*, the first work he ever recited in public,[4] indicated that he was a complete agnostic. This was the attitude which the Hippocratic physicians were taking up about health. 'No illness', said one of them, 'is more divine or more human than any other.'[5]

That is very much the approach of Thucydides. Indeed, he may well have been, at heart, an atheist. But, if so, he preferred not to say so; even Anaxagoras had been prosecuted at Athens for impiety. What emerges from the History instead is a sober, unprejudiced, undogmatic agnosticism. The Plataeans, the Melians, Nicias, all appeal to the gods. But they might have saved their breath for all the good it does them. In other words, if the gods exist, the historian cannot see how they operate. Causes, to him, are entirely human. It was indeed a momentous decision to humanise history.

His attitude to oracles, therefore, is profoundly different from that of Herodotus. Like blood-guilt and blasphemy, they were respected not as divine manifestations but as influences on what people thought and did – for such an influence oracles undoubtedly were. But Thucydides is not totally detached when he writes of this subject, since he evidently felt a personal distaste for soothsayers. He provides sarcastic notes about prophecies that were ineffective or prudently ambiguous or rehashed by public opinion.[6] There is also a touch of irony – and it is not the pious dramatic irony of Herodotus – in his suggestion that an oracle came true in exactly the opposite sense to what was expected.[7] The view of Thucydides on the whole matter is expressed once and for all by his comment on an oracle which had pronounced that the war would last for thrice nine years. This, he said, was the one and only instance in which people who put their faith in oracles were justified by the event.[8] The law of averages had finally allowed an oracle to be fulfilled.

Men get landed, it is true, with Fate or Necessity (*Ananke*). But this is not so much destiny as the unavoidable result of a chain of events:

something they have brought upon themselves by what they have done.[9] 'Those that take the sword may perish by the sword,' as Andrewes expresses it, 'but only if they are defeated.' Probably there is yet another correspondence with Democritus here, for when the Thracian philosopher said 'nothing occurs at random, but everything for a reason and by necessity'[10] he seems to have been thinking on similar lines. Democritus also had much to say about Chance, the unexplained factor he invoked to account for the original formation of the world from atoms in the void. But in regard to human affairs he declared that 'Chance is a bogey invented to excuse stupidity',[11] and Thucydides offers a similar suggestion when he makes Pericles say, 'we commonly blame Chance for whatever belies our calculation'.[12]

He is fascinated by Chance; by the sort of horrible accident that caused a totally unnecessary and unexpected massacre of all the inhabitants, including the school-children, at the small Boeotian town of Mycalessus.[13] What brought that about was no divine power; on such an occasion Chance denotes those aspects of a situation which men, with their limited ability to plan, prove incapable of anticipating or controlling.[14] In the same spirit Hippocrates was identifying the health-factor that did not yield to scientific analysis. Here are up-to-date, secularised versions of Homer's confrontation of human intelligence and bravery with factors which cheat them of their purposes. Foresight and Chance are continually at war with one another, and the latter often prevails. It did so, for example, in circumstances of sheer bad luck, when Chios, having behaved with praiseworthy caution during the revolts against Athens (411), did not escape suffering all the same.[15]

Bad luck seemed all too likely to prevail over judgment, because Thucydides' experience of life had made him gloomy. It is true that progress was possible, if men behaved sensibly; and in the material field, as his survey of the remote past shows, Thucydides was quite aware that there had been material advances.[16] Philosophers had admitted as much;[17] Protagoras pointed out that such upward developments were a matter of historical fact. But it was also well known that human designs are apt to go wrong, and nobody knew this better than Thucydides, who stands right at the centre of the ancient tradition of historical pessimism (p. 48). At just about the time when his work was being completed, the last play of Sophocles, the *Oed ipusof Colonus* (*c.* 401), gave immortal expression to the same view.[18] For Chance is usually too much for feeble human beings.

In a war, accident is more prominent than ever. The blows one side receive from it are obviously a windfall to their opponents. At Pylos, for example, the Athenian success and Spartan disaster came from an attack which Thucydides represents (we cannot control his version) as a casual affair largely prompted by luck.[19] Chance defeats foresight once again. The absence of the latter has abased the Spartans, and the presence of the former has given the Athenians a victory. And this whole course of events seems to the historian typical of the accidents that proliferate in war. Not only is any single battle hazardous and confused, but the whole course of hostilities turns out quite differently from anyone's expectations, owing to the accidental factors that intervene. Events can evolve as stupidly as the designs of men.[20] When the Spartans were considering whether to fight, the Athenian delegation warned them of this. 'Think of the great part that is played by the unpredictable in war. . . . The longer a war lasts, the more things tend to depend on accidents. Neither you nor we can see into them: we have to abide their outcome in the dark.'[21]

And above all, as Euripides also declared in his *Trojan Women* (415), war tends to produce conditions in which the human mind loses its balance and its standards of conduct. There is nothing inevitable or irrestible about this, in the sense of the gods fuddling people's wits. But it is inevitable all the same – in the sense that a law of human psychology makes such things happen. In the conditions produced by war, every man acts for himself and not for his country, which is soon convulsed by malevolent, destructive faction warfare.

And so in Book III, Thucydides digresses and applies his most refined speech-technique (p. 92) in order to provide an unequalled analysis, as valid in our day as in his, of the internal struggle which broke out in one of the Greek city-states, Corcyra (Corfu). A pattern for similar disintegrations elsewhere, it foreshadowed the civil strife which helped to bring down Athens. To fight for power was human nature (p. 108), but in wartime, with the major powers egging on the political parties in one state after another, the whole process got out of hand; and rivers of blood started to flow. Thucydides' expert concern for group psychology gives him a special interest in the gradual decline of conduct that causes such disasters and is accelerated when they occur.

One accompaniment of the process is an inversion of values, mirrored in a turning upside down of the normal significances of language: 'To fit in with the change of events, words, too, had to change their usual meanings. What used to be described as a thoughtless act of aggression was now regarded as the courage one would expect to find in a party member. . . . Anyone who held violent opinions could always be trusted, and anyone who objected to them became a suspect.'[22] This explanation of how the infernos of political hatred completely transposed the use of words has a modern ring. But it was also very much in keeping with the fiction-puncturing questions that were being asked at the time by contemporary sophists and by Socrates. Such an approach came particularly easily to Thucydides because, in his determination to strip off any trace of comforting illusions, he was always ready to pounce observantly and ruthlessly on the blatant contrasts between what men and parties and governments profess and what they do.

The Corcyraean horror is the last of three set-pieces in the superb central section of Thucydides' account of the Ten Years' War, representing his most serious thoughts. Before this account of internal strife came the no less harrowing descriptions of the vengeance taken by Athens and Sparta on smaller places that had resisted them, Mytilene and Plataea respectively.

These incidents raise a different political problem of equal urgency, the question of imperialism. In connection with Pericles it was observed that, whereas a veil is drawn over the early aggressive part of his career, the Funeral Speech does suggest that Thucydides felt admiration for the Athens which these imperialistic activities had created (p. 96). The unprecedented brilliance of that world gazes out at us even today from the ruined yet immensely nostalgic temples of the Acropolis. No culture, said Spengler, has ever adored another so passionately as the Western world has adored the ancient Greeks; and what has been admired is the Athens of the Funeral Speech, with its freedom and ease, its cultivation of 'refinement without extravagance and knowledge without effeminacy'. 'I declare', cried Pericles, 'that our city is an education to Greece. Fix your eyes every day on the greatness of Athens as she really is, and fall in love with her.'[23]

He professed openly, according to Thucydides, that the money for all this came largely from the subject states. The magnificent use that Athens made of these funds is the practical justification for its empire. But there is another reason, too, why the Empire is justifiable, and that, we are told in terms that seem surprisingly frank, is because it is natural for men to want glory and dominion.[24] Whether this is Pericles or Thucydides speaking, we do not know, but the historian certainly believed that the drive to power is natural, for individuals and communities alike. If, therefore, a state is strong enough, its growth at the expense of others is inevitable and even justifiable. It has always been a rule that the weak should be subject to the strong; Thucydides says so again and again.[25] Even the moderate Syracusan statesman Hermocrates, of whom he approves, conceded that the designs of Athens in Sicily have to be pardoned, because it is in the nature of human beings to try to rule wherever they find there is no adequate resistance in their path.

At this time, the sophists were analysing the scope and significance of force in human activities, either measuring it up against justice or explaining that the two things merged. In Athens, there were, it is true, many stories of generosity and protection of the weak. But the display of such qualities was restricted by the interests of the State. Thucydides only attaches a subordinate role to justice, dismissing it as generally irrelevant.[26] Pericles, in the speeches ascribed to him, avoids paying any attention to the conventional theme of Athens as champion of liberty and the oppressed. Instead, he praises power. And the logical deduction, often repeated in the pages of Thucydides, is that empires cannot voluntarily stop, because to relinquish them is perilous and suicidal. As the Athenians explained to the Spartans, 'At first, fear of Persia was our chief motive, though afterwards we thought, too, of our own honour and our own interest. Finally there came a time when ... it was clearly no longer safe for us to risk letting our empire go, especially as any allies that left us would go over to you.'[27]

Here again there is no lack of frankness. The Corinthians pointed out to their Spartan allies that all this imperialism was a product of the Athenian temperament. 'If they aim at something and do not get it, they think they have been deprived of what belonged to them already; whereas, if their enterprise is successful, they regard that success as nothing compared to what they will do next. ... In a word, they are by nature incapable of living a quiet life themselves, or of allowing anyone else to do so either.'[28]

The historian does not let us know whether he thinks these Athenian characteristics, in themselves, are good or bad. To him, as to Sophocles, the answer depends on how the quality is used.

> Many the wonders, but nothing walks stranger than man.
> Clever beyond all dreams
> The inventive craft that he has
> Which may drive him one time or another to well or ill.[29]

But Democritus, in his ethical work *On Cheerfulness*,[30] is disposed to see the potentially bad side, for he warns against the evils of restless activity. And Thucydides himself, at a later stage in his work, has a word of praise for the *caution* of Chios, the passive opposite of Athenian hustling (p. 105).

He is also well aware that many people found this Athenian characteristic unlovable. For all his admiration of Athens, he emphasises at length the extreme unpopularity of its rule and the passionate desire of the subject cities, or rather of their ruling classes, to revolt.[31] Indeed, for dramatic reasons, he probably overpaints this picture, and exaggerates the corresponding hopes of liberation that were centred upon Sparta. Thucydides loves contrasts of this kind. He also wants to avoid the well-worn, standard oratorical praises of Athens. And his severe view of Athenian rule was no doubt influenced by what he heard, during the years of his banishment, from his country's enemies and its even more embittered exiles.

These beliefs about imperialism are brought out with ruthless candour in the discussion of Melos in Book v (416 BC). That little island, originally colonised by Sparta, had refused to pay tribute to Athens.[32] In the dialogue which Thucydides devotes to the occasion, Athenians and Melians are debating what should happen next. In a case like this, when relations between states of wholly unequal power were concerned, the Athenians, who were about to reduce Melos to subjection, dismissed justice as irrelevant. In the mouths of the Melian representatives, on the other hand, are placed arguments, perhaps rather original and unusual in this age,[33] supporting fair play in inter-state dealings. But the Athenians, in the circumstances, will have nothing of this.

You know as well as we do that, when these matters are discussed by practical people, the standard of justice depends on the equality of power to compel, and that in fact the strong do what they have the power to do and the weak accept what they have to accept. . . . We know that you or anybody else with the same power as ours would be acting in precisely the same way.[34]

Some contemporary sophists were maintaining that might is right.[35] But that is not quite the point which these spokesmen of Athens wanted to make. They were reflecting another and rather more subtle sophistic argument by maintaining that the question of justice does not enter into the matter at all unless there is equal power on both sides to enforce it.

There was a tragic irony in this warning against deceptive hopes uttered by the Athenians at a time when they themselves were about to launch confidently on the Sicilian expedition. And there was tragedy in the brutal annihilation of the Melians by Athens, so soon to be followed by the obliteration of the Athenian army in Sicily. These were human tragedies, not divine (p. 102), and they were brought about by unwisdom. Thucydides evidently agreed that the facts of life are as the Athenian delegates said they are. But he had already pointed out the practical perils of treating people as badly as this when he scathingly condemned the cruelties of Cleon and saw them as contributions to the ultimate catastrophe (p. 98).

Cleon, the sort of man who produced disaster, is presented as a demagogue – a much more extreme democrat then Pericles.[36] For, although the government presided over by Pericles had been a democracy in name, Thucydides remarks that it was really coming to be ruled by its first citizen.[37] And we are told how well he did it. A strong guide of the State was an appropriate solution for the problems of a people at war. Thucydides was probably aware that Protagoras, too, felt able to offer arguments in favour of a 'wise monarch'.[38] The historian himself was a man who, like most educated people with aristocratic connections, approved of democracy if, and only if, it did not go too far.

He admired democratic institutions and manners because they were the source of Athenian strength. What he found particularly useful in this system was the rule of law, which Herodotus had likewise admired,[39] and he approved of the high conception of civic duty enunciated by Pericles as a speciality of the Athenians, and indeed attributed to them even by their enemies. 'As for their bodies, they regard them as expendable for their city's sake, as though they were not their own; but each man cultivates his own intelligence, again with a view to doing something notable for his city.'[40] This attitude, like the equality of opportunity which went with it, appealed to Thucydides. And it was also of practical value, because the existence of a democracy at home prevented the bulk of the populations in other cities from associating themselves with the anti-Athenian feelings of their own leading men (p. 109).

On the other hand he feels the utmost contempt for demagogic leaders like Cleon, because he hates the fickleness of the mob they played up to.[41] Having, then, so exceptionally little sympathy for the common man, he might be expected to prefer the sort of closed oligarchy his kinsmen had conducted in the past. However, this does not appeal to him either. He is able to appreciate that government by the few had served Sparta well.[42] But there conditions were peculiar, and at Athens he will have none of it. He adopts a very critical view, therefore, of the oligarchical government of the Four Hundred at Athens (411). For one thing it was not likely to impress the allies.

The states in the Athenian alliance, he said, saw no reason to suppose that they would be any better off under the so-called upper classes than under the democracy, considering that when the democracy had committed crimes it had been at the instigation, under the guidance, and usually for the profit, of these upper classes themselves. With these classes in control, people could be put to death by violence and without a trial, whereas the democracy offered security to the ordinary man and kept the upper classes in their place.[43]

And he himself agreed that there were many objections to oligarchy. A typical example was the disagreeable personal animosity – much nastier than anything under a democracy – which arises when people under an oligarchical government do not get the jobs they want.[44] Although the Four Hundred included men such as Antiphon whose talents, as far as the interests of the State were concerned, seemed to outweigh his faults (p. 100), oligarchs tend to be self-seekers and traitors.

It was a very different matter when the Four Hundred were overthrown by the Five Thousand. Control was now lodged, for a short

III

time, in the hands of a reasonably large quantity of men belonging to the upper property-classes and limited to people over thirty years of age. This development, which was accompanied by the abolition of pay for office, inspires the historian to utter an approving word. 'During the first period of this new regime the Athenians appear to have had a better government than ever before, at least in my time. There was a reasonable and moderate blending of the few and the many, and it was this, in the first place, that made it possible for the city to recover from the bad state into which it had fallen.'[45] This unusually cordial statement might seem to contradict his earlier praise of the quite different Periclean regime, which, although under strong direction, had been a much wider democracy. In those days the sailors had played an active part, and Thucydides seems to have regarded that as a good thing,[46] whereas under the Five Thousand they were excluded. Perhaps what he is saying is that the former system had worked under Pericles, but now, in the absence of his guidance, the new arrangement was better.

The leading spirit of the Five Thousand was Theramenes. A controversial figure, he was criticised for his political gymnastics. But like Antiphon he is praised by the historian for his cleverness, that quality which Thucydides so much admired. And the two men had something else in common as well. For Theramenes, as Aristotle later remarked, was ready to serve under any and every constitution; and Thucydides' approval was increased by the fact that he, too, did not attach great significance to constitutional forms. They were a fashionable subject of study, however, and essays on constitutions had begun to appear recently (p. 44). The anonymous author of one short pamphlet, known as 'The Old Oligarch (? 443), objected, like Thucydides, to advanced democracy. But he ironically explains, apparently to a foreign opponent of the system in question, that at Athens it would be far from easy to overthrow. Here is a writer not only more conservative than Thucydides, but for once more caustic as well. But that is because the historian does not think it worth while to become caustic about constitutional issues. The claim by Friedrich Dahlmann, in 1848, that his German constitution proposed 'with a few incisive paragraphs to heal the ills of a thousand years' would have seemed to him ridiculous.

What was needed, instead, was to study politics – the behaviour of politicians under whatever system they might find themselves. And so Thucydides, with his fierce and profound interest in the performances of these politicians, imposed on the world the idea that the only history worth having is political and at least politico-military history. The nineteenth century was particularly indebted to this idea, and it was then that Seeley wrote: 'history is past politics, and present politics future history'.

7

The Methods of Thucydides

BEING, therefore, a political historian, Thucydides was not an economic historian, at least not in any modern sense of the term. Indeed, it was not possible for him to be anything of the kind. The data needed in order to write such history were not there to be collected, or at least never *were* collected; and in any case historians had different aims. Nevertheless, Thucydides was thoroughly well aware of the importance of the economic factor. Writing, for example, about early Greece, he stresses its lack of material resources. He also emphasises that the power of the Athenians depended on financial strength; and he gives a detailed survey of their assets at the beginning of the Peloponnesian War. However, he decided that the war's main underlying cause was not economic at all, but political. It was not the commercial jealousy of Corinth. This, it is true, sparked the hostilities off. But the real, basic cause was Sparta's political fear (p. 80).

This is a period for which we do not possess many external counter-checks upon whatever information the hazards of fortune have left us. For the most part, therefore, what Thucydides tells us, or chooses not to tell us, cannot be corroborated from any other source. Since, then, like other ancient historians, he could not, or would not, write an economic history of his times, we cannot do so either. But we do happen to have many fragments of Athenian quota lists or tribute lists. They indicate the annual sums due from every tribute-paying member of the Delian (Athenian) League to the Treasury of Athena at Athens. These lists were usually published on tablets of wood, but the records of the quotas from 454/453 to 415/414 were fortunately inscribed on stone.

These documents show us some of the financial facts that Thucydides has chosen *not* to tell us. He has not, for example, let us know that tributes were raised in 425-424. The fact that such an increase took place implies that reserves had been low. Yet he has not mentioned this consideration as an argument in favour of peace during the debates on the subject in 423 or 421. Like other ancient historians, he felt no obligation to study epigraphy, or numismatics either. Nor, for that matter, does he bother to mention that, since empire meant arteries of trade, the war-party were the merchants of the Piraeus. Thucydides ruled, as a modern historian would not have ruled, that a description of such matters was irrelevant to his plan. Major developments regarding Persia are also omitted, and so are internal political changes, when they do not seem relevant to his over-all design. This rigorous selectivity means that he has given us a history which is almost unique for the large ranges of events and developments which it does *not* tell us – and which we consequently do not know.[1]

His work, instead, is unparalleled for its rigorous structure, for the intense concentration of its impact. This rigour imposes its own pattern on what he writes, fitting the narrative into the mould he himself has constructed. His ruthless elimination of items held to be irrelevancies has made his work one of the shortest of the great historical masterpieces, but it has also left us with no possibility of examining his conclusions or forming alternative opinions for ourselves.

Anaxagoras declared 'that which appears is an earnest of what does not', and the same might be said of Thucydides' historical method. This process of simplification is diametrically opposed to the practice of writers such as Proust, who prefer to preserve every aberration and meander. It is also opposed to the methods of Herodotus, for whom Thucydides shows little sympathy (p. 78). The younger man was the hedgehog to the older man's fox: 'the fox knows many things, but the hedgehog knows one big thing'.[2] When they both described Thrace and Macedonia, for example, the picturesque incidental details of Herodotus are wholly lacking in Thucydides, who limits himself to what he regards as essentials.[3] He is always on the look out for generalisations, disengaging any factor likely to repeat itself and converting it into a timeless abstraction, just as contemporary sculptors were isolating the permanent elements in people's faces.[4] With powerful repercussions on the whole future of historical writing, as Arnaldo Momigliano says, 'Thucydides carefully read (or listened to) his Herodotus and decided that the Herodotean approach to history was unsafe. . . . Thucydides did not believe there was a future in Herodotus' attempt to describe events he had not witnessed and to tell the story of men whose language he could not understand. . . . He was insensitive to Herodotus' bold attempt to open up the gates of the past and of foreign countries to historical research. He was setting up stricter standards of historical reliability, even at the risk of confining history to a narrow patch of contemporary events.'

In order to maintain these standards, Thucydides shows iron restraint. For page after page he offers no moral judgments. Men, he seems to tell us, are bound to act in their own interests, and cannot therefore be blamed. He seeks to emphasise his objectivity by writing of himself in the third person, like Julius Caesar. Never is his detachment more remarkable (and deliberate) than when he is describing the events which led to his own failure and exile. It is true that Cleon, who bore a share of blame for the entire situation, is disparaged. But the enemy commander Brasidas is one of the men Thucydides admires – unless that is a subtle form of self-defence, because his excellence makes Thucydides' failure against him the more excusable. At any rate the outcome, the most wretched and decisive event of his life, is described by the historian with almost superhuman brevity and restraint: 'it happened that I was banished from my country for twenty years after my command at Amphipolis'.[5]

That is a characteristic manifestation of his continual attempt to look at events steadily and in due proportion. But in these post-Freudian, post-Marxian days we know that impartiality is impossible to attain. And certainly Thucydides does not, in fact, attain it. For one thing, in spite of his rejection of divine anger, he is not as consistently amoral as the truly impartial man would have to be. For the disintegration of Corcyra racked in civil strife, the demoralisation of Athens shattered by the plague, do not, in reality, leave him cold, but cause him distress. And these signs of humanity are rather more than a concession to the conventional scruples of his readers; he sounds a compassionate man.[6] Like Descartes, he thought, or claimed to think, that he had stripped himself of every preconception. But in fact he does not ally himself with the complete moral nihilism favoured by some contemporary sophists. Instead, he stands about half-way between that totally negative point of view and the coherent application of ethical standards to political behaviour.

Thucydides, then, betrays his claims to impartiality by allowing a certain amount of moral bias into his story. He also has powerful prejudices and obsessions. Some he is at pains to hide. Others, such as his detestation of Cleon, are unconcealed. Infrequently, but all the same decidedly, he offers personal interventions and views,[7] erupting from strong inner tensions which 'broke through impersonality', as M.I. Finley remarks, 'into savage whiplash comments'. His severe selection of material is in itself, as it cannot fail to be, an inevitable expression of choice and partiality. The consequent absence of a balanced picture prompted from Cobden the anguished cry, 'A file of *The Times* newspaper is worth all the works of Thucydides.' But *The Times*, too, as readers of *Pravda* will tell you, is not wholly without its partialities. Nor is *Pravda*; newspapers are all alike inevitably unobjective, and so are historians.

Yet, whatever his partialities, the historical method of Thucydides remains something gigantically impressive – and something new. Or rather, it is an extension of Herodotus with the addition of more determinedly systematic effort and a good many grains of salt. He was also in a position to benefit from certain researches which had not been available to Herodotus. He knew, for example, of the chronological improvements of Hellanicus (p. 77). The outbreak of the war is most meticulously dated, not by one calendar reckoning, but by three: those of Athens and Argos and Sparta.[8] The fact that these cities used thoroughly diverse ways of reckoning the passage of time illustrates the almost unimaginable chronological problems which faced Thucydides. Inevitably, he failed to date certain events satisfactorily.[9] But his attitude to such problems was acute and critical. For example, a purely annalistic arrangement seemed to him insufficient – one of his criticisms of Hellanicus – and so he dated the events of the war by summers and winters.[10]

In order to defend his methods of collecting information, Thucydides notes that throughout the whole twenty-seven years of the war he was a man of mature age capable of finding out the truth.[11] And he described the procedure that he followed.

With regard to my factual reporting of the events of the war I have made it a principle not to write down the first story that came my way, and not even to be guided by my own general impressions. Either I was present myself at the events which I have described or else I heard of them from eye-witnesses whose reports I have checked with as much thoroughness as possible.[12]

As a personal observer he possessed an advantage over Herodotus, because until his exile he had taken a more prominent part in events. Thucydides was a soldier like Aeschylus who fought at Marathon, and a general like Sophocles who helped suppress a revolt at Samos (440). At several points in Thucydides' narrative there are touches which suggest first-hand observation.[13] As for the obtaining of information at second hand, he stresses what a difficult task this was. For 'different eye-witnesses give different accounts of the same events, speaking out of partiality for one side or the other or else from imperfect memories'.[14] Although Thucydides never names his informants, he sought them out in a highly conscientious way – interrogating Plataeans, for example, about the siege of their town, and consulting Spartans as well as Athenians about Pylos. He notes a beneficial result of his exile in the opportunity it gave him to consult Peloponnesian informants.[15]

Moreover, although he makes no use of the tribute lists (p. 115), he does cite eleven other documents textually. Not all, however, are genuine,[16] and one conflicts with the narrative.[17] It has been suggested that this material would have been further assimilated had Book VIII been finished (p. 86), and a similar point has been raised in connection with Book v which contains the text of the Peace of Nicias. Although it would never have occurred to Thucydides that written records are a primary source for history, he is one of the very few surviving Greek historians to have utilised documents in such a way. Not all his research methods, however, have as modern an air as this. For example, the indication of rival versions is infrequent – as infrequent as any explanation or identification of the evidence that has been employed.[18] Certainly, his way of carrying out an enquiry represented a huge advance in efficiency on anything that had gone before. And yet, he does not lift more than a corner of the veil. As Bury rightly concluded, 'the secret of his critical methods may be said to have perished with him'.

Factual truthfulness was not, perhaps, the dearest of things to most Greeks. But it is evident that Thucydides, granted his conventions and prejudices, attached an unprecedentedly high degree of importance to the truth. Contemporary sophists may not have instilled in him a very keen interest in questions of moral right and wrong, but he did derive from them the sharpest desire to distinguish between what was true and false.

He also owed quite a lot of his scientific method to contemporary advances in natural science. Euripides was praising such researches,[19] and Thucydides has much in common with the most famous of all physicians, Hippocrates of Cos, whose influence reached its peak during the Peloponnesian War. This influence is very apparent in the historian's detailed account of the terrifying plague at Athens.[20] To facilitate prognosis, the Hippocratics were at pains to describe the course of a disease accurately, and Thucydides' descriptions are of the same meticulous and analytic nature. The plague was particularly important to him, first, because he caught it himself, and secondly, because it was an excellent example of that typical sort of historical phenomenon which falsifies all calculations (p. 105). Furthermore, prognosis was just what he was interested in; he regarded it as the chief quality of a statesman (p. 95). Hippocrates was taught by a Greek from Thrace[21] where Thucydides lived – and was said to have died in northern Greece, at Larissa.

In his descriptions of battles, the historian may well seem to have declined from this scientific ideal. These accounts include much detail and display evident personal experience and expertise, and yet, like the battle-pieces of most other ancient writers, they are suspiciously unreal and repetitive. Perhaps Greek battles may have possessed a somewhat repetitive character. But Thucydides all too often leaves the purpose as well as the conduct of an engagement obscure and unexplained.[22] This is partly because he only mentions military technicalities when they explain a general principle,[23] or when a ruse or a mistake creates a dramatic situation; the dramatic and psychological elements are what he wants to emphasise.[24] Another reason, however, and one which was appreciated by

Herodotus and Tolstoy, was the fact that battles *are* obscure. A night engagement offers Thucydides an extreme example of this state of affairs: 'In daylight those who take part in an action have a clearer idea of it, though even then they cannot see everything, and in fact no one knows much more than what is going on around himself. But in a battle by night . . . could anyone be sure of what happened exactly?'[25] For when Thucydides finds it impossible to discover the truth, he is not afraid to say so. This applies to historical times, but it is also very relevant to his survey of ancient epochs in Book 1.

I have found it impossible, because of its remoteness in time, to acquire a really precise knowledge of the distant past or even of the history preceding our own period. . . . People are inclined to accept all stories of ancient times in an uncritical way – even when these stories concern their own native countries.[26]

This was indeed a promising beginning, and its promise is fulfilled by an account of early history which is a highly professional reconstruction on the basis of the fashionable criterion of probability.

Thucydides warns hearers and readers that they may find there is not much romance in his work.[27] But, in fact, all that can be said against him is that he does not go far enough towards cutting it out. For example, he tries to tidy up Homer and eliminate his 'exaggerations', thinking that this removal of unlikely accretions has reduced myths to history, and failing to appreciate the purely fictitious character of so much of the epic material.[28] This was common practice among ancient historians, and Herodotus had proceeded in the same way – though he did not attempt quite so laboriously to extract a kernel of fact. Nevertheless, this section of Thucydides' work contains a masterly and unusual account of material progress (p. 114), and it also includes thoroughly 'modern' archaeological deductions from the contents of ancient graves.[29]

Historical sources for this antique epoch were of course non-existent – that is to say, they were almost limited to what the poets had handed down. However, there was a history of the heroic age by the contemporary sophist Hippias of Elis, a man who was alive to the relativity of custom at different places and epochs.[30] For the later periods, and especially the Fifty Years that followed the Persian War, Thucydides may have drawn upon Antiochus of Syracuse, whose account of Sicily down to 424 BC was the first history of the western Greek world, and, in part, a contemporary history at that. But apparently no general history of the Fifty Years existed, except the brief and not wholly satisfactory chronicle of Hellanicus, and Thucydides' account of the rise of the Athenian Empire during that period not only provides an apt introduction to the principal theme but is as much of a pioneer *tour de force* as his account of more ancient times.

Yet, in an age when the keeping of records was extremely scrappy, the material for the diplomatic and social history of the decades preceding the Peloponnesian War was already irrecoverably lost at the time when Thucydides wrote. And even when information *was* available he does not always give it to us, because of his rigorous selectivity. For example, relations with Persia are skimped: there is no stress on the anti-Persian tasks of Athens' Delian League, and the Peace of Callias (449) which put an end to hostilities with Persia is ignored. For Thucydides did not regard it as part of his task to imitate Herodotus and write about Hellenic conflicts and relationships with the Persian Empire: he only mentions Persia when he has to. This shows a particularly strong degree of self-imposed restraint, because Thucydides, an exile, was in a good position to obtain documents and information from the borderlands between the Greek and Persian worlds, and in fact did so to good effect.

Furthermore, he had no racialist reasons for discriminating against the Persians. On the contrary, like other people of this time (p. 46), he felt detached from the old emotional hostility towards them. His views were not far from the rising cosmopolitanism of contemporary sophists.[31] Moreover, his northern connections had given him a considerable interest in non-Greeks, as he showed by a digression on his father's country Thrace (of which, like Herodotus, he had an exaggerated opinion)[32] and by remarks indicating his approval of King Archelaus of Macedonia, a country which was not regarded as truly Greek, although its monarch claimed to be.[33]

Many a comment of this kind shows how easily Thucydides rose above petty chauvinisms. Yet his main subject was still Greece, and no one has equalled the penetration with which he analysed Greek society at its zenith. Nor has anyone ever probed the motives of men with greater rigour and intensity. It was for this reason, in spite of all Herodotus had achieved, that David Hume wrote: 'the first page of Thucydides is the beginning of all true history'.

3

The Later Greeks

8

Xenophon

AFTER the death of King Darius II of Persia (424–405 BC), the succession of his elder son Artaxerxes II Memnon was contested by the younger son Cyrus. Returning to Asia Minor where he had been ruling as viceroy, Cyrus began to collect a force of mercenaries from among the Greek soldiers who were footloose at the close of the Peloponnesian War. Ostensibly the recruiting was designed for operations against recalcitrant tribesmen in the centre of the Anatolian peninsula. But its real purpose was to march deep into the continent in order to overthrow the prince's elder brother. And so in 401 the Greek army of the Ten Thousand left Sardis on its way through southern Anatolia towards Mesopotamia.

The story of the expedition, the *March into the Interior (Anabasis)*, was told by one of the Greek commanders, the young Athenian Xenophon (*c.* 430–?350s BC). The work was later divided into seven books. In the first, an account is given of the inland march of the Ten Thousand, followed by the engagement at Cunaxa, forty-five miles from Babylon. Cyrus was killed in the battle; and soon afterwards, twenty-four of the principal Greek leaders were trapped and put to death, owing to the treachery of the Persian Tissaphernes. The Greek army then appointed Xenophon as one of the new generals, under the Spartan Cheirisophus. These events are discussed in the second book, and the next two are devoted to the withdrawal of the Greeks in the direction of their homeland, through

125

Mesopotamia, Kurdistan and Armenia, as far as the Black Sea.

The next two books deal with the rest of their journey. They set sail on the Black Sea and then proceeded by land across northern Asia Minor, until they reached the Bosphorus. Xenophon describes and justifies his methods of leadership over an army that had become truculent and undisciplined; after the death of Cheirisophus, he took sole charge. The final book tells how the force was brought over to Byzantium, a city then under Spartan control. With difficulty Xenophon succeeded in persuading his men not to sack the place (400). After he and the six thousand Greeks who were all that remained had spent the winter in the service of a Thracian brigand-prince, Seuthes, they were enlisted by two officers of the Spartan Thibron to fight against Tissaphernes in coastal Asia Minor. When they had got as far as Pergamum, Xenophon took a few men and attacked the stronghold of a wealthy Persian landowner Asidates, capturing him and his family and his possessions, and securing a huge amount of plunder. Then Thibron took the force over.

Xenophon was about twenty-nine at the time of the expedition. But he seems to have been over fifty when he described it in his *Anabasis* (*c.* 379).[1] This, his most famous work, is a fresh and vivid account of an enterprise in which he had played a leading part. Rarely has a good story been told so well by a major participant. One of the passages that has remained in the memory of the Western world is his description of the moment when the weary column, after its long retreat through inhospitable lands, reached the heights above Trapezus (Trebizond), and first caught sight of the sea, which meant so much to any Greek.

When the men in front reached the summit and caught sight of the sea there was great shouting. Xenophon and the rearguard heard it and thought there were some more enemies attacking in the front. . . . However, when the shouting got louder and drew nearer, and those who were constantly going forward started running towards the men in front who kept on shouting, and the more there were of them the more shouting there was, it looked then as though this was something of considerable importance.

So Xenophon mounted his horse and taking Lycus and the cavalry with him, rode forward to give support, and, quite soon, they heard the soldiers shouting out 'The sea! The sea!' and passing the word down the column. Then certainly they all began to run, the rearguard and all, and drove on the baggage animals and the horses at full speed; and when they had all got to the top, the soldiers, with tears in their eyes, embraced each other and their generals and captains.[2]

The only thing that jars slightly in the adventure stories of the *Anabasis* is the continual rightness of Xenophon's own behaviour as presented by himself. He justifies every one of his decisions with great care, and the general picture that is presented savours of complacency: 'While Xenophon was having breakfast two young men came running up to him. Everyone knew that it was permissible to come to him whether he was in the middle of breakfast or supper, or to wake him from his sleep and talk to him, if they had anything to say which had a bearing on the fighting.'[3] Some of these self-complimentary reminiscences may have assumed a more golden hue over the years, since Xenophon had waited for so very long before publishing his version; and in any case he was somewhat romantically inclined. The frequent self-justification is also intended as a reply to a much more critical account, now no longer extant, written by another of the mercenary captains on the expedition, Sophaenetus of Stymphalus. In order to make his own interpretation of events look more objective, Xenophon first published it under a fictitious name.[4]

He was not, apparently, able to get a general view of the disastrous Battle of Cunaxa which brought the hopes and life of Cyrus to an end. The engagement is excitingly enough described in terms suitable for the recitation for which the passage was destined, but its narration suffers from the defects which are so typical of ancient accounts of battles. Xenophon did, it is true, evidently hear Cyrus give an order,[5] which was not properly obeyed, but his knowledge of other features of the encounter is owed to a Greek who was the Persian court doctor, Ctesias of Cnidus. Just before Cyrus was killed he wounded Artaxerxes in the chest, and the Cnidian doctor is quoted as claiming to have dressed the wound himself. Ctesias wrote an extensive history of Persia[6] in a sensational, credulous fashion which foreshadowed the romantic historical novel, and some of the documents he cited in the work may have been invented by himself.[7] While censuring the ignorance of Herodotus, Ctesias includes ethnographical data according to his tradition, and some use may have been made of this information in the *Anabasis*.

But Xenophon's own experience and observations provide the same sort of picturesque material. Here, for example, are the drinking-habits of an underground village in Armenia.

There was barley-wine in great bowls. The actual grains of barley floated on top of the bowls, level with the brim, and in the bowls there were reeds of various sizes and without joints in them. When one was thirsty, one was meant to take a reed and suck the wine into one's mouth. It was a very strong wine, unless one mixed it with water, and when one got used to it, it was a very pleasant drink.[8]

One of Xenophon's principal interests was hunting – a vital food-gathering activity in the ancient world – and he had good opportunities to indulge this taste during the march. On the right bank of the Euphrates, for example,

Wild asses were very common and there were many ostriches also there were bustards and gazelles. . . . In the case of the wild asses, it was impossible to catch them except by stationing the horsemen at intervals from each other and hunting in relays. No one succeeded in catching an ostrich. Indeed the horsemen who tried soon gave up the pursuit, as it made them go a very great distance when it ran from them. It used its feet for running and got under way with its wings, just as if it was using a sail.[9]

Xenophon himself wrote a textbook on this subject of hunting.[10] Like other men with such tastes, he also held strong views on the desirability of good old-fashioned order and discipline, and indeed his ideas of sound government often seem to boil down to this. He was deeply impressed, for example, when Cyrus' waggons had got stuck in the mud, and the prince ordered the leading Persian noblemen to give a hand.

Then certainly one saw a bit of discipline. Wherever they happened to be standing, they threw off their purple cloaks and rushed forward as though it was a race – down a very steep hill, too, and wearing those expensive tunics which they have, and embroidered trousers. Some also had chains round their necks and bracelets on their wrists. But with all this on they leapt straight down into the mud and got the waggons on the dry ground quicker than anyone would have thought possible.[11]

But in spite of all his emphasis on discipline Xenophon has great sympathy for the ordinary soldier, whose day-to-day existence receives unique attention. Indeed, so great is his interest in the rank and file that he was criticised for being too sympathetic to them. The very human disagreements that occurred in the course of the expedition give an excellent picture of how the Greek way of life actually operated in practice, with its incessant talk and argument and clash of personalities. People's characters were of absorbing interest to Xenophon, and the acutely observed sketches summing up Cyrus and the Greek leaders[12] foreshadow the biographical enterprises on which he was going to embark in later years.

The *Anabasis* also looks towards the future in another way. This Greek penetration far into the interior of the Persian Empire was a sort of rehearsal for Alexander the Great. It made Persia's strategic weakness apparent, and it showed that a pan-Hellenic invading army was not beyond the bounds of possibility. Xenophon also anticipated Alexander and his successors by his plan to found a pan-Hellenic city on the south-east shores of the Black Sea. But the project came to nothing, since the idea of settling there did not appeal to his troops.

These various themes were further developed in his subsequent writings. Another twenty years passed before he approached the completion of his principal historical work, the *Greek History* in seven books. This began where Thucydides had left off (411), and continued until the year 362.

The first book, and part of the second, continue Thucydides' story of the Peloponnesian War until the final defeat of the Athenians by Lysander of Aegospotami on the Hellespont (405), followed by their capitulation in the next year. Then comes an account of the oligarchic revolution which placed the pro-Spartan Thirty in power Athens, and a description of their fall. A new phase begins with the third book, which, after briefly mentioning the events described in the *Anabasis*, describes the dominance of the Spartans and the campaigns they undertook against the viceroys of Persia in Asia Minor. In 395, with Persian encouragement, an anti-Spartan coalition was formed among the Greek states, and Lysander died. In Book IV the main part is played by Agesilaus, king of Sparta. After conferring with Pharnabazus, the Persian ruler of north-western Asia Minor, he returned to Greece where, at Coronea in Boeotia, he inflicted a defeat on the coalition (394). The Thebans had fought well against them, but after Coronea no enemy dared to face a Spartan army in pitched battle for another twenty years. Agesilaus also fought at Corinth and in north-western Greece and Argos, while Spartans and Athenians resumed hostilities against one another at sea (391–388). Book v tells how the Persians were persuaded by the Spartan general Antalcidas to agree to the 'King's Peace' (386). Athens and its allies were compelled to agree, and the subjection of the Asiatic Greeks to Persia was sealed.

Next the Spartans surprised, seized and garrisoned the citadel of Thebes (382), creating much disillusionment among Greeks who had hitherto been supporters of their cause. In the following year, after a prolonged siege, they reduced Olynthus in Thrace, disbanding the Chalcidian League over which it had presided. But rivals to Spartan domination were coming forward. The sixth book describes a transitory new power under Jason of Pherae in Thessaly. Some temporary successes were registered by Athens, which had formed a second League disclaiming the imperialistic ambitions of the previous century. The Athenians were now supporting Thebes, which, inspired by their leader Epaminondas, won the battle of Leuctra, and thereby eliminated Spartan influence from central Greece (371). When, however, they pressed on into Sparta's own homeland of Laconia, Athens decided to change its line and help the Spartans against their invaders. Book VII describes the brief period of Theban hegemony, leading up to the battle of Mantinea (362) in which Epaminondas, though again victorious against the Spartans, was fatally wounded, so that Thebes never proved able to assert itself again.

During the greater part of this period Xenophon was estranged from his native Athens. After the conclusion of the expedition described in the *Anabasis*, he had enrolled under the Spartan king Agesilaus.[13] Then, accompanying Agesilaus to Greece, he witnessed the battle of Coronea and indeed probably took part in it, fighting on the Spartan side against his fellow-Athenians and their Theban allies. Accordingly, Athens sentenced him to exile,[14] and he went to Sparta where he was joined by his wife and sons. A few years later the Spartans gave him an estate at Scillus near Olympia. However, Elis, to which the region had belonged, resumed occupation of Scillus after Sparta had been defeated at Leuctra, and so Xenophon lost his property. He took refuge at Corinth, but in *c.* 369 Athens, which had now made an alliance with the Spartans, rescinded his banishment. He sent his sons to serve in the Athenian cavalry, and one of them fell fighting against the Thebans at Mantinea. Whether Xenophon himself returned to Athens, and if so for how long, is uncertain. But Corinth is said to have been the place of his death, which probably occurred after 355. His *Greek History* had still been unfinished as late as 358.[15]

The first part of the work, extending down to the end of the Peloponnesian War (404), is distinct from the remaining books. Xenophon was one of several writers who deliberately attempted this task of continuing Thucydides.[16] Like the others, however, he is not in the same class as their forerunner and master. For one thing, he has moved away from the Attic way of speech, the medium of fifth-century masterpieces, to a more relaxed and less distinctive language, anticipatory of the common tongue of later Greece (*koine*). Because of his long absence from Athens, this style came more easily to him; but, although it has the advantage of greater lucidity and is therefore much easier to read, it altogether lacks the tension and brilliance of the earlier historian.

Moreover, as Xenophon's banal remedies for moral and social evils indicate,[17] he is vastly inferior to Thucydides in intellectual depth – and his reliability has been discredited by the discovery of a papyrus giving conflicting and evidently better versions of some of the events he describes (p. 427, n. 16). There is, inevitably, an anticlimax – or at least a change of direction into less challenging paths.

Nevertheless, this country gentleman who liked a good story was by no means an ordinary person. Pious and superstitiously attentive to omens, yet a practical man of affairs, he was uninterested in the basic causes of events, but a keen enough calculator of situations. Philanthropic yet egotistical, reactionary, un-self-conscious, optimistic about life and human nature, and above all versatile, he was the best of mirrors to his times.

Xenophon also possesses a special expertise rare in ancient historians; he knows about military affairs. It is true that contemporary specialists added a professional touch which he could not claim.[18] But he possessed a profound understanding of cavalry tactics, and was, indeed, the author of an essay on the duties of a cavalry commander. Appended to it is a treatise on horsemanship, the earliest complete work of its kind which is still in existence.

But his special attraction lies in his talent for the succinct and rapid description of exciting events. Xenophon's effective treatment of single episodes and scenes anticipates a later and more deliberately dramatic school of writing (p. 137). His pictures remain in the memory: the return of exiled Thebans, the speeches of Critias and Theramenes in his account of the oligarchic Thirty,[19] the trial of the moderate Theramenes and his execution with a joke on his lips (404).

Xenophon is again at his best describing Athens at the moment when the Athenian ship the *Paralus* brought the city the news of the fatal defeat at Aegospotami.

> It was at night that the *Paralus* arrived at Athens. As the news of the disaster was told, one man passed it to another, and a sound of wailing arose and extended first from the Piraeus, then along the Long Walls until it reached the city. That night no one slept. They mourned for the lost, but more still for their own fate. They thought that they themselves would be now dealt with as they had dealt with others.[20]

The writer of such words evidently felt for Athens in its distress. Yet, like Herodotus and Thucydides, he was an exile; and this gave him a wider view. In particular, as his career showed, he resembled many other upper-class Greeks in feeling a profound admiration for Sparta. At one point in the *Anabasis* we find him, as an Athenian of a sort, engaging in heavy *badinage* about the characteristics of the two peoples with a Spartan fellow-officer.[12] He even found something attractive in the 'laconic' witticisms and cruel practical jokes that passed for a sense of humour among the Spartans.

Being a man whose patriotic feelings for his own city had become so diluted, he felt content, at first, to see Sparta take charge after the Peloponnesian War. The idea that, in a changing and expanding world, landlocked Sparta was very soon going to become out of date would have been quite strange to him. Another of these old-style city-states was Thebes, which now had its moment of glory (p. 130). Xenophon greatly prefers Sparta to Thebes, whose leader Epaminondas he pointedly ignores. Nevertheless, when Sparta seized the Theban acropolis he was deeply shocked, and, although he sent his son to fight and die for the Spartans, his own sympathies towards them become more tepid and critical. This change of attitude is apparent both in the *Greek History*[22] and in a work on *The Constitution of the Spartans*, where a laudatory account eulogising the city's legendary founder Lycurgus (and assuming that he had possessed the views held by Xenophon himself) terminates in a censorious chapter prompted by disgust at the Spartan aggression.[23]

But before disillusionment had set in, Xenophon, who liked a colourful personality and a hero, found both in the Spartan monarch Agesilaus. One of the most picturesque scenes of the *Greek History* points the conventional contrast between Spartan austerity and Persian luxury by describing the meeting between Agesilaus and the satrap Pharnabazus.

Agesilaus and his escort of thirty Spartan officers were lying on the grass waiting for the Persians. Pharnabazus appeared dressed in clothes that would have been worth a lot of gold, and then his servants came forward to spread down for him the kind of soft rugs on which Persians sit. However, when Pharnabazus saw that there was no sort of ostentation or finery about Agesilaus, he was ashamed to make a display of his own luxury and lay down on the grass too, just as he was.[24]

After the death of Agesilaus (360), Xenophon wrote his praises in a composition which marks a new stage in the biographical type of literature which had gradually been developing. A man of marked though limited ability, the king had been quick-witted and romantic, a better tactician than strategist, narrow in his loyalties and thoroughly Spartan in his failure to appreciate sea-power. However, as Xenophon himself indicates,[25] carping criticism is not to be expected in an essay of this sort. It is a panegyric, a prose adaptation of the type of poem known as an *encomium*. Originally this had been the name of the triumphal song with which a victor in the games was led back in procession to his home, and then the term was extended to eulogistic writings in general. Xenophon again expressed this taste for hero-worship in a dialogue featuring King Hiero I of Syracuse (478–466),[26] who had extended his city's power over most of Sicily. There is also a long, dull, romantic, biographical story of the first king of Persia, *The Education of Cyrus* (559–529),[27] who is made to embody the historian's own concepts of the perfect ruler, including an officer-and-gentleman attitude towards education which is ostensibly Persian but is really based on traditions about Sparta.[28]

Similar ideals are attributed, by Xenophon, with dubious authenticity, to Socrates. A lot of information about him, much of it equally debatable, is included in his *Memoirs* devoted to this subject (360s BC; the usual title, *Memorabilia*, dates from AD 1569). This is not exactly a Life but a series of reminiscences. Xenophon had known the man[29] but was hardly a real pupil, and Socrates had died over thirty years before without leaving any writings. He appears in this work as a prosaic figure who displays a robust, paradoxical common sense, often in unexpected ways. The trial which led to his execution, as described here, has little in common with Plato's famous account in the *Apology*. The latter work is largely fictitious, and it is just as hard to believe the version of Xenophon. It is intended as a reply to current attacks on Socrates' memory.[30] Xenophon's descriptions of him were probably drawn, in large part, from an extensive literature that has not survived. Yet the *Memoirs* may well have been the most important biographical or semi-biographical work that had so far appeared. The whole idea of biography was greatly encouraged by the colourful, original, tantalising personality of Socrates, which people were eager to reconstruct from their own various imaginative and partisan points of view.

Every one of Xenophon's works shows, in varying fashion, this preoccupation with life-stories of men – an interest which he extends also to women.[31] During the same years the orator and educationalist Isocrates (436–338 BC) was displaying a similar tendency, and the two writers must have exercised some influence upon each other. Biography, of a sort, was now under way. The idea that men's deeds must be recorded was as ancient as literature itself, but it was not until the fifth century BC that prose memoirs, and sketches of politicians, had begun to come into fashion (p. 20).[32] Now, after the concentration of the sophists and Euripides and Thucydides upon individual personality, the fashion was gaining ground. It is true that unmixed biography was not usually regarded by the ancients as a part of history (p. xiv) – a down-grading for which its origins from encomium were partly responsible. There is, certainly, a great deal of history which ancient biographers deliberately ignore, but the same might be said of the historians. Nevertheless, from now on they generally considered character sketches and biographical facts to be part of their business. Moreover, biography itself, regarded as a separate genre, began to make headway on its own account. In these developments Xenophon, like Isocrates, assumes particular importance. But his effect on the evolution of the art also had its harmful side, because his moral preoccupations induced him to concentrate Greek biography on the question how well this or that individual conformed to a preconceived pattern of ideal behaviour.

9

The Dramatic Historians

THE fourth century BC should have been propitious to history because it was an age of such unparalleled changes. Xenophon's emphasis on the desirability of strong leadership was soon given forcible practical expression by Philip II of Macedonia (359–336). Reducing Greece to virtual subordination, he ushered in the Hellenistic epoch during which the city-states, with a few exceptions such as Rhodes, no longer possessed any real independence of action.

Efforts by these states, after the death of Philip, to regain a free hand were crushed by his son Alexander, who then drove east, repeating on a vast scale the move against Persia in which Xenophon had participated. The annexation of the entire Persian Empire gave Alexander the greatest territory that any ruler west of China had ever possessed. After his death (323), followed by half a century of confusion, three huge successor states held the field: the Antigonids in Macedonia, the Ptolemies (Lagids) in Egypt, and the Seleucids in Syria and the east. Each of these empires controlled an ever-shifting pattern of dependencies. During the third century BC, a large part of Asia Minor split off from the Seleucid realm to form the kingdom of Pergamum. The mainland of Greece, which had been the target of competition between the great powers, witnessed the formation of two federal groups of city-states, the Aetolian and Achaean Leagues, dominating central Greece and the Peloponnese respectively.

Meanwhile, during the early years of the same century, the Romans had become masters of the whole of central Italy. They were therefore bound to clash with the Greek cities in the southern part of the peninsula. Conflict was also inevitable with Carthage, originally a Phoenician colony and now the leading western Mediterranean power, with a large foothold in western Sicily. A monarch of the Greek borderlands across the Adriatic, Pyrrhus of Epirus, did not succeed in establishing himself in south Italy and the Sicilian territories across the strait. Not only did he fail to dislodge the Romans but he left them more powerful than before. And so the stage was set for the direct confrontation between Rome and Carthage.

But a vital chapter of ancient historical writing, a series of vital chapters, is missing. For the Greek historians of this entire period are lost. However, it is at least possible, by collecting and assessing references to their works in other writers, to attempt a fairly confident reconstruction of their principal aims and characteristics.

The most eminent among them were all affected by Xenophon's contemporary Isocrates, the Athenian orator and educationalist. For he was the chief creator of rhetoric as a distinct science. In pursuance of the ideas of Gorgias, he developed the profoundly influential idea that language should be adjusted and modelled in such a way as to subjugate readers to the writer's will. His words must be calculated to cause pleasure by every available means. Yet his purpose in doing so should not be purely hedonistic. On the contrary, his duty is to provide, and commend to his public, instruction of a more unequivocal kind than Herodotus or Thucydides had ever attempted, and to supply it on a more systematic and far-reaching scale than the rather casual uplift of Xenophon.[1]

The historians who accepted these ideas had consequently entered a new phase. It was now their business to supplant the poets as popular teachers.[2] Yet at the same time rhetoric was bound to compete strongly, and often contradictorily, with the claims of veracity. The latter quality was too easily interpreted as being of only secondary and relative importance.[3] For example, this was manifestly the case with the nostalgic glorifications of the Attic past in which Isocrates and other orators indulged.[4] It was equally true of the encomia, sometimes including deliberate deviations from the truth, which gave

Isocrates, like Xenophon, a somewhat equivocal role in the history of biographical writing (p. 134).[5]

Ephorus of Cyme, who was born soon after 400 and died in 327 BC, studied under Isocrates but did not attempt his elaborate manner, though he derived from him a taste for heavy moralising.[6] Many criticisms were launched at his history, which, although a vast and erudite work of synthesis, was evidently vulnerable on several grounds.[7] However, it is now almost entirely lost.[8] Our view, therefore, of Ephorus, as of most historians in this and the following epoch, must inevitably be coloured by their successor Polybius, whose work, extant in part, will be the subject of the next chapter. For Polybius devoted an unusual amount of space to the analysis of his forerunners, often in sharply critical terms. He begins with a prejudice against Ephorus, because the latter had apparently slighted the musical talents of Polybius' native land Arcadia.[9] Nevertheless, though he regards Ephorus' descriptions of land warfare as defective he is prepared to admit the good quality of his descriptions of sea-battles.[10] He also devotes unusual words of praise both to the style of Ephorus (although surviving fragments show it to have been poor) and to his welcome recognition that history and oratory are not the same thing.[11]

Most praiseworthy of all, however, in the opinion of Polybius, is Ephorus' choice of theme, which purported to be a universal history of Greece.[12] The concept was derived from the pan-Hellenism of which Isocrates, following up the intellectual destruction of city-state barriers by the sophists, had become a pioneer exponent.[13] Pan-Hellenic tastes were establishing a standard Greek language (p. 131). They were also encouraging a kind of history which, at least as far as the Greeks were concerned, did increasingly deserve to be described as universal. Here, however, Polybius for once errs on the side of being overcomplimentary. For Ephorus was not, in fact, really universal – even on the limited, pan-Hellenic, scale at which he aimed. It is true that he envisaged the history of the Greek peninsula as a unity. Nevertheless, rather than attempt a synoptic view, all he did was to collect and juxtapose particular histories of the various city-states without any serious attempt at welding them together.[14]

The second of the principal fourth-century historians was Theopompus of Chios (c. 378–305). Again, except for a considerable number of fragments, his works are lost. He, too, was probably a disciple and certainly a supporter of Isocrates. He was also an adherent of his master's insidious views on history, which he demonstrated in a summary of Herodotus, then in a *Greek History* (down to 395) which was one of several continuations of Thucydides,[15] and next in a life of King Philip II of Macedonia. The first of these works indicated that Theopompus modelled himself on Herodotus' taste for anecdotes, digressions and travels.[16] The *Greek History*, written in *c.* 350, was a political polemic against Thucydides, supporting Sparta,[17] blaming the Peloponnesian War on the Athenian democracy[18] and expressing hatred of all democratic governments. The *Life of Philip*, full of enormous digressions,[19] recognised that the power of Macedonia, through its king, had provided a unifying principle which started a new epoch of world history. Theopompus exalted the monarch as the man who placed Isocrates' pan-Hellenism on the map and put it into practice.[20] However, he criticised Philip's private life, on the grounds that this caused his death and all the confusion it created.[21] Later on, Polybius was disgusted by these attacks on the monarch who had not only shown kindness to his own country Arcadia, but had also, in his view, saved Greece from Spartan oppression.[22] He likewise blamed Theopompus for neglecting the period of history just before Philip II, and for writing a history round a man rather than round Greece.[23] This seemed to him to be carrying the trend to biography too far. Nevertheless, in seeing Philip as the herald of a new world of large monarchies, Theopompus showed better judgment than his disapproving successor.

Polybius also rebuked him for self-contradictory, coarse and undignified extravagance of language.[24] Theopompus was notorious for the violent and temperamental manner in which he concentrated on people's private lives, launching ferocious charges of luxury and vice, and presenting disclosures of the secret wickedness that so often lurks beneath apparent virtue[25] – a theme which later historians, particularly Romans, imitated in abundance. Although remarkable for wide research, he was prepared to invent his own myths and fables and incredible stories. Indeed, he even boasted of this,[26] citing his teacher Isocrates who had used myths as a rhetorical device to point a moral or an argument. In order to attract readers, Theopompus aimed at the Isocratean type of rhythmical, rhetorical prose.[27] Our loss of his writings has deprived us of spicy, individual, versatile works,[28] though they were not, apparently, histories of the very first order.

The third of the important fourth-century historians, whose output has again almost entirely disappeared, was Timaeus of Tauromenium in Sicily (*c.* 356–260 BC).[29] Fleeing from his native island for political reasons, he settled in Athens (317 or 312 BC) and studied rhetoric under a pupil of Isocrates. Then he wrote an extensive History, largely concerned with Sicilian affairs but including events in Italy, Carthage and Greece down to *c.* 264 BC.[30] A writer whose extremely severe, cranky and irritable criticisms of other historians – sharply indicated in each case by name – earned him the title of the Fault-Finder,[31] he became, in his turn, the target of a prolonged and savage onslaught from Polybius. 'Timaeus, who is so fond of criticising others for trifles of this sort, has totally neglected the business of making personal inquiries which is the most important element in writing history. . . . He is blinded by prejudice.'[32] He is further accused of extreme credulity and a 'womanish love of strange events'.[33] Although Polybius is bound to admit that the very considerable reputation of Timaeus makes it necessary to take him seriously,[34] these criticisms go on and on until they have filled almost an entire book. Almost no unpleasant thing that could possibly be said is omitted.[35] But the gist of the entire attack is that Timaeus failed to participate in events, as every historian should (p. 161). Instead, says Polybius, he was just a professional and a bookworm who wrote his whole history far away from where things happened, sitting in his study and his library, so that the result is a great deal of pedantry and legend, something utterly remote from reality.[36]

Timaeus appeared to Polybius, who likewise aspired to write about the west, as a dangerous competitor who had stolen some of his thunder before he was born. Indeed, Timaeus, together with a predecessor Antiochus of Syracuse, has a very good claim to be regarded as one of the pioneers and founders of Western history. He also possessed the distinction of being the first historian who took an interest in Rome, which was Polybius' speciality. This uncomfortable situation, inevitably involving all subsequent writers in a certain dependence on Timaeus' account, was all the more apparent to Polybius because he had to start his account of the western Mediterranean where his predecessor had stopped; he had been left with no alternative.[37] To the later historian, a keen supporter of the Achaean League (p. 155), Timaeus' old-fashioned incomprehension of these federalisms was irritating. His famous, elaborate literary style,[38] and his sense of humour, also invited jealousy.[39] At the same time, there were evidently faults in Timaeus which it was legitimate enough to point out – his uncritical and clumsy approach, his over-pious love of marvels and providential coincidences, his childish commonplace and moralising platitudes, his love of trivialities which got him called an 'old rag woman', and his many inaccuracies, quite as great as those of the historians whom he himself accused of the same weakness. These were all qualities which kept Timaeus out of the highest rank of historians. But his collection of a mass of historical and ethnographic information, and his efforts to synchronise chronologies – notably those of Rome and Carthage – were made use of by many of his successors.[40]

Older than Timaeus, a little younger than Ephorus and Theopompus, was Aristotle of Stagirus in the Chalcidice (384–322 BC), whose immense life-work left permanent repercussions on history, as it did on every kind of study. His *Constitution of Athens* belonged to a fashionable genre,[41] and his *Politics*, too, obviously had historical implications.[42] The *Poetics* contain a famous distinction between poetry which tells what might happen (universal truths) and history which tells what has happened (particular facts). 'For this reason poetry is something more philosophical and more worthy of serious attention than history.'[43] Such a point of view scarcely encouraged men of major intellect to become historians, but it did at least focus attention once again on factual truthfulness as the leading criterion.[44] However, despite wider modern claims, the main effects of Aristotle on the historical writers just after him came from his general stimulation of scientific research, and from the refinement of specialist techniques and terminology which his activities and attitudes produced. In a more specific sense, he also exercised great influence on the biographical aspects of historical writing which Xenophon and Isocrates had recently developed. Aristotle and his followers the Peripatetic school, though generally believing that people were born with their characters ready-made, showed a keen interest in the various patterns of behaviour[45] and in their relation to free will.[46] These themes were bound to intensify biographical study.

So, of course, did the obvious need to chronicle and embroider the sensational life-story of Alexander the Great – which was practically synonymous with the history of his times. The many Greek 'biographers' of Alexander, now lost, evidently ranged all the way from fact to legend.[47] One of the most notable students of the king's career was Aristotle's nephew Callisthenes of Olynthus. Polybius, however, unkindly remarked that he deserved the death by torture that befell him at Alexander's hands (327) – since the biographer had inexcusably supported the un-Greek tendency to deify the king.[48] Nor can the same critic have approved of Callisthenes' abandonment of Greek history, in the accepted sense of the term, in order to write about the deeds of one man. This was in the tradition of Theopompus, who had seemed to be at fault for centring his work on Alexander's father Philip II. Moreover, Callisthenes was prepared to illustrate his theme by including speeches which possessed no basis in fact (p. 160).

After the death of Alexander, there was a clash between the factual and fictional types of historian. They were represented, respectively by Hieronymus of Cardia (died *c*. 250)[49] and the tragic, emotional, melodramatic Duris of Samos (died *c*. 270).[50] Their works have vanished, but the latter school, which criticised Ephorus and Theopompus as insufficiently vivid,[51] elicited severe remarks from Polybius. This censure is particularly directed against one of Duris' pupils, Phylarchus of Athens. Phylarchus, who wrote an extensive history dealing with the years between 272 and 220, is accused of falsifying speeches and wallowing in shameless sensationalism.[52] He is jeered at for imagining he was some sort of a tragic poet, with all his sob-stuff about captured cities, clinging, dishevelled women, weeping children and pathetic aged parents.[53]

Even when allowance is made for exaggeration, the criticism must have been basically sound. The glamorous standards which Phylarchus had taken over from Duris just would not do for a serious historian, however excellently they would suit what we should now call a historical novelist – or however well they might do for Livy (p. 236). No doubt there was much to be said for Phylarchus' spirited style, but the complaints of his stage machinery and touching, fabricated scenes are corroborated by other writers.[54] He was also vigorously moralistic and partisan, exhibiting dislike both for Macedonia and the Achaean League,[55] so that the comments of the League's adherent, Polybius were given added sharpness by personal and political bias.

Worst of all, Phylarchus had ventured to criticise Aratus of Sicyon (d. 213), the guiding spirit of the League, who was Polybius' hero (p. 155). Aratus himself left an important record, his *Memoirs*, extending down to the year 222.[56] This work played a significant part in subsequent history, because it was the prototype of many Greek and Roman autobiographical works. Its author himself fulfilled a major role in historical events. However, the Memoirs were not so reliable and objective as Polybius claimed.[57] Even Aratus, as his admirer is compelled to admit, was not exempted from the general rule that men were sometimes prevented by circumstances from uttering or writing their true opinions;[58] and surviving fragments show an oratorical note of bias and rancour. Another author of the same period was Fabius Pictor, a Roman senator who fought in the Second Punic War and wrote a history of Rome which expounded to the Greeks, in their own language, the Roman tradition of good faith and loyalty. This was a tradition that greatly impressed Polybius, who uses Fabius and praises him, adding, however, that he must not be swallowed whole just because he is a Roman senator, a fact which has made him excessively chauvinistic.[59]

Polybius, then, throws a vivid though often disapproving light on the writings of his predecessors, and we have had to pay special attention to what he says because their works have not survived. The time has now come to investigate this acute but censorious man in further detail.

10

Polybius

POLYBIUS of Megalopolis in Arcadia (*c.* 200–118 BC) wrote a *Universal History* in his native Greek. We are told of the stages by which Rome had gained its dominion over the whole civilised world, achieving supremacy first over the western and then the eastern Mediterranean during the fifty-three years 220–168 BC. Polybius then goes on to describe the aftermath of those events, down to 144. The work is divided, by himself, into forty books. Of these, five have been preserved in their entirety. From the rest, we have excerpts of varying size, including a large part of Book VI, substantial portions of VII–XVI, and smaller extracts and fragments from most of the others.[1] Nearly a third of the whole history has survived.

The first book begins with an explanation of the supreme significance of the subject. There follows a sketch of the first Roman interventions among the Greek city-states of south Italy during the early third century BC. Some of these states appealed to the Carthaginians, who were Rome's competitors for the control of the western Mediterranean. This situation led to the First Punic War (264–241), which in spite of terrible losses was finally won by the Romans. Book II tells of the subsequent rivalry in Spain between the Romans and Carthaginians, who were led first by Hamilcar (d. 229/8) and then by his son-in-law Hasdrubal, followed after his death (221) by Hannibal who was Hamilcar's son.

The third book describes the outbreak of the Second Punic War, the most serious war in which Rome had ever been engaged.[2] An account is given of Hannibal's crossing of the Alps into Italy, followed by his victories over the Romans at the rivers Ticinus and Trebia and then at Lake Trasimene and Cannae (218–216). Book IV is mainly concerned with Greek affairs, and contains a long geographical digression on the advantages of the site of Byzantium (Constantinople). The next book describes how King Philip v of Macedonia (238–179 BC) concluded a treaty with Hannibal which led him into hostilities against the Romans and thus helped to bring about their subsequent intervention in eastern affairs. The sixth book breaks off the story to discuss state constitutions and their relative merits. Polybius explains why he believes that the Roman constitution is the best, and why it comprised a major cause of Rome's greatness. The military system of the Romans is also analysed.

In Book VII the year 215 marked the beginning of an annalistic treatment. Henceforth events in east and west are described year by year, with deviations when necessary. Usually a whole or half Olympiad (four-year period) fills each book. Books VII–XV continued the Second Punic War to the climactic victory at Zama by Scipio the elder. The account is interrupted, in Book XII, by the prolonged attack on the historian Timaeus (p. 140), which gives Polybius an opportunity to explain his own views about historical writing. Thus XII, like VI, marks a break which represents a division of the first part of the work into groups of six books, though later the groups vary in length.

Book XVI starts to recount the Second Macedonian War (200–197), and two books later there is a description of a confrontation in 198 between Philip v and Flamininus, the Roman general who subsequently defeated the monarch and announced the unreal 'liberation' of Greece. The work then went on to describe Rome's decisive rebuff to the Seleucid imperialist Antiochus III at Magnesia in Asia Minor (190),[3] followed in Book XXVI by the equally conclusive victory at Pydna over Perseus, King of Macedonia, Philip's son (168).

Polybius then carried out his supplementary plan, and described the events of the twenty-four years subsequent to Pydna. Books XXX–XXXV deal with the events of the next few years, and surviving excerpts include, in XXXI, a full portrait of Scipio Africanus the younger (Scipio Aemilianus). There was a geographical interlude in the lost Book XXXIV. The final books gave an account of Scipio's conquest of Carthage in the Third Punic War, and the sack of Corinth and destruction of the Achaean League by the Romans in the same year 146. The work concluded with the events of the two following years, and culminated in a sort of chronological recapitulation or index.

Polybius' birthplace the 'Great City', *Megale Polis* or as the Romans called it Megalopolis, had been founded between 370 and 362 under the influence of the Theban Epaminondas. Standing in a splendid setting on a plain ringed by mountains, it was designed to be the centre of an Arcadian League which should serve as a counterweight against Spartan influence in the Peloponnese. Forty villages were absorbed into the new foundation and most of the people of Arcadia became its citizens. Then, in 235/4, Megalopolis joined the much larger Achaean League, at that time controlled by its first great leader Aratus (p. 143), and was made the meeting-place of the federal Senate and Assembly. Destroyed by the Spartans, the city was restored by the second Achaean hero, Philopoemen of Megalopolis, who abolished the military power of Sparta (188). Three centuries later the place was already a heap of ruins. The fragments which still survive include traces of the senate-house, and the remains of the largest theatre in Greece.

Polybius, himself the son of a politician of the Achaean League, was chosen as a youth to carry the ashes of Philopoemen to their grave (183). Shortly afterwards he wrote the life of the dead statesman, and carried on his policy of insistence that the Achaeans should be as independent as possible of their Roman protectors, and should take every possible step to retain a predominant position in the Peloponnese. In 169–168 Polybius held the federal post of Cavalry Commander, the second most important office in the League.

However, during the war which ended in the conquest of Macedonia by the Romans (168), his party had shown Macedonian sympathies. Consequently, he and a thousand other Greeks were ordered to Rome. Ostensibly they were summoned for examination, but they were detained for many years without trial. Polybius himself, however, was protected by the famous Lucius Aemilius Paullus, conqueror of Macedonia, and by his son Scipio Aemilianus with whom he formed a close friendship.[4] Although Polybius was able to travel within Italy,[5] we do not know whether he could temporarily go outside the country or not. At any rate, an application to permit him to go back and live in Greece was turned down. It was not until 152 BC that the 300 survivors of the 1000 internees were allowed to go home. Polybius would have been able to go with them; but he refrained from doing so. Instead, he almost certainly accompanied Scipio Aemilianus to Spain in 151–150 when the latter served against the Celtiberians (centred on Numantia) whose final downfall Scipio was to encompass eighteen years later. Then, after a brief visit to Greece, Polybius was with Scipio again in north Africa, and witnessed his destruction of Carthage.[6]

Meanwhile the Achaean League, egged on by the returned deportees who were given a free hand by a pro-Roman leader's death,[7] had incurred the wrath of Rome, with fatal results. Destroying its principal member-city Corinth, an action which marked a terrible and decisive stage in their relations with Greece, Rome also abolished the League itself. Polybius, by now a man of some importance in the eyes of the Romans, was requested by them to supervise the extensive administrative changes that such a step required. These changes involved the establishment of a direct, separate relationship between the Roman government and the individual cities which had formerly belonged to the League. Polybius regarded this difficult and delicate task as the finest achievement of his career.[8]

He outlived these events by a quarter of a century, writing and adding greatly to the travels he had already undertaken. The extensive journeys of his long life included a crossing of the Alps,[9] visits to Alexandria and Sardis and Numidia and Gaul and perhaps Spain,[10] and an exploration of the African coast which took him out into the Atlantic Ocean and up the west coast of Portugal (146). He was very proud of these journeys, and there was some justification for his epitaph at Megalopolis which declared that he 'had wandered over every land and sea'.[11] He was killed, so it was said, by a fall from his horse at the age of eighty-two.[12]

Polybius' *History*, in the form in which we possess it, is the fruit of his enforced leisure at Rome. Some of his material on Achaean affairs may already have been more or less prepared before he arrived in Italy.[13] But that is doubtful, and in any case he appears to have got to work on the major part of the book soon after his internment began. References to Roman events suggested that he had published the first four or possibly five books before 150,[14] and Book XI, relating to constitutional matters, probably came out with them. By that time he may have written as far as the end of the Second Punic War (202 BC; up to XVI, except perhaps XII), appropriately publishing this material while the Third and last war of the series was being fought (147–146).

His original intention had been to terminate his work with the victory over the Macedonians (168, Book XXVI) which placed the whole of the eastern Mediterranean under Roman control. But then the almost simultaneous destructions of Carthage and Corinth (146) made him decide to carry on the story to those epoch-making events and what came immediately after them, 'because of the scale of the operations therein and the dramatic nature of what happened, and above all because I was not only a witness to most of the events but took part in some and administered others'.[15] That observation, like certain others, was inserted in books that had already been written, in order to explain the new plan and add further emphasis to the general theme of Rome's rise to supremacy. But the revisions were not systematic, since there still remain a number of passages which presuppose that Carthage was still in existence. The thorough revision of an ancient book presented practical difficulties (p. 31), and in any case, as Ernst Badian remarks, 'perhaps rightly, he saw no need to eliminate or amend, as a modern scholar might, any reference or part of his discussion that no longer reflected topical reality'. All the same, Polybius apparently continued, throughout his life, to insert additions and corrections here and there. A sort of obituary note in the last narrative book (just before the final summing up)[16] suggests that the whole work, incorporating these amendments, was published after his death.

He gives powerful reasons for selecting as his principal theme the expansion of Roman power over the whole Mediterranean world (220–168 BC):

There is, I trust, no one so sluggish and dull as not to be curious how, and because of what qualities in Roman government, practically the whole inhabited world in less than 53 years fell completely under the control of Rome – the like of which, it will be found, has never happened before.[17]

These events were of unprecedented significance because the whole huge territory of the Mediterranean and middle east – the whole inhabited world as he calls it, or at least almost the whole civilised Western world – had become one. 'The wider the circle is,' said Edward Meyer, 'over which the effects of a historical event extend, the more important it is.' By this standard Polybius' subject, as he declares, was exceptional and unique.[18]

In this situation the only serious kind of history that could be written seemed to be the universal synoptic kind, because this alone corresponded objectively with the actual situation which had come into being in the contemporary world. Evidently the claim to write this sort of history had been advanced before, because Polybius refers to such endeavours – though only to discuss them as flimsy and insufficiently comprehensive. It is true that he praises a predecessor, Ephorus, for making a similar attempt when dealing with a period before the Roman unification, and indeed he praises him rather more than he deserves (p. 138).[19] Nevertheless, Polybius claims that he himself is a pioneer in the enterprise he is undertaking.

No one in my time has essayed a systematic world history; had anyone else done so, I should have been much less ambitious to undertake this task. . . .[20] I have set my hand to write, not narrowly limited affairs as my predecessors did – for instance, the affairs of Greece or Persia – but rather those occurring everywhere in the known parts of the inhabited world.[21]

This, says Polybius, was a form of historical activity infinitely superior to the mere construction of narrow specialised studies – which inspire in him a decided animosity.

Those who think that they can gain a sound view of history as a whole from historical monographs seem to me to make the same mistake as would those who gazed on the dissected limbs of some body that was once animate and beautiful, and fancied that this was as good as seeing the life-force and beauty of the creature itself. . . .

To the degree that learning surpasses mere listening, to that same degree I consider my history to surpass the total contribution of all the separate monographs.[22]

For detailed theses of that kind put things out of perspective, obscure causes and effects, and encourage exaggerations and sensationalisms which a wide canvas makes it easier to avoid.[23] Consequently,

Polybius feels nothing but contempt for specialised works on genealogies, foundations and kinship ties. He considers them fit only for antiquarians[24] – whose differentiation from serious historians, a very influential distinction in later Europe, had already become canonical (p. 389). For narrow efforts of that kind do not really get one anywhere, he says. It is only a truly universal history, such as he was trying to write himself, that can give a correct idea of the all-important causes and effects which are essential if one is going to try to assess the true significance of events.

The possibility of taking this broader view had been created by the completely new state of affairs brought about by Rome. The Romans had seized the opportunities that history and geography had combined to provide, and Polybius proposes to give us a rational account of how this came about. 'It was not by an act of chance, as some of the Greeks suppose, nor by spontaneous action, but through quite reasonable causes that the Romans . . . achieved their aim.'[25] At the same time, however, the historian advises us that he is going to adopt an objective attitude to the Roman phenomenon: he is not disposed to regard success as the sole criterion of history. 'Judgments about the victors or the vanquished cannot be final when they are based simply on their achievements alone. . . . For obviously, evidence of what happened afterwards will make it clear whether the dominion of the Romans is to be shunned or, on the contrary, welcomed.'[26] As a result of this unbiased attitude, his judgment of Rome was finely balanced. He greatly admired the old Roman spirit which had triumphed by 'the discipline of many struggles and troubles, and the continual choice of the best in the light of experience gained in disaster'.[27] Moreover, even in his own day, he was still enormously impressed by the best representatives of Rome, men such as Scipio Aemilianus[28] and other eminent personages who, like Scipio, had given him their friendship. Polybius thought the traditional immunity of Romans to bribes was a wonderful thing (p. 154)[29].

He also felt a great admiration for the Roman constitution, and devotes an entire book (VI) to explaining why. Extending his 'science' of prognostication to this field (p. 155), he is clearly very pleased with the result. In the first place, he strongly shares the Greek conviction, based on the moral and educational value of laws, that national constitutions are all-important; the fate of states is completely bound up with them. And so he decided that the constitution of the Romans, too, was the key to their successes. He knew it was the product of many struggles and experiments.[30] Yet he scarcely appreciated that what had really made Rome powerful was its flexibility and capacity for growth.[31] Instead he regarded the Roman constitution as the decisive factor which had raised the country to supremacy.

He believed that this constitution had achieved such a special degree of excellence because it incorporated a perfect balance between the various elements of political life.

From a date 32 years after Xerxes' invasion of Greece, the Roman constitution was one of those that are continually being further improved in detail; it reached its best and perfected form at the time of the war with Hannibal. . . . Not even a native citizen could declare with certainty whether the state, taken as a whole, was aristocratic or democratic or monarchic.[32]

In fact, however, this alleged balance was not so evenly poised as Polybius maintained. For the Roman system inevitably favoured conservatism. Indeed, all these 'mixed constitutions' are more oligarchic than anything else. And it is therefore no accident that Polybius approved of them: because what really impressed him was the oligarchic and stable element in the Roman State – the majesty of the Senate.

His admiration of the Roman constitution is so great that he compares it favourably to other alleged mixed systems, including those of Carthage [33] and the Dorian city-states of Crete, and, on the Greek mainland, particularly Dorian Sparta. The 'mixed' formula had already been applied to Sparta by Greek thinkers,[34] and at Rome the same idea had recently been developed by Cato the elder, again, it appears, with a Roman as well as a Carthaginian comparison (p. 170). Such analogies are not very valuable, because the classification seems too schematic to fit even one individual state, let alone several. But one is left with the strong suspicion that what Polybius privately has in mind, as an example of a mixed constitution, is his own Achaean League. Indeed, he seems to be thinking of it as a *model* for contemporary Rome, though he does not mention this conception explicitly, since it would have been tactless to do so after the Romans had forcibly dissolved the League.

It would be of importance to discover what Polybius felt about the future prospects of Rome's constitution, since this ought to show where this acute observer really thought Roman imperialism was leading. But the answer that we get is somewhat equivocal. His survey has not survived in all its complexity, but enough has remained to indicate that its argument is contradictory and puzzling. In spite of its great influence on subsequent European thought, this analysis shows him not, as he supposed, at his best but at his worst. The various traditional Greek ideas which he introduces, 'mixed constitution', cycle of constitutions, and natural law of decline are uneasy and indigestible in combination. The main interest of Polybius' treatment lies in his application of these ideas to the vast phenomenon of Rome. It had often been maintained that a natural process of retribution makes decline and catastrophe the inevitable destiny of every mortal thing (p. 48),[35] and it was easy to infer from this that all phenomena proceed in cycles.[36] If that is so, the cyclical formula is applicable to constitutions: they are bound ultimately to fall. Yet the Romans, according to Polybius, had obtained exemption or at least a moratorium from this doom, since the emergence of their mixed constitution in the fifth century BC had enabled them to arrest and suspend the downward cyclical process, 'owing to the principle of equivalence of forces'.[37]

As long as this balance lasted, there was no reason why the suspension should not persist. But would the balance last? Did Polybius, that is to say, believe that Rome would continue to escape from the law of decline? His answer is rather confused and confusing. Being less interested to develop the cyclical theory than to stress Roman longevity and the self-correcting tendencies which had, at least for the present, applied the desirable brake, he is able to refrain discreetly from giving an unambiguous verdict. We know too little, he says, about Rome's earlier institutions to be able to deduce from them with any confidence what is going to happen in the future.[38] Most of his own observations about the early Romans are lost.[39] Nevertheless, he does make it pretty clear that he felt that even Rome must succumb in the end to the mob-regime which upsets such balances and produces collapse. For he repeatedly and emphatically quotes the rule that this is what happens to states, and Rome is not to be an exception. In his eyes it was not destined for eternity.[40]

Polybius was, by nature, inclined to favour this pessimistic sort of view, because he believed the old Roman excellence to be already, to some extent, a thing of the past. Like later writers, he saw the eastern wars of the second century BC as the causes of this moral decline (p. 229). When he had been a young man, he and his friends adopted a detached or critical attitude towards current Roman policy. This earned him and them deportation, and his exile began with 'utter loss of spirit and paralysis of mind'[41] which was unlikely to make him love the Romans so much that he wanted to throw all historical rules overboard in their favour.

As a result, he treats Hannibal, for example, with a fairness notably deficient in the Roman tradition:[42] 'When a man takes on the character of a historian, he will often have to praise and glorify his enemies in the highest terms, when their actions demand it, and often criticise and blame his dearest friends in harsh language, when the errors in their conduct indicate it.'[43] Although Polybius did not approve of making history into biography (p. 139), he inherited a measure of the biographical preoccupations that had developed over the past three centuries. Consequently he could not help taking an interest in the strength of personality which had been so manifest in Hannibal.[44] His admiration for this quality helped him to put into practice the general principle of balance enunciated above, and thus to attain an unfamiliar degree of objectivity. In accordance with the same principle, his remarks about Roman policy in the 160s and 150s modify their generally favourable verdict by a good many censorious remarks.[45] From then onwards, it is true, his sympathies are increasingly with Rome. Nevertheless, just as he had been willing in the Second Punic War to see the good side of Hannibal, so again before the Third Punic War he openly sets out the arguments put forward by the Carthaginians.

The hostility which the Achaeans were now showing towards the Romans (p. 147) was the product of League policies which Polybius now deplored. Nevertheless, Rome's destruction of the entire federal entity must have come as a terrible shock to him. No doubt this was partly assuaged, human nature being what it is, by the fact that he personally was called in by the Romans to organise the subsequent settlement. By agreeing to do so, he became an early exponent of the type of Greco-Roman literary man who chose to collaborate with the conqueror – interpreting Rome to Greece, explaining that the

Empire had come to stay and could not be resisted, and indicating that this was such a vast historical design that it absolved his own compatriots from any slur of failure or impotence. Another Greek friend of Scipio Aemilianus, who again sought to reconcile his countrymen to Roman rule, was the Stoic philosopher Panaetius of Rhodes (*c.* 185–95 BC). The founder of Stoicism, Zeno of Citium in Cyprus (*c.* 300 BC), had concluded that since every man possesses a share of divine spark we are all brothers, and are therefore bound by a moral imperative to treat one another decently. Panaetius adjusted these ideas of human brotherhood to the requirements of the Roman aristocracy, and declared that the Empire was beneficial to rulers and ruled alike. And he was followed by Posidonius of Apamea, who actually declared that the Roman Empire and the ideal Stoic world-state were identical.

Polybius, true to his reserved attitude towards success stories, was not prepared to go to quite those lengths. Nor could he, like Thucydides, bring himself to conclude or imply that self-interest and aggression are inevitable and therefore acceptable. On the contrary, he clearly indicates that ethical standards, and moderate ways of behaving, must be maintained. They are morally desirable; they also pay good dividends. And one of the reasons why he admired Rome so much was because he believed this was the code it had followed in the past.[46]

All the same, Polybius never forgot he was a Greek. He even, explicitly, reserved the right (which other historians have assumed surreptitiously) to show partiality to his own fellow-countrymen – provided, he adds a little perplexingly, that nothing is said contrary to the facts.[47] Certainly he appreciates the faults of the Greeks very clearly, blaming the depopulation of their land on their own selfish exploitation, and comparing their honesty very unfavourably with that of the Romans (p. 150).[48] Nevertheless, his work contains many signs of attachment to his own region and locality. His decision to follow Timaeus and base his chronology on Olympiads and Olympic Years was a direct consequence of his Peloponnesian origin (though this procedure bisected the campaigning-seasons and had to be modified, in the interests of comprehensibility, by Roman and other systems).[49]

But, above all, he shows a strong patriotic bias towards his native Arcadia[50] and towards the Achaean League and his own party within the League. These attitudes powerfully influence his views about earlier historians (p. 139). Achaean politicians, too, who had opposed his father and himself are naturally deplored; though, after the dissolution of the League, he refused to accept the property of one of these opponents when it was offered to him.[51] When speaking of the admired Achaean leader Philopoemen, he makes a conscious and explicit attempt to be impartial, pointing out again that history is not the same thing as panegyric.[52] On the other hand, his pro-Achaean alignment makes him deeply hostile to the rival Aetolian League, and he hates King Cleomenes III of Sparta who seized Megalopolis.[53] Here the memoirs of the Achaean statesman Aratus are uncritically accepted. Achaea, in return, recognised the sympathy and practical services of Polybius by numerous statues and monuments in his honour.

Thucydides had indicated that his work was intended as a permanent possession which would be of value to those who studied it. Polybius echoed the claim, adding more explicitly that his own work is designed to provide instruction. He asserts over and over again that history, in the way that he has written it, can be useful. 'Even if our current affairs are prospering, no sensible person could reasonably be certain about the future by inferring from the present. It is on this basis that I declare an understanding of the past to be not only pleasant but actually necessary.'[54] This utility may recently have been reasserted by Cato (p. 170), but clearly it was not regarded as self-evident, for Polybius labours the point. His history is not merely intended to be a general guide. It is actually designed as a sort of manual, which will help public figures to act rightly. To predict it, and also to deal with it. Those who have read their Polybius are supposed to be equipped with the means of coping scientifically with any emergency that may arise,[55] improving themselves by studying other people's calamities rather than experiencing them in person,[56] and resisting and counteracting the natural tendency of all things to deteriorate. He felt that his own achievement in settling Achaea after 146 had proved this point. Even in almost hopeless conditions, men in public life can find the right course if they work on the right assumptions, based on historical experience. And he is continually astonished and annoyed at people's failure to learn from history.[57]

The lessons are concrete, practical ones. Interest in the past for its own sake, or as the subject-matter of pure scholarship, is conspicuous by its absence.[58] Moreover, the claim to timeless universality is overlaid by a good deal of direct advice to contemporaries.[59] In spite of the deliberate echo of Thucydides, this unsparing, rather hectoring didacticism, with its numerous personal and subjective interventions, presents a great contrast to the older historian's indirect, artistic and dramatic approach. Polybius' work, more than any other ancient writing that has survived, is deliberately and openly a case-book for politicians, rather as the Chinese history which came into being a generation or two later was intended to train civil servants.[60]

Because of this overriding and constantly expressed instructive aim, even the relatively limited portions of Polybius that have survived are hard to get through. It is true that, in citing the conventional contrast between the pleasurable and the useful, he says he wants his work to be the former as well as the latter, recognising that a literary work ought to be attractive. And indeed, when he wants to tell a good story, he can do so, especially when lessons are out of the way and he is content to use simple and straightforward methods. For example, his account of the escape of the Syrian prince Demetrius from Rome (162), an adventure in which he himself personally assisted, is vivid and authentic.[61] Moreover, he shows artistic skill in devising his over-all structure, breaking off, for example, to talk of Roman institutions just at the time when readers, shocked by the setbacks in the Second Punic War and excited by Rome's determination to resist, are ready and eager to learn what the city and people were like in those days.

There is also some evidence of a progressive attention to grammar and style. On the whole, however, his language has the flat and prosy verbosity of a government department. Unlike almost any other notable literary product of antiquity, it is actually improved by a good translation. After all, Polybius himself said that the aim should always be commensurate with the effort.[62] He may have been theoretically aware that one must write attractively, but he was really out not to amuse but to teach. So evidently he did not exert himself to the utmost to write good Greek. But here his skill, or his psychology, was deficient; if he had written better he would have been a better teacher. He himself is uncomfortably aware that the length of his work makes it tough reading, though he declares it to be wrong that people should take this view – because it is he, and not the writers of shorter books, who is giving the true causes of events.[63]

For causes are the essence of his history and the basis of its value. Descriptions of events which do not take them into account are not enough. For what is the good of a statesman who cannot reckon how, and why, and from what source each event has originated?[64] Polybius' own claim to discern and demonstrate such causes is based on 'science and art', that is to say on the efficiency of his own, modern type of history,[65] assisted by the speeches inserted in his work, which were designed to clarify causation.[66] His method is explicitly stated to depend upon the adoption of a scientific and technical point of view. Like Thucydides, he is inspired by the achievements of science, and consciously revives the analogy of medicine;[67] and he has the advantage over Thucydides that further centuries of rich historical experience have now gone by.

His consciousness of this long and enigmatic past warned Polybius that the historian's power to reconstruct causes is subject to profound limitations. This modest attitude, which agreeably conflicts with some of his more priggish assertions about other matters, is summed up by repeated appeals to the concept of Chance.[68] He uses the term incessantly, to denote everything in his theme that is imponderable, irrational and uncontrollable. In his first three books alone, the word 'unexpected' appears on no less than fifty-one occasions.

As in other ancient writers, Chance is interpreted in various ways. But Polybius believes it to merit particularly serious treatment in an instructive work such as his own, because its identification as an operative factor will teach the reader how to bear the vicissitudes of his own life with a more philosophical endurance. Half-personified, Chance is occasionally just a punisher of wrongdoing;[69] but innocent people are equally likely to get hurt.[70] It is as much a part of man's endowment as his looks or mental gifts. It produces, even seems to delight in, coincidences, contrasts, reversals.[71] And reversals mean downfalls, because success cannot last.[72] Here again, as in Thucydides, is the language of tragic drama, retained by a man whose ways of thinking were alien from those of the dramatists.

These seemed good reason to ascribe the Romans' seizure of power to Chance. Nevertheless, there are also perfectly rational, identifiable causes for their emergence. So there are, indeed, for every other phenomenon as well.[73] Indeed, the identifiable causes are precisely what produce the unexpected developments grouped under the general heading of Chance.[74] To attribute to Fortune what is really the product of human action is a mistake.[75] Yet the two sorts of cause are frequently interconnected, and the best thing, therefore, is to cite rational causation and Chance at one and the same time. Chance is the producer of the play,[76] but inside the grand production man can control the sub-plots and scenes. And Polybius goes on to add, in the spirit of the Stoics, that man is also in a position to control his own inward temper with which he faces events.

Sometimes Chance may be merely another way of saying Providence. True, when you can discover the material reason for something, you are not entitled to introduce any supernatural agency.[77] All the same, a transformation on the scale of the rise of Rome must be providential[78] – a comfort for the humiliated Greeks.

You are warranted, that is to say, in ascribing inexplicable developments and events to the gods. You can ascribe to them also the human states of mind that are the springs of action. But myths are to be avoided by historians,[79] and miracles do not happen. Stories of such things, however, are permissible so long as they do not go too far.[80] And indeed the whole paraphernalia of religion is justifiable, because the masses are so unstable that they need it.[81] This doctrine, with its anticipation of the Marxist 'opiate of the people', was coming into vogue in official Roman circles. Or rather, it had long prevailed there, and was now receiving articulate expression.

Causation, then, is the product of analysable events modified by a strong unpredictable element. This is an elaboration of the rationalism of Thucydides. And Polybius chose to take the analogy with his great predecessor further still. Thucydides had devoted his full talent for the investigation of causes to his main subject, the encounter between Athens and Sparta. Central to Polybius' theme, also, is a war – the Second Punic War, in which the Romans finally defeated Hannibal.

Thucydides had distinguished between the immediate and ultimate causes of hostilities. Polybius borrows this distinction, but adds a

third element, the 'first overt act' (*arche*).[82] Speaking with characteristic acidity about writers who fail to distinguish this additional
factor, he goes on to make a triple diagnosis on these lines he has
indicated, both of Alexander's Persian war and of Rome's war
against the Seleucid Antiochus III. His analyses are a little far-
fetched; Xenophon's eastern expedition, for example, had a certain
significance (p. 129), but it is strange to find it actually described
as a 'first cause' of Alexander's war. The formulations are meticulous
but they simplify and schematise, and they do not go deep. The
improvement on Thucydides is just not there. Polybius' ideas of
causes are rather crude and dogmatic, showing a certain lack of
insight into the historical process. He is not, for example, concerned
with the degree to which the Romans were, or were not, aggressive
imperialists, or interested to know what drove them on. Nor has he
got the imagination to penetrate to Thucydides' profound levels of
humanity. Moreover, the older historian could never have descended
to the anticlimaxes and banalities which recur from time to time in
Polybius' work.

Just as he likes to elaborate on Thucydides' theories of cause and
effect, so he also repeats, again at increased length, his forerunner's
emphasis on the truth.[83] What Polybius aims at is 'pragmatic'
history – serious, systematic, interpretative treatment of matters of
fact.[84] If history is to teach efficiently and reliably, the first essential
is that the account should be true. Indeed, 'just as a living creature is
completely useless if deprived of its eyes, so if you take truth from
history, what is left but an unprofitable tale?'.[85] Though minor
errors are excusable – especially in an extensive work – the deliberate
failure to make oneself into a competent historian is unforgivable.[86]
And so is deliberate distortion.[87]

Polybius specifically extends this doctrine to speeches, of which
about fifty appear in the surviving portions of his work. Their purpose
is to illustrate causes and effects, 'summing up events', as F.W.
Walbank points out, 'and holding the whole history together'. The
historian, Polybius declares, must record what was really said,
however commonplace.[88] There is a new stringency in this statement
of what speeches ought to do. More clearly than any previous
writer, Polybius was making an explicit stand for truthfulness in
regard to this vital element in ancient historical writing. He did so
all the more sharply because some of his predecessors had allowed

themselves an almost complete abandonment of any such criterion, one of them, Callisthenes, even pronouncing, in the spirit of 'the appropriate' stressed by his uncle Aristotle, that what a speech in a history had to do was to hit off the character – to match the oratory to the person and the situation.[89]

Having stated the ideal, however, Polybius fails to live up to it. On certain occasions he admits he has selected and abbreviated.[90] Besides, his most elaborate speeches, those intended to possess special significance, are worked over and worked up[91] – to say the least: for sometimes whole orations, notably those of Hannibal and the consul Publius Scipio in 218, are obviously fictitious from beginning to end. What Polybius really wanted to achieve by such speeches was to provide the sort of arguments which converted people from one cause to another. This seemed to him a good way of illustrating the dynamic interactions between one individual, or one group of individuals, and another. 'A single well-timed speech by a trustworthy person often turns men from the worst courses and incites them to the best.' Exact fidelity, then, was less important than psychological cogency.

And yet, there are those unprecedentedly sharp statements about truthfulness. Like his explanation of the causes of the war, they represent an extension, or a more emphatic assertion, of Thucydidean doctrines. And the attention to Thucydides is carried further still.

First, Polybius agrees with him that the only history is contemporary or near-contemporary history, The historian must be able to consult actual participants.[92] It is no more possible to become a historian by studying documents than to become a painter by looking at the works of earlier artists.[93] The analogy between the two sorts of activity is a false one, since a historian does not read books as models but as sources. But the pronouncement in favour of contemporary history was not out of line with most historical thinking, both of his own and of earlier times. As to the definition of what 'contemporary' means, Polybius chose 220 BC as the beginning of his main period because eyewitnesses could not be examined for any happenings before that time.[94] He had many opportunities, while at Rome, of meeting the stream of envoys and hostages that came to Italy, and he went to great lengths to interview men who had taken part in important events.

But this was not nearly enough for him. The eye, he said, is far more accurate than the ear,[95] and he regarded it as essential that the historian should have participated personally in the circumstances he described.[96] That is what Thucydides had done, and Polybius, too, played an active role in the happenings of his times. The failure to do likewise, he believed, was what had made his predecessor Timaeus so futile (p. 140). To be a historian it is necessary to have been a politician and military commander oneself. As one would expect from Polybius who was the author of a tactical handbook (now lost), this meant in his case that his battle-pieces are generally clear.[97] Moreover, he adds a prolonged account of the Roman army.[98] This contains a description of camp layouts which is, admittedly, tantalisingly inadequate.[99] But the account is supplemented by an explanation of Roman signalling that is actually based on inventions of his own.[100]

Not only must historians have occupied leading positions in public events, but Polybius regards his other sort of personal experience as equally indispensable – that is to say, his travelling. In this respect, he is the heir of Herodotus even more than of Thucydides, and it was an achievement to have blended the two traditions. To Polybius, the elements in historical research are three. Political experience is one, and written documentation is another; and the third 'consists in inspection of various cities and places, rivers, lakes, and generally the particular features and distances on land and sea'.[101] He had a sharp eye for the lie of the ground, and always insisted on the importance of accurate geography to the historian. Like an eighteenth-century *savant*, he was conscious that the opening up of the world had provided new opportunities for getting at the truth.[102] He wrote a work – probably a separate essay – *On the Habitability of the Equatorial Region*.[103] And he obtained great satisfaction from his own travels, especially his voyage of discovery into the Atlantic (p. 147). So keen was he to be regarded as the second Odysseus that the geographer Pytheas is fiercely attacked (*c.* 310–306): there must be no western explorations other than his own.[104] Consequently, his work offers many digressions on geography.[105] And there was even a whole book on the subject, the lost XXXIV, including detailed accounts of his journey in Spain. Polybius' knowledge of geography is not, in fact, up to recent Alexandrian standards.[106] But he was very insistent on comprehensibility. Just as chronology has to be clear and under-standable (p. 154),[107] so, also, the geographical digressions strike a further blow for the same cause of popularisation: it is useless, he rightly says, to mention strange places unless these are brought into relation with the knowledge of the reader.[108]

Political experience, then, and geographical observation are two of the elements which Polybius requires in a historian. His third requirement is the utilisation of written records. He employed archives and documents wherever he could get access to them, chiefly in Rome[109] but also elsewhere.[110] In this field his greatest suc-cess, of which he was very proud, was the discovery on the south Italian promontory of Lacinium of a bronze tablet listing Hannibal's army. He seems to suggest that no historian had ever seen the inscription before.

As regards his literary sources, our information is extremely deficient.[111] Because of the vastness of his project, he clearly had to use written evidence throughout. Yet he does not seem to have been very well read. With regard to philosophy, for example, he is capable of using the word 'unphilosophical' as a term of abuse, and yet his own studies in the subject were evidently slight. Indeed, the way in which he refers to earlier authors, in whatever field, makes it probable that he drew upon one of the books of collected quotations that were available for this purpose.

At one point he adopts an appreciative and indeed deferential attitude to his forerunners: 'We should not find fault with writers for their omissions and mistakes, but should praise and admire them, considering the times they lived in, for having ascertained something on the subject and advanced our knowledge.'[112] This, however, proves to have been a very strange pronouncement for Polybius to have offered, since, as we have seen at some length, he conspicuously fails to act in accordance with it. Historians customarily criticised their predecessors, but the attitude adopted by Polybius is remark-ably and unpleasantly sharp. Perhaps this tone would not have seemed so unusual if more works by Hellenistic historians had survived. For this was a time when criticism was violent. Standards of truthfulness were unsteady – and productive of furious disputes. Like others who engaged in these quarrels, Polybius accepted the convention that they were part of the game. But his ferocity was not purely conventional, for he felt very strongly on the subject and wanted to defend his views. Consequently his claims to intellectual tolerance were cancelled out by an equally marked tendency to indulge in resentful abuse and self-justification. This duality some-times appears in a schizophrenic form when the same author is disagreeably attacked at one point, and courteously praised at another. Polybius is prepared to admit that many things prevent writers from expressing themselves quite frankly. He appreciated that this was true even of his hero Aratus (p. 143). All the same, he claimed to regard it as a public duty to correct other historians. Thucydides lies outside the range of his censure. This is partly because he was too remote in date to attack jealousy or provide a suitable target. Besides, although Polybius knew so much about his historical principles, it seems doubtful whether he had actually gone to the length of *reading* him. The passages with which he was familiar could well have been culled from intermediaries (p. 162).[113] But in any case it would not have been proper to criticise Thucydides, because Polybius knew himself to be affected by his attitude and approach, and believed that the two of them stood for the same historical ideas and ideals. For both desired to impart instruction, and both directly participated in events.

However, a great period of time, nearly three eventful centuries, had passed since Thucydides; and Polybius, not unnaturally, felt greater concern about writers of more recent date.[114] Of Xenophon little need be said, since although Polybius mentions him (and indicates a disagreement) there is no important debt or clash to record.[115] Since then, however, a great many people had written histories, although they are all now lost. For one thing, there had been a large outcrop of the specialist monographs to which Polybius objected so strongly (p. 149). But there had also been quite import-ant, indeed major, historians since Thucydides and Xenophon. Polybius made great use of their writings, but largely conceals this fact by telling us how little he thought of them, and particularly of Timaeus (p. 140).

As we have seen, his reasons for this depreciation fall into two main categories. First, there were partisan reasons. He took marked exception to critical comments about his native Arcadia, or his Achaean League, or its admired leader Aratus. But there was also a second and more objective reason for his disapproval of the fourth- and third-century historians. It seemed to him that Timaeus and Phylarchus and the rest had degraded history into mere sensational, quasi-historical romance.

Polybius obviously does not quite do them justice. Their way of writing, for example, must often have been much more attractive than his own. And yet, as far as we can tell, there was a good deal to be said for his view. His nagging manner, however – which led him, for example, to write to contemporary historians explaining where they had gone wrong[116] – inspires irritation. Nor was he always free from partiality or untruthfulness. Yet in such an enormous pioneer work the imperfections to which humanity is liable are hard to avoid. Polybius did avoid the worst of them: a lot of the snares into which one after another of his predecessors since Thucydides had fallen were safely shunned.

Even if he could not always reach the heights, his eyes were always fixed in that direction. In spite of all hindrances, he possessed a genuine and indeed passionate admiration for the truth. He was diligent and shrewd. He could see most things in proportion, and except when he embarked on fields which did not suit him (such as studies of constitutions), he was well able to comprehend what he saw. 'In history', said Theodor Mommsen, 'his books are like the sun.' Their contrast to the preceding and following darkness is, in part, due to the accident which has preserved large portions of his work, but not more than fragments of any other historian for nearly three centuries before him and a century afterwards. But the contrast is also an objective matter: because it can confidently be surmised that, even if all these writers had survived, Polybius would still have been outstanding among them.

4

Latin Writers
of the Republic

II

Cato the Censor
and after

THE keeping of records had early been a feature of the Roman State. Since the Government could take no action without first formally ascertaining the will of the gods, these records were a matter for the religious authorities, and the annual register was kept by the board of priests. As Cicero makes a speaker in one of his conversation-pieces remark:

History began as a mere compilation of annals; on which account, and in order to preserve the general traditions, from the earliest period of the City down to the pontificate of Publius Mucius Scaevola [130 BC], each high priest used to commit to writing all the events of his year of office, and record them on a white surface, and post up the tablet at his house, so that all men might have liberty to acquaint themselves therewith. And to this day those records are known as the Pontifical Chronicles.[1]

How early such records began to be kept is uncertain. If any existed before the sack of Rome by the Gauls (c. 390), they may have been destroyed at that time. But in any case notices dating from that antique period could not have been more than bare lists of annual officials and events. Besides, whatever their epoch, the earliest of such lists were merely written on slates, from which the successive annual entries were wiped each year with a wet sponge (tabulae

167

dealbatae). Subsequently, the inscriptions were transferred on to stone; but it may only have been in *c.* 300 that there appeared this permanent sort of documentation, converting ephemeral publications into chronicles.

These chronicles moulded future Roman historical writing, which was frequently cast in the form suggested by the pontifical records. This was an annalistic form, divided according to the officials, and especially the consuls, who held office year by year. This type of framework had the disadvantage of inhibiting the larger view, but it saved Romans from the complexities and quick-sands of chronology which had been such a nuisance to Greek historians. It also gave Roman history a special character of its own, because it meant that, whereas Greek history had sprung from geography and human behaviour, its Roman counterpart began with politics and the State. Nor, in their mature form, were the pontifical chronicles by any means limited to lists of officials. They took note of all events in which the board of priests took ceremonial action – elections, the passing of laws, the building of temples, the conduct of wars, the celebration of Triumphs, the appearance of omens. Cato the elder scoffed at these priestly annals for even including notes on famines and eclipses.[2]

They were by no means the only record Rome possessed. Treaties were preserved, and no doubt all laws as well, at least as long as they remained in force. Furthermore, individual noble families are very likely to have kept particulars of the achievements of their ancestors.

The war fought against the Epirot invader Pyrrhus, early in the third century BC, did not prompt any Romans to write literary accounts of the operations. They were not yet ready to write even historical verse, much less historical prose which, as in Greece, came later. But then Naevius (*c.* 270–201) not only wrote historical Latin plays but, after fighting in the First Punic War, composed an epic poem about its military and naval encounters. He employed the Latin language and a national metre, and produced a poem which is shewn by its surviving sixty-five lines to have been crude yet also vigorous. Next, Ennius of Rudiae in Calabria (239–169 BC) included among his many poetic works a highly influential Latin epic, *The Annals*, giving an account of Roman history to 171 BC, with a biographical trend which included admiration of Rome's enemy

Pyrrhus for his chivalry.[3] Five hundred and fifty hexameter lines of the poem survive.

An older contemporary of Ennius was Fabius Pictor (p. 143), a historian and senator who was the author of a history of Rome. He wrote in prose; but the prose was Greek. The work is lost, and we do not know whether he wrote it before or after the victorious conclusion of the Second Punic War. But in any case Pictor fits into the pattern of the Greek literature as one of the many foreigners, including priests in Babylonia and Egypt,[4] who saw Greek as the only civilised literary language, and used it to write the histories of their native lands. Although the pontifical chronicles were presumably available for writers who attempted historical accounts of Rome, they did nothing to make good the deficiency of any convention of literary prose, which existing traditions of oratory and law scarcely counterbalanced (p. 171).[5] Besides, Latin did not reach a large enough audience.

Fabius seems to have expected that other leading Romans would read his work,[6] but he was mainly writing for Greeks, in order to explain to them, in terms which seemed over-patriotic to Polybius, the admirable moral code which allegedly dominated Roman public and private life. The fact that Fabius used both Olympic dates and consular years as chronological indications illustrates his intermediate position between the two cultures. In keeping with his use of the Greek language, he provided the sort of mythological and other material which was to be found in Greek foundation-monographs and the like.[7] Yet he was also a nationally minded Roman and adopted the annalistic framework of Roman tradition. And Fabius likewise established the long-lived custom by which men who, like himself, were leading Romans were regarded as the proper people to write Roman history. This doctrine, which met with the approval of Polybius, meant, in effect, that future historians were usually senators.[8]

The man who took the pioneer step of writing a Roman history in Latin instead of Greek was Cato the elder, who was born in 234 BC. Fighter in the Punic War, senior officer, statesman, public speaker, moralist, expert in agriculture and law,[9] he was one of the most colourful, encyclopedic and complex personalities of the Roman Republic. The loss of his *Origins*, a history of Rome down to the last year of his life, means that our whole idea of the development of Latin historical writing remains fragmentary. But 143 excerpts survive, and, brief though these mostly are, they enable us to obtain some appreciation of the character of the work.

The earliest known history in the vernacular, Cato's *Origins* consisted of seven books. The first three corresponded with the title, being concerned with the beginnings of Rome and other Italian towns, and their most ancient history. The fourth book, which has a fresh introduction, contained material less relevant to the designation of the work,[10] since its contents comprised the First Punic War and the initial years of the Second. Book v carried on the story at least as far as Rome's victory over Macedonia (168). The two final books dealt with the last nineteen years of Cato's life, down to a few months before his death (149). The *Origins* seem to have been published posthumously.

Cato's attitude to Greece was ambivalent. His political attitudes were anti-Hellenic, and like his younger contemporary Polybius he took a low view of many aspects of the Greeks of their time. He was deeply disturbed by the rapid invasion of Rome by these inferior manifestations of Hellenism, and his message to the Romans was that their own tradition, as exemplified by their constitution, which Polybius also so greatly admired, was sounder and better. And yet the name of his history, a translation of the 'Foundations' which formed the title of so many Greek monographs (p. 20), is symptomatic of another side of the question. For Cato, while anti-Hellenic, was also a Hellenist. Plutarch said that he only started learning Greek when he was eighty, and yet the whole presentation of his work, though its language is Latin, owes as much as the writings of Pictor to the Greek tradition. From Greece comes Cato's interest in national constitutions, and in geography and ecology and human life and customs; and his narrative style is reminiscent of Xenophon. It appears that the *Origins* contained an assertion of the utility of history,[11] which may well be the source of Polybius' similar declaration, unless they were drawing on a common authority (p. 155).

This is not yet the balanced Greco-Roman humanism of Cato's political opponent Scipio Aemilianus, whose salon of learned Greeks and Romans included Polybius. Cato, too, was prepared to encourage the Hellenising epic poet Ennius – though he did not hold a very high opinion of him – but he did this because he wanted to show the Romans that they could get along without Greece. Usually he is accurate and willing to admit ignorance.[12] But in order to prove this nationalistic point he fabricates a custom of ballad-singing at ancient Roman banquets,[13] so that his compatriots could feel that their tradition comprised a patriotic counterpart to Homer.

But the best way he could place the Romans alongside Greece, or above it, was by writing books which were Greek enough to enable the originals to be dispensed with. He goes out of his way to link the beginnings of Rome with the best of Greece. Even the Roman austerity that he glorified is given a Spartan origin, by way of the Sabines as intermediaries. Moreover, Cato's Latin diction, rugged, varied, vivid and astonishingly rich for this early date,[14] is not altogether free of Greek rhetorical devices. And he was detached enough from the Roman tradition to scoff at the trivialities of the pontifical annals. He adopted, it is true, their year-by-year chronology, but merged it with a method of arrangement by subjects which he had learnt from the Greeks.

Greek in derivation, again, was his inclusion of speeches.[15] But here was a novelty, because some of them were speeches he had delivered himself and so his own words (as well as his deeds) figured largely in the later books of the *Origins*. For Cato embodied in his life the fact, which had now become evident, that Rome was quite as addicted to the practice of public speaking as the Greeks – and before long they were just as deeply absorbed in the theory as well. A hundred years after Cato's death more than a hundred and fifty of his speeches were still available.[16] The traditions of oratory and law on which they were based meant that there had, no doubt, been some sort of literary prose before him (p. 169). But Cato was the first Roman to study the use of his own language seriously. Eloquent, incisive and witty, the possessor of a vituperative tongue, his political career brought him to trial no less than forty times. It was his custom to plead in his own defence. He spoke with torrential vigour, and was invariably acquitted.[17]

Cato was out of line with the traditional aristocratic thought of Rome. Himself an upstart 'new man' – belonging, that is to say, to a family which had never before gained a consulship – he claimed that he wanted to strengthen the ruling class; but only by purging it of its ills and subjecting its members to unremitting censure. Such criticisms figured largely in the later books of his *Origins*, and his own speeches which appear in them attack the nobles for greed and oppression. Cato blames early writers for glorifying their families. He himself reacts so strongly against bestowing individual praise that he suppresses the names of Roman generals altogether. In the First Punic War the Carthaginian elephant Surus is singled out for mention!

Furthermore, Cato was far ahead of the narrow metropolitanism of contemporary senators in his attitude towards Italy. Himself a product not of Rome but of rural Tusculum, he regarded not merely the capital but the whole of Italy as his subject, displaying a liberal conception of the entire peninsula as a unit.[18] This theatrical, red-haired, hard-headed dynamo of energy was a reactionary in some ways, but in others he was an innovator. He was also a man with a keen eye for business, and he built Rome's earliest banking-centre.[19]

Cato's example inspired other writers to attempt their own large-scale annalistic renderings of Roman history.[20] But soon afterwards a decisive stage was marked by the appearance of the Annales Maximi, in eight books. This collection seems to have comprised a version of the priestly chronicles involving much systematic reconstruction of their contents, together with those of other early archives. Moreover, the new publication went as far back as epochs involving legendary speculation.[21] This ambitious project, which exercised a permanent effect on Roman historical writing, was sponsored by Publius Scaevola, chief priest for a decade or more after *c.* 130 (p. 167). Much, or at least some, of the lore contained in the Annales Maximi had probably been available earlier to any senator who wished to write history. But now this material was far more accessible, and attracted correspondingly greater interest.

The task of the Latin writers who followed was to apply their knowledge of Greek historical and rhetorical theory and practice to all these data. What they did, in the words of A.H.McDonald, was 'to elaborate the ceremonial form and expand the records in the light of senatorial constitutionalism, legalistic antiquarianism, and family interests. . . . This led to inaccuracy, invention and tendentious falsification.'[22] The temptation to fabricate was all the greater because the Annales Maximi were published at a time when Roman politics were entering upon a new phase of ferocity and tension.

This grimmer period was inaugurated by the brothers Tiberius and Gaius Gracchus (d. 133, 121), whose efforts to induce the Senate to accept reforms led to their violent deaths. Hitherto politics had been a matter not of parties but of ever-changing groups. But one consequence of these developments was the gradual crystallisation, among the nobles, of two schools of political thought. There were still continual shifts in personnel, but on the whole a division was now to be seen between the men favouring senatorial traditionalism (the 'optimates') and those who were prepared to appeal over the Senate's head to the Assembly of the people (the 'populares'). That body had previously accepted a docile role – which had been confirmed by the Senate's success in the Punic Wars. But now it increasingly showed that it was prepared to do so no longer.

The new partisan atmosphere stimulated writers to pursue the paths of savage argument and controversy which Cato had indicated – and to pursue them in relation to the contemporary history which he had made possible as a literary theme. Gaius Gracchus himself pointed the way by writing a propagandist biography of his own brother, on the lines of Polybius' essay on Philopoemen (p. 155). His opponents likewise buckled to the task.[23] This type of writing came all the more readily to the Romans because they were accustomed to semi-biographical forms. The most influential of these was a variant of the Greek encomium (p. 133), consisting of eulogies of deceased personages which it was customary to deliver at funerals,[24] write down[25] and preserve in the family home. Romans were also addicted to obituary inscriptions, which as time went on became more and more elaborate.[26]

But the most important historian working at this period drew more upon Greece than upon these native traditions. He was Coelius Antipater, who wrote after 121 BC. His subject, however, was not contemporary history but the Hannibalic War. And the special feature of his contribution, in so far as the disappearance of his work enables us to reconstruct its character, was not so much the analysis of a political point of view – he was unusually impartial – as a more sophisticated display of Greek methods than anyone had applied hitherto. One example of this aptitude was his choice of subject, which introduced Rome to the Greek sort of historical monograph. Other innovations, he claimed, included greater accuracy (modified, it appears, by a taste for sensationalism) and a more careful sort of prose.[27] His style caused him to be the first historian admired for his literary qualities by Cicero, though the orator uses somewhat guarded terms.[28]

The next stage was the acclimatisation to Rome of the sort of autobiographical memoir that Aratus had written in Greek. Roman memoirs are almost totally lost. But it is clear that the phenomenon played a more significant part than it had ever played in Greece – although Cicero comments that already in his time the earliest specimens had no readers any more. The conservative politician Marcus Aemilius Scaurus (consul in 115 BC) wrote his memoirs which no doubt had a political axe to grind, and a further autobiographical writer was another statesman of a similar way of thinking, Marcus Rutilius Rufus. Rutilius was a versatile phil-Hellene who had played a part in one of the principal dramas of the age, when the war against Jugurtha of Numidia enabled the 'new man' Gaius Marius to supersede the aristocratic commander Metellus through the direct action of the Assembly undertaken in defiance of the Senate. Rutilius had stayed on in Africa, and subsequently he raised and trained the army which Marius used to repel the German invaders of Italy (102–101).

Another pro-senatorial writer was Catulus. Poet, philosopher, orator and popular mythologist, he was the author of numerous literary works including a memoir on his own consulship (102) composed in a Latin version of Xenophon's style. Catulus was even more prominent than Rutilius in the midst of events. Having served as Marius' fellow-commander against the Germans, he helped to repress the 'popular' Saturninus in 100 and fought against rebel Italians in the Social (Marsian) War (91–89), finally succumbing to the followers of Marius.

The career of Marius was largely responsible for a new phase in which generals began to attract to themselves the loyalties which soldiers had previously owed to the State. Civil war broke out because Marius and a younger man, Sulla, were competing for the command against Rome's enemy Mithridates VI of Pontus in Asia Minor. Sulla violently asserted his right to the appointment, leaving Marius to conduct an orgy of massacres at home. But Marius died (86), and Sulla, victorious against Pontus, returned to Italy to exact bloodthirsty vengeance against the Marian faction (82–81). His appointment to the ancient emergency office of dictator carried with it unprecedented powers without limit of extent or duration which heralded the collapse of the Republic. However, Sulla himself, after undertaking a whole series of administrative measures to bolster up conservative interests and institutions, abdicated, and died in the following year (78).

At that time he had almost, but not quite, finished his own autobiographical memoirs or *Acts*.[29] Edited and published after his death by a former slave, this was a lengthy composition of twenty-three books, going back to the origins of his own family and perhaps beyond,[30] and ending (by a posthumous addition) with the prediction of his imminent death. The surviving fragments of the work, said H.J. Rose, 'show that its loss is to be regretted, not so much as a trustworthy historical document, for its author was capable of amazing inventions,[31] but as throwing a light on one of the most extraordinary characters in history, a blend of ruthless and single-minded efficiency with a confidence in his own good fortune which amounted to gross superstition'.

In these memoirs, we learn from Plutarch,

Sulla wrote that, when he considers all those occasions on which he appears to have made wise decisions, he finds that the most successful actions were those upon which he entered boldly and on the spur of the moment rather than after due deliberation. He says too that he was born with natural endowments not so much for war as for Fortune – and from this it appears that he attributes more to Fortune than to his own superior ability. Indeed, he makes himself a pawn in the hand of Providence.[32]

In other words, Sulla was pointing towards a long future by showing all his deeds as the working out of destiny, so that he himself appears as a leader enjoying superhuman guidance. The lesson was not lost on Caesar, who developed the personality cult further – and learnt other lessons also from Sulla's career, remarking that he had been fatuous to abdicate. Sulla also looked ahead to Caesar by refusing to employ the literary and learned ornaments of the Greeks for his memoirs, although he himself had received an elaborate education. Instead he wrote in straightforward Latin,[33] suitable to the 'raw material of history' which this propagandist composition made itself out to be.

Like most absolute rulers, Sulla also managed to find writers other than himself who were prepared to write history his way. The clever young historian Sisenna, in a long description of the Social and Civil Wars, seems to have adhered pretty closely to his views. Sallust later called him the best and most careful of the men who had written about Sulla, but censured his bias in the great man's favour.[34] Sisenna's manner of writing is shown by surviving fragments to have been verbose, archaic and affected. Yet it later seemed to Cicero a great stylistic improvement on the crude efforts of the past – though still nothing like good enough. It is significant of Sisenna's approach that he translated spicy romances ('Milesian tales'), and explicitly based his historical method on a sparkling but unreliable Greek writer of the third century, Clitarchus of Alexandria (p. 431, n. 47).[35]

This allegiance was typical of the historians of the Sullan epoch. They went in for an attractive novelistic presentation laced with much antiquarian legendary detail which displayed a false appearance of authenticity. At worst these 'later annalists' apparently sank to very dim depths of barefaced falsification, quite down to the standard of the most mendacious among the Greeks. Yet their dramatic presentation exercised great influence on later historians such as Livy.[36] Such writers, when they were describing battles, grossly exaggerated the losses of the enemy, and the triumphs of their own side. Besides, not being members of the Senate as so many of their predecessors had been, they lacked easy access to official records. So they made up for this deficiency by the uninhibited invention of alleged documents and archives.

A more serious author, Macer (d. 67 BC), claimed to be using a hitherto unemployed source for early Roman history. This was a collection of books supposedly going back to the fourth century BC, which was written on linen (*libri lintei*) and contained antique lists of senior officials and perhaps records of other matters also. These mysterious documents, said to have been preserved in the temple of Juno Moneta,[37] need not be dismissed as forgeries fabricated by Macer.[38] But it is unlikely that they went back to the fourth century; they may not have been more than a hundred years old. Nevertheless, it was the discovery of the Linen Books which stimulated Macer to become the first senator for about two generations to write a major history.

While showing the usual favour to early members of his own family,[39] he must, on the whole, have reflected the 'popular' point of view. For although Macer was a former supporter of Sulla, he was

one of those politicians who had turned against the dictator's reactionary system after his death. A similar 'democratic' line, later, was
followed first by Pompey and then by Caesar, both of whom used
anti-conservative programmes as a means to secure individual power
for themselves.

Such were the sinister aims of Caesar which the orator Cicero (106–
43 BC) devoted his life to opposing. Pompey he could never regard,
or at least not for long, as possessing such ambitions to any dangerous
extent. Cicero's growing devotion to the conservative cause (finally
espoused by Pompey) was one reason why he described Macer as a
ridiculous writer.[40]

Conscious of the need to record his own times, Cicero was profoundly interested in history. Yet his voluminous output did not include anything historical in the strict sense of the term. A partial
exception, although heavily self-justificatory in character, was a
memorandum relating to his own famous, controversial consulship
of 63 BC, in which he suppressed the conspiracy of Catiline. But this
essay, which violently attacked Caesar, remained a secret until after
his death. It has now disappeared,[41] and it remains uncertain, therefore, whether the biographer Nepos was right to declare that history
may have had more cause than the Republic to lament Cicero.[42]

In spite of this sparseness of his own purely historical writings, the
spokesmen in Cicero's dialogues have a great deal to say about the
past, and a great deal more about how history ought to be written.
First of all there are the usual impeccable insistences on the truth. In
words attributed to the orator Marcus Antonius, the grandfather of
the triumvir,

Who does not know history's first law to be that an author must not
dare to tell anything but the truth? And the second that he must make
bold to tell the whole truth? That there must be no suggestion of partiality
anywhere in his writings? Nor of malice?[43]

History is 'the witness of the age, the light of truth, the life of the
memory, the instructress of his life', and its devotees must exclude the
fabulous and distinguish carefully between legend and sober history.[44]

Elsewhere Cicero adds that earlier historians, notably Macer, had
failed in this respect. He also blames the speeches in praise of eminent
men which were preserved in the archives of Roman families: 'By

these laudatory speeches our history has become quite distorted. For much is set down in them which never occurred, false triumphs, too large a number of consulships, false relationships . . . as if I, for example, should say that I was descended from Manius Tullius the patrician!'[45]

Nevertheless, he himself urged a contemporary historian, Lucceius, to write about his own famous consulship in precisely this eulogistic style: 'So I will blatantly ask you to celebrate my exploits with even more enthusiasm than you perhaps feel, and in this case to disregard the principles of history. . . . Indulge your affection for me a trifle more even than strict truth would allow.'[46] However much importance Cicero may have attached to the truth, he is here suggesting this was an occasion for applying to one person, and a single noble theme, the techniques not so much of a historical work as of a moving stage-play which dramatically records ups and downs. He is asking Lucceius to apply the traditional standards of encomium which, as he indicates elsewhere, are not the same as those of history.[47] In other words, the political situation was so grave, and his own career in such peril (owing to the feeling against his execution of the Catilinarian conspirators), that he felt praise took priority over truth; though Lucceius, who failed to respond, may not have agreed. Cicero, then, is guilty of wanting to stretch the truth – with whatever degree of extenuating circumstances a politician in a jam may be held to deserve.

It was in this same spirit that he asked the distinguished Greco-Syrian historian Posidonius (*c.* 135–50 BC) – who equated the Roman Empire with the Stoic world state (p. 154)[48] – to write the history of that controversial consulship of his. Posidonius had already composed a eulogy of Pompey (now lost) but he was no more willing than Lucceius to take on Cicero's consulship. And so he produced the tactful reply, showing a touch of the ironical humour for which he was known, that the memorandum with which Cicero had accompanied his request was already such a masterpiece in itself that it could not be improved upon by anyone else. Later, Cicero, who possessed a very Roman aliveness to the biographical aspects of history,[49] himself embarked on the field of panegyric, writing a highly tendentious eulogy of his deceased political opponent Cato the younger. This tract in favour of Republicanism earned a strong counterblast from Caesar.[50]

These two pamphlets have not survived, but they were evidently mere politics, not the truthful history for which Cicero expressed such admiration. A partial explanation of this apparently contradictory approach, in which theory and practice seem so much at variance, can be derived from what he says about earlier Latin historians. For one thing, it turns out that the truth he so warmly praised is a matter of moral attitude more than professional expertise or factual accuracy. Secondly, what really interested him most of all was style. As he makes his friend Atticus say in the *Laws*, none of these historical writers, so far, have really been any good – Sisenna was the best, but even he had fallen far below the desired standard (p. 176).[51] What he means by this, however, is that they had all been defective not so much in substance as in the manner in which they wrote. Though impressed, as a patriot, by the quaint archaic majesty of the old Roman historical tradition, it leaves him cold as a stylist, for he is a devotee of that Greek school of historical writing which insists that history must be well written: meaning by this that it must be written by experts in the theories and devices of rhetoric. That was the teaching of the school of Isocrates, and Cicero vigorously praises its chief practitioners.[52]

In other words, history exceeds all other branches of literature in its closeness to oratory – a view which had a marked effect on subsequent Roman historical writing, and was soon to be given the fullest expression by Livy (p. 224). Cicero gives downright and highly articulate utterance to the ancient view that history is quite as much a matter of style as of facts – or, it must be feared, perhaps even more so, since in the *Brutus* we hear Cicero, 'smiling', make the remark that 'the privilege is conceded to rhetoricians to distort history in order to give more point to their narrative'.[53]

He follows up this theme with a further argument. Just as the orator needs to know his history,[54] so conversely the only historian who can give his work an appropriate style is the person who has been trained in these oratorical studies which stood at the centre of Roman public life and education. 'History, which bears witness to the passing of the ages, sheds light upon reality, gives life to recollection and guidance to human existence, and brings tidings of ancient days; whose voice but the orator's can entrust her to immortality?'[55] Men of eloquence, Cicero urges, must take a rest from litigation and the Forum, as they used to in Greece, so that they can turn instead to the task of historical writing.[56] They are required for what he calls the 'building up' of history,[57] which needs the fully developed kind of prose composition practised by public speakers.[58] True, a historian must aim at a more smooth and flowing style than speakers in court habitually employ.[59] All the same, as Cicero is glad to remind us, the Greeks had actually classified history as a kind of oratory; they had called it the 'show-piece' (epideictic) branch of the art.[60]

A mind of great power was needed to rescue Roman historical writing from the picturesque insincerities which now seemed to have become its future destiny.

12

Caesar

By suppressing Catiline's wild men while he was consul, Cicero believed he had saved the Republic. But the whole incident took place while the most powerful man in the Roman Empire, Pompey, was away in the east, putting an end to Rome's persistent foreign enemy Mithridates of Pontus. When Pompey came back, the Republic which Cicero wanted to save was suppressed by the ominous First Triumvirate. For in this pact the three most powerful men in Rome – Pompey, Crassus and Caesar – joined forces to establish a virtually dictatorial control over the State.

Removing the highest decisions out of the hands of the noble cliques who had hitherto dominated the Senate and the State, the triumvirs transferred all power into their own hands. Caesar's share was the consulship of 59 BC followed by a major provincial command. Indeed the one necessitated the other, because the agrarian legislation (redistributing land) and high-handed, violent conduct by which he served the interests of his fellow-triumvirs and himself so outraged conservative opinion that his freedom and his life would not have been safe if he had thereafter relapsed into the status of a private citizen. In preparation, therefore, for the moment when he would no longer be consul, he got himself appointed governor of the two Gauls (southern France and northern Italy) and Illyricum (Dalmatia). Then, in 58, confident that all conservative opposition at Rome would be paralysed by the gang-warfare he himself had arranged, he set out for the Gallic War which was destined to occupy the next eight years of his life.

That part of his *Commentaries* relating to the Gallic War consists of seven books describing the first seven of the eight annual campaigns (58–51 BC). In these operations he conquered central and northern France and established the Roman frontier on the Rhine, as well as conducting two expeditions across that river and two across the channel to Britain. In the first book, after discussing the customs and institutions of the Gauls and Germans, he deals with the fighting of 58 BC against the Helvetii – Celts of Switzerland who were seeking to migrate to Gaul. Then he reports the campaign against the German Ariovistus who had seized lands belonging to the Sequani (Saône) – the weaker of the two leading tribes of central Gaul, the other being Rome's traditional allies the Aedui. The second book tells of the following year, which witnessed desperate fighting against the Nervii, one of the Belgic tribes inhabiting northern France and Belgium. Book III describes the naval warfare which reduced the Veneti of Brittany. An expedition of Publius Crassus (son of the triumvir) against the Aquitani of south-western Gaul is also recorded.

The fourth book (55 BC) recounts Caesar's annihilation of two immigrant German tribes the Usipetes and Tencteri, and his subsequent bridging of the Rhine and brief demonstration of force on the other side of the river, intended to impress those remoter German peoples known as the Suebi. Then followed his almost equally short-lived first landing in Britain. Book V narrates the second expedition to Britain in 54, and, back in Gaul, the ambushing of a Roman camp by Ambiorix of the Belgic Eburones during the winter. The subject of the sixth book is Caesar's re-establishment of order in northern France, followed by a second crossing of the Rhine. Book VII, the climax of the work, tells the story of the Great Revolt of 52 BC, led by Vercingetorix of the central tribe of the Arverni. Caesar records his setback at the hands of Vercingetorix at Gergovia (Clermont-Ferrand), followed by the final defeat and capture of the nationalist leader at Alesia (Alise-Ste-Reine).

Caesar's work ensures that we know more about his Gallic War than any other military operations of the ancient world. This is the only contemporary narrative of a major Roman foreign war that has come down to us – and it is written by the principal commander

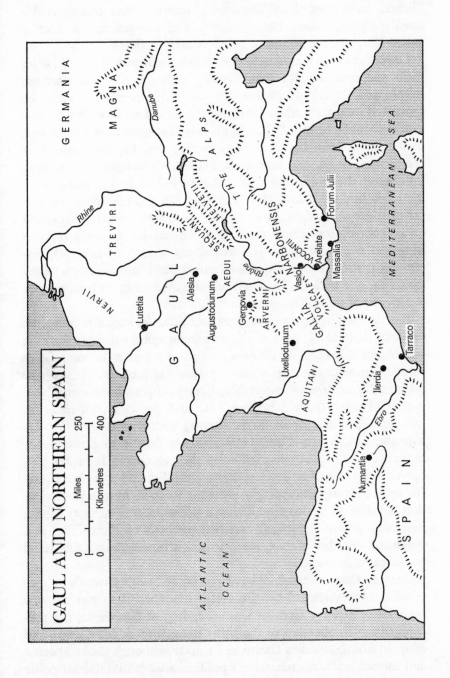

GAUL AND NORTHERN SPAIN

himself. In the words of Theodor Mommsen, 'the enormous difference between these Commentaries and everything else that is called Roman history cannot be adequately realised'.

Caesar writes in a masterly style, a pure unrhetorical sort of Latin, lucid and compact like Attic Greek, made up of words that are simple and unerringly chosen. 'As the sailor avoids the rock,' he remarked in a grammatical treatise, 'so should you avoid the word that is obsolete or rare.'[1] The Latin title *Commentarius* is a rendering of the Greek term that had been used to describe the memoirs of the dictator Sulla, and that work, like Sulla's straightforward style, influenced the man who was going to follow in his footsteps as dictator. But the *Gallic War* was also a series of reports from a commander in the field. In this sense the name suggests memoranda or notebooks, something more than official log but not quite a historical commentary in the traditional sense – a general's dispatches certainly, but dispatches embellished with orations (even including one by a Gallic rebel) and augmented by at least a spare sufficiency of other background.

But that is a deceptively modest description for such a masterpiece as Caesar's book. It is, in fact, something quite original, since he was consciously creating his own genre and a new style, unafraid of comparison with the mighty literary names of the past. He was also taking sides, as Roman writers often liked to do, in a historiographical battle inherited from Athenians four and five centuries ago, but now reverberating again in the literary circles of Rome. For this was the time when Cicero was showing favour to those Greek historians of the past who, following the precepts of Isocrates, had opted in favour of a flowery, rhetorical, didactic style of writing (p. 137). Caesar's exceedingly different work is, by every implication, a criticism of this school, and a declaration of support for the practical, personal, factually verified methods of Thucydides and Polybius[2] – neither of them mere armchair historians, but first-hand participants in events.

Because Caesar's work did not correspond with Cicero's picture of what history should be, the orator described it as just the raw material of history. Here he was accepting, at face value, the self-deprecating implication of the title *Commentaries* which Caesar had adapted from Sulla. But Cicero and Caesar, although they suspected and indeed loathed each other's politics, always maintained polite literary relations, and Cicero extends his remarks beyond this apparently slighting suggestion in order to introduce a very warm tribute.

Admirable indeed! The *Commentaries* are like nude figures, straight and beautiful; stripped of all ornament of style as if they had laid aside a garment. His aim was to furnish others with material for writing history, and perhaps he has succeeded in gratifying the inept, who may wish to apply their curling irons to his material; but men of sound judgement he has deterred from writing, since in history there is nothing more pleasing than brevity clear and correct. . . .[3]

Caesar's general Hirtius, who was allotted the daunting task of rounding off the *Gallic War* with a final eighth book,[4] emphasised not only the articulate excellence of Caesar's style, but the facility and speed of his composition. 'My admiration for his writing', said Hirtius, 'is greater even than other people's. They appreciate the high standard of his writing. I know more – how easily and how quickly he wrote.'[5]

The *Commentaries* do not entirely consist of direct narrative, or even of narrative enlivened by speeches. There are also ethnographical digressions, in the oldest historical tradition. These are of peculiar interest to the modern peoples of Western Europe, whose fortunes were moulded by Caesar's deeds. Considerable information is given about the institutions of the Germans,[6] and about events and customs in Gaul, and in Britain as well.

In Britain far the most civilised inhabitants are those living in Kent (a purely maritime district), whose way of life differs little from that of the Gauls. Most of the tribes in the interior do not grow corn but live on milk and meat, and wear skins. All the Britons dye their bodies with woad, which produces a blue colour, and this gives them a more terrifying appearance in battle. They wear their hair long, and shave the whole of their bodies except the head and the upper lip. Wives are shared between groups of ten or twelve men. . . .[7]

But these digressions remain subordinate to the fast movement of the whole story, and it is best to read the *Commentaries* as rapidly as they were written. Caesar's deeds, whether stirring or horrible, still speak for themselves as freely as when he recorded them. Unlike most other classical historians, he is less interested in characters and personalities than in actions. Comments on what happened, and discussions of why it had happened, are restricted, except when he desires to make some forcible point.[8] Strategies are rarely explained beforehand; they are left to be unfolded as situations develop.[9] Praise and blame, too, are pared to a minimum.[10] And yet the down-to-earth, rather beastly tale is penetrated with occasional, unexpected personal touches, subtly selected to arouse interest and sympathy.[11] And there are sudden flashes which raise the work to formidable literary heights.

Caesar is inclined to devote greater detail to happenings at which he was not present than to those in which he participated himself. This may have been because he was the sort of man who derives keener artistic stimulus from what he reads than what he sees or does. Or perhaps, when he had not been an eyewitness, he applied less strict standards of accuracy. Pollio (76 BC–AD 5), who served under him and later wrote an important history of the Civil Wars (now lost),[12] included among his notoriously severe literary judgments[13] a criticism of Caesar's excessive credulity towards the reports of his subordinates.

Asinius Pollio thinks that the *Commentaries* were put together somewhat carelessly and without strict regard for truth; since in many cases Caesar was too ready to believe the accounts which others gave of their actions, and gave a perverted account of his own, either designedly or perhaps from forgetfulness; and he thinks that he intended to rewrite and revise them.[14]

If Caesar, confronted with so many dispatches, accepted some of them too readily,[15] or if his phenomenal memory was occasionally at fault, it would hardly be surprising. But Pollio's observation also suggests the possibility that he inserted deliberate distortions. This raises the whole question of the reliability of the *Commentaries*. The ever-present dangers of bias, conscious or unconscious, are obviously accentuated when the historian himself is the leading actor on the stage. Nor should the reader's suspicions or reservations be lulled by the seemingly objective impersonality with which Caesar, like Thucydides and Xenophon, writes of himself in the third person.

His book had an eye on posterity. But it was mainly written for his own contemporaries – for the Roman governing-class from which, thoughout these long years in Gaul, he never took his eyes. He went into the war with a storm of criticism already around him, and, as the hostilities proceeded, he was criticised a great deal more. In one of the dramatic speeches which illuminate his narrative, he makes the German chieftain Ariovistus refer to this hostility at Rome: 'If I killed you, there are plenty of nobles and politicians in Rome who would thank me for it; I know this, because they themselves commissioned their agents to tell me so. I could make them all my grateful friends by putting an end to you.'[16] Caesar's purpose in including this passage is to imply that all his good work in the field was being undermined by treachery at home. And indeed the principal purpose of the *Commentaries* was to provide a counterblast to this opposition in the capital. It would, no doubt, have been over-optimistic to expect to silence his most ferocious Roman opponents. But he saw a good chance of winning over the numerous floating voters. An immense barrage of publicity was kept in motion to achieve this,[17] and the *Commentaries* formed an important part of the campaign.

Caesar evidently felt that his public would, on the whole, have no objection if he conducted the most frightful massacres among his and their foreign enemies. And he was no doubt right in this assumption. He therefore proudly indicates that his unprovoked attack cost the Helvetii more than a quarter of a million lives, among them many non-combatants (58).[18] More blatant and brutal still is the account of his deliberate annihilation of the German immigrant hordes in 55.

There was also a great crowd of women and children in the German camp – for they had brought all their families with them when they left home and crossed the Rhine. These began to flee in all directions, and were hunted down by the cavalry which Caesar sent out for the purpose. ... A large number were killed, and the rest plunged into the water and perished, overcome by the force of the current in their terror-stricken and exhausted state.[19]

This was too much for the younger Cato, who protested at Rome that divine retribution must surely be on its way. Caesar, he declared, should be handed over to the Germans to atone for such infamous treachery. His objections were not so much humanitarian as political, or rather, like so much else in Rome, politico-religious, since the breach of faith was a matter of religion. Cato's complaints fell on deaf ears. But in recording a later atrocity, Hirtius feels obliged to accompany his account by the nauseating suggestion that it was the act of a merciful man (51).

Caesar saw that his clemency was so well known that no one would think him a cruel man if for once he took severe measures. So he decided to deter all others by making an example of the defenders of Uxellodunum. All who had borne arms had their hands cut off and were then let go, so that everyone might see what punishment was meted out to evil-doers.[20]

However, in this war, his 'clemency' was merely a side-issue. What he really wanted to get across to enemies or doubters at Rome was something different, namely the patriotic correctitude, indeed inevitability, of all his actions, and their absolute conformity with the mandate entrusted to him by the Government of Rome. For example, his action against the Helvetii in 58 might very well, if left unexplained, have looked like sheer aggression, undertaken for the sake of military glory. It might also be censured (though there were legal pros and cons to this argument) as an excursion beyond the Roman frontiers, such as Roman governors were forbidden to undertake. So we are told that, in fact, there were cogent reasons for the military operation. 'Caesar saw that it would be very dangerous to the Province [Narbonese Gaul] to have a warlike people, hostile to Rome, established close to its rich cornlands, which were without natural defences.'[21] This assertion, like so many others in the *Commentaries*, has a disarming air of uncontroversial sweet reason.[22] As Hirtius remarked, Caesar possessed 'the surest skill in explaining his own plans'. It is usually extremely hard to fault him on facts. The way in which he demonstrated how right he was in everything he did was not by lying. An occasional distortion or exaggeration might well pass unchallenged. But downright lies could all too easily be caught out: because, after all, Caesar was by no means the only Roman who wrote home from the Gallic campaigns – and eventually returned home, too.

The speeches inserted in the *Commentaries*, it is true, sometimes have the fictional appearance familiar from earlier historians. They do not look anything like word-for-word reports. Nor, in all probability, were they all addressed (in whatever form) to the very large throngs of soldiers who were often supposed to be their audiences. Yet this method of narration was not, in itself, an attempt to draw wool over anyone's eyes. It was, rather, a means of painting in backgrounds and motivations – a convention which readers of the day, like readers in previous centuries, would understand. Moreover, these orations sometimes allow even Caesar's most determined enemies to utter arguments as convincing as any that the cleverest barrister could have devised on their behalf. For the story, he felt, would not have had a sufficiently telling dramatic impact without the inclusion of the other side's case.

He enlarges with a certain element of self-dramatisation, not too indiscreet and no doubt accurate enough, upon his own fabulous ascendancy over his troops. The legionaries are referred to with an instinctive, sympathetic affection which permits 'citations' of special acts of gallantry by individual soldiers. One of the effects of this ascendancy, an effect of which we are reminded from time to time, was the importance of his own magic presence.[23] We also hear of the specular personal interventions which decided the fate of battles.

As the situation was critical and no reserves were available, Caesar snatched a shield from a soldier in the rear (he had not his own shield with him), made his way into the front line, addressed each centurion by name, and shouted encouragement to the rest of the troops, ordering them to push forward and open out their ranks, so that they could use their swords more easily.[24]

Caesar sees history as a panorama full of dramatic reversals,[25] and so, remembering Sulla's almost mystic attention to Fortune (p. 175), he too believes to an abnormal extent in the luck which wins these charismatic successes for himself.

Specific self-criticism, not unnaturally, fails to find a place. Indeed, when things went wrong, as they did at Gergovia (52), Caesar is at pains to point out that the military rebuff was caused not by any fault of his own but by the hasty, disobedient actions of junior officers and men: 'The next day Caesar paraded the troops and reprimanded them for their rashness and impetuosity. They had decided for themselves, he said, to advance farther and attack the town, neither halting when the retreat was sounded nor obeying the military tribunes and generals who tried to restrain them.'[26] We have no means of telling whether this diagnosis of the defeat is correct. It may, instead, conceal some miscalculation on the part of Caesar himself, which he found it preferable to blame on his subordinates.[27]

But self-blame is never a conspicuous feature in the memoirs of any general, and it is scarcely likely to be prominent in a work specifically designed to justify Caesar politically to the people who mattered at home. Good propaganda, directed to such a purpose, is careful in its selective window-dressing, and the *Gallic War* is among the most potent works of propaganda ever written.

The persuasive element seems particularly strong in the initial sections, which relate to a time when the need for it was greatest. This portion of the work, like each of the annual reports that follow, appears to have been completed soon after the end of the year with which it deals. When the various books were published is another problem. Perhaps they were shown to leading Romans year by year as each was written, in order to win support during the successive political crises and elections that took place in Caesar's absence. But in any case the work subsequently came out as a whole, at a time when the war was well advanced or perhaps complete.

While the Gallic War had still been under way, the alliance formed by the members of the First Triumvirate against their conservative, Republican, political enemies held together for a time. Later on, the agreement showed signs of cracking, and then it was cemented together again at the Conference of Luca (Lucca) in 56. Thereafter, however, several things happened which caused relations between the triumvirs to break down. One of these events was the death of Julia, who had helped to keep her father Caesar and her husband Pompey on tolerably good terms with one another. Next, the defeat and death of the third triumvir, Crassus, fighting against the Parthians in Mesopotamia (53), brought the two men into a more perilously direct confrontation.

The question of Caesar's future raised a particular difficulty, and it was this problem, before long, which proved insuperable. He wanted to make sure, when the end of the war arrived, that he would be able to move straight from his command to a second consulship in Rome. It was essential to avoid an interval of private status, which his political enemies would undoubtedly use to cause his ruin. The conservatives, however, were convinced that once at Rome he would use his position and his army to seize supreme, dictatorial power. Gradually, they persuaded the hesitant Pompey that they were right; and at the beginning of 49 he agreed to become their military leader.

And so, when two tribunes of the people bringing messages from Caesar were expelled from Rome, their master took the fateful step of conducting the advance guard of his army across the Rubicon, the stream which divided the north Italian part of his province (Cisalpine Gaul) from metropolitan Italy. The Civil War had begun.

The first two years of the fighting, in Italy, Gaul, Spain and the Balkans, culminated in the defeat and death of Pompey. Next followed campaigns by Caesar in Alexandria and Asia Minor. Then he went on to north Africa and Spain in order to overthrow Pompey's sons and lieutenants. These four campaigns subsequent to Pompey's death, two against foreign states and two against surviving Pompeians, are described for us by anonymous officers of Caesar.[28] The operations during the first two years, down to a short time after Pompey's murder by the Egyptians, were narrated by Caesar himself. This is the second part of his Commentaries, called the *Civil War*.

It is divided into three books. The first opens with the debates in Rome preceding the war, and explains how the intransigence of his enemies compelled Caesar to cross the Rubicon and launch his lightning invasions of Italy. Pompey evacuated Rome, and soon afterwards sailed away to the Balkans; an attempt at resistance by Ahenobarbus at Corfinium had proved futile. Leaving forces to reduce Massilia (Marseille), Caesar proceeded to Spain, where he forced the Pompeian leaders Afranius and Petreius to surrender near Ilerda (Lerida). Book II describes the fall of Massilia and the destruction of the army of Caesar's lieutenant Curio in north Africa.

The third book tells how first Caesar and then his lieutenant Antony succeeded in crossing over from Italy to Greece to confront Pompey (48). After a serious repulse outside Dyrrhachium (Epidamnus), Caesar won an overwhelming victory at Pharsalus in Thessaly. Pompey fled to Egypt, where he was assassinated by supporters of the young King Ptolemy XIII. Caesar, arriving immediately afterwards, announced his intention of mediating between Ptolemy and his sister and fellow-monarch Cleopatra, with whom the boy's government was at war. Ptolemy's army occupied the greater part of Alexandria and forced Caesar to join battle with them. Soon after hostilities had begun, the work breaks off.

The *Civil War*, like the *Gallic War*, exploited Caesar's incomparable talent for depicting his own actions and motives in a favourable light. The date of publication is again disputed. It is likely, however, that each annual instalment became known among leading Romans soon after the events it described. This had also, perhaps, been the case with the *Gallic War*, and here again the supposition seems to be confirmed by the unusually emphatic note of self-justification in the account of the initial campaign. Throughout the work runs the contention that Caesar's enemies, by their insistence on pursuing a personal vendetta, had forced on him a war he never wanted.

All the friends of the consuls, all the adherents of Pompey, and all those with old grudges against Caesar were mustered in the Senate. Their numbers and the uproar they made intimidated the timorous, made up the minds of the waverers and robbed the majority of the power to decide freely. . . . Cato was stung by his defeat at the elections. Lentulus was actuated by the size of his debts. . . . Scipio had a dread of the law courts. . . . Pompey was reluctant to let anyone stand on the same pinnacle of prestige as himself.[29]

The other side, of course, could have demonstrated Caesar's dubious past and suspect aims with equal effectiveness, if only they had possessed the literary artist to do the job. But Caesar was at least justified in describing his real enemies as a small minority of senators, whether they should be described as reactionaries or Republicans, who had forced their uncompromising policy on the rest.

Although anger and scorn are not far beneath the surface, the lucid, concise calmness of the *Civil War* is calculated to form an impressive contrast with the hate-ridden gossip which was raging against him. The emphasis on peacefulness is almost feverish. Caesar insists that he is fighting not to destroy his enemies but to reconcile existing differences with as little bloodshed as possible. In February 49, his stated war-aims included the freeing of the Roman people from oppression by a small clique, and the restoration of the tribunes of the people who had been illegally driven from the city. He thought it absurd to say that he was the revolutionary and that the constitution was upheld by Pompey, whose career, starting with a murderous youthful phase, showed that precisely the opposite was the case. As for himself, the conqueror of unprecedently vast territories for Rome, all he claimed was that he should be rescued from undeserved humiliation at the hands of his foes. 'I merely want to protect myself against the slanders of enemies, to restore to their rightful position the tribunes of the people, who have been expelled because of their involvement in my cause, and to reclaim for myself and for the Roman people independence from the domination of a small clique.'[30] Caesar's assertion that he must protect himself was not only a practical matter. It was also based on a consideration of the greatest importance to an aristocratic Roman: his honour or prestige, in Latin *dignitas*. 'It pained him', he says, 'to see the privilege conferred on him by the Roman people being insultingly wrested from him by his enemies.' And the reason why this was so painful was because 'prestige has always been of prime importance to him, even outweighing life itself'.[31]

But Caesar's prestige would be defended by Caesar's fortune: and there was something more than normal or ordinary about this mysterious quality. Fortune had already stood him in good stead in the Gallic War, when he revived Sulla's emphasis on the concept (p. 189). And now – although human endeavour, especially by Caesar, could lend a helping hand[32] – the same agency sometimes showed its hand again in near-miracles. Such, for example, was the change of wind which enabled Antony to get across the Ionian Sea and join him in the Balkans in early 48: 'As soon as they entered harbour, by an unbelievable stroke of luck the wind, which had been blowing from the south for the past two days, veered round to the south-east. This could be regarded as a sudden reversal of fortune.'[33] And the same point is elaborated elsewhere: 'Fortune, whose power is very great in all spheres, but particularly in warfare, often brings about great reversals by a slight tilt of the balance.'[34] Certain disagreeable happenings, such as the mutiny of his soldiers at Placentia (Piacenza) in 49, are omitted from the narrative altogether. But Caesar is glad enough to let us know when his battles hung in a precarious balance, which often only at the last moment, after extreme emergencies, tilted in his favour.

This attitude to Fortune, and the knowledge of the help it had given him, made Caesar feel a certain contempt for his enemies. Contempt, for example, seemed to be at the root of a new policy of clemency, which had been talked about before but was now extended, amid much publicity, to Roman foes such as Ahenobarbus who fell into his hands.[35] Nor, if he had not despised his opponents, would he have alienated most of his own class by declaring that the dictatorship, first assumed temporarily five years earlier, was henceforward going to be his possession in perpetuity. For this step, taken in February of 44, was the negation of the Republican constitution, since it meant that the members of the other hereditary leading families would continue for the duration of his life to be deprived of their traditional pickings. Moreover, the situation was all the more offensive because he was about to leave for the east to fight against the Parthians. This meant that he would be away for an indefinite period, during which senators would have to queue up for favours in the anterooms of his henchmen at Rome. The victor of the Gallic War and the Civil War remained careless of this possibility. When he had time to think of it at all, he put his trust in the Fortune which had brought him so far. On the Ides of March, it deserted him, and the State was left in leaderless confusion.

13

Sallust

THE murder of Caesar was not followed by the restoration of the Republic. What came instead was a new round of civil war. The men who had killed him, Brutus and Cassius, were compelled to depart for Greece. At home, the young Octavian – the future Augustus – whom Caesar's will had named his son and major heir to his personal possessions, clashed with Caesar's lieutenant Antony, and was supported by Republicans such as Cicero. However, after the two factions had come into conflict at the battle of Mutina (Modena) in 43, Antony and Octavian united with another Caesarian leader, Lepidus, to form the Second Triumvirate. This compact, which unlike the First Triumvirate was an official Act of State, gave the three men joint dictatorial powers and ensured that the free working of the Republic should not be restored. In the following year, Brutus and Cassius were overwhelmed by the triumvirs at Philippi in Macedonia and lost their lives.

Such were the circumstances in which Gaius Sallustius Crispus about (86–*c*. 34 BC) decided to write about some of the events, during the past seventy years, which had led to this grim situation.

His first historical work, probably written shortly after Philippi, was an account of the conspiracy which Catiline had launched against the Roman State more than twenty years earlier. Sallust begins by announcing his own retirement from politics. Then he explains that he has chosen this subject because Catiline's crime was an unprecedented one, which had faced the Roman State with an entirely new kind of threat. A description of Catiline's character is followed by a survey of Rome's early history and subsequent moral decline. Then comes an account of Catiline's (alleged) first attempts at revolution (66–65 BC); and we are given a character-sketch of the debauched noblewoman Sempronia who became one of his supporters.

After his failure at the consular elections in 63, Catiline's projects assumed an even more desperate character, and the historian describes how he started forming private armies in various parts of Italy, and planning murder and arson in the capital itself. Taxed with these plans by the consul Cicero, Catiline walked out of the senate-house and left Rome to join his camps at Arretium (Arezzo) and Faesulae (Fiesole). After indicating Italy's miserable condition, which had won the revolutionary cause many adherents, Sallust goes on to describe how the conspiracy was disclosed to Cicero by Gallic tribesmen on a visit to Rome, who reported that their loyalty had been tampered with by the plotters.

Five leading Roman noblemen were found to be implicated. They were placed under arrest, and the Senate discussed what their fates should be. The speeches made by Caesar and Cato during the debate are reported by Sallust at length. Caesar argued against the execution of the conspirators, suggesting that they should instead be confined for life in Italian municipalities. Cato, on the other hand, demanded their execution; and his view carried the day. The characters of the two speakers, regarded by Sallust as the outstanding personalities of his time, are described and contrasted. The consul Cicero arranged the execution of the plotters, and at the beginning of 62 BC Catiline himself was cornered and killed at Pistoria (Pistoia) in northern Etruria.

Sallust's second historical monograph (*c.* 41–40 BC) goes further back in date. Its subject is Rome's war of 111–105 BC against Jugurtha the king of Numidia, which is eastern Algeria today. The author begins by justifying the writing of history as an activity preferable to a politician's career. He points out that the *Jugurthine War* deals with an especially important theme, first because of the hard-fought battles and their varying fortunes, and secondly because the war witnessed and created the first challenge by Romans to the arrogance of their own aristocracy.

Sallust goes on to describe Jugurtha's early life, his rise to power, and his defiance of Rome (116–112 BC). After diplomatic exchanges, in which the conservative leader Scaurus allegedly played a discreditable part, Rome finally declared war on the king. But as a result of the corruption of senior Roman officers, the operations came to nothing. Jugurtha then visited Rome to plead his case (110). After organising the assassination of a rival, he was expelled and the fighting was resumed. The Roman commander Metellus, who belonged to the greatest family in Rome, won victories. Yet he suffered defeats as well, and proved unable to finish off the war.

The turning-point came when his lieutenant Marius, a 'new man', returned to Rome and stood for the consulship. In spite of aristocratic opposition, he was elected with enthusiastic popular support. His first step was to widen army recruitment by accepting volunteers from the poorer classes. Appointed to replace Metellus, he wore down Jugurtha in three campaigns (107–105), and forced the king's ally, Bocchus I of Mauretania, to ask for peace. Marius' lieutenant, Sulla, persuaded Bocchus to betray Jugurtha, who was ambushed, delivered to Sulla, and handed over by him to Marius.

This was the time of the invasions of the Empire by the Germans; and the book ends by describing how, once the Jugurthine War had been won, Marius was again elected consul in order to deal with the new menace that had arisen in the north.

Sallust started his *Histories*, his greatest literary achievement, in about 39 BC. The work only survives in fragments, including four speeches, two letters and about five hundred small extracts that have been preserved by various means. The five books of the *Histories* covered the period from 78 BC to the early sixties. He may have intended to add further books carrying the story down to 60, or possibly even to 51 or 50. But, if so, his death prevented the completion of the plan.

A prologue on earlier Roman history argued that stability had vanished from the State when there was no longer anything to fear from Carthage; then party politics began, with all their dishonesty and corruption. The first book went on to deal with the year 78 BC in which Marcus Aemilius Lepidus (father of the triumvir) had staged an abortive revolt against the conservative system established by Sulla. Sallust makes Lepidus deliver a violent harangue against Sulla, ostensibly at a time when the latter had abdicated from the dictatorship but was still alive.

The rest of the book was concerned with Sertorius, an adherent of the Marian party who had taken refuge from Sulla in Spain. There, from 80 BC onwards, he raised the greater part of the peninsula against the dictator and his government. Book II told of the death of Lepidus in Sardinia (77) and the dispatch of Pompey, the major figure in the *Histories*, to fight against Sertorius in Spain. The third book described Sertorius' downfall and death (72), the dispatch of Marcus Antonius (father of the triumvir) to the east with a special command against the pirates (74), the beginning of the slave revolt of Spartacus (73–72), and the first successes of the conservative general Lucullus against Mithridates of Pontus. Book IV continued this story of victory. But the final book (which was probably left incomplete) began with Lucullus' first military setback, and went on to describe the Roman debate which, against violent conservative opposition, gave Pompey the command in his place (67).

Sallust's home-town Amiternum (San Vittorino) lay in a rich plain north-east of Rome. This region in the heart of the Abruzzi was an area traditionally noted for its stern Sabine austerity.[1] But the local nobility of the place, to which the Sallustii presumably belonged, was thoroughly Romanised by the time the historian was born. There are stories of his youth, mostly discreditable but perhaps legendary. No solid facts are known about him until he became quaestor at Rome in 55. Then, as tribune of the people in 52, he opposed Cicero's defence of the political gangster Milo on the charge of murdering his 'popular' counterpart Clodius.[2] In 50 Sallust was one of many people expelled from the Senate by the censors. It was alleged that he had committed adultery with Milo's wife,[3] but there were probably grudges against him because of the anti-conservative line he had adopted during his tribunate.

In the subsequent civil war between Caesar and Pompey, Sallust again opposed the conservatives, taking the side of Caesar who restored him to senatorial rank. He held commands in Illyricum (Yugoslavia) without much success, and failed to suppress a mutiny in Campania (47). But as praetor in the following year he fought well against the Pompeians in north Africa, and was rewarded with the governorship of the province of Africa Nova, into which the greater part of the Numidian kingdom was converted after the campaign. On his return to Rome he was prosecuted for extracting illegal gains from his province. Caesar did not bring him to trial, but Sallust retired from public affairs. He spent the remaining eleven years or so of his life on the large properties he had acquired, including the magnificent Sallustian Gardens where emperors were later glad to live.[4]

Whether his retirement was purely voluntary seems doubtful; and it may well be that he was never offered any further employment. He would have been eligible for a consulship in 43, but the arrangements for future appointments which Caesar made before his death did not include Sallust's nomination to a post.[5] In any case, even if his political career was not halted in Caesar's lifetime, it came to an end with his death. Could he, if he had wished, have continued to serve under Octavian or Antony or Lepidus? We cannot be sure. In his writings, apparent analogies between the young Octavian and the murderous young Pompey, and certain indications about the parents of Antony and Lepidus, suggest that he felt malevolently towards all three members of the Second Triumvirate.[6] There are other oblique sneers at the régime as well (p. 202). And so Sallust never went back to state affairs. Instead he turned to the writing of history – possibly in late 44, when politics looked particularly turbulent and gloomy.

However, his own version of why he had retired is a grave and austere one, based on the conclusion, not altogether free from the taste of sour grapes, that public life is an unsatisfactory way of spending one's time: 'Among those occupations which belong to the world of action, it is my opinion that magistracies, military commands, and indeed all kinds of public appointments, in our own epoch at any rate, have the least to recommend them.'[7] So that, according to Sallust, was why he decided to abandon his official career: 'At last, after passing through many sufferings and dangers, I achieved a state of peace of mind and decided to spend what remained of my life far removed from public affairs. But I did not intend to idle away this precious leisure.'[8] There are echoes of Plato and other philosophers here.[9] Not for Sallust the characteristic, unintellectual pursuits of a typical upper-class Roman's retirement.

'I did not intend . . . by taking up agriculture or hunting to lead the kind of life which is fit only for slaves' (p. 203, n. 26). On the contrary, he proposed to go on serving Rome – but not by taking another job: 'My choice was made not through any desire to lead an easy life, but on the merits of the case, and further that our country may well benefit more effectively from my retirement than from the activity of others.'[10] The way he could help best, he felt, was by turning to history. Even when events are not outstandingly remarkable in themselves, a historian is capable of shedding illumination upon them.

The exploits of the Athenians were certainly great and magnificent enough in my estimation, and yet perhaps somewhat less important than fame has made them out to be. But because Athens produced historians of genius the achievements of her citizens are celebrated throughout the world as the greatest of all time.[11]

Whereas the subjects Sallust himself has chosen, he declares, are very far from insignificant: on the contrary he finds them to be of altogether special significance. The conspiracy of Catiline was 'a criminal enterprise which I consider specially memorable as being unprecedented in itself and fraught with unprecedented dangers to Rome'.[12] The *Histories* dealt with an even more momentous theme. Its aim was nothing less than to elucidate and explain the whole process of national collapse of which the Catilinarian plot was such an alarming symptom. Moreover, the *Histories* began with the dangerous moment of civil strife following the disappearance of the dictator Sulla. This had a painful relevance to the years in which Sallust was writing. For now another dictator, Caesar, had just vanished from the scene. Again the future looked highly unpleasant – with further tyranny not merely in prospect but already firmly clamped upon the State.

But Sallust's principal diagnosis of the reasons why the Republic had declined is contained in the prologue of his *Jugurthine War*. Although farther back in time, the subject was again deeply relevant to contemporary happenings: 'The war which the Roman people waged against Jugurtha . . . was the first occasion upon which the arrogance of the Roman aristocracy received a check. It marks the beginning of a conflict which was to throw all Roman institutions, human and divine, into chaos.'[13] The war against Jugurtha, that is to say, had brought about that crystallisation of two warring factions, *optimates* and *populares*, which is seen by Sallust as the main cause of the break-up of the Republican institutions. In a spirit of nostalgia which for all its exaggeration contained a grain of truth, he pictured the early phases of Rome's history, the centuries which had witnessed its major triumphs, as a Golden Age – because at that time no such division had existed: 'The utmost harmony and the least possible avarice prevailed between the citizens – they strove to outdo one another only in merit.'[14] It had become a moral commonplace to detect the decisive point of later decline at some point or other of the second century BC. As for Sallust, he saw the year 146 BC, when the annihilation of Carthage freed Rome from its fear of foreign enemies, as a critical moment of deterioration which had given birth to the internal political evil: 'Down to the time of the destruction of Carthage, the Senate and the Roman people shared the government of the state in a spirit of harmony and moderation. . . . But once this fear had been lifted from men's minds, it was not long before pride and wantonness took its place.'[15] More specifically, the fall of Carthage had been followed by the age of the Gracchi, in which the supremacy of the Senate was first challenged. Ungovernable passions were released on both sides. Human nature loves not only liberty but power;[16] and so, in accordance with this inexorable demand,

The aristocrats now began to exploit their rank and the people their freedom, each from their own selfish ends, and each man proceeded to seize, plunder and rob on his own account. In this way the Romans became divided into two parties, and the state which had hitherto united their interests was torn asunder.[17]

Modern research has tended to blur the edges of this sharp, twofold division between two parties, that is to say, two sections of the governing class, conservative and radical. At most times there was, instead, a continually changing pattern of various loose political coalitions and warring groups. Yet at times the dichotomy assumed a more clear-cut shape. It did so in the time of the Gracchi, and the process repeated itself during the last convulsive years of the Republic. Then it was Pompey, Crassus and Caesar who claimed to stand for the 'popular' cause against the conservatives. But their claims, says Sallust, were just eye-wash. So were those of everybody else. The ambitions of every politician were purely selfish: 'All those who followed a political career from the consulship of Pompey and Crassus [70 BC] used high-sounding phrases. . . . But behind this facade of public concern each one was striving to win power for himself. . . . Both sides exploited any advantage ruthlessly.'[18] Although Sallust is speaking of the men who subsequently formed the First Triumvirate, what he has in mind is the *Second* Triumvirate of his own time. The degradation of the parties, which had been so conspicuous a feature of those earlier decades, had been the direct cause of this new and current despotism. When Sallust used the phrase 'the domination of the few' in relation to the years about which he was writing, the words possessed a topical significance, in keeping with his sour innuendoes against the second batch of triumvirs (p. 199).[19] But he chooses, no doubt from necessity, to speak of them indirectly, through the mirror of the previous generation, when the seeds of the sordid circumstances of his own day had been sown, with one side as much to blame as the other.

For Sallust, as Sir Ronald Syme observes, had a 'keen and unfriendly insight into human behaviour, a flair for hypocrisy and fraudulence in all their varied manifestations'. He is well aware that a historian who criticises the faults of others will be accused of mere envy and ill-will;[20] and there must have been many who found his strictures severe. But he lashed out all the same.

The history of the Republic had basically been the history of the conservative aristocracy. Sallust, for all his wealth, was a 'new man', and felt the utmost distaste for the traditional governing class. Long ago, certainly, in the supposed Golden Age of Rome, its members had been the creators and saviours of the State: 'After much reflection I came to the conclusion that the secret of these [early] successes lay in the valour, amounting to heroism, of a small number of citizens.'[21] But now, he felt, the Roman nobility had become detestable. It was guilty of mediocre incompetence, and above all of sheer venality and greed. This is one of the main themes of the *Jugurtha*, in which the senators of Rome are depicted as thoroughly liable to corruption by the money of this Numidian foreigner: 'The king's lavish gifts to his friends and to other men who at that time wielded influence in the Senate . . . produced such a change of heart that the nobility's attitude promptly veered from one of extreme hostility to keen support and goodwill.'[22] The point is summed up by an epigram attributed to the monarch himself, at the conclusion of his visit to Italy in 110: 'After Jugurtha had left the gates behind him, it is said that he more than once glanced back at Rome and finally remarked, "A city for sale! It will not last long, if it ever finds a buyer!" '[23] How fair this accusation is we cannot say. Probably it is exaggerated – senators had more sensible reasons for hestitating to fight Jugurtha than Sallust chose to believe.[24] But certainly the Senate contained some members who were prepared to accept money from the king: and they may even have been fairly numerous. The foreign policy of such men is denounced as cunning and dishonest.[25]

So sharply does the historian dislike this hereditary ruling group into which his riches had almost (but not quite) brought him, that he even sneers at its traditional pursuits of hunting and farming (p. 200).[26] He refuses to call the conservative group by the name they chose for themselves, 'the best men' (*optimates*), preferring to describe them as a faction (*factio*). Their enemies, the 'popular' politicians, belonged to the governing class just as much as their adversaries, but the degree of support they attracted among the citizenry at large seemed to invite comparison with the ancient battle between the patrician and plebeian order.[27]

Sallust is the more ready to make this sort of comparison because his anti-conservative attitude is accompanied by an unusual appreciation of the miseries of the poor. This is expressed in the vivid phrases attributed to the democratic politician and historian Macer: 'You have given up everything in exchange for your present slothfulness, thinking that you have ample freedom because your backs are spared, and because you are allowed to go hither and thither by the grace of your rich masters. Yet even these privileges are denied to the country people. . . .'[28] The same points of view had already emerged strongly in the *Catiline*. There, the attacks on the upper class are attributed to the younger Cato – a piquant touch, since he became its leader. And the same theme is developed by the villain of the piece, namely Catiline himself. His build-up by Sallust as a great revolutionary is exaggerated. But there is more to be said for the historian's opinion that Catiline was the product of a moral breakdown induced by the bad government of the nobles. And what he is made to say about the glaring differences of wealth between the social classes carries the ring of conviction.

Can any of you, who calls himself a man, tolerate the idea that these creatures should pile up their wealth, which they then squander by building out into the sea or levelling mountains, while we are without the means to buy even the barest necessities? . . . There is nothing left to us except the air that we breathe. . . .[29]

Sallust stands almost alone among ancient historians when he lays this emphasis on the widespread impoverishment and discontent prevailing in Italy, the problem which had anguished the Gracchi and had been exacerbated still further by the Social and Civil Wars. We seem to be listening to an anticipation of the Marxist class-struggle. When so many Roman writers supported the oligarchy, it is of value to read Sallust's anti-establishment view.

Nevertheless, when he comes down to the individuals who had played their parts in these troubled years, he refrains from schematic contrasts between good men and bad. In the *Jugurtha*, nobles such as Scaurus and Metellus confront the 'new man' Marius who successfully flouted their power. But we are not offered anything like a simple decision in favour of the latter. It is true that the historian writes about Scaurus with a severity which is perhaps excessive. But he is remarkably just to Metellus, who is shown to have come close to winning the war. Metellus, we are told, possessed the old virtues of incorruptibility and fairness. His only fault was his equally traditional arrogance, which played into Marius' hands. Certainly, we are given a conventional conflict of types. But it is not between a bad man and a good one: it is between a proud noble and the able parvenu, in whose hands, at the end of the *Jugurtha*, lies the whole future of Rome, as the Italian peninsula is menaced by German invasion.[30]

In order to give point to the dramatic picture, the rise of Marius is depicted as a process speedier and smoother than in fact it was. Nevertheless, just as Metellus is not painted too black, Marius is not excessively glorified. On the contrary, he is shown to have been over-ambitious. Moreover, another *popularis*, Gaius Memmius, who led the agitation against the conservatives in 111, is regarded with positive disfavour, emerging as a mere irresponsible demagogue.

It is true that Sallust allows himself to use the political catchwords of the *populares* when he is attacking the other side. Yet he is not by any means wedded to the popular cause. Not only did Marius have his faults; but the popular politicians who came after him were a good deal worse: 'Even our self-made men, who whenever they triumphed over the nobility in earlier times did so through solid merit, now no longer strive for power or prominence by honest means.'[31] Party strife, then, is firmly blamed on both sides alike. Each of the two factions exploited any and every advantage ruthlessly.

Caesar, who had claimed to be the most 'popular' of all, has sometimes been regarded as the hero of Sallust's *Catiline*. On this interpretation, the essay was written to counteract current attacks on his memory.[32] But further inspection shows this to be an oversimplified view. Certainly, Caesar's great gifts are displayed (in a somewhat depersonalised fashion). But he is placed in the most deliberate juxtaposition with the ultra-conservative Cato the younger. Sallust admires Cato just as much as he admires Caesar – with another look over his shoulder at the current triumvirs, because Cato stood for everything they hated.

Cato and Caesar were two men of opposite political ideals, who in Sallust's view stood head and shoulders above all other people of their day: 'In my own time two men appeared who towered above their contemporaries, though their characters presented the sharpest of contrasts, namely Marcus Cato and Gaius Caesar.'[33] By implication, they towered even more outstandingly above their successors, the new triumvirs, under whom Sallust was living in wealthy but jaundiced retirement. Indeed the two men both stood, in their different ways, for an old order which had gone. It had not been a very desirable order, because no one, not even these talented men, had been able to save the State. Yet it had been a system which at least produced two such formidable personalities, whose gifts were all the more conspicuous amid the surrounding ruin.[34] And so they are brought together by describing the two sharply contrasting orations which they allegedly delivered during the debate on the doom of the arrested Catilinarians.

The speeches are too Sallustian in style to be anything like what either speaker can have actually said. However, the versions we are given may well represent the substance of the words spoken on this historic occasion. The arguments placed in the mouths of the two men possess a peculiar piquancy, involving an ironical reversal of their careers. For Caesar appears as the constitutionalist, and Cato, usually a fanatical stickler for the law, is seen here as a man all too ready to override legalistic considerations, in what he considered to be the larger interests of the State. Finally, the speeches are supplemented by careful and vivid sketches of the characters of the two speakers. Further emphasis is thus laid upon the different, contrasted kinds of Roman excellence they embodied.

The whole picture comes as a surprise to anyone who has read the consul Cicero's Catilinarian orations, in those magnificently eloquent versions which were released to the public three years after they were delivered. To the first of those speeches, in which Cicero warned the Senate how perilous Catiline was, Sallust does justice. He does not quote the speech; he does not need to, because it had been published. But he refers to it in generous terms: 'It may have been that Cicero was inspired by fear of Catiline's presence or was carried away by sheer indignation. At any rate he delivered a brilliant speech, which proved invaluable to his country, and which he later wrote out and published.'[35] Yet the subsequent debate about the captives emerges from the pages of Sallust and Cicero in unrecognisably divergent terms. Cicero's Fourth Catilinarian Oration shows how he himself, as presiding consul, gave a decided turn to the proceedings. Sallust, on the other hand, treats the speeches of Cato and Caesar as the highlights, and purports to reproduce them in full: whereas all that he says about Cicero is that 'the consul consulted the senate as to what should be done with the prisoners'.[36]

Here is another example of Sallust's subtle, detached, ambivalent attitudes to politics. Cicero would have been far from pleased with this treatment; and indeed he and Sallust stood for conflicting conceptions of politics, history and literary style alike (p. 213). Nevertheless, it would not be right to conclude that the historian is subjecting his memory to attack.[37] Nothing would have been easier or more advantageous than to do so under the Second Triumvirate. Classifying Cicero among their worst political enemies, the triumvirs had recently had him tracked down and put to death (43). But Sallust, estranged from the current sources of power, was not prepared to play the triumvirate's game. He will not, it is true, let Cicero fill the centre of the picture. But he allocates him a firm, if limited, quota of praise.

Mordant, censorious and disllusioned, Sallust saw Chance at work everywhere. Yet this was not the exciting, favouring Fortune of

1 Egyptian official history: King Ahmosis or Aahmes (sixteenth century BC) informs his wife of his intention to pay additional honour to the memory of his ancestors.

2 Hittite official history: decree of King Telepinus (c. 1500 BC) from his capital Hattusas (Boğazköy in Turkey), prefaced by a long historical preamble. Vorderasiatisches Museum, Berlin.

3 Relief of Mesha, King of Moab, mid-9th century BC, telling of his wars against Israel. These events are not described in the Bible.

4 Babylonian official history: cylinder of King Cyrus, recording his capture of Babylon without a battle (536 BC), and pointing out that he sent prisoners from Babylonia (no doubt including the Jews) back to their own countries.

5 Herodotus and
Thucydides: a double
bust symbolising the
two main schools of
ancient and European
history. National
Archaeological
Museum, Naples.

6 King Leonidas.
Herodotus tells how
he held the narrow
pass of Thermopylae
against the Persians
for three days, dying
with his three hundred
fellow-Spartans
(480 BC) and a
contingent from
Thespiae in Boeotia.
Sparta Museum.

7 Illustrating one of the stories told by Herodotus: King Croesus of Lydia, after his overthrow by the Persians, is placed on a funeral pyre (Apollo sent a rainstorm to put the flames out). Red-figure amphora from Vulci in Etruria. Louvre, Paris.

8 A large silver coin of Syracuse (*c.* 410 BC). The captured arms beneath the chariot celebrate the destruction of the Athenian expedition described by Thucydides. British Museum.

9 Electrum (pale gold) coin of Cyzicus (Bal Kiz in Turkey) with an early coin-portrait, probably depicting an eminent local citizen: issued in *c.* 350 BC, at a time when interest in human personality was stimulating biographical writing by Isocrates and Xenophon. British Museum.

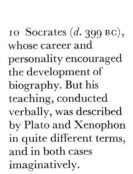

10 Socrates (*d.* 399 BC), whose career and personality encouraged the development of biography. But his teaching, conducted verbally, was described by Plato and Xenophon in quite different terms, and in both cases imaginatively.

11 Coin of Alexander the Great (336–323 BC). The many Greek biographies of Alexander, now lost, ranged all the way from serious factual treatment to wholly fictitious legend. British Museum.

12 Ptolemy Soter, who became King of Egypt after Alexander's death, wrote an account of Alexander's campaigns based on his own recollections and official records. Ny Carlsberg Glyptothek, Copenhagen.

13 Megalopolis in
Arcadia: the birthplace
of Polybius.

14 The historian
Polybius shown on a
relief at Cleitor (near
Calavryta in Arcadia)
dedicated in the third
century AD by Titus
Flavius Polybius who
claimed to be his
descendant. The relief
is now almost destroyed,
but this photograph is of
a cast made before the
damage was done.

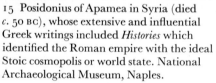

15 Posidonius of Apamea in Syria (died
c. 50 BC), whose extensive and influential
Greek writings included *Histories* which
identified the Roman empire with the ideal
Stoic cosmopolis or world state. National
Archaeological Museum, Naples.

16 Julius Caesar commemorates his GallicWar:
trophy and prisoner, *c.* 49 BC. British Museum.

17 Masada near the Dead Sea. Scene of the last resistance of the Jews (AD 73), harrowingly described by Josephus.

18 Livy's admiration for patriotic, family history and legend had already been prominent on the coinage long before his time. Here Brutus portrays two of his alleged ancestors who fought tyrants. British Museum.

19 The Triumphal celebration after the fall of Jerusalem, described by
Josephus. This relief from the Arch of Titus, captor of the city, shows the
booty from the Temple, including the table for the shew-bread, the
trumpets and the seven-branched candlestick (Menorah).

20 Water-pipe from Deva (Chester), with the name of Rome's governor
Agricola, the father-in-law of Tacitus who wrote his eulogistic biography.
Agricola's name is to be seen three-quarters of the way along the inscription.
Chester Museum.

21 Bronze head, formerly gilded, of Tiberius, the central figure of the *Annals* of Tacitus. National Museum (Terme), Rome.

22 The Lion of Chaeronea in Boeotia, central Greece, the birth-place of Plutarch. It originally surmounted the collective grave of 214 soldiers of the Theban Sacred Band who fell fighting against Philip II of Macedonia in 338 BC.

23 Hadrian (AD 117–138), who employed as a secretary and then dismissed from his service the biographer Suetonius. Bronze statue in Museum of Antiquities, Istanbul.

24 Nero (AD 54–68), whose fantastic reign is dwelt upon by Tacitus and Suetonius. The official interpretation of events, displayed on magnificent coins, gives a very different picture: here is a triumphal arch commemorating successes in Armenia. British Museum.

25 Theodosius I (*d.* AD 395), in whose last years, darkened by a pagan rebellion, the completion of Ammianus' *History* was a delicate matter. Silver missorium found at Almendralejo (Badajoz), Spain. National Archaeological Museum, Madrid.

26 'Sallust the Writer', SALLVSTIVS AVTOR, recalled on a bronze 'contorniate' – prize or memento of the Games – more than four hundred years after his death.

INCIPIT LIBER GAII CESA
RIS BELLI GALLICI IVLIA
NI DE NARRATIONE
TEMPORVM

Incipit liber Suetoni

Gallia est omnis divisa in partes tres. Quarum unam in colunt belgae. aliam aquitani. tertiam qui ipsorum lingua cel tae. nostra galli appellantur. hi omnes lingua institutis legibus inter se differunt. Gallos ab aquitanis garumna flumen. a belgis. matrona et sequana dividit. horum omnium fortissimi sunt belgae. propterea quod a cultu atque humanitate provinciae longissime ab sunt. minimeque ad eos mercatores saepe commeant. atque ea quae ad effeminandos animos pertinent important. Proximique sunt ger manis qui trans rhenum incolunt. quibus cum continenter bellum ge runt. qua de causa. helvetii quoque reliquos gallos virtute precedunt. quod fere cotidianis proeliis cum germanis contendunt. cum aut suis finibus eos prohibent. aut ipsi in eorum finibus bellum gerunt. Eorum una pars quam gallos optinere dictum est. initium capit a flumine rhodano. continetur ga runna flumine. oceanum finibus belgarum attingit. etiam ab sequanis et helvetiis flumen rhenum vergit ad septentriones. Belgae ab extremis galliae finibus oriuntur. pertinent ad inferiorem partem fluminis rhe ni. spectant in septentrionem et orientem solem. Aquitania a garun

27 The first page of Caesar's *Gallic War*, ninth or tenth century: the earliest extant text. University Library, Amsterdam.

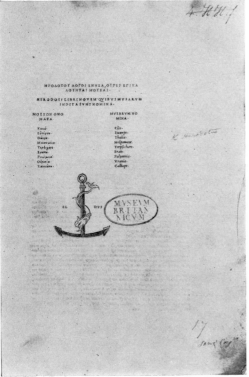

28 Title-page of manuscript of Sallust, *Catiline* and *Jugurtha*, Florence, 1466. British Museum.

29 From the Aldine edition of Herodotus, published by Aldus Manutius (Teobaldo Mannucci) at Venice in 1502.

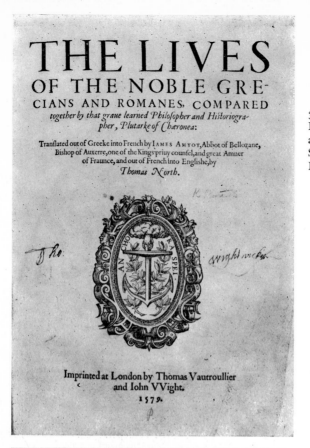

Caesar, but a capricious symbol of life's unfairnesses.[38] For Fame and Glory had not remained with Sallust, at least not in his public life: which was sad, since they were what he regarded as the whole aim of human endeavour. 'The truth is that no man really lives or gets any satisfaction out of life, unless he devotes all his energies to some task and seeks fame by some notable achievement or by the cultivation of some admirable gift.'[39]

This Fame could only be won by the *virtus* that had stood Rome in such good stead in ancient times. For Sallust, whatever his own moral defects may have been, was intensely moralistic. The ethical pre-occupations of earlier Greek and Roman historians reached their climax in his work. Economic and political issues appeared to him in moral terms: indeed the terms political, economic and moral seemed synonymous. Yet the 'virtue' he had in mind was wider than the old Roman aristocratic ideal because, like the same criterion in Thucydides, it was a matter of brain no less than of character. This brain-power could operate in any profession or class. As part of a general contrast between appearances and realities, to which Sallust reverts again and again, it is often contrasted with bodily externals.

> The man who sets out to achieve fame ought to rely upon his intellect far more than upon his physical prowess. . . . At last men learned by the hard test of action and danger that in warfare it is the intellect which emerges supreme. . . . Every human activity that we survey, whether it be agriculture, navigation or architecture, depends upon a directing intelligence.[40]

This stress on intellect, combined with Sallust's ethical preoccupations, endows his portrayal of individuals with a special and emphatic significance. At the time when he was writing, biography was exceedingly fashionable. Incorporating all the Greek ideas on the subject, it had blended them with the special Roman traditions which favoured the development of the art (p. 168). The monographs of the mid-forties BC had been merely tendentious (p. 178).[41] But the *Images* (*c.* 39 BC) which comprised one of the numerous works of the polymath Marcus Terentius Varro of Reate (Rieti) (116–27 BC) were evidently more balanced pieces of work; and indeed they constituted a literary landmark.[42] This collection contained seven hundred biographical pictures of Greek and Romans, each with an introductory epigram. But unfortunately the *Images* are lost, and we can only judge

207

the period by the feeble *Lives* of Cornelius Nepos (*c.* 99–24 BC).[43] A number of these have come down to us,[44] the most distinctive being a study of Cicero's friend Atticus, written while Atticus was still alive (*c.* 34).[45] Nepos concedes that biography is less systematic and dignified than history and knows that his readers will not be high-powered.[46]

This dignity of history means a great deal to Sallust; and yet for him, too, as for the humbler biographers, individuals stand at the centre of the stage. Their characters are built up not so much by formal obituaries as by swift, incisive sketches, selecting actions and speeches which show people gripped by strong passions and plunged in sharp, violent conflicts with one another.

The shadow of Sulla's personality hung heavily over the last years of the Republic. Explaining that he will not have occasion to deal with him elsewhere (though his heritage could not fail to play a prominent part in the *Histories*), Sallust devotes one of his set pieces to this man. He describes Sulla's superior intellectual powers, and his equal appetites for glory and pleasure; his eloquence, shrewdness and capacity to make friends; his generosity, too – combined with a gift for dissimulation which appealed to Sallust's interest in what lies behind outward masks, because Sulla 'was deep beyond belief in his capacity for disguising his intentions'.[47]

He had devoted his gifts to an attempt to shore up the aristocratic system. It was Catiline's aim, on the other hand, to shatter it by violence. Sallust's delineation of this swashbuckling figure is too much like the picture of a villain in a melodrama; though there is a redeeming pathos in his brave death in battle: 'Catiline himself was found far ahead of his men amid a heap of the enemy's dead. There was still breath in his body, and his face wore that expression of savage courage which was so characteristic of him in his lifetime.'[48] Catiline had been a success both with young men and with women. One of the most original features of Sallust's portrait gallery is a full-scale account of his astonishing adherent or female counterpart, Sempronia, who recalls the part women were now playing in Roman public life and foreshadows memorable character-studies of empresses during the centuries to come.

Among his supporters was Sempronia, a woman who had committed many crimes which were audacious enough to be the work of a man. Fortune had been generous to her, not only in her noble birth and exceptional beauty, but also in the character of her husband and her children. She was well read in the literature of Greece and Rome, could sing, dance and play the lyre with more talent than an honest woman needs, and possessed many of the other accomplishments which enhance a life of luxury. Modesty and chastity, on the other hand, were qualities for which she had little use, and it would have been hard to say whether she was more careless of her money or her reputation. Indeed so little could she control her passions that she was most often the suitor in her love affairs.

Even before the time of the conspiracy her extravagance and lack of money had launched her on the downward path, so that she had often broken her word, forsworn money placed in her charge, and acted as an accomplice in murder. Yet in spite of all this she was a woman of exceptional gifts. She could write verses and hold her own in repartee, while her talk could be modest, tender or wanton as she chose, and to sum up, her personality combined wit and charm to a remarkable degree.[49]

How far such a picture was true is another matter. For the stylistic brilliance of Sallust is not equalled by his precision in regard to facts. It is very easy to offer a catalogue of his faults as a historical source. All three of his writings begin with gross chronological distortions, and continue with an almost unbroken series of unproven rumours and vague or irrelevant generalisations. The *Jugurtha* gives a dubious account of the origins of the war (p. 197), and freely rearranges events in order to argue that the king's character was the principal cause of the breach. The account of the early history of Africa, although Sallust claims to have taken it from a king of Numidia, and although he was governor of that country himself, is almost worthless. Descriptions of fighting, too, are stronger on colour than on fact. They are patchy, unevenly proportioned, and careless about numbers, dates, geographical locations and distances. The historian offers the conventional excuse that battles *are* chaotic and chancy.[50] But he certainly does nothing to make them any clearer.

The *Catiline* offers a gravely twisted version of a 'first conspiracy' in 66–65. Or indeed the account may be wholly fictitious. The events of a few months are extended over a period exceeding a year; and the secret deliberations of the plotters are presumably invented. The *Histories*, too, is deficient in judgment, notably in the view that internal peace had prevailed between the Second and Third Punic Wars. For his historical interpretations become even more remote from any

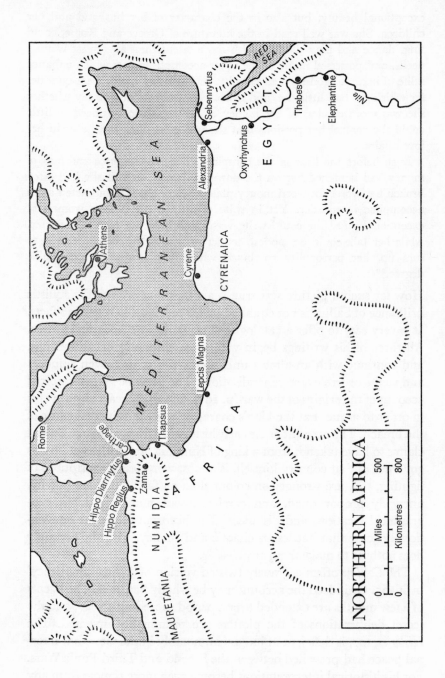

NORTHERN AFRICA

probable facts as the subject recedes into the past. Rhetoric takes over. Sallust was, as it happens, not much of a public speaker himself. But it is understandable that two hundred years later the Roman writer of a historical handbook, Granius Licinianus, should have expressed the opinion that he ought to be read not as a historian but as an orator.[51]

And yet his literary gifts were outstanding. Here is an extreme version of the familiar dilemma of ancient historiography. It was supposed to achieve both accuracy and style at the same time: and Sallust asserts, quite rightly, that the combination and reconciliation of these two qualities was the principal difficulty a historian had to face.[52] He himself, however, tilts the balance violently in one of these two directions, since he is shaky about the facts but a writer of masterpieces which have captivated the world.

Indeed, accuracy does not enormously concern him. That was a matter for less ambitious works such as biographies or memoirs or 'commentaries'. His task as a historian was rather to select, and dramatise, and present his material with impressionistic force. And so in the *Jugurtha*, as Syme says, 'Sallust offers a picture of African warfare valid in any age. Vivid phrases call up the desert, the scrub, the broken country, the elusive enemies, thirst and fatigue, treachery and murder. In this matter, the merits of Sallust are patent and acknowledged.'

His success is partly due to expert organisation of his material. Small incidents are cunningly linked together into units, and each part grows irresistibly to a conclusion – which in turn looks ahead to subsequent events. The supreme example of Sallust's skill is his *Catiline*. Every possible advantage is taken of the striking, tragic theme to create an elegant, close-knit, diversified structure, leading steadily up to a climax. That was Sallust's way of acclimatising the monograph to Rome. If more of his *Histories* had survived, we should surely have to admire his management of great exciting episodes. They had never been used so extensively in Roman history before, and Sallust must have organised them in clever subordination to a major, sweeping plan, with each book ending on a powerful climactic note.

This sort of design, even in the smaller works, depended partly on the use of digressions, artfully contrived to place the narratives in their broader historical setting. In the *Catiline* the digressions on personalities, affairs in Rome, public ethics and statesmanship are distributed so as to give maximum effect to the gradual mounting up of tension. The *Jugurtha* contains geographical as well as historical digressions, and these sometimes contain smaller set pieces within themselves. In the *Histories*, this treatment is extended from north Africa to various regions of the east, in which Sallust himself may have served on the staff of some Roman general.[53]

Narratives and descriptions alike move with his famous 'immortal speed'.[54] But this is far from the lucid brevity of Caesar. Unlike him, Sallust is at pains to avoid everything that is straightforward and simple. Instead, incurring the disapproval of the contemporary historian Pollio,[55] he strives after an archaic epigrammatic abruptness, carried to the point of obscurity.[56] But what is uppermost in Sallust's mind is a deliberate contrast between this skilful disharmony and the ample smoothness of Cicero. It is a contrast designed to mirror trenchant criticism of an oratorical style which he considered pompous and a political style which savoured of time-serving hypocrisy. It was fortunate for Cicero that Sallust disliked Cicero's enemies the triumvirs quite as much as he disliked Cicero, or more – and that he regarded his career as more or less irrelevant to the interesting revolutionary trends of the time. For these reasons he is content to neglect rather than attack the orator's actions and pretensions in regard to the Catilinarian conspirators (p. 206).[57]

A Roman writer who seemed to Sallust a great deal more attractive than Cicero was the earliest of the Latin historians, Cato the Censor. This admiration came all the more easily because he also attached so much significance to the Censor's great-grandson Cato the younger (p. 205). Sallust praised the elder Cato as the most eloquent of Romans;[58] and indeed he was taxed with appropriating archaic words from that source.[59] But probably he borrowed turns of speech quite as much as words. What appealed to him was the old man's pithy gift of epigram, especially when this was devoted to praise of the old Roman *virtus*. Sallust liked his criticisms of the senatorial class, too, and his attacks on its idle sloth and vice.[60]

Imitation of Cato the elder also seemed to Sallust the best way to produce a Latin copy of the historian whom above all others he selected as his model. This was Thucydides. His desire to be the Roman Thucydides was noticed by Velleius,[61] writing history two generations later. It is apparent in many a deliberate echo, including direct verbal reminiscences of the Greek historian's analysis of civil strife. Sallust's old-fashioned severity of diction, and the concentrated, broken abruptness of his style, are deliberately Thucydidean. So is his solemn stress on the power of intelligence (p. 207). Above all, there is the same pervasive feeling of alienation from the public affairs in which, like his Greek forerunner, he had played a role of some importance before being cast aside. Sallust was all the more ready to cite Thucydides as his exemplar because Cicero, whose literary methods he so greatly disliked, had criticised the Athenian as a model for oratory. On the other hand it was over-patriotic of the literary critic Quintilian to place the two historians on the same level.[62] Sallust was a brilliant writer, but his sceptical demolition-work fell far short of his mighty predecessor's profound analyses.

All the same, something new had been achieved at Rome. Only a short time before, Cicero was complaining that Latin history had never seen a master whose style was capable of doing justice to the subject (p. 179). Now it had one – though Cicero would have hated the result. The future lay between the Ciceronians, rotund and bland, and the disillusioned and biting Sallustians.

5

The Two Faces
of Empire

14

Livy

THE Second Triumvirate, on which Sallust cast so jaundiced an eye, pursued its dictatorial way until one of its members, Lepidus, was forced into retirement by the others (36 BC). Soon afterwards, the relations between the two survivors deteriorated, and in 31 Octavian defeated Antony and Cleopatra in a naval battle at Actium off north-western Greece. On their deaths in the following year, he became sole ruler of the Roman Empire, and established a new sort of auto-cratic régime. Calling himself Augustus, a name with antique religious associations, he spent the remaining forty-five years of his life transforming the Roman administration into an organism capable of bearing its huge responsibilities. Because he controlled the army and the revenue, his authority was unchallengeable. Yet describing his own position by the term *princeps* – which lacked dictatorial trappings – he interpreted his powers as ostensibly renewable. Every outward Republican form and institution was resuscitated and en-couraged. A few aristocratic conspirators were sharply suppressed. But, since Augustus had ended the long civil wars and brought peace, most people were content with autocracy when it 'restored the Republic', that is to say, the public organs of the traditional State.

For good measure, Augustus displayed the antiquarian spirit, which had now become fashionable, by rebuilding many Republican temples and cherishing numerous early traditions. The climax was reached in the ancient Secular Games (celebrating the passing of a century in the life of Rome), which were revived and celebrated in 17 BC. The poet chosen to compose the Secular Hymn was Horace. The same Augustan brand of patriotic antiquarianism is also greatly to the fore in other poets who, like him, belonged to the circle of the emperor's adviser Maecenas, especially Virgil and Propertius.

The outstanding historian of the Augustan age was Titus Livius of Patavium (Padua), who lived from 64 or 59 BC to AD 12 or 17. His *History of Rome* was written in Latin and filled 142 books. Thirty-five of these survive, namely I–X and XXI–XLV, covering the periods 753–243 and 219–167 BC respectively. From the lost books we have fragments and excerpts; and there are two sets of abridgments.

The work was roughly divided into decads, or groups of ten books, each of which in turn subdivides into two halves or pentads. The preface expresses confidence in the grandeur of the subject, diffidence about the author's ability to handle it, a lament for the recent decline of Rome, and a warning about the unverifiable nature of its earliest history. The first book deals with the story of Aeneas and the period of the Roman kings (traditionally 753–510 BC), culminating in the establishment of the Republic and the appointment of the first pair of consuls. Book II (509–477 BC) tells the sagas of Horatius on the bridge, the heroic maiden Cloelia, the secession of the plebeians, the career of Coriolanus, and the defeat by Etruscan Veii on the Cremera. The subjects of the third book include the dictatorship of Cincinnatus, the Law of the Twelve Tables (451–450), the rape of Verginia by Appius Claudius the Decemvir, and his downfall. Book IV describes the death of the would-be tyrant Spurius Maelius (440–439?) and the seizure of Fidenae from Veii. The principal themes of Book V are the destruction of Veii by Camillus (396) and the brief capture of Rome by the Gauls (390).

The sixth book is concerned with wars against Volscians and Etruscans and constitutional struggles, and the seventh with the election of the first plebeian to the consulship (366), the myth of Curtius who leapt into a chasm in the Forum, and various campaigns leading up to the first Samnite War (343). This war inaugurated nearly half a century of massive hostilities against the Samnites, who were the principal rivals of the Romans in the Italian peninsula. One of the heroes of Book VIII, however, died fighting against Rome's neighbours the Latins. This was Publius Decius Mus, who sacrificed

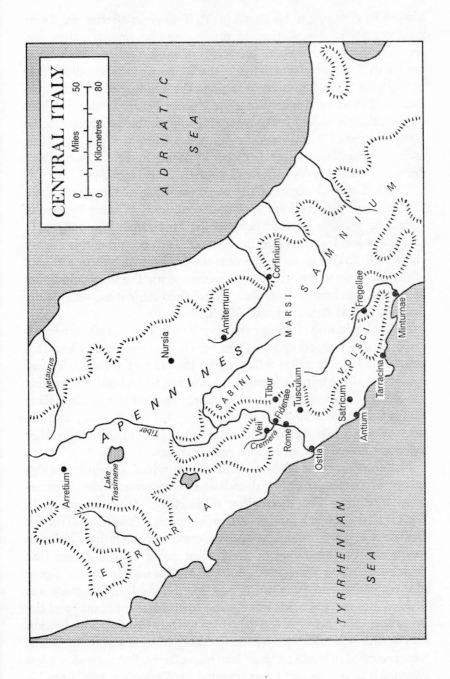

himself by charging to his death (340). Two years afterwards, Rome finally defeated the Latins, incorporating the smaller states and reducing the larger ones to the status of subject allies. Livy's ninth book tells of the disastrous defeat of the Romans at the Caudine Forks (321, in the Second Samnite War), and the building of the first aqueduct and road by Appius Claudius Caecus (312). Lucius Papirius Cursor, described by Livy as a general comparable to Alexander the Great, retrieved the situation against the Samnites (309), and the main theme of Book x is their defeat by Rome in a third war, which decided the destiny of central and southern Italy (298–290).

The lost second decad of the work was divided into two halves. One reached the termination of the hostilities with King Pyrrhus of Epirus (272), and the next covered the First Punic War (264–241) and the events leading up to the Second. The account of this mighty clash (208–201) is given in the next ten books, which form a climax of the *History* in so far as it has come down to us. The story culminates in the comparison of Hannibal with Scipio Africanus, who finally defeated him at Zama in north Africa.

At the beginning of Book xxxi Livy inserts a new preface, necessitated by the vast ocean of affairs which now confronts him. This pentad and the two that follow cover the wars of the early second century bc. One brings the story down to 192 when hostilities against the Seleucid Antiochus iii were beginning, another to 179 when King Philip v of Macedonia was succeeded by his son Perseus, and the next to 167 when Aemilius Paullus celebrated his Triumph after defeating Perseus in the previous year at Pydna.

Nothing that came afterwards has now survived, except in abridgments. The arrangement by decads and pentads was evidently somewhat modified. The destruction of Carthage (146) appeared in Book li, the breach of the old aristocratic régime by Tiberius Gracchus in lvii, the defeat of the German invaders by Marius in lxviii and the beginning of the Italian revolt against Rome (the Social or Marsian War, 91 bc) in lxxi. Marius was the central figure of three books, and Sulla of the two that followed. Sulla's story was divided into two parts, his war against Mithridates of Pontus and the brutalities that accompanied his return to Italy (83–82). The division into decads was reasserted by the deaths of Marius and Sulla, which were recorded in Books lxxx and xc respectively. But thereafter a less symmetrical arrangement was reverted to. Caesar's career, from his first consulship (59) to his end, occupied Books CIII to CXVI, with Pharsalus and Pompey's murder in CXI and CXII respectively. The last eight of these fourteen books were at some point given the separate title of the *Civil Wars*.

The next five books were limited to the twenty months following the Ides of March. This period of internal strife, like the struggles of the immediately preceding years, must have been dealt with in great detail. The battle of Actium (31 BC), in which Octavian (the future Augustus) defeated Antony and Cleopatra and became the master of the Roman world, was described in Book CXXXIII. The next book, when it reached the year 29 BC, seems to have included a passage indicating that what followed thereafter was a sort of epilogue supplementary to Livy's original intention. The résumés of Books CXXXVI and CXXXVII are missing, but it is clear that their main emphasis was on frontier operations. The principal commanders in these wars included the emperor's step-sons Tiberius and Drusus the elder. The death of the latter in 9 BC was reached in the final book.

One of the most astonishing features of Livy's *History* was its gigantic size. This also explains why so much of it is now lost. As the poet Martial declared, his entire library did not have room for the whole work.[1] Its range extended over 744 years, and it is not surprising that the author was increasingly daunted by the immensity of his task.[2]

In order to perform his achievement, he had to publish three or more books annually, year after year, for forty years. Book I was probably published first, since it is followed by a fresh introduction. This initial book seems to have been composed in the early period of Augustus' sole rule, between 27 and 25 BC. The next four may have been published together, because they are separated from what comes after by a new preface. Books VI–X seem to have been written before 20 BC, since no cognisance is taken of a major event of that year, the recovery by Rome of the military standards Crassus had lost to the Parthians thirty-three years earlier. Then followed book after book, in unremitting, inexorable abundance. The last twenty (starting with the events of 43 BC) were not published until after the death of Augustus (AD 14) – which may or may not have preceded the death of Livy himself. But it is possible that this final portion of the work had been completed some years earlier.

Livy's life was exceedingly quiet. He was the very opposite to history-writing men of action like Thucydides and Xenophon and Polybius. Patavium, his home-town, may not have seen very much of him.³ He received his education in rhetoric there, and went in for some equally Ciceronian activity as a literary philosopher. But at some quite early stage he moved to Rome, where he was admitted to the circle of Augustus. He gave recitations of his own work, and offered encouragement to the historical studies of the emperor's young relative Claudius, who was later to occupy the imperial throne himself.⁴

But Livy spent most of his life reading and writing. He is the only Roman historian who never held any office of State which would take him abroad or enable him to travel freely. How much he travelled in a private capacity we cannot say; but probably not much. As a historian, however, he acquired a certain reputation during his lifetime.⁵ Before Livy, this clear-cut division between studious writer and man of action would not have been practicable, since the relatively small number of Italians who possessed an education had all been needed for public affairs. Livy is the prototype of the nineteenth-century historian who never saw a shot fired in anger.

If the first remarkable feature of Livy's work was its sheer size, the second was its marvellous evocation of the greatness of his adoptive country, Rome.

> Whether I am successful or not, it will give me satisfaction to have done my part, to the best of my ability, in contributing to the record of the greatest people in the world. . . . Now, unless my passion for the task I have undertaken is blinding me, no state has ever possessed more abundant greatness, higher principles, and nobler examples than Rome.⁶

Livy is unique because he shows us so eloquently how the Romans, at the time when their imperial civilisation was at its height, thought about the past that had created this mighty phenomenon. They, and he, profoundly revered their national tradition, and the bygone days in which their ancestors had overcome the many perils and trials which had made them physically and morally capable of the leadership of the world. Even after their most crushing defeat by Hannibal at Cannae (216 BC), Livy finds them to be endowed with a toughness and stability which, in the end, were bound to prove irresistible.

Neither the defeats they had suffered nor the subsequent defection of all these allied peoples moved the Romans ever to breathe a word about peace. So great, in this grim time, was the nation's heart, that the consul, fresh from a defeat of which he himself had been the principal cause, was met on his return to Rome by men of all conditions, who came in crowds to participate in the thanks, publicly bestowed on him, for not having 'despaired of the commonwealth.' A Carthaginian general in such circumstances would have been punished with all the rigour of the law.[7]

As an appropriate setting for the grandeur of his subject, Livy employs the annalistic framework of his Roman predecessors (p. 168). His own contribution is the insertion, within this framework, of major episodes or scenes or sequences of scenes. If Sallust's *Histories* had survived, we might have found something of the same sort (p. 211). But Livy's descriptions possess a literary, rhetorical brilliance which is all his own, and which, indeed, no other historian has ever equalled. Some critics have seen fit to attribute the dramatic colour of these pictures to his Venetian temperament, comparing Titian and Tintoretto, or more realistically citing his own contemporaries in Roman Venetia who were producing an individual school of sculpture. At all events the colour is deep and strong, brightening stretches of straightforward narrative with great set pieces perfectly adapting the pathetic or horrific traditions of Hellenistic historical writing to the noble qualities of the Latin language.

One of the most dramatic and significant events of all time was Hannibal's invasion of Italy (218 BC). It enables Livy's talents to find their fullest expression. Already before the invader reaches Italian soil the excitement begins, when the Gallic tribe of the Volcae, attempting to block Hannibal's passage at the Rhône, is taken in the rear by a Carthaginian detachment.

The Gallic warriors came surging to the river bank, howling and singing as their custom was, shaking their shields above their heads and brandishing their spears, in spite of the menace which confronted them of those innumerable hostile craft – rendered yet more alarming by the roar of the stream and the cries of the soldiers and sailors struggling to overcome the fierce current and the shouts of encouragement from their comrades awaiting their turn to cross. All this was bad enough. But suddenly, from behind, a more terrible sound assailed their ears – the triumphant shout of Hanno's men.[8]

The subsequent crossings of the Alps provide an unforgettable succession of vivid scenes, as Livy brings before our eyes the grimness of nature, the stumbling horses, the agonising descent over the newly fallen snow, and Hannibal's magical influence over his men even in the most terrible conditions.

The dreadful vision was now before their eyes; the towering peaks, the snow-clad pinnacles soaring to the sky, the rude huts clinging to the rocks, beasts and cattle shrivelled and parched with cold, the people with their wild and ragged hair, all nature, animate and inanimate, stiff with frost. . . .

In the narrow pass the marching column was rapidly losing cohesion. There was great confusion and excitement amongst the men, and still more among the terrified horses, as the tribesmen came swarming down the rocky and precipitous slopes, surefooted as they were from long familiarity with their wild and trackless terrain. . . .

Terrified by the din, echoing and re-echoing from the hollow cliffs and woods, the horses were soon out of control, while those which were struck or wounded lashed out in an agony of fear. . . . In the confusion many non-combatants, and not a few soldiers, were flung over the sheer cliffs which bounded each side of the pass, and fell to their deaths thousands of feet below. But it was worst for the pack-animals. Loads and all, they went tumbling over the edge almost like falling masonry.[9]

In his treatment of these major episodes Livy owes something to Sallust. He is indebted to him for stylistic features as well, and particularly for the vigour and variety of his expression. For any Augustan historian such a debt was almost inevitable. And yet Livy stands, and intends to stand, for totally different things to his predecessor. It is not surprising to learn that he expressed disapproval of Sallust[10] – though the two men were obviously compared, not always to Livy's advantage.[11] Whatever detailed borrowings Livy may have permitted himself, the broad, urbane, ornate flow of his language, described as a pure milky abundance or rich creaminess (*lactea ubertas*),[12] is in itself an implied correction of Sallust's abrupt, archaic mannerisms. This fuller style harks back instead to the rotundity of Cicero, the good Republican with proper opinions on the emotive value of history, whom Livy, we are told, urged his son to read with special care.[13] The historian and critic Pollio, who had political reasons for disliking Livy's home-town (p. 233), sneered at the historian for 'Patavinity',[14] regarding this high-flown diction, and probably the romantic view of history it enshrined, as un-smart and provincial.

For elevated emotions and thoughts were what Livy was at pains to provide. A psychological historian before everything else, he was already noted in ancient times for his unique capacity for revealing people's inmost feelings and attitudes and adapting his treatment to different themes and persons.[15] One after another, his episodes are transfigured and heightened by his interest in human motives – emotional rather than intellectual – and particularly by his concentration on the excitements which sway multitudes in times of crisis. Thucydides had been the master of this art. But he had also, on occasion, called attention to such matters as the technical aspects of sieges (p. 118). So had Polybius, for example while he was writing of the siege of Syracuse in 211 BC.[16] When Livy, however, writes of the same event, all material of any military value is thrown aside in order to dwell on the agony and bravery and desperation of the besieged.[17]

Again, in the early conflict between the patrician and plebeian orders, it is scarcely possible to reconstruct the course of the various negotiations. But we are left in little doubt concerning the atmosphere of the struggle. It is revealed by a hundred expert touches. Livy particularly specialises in recounting what people underwent and suffered as they reacted to events. That is the main theme of Hannibal's battle on the Rhône (p. 223). The terror felt by the Gauls is palpable, and so is the pity felt by the author, for Livy feels deeply for the plight of the distressed. 'Of the emotions and sufferings of those who were caught up in one or other of the great crises of Roman history,' as J.B. Bury said, 'he wrote with brilliant liveliness and sympathy.'

The contrast between his methods and those of Thucydides is illustrated by Livy's account of the sickness which struck down both besiegers and besieged at Syracuse. Echoes of the earlier historian's account of the Athenian plague are inevitable and deliberate. But whereas Thucydides had offered a clinical analysis of the symptoms (p. 119) Livy concerns himself with the misery and pathos of the situation.

It was autumn, and the region naturally unhealthy. . . . The intolerably intense heat affected almost everyone in both camps. First men fell ill and began to perish because of the unhealthiness of the season and region. Then the disease spread. . . . Every day there were burials and deaths before men's eyes, and day and night lamentation was universally heard. Finally they became so accustomed to and brutalised by their evil fate that they not merely refrained from escorting the dead with tears and customary mourning, but did not even carry them out to burial. There the corpses lay in full view of those awaiting a similar death; and so, through fear and disease and the deadly odour, the dead bodies brought to destruction the sick, and the sick the healthy. Some preferred to die by the sword, and rushed unaccompanied into the enemy guard-posts.[18]

Every effort, then, is made to ensure that we shall share the feelings of the multitudes struck by plague or battle or crisis. With individuals it is the same; we are constantly brought into just the same sort of contact with them. 'Livy perpetually seeks', says P.G. Walsh, 'to communicate with the minds of the past, to relive their mental and emotional experiences.' And above all, reasonably enough in the circumstances of the ancient world, it is the leaders who are regarded as important – the men who make the decisions (p. 58). The practice of obituary notices, rare in Thucydides and Sallust, is extended.[19] Further critical comments, too, are briefly inserted at the beginning or end of a unit. Yet it is rare for Livy's own personal judgments to be intruded. In general, he prefers the indirect methods of tragic drama. We learn about people by hearing what other people think of them, and by discovering the effects of their actions on what someone else subsequently does.

With this purpose in mind, the ancient contrivance of the speech is cleverly exploited. It is true that speeches only occupy 12 per cent of the surviving parts of the *History* – not more than half the proportion of Thucydides. Nevertheless, 407 of Livy's speeches are extant, including sixteen of considerable length. These orations invariably form integral and carefully planned features of the general design, and they attracted special admiration in ancient times.[20] Elaborately rhetorical in construction,[21] they are often unnatural, and obviously unrelated to anything that could actually have been said. Yet they show real insight into the mainsprings and motives of human character.

The speeches are also adept in their presentation of contrasting personalities. All too frequently, however, the contrasts are just simple moralising distinctions between Livy's ideal Roman virtue and the evil forces with which it had to contend. All national types are stereotypes – Gauls are unreliable and gutless, Numidians lustful,

Campanians luxurious, Carthaginians treacherous. And almost all individuals are heroes or villains. As for the heroes, Scipio Africanus the elder or Marcellus five times consul, or Titus Flamininus the liberator of Greece, Livy has brought their glory to life, but not their personalities. The less desirable features of these are glossed over. His portrait gallery is like the row of statues of Rome's triumphant generals which Augustus erected in his Forum, each inscribed with the victor's name and the details of his career.

Livy presents a classical confrontation between the elder Scipio Africanus and Hannibal (202 BC). Their meeting is accompanied by a symmetrical exchange of discourses which, like all the rest of the incident, is manifestly fictitious: 'Exactly half-way between the opposing ranks of armed men, each attended by an interpreter, the generals met. They were not only the two greatest soldiers of their time, but the equals of any king or commander in the whole history of the world.'[22] The situation is fabricated, but the estimate is interesting, because Hannibal emerges as a very unusual figure to appear in the pages of Livy. Most of his characters are plain black or white. Hannibal, on the other hand, though he cannot be a hero – since he is the arch-enemy of Rome – is by no means regarded as an out-and-out villain. Instead, Livy attempts a more balanced judgment, like Polybius before him. Indeed, Livy's picture of Hannibal has been compared to Virgil's contemporary representation of Rome's mythical foe Turnus, who seems to many readers to have stolen the emotional thunder of the less exciting official hero Aeneas.

Very soon Hannibal no longer needed to rely upon his father's memory to make himself beloved and obeyed: his own qualities were sufficient. . . . Reckless in courting danger, he showed superb tactical ability once it was upon him. His time for waking, like his time for sleeping, was never determined by daylight or darkness. When his work was done, then, and then only he rested, without need, moreover, of silence or a soft bed to woo sleep to his eyes.

The rather conventional catalogue of virtues continues. But then Livy, less impartial than Polybius after all, cannot refrain from incorporating the slurs which formed part of the orthodox Roman tradition: 'So much for Hannibal's virtues – and they were great. But no less great were his faults; inhuman cruelty, a more than Punic perfidy, a total disregard of truth, honour and religion, of the sanctity of an oath and of all that other men hold sacred.'[23] However,

Livy's Hannibal remains a complex figure, with balancing features. But this duality in the character of a single individual only appears very rarely in his pages. On the whole, simpler presentations of character served his purpose much better. This purpose was to illustrate moral qualities, and to show their decisive impact on events. He says so clearly in his preface, with the observation, hallowed by antiquity, that history does us a good turn by setting all its varied lessons luminously on record for our attention.[24] And so Livy's aim was to lead men to avoid the evil and choose the good, by exhibiting the nature and consequences of both. The result is, as R.M.Ogilvie says, that 'time and again episodes are given a self-contained unity by being turned into moral parables.'

In particular, the morality very often assumes a patriotic form. Livy's patriotism was partly inherited from his sources, but it is also, quite evidently, based on intense personal convictions. It strikes far too uncritical a note, and has contributed to the chauvinistic brands of history which have played havoc in our own times. The account of the earlier Republic is largely one long narration of traditional Roman virtues. Camillus, saviour of Rome in the early fourth century BC, is even credited with declaring how nicely the ancient Romans had waged their wars: 'War has its laws as peace has, and we have learned to wage war with decency no less than with courage.'[25] Livy lacks the insight of Thucydides or Sallust into the degradations of war, and his assessment falls ludicrously wide of the savageries perpetrated by the Romans for century after century. But he goes further still, and declares that Rome is morally entitled to rule other nations.[26] Here, like Cicero before him, he was able to borrow gladly from accommodating Greek philosophers (p. 178). At the same time he had to bear in mind rival Greek or Greek-inspired schools of history which continued to see the third and second centuries BC from a Hellenic and sometimes anti-Roman standpoint.[27] But he noted such views only for the purpose of implicit correction.

On several notable occasions, Livy deliberately departs from Polybius in order to distort history for national reasons.[28] In order to show Rome in a better light, he grossly falsifies the crisis that led to the Second Punic War, adopting a version which placed the siege of Saguntum in 218 instead of 219. Perhaps Livy owed the fabrication to Fabius Pictor (p. 143). 'The motive for such distortion', says Walsh, 'was to minimise Rome's neglect of her ally by emphasising the alleged suddenness of the attack upon and capture of Saguntum, and by implying that Rome had no time to send help.' Moreover, the preceding Carthaginian operations are twisted, with much invention of speeches, in order to brand the enemy as the aggressor.

Patriotism often merges into internal political prejudices. These were partly due to the highly partisan character of the family records used by Livy's sources, which glorified their own houses at the expense of others. He is well aware of the mendacity of such archives.[29] But this does not prevent him from denigrating the house of the Claudii because he inherited the prejudice from Fabius Pictor, whose family was against them.

More often, however, Livy's views on home politics take the form of a straightforward bias toward conservatism and the senatorial cause. In writing of the Second Punic War, which moved him more than any other event in Roman history, Livy felt sure that no one could fail to be impressed by the solid achievement of senatorial rule (p. 222). The theme is never far away. As he looks back to the times when the oligarchy firmly controlled finance, foreign and military affairs, and religion, the Senate is heavily idealised. Agrarian laws, of all dates, come in for criticism owing to unhappy memories of the 'popular' agrarian legislation of the first century BC, notably during the first consulship of Caesar (p. 181).

And so the historian falls in firmly with a tradition which had nothing too bad to say for second-century leaders such as Gaius Flaminius, Marcus Minucius Rufus and Gaius Terentius Varro. All these were men who had been helped on their way by popular acclamation: 'Gaius Flaminius slipped away to his "province" before his formal investiture. The revelation of what he had done made the Senate, already angry, much angrier: "Flaminius" – such was the cry – "is now at war not only with the Senate but with the gods."'[30] It was a commonplace to attribute the beginnings of moral decline to some date during the second century BC, and Livy was one of those who selected, as the key moments in the process of deterioration, firstly the years 189–8 'when luxury was introduced owing to an influx of Galatian booty', and secondly the attempts of the Gracchi to introduce democratic reforms.[31] He held that Marius, the popular nominee, had subverted the State, by craft and then by violence.[32]

As to Sulla, Livy deplored his cruelty, but admired his achievement in repairing the ancient system.[33]

His judgments about more recent times, in so far as we can reconstruct them from epitomes and quotations, introduced a number of significant points. Although he attacked the First Triumvirate and did not exempt Pompey from criticism, he sought to counteract Sallust's extremely unfavourable picture by glossing over his youthful brutalities. Indeed Augustus called Livy 'the Pompeian',[34] because, when it came to the Civil War, he favoured Pompey as champion of of the lawful senatorial government. With regard to Pompey's enemy Caesar, the historian expressed doubts whether 'his birth was of more benefit to the State than if he had never lived'[35] – an attitude comparable to ambiguous observations by Virgil. The younger Cato's greatness, on the other hand, lay beyond the reach of praise or blame,[36] and Livy refrained from censuring Cassius and Brutus, 'describing them in language appropriate to distinguished men'.[37] These discussions of what was still within living memory dealt with the matters which must have interested him most, and probably inspired his best work. 'I should be glad', said Bolingbroke with some justification, 'to exchange what we have of this history for what we have not.'

Livy's treatment of Cicero was carefully balanced. While the orator's human weaknesses are admitted, he is handsomely praised, although Augustus was hostile to his memory. His end, says Livy, was a tragedy, though he feels obliged to add that it was the only one of his adversities that Cicero bore well – and that, if he had had a chance, he would have treated his enemies just as badly as he was treated himself.[38] Nevertheless, he concludes, the orator was a man of real greatness; which is not a surprising verdict since Livy was thoroughly Ciceronian in his political and literary views alike (p. 224).

The only personage of the first century BC to whom he showed uncompromising hostility was Antony, enemy of the constitution and lover of the foreign woman Cleopatra. In his treatment of the struggle of Antony and Cleopatra against Octavian, the future Augustus, Livy was wholeheartedly on Octavian's side. Yet the sections on the Augustan age which followed were by no means mere adulation. Admittedly the treatment of certain figures in earlier parts of the history, such as Romulus and Camillus and Decius and Scipio, is influenced by phrases relating to ideal leadership which were current in descriptions of Augustus.[39] It is also evident that, after the prolonged horrors of one civil war after another, Livy, like contemporary poets, must have felt that the Pax Augusta was a marvel which showed Rome's divine destiny at work. He is also likely to have utilised certain of Augustus' own writings, now lost, notably his autobiography (*On his Own Life*) which filled thirteen books and extended to 25 BC, the date of its publication.[40]

Nevertheless, Livy's handling of the first century BC makes it clear that specific Augustanism affected him less than it influenced Virgil and Horace, not to speak of more adulatory writers. In fact, he was by no means one of the emperor's most wholehearted supporters. As far as we can tell from the abridgments, his work contains no explicit approval of the widespread reforms in which Augustus was engaged during the years round 28 BC.[41] On the contrary, Livy shows notable caution about the feasibility of anything of the kind. 'Our defects are unendurable to us – and so are their cures' (p. 233).[42] However, this attitude of apparent detachment towards current developments, combined with nostalgia for the old Republic, was not as anti-Augustan as it looks at first sight. On the contrary, it was facilitated by Augustus' own claim that he was not, formally speaking, an autocrat at all, but the restorer of the old Republican institutions. After the torments of previous decades most people found this fiction acceptable, bearing in mind that the size of the Empire meant that any authentic revival of the past system was impracticable. It was therefore politically possible, and legitimate, to profess an antiquarian form of Republicanism. Indeed, as time went on, the atmosphere of Augustan society seems to have become increasingly Republican and aristocratic.

Livy was therefore free to pursue his Ciceronian idealisation of the free, senatorial State. It is, however, possible that he pursued this theme a little too far for comfort. For the fact that his last twenty-two books, dealing with the period 42–9 BC, were not published until after Augustus' death (p. 221) suggests deliberate postponement – perhaps because of his sceptical remarks about 'cures', or possibly in view of his relatively sympathetic attitude towards Brutus and Cassius. He seems to have been conscious of the need for care. The epitomes suggest that a full discussion of controversial agrarian laws of the first century BC (p. 181) was avoided, and that the delicate home affairs of Augustus' own time (which included acute tensions and alleged plots) were likewise rapidly passed over.

Soon after 9 BC the régime ran into dynastic troubles, which may have caused Livy's hopefulness to dwindle further. Outstanding among these troubles was the temporary estrangement of the emperor's surviving stepson and chief lieutenant Tiberius, because he felt he had been unjustly passed over (6 BC–AD 4).[42] This placed Livy in a serious dilemma. He had adopted a tradition hostile to Tiberius' difficult family the Claudii (p. 229). Yet it seems that the missing books devoted high praise to the prince's wars on the northern frontiers. As regards the latest embarrassments, it might prove, indeed in view of his later succession to the throne it would have proved, most imprudent to blame Tiberius in any way. At the very least any discussion of the matter could only introduce a jarring note; about these high and inflammable troubles silence was the only possible course. And so it was probably during this awkward period that Livy decided not to continue his history beyond 9 BC. As he himself observes, 'the nervousness felt by the historian who deals with contemporary happenings, even if it does not cause lapses from truthfulness, can be a worrying thing'.[43]

Official Augustan propaganda, as displayed for example on the emperor's coins, liked to see the new order as a return to the Golden Age. Contemporary poets support this conception. And yet strangely enough, and it would seem contradictorily, they still find it possible to adhere to the ancient convention that everything is getting worse all the time (p. 152). Thus Horace, for all his pro-Augustan views, echoes the pessimism of the Greek poet Aratus of Soli.

> Degenerate sires' degenerate seed,
> We'll soon beget a fourth-rate breed.[44]

Livy adopts a rather similar contradictory approach. He offers one patriotic pronouncement about contemporary Rome, praising the prevalent love of peace and care for national harmony.[45] But the preface to the whole work, even if partly conventional and also somewhat juvenile, is remarkable for its gloom at a time when Augustus was attempting a far-reaching and comprehensive social revival.

Contemporary history displays our nation suicidally eating up its own mighty resources. Let it be noted how the moral rot started, how standards were gradually sapped, then crumbled more and more ominously, and finally began to collapse into utter ruin. That is the stage we have now reached. Our defects are unendurable to us – and so are their cures. . . . From unlimited self-indulgence has come a longing to pursue vicious extravagance to the point of personal and universal annihilation.[46]

Like the poets, Livy looked back in shame and horror at the two decades before Augustus. But his backward gaze is so riveted on these evils that, in so far as we can judge from surviving portions of the work, there was no emphatic echo of Virgil's pronouncement that Rome has been given empire for all eternity. Polybius had skirted round the question of an eventual downfall, with no sign of any positive declaration that it could be avoided (p. 152). Livy is unlikely to have discussed the matter. He is not a thoroughgoing pessimist like Sallust, because he believes more sincerely than his predecessor that a revival of the old virtues really *could* restore Rome. But he offers no indication that the decline has been halted yet.

His strongly Republican conservatism was in keeping with the characteristics of his own town, Patavium. North Italy (Transpadane Gaul) was increasingly coming to be regarded as the home of the old Roman virtues, and Patavium in particular, which was enjoying a period of great prosperity, retained the strict moral outlook of older times. In spite of Caesar's favour towards the territory, which he valued very highly for its manpower and wealth, its Republican sentiments remained strong. Mediolanum (Milan) continued to cherish statues of Brutus and Cassius even after Augustus had become master of the world, and Patavium defied Antony in 43 and was consequently persecuted by Pollio.[47] That was in Pollio's capacity as Antony's general. In his role of literary critic, too, he sneered at Livy's 'Patavinity' (p. 224). Livy was, indeed, loyal to his native land, giving special prominence to its legendary origins and inserting favourable allusions to the region whenever opportunity offered.[48] There were a number of things that specially attracted him about his native city. It paid a special tribute to harmony between various orders and interests by giving a board of priests the name 'Concordiales'. In the same spirit of toleration, Livy lays continual stress on civic concord, applauding at every juncture what he regarded as reasonable compromises, though these, as reformers so often complain to be the case with moderates, generally meant the retention of the *status quo*.

Livy's origins from Patavium, and the misfortunes the place

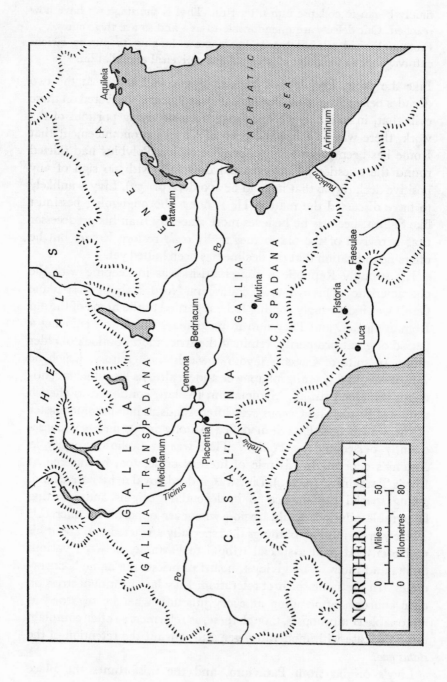

NORTHERN ITALY

suffered in the Civil War, inspired him with sympathy for Italian towns and tribes. We should have been likely to find the same thing in the elder Cato, another municipal townsman, if his writings were extant; but it is exceptional in surviving historians. No doubt Livy's Italian feelings obtained expression in his account of that terrible civil upheaval, the Social or Marsian War, which had taken place barely a quarter of a century before he was born. The same breadth of view causes him to provide extensive and invaluable information about the settlements planted by the Romans in various parts of Italy, for example during the first three decades of the second century BC.

Livy appreciates the economic significance of these colonies. Indeed, he is alive to economic considerations in general. He is at pains to indicate the financial effects of the battle of the Metaurus, in which Hannibal's invading brother Hasdrubal met his end (207 BC).[49] He includes many particulars of matters such as building-policy and transportation. Indeed, in regard to the whole question of the national revenue, 'the comprehensiveness of Livy's account', as Walsh observes, 'surpasses in breadth that of other ancient historians'.

It is possible, then, to find points in his favour as a scholarly researcher. He listed many details conscientiously. And yet it must be added that his narrative often bears only the slightest relation to any events that are at all likely to have occurred.

When military history was the theme, Sallust had echoed the conventional excuse that descriptions of battles must needs be vague because they were, in fact, very mixed-up affairs. Livy repeats the excuse, adding a new and characteristic note of his own.

> The din of the mêlée was so great that not a word either of exhortation or command could be heard. . . . In that enveloping mist, ears were a better guide than eyes: it was sounds, not sights, they turned to face – the groans of wounded men, the thud or ring of blows on body or shield, the shout of onslaught, the cry of fear.[50]

This determined attempt to lead the reader away from mere technicalities to the emotional reactions which interested Livy so much more cannot conceal the fact that he was exceedingly ignorant of military affairs. No doubt his cloistered existence had much to do with this, and kindly critics have suggested that it is surprising he got so much right as he did. At any rate, his battles, even more than those of earlier historians, bear a generic resemblance to one another which is more than suspicious.

Geography and topography, too, are so confused that to this day we cannot tell the route by which Hannibal entered Italy.[51] Speeches, diverging completely from anything that might have been said, are inserted, for literary reasons, on historically inappropriate occasions.[52] In 191 BC, a fictitious Assembly is introduced to exploit the historian's talent for crowd scenes. Moreover, these orations are often crammed with anachronisms, as though, it has been said, 'he was painting members of the Witenagemot in the costume of the House of the Commons'. Throughout the entire work, falsifications in the interests of patriotism or conservatism or dramatic effect abound.

Material which had appeared in the Annales Maximi (p. 172) was known to Livy, but probably only at second hand. He did not feel it was part of his job to consult such records himself.[53] When a document is quoted, it is transformed into the proper literary diction of history.[54] He accepted Augustus' disingenuous word for the contents of one ancient inscription[55] – a course difficult for him to have avoided, it is true, and followed (whether from carelessness or intent) by an implicit contradiction later on.

But almost nowhere is there any criticism of sources. Sometimes, admittedly, Livy shows good sense in choosing between them.[56] And on other occasions he is right to leave the issue in doubt. He has occasion, for example, to refer to two historians of the first century BC, Tubero and Macer, and to the Linen Books, or *libri lintei*, which were dubiously ascribed a venerable antiquity (p. 176). 'Both of these writers', he says, 'quote the authority of the Linen Rolls. Macer chooses unhesitatingly to follow them, Tubero admits to uncertainty. So we must leave it in doubt – the mists of antiquity cannot always be pierced.'[57]

This refusal to judge, noted in ancient times as a special characteristic of Livy,[58] is praiseworthy up to a point. But to a modern historian it seems a little too prompt, exonerating him from coming to conclusions on vital matters. Since he wrote so much and so quickly, it was impossible for him to approach the standards of source assessment that had been achieved by the best of the Greek historians.

Livy does not invoke his authorities by name except when a controversial matter is at stake. But it seems likely that he adhered more or less faithfully to one source at a time over a considerable period, occasionally recording, as a sort of footnote, a contradictory tradition from another source, or an opinion of his own. When no such relatively clear-cut procedure is possible, he is inclined to bring in two or three writers of contrasting views, moving from one to another without any attempt to conflate or judge or reconcile their opposed opinions. In some cases he will incorporate contradictory versions from two or more sources, and even describe the same event twice over in different terms.

When he quotes varying estimates of the size of Hannibal's army, one of them is derived from an inscription which Polybius had actually seen (p. 162). Yet Livy does not think it worth while to refer to the point, nor does he express preference for the authenticated version. Nevertheless, for long stretches of narrative, especially during the years 201–167, he follows Polybius closely, though he only names him once – in brief but complimentary terms.[59] On sixteen occasions he appends alternative versions to the Polybian tradition.[60] While scrupulously reproducing much of the earlier writer's detail, he alters and falsifies him in order to dramatise; and at least five times he grossly mistranslates the Greek. In accordance with his own tendency towards patriotic distortion, Livy adjusts Polybius' evidence about Scipio and Titus Flamininus, which was already complimentary enough, in order to make them into more orthodox representatives of Roman virtue.

For portions of the work which Polybius had not covered, he apparently continued, for the most part, to use one source at a time, drawing in turn upon a number of Latin predecessors, bad or less bad.[61] In the absence of systematic references to their names, it is not always easy to see who they were. But obviously they provided ample fuel for his nationalistic and conservative emotions and prejudices.

The emperor Caligula may have been unduly unappreciative in describing Livy as verbose and careless.[62] Yet, all in all, we have to agree with the verdict of Quintilian, who expressed a similar sentiment in more judicious terms. Livy's style, he observed, 'is hardly of a kind to instruct a listener who is looking not for beauty of exposition, but for truth and credibility'.[63] He had a taste for the truth, it has been said: but no passion for it.

However, when we criticise these shortcomings, we are asking for something which Livy did not really claim to provide. He is closer to expansive popular historians than to the modern research scholar. As Ogilvie points out, he resembles Sir Walter Scott, writing at a time when there was 'a widespread interest in the past, unaccompanied by widespread or specialist learning'.

This aspect of Livy is of course particularly apparent in his early books, in which he deals, like various other contemporary writers,[64] with remote and misty epochs in the story of Rome. He strongly defends the admission of this sort of material into his history. In the first place, it is included out of deference to Romans of the past. The recognition that the recording of portents and prodigies had become unfashionable causes him to define this principle: 'Not only does my own mind, as I write of old-time matters, become in some way or other old-fashioned, but also a certain conscientious scruple keeps me from regarding what those very sagacious men of former times thought worthy of public concern as something unworthy to be reported in my history.'[65] In his preface, he offers another reason for including these legendary happenings. Their narration, he says, is an agreeable escape and relief from the miseries of his own age (p. 232). But in fact this type of material appealed to him for a much more positive reason. He shared the contemporary antiquarian taste very strongly. One of his most powerful instincts was a sentimental emotional admiration for the glorious native traditions of Rome. In consequence, he became the most brilliant and influential eulogist the city and empire ever had the good fortune to produce.

Of the legendary character of his material he is extremely well aware. From time to time, as the great old stories follow one another, due provisos about their fabulous character are added. For example, an omen dramatically foretelling the fall of Veii (396 BC) prompts him to remark: 'Personally I am content, as a historian, if in regard to things which happened so many centuries ago probabilities are accepted as truth.'[66] And he adds that he does not take the tale seriously as historical fact. The prefatory remarks of the whole work had already contained a warning that the stories he is going to tell do not belong in any strict sense to factual history.

Traditions relating to the period before the foundation of the city was carried out or contemplated I propose neither to establish nor to refute. They belong to poetic fiction rather than to the authentic records of historical fact. . . .

Prehistory is allowed the indulgence of blending the doings of men and gods in order to make the origins more impressive. And if any country is entitled to sanctify its beginnings by attributing them to divine action, that is true of the Romans.[67]

In this passage, Livy is specifically referring to the age before Rome was even founded. But the words are equally applicable to any of the earliest centuries after the city's foundation. Livy is a prose Virgil who has given these distant tales eternal life. A characteristic example is the holding of the bridge by Horatius against fearful odds. This is one of the sagas which Livy has no intention of vouching for as real history. 'It was a noble piece of work,' he says, 'legendary maybe, but destined to be celebrated in story through the years to come.' And it owed this perpetuation largely to Livy's own account.

Once more Horatius stood alone; with defiance in his eyes he confronted the Etruscan chivalry, challenging one after another to single combat. . . . With a fierce cry they hurled their spears at the solitary figure which barred the way. . . . The Etruscans moved forward, and would have thrust him aside by the sheer weight of numbers, but their advance was suddenly checked by the crash of the falling bridge and the simultaneous shout of triumph from the Roman soldiers who had done their work in time. The Etruscans could only stare in bewilderment as Horatius, with a prayer to Father Tiber to bless him and his sword, plunged fully armed into the water and swam through the missiles which fell thick about him safely to the other side, where his friends were waiting to receive him.[68]

That is splendid myth. Other stories, notably those relating to the career of Coriolanus, again bear the marks of Greek mythological origins. So do the birth and death of the first king Romulus, who is merely a personification of Rome invented according to the fashion of Hellenic 'foundations'.[69]

The Horatius story has just been described as myth. Or was it, instead, legend, using that term to mean material in which there was a grain of original truth? When we came down to this difficult task of trying to find out where (if anywhere) the grains of truth in these stories lie, it is obviously necessary to make many allowances and subtractions – casting a sceptical eye on the self-glorifying traditions of the great Roman families, traditions which were still being imaginatively amplified and slanted as late as the first century BC. And yet, once the inevitable adaptations have been made, an

239

immense amount of truth has been shown to be lurking in Livy's words. Modern archaeologists are the people who have demonstrated this, and the truths that emerge are often unobtainable from any other source but Livy.

For example, his indication that the kingship of Rome fell for a considerable period into the hands of the Etruscans, who dominated the country north of the Tiber, has been substantially confirmed by excavators. His date of 616 BC for the first Etruscan king may be a little too early, but not very much; and the names Tarquin and Tanaquil, which figure so largely in his account, have been found on inscriptions in tombs.[70] He identifies Etruscan origins for certain Roman institutions.

Some have fancied that Romulus made the lictors twelve in number because the vultures, in the augury, had been twelve; personally, however, I incline to follow the opinion which finds for this an Etruscan origin. We know that the State Chair – the 'curule' chair – and the purple-bordered toga came to us from Etruria; and it is probable that the idea of attendants, as well as, in this case, of their number, came across the border from Etruria too. The number twelve was due to the fact that the twelve Etruscan communities united to elect a king, and each contributed one lictor.[71]

Such comments, even when vulnerable in detail, display a remarkable power to divine the probabilities of those antique times. The obstacles that had to be overcome before any conclusions at all could be reached about the remote past were enormous. The auxiliary techniques of history were almost non-existent: it is only in our day that archaeologists have illuminated the early epochs of Italy. Livy was also embarrassed by a wish on the part of his readers – a wish, moreover, that he himself shared – to get on to the excitements of the later Republic. Nevertheless, he still chooses to dwell on the early periods, perseveringly attempting to detect in them the seeds of later Roman constitutional, judicial and especially religious procedures. He deliberately quotes myths in order to provide the archetypes of such practices,[72] or to explain (not always self-consistently) the sanctity of famous places.[73]

He manages, like many others before and after him, to combine a considerable tendency towards rationalism with an earnest approval of religious practices. Religion, in Rome, was mainly public, and Livy supported Polybius' advocacy of its performance on the grounds that this was good for public morale (p. 158). He never missed an opportunity to stress ancient religious observances, especially if they are edifying.[74] But his attitudes to religion are as equivocal as his attitudes to legend, with which, indeed, religion continually merges. It was a legendary portent which inspired the apologetic statement that such things must be included because they were venerable features of tradition (p. 238): and other divine signs prompt him to a further disclosure of his religious position.

Many prodigies were reported [206 BC]. The temple of Jupiter at Tarracina and of Mater Matuta at Satricum were struck by lightning; no less alarming at the latter town was the spectacle of two snakes gliding in through the door of the temple of Jupiter; from Antium came a report that the ears of grain seemed to have blood in them as they were being cut; a two-headed pig was born at Caere, and a lamb with both male and female organs; at Alba two suns were said to have been seen; there was a light in the night sky at Fregellae; in the country near Rome an ox talked, and the altar of Neptune in the Circus Maximus poured with sweat.[75]

These alleged omens could be defended as history on the grounds that they influenced people's feelings, thoughts and actions. And Livy, in fact, refrains on this occasion from going any farther, for he is careful to point out that he does not necessarily believe this weird catalogue to have shown the hand of any god at work: 'it was inevitable that, in critical times like these, men should attribute everything that happened, whether favourable or adverse, to divine agency'. Nor is this the only occasion on which he shows a sceptical spirit.[76] At other times, however, he does show some measure of belief in divine warnings of just the same sort.[77]

His verdict, then, is ambiguous. 'He sees the prodigies', says Walsh, 'as possibly symptomatic of a disordered universe, portending future disaster.' Such happenings *may* convey a sign from heaven. This had been the view of Posidonius, the encyclopedic Greek historian who died when Livy was a boy. Posidonius had derived this attitude from a modernised brand of the Stoic belief in a provident government of the universe. Livy, himself, does not employ any particular philosophy as a metaphysical framework. Nevertheless, like Cicero and many other educated Romans, he was sufficiently imbued with a generalised version of Stoic ideas to adopt the same cautious but not invariably sceptical approach towards these supposed portents.

A similar ambivalence between normal and numinous, between piety and rationalisation, had appeared in his pages on the occasion of a plague in the fifth century BC. The Senate ordered a national act of prayer; and the pestilence came to an end. 'Every shrine was packed; in every temple women lay prostrate, their hair sweeping the floor, praying to the angry gods to grant them pardon and put an end to the plague. It may be that the prayers were granted; in any case, the sickly season was now over. . . .'[78] These equivocations have led to the most varied modern interpretations of Livy's own personal views about religion. The word 'Fate' appears particularly often among the supernatural sagas of his first decad.[79] Later, when we come to historical times, this sort of Stoic determinism seems farther from his thoughts. Sometimes he refers to Fate, and sometimes to the gods; he does not distinguish sharply between the two conceptions. But it would be a mistake to conclude, because of his scepticism about certain divine manifestations, that he is sceptical about the existence of the divine power itself. No doubt some of his references to religion are little more than tributes to the unmistakable role played by religious belief in the achievements of Rome. Yet he himself, being a believer that divine interventions *can* occur, lays emphatic stress upon the need for a right relationship between men and gods. That right relationship is just what *religio* means: and the exchange of speeches between Scipio's father Publius and Hannibal before the Carthaginian victory of the Ticinus (218) contrast that *religio* with Hannibal's reliance on mere Fortune – a reliance which will ultimately bring him down.[80]

Livy's use of the phrase the 'benignity of the gods' recurs no less than sixteen times in the surviving portions of his work. It must signify that he saw his myths and fables, and probably even his gods themselves, as symbolically representing a divine order of things by which men's lives are directed. This, surely, was what had saved Rome in early days, when the city was encompassed simultaneously by external and internal war and by disease. Conversely, the Gallic invasion was a way of testing and proving the Romans, and indeed, almost in Jewish fashion, of chastising them for their faults.

Rome survived such tests, and was divinely appointed to rule the world; and, by the same token, its history was appointed to instruct the human race.

15

Josephus

THE next ancient historian of distinction, Josephus, takes us from Latin back to Greek, from the conquerors to the conquered, from a chair-borne view of events to a position on the stage. We also move from the capital of the Empire to a point at its eastern periphery; namely Judaea, roughly corresponding with the modern Israel.

Persia had allowed the Jews to rebuild Jerusalem in the fifth century BC (p. 13), and the country remained subject to the Persians until their empire was destroyed and taken over by Alexander the Great (332). After the death of Alexander, Judaea formed part of the dominions of the Ptolemies of Egypt. Then it passed, after various vicissitudes, to the Seleucids who were based on Syria and Mesopotamia (202). They tried harder than the Ptolemies to assimilate this border province to the Greek or Hellenised regions of their empire, and found support among sections of the Jewish ruling class.

But when the Seleucid Antiochus IV Epiphanes dedicated Jehovah's Temple to Olympian Zeus (167), a nationalist and religious rebellion broke out. Priests-kings of the house of Hasmon, notably Judas Maccabaeus, created the Hasmonaean (Maccabee) line which won independence for Judaea for the first time for over four hundred years, and for the last time until the twentieth century AD. In the years around 100 BC there was, for a short time, a Greater Judaea, comprising a wide surrounding region. In 63, however, the whole country fell to the Roman armies of Pompey, who stormed Jerusalem and slew the priests at their altar.

Rome did not annex the country, but established its Jewish nucleus as a minor dependent state under the Hasmonaean John Hyrcanus II. He was subsequently stripped of his temporal powers, but recovered them after sending help to Caesar in Alexandria (p. 191). The contingent was commanded by his vizier Antipater, a man from Idumaea (Edom), where the people had been forcibly converted to Judaism in the previous century. After a brief interval of Parthian suzerainty, Antipater's son Herod the Great ruled as king of the Jews, with the support first of Antony and then of Augustus (40–4 BC). A monarch of ruthless efficiency, and a munificent builder and patron, Herod was keen on Greek culture, yet he also championed the Jews of the Dispersion. At home, he was the mass murderer of his own family. After his death, ten years of squabbling between Herod's sons were followed by the annexation of Judaea, which became a minor Roman province. (This took place in the fifth year after the date which has been officially associated with the birth of Jesus. But the Christian era was only fixed in the sixth century, and the actual date when he was born is disputed.) The governors of the new province, who were loosely supervised by the governors of Syria, only ranked as procurators – Romans not of senatorial but of knightly rank. Under Augustus' successor Tiberius, one of these procurators was Pontius Pilate (AD 26–30), under whom Jesus was crucified.

Tension between the Jews and their rulers, already high because of numerous grievances, reached boiling-point when the next emperor Caligula (37–41) ordered his own statue to be set up in the Temple. At this juncture, however, Caligula was murdered, and Claudius (41–54) reconverted Judaea from a Roman province into a dependent kingdom. Its prince was now Herod's grandson Agrippa I (Herod Agrippa), who had intervened to avert Caligula's proposed desecration. When Agrippa I died in 44, his son Agrippa II was given a client state between that country and Syria-Phoenicia.[1] But in Judaea the provincial régime of the procurators was restored, and during the remaining years of Claudius and under Nero (54–68) relations between ruler and ruled went from bad to worse. Finally, in 66, open revolt broke out. The governor of Syria, Gaius Cestius Gallus, intervened but failed to capture Jerusalem, suffering a reverse at Beth-Horon. Then Nero sent his general Vespasian to crush the revolt. Accompanied by his son Titus, Vespasian entered Galilee, north of Jerusalem, but operations were twice delayed owing to the convulsions of the Year of the Four Emperors (69), which culminated in Vespasian gaining the throne. Titus stayed behind to reduce Jerusalem in the following year, though a few other fortresses still resisted.

The revolt, and particularly the capture of Jerusalem, had been accompanied by appalling hardship, brutality and loss of life. The Temple was burnt down and its worship abolished, and the tax which every Jew had paid to its funds was transferred to Jupiter Capitolinus. The rebellion continues to this day to exert a profound influence on the politics of the middle east.

Its story is told us in Greek by the man who had commanded the Jewish rebel forces in Galilee, Josephus the son of Matthias (Yoseph ben Matatyahu). He was born in AD 37/8 and died at an uncertain date after AD 94/5. His *Jewish War* is divided into seven books and 110 chapters, though these divisions are not necessarily the author's own. The work was the offshoot of a larger project: 'I had, when writing the history of the war, already contemplated describing the origins of the Jews and the fortunes that befell them. . . . However, since the compass of such a theme was excessive, I made the War into a separate volume.'[2] According to the tradition established by the earliest Greek historians, the preface describes the war he has chosen to deal with as the greatest upheaval of all time. The rest of the first book is introductory, surveying Jewish history from the time of Judas Maccabaeus, with a long survey of the reign of Herod the Great. In the second book the introduction continues with an account of Herod's sons and the two periods of Roman annexation which finally led to the open hostilities of AD 66. We are also told how, after their outbreak, the Jewish authorities appointed Josephus governor of Galilee, the northern frontier-province of Judaea. Book III records the arrival of the future emperor Vespasian and his son Titus, and their southward advance. Compelled to surrender to the Romans, Josephus tells how he became their prisoner – and subsequently their favoured collaborator. The book also contains geographical descriptions of the various regions of Palestine, and an analysis of the Roman army.

Book IV describes the Jewish factions in Jerusalem and their alleged atrocities against one another. The accession of Vespasian to the imperial throne is then reported. The next two books give a detailed account of the siege and capture of the city by Titus, followed by the burning of the Temple (70). The last book contains the story of the subsequent mopping-up operations, including the heroic defence of Masada which did not fall for another three years.

Josephus was very proud of the eminence of his Jewish family. His father was a well-known member of the highest priestly aristocracy, and his mother possessed royal Hasmonaean blood.[3] His native tongue, like Jesus Christ's, was Aramaic, the Semitic language which had become the official speech of the Persian Empire and had expanded enormously throughout the middle east. Josephus received the best education a priest's son could obtain, and claims, without undue modesty, to have been a child prodigy.[4] When he was sixteen, he had to decide which Jewish sect he should belong to. He tried all the three[5] principal groups (Pharisees, Sadducees and monastic Essenes), and then joined the Pharisees and became a priest at Jerusalem. In about AD 64 (shortly before the traditional dates for the martyrdoms of Peter and Paul) he went to Rome in order to intercede for some fellow-priest who had been arrested. His mission was successful, owing to the good offices of Alityrus, a Jewish actor who belonged to the entourage of Nero. Assistance was also received from the emperor's wife Poppaea, whom he reported to be favourably inclined towards Judaism. She presented him with liberal gifts, and he left the capital with friendly feelings towards the Romans.

He returned to Judaea to find the rebellion was already gathering force.

To the ordinary Jew [says Arnaldo Momigliano] the duty of paying tribute to the Romans, the sight of the Temple commanded by the Roman garrison in the neighbouring Tower of Antonia, the thought that the vestments of the High Priest were in Roman hands, and the knowledge that the traditional administration of justice was limited by the intervention of the Roman governor, which was inevitable in spite of the large share left to Jewish courts – all these things were a continual offence. The complete lack of understanding and consequently of tolerance that most of the Jews evinced for the Romans was matched on the Roman side. . . . It was a conflict between the Jewish ideal of a state subordinated to the national religion, and the cosmopolitanism of Imperial Rome in which religion itself was subordinated to the State.

The Jewish cause, however, was far from united. The Pharisees had split into right and left wings. The first of these groups, to which Josephus had decided to belong, differed at this time from its former rivals, the Sadducees, on certain doctrinal matters only, and had abandoned its political role. The left wing of the Pharisees, on the other hand, became the secret revolutionary network of the Zealots. They possessed a considerable following inside the cities, and an outlawed underground movement in the countryside. They were also assisted by a large number of more lukewarm anti-Romans, who did not dare to refuse to help. Declaring that there was no ruler but God, and, on a more practical level, that the tax-collectors of the Romans must be expelled from the country, this secret organisation was stimulated by Messianic beliefs. Josephus says nothing of these, because he refuses to allow the Zealots any theological significance. He assails them with every sort of abuse, blaming them savagely for the ruin of Israel.[6]

For Josephus was convinced that going to war had never done the Jews the smallest good. 'Warfare has never been allowed our nation. Our fighting is always followed by defeat.'[7] Instead, paraphrasing the Old Testament, he adhered to the anti-Zionist, supernationalist, cosmopolitan belief 'that the whole world is proposed to be your place of habitation for ever'.[8] He did not, therefore, feel that the faith of Israel was irrevocably associated with its soil.

Passing from the general to the particular, he saw that the present revolt was doomed to failure.

All over the city they were forging missiles and suits of armour, most of the young men were receiving haphazard training, and there was tumult everywhere. Among the more stable, however, there was utter dejection; many saw only too well the approaching calamity and openly lamented. . . . The whole condition of the city before the arrival of the Romans proclaimed the coming destruction.[9]

By airing these defeatist views, Josephus courted extreme peril. He was compelled to take refuge in the Temple. Other leading priests, who agreed with his policy, were equally powerless. It was believed by these people that the intervention of the Roman governor of Syria, Cestius Gallus, would bring the rebellion to an end; and clearly that is what they hoped. But instead Gallus was unexpectedly repulsed from the gates of Jerusalem and defeated at Beth-Horon. This success over one of the highest Roman officials enormously encouraged the war party among the Jews, and was therefore, according to Josephus, a catastrophe: 'This reverse of Cestius proved disastrous for our whole nation, for the advocates of the war were so elated with this success that they entertained hopes of remaining victorious to the end.'[10] This elation, however, was soon modified by two developments: a murderous wave of anti-Semitism which spread through Syria, and the unmistakable imminence of Vespasian's penetration into Galilee. In Jerusalem, the temporary ascendancy of a moderate group[11] enabled Josephus to emerge from hiding, and the Jewish leaders who were now in charge of the city sent him to take command of troops in Galilee. In the *Jewish War* he implied that his mission was to organise resistance against the Romans,[12] although later, as a Roman pensioner, he preferred to say that his aim had been to deceive and pacify Jewish 'robbers' or extremists (p. 266).[13] The dispatch of a pro-Roman to hold this post shows that the authorities now in power at Jerusalem felt little desire for an all-out war against Rome.

The towns of Galilee were split into many different parties, and Josephus met with much opposition from his fellow-Jews. This was especially notable at the fortress of Gischala, where a chaotic situation prevailed: Josephus made a ferocious enemy of a local leader named John, whom he describes in terms of unmeasured abuse (borrowed from Sallust's attacks against Catiline). On the approach of Vespasian, Josephus' large army melted away, and he took refuge in the fortified town of Jotapata. This withdrawal by Josephus into what the Roman commander called 'this prison'[14] does not look as if he intended to offer a very determined resistance. However, he stresses the efficiency with which he conducted the defence of the town, using boiling oil, covering his messengers with sheep-skins to disguise them as dogs, and plastering the enemy's gangways with a boiled mash of the clover-like herb fenugreek, on which the attackers slithered helplessly.

And so Jotapata held out. As the siege tightened, however, Josephus became convinced it was no use carrying on. And so, together with certain fellow-members of the upper class, he decided to desert his post, and to leave the rest of the defence force to its fate.

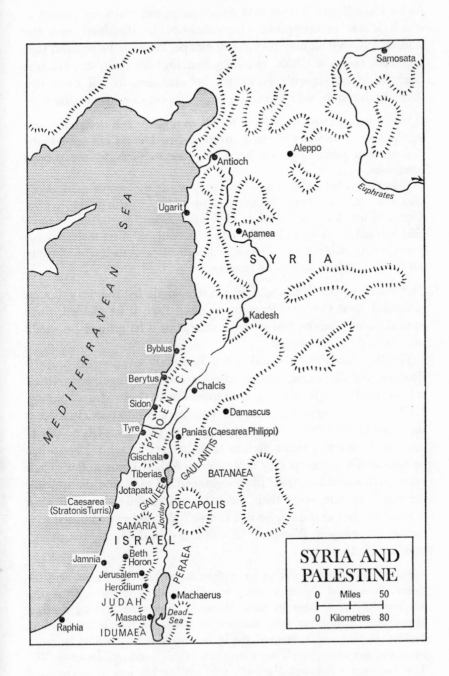

SAMOSATA

Aleppo

Antioch

Euphrates

Ugarit

Apamea

S Y R I A

Kadesh

Byblus

Berytus

Chalcis

Sidon

Damascus

Tyre

Panias (Caesarea Philippi)

Gischala

GAULANITIS

Tiberias

BATANAEA

Jotapata

GALILEE

Caesarea
(Stratonis Turris)

DECAPOLIS

Jordan

SAMARIA

I S R A E L

Jamnia

Beth
Horon

Jerusalem

PERAEA

Herodium

Machaerus

J U D A H

Dead
Sea

Raphia

Masada

IDUMAEA

MEDITERRANEAN SEA

PHOENICIA

SYRIA AND PALESTINE

0	Miles	50

0	Kilometres	80

As he himself put it with that devastating, self-revealing frankness which is one of his special characteristics, he discussed with the leading fellow-Jews how they could escape, because 'he realised that the town could not hold out long and that his own survival was doubtful if he stayed'. However, he manages to tell even this discreditable story with the usual abundant pats on his own back.

> Josephus concealed his anxiety for his own safety and declared it was for their sakes he was arranging to leave. . . . He did not see how by staying with them he could be of any use to them in the present conditions. . . .
>
> This appeal fell on deaf ears; it simply made the people more determined to hold on to him. Children, old men, women with infants in arms wept and fell down before him. They all grasped him by the feet and held him fast, imploring him with sobs to remain and share their lot – not through envy of his escape, I think, but in the hope of their own; for they felt perfectly safe so long as he remained.[15]

The effect of this self-praise is a little spoilt by the very honest admission that follows: 'Josephus realised that, if he yielded, these appeals would be the end of the matter, but if he refused he would be watched.' So he stayed.

Finally, after the siege had lasted for nearly seven weeks and the situation was desperate, the defenders agreed to die together in a mass suicide-pact: and Josephus agreed to be one of those who would die. He had been against this plan, but was coerced into participation at the point of the sword – 'although', he says, 'the others felt unable to press their weapons home against their beloved general. Even when he was at his last gasp they still respected their commander. Their arms were enfeebled, their blades glanced off him, and many while thrusting at him with their swords spontaneously lowered their points.' Be that as it may, he was compelled to associate himself with the terrible project. However, he succeeded in deceiving the others, and survived.

> Putting his trust in divine protection he staked his life on one last throw. 'You have chosen to die', he exclaimed. 'Well then, let's draw lots and kill each other in turn. Whoever draws the first lot shall be dispatched by number two, and so on down the whole line as luck decides. In this way no one will die by his own hand – it would be unfair when the rest were gone if one man changed his mind and saved his life.' The audience swallowed the bait, and getting his way Josephus drew

lots with the rest. Without hesitation each man in turn offered his throat for the next man to cut, in the belief that a moment later his commander would die. Life was sweet, but not so sweet as death if Josephus died with them.

But Josephus – shall we put it down to divine providence or just to luck? – was left with one other man. He did not relish the thought either of being condemned by the lot or, if he was left till last, of staining his hand with the blood of a fellow Jew. So he used persuasion, they made a pact, and both remained alive.[16]

Self-preservation is a natural instinct. But no one else has ever told so openly and complacently how, in tragic circumstances, he tricked his own courageous people in order to save himself. It would indeed be difficult, as Heinrich Graetz said in his *History of the Jews*, to believe all the instances of craft and duplicity on the part of Josephus, 'had he not himself dwelt upon them with unexampled shamelessness'. Or, to quote his own words, 'In this predicament, his resourcefulness did not fail him'.

He was taken to the Roman camp as a captive. Soon afterwards, however, he was set free, visiting Alexandria in the company of Vespasian and witnessing Titus' siege of Jerusalem as an observer. When, finally, the Romans closed round the walls, the Jews within were rent by internal disunity. Josephus, eager at every point to vilify the defenders, is at pains to stress these dissensions, emphasising also the ferocity which accompanied them. According to him, this compared unfavourably with the 'clemency' of the Romans (p. 256). Inside the city, the moderates were no longer in charge, and two rival resistance movements were fighting against each other for control. One was led by Josephus' enemy John of Gischala, and the other by Simon bar Gioura ('son of a proselyte') who had gained a reputation by the capture of Hebron and other commando actions against the Romans. However, in face of the final menace, the two groups finally came to an agreement.

Many times Josephus went round the walls, urging the population to surrender; 'pleading with them,' records G.A. Williamson, 'while the tears ran down his face, to yield to the merciful Roman whose one desire was to end their agony'. And so the greatest of Jewish historians became a traitor to his people at its most critical hour. Or, to say the least, he was unheroic in seeing the advantages of collaboration so clearly – though it would be much harder to say, in the light of cold reason, that he was wrong in supposing that the insurrection had no chance whatever of success.

At last the city fell to Titus, in circumstances of unrelieved horror.

Those who perished in the long siege totalled 1,000,000. . . .[17] Every man who showed himself was either killed or captured by the Romans, and then those in the sewers were ferreted out, the ground was torn up, and all who were trapped were killed. There too were found the bodies of more than 2,000, some killed by their own hand, some by one another's, but most by starvation. So foul a stench of human flesh greeted those who charged in that many turned back at once. Others were so avaricious that they pushed on, climbing over the piles of corpses; for many valuables were found in the passages and all scruples were silenced by the prospect of gain.

Many prisoners of the party chiefs were brought up; for not even at their last gasp had they abandoned their brutality. But God rewarded them both as they deserved. John, starving to death with his brothers in the sewers, after many scornful refusals at last appealed to the Romans for mercy, while Simon, after battling long against the inevitable, gave himself up. John was sentenced to life-imprisonment, but Simon was kept for the triumphal procession and ultimate execution.

The Romans now fired the outlying districts of the town and demolished the walls. So fell Jerusalem in the second year of Vespasian's reign, on the 8th September – captured five times before and now for the second time laid utterly waste.[18]

The conquerors officially treated the war as over, and Vespasian and Titus returned to Rome and celebrated a magnificent Triumph (71). Simon, we saw, was executed, John condemned to imprisonment. Reliefs on the Arch of Titus at Rome still display the spoils: the table of the shewbread, the trumpets and the great seven-branched candlestick, the Menorah, which, despite varied rumours, has never been seen since. Yet the war was not, in fact, finished, since three of the powerful fortresses built by Herod were still unconquered. The resistance of Herodium, south of Jerusalem, was brief. Machaerus in Transjordan held out longer. Masada above the Dead Sea's western bank, towering above a sheer drop of more than 1300 feet, endured under Eleazar ben Yair until April of the year 73. Josephus gives a harrowing account of how the last 960 survivors of Masada destroyed one another; only two women and five small children hid themselves and survived. It is astonishing that he could write with such uninhibited eloquence about this suicide pact after he had evaded another and let his comrades die (p. 251). Some of his descriptions of what happened at Masada, including Eleazar's lengthy exhortations, are exaggerated or invented, even if one of the survivors, his informant, was a relative of Eleazar, 'superior to most women in intelligence and education'. But the basic facts are probably as Josephus told them. Recent excavations have revealed the charred sandals of small children, and a potsherd bearing Eleazar's name. This may have been one of the lots drawn at the final moment of catastrophe to appoint ten of the defenders who would put the rest to death.

Meanwhile, however, Josephus was safely out of the way. After the capture of Jerusalem he was given a piece of land outside the city, and he persuaded the Romans to release some of his friends.[19] Then he proceeded to Rome, where he was awarded Roman citizenship, taking the imperial family name, Flavius, in the same way as an ex-slave might assume the name of his master. He was also given a pension and a residence. After the siege of Jotapata he had married a prisoner of war from Caesarea ('at the command of Vespasian'), but while he was at Alexandria with Vespasian he divorced her in favour of a woman of that city. In Rome, he wedded an aristocratic Jewish heiress from Crete. His Alexandrian and Cretan wives presented him with three and two sons respectively. What happened to his parents we do not know. They may have perished in the siege of Jerusalem.

Safely established in Rome, Josephus spent the last five years of Vespasian's reign writing the *Jewish War* (c. 74-9).[20] However, the Greek text which has come down to us was not the original edition. As he indicates in the preface, that had been in Aramaic. It was intended for Parthians, Babylonians, southern Arabians, Mesopotamians and Assyrians. That is to say, the work was originally written for the numerous eastern Jews, ancestors of their communities today, who had remained scattered abroad in the Dispersion and had never returned to Palestine, becoming augmented meanwhile by local converts to Judaism. The Mesopotamian brethren, Josephus indicated, had been suspected of wanting to join the insurrection, and his work was intended to inform them accurately of its causes, the sufferings it entailed and its disastrous conclusion. He wrote, then, in the Roman interest, to ensure that these people should accept the *fait accompli* of the destruction of the Temple without fomenting discontents along the borders of the Empire.

The version that has survived, however, is a second, Greek edition,[21] which he prepared 'for the sake of such as live under the government of the Romans'. It was designed for the educated, Hellenised Jewish upper class – and he also specifically names important Romans among his readers.

Josephus was aware that his Greek was shaky. Nearly twenty years later, he remarked that he had taken great pains with the literature and grammar of the language, though he admitted that his pronunciation was still imperfect.[22] At any rate, he employed helpers to assist him with the *Jewish War*: 'In the leisure which Rome afforded me, with all my materials in readiness, and with the aid of some assistants for the sake of the Greek, at last I committed to writing my narrative of the events.'[23] He himself gives us to understand that this new version was a *translation* of the Aramaic original. But numerous references to classical literature, including echoes of Thucydides and Sophocles and others (not to speak of Sallust, Virgil and Livy, whom he certainly cannot have read), necessitate the conclusion that his collaborators modified and amplified the Aramaic edition. If Josephus composed a complete first Greek draft (as may be doubted), they must have polished it up and radically altered and improved it. His Greek, or rather theirs, is a vigorous literary Attic, usually but not always clear, with an enormous vocabulary, and much adroit antithetical argument in the speeches.

What the Aramaic book was called we do not know. But the title *The Jewish War*, which Josephus gave the Greek edition, is what a Roman but not a Jew would have been likely to call the war. It shows the pro-Roman bias of the work. In his preface he attempts to grapple with this question of bias. While laying due emphasis on Roman power, genius and glory, he does not propose, he says, 'like other writers who claim to be writing history', to disparage the actions of the Jews. For that, surely, would be no sort of compliment to the grandeur of Rome. Conversely, he stresses the might of the Roman army, not only to deter those who may be tempted to revolt, but to console the people who have been vanquished by so

great a force.[24] This is a more explicit version of Polybius' explanation to the Greeks that Rome was irresistible. Josephus also pro-
claims the harsher conviction that the tragic fate of the Jews was no
more than they had deserved. From outside the walls of Jerusalem he
harangued the besieged population with the words: 'I know that
the Almighty has abandoned the holy places and stands now on the
side of your enemies!' Looking back, he took the same view of
Pompey's destruction of the Temple in 63 BC. The Jews who had
then been subjected were people who did not deserve to be free.[25]
Then and now, the Roman conquests were providential, for 'without God's aid it would not have been possible to consolidate so
great an empire'.

This eulogy of Rome was inseparably blended with praise of the
Flavian dynasty which had welcomed and financed his own collaboration. Josephus reports (and the story is confirmed from Roman
sources[26]) that he was originally spared by his captors because,
immediately after falling into their hands, he had declared to
Vespasian that he was destined to become emperor of Rome. There
were many current prophecies, in the Biblical tradition, indicating
that rulers of the world were destined to come out of Judaea. The
Messianic Zealot movement took over these forecasts for its own
purposes. But they were also applied to Vespasian and his sons.[27]
The Rabbi of Jerusalem Johanan ben Zakkai, who managed to
leave the besieged city and come to Vespasian, made pronouncements on similar lines.[28]

Josephus' piece of intelligent anticipation stood him in good
stead with Vespasian and Titus. He refers, in his later works, to his
utilisation of their official reports or commentaries,[29] and it is likely
enough that these were employed for the *Jewish War*. At all events
his many items of precise information about the military affairs of
the Romans evidently came from an official source. Not unnaturally,
he adopts Vespasian's interpretation of events against his enemy
Vitellius in the Year of the Four Emperors.[30] Then, when we come
to the Jewish War, Josephus has no criticisms to offer when Vespasian
ties men up and throws them into the Dead Sea alive as an experiment, or lures 38,000 Jews to the town of Tiberias to be sold as
slaves or butchered.

But he reserved the fullest resources of his adulation for Titus, who
employed him as interpreter and intermediary during the siege of

Jerusalem. Josephus depicts Titus as a paragon in every possible respect. This involves a good deal of special pleading, indeed lying. Not only is the most improbably pseudo-Jewish, monotheistic language put into Titus' mouth, but his alleged unwillingness to destroy the Temple appears to be quite untrue.[31] And Josephus' assertion that, in contrast to the savagery of the Jews towards each other, the Romans showed them clemency is contradicted by his own account.

While he remained at Caesarea Titus celebrated the birthday of his brother in the grand style, reserving much of his vengeance on the Jews for this notable occasion. The number of those who perished with wild beasts or in fighting each other or by being burnt alive exceeded 2,500. Yet all this seemed to the Romans, though their victims were dying a thousand different deaths, to be too light a penalty. . . . At Berytus [Beirut] vast numbers of prisoners perished in the same way as before.[32]

Josephus' indifference to this brutality need cause no surprise, because he himself was revoltingly cruel. When there was trouble at Tiberias, and a young man named Clitus became known as an extremist leader, Josephus had ordered both his hands to be cut off. But then, he flattered himself, he showed great generosity in permitting the youth to keep one of his hands, and allowing him to cut the other one off himself.[33] (In a later publication he inserts an improving address that he delivered to Clitus on this occasion.) So the savagery of Vespasian and Titus did not worry him. Indeed, Titus is invariably depicted as an irreproachable fairy prince.

And Titus reciprocated by associating himself with the favours which his father extended to the historian. He gave the *Jewish War* his imprimatur, and issued instructions that it should be published: 'So anxious was Titus that my volumes should be the sole authority from which the world should learn the facts, that he affixed his own signature to them and gave orders for their publication.'[34] Many Roman participants in the campaign received presentation copies of the *Jewish War*, but the first recipients were Vespasian and Titus.[35] Josephus also showed forethought by praising Titus' younger brother Domitian, who in due course, after he had succeeded Titus on the throne, awarded him further honours.[36]

Although the *Jewish War*, as it has come down to us, was detached from what would have been a larger work (p. 245), it nevertheless contains an introductory survey of more than two hundred years of Jewish history. Through this tangle Josephus, after the embarrassments of his own career, wends his way with some discretion, but also with a certain degree of frankness. For example the Hasmonaeans (Maccabees) might well have been adversely regarded as the prototypes of the rebels. Yet, being related to them by marriage, he finds it possible to speak of them with approval. Herod is treated unevenly, but at considerable length – proportionally far greater length than is devoted to later periods, because there was more written material about his career (p. 263). It was desirable, in this connection, not to say anything that would offend Herod's great-grandson Agrippa II whose domains bordered on Judaea. The goodwill of this prince was important to Josephus, because Agrippa was habitually treated as a spokesman of Jewish interests at the Roman court. Besides, his sister Berenice (with whom he was said to have an incestuous relationship) was for a long time the highly favoured mistress of Titus. She lived with him openly during her stay in Rome in 75, though he was more evasive when she paid a further visit to the capital four years later.

Agrippa, whose ancestors had been Idumaean converts, was eager to be regarded as a true Jew, and stood in particular need of such justification because the rebellion had seen him on the side of Rome. He must have been pleased with Josephus' desire to be helpful because he wrote the historian 'sixty-two letters testifying to the truth of the record'. In one of these letters, Agrippa remarked that he had read the book with great pleasure. 'You seem to me', he added, 'to have written with much greater care and accuracy than any who have dealt with the subject before. Send me the remaining volumes.' In another letter he offered what sounds like a more equivocal compliment: 'From what you have written you appear to stand in no need of instruction, to enable us all to learn everything from you from the beginning. But when you meet me, I will myself by word of mouth inform you of much that is not generally known.'[37] If that contains a veiled criticism, Josephus evidently did not notice it. He tells us that copies of the *Jewish War* went not only to Romans but to 'many of our own men who understood Greek learning, including the admirable King Agrippa'. Elsewhere he remarks, 'I sold copies to a large number of my compatriots'.[38] It is not known whether Agrippa got his copy free or not.

Examples have already been quoted to indicate how Josephus' various political preoccupations, as well as a relentless taste for self-praise, got in the way of telling a truthful story. Such instances could easily be multiplied. His villains are more than black, and his heroes are paste-board saints, very different from some of the flesh-and-blood personages of the antique Jewish historical tradition.

On factual matters he is variable. Though siege tactics are well described, his battles tend to be melodramatic set pieces of the kind that have so often been encountered in the pages of his Greco-Roman predecessors. Moreover, even when politics are not involved, Josephus is a great exaggerator, especially of figures and statistics. Mount Tabor is a plateau nearly two miles long, 1800 feet above the sea. In Josephus, these totals become three miles and 20,000 feet respectively.

He is also an inventor. It was traditional to fabricate speeches, but he does so with particular lavishness. The horrors of Jerusalem and Masada were no doubt dreadful enough to stand in no need of exaggeration. And yet his details still manage to have a conventional literary ring. Was it true that messengers covered themselves with sheepskins to look like dogs (p. 248)? Or that a missile hit a pregnant woman and shot her child out of her body for a hundred yards? Did a stone used as a projectile really knock a man's head off and fling it like a pebble more than six times that distance?

And yet to leave the matter there would be misleading. Josephus' numerous digressions, though often irrelevant except as background in the very widest sense, bear the stamp of personal and often accurate knowledge. Some of his topographical descriptions, for instance at Masada, have been confirmed by excavations. His account of the Temple at Jerusalem, too, even if it cannot be squared completely with archaeological conclusions, is both earlier and more reliable than any Hebrew authority.

Indeed Josephus is virtually our only source for a profoundly important chapter of history. He adds enormously to our information. Where his personal prestige was not involved and his taste for hyperbole not enlisted, he tells a knowledgeable, exact and comprehensive story, and tells it conscientiously and fascinatingly. Indeed, even his impregnable opinion of himself has an advantageous effect on his truthfulness, for it makes him confess freely to courses of action which a less complacent and more squeamish historian would have hesitated to record. Assisted by this powerful vein of frankness, which goes far to counterbalance his other aberrations, Josephus' narratives are, for the most part, both illuminating and reliable. They had to be, since they would be read by important people who had actually played a leading part in events. What he says about earlier writers of contemporary history applied to himself: 'it was impossible to depart from the truth without being detected'.

Undeterred by the shortcomings imposed by his own political necessities, he goes on to enlarge with some passion upon the conventional assurance that a historian has got to be truthful. 'I am determined to respect the truth of history, though it has been neglected by the Greeks. . . . To those who took part in the war or have ascertained the facts I have left no ground for complaint or criticism. It is for those who love the truth, not those who seek entertainment, that I have written.'[39] His stress on the search for truth is emphatic and repeated.

As we have seen, these assurances clash with blatant falsifications. Yet they are also to some extent warranted by his unusually workmanlike approach. Josephus' strongest card is the fact that he had participated himself. Like Thucydides and Xenophon and Polybius before him, he is able to claim the great advantage of having played a prominent role in so much of what happened. And like Polybius, he castigates those who write without ever having stirred from their own homes.

We have actually had so-called histories even of our recent war published by persons who never visited the sites nor were anywhere near the actions described, but, having put together a few hearsay reports, have, with the gross impudence of drunken revellers, miscalled their productions by the name of history. I, on the contrary, have written a veracious account, at once comprehensive and detailed, of the war, having been present in person at all the events. I was in command of those whom we call Galileans, so long as resistance was possible; after my capture I was a prisoner in the Roman camp. Vespasian and Titus, keeping me under surveillance, required my constant attendance upon them, at first in chains. Subsequently I was liberated and sent from Alexandria with Titus to the siege of Jerusalem.

During that time no incident escaped my knowledge. I kept a careful record of all that went on under my eyes in the Roman camp, and was alone in a position to understand the information brought by deserters....[40]

These unusual opportunities gave Josephus some justification for claiming that he not only sought to pursue the truth, but was able to produce something truly valuable in the process. 'The real worker is not the man who merely changes the order and arrangement of another man's work, but the one who has something new to say and constructs a historical edifice of his own. I myself have gone to great trouble and expense, though an alien. . . .'

And yet, because of the deep flaws in his personality, we find ourselves reluctant to believe what he says. But is this fair or right? 'Dislike of an author as a person,' as Moses Finley points out,

no matter how extreme, need not carry over to his work, at least not in the same measure. . . . Josephus was a good writer, sometimes almost a great one, after all. Even if his books are judged most harshly as accurate historical writing, they remain valid as testimonies. . . . Josephus has surely captured the tensions, the brutality, the religious fanaticism, and the intense horror of the war – he has that right even when his 'facts' are most fictitious and distorted. For obvious reasons, that particular struggle retains an interest, nearly two thousand years later, unique among the many wars fought by and against the Romans. And so Josephus had greatness thrust upon him.

Jerome saw him as the Greek Livy. That did both historians an injustice. The prejudices and distortions of Livy, though powerful, are less urgent and shocking than those of Josephus. But that is because Livy was a historian who stayed at home, whereas Josephus stood right in the middle of one of the most terrible wars of repression that the world has ever seen.

The much wider project of which the *Jewish War* was an offshoot (p. 245) took shape as his second major work (*c.* 93–4). It is known to us as the *Jewish Antiquities*, though he himself called it the *Archaeologia*.[41] This work is in fact a history of the Jewish race, right from the Creation up to AD 66, the year in which the rebellion began. Altogether this account had taken Josephus eighteen years to write. It fills twenty books of Greek – as long as the entire canon of the Jewish scriptures put together.

The first ten books more or less follow the Old Testament narrative. The story of Moses is given in Books II–IV, VII is devoted to David, and the three books that follow carry the story to the death of Ahab, the captivity of the Ten Tribes of Israel, and the conquest of Babylon and Assyria by the Persian king Cyrus (539). Then the next three-and-a-quarter centuries, down to the death of Judas Maccabaeus, are compressed into only two books. Books XIV and XV recount Pompey's sack of Jerusalem, Antipater's assistance to Caesar, and the rise of his son Herod. The next two books continue to dwell on the reign of Herod, which is described in much greater detail than had been devoted to it in the *Jewish War* (p. 257). Book XVIII opens with the conversion of Judaea into a Roman province, and the final pair of books describes the fortunes and policies of successive Roman governors, down to the fatal deterioration.

The *Jewish Antiquities* are dedicated to a certain Epaphroditus, perhaps identifiable with a learned Greek grammarian and freedman, Marcus Mettius Epaphroditus of Chaeronea, who possessed a library of 30,000 volumes and died in the later nineties. The *Antiquities* were a work of piety to the Jews. Even if Josephus had deserted their political cause, he did not feel himself a renegade. His main purpose, therefore, was to assert the antiquity of Israel, and its lofty religious and ethical standards, and its place among the nations. In the same spirit, for centuries, men had written in Greek to praise their own peoples, Mesopotamians, Egyptians and Romans (p. 169).[42] And so Josephus, too, following up certain earlier Jewish writers in Greek,[43] now sought 'to reconcile other people to us and to remove any reasons for that hatred which unreasonable men bear towards us. As for our customs, no nation observes the same practice as another; in nearly every city we encounter different ones. But Justice is a universally admired practice and adventageous to all men equally, whether Greek or barbarian. And for justice our laws have the greatest regard. These laws, therefore, if we observe them rightly, make us charitable and friendly towards all men. For this reason we have a right to expect similar treatment from others. . . .'[44]

And Josephus asserted the superior antiquity not only of the Jews themselves, but of their historiography. Although Hebrew writers had rarely, except in minor matters, attempted a secular approach, something could be said in favour of this claim. But there had not, hitherto, been any such continuous account available to the Greek-speaking neighbours of the Jews. That is what Josephus now sought to supply. Grounding the authenticity of the Hebrew tradition on the descent of the Biblical text through many centuries, he makes it his task to retell the Bible story. But he supplements it by numerous small deviations, due to alternative traditions or glosses derived from earlier Jewish historians[45] and theologians and Pharisaic scholars. Moreover, the Bible is patriotically doctored; awkward features such as the Golden Calf are omitted.

Roman opinion is also borne in mind. Although the *Antiquities* are less aggressively pro-Roman than the *Jewish War*, some adjustments have been made with an eye on possible Roman reactions. For example, Daniel, interpreting Nebuchadnezzar's dream, had spoken of the fourth kingdom of 'iron mixed with miry clay' – which would be destroyed by another monarchy. But Josephus prudently omits the point,[46] because this and similar stories were being currently echoed as prognostications of the fate of Rome.

His standard of Biblical interpretation is poor. So is his grasp of comparative religion. It is interesting, however, to see Greek doctrines of Fate and human responsibility blended with the Hebrew tradition of free will. Indeed, they are tacitly treated as part of Jewish doctrine.

We must indeed assume that man's actions are predetermined by some inevitable necessity, which we call Fate, because nothing is done without it. This view, however, should be weighed against the one which attributes events in part to ourselves and holds man reponsible for the conduct of their lives – which is the teaching of our ancient law. . . .[47]

In many such allusions to the Greek concepts of Fate, Fortune, and Nemesis, Josephus shows a paganised outlook. But there is little merit or accuracy in his comparisons between Jewish sects and Greek philosophical schools.[48] Serious efforts to give his religion an underpinning of Greek philosophy (notably by Philo Judaeus of Alexandria, who also described his mission to the emperor Caligula) made no impression on him. Nor, indeed, was his Judaism at all profound: in the *Jewish War* the Synagogue only obtains a single mention.[49] For Josephus as for many Romans, religion was all on the surface, a matter not of emotional excess but of accurate ceremonial. The lesson of history was that 'those who follow the will of God *and do not venture to break his excellent laws* are offered felicity for their reward'.[50]

The post-Biblical sections of the *Antiquities* form the most valuable part of the work, because they deal with many events that are elsewhere recorded inadequately or not at all. But they also contain a number of fabrications. Among these is a long, anachronistic story of an alleged visit to Jerusalem by Alexander the Great, presented as a supporter of Judaism and an enemy of the Samaritans, whom Josephus like other Jews deplored.[51] The two centuries preceding the Hasmonaeans are skimped, because there were no proper sources.[52] The treatment of Herod contains strange inconsistencies, and notable contradictions of what had been said in the *Jewish War*. These anomalies are based on the imperfect assimilation of two schools of thought, one comprising servile flattery of Herod and the other incorporating a hostile tradition. At times, Josephus still mirrors the eulogistic attitude, since he makes great use of a *Universal History* by Nicolaus of Damascus, who had been Herod's court-historian.[53] Yet, on other occasions, we find a more detached or even hostile point of view than had been apparent in the *Jewish War*. He also regrets the supersession of his kinsmen the Hasmonaeans by the family of Herod (p. 244).[54] Possibly a number of these more critical points date from a second edition of the *Antiquities*, published after the death of Herod's descendant Agrippa II.[55]

The work also contains references to Jesus Christ, John the Baptist and James the brother of Jesus.[56] Although these allusions have naturally attracted keen interest, they are disappointingly uninformative, considering that Josephus lived in the homeland of Christianity throughout its formative years. Besides, the remarks about Jesus, and probably portions of the other passages as well, do not in fact go back to Josephus at all, but are insertions by a later hand.

The *Antiquities* also allude to specifically Roman events. In particular, there is a long account of the murder of Caligula and the accession of Claudius (AD 41), events missing from our surviving texts of Tacitus. The character of the secretive Tiberius, too, is illustrated by many private talks, emotions, prayers and thoughts which Josephus either invented himself or derived from an over-imaginative Roman source.[57] It is also difficult to see how he can have known what King Monobazus of Adiabene did in the darkness with his sister-wife. 'As he was in bed with her one night he laid his hand upon his wife's belly and fell asleep, and seemed to hear a voice, which bade him take his hand off his wife's belly, and not to hurt the infant that was therein.'

Nevertheless, Josephus continued to profess a stern regard for the truth. He foreshadows Tacitus in his equal severity towards both types of imperial historian, the flattering sort 'who, as a result of being well-treated by Nero, neglected to tell the truth', and the opposite category 'who detested the emperors and, from sheer hatred, behaved so outrageously with their falsehoods that they deserve severe criticism' (p. 294).[58]

During the years between the *Jewish War* and the *Antiquities*, his life at Rome had not gone smoothly. In 73, on the occasion of a Jewish insurrection in Cyrene, a weaver there named Jonathan, one of many co-religionists who had a grudge against Josephus, denounced him to Vespasian as an instigator of this revolt. However, the historian was cleared by the intervention of Titus, and was even granted another estate in Judaea, while Jonathan was tortured and burnt alive. From time to time there followed other similar denunciations of Josephus, again brought forward by Jews alienated and shocked by his record. These attacks were all successfully warded off. Nevertheless, very soon after the publication of the *Antiquities*, or as an actual appendage, he decided to supplement it by a further work. This addition or epilogue, written in a somewhat unpolished style and apparently without the aid of helpers, is described as his *Life*, though it is not, in fact, a balanced autobiography since nearly nine-tenths of the contents consist of a defence of his conduct in Galilee in AD 67 which had led to his change of allegiance (p. 251).

Josephus makes it clear that there was a special reason why he felt the need to produce a new account of this phase of the war. It was because another writer had now published a version hostile to Josephus, evidently charging him with being partly responsible for the rebellion of 66–70. In the oppressive last years of Domitian (81–96), when these accusations were launched, they could be extremely perilous. Fortunately, Josephus had flattered Domitian and enrolled him among his patrons. But the emperor had become a very violent and suspicious man, and now that his father and elder brother, Josephus' principal protectors, were dead, it was particularly necessary to argue that he had really been on the Roman side from the very beginning.

The unfriendly book which caused him so much anxiety was the work of a certain Justus of Tiberias in Galilee. His emergence to undertake this task was particularly awkward because Justus, like Josephus, had actually been present at the events he was describing. During the period of Josephus' Galilean command Justus had acted as the leader, in his home-town, of a party which, although not extremist in tendency, brought him into acute collision with Josephus. The grudge had persisted. Justus' work, which was another *Jewish Antiquities* from Moses to his own day,[59] has not survived. But it was still extant in the ninth century, when it was known to Photius of Byzantium. He quoted a view that it was pure invention. Yet that idea may have originated from Josephus, and Justus evidently ranked with him as one of the leading Greco-Jewish historical authors.

Explaining the reasons for his own counterblast, Josephus claims that it is virtuous of him to write again 'while there are still living such as can either prove what I say to be false, or can attest that it is true'.[60] Yet the holocaust of leading Jews during and after the war – including the victims of the suicide pact from which Josephus had made his escape – meant that, in fact, there were very few survivors who were in a position to contradict anything that he said. So he must have felt that the survival of this isolated observer was really bad luck. Whether Justus was still alive when the refutation was published we do not know. At all events Josephus unleashed a torrent of abuse upon his head, calling him a spiteful ignorant liar on a par with people who were forgers of contracts – a nasty dig since Justus, after enjoying the protection of Agrippa II on charges of rebellion, had subsequently been dismissed by the monarch for forgery.

Josephus goes on to say that it was not himself but Justus who, as far as Tiberias was concerned, had fomented the revolt.

How then, Justus – if I may address him as though he were present – how, most clever of historians, as you boast yourself to be, can I and the Galilaeans be held responsible for the insurrection of your native city against the Romans and against King Agrippa, seeing that, before I was elected by the general assembly at Jerusalem to the command of Galilee, you and all the citizens of Tiberias had not only resorted to arms, but were actually at war with the towns of the Syrian Decapolis? It was you who burnt their villages. And your servant fell in the engagement on that occasion.[61]

Besides, he points out, Justus had lacked his own opportunities to discover the true facts – opportunities provided him by the Romans: 'The facts are recorded in the *Commentaries* of the Emperor Vespasian ... you were neither a combatant nor had you perused the *Commentaries* of [Titus] Caesar, as is abundantly proved by your contradictory account.' Whereas Josephus himself, on the other hand, in order to refute the calumnies of Justus, now claimed to be bringing forward hitherto unpublished information. Why then, people would ask, had he not produced this information before? The explanation, he says, lies in his sheer niceness of character.

Being therefore now compelled to defend myself against these false allegations, I shall allude to matters about which I have hitherto kept silent. My omission to make such a statement at an earlier date should not occasion surprise. For, while veracity is incumbent upon a historian, he is none the less at liberty to refrain from the harsh scrutiny of the misdeeds of individuals, not from any partiality for the offenders, but because of his own moderation.

In effect, what Josephus was now doing, at great length, was to explain that he had not really been an anti-Roman commander in Galilee at all. He had been sent by the Jerusalem Assembly (Sanhedrin) as one of three commissioners to pacify and disarm Jewish extremists. His mission was to wait and see what the Romans were going to do, keeping his arms in reserve against any emergency. Then, however, he was suspected of treachery by his fellow-Jews, and four commanders were actually sent to try to supersede him. This meant that he had to commit himself to an anti-Roman position, and was obliged to stand siege from Vespasian at Jotapata. Before that, as we are told with renewed emphasis, he had continually protested against the madness of the insurrection. And the wickedness of the arch-rebel John of Gischala is brought home to us in even more virulent terms than before.[62]

In one way Josephus' account of his Galilean command in the *Life* may be more accurate than what he had said in the *Jewish War*. For he is at least forced to abandon the role of the great general: since Justus had been there to see, or at least near enough to know. On the other hand, the *Life* is evidently disingenuous in its interpretation of the official duties that had been assigned to him in Galilee. It is probable enough that he had undertaken the job more or less under compulsion and that his execution of his functions was lukewarn even before he turned traitor. The appointment of a man with his sympathies showed that the Jewish authorities in power at that particular time were not very keen on the idea of a war against the Romans (p. 248). But the purpose of his command was surely to stave off and stop their invasion.

The *Life* was followed, perhaps almost immediately, by another work answering further attacks. This time they had been directed not against his personal conduct, but against his literary work, with the *Jewish Antiquities* as a particular target.[63] The hastily but skilfully written pamphlet which now emerged is known to us by the title *Against Apion*, because the second of its two books contains refutations of a long-dead Greco-Egyptian grammarian of that name. In the reign of Caligula (37–41), Apion had led a deputation from Alexandria to Rome to protest against the Jews. He had also published anti-Semitic writings which circulated widely at Rome; and Josephus is happy to report that he came to a miserable end.[64] Manuscripts call the work 'Concerning the Antiquities of the Jews: against Apion', but the Alexandrian theologian Origen gave it the shorter name *Concerning the Antiquities of the Jews*.[65] This is a more appropriate title, since the critics (now lost) whom Josephus is rebutting evidently included some who were a good deal more recent than Apion. For the wide range of unfriendly writers whom he sets out to contradict not only went back to Egyptians of earliest Alexandria,[66] but included 'authors of scurrilous and mendacious statements' who were evidently his contemporaries.

This most famous of all justifications of Judaism, constituting a passionate expression of pride in Josephus' ancestry and beliefs, seems to be directed towards Jews of the Dispersion (rather than Palestinian Jewry) whose faith, subjected to the hostile barrages of Apion and his like, might become lukewarm. His arguments bring the controversy up to date by refuting current charges of anti-social, unpatriotic behaviour. But the main purpose of the work is to emphasis the timeless, universal validity of the Hebrew moral and legal codes.[67] Particular stress, too, is laid on the venerable antiquity of Judaism, in comparison with the Greeks. It is also pointed out that a direct consequence of this antiquity is the greater seniority of Jewish historical writings (p. 11).

My first thought is one of intense astonishment at the current opinion that, in the study of primeval history, the Greek alone deserve serious attention, that the truth should be sought from them, and that neither we nor any others in the world are to be trusted. In my view the very reverse of this is the case. . . .

In the Greek world everything will be found to be modern and dating, so to speak, from yesterday or the day before. Surely, then, it is absurd that the Greeks should be so conceited as to think themselves the sole possessors of a knowledge of antiquity and the only accurate reporters of its history. . . . While, then, for eloquence and literary ability we must yield the palm to the Greek historians, we have no reason to do so for veracity in the history of antiquity, least of all where the particular history of each separate foreign nation is concerned. . . . Our records contain the names of our high priests, with the succession from father to son, for the last two thousand years. . . .

We have given practical proof of our reverence for our own Scriptures. For, although such long ages have now passed, no one has ventured either to add, to to remove, or to alter a syllable. And it is an instinct with every Jew, from the day of his birth, to regard them as the decrees of God, to abide by them and if need be, cheerfully to die for them. Time and again ere now the sight has been witnessed of prisoners enduring tortures and death in every form in the theatres, rather than utter a single word against the Laws and allied documents.

What Greek would endure as much for the same cause?[68]

6

Tacitus

16

Tacitus and the Empire

THE three emperors of the Flavian dynasty who helped Josephus were also those who gave his younger contemporary, Tacitus, an official career. Cornelius Tacitus was born in AD *c*. 56–7. We know little or nothing of his origins. Indeed, it is not even known whether the first of his three names was Publius or Gaius. His family may have come from the south of France – perhaps from Vasio (Vaison),[1] or from his father-in-law's home-town Forum Julii (Fréjus). It is also possible that they originated from northern Italy (Cisalpine Gaul). Tacitus' father *may* have been an imperial agent (procurator) of that name at Augusta Treverorum (Trier) or Colonia Agrippina (Cologne),[2] and paymaster-general for the armies on the Rhine. But again we do not know for certain. At all events the historian was a member of that upper class from the western provinces which found new prospects opening under the imperial régime.

When the death of Nero was followed by the bloodstained year of the Four Emperors (69),* Tacitus was only a boy. 'I have no wish to deny', he said, 'that my career owed its beginning to Vespasian [69–79], its progress to Titus [79–81] and its further advancement to Domitian [81–96].'[3] Under Vespasian he held the junior office of quaestor and probably served as a legionary officer in one of the

---

* Galba, Otho, Vitellius, Vespasian.

provinces (?*c.* 76). But the greater part of his c ~rial career took place under Domitian, when he became praetor an .nember of a priestly board (88). Moreover, like almost all other contemporaries of his rank, he probably commanded a legion at some time. This may have happened in 89–93, since he tells us he was absent from Rome for four years at that stage.

Josephus was another who had been favoured by Domitian, though he may have become anxious about that emperor's attitude. On Tacitus the black last years of the reign, a period of unhappiness and terror for high officials, exercised a traumatic effect. Yet he survived to enjoy the consulship in 97, during the brief reign of Nerva (96–8); he may already have been destined for the post by Domitian. And then, finally, under Trajan (98–117), he held the governorship of the greatest of Roman provinces, Asia (western Asia Minor), the climax of a senator's career. Probably he lived on into Hadrian's principate that followed (p. 450, n. 7).

Yet his life under Domitian, a life of promotions but harrowing anxieties, was what remained most firmly fixed in his mind and heart. His earliest historical essay illuminates important aspects of the reign. This was a Life of his father-in-law Cnaeus Julius Agricola of Forum Julii (AD 40–93). Published in AD 98, the work opens with references to the perils of biographical writing during the tyranny of Domitian. And indeed, adds Tacitus gloomily, even in the happier times of Nerva and Trajan there still lingers on a certain hostility towards good men. The main section begins with an account of Agricola's parentage and early life, leading up to his appointment as governor of Britain (77/8). Next comes a long digression giving an account of that country and a sketch of its relations with Rome up to the time of Agricola's arrival. Mention is made of the reconnaissances of Julius Caesar (p. 182), the conquest of the southern part of the country by Claudius (43–8), and the rebellion of Boudicca or Boadicea (60). Then follows a description of Agricola's successful campaigns, culminating in the defeat of the Caledonians (Scots) at the unidentifiable site of Mons Graupius (83/4). There is also a reference to the circumnavigation of north Scotland by the Roman fleet. The next part of the biography tells of Agricola's recall by the suspicious Domitian, followed by retirement and death. The epilogue sums up his career and high character, and expresses satisfaction that he was spared the sight of Domitian's worst atrocities.

A little more than a decade after the appearance of the *Agricola*, Tacitus brought out his first major publication, the *Histories* (*c.* 109). It had already been talked about for several years,[4] during which selected passages were recited and the earlier portions may have been published separately.[5] The work has no manuscript title and we do not know its original name. Consisting perhaps of twelve books, it covered the period of Tacitus' youth and early maturity, from the Year of the Four Emperors to the death of Domitian.

The first four books and part of the fifth are all that survive. Book I indicates the situation at the death of Nero (68) and describes the early part of the following year, including the death of Galba, the accession of Otho and the movement of Vitellius' generals from the Rhine towards Italy. The second book indicates the presence in Syria of the fourth contestant, Vespasian, and then describes the defeat of Otho by the Vitellians at the first battle of Bedriacum (near Cremona in north Italy) and his subsequent suicide (April 69). While Vespasian declared himself emperor, Vitellius arrived south of the Alps and then proceeded to Rome. The third book tells of the second battle of Bedriacum in October, at which Vespasian's general Primus defeated the Vitellians. Primus then marched on the capital, and Vitellius was put to death (December 69). Book IV, after noting the confusion that prevailed in the Senate, gives an account of a revolt on the northern frontier by Civilis, a Batavian (German) who was supported by Gallic tribes. Mention is also made of omens announcing the imperial destiny of Vespasian (p. 255). The portion of the fifth book that is still extant gives a brief account of the Jews, whose rebellion Vespasian and his son Titus had crushed, and describes the suppression of Civilis' revolt by the Roman general Cerialis (70).

The contents of the lost remainder of the work are still, to some extent, conjectural. Books V and VI probably brought the story down to Vespasian's death (69), thus completing a group of six books (hexad) – which falls into halves, comprising the civil war and the reign of Vespasian respectively. The second hexad can then be regarded as having covered the reigns of Titus and Domitian (VIII–XII). This section, too, may well have been divided into halves, the first recounting the sound internal situation left by Vespasian and the peaceful successions of his sons, and perhaps proceeding as far as Domitian's wars on the Danube (88), and the second describing the subsequent military failures. These were followed by the series of purges which continued for the rest of his life and must have formed highlights of Tacitus' account.

His last and greatest masterpiece, the *Annals*, was published shortly before or after the death of Trajan (117). An alleged reference to events of 116 could, in fact, have been written earlier.[6] But it is probable, though not quite certain, that there are allusions to the principate of Hadrian.[7]

For his subject-matter, Tacitus chose to go back to the years that had preceded the events narrated in the *Histories*. For it was at that earlier time, under the successors of Augustus, that he detected the origins of the evils he himself had experienced. The *Annals* described events from the beginning of Tiberius' reign (AD 14) to a point in 68, soon after the death of Nero, the last emperor of Augustus' dynasty. Tacitus himself seems to have called his work ' From the Death of the Divine Augustus'. Of the eighteen books which it apparently contained, we have most of I–IV and XI–XVI: parts of V, XI and XVI are missing. The extant account ends at 66. It is likely that the work was divided into three main sections, each consisting of six books, as in the *Histories*.

The first of these hexads covered the reign of Tiberius (AD 14–37), dividing it in two equal parts. The latter section, when the emperor had displayed his true colours (p. 286), displays a more mournful picture than the former. Book I opens with a sketch of previous Roman history, and a summary of Augustus' reign, including a survey of people's opinions about the future. The remaining portion of the book, although (as always) chronicling a wide variety of events occurring in each year, is mostly concerned with mutinies on the northern frontiers and the first German campaigns of Tiberius' popular nephew and adopted son Germanicus (AD 15). Book II continues the account of these wars until Germanicus' transfer to the east and his death at Antioch (19), followed in the next book by the trial and suicide of Cnaeus Piso who had been his opponent and was suspected of having murdered him. A serious rebellion took place in Gaul (21). The fourth book refers to the sinister ascendancy of Tiberius' chief minister Sejanus and the outbreak of the first treason trials, while the fifth tells of the death of the emperor's mother Livia (29). Sejanus' downfall and death (31) are missing. Book VI recounts the aftermath, and goes on to emphasise the glumness and debauchery of Tiberius, who was now in retirement at Capreae (Capri). We are then told of the unhappy ends of other imperial personages, followed by the death of the emperor himself.

The second hexad, of which the greater part is lost, is likely to have comprised two books on the eccentric reign of Caligula (37–41), and four about Claudius (41–54), with emphasis, no doubt, on the strange and ludicrous circumstances of his accession. Probably the missing portions also noted a subsequent deterioration of Claudius' conduct (from *c.* 49), like the earlier decline of Tiberius. The surviving part of Book XI describes the excesses and downfall of the emperor's wife Messalina (47–8). The twelfth book, which includes the events of six years, tells how he married Nero's mother Agrippina, and was poisoned by her agent.

The third section of the *Annals* covers the reign of Nero (54–68), another emperor whose behaviour decisively worsens. The thirteenth book indicates the weakening of Agrippina's influence, and Nero's murder of his step-brother Britannicus (55). The historian then passes on to the campaigns of Corbulo in the east (58). The highlights of XIV are the assassination of Agrippina by her son, his public exhibitions as a charioteer, the revolt of Boudicca in Britain (61), and the initiation of a reign of terror including the murder of Claudius' daughter Octavia. She was succeeded as Nero's wife by Poppaea. The fifteenth book resumes the account of Corbulo's eastern campaigns and describes the Great Fire of Rome (64) – for which Nero blamed the Christians – and the conspiracy of Gaius Piso against the emperor in the following year. In Book XVI a series of persecutions leads up to the death of the Roman senators who led the Republican, philosophical opposition to the régime, Thrasea Paetus and Barea Soranus (66).

With the suicide of Thrasea the *Annals* break off. The missing part of the sixteenth book, and the two books which followed, must have dealt with the further casualties from Nero's increasing savagery. Then they presumably described his tour of Greece, the Jewish rebellion which was the subject of Josephus, and the revolts of Vindex and Galba which caused Nero's death. The *Annals* may have ended at that point. But more probably they continued until a later month of the year 68, when Galba's short-lived administration was almost at once threatened by Nymphidius Sabinus, the commander of his guard.

Tacitus also wrote two other works which are of interest to historians, though not primarily of a historical character. After receiving an elaborate rhetorical education, he had started life by embarking on a successful and famous career as orator, recorded by his literary friend Pliny the younger.[8] None of Tacitus' speeches have come down to us, but one of his writings – if, as is highly probable, its ascription to Tacitus' authorship is correct[9] – deals explicitly with the subject. This is the *Dialogue on Orators*. Four historical characters, two lawyers and two literary men, are discussing the claims of oratory against other branches of literature, and considering the reasons why eloquence had deteriorated since Cicero's death. One reason indicated for the decline was that this sort of impassioned disputation had much less part to play under emperors than amid the clashes of the outgoing Republic. The *Dialogue* claims to be reporting a discussion that took place in about AD 75. But it is dedicated to Lucius Fabius Justus (not Josephus' enemy Justus), who was consul in 102, and the treatise was probably published during his consulship or not very long afterwards. It is relevant to the historical works of Tacitus, since they too display his life-long interest in oratory (p. 292).

Four years before the consulship of Justus, Tacitus had written another monograph which likewise, though in a different way, led up to his major historical compositions. It was a geographical and ethnographical study, *On the Origin, Geography, Institutions and Tribes of the Germans*, generally known as the *Germania*.[10] This survey of the peoples of central Europe seems to contain traditional moral contrasts, or implied contrasts, between the decadence of Rome and the crude vigour of the teeming peoples beyond the Rhine, idle and drunken though they were.[11]

Writing at a time when Trajan, in the year of his accession, was occupied in major military operations against the Germans, Tacitus sees them, despite their relative lack of organisation, as a grave potential threat to Rome, even graver than the Parthians in the east.[12] This estimate was no doubt intended as a tribute to the importance of Trajan's campaigns. But it was also prophetic. Less than seventy years later it began to be clear to everyone that the Germans were the greatest of all external menaces to the security of the Empire.

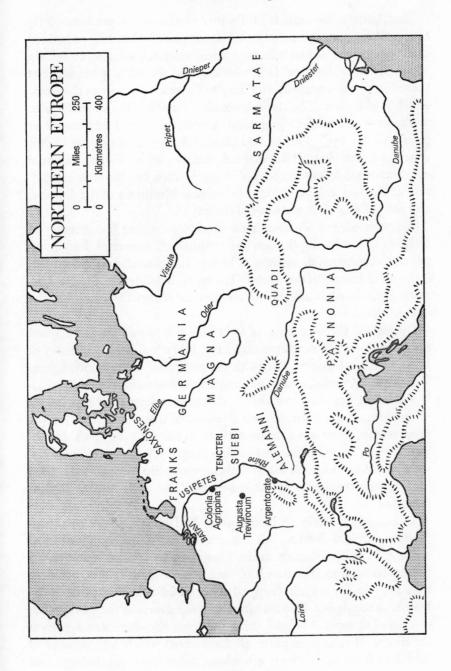

The *Agricola*, the earliest of Tacitus' works with a predominantly historical content, appeared in the same year.[13] This, too, contained much geographical and ethnographical material, relating to Britain where Agricola, Tacitus' father-in-law, had served as governor. But these descriptions are only auxiliary to the main purpose of the work, which is eulogistic. The *Agricola* recalls a familiar Greek and Roman tradition – the semi-biographical, oratorical, moral encomium or panegyric (p. 133). Tacitus had himself delivered an oration of that type at a funeral in 97.[14] But in the *Agricola* he endows the conventional exhortations to follow a model of virtue[15] with a flexible artistic structure of his own, taking account of the new conditions of the Empire, and the political circumstances of the day.

Every oratorical resource is devoted to attacking the memory of Domitian, and by implication the attitude and career of Trajan are praised. A substantial amount of history is included, and indeed this is the main feature of the work.[16] The trend is deliberate, for the *Agricola* is announced as a first instalment of the *Histories*,[17] which was the next work to come.

During the three-quarters of a century and more that had elapsed since the deaths of Augustus and Livy, there had been a number of Latin historical writers. But, with the exception of the minor figures Velleius and Curtius, almost nothing they wrote has survived (p. 294). It is possible, however, to conclude that the suspicions and oppressions of emperors had inhibited their freedom of utterance. And, for the same reason, there was a brain-drain from history to fashionable subjects such as the description of foreign peoples. Nevertheless, between them, these historians of the first century AD must have added a good deal to the traditions of subject-matter and style which Tacitus inherited.

In his major works he incorporates and blends, in his own profoundly original fashion, all the traditional features of historical writing. First, the Roman strain, illustrated by a basic year-by-year presentation, with the consuls of each year named. It is no accident that his climactic work dropped its original title and came to be known as the *Annals*. Tacitus himself, in the course of the work, refers to it by that word,[18] besides using the term elsewhere as a synonym for history. He also exemplifies all the interests which the Romans had inherited from the Greeks: ethnology, biography, psychology, and rhetorical types and situations. His battle-scenes all too often come into this last category, because, according to traditional practice, they frequently create more factual problems than they solve. There is also a continuous exploitation of emotional effects, aiming at pathos and emphasising the tragic and terrible character of events.

Ethical purpose is likewise never absent from Tacitus' mind. The sequence of events on which he chooses to focus his attention provoked the sternest moral reflections. To him, as to Sallust and Livy and many others, disaster seemed due to vice: and he saw it embodied in the history he was recording. Although, sometimes, the picture is over-laid by a tendency to fatalism (p. 303), good and evil are persistently emphasised and contrasted, in conventional sentiments endowed with striking turns of phrase. 'It is from such studies – from the experience of others – that most men learn to distinguish right and wrong, advantage and disadvantage. Few can tell them apart instinctively.'[19] And so it is 'a historian's foremost duty to ensure that merit is recorded, and to confront wicked deeds and words with the fear of posterity's denunciations'.[20]

That had been the tendency of ancient historical writing for centuries past, and it corresponded with the predilection of Tacitus' own mind. It gave him, like his predecessors, a lofty conception of his task, and made him regard history as an elevated and exalted activity. He is aware that the evil in what he has to record outweighs the good; and he sees that this makes for a grimness which earlier historians, with all their exciting battles and heroic deaths in the field, had been in a position to avoid. He himself, too, in the *Histories*, had been able to strike a more stirring note, though the battles he described there were hateful because they were fought by Roman against Roman.

Even the home affairs earlier historians had been called upon to discuss were more glorious than those which he now had to deal with.[21] Moreover, these metropolitan events have to loom more largely in his account than theirs; and he finds them circumscribed and depressing. All the same, his concentration on happenings at Rome derives from a deliberate choice. For Tacitus remains heir to the traditional, centripetal view of Roman history. The very first words of his *Annals* are 'the city of Rome'. For the city was still the seat of political power; and politics is his subject. Although he includes much social material and is well aware of the economic factor, Tacitus is primarily a historian of Roman politics.

This imposes a limitation on his handling of provincial affairs. He does not, for example, concern himself very seriously with exotic phenomena such as the Jews and Christians, who are both described in the most inadequate fashion.[22] And yet the provinces are by no means ignored. The *Histories* is largely staged outside the capital, and so is one-third of the *Annals*. For example, the province of Asia, where Tacitus had been governor, is an area in which he often shows an interest. His inadequate picture of other important territories, such as Spain, may well have been remedied, to some extent, in the parts of his work that have not come down to us.[23] The *Agricola* has much to say about Britain: 'I would add but a single word, that nowhere has the sea more influence. It gives to many of the rivers a tidal character. Nor merely do the incoming tides wash the shores and ebb again, but penetrate the land deeply and invest it, and even steal into the heart of hills and mountains as though into their native element.'[24] In the *Germania*, this sort of ethnographical material had, of course, predominated, and the *Histories* and *Annals* continued to show a special concern for the northern frontier, which Tacitus regarded as vitally important (p. 276) and evidently knew personally. Though sometimes out of date with his information, he felt obliged to complain of the neglect of this area by Greek historians.[25]

Gaul and Germany, where there were dangerous risings in AD 70, provide him with the opportunity to give a balanced verdict on Roman imperialism. Its debit side is remorselessly listed by the rebel leader Civilis.

The levy was by its nature a heavy burden, but it was rendered still more oppressive by the greed and profligacy of the recruiting sergeants who called up the old and unfit in order to exact a bribe for their release, while young, goodlooking lads – for children are normally quite tall among the Batavians – were dragged off to gratify their lust. . . . Civilis catalogued the wrongs, the depredations and the other ills of slavery. . . . The Batavians were at the mercy of prefects and centurions who, when glutted with spoil and blood, were replaced by others looking for fresh pockets to pick and new labels for plunder.[26]

On the other hand the Roman general Cerialis points out the advantages of the Empire to its subjects.

Throughout the whole of Gaul there were always despots and wars until you passed under our control. We ourselves, despite many provocations, imposed upon you by right of conquest only such additional burdens as were necessary for preserving peace. Stability between nations cannot be maintained without armies, nor armies without pay, nor pay without taxation. Everything else is shared equally between us.[27]

With a favourable eye on the current aggressive policy of Trajan, Tacitus blamed Tiberius for adhering to the policy of non-expansion that had been the final advice of Augustus. But when the historian adopts this attitude he is considering the advantage not of the provinces but of Rome. As usual, he sees the matter from the point of view of the capital. The emperor into whose reign he may briefly have lived, Hadrian (AD 117–38), was to develop the idea of a Roman Commonwealth in which the provinces enjoyed a proud role as constituent parts, anticipatory of a gradual process of decentralisation and foreshadowing also the nation states which were to develop four centuries later. Tacitus, however, may well be implying a criticism of this sort of conception, if not in direct relation to the policies of Hadrian, at least because such ideas were in the air.

It is upon the capital, then, that the lurid spotlight is generally directed. When we read of the faults or fate of an occasional visitor or governor in the provinces, Rome is always in mind. And Tacitus, thinking of Rome, thinks of its emperor. Indeed the provinces, too, are mainly seen as parts of the immense structure which conferred on its ruler the heaviest responsibility that any man has ever had to bear, with the possible exception of modern presidents of the United States. Since, therefore, the emperor was all-important, the highest and most meaningful drama centred on the glamorous, sinister imperial court. The traditional framework of Roman year-by-year narration is used for an incisive analysis of this new sort of absolute power. The point that the emperor, in the end, decided everything is made incessantly. It is emphasised at the very outset of the *Annals* in a brief recapitulation of the reign of Augustus. 'He gradually pushed ahead and absorbed the functions of the senate, the officials and even the law. Opposition did not exist. War or judicial murder had disposed of all men of spirit. Upper-class survivors found that slavish obedience was the way to succeed, both politically and financially.'[28]

Yet the autocracy of Augustus was nothing to the ruthless despotism that followed. This had a thousand ramifications. For instance, there was an end to free speech. Tacitus politely claimed that his own happier age had reversed this tendency (p. 298), but his claim does not carry complete conviction, since the resources of imperial propaganda were, and remained all-pervasive. Even as far back as Augustus, its pronouncements had been thoroughly disingenuous. The impressiveness of his Republican façade had only meant that the slave-state, which was to grow out of this régime, would be all the more loathsome.[29]

Here again is Sallust's favourite credibility gap, the contrast between promise and performance. This time it is applied to the new dilemma between liberty and adulation. But, in any case, was there a need for free speech any longer? As the *Dialogue on Orators* had suggested, 'what is the use of one harangue after another on public platforms, when it is not the ignorant multitude that decides a political issue, but a monarch who is the incarnation of wisdom?' (p. 276).[30]

Wisdom; or the contrary. For rule by one man, though it may well have become inevitable (p. 295), was utterly hazardous. Tacitus' temperament and knowledge of affairs make him aware that any person is, and always has been, unreliable. This is as true of an emperor as of anyone else. Now, therefore, that the State is unified under an omnipotent ruler, human happiness hangs by a thread. When the emperor is a bad man, and rules badly, there is misery. Oppressive rule comes from the moral degeneracy of the ruled who have lacked the capacity to assert their claim to a better system. And then the oppression resulting from their incapacity causes the degenerative process to proliferate further. Tacitus continually reiterates a series of interlocked themes to illustrate the insidious increase of oppression and degeneration alike.

He may hope, against his better judgment, for a ruler who will not be too rapidly spoiled by power.[31] Yet it seems that he is not really able to believe that an autocrat *can* be good. For he constantly stresses the evils of rule by one man. This conviction is the central point of his philosophy. It seems to him, as it seemed to the nineteenth-century historian Lord Acton, that no man's character, however strong, can stand up against the corrupting effects of absolute authority. Tiberius, a Roman nobleman is quoted as saying, was a man of great experience, and yet even he had been transformed and deranged by autocratic power[32] – or rather, as Tacitus himself preferred to think, autocratic power had caused the latent flaws of his personality to emerge (p. 286). Consequently it was under Tiberius that freedom suffered some of its most damaging losses, including a fatal succession of treason trials.[33] That is why Tiberius is the dominant figure in the *Annals*.

17

Tacitus and the Emperors

IN dealing with his overwhelmingly weighty theme, Tacitus claims he is unmoved by indignation or partisanship, since 'partiality and hatred towards any man are equally inappropriate in a writer who claims to be honest and reliable'.[1] Moreover, in his own case 'the customary incentives to these biases are lacking'.[2] Such protestations were conventional, though Tacitus, as so often, expresses such well-worn material in vivid personal terms. Indeed, his words reflect sincere feeling, for after reading his work it is impossible not to believe that he meant what he said. Yet he deceived himself. In particular, his gradually constructed estimate of the emperor Tiberius (AD 14–37)[3] the most famous and detailed of the character-studies which abound in the work, by no means seems to us free from indignation and partisanship.

Tiberius had died nearly eighty years before Tacitus wrote about him. Even looked at in isolation, without reference to what happened afterwards, the events of the reign could be interpreted as indicating a significant advance towards complete autocracy (p. 282). But the venomous attitude of Tacitus also reflects the fact that he himself, at the time when he was creating the picture of Tiberius, had lived through the régime of Domitian (AD 81–96). For here was another sombre tyrant whose oppression of senators, especially during his last three years, was more terrifying still. Under Domitian,

The Mediterranean swarmed with exiles and its rocky islets ran with blood. The reign of terror was particularly ruthless at Rome. Rank, wealth and office, whether surrendered or retained, provided grounds for accusation, and the reward for virtue was inevitable death. The profits made by the prosecutors were no less odious than their crimes. Some helped themselves to priesthoods and consulships as the prize of victory. Others acquired official posts and backstairs influence, creating a universal pandemonium of hatred and terror. Slaves were suborned to speak against their masters, freedmen against their patrons, while those who had not an enemy in the world were ruined by their friends.[4]

The mental disturbance that the memory of those harrowing times caused Tacitus was all the worse because his own promotions under Domitian were evidently on his conscience.

Assuredly we have furnished a signal proof of our submissiveness; and even as former generations witnessed the utmost excesses of liberty, so have we witnessed the extremes of slavery; wherein our inquisitors have deprived us even of the give and take of conversation. We should have lost memory itself as well as voice, had forgetfulness been as easy as silence.[5]

He is writing these words in painful recollection of his own tenure of the praetor's high office during Domitian's reign (88). And not only did he accept that post, in addition to a priesthood in the same year, but he was also in the capital during the exceptionally disagreeable final years of the reign. It may even have been Domitian who nominated him to the consulship which he held during the brief principate of Nerva that followed (p. 272). Nor, afterwards, could he claim that he had taken part in the final, successful plot against Domitian, or, for that matter, in earlier conspiracies either.[6] Worst of all, while Domitian was striking leading men down it must have been difficult or impossible for someone of Tacitus' high rank not to acquiesce in purges that fell on people very close to himself.

Consequently, he remained obsessed by the real or imaginary Domitians of past history. Domitian had expressed admiration of his imperial predecessor Tiberius, showing that the analogy came readily to mind. The treason trials of Domitian could be held to have originated in Tiberius' trials; and Tacitus came to form the opinion that Domitianic evils in general had their roots in the time of Tiberius. In fact, however, Tiberius' senators had been far less servile and oppressed than those of Domitian. Nowadays it seems to us that Tiberius was a gloomy but honest ruler – a man who owed many of the tragedies of his reign to an inability to conduct personal and public relations. Tacitus' study, says A.H. McDonald, 'exaggerates a mixture of genuine hesitation and conventional reluctance'. Augustus, in erecting his elaborate oligarchic fictions, had shown far greater dexterity. Indeed, his success depended very largely on the delicate manipulation of people, individually and in the mass. The morose Tiberius lacked this light touch. The task of making a success of his relations with other people was not one that he tackled with any keenness. He was either too difficult or too honest.

Yet Tacitus regards him as anything but honest. His family, the Claudii, had a sinister, tyrannical reputation in the eyes of senatorial historians (p. 232). Tiberius, admittedly, might not seem quite to fit into this picture. But that, according to Tacitus, was because of his profound hypocrisy: 'What he said, even when he did not aim at concealment, was – by habit or nature – always hesitant, always cryptic. And now that he was determined to show no sign of his real feelings, his words become more and more equivocal and obscure.'[7] Vigilant as ever to note the discrepancies between fact and impression, Tacitus does not cease to stress the duplicities and concealments of the complex, saturnine Tiberius. In a series of malevolent assessments, this dissimulation is one of the factors that makes him look like a stock tyrant of ancient tragedy – the sort of cunning, ruthless, suspicious, sensual figure, dependent on evil advisers, who had probably figured in the lost poetic tragedies of the Roman Republic, and reappeared in the plays of Seneca the younger (d. AD 65), from whom Tacitus adapted a large element of melodrama (p. 293). To the indignation of most modern historians, Tiberius' mother also, the empress Livia, emerges as a fearful intriguer and multiple murderess with an itch to dominate, 'a catastrophe to the nation as a mother and to the house of the Caesars as a step-mother'.[8] Sallust had shown that female personalities were worth studying, and Tacitus pursued the idea on a formidable scale. Consider, for example, his enquiry into why Tiberius spent the last eleven years of his life at Capreae. Was this because of his sinister adviser Sejanus? Or was it for some other reason? Was it, perhaps, because of Livia?

Like most historians, I attribute his withdrawal to Sejanus' intrigues. Yet since he maintained this seclusion for six years after Sejanus' execution [AD 31], I often wonder whether it was not really caused by a desire to hide the cruelty and immorality which his actions made all too conspicuous. It was said that in old age he became sensitive about his appearance. Tall and abnormally thin, bent and bald, he had a face covered with sores and often plaster. His retirement at Rhodes had accustomed him to unsociability and secretive pleasures.

According to another theory he was driven away by his mother's bullying. To share control with her seemed intolerable, to dislodge her impracticable – since that control had been given him by her. For Augustus had considered awarding the empire to his universally loved grand-nephew Germanicus. But his wife had induced him to adopt Tiberius instead. The Augusta [Livia] harped accusingly on this obligation. And she exacted repayment.[9]

Here it has proved possible to denigrate Livia along with her son, killing two birds with one stone. In order to destroy both their reputations more effectively still, their young, attractive kinsman Germanicus (d. AD 19) is portrayed as a brilliant princely paragon who can do no wrong. The picture is rather dull, because that is what Tacitus, despite himself, found good men to be. Germanicus' war in Germany, intended like his character to reflect the reigning monarch Trajan, is depicted in glowing colours which almost conceal the expensive uselessness of the operations.

It was a tradition of ancient biography and psychology that people's inborn characters remain with them unchanged, and that, if there does seem to be a change, it is only a revelation of pre-existing but hitherto latent features (p. 318). Consequently the fact that Tiberius seemed better at first, and then apparently deteriorated, is regarded by Tacitus as deceptive. It merely suggests to him that, whereas the emperor's nature was fundamentally vicious, this only became evident by degrees.

His character had its different stages. While he was a private citizen or holding commands under Augustus, his life was blameless; and so was his reputation. While Germanicus and Drusus still lived, he concealed his real self, cunningly affecting virtuous qualities. However, until his mother died there was good in Tiberius as well as evil. Again, as long as he favoured (or feared) Sejanus, the cruelty of Tiberius was detested, but his perversions unrevealed. Then fear vanished, and with it shame. Thereafter he expressed only his own personality – by unrestrained crime and infamy.[10]

One school of thought maintained that Tiberius was corrupted by power (p. 282). Tacitus was tempted by the view. Nevertheless, on the whole, he still preferred to maintain that the emperor had always been corrupt, but that it was absolute power, with no one to check him, which made the full horrors of his personality come out into the open.

The characters of very powerful people, who ruled the world, provided the themes on which Tacitus wished to concentrate. And every resource at his disposal is devoted to painting this picture of Tiberius. One of his favourite devices is the damning 'aside'. He also utilises every possible sort of hint to imply the worst. Sometimes these innuendoes assume far-fetched forms. Tiberius' refusal of excessive adulation, one would have thought, was a good thing – especially in the eyes of Tacitus. But no: although, as often, the opinions are attributed not to the historian himself but to the man in the street: 'Even in private conversation, Tiberius persisted in rejecting such veneration. Some attributed this to modesty, but most people thought it was uneasiness. It was also ascribed to degeneracy, on the grounds that the best men aimed highest. . . .'[11] The same damaging effect is also achieved by the apparently innocuous method of quoting various explanations of an event, and then *denying* the worst of them. For example, Tiberius' son Drusus the younger showed an embarrassingly sadistic excess of enthusiasm for gladiatorial shows.

Drusus was abnormally fond of bloodshed. . . . Tiberius himself kept away. Various reasons were given – his dislike of crowds, or his natural glumness, or unwillingness to be compared with Augustus, who had cheerfully attended. It was also suggested, though I would scarcely believe it, that he deliberately gave his son a chance to show his forbidding character – and win unpopularity.[12]

'Motives are complex,' says Kenneth Wellesley. 'Will it not be better, where so much is dark, to leave the reader to ponder?' Yet perhaps there is no smoke without fire, and somehow or other, despite the denials, the possibility that Tiberius may have acted from these malevolent motives has been implanted in our minds. The technique recurs when Drusus dies and Tacitus explains that we must not accept the rumour that Tiberius murdered him. If the historian had refrained from mentioning that such a rumour was going round, we should not have thought of accepting it. Indeed, we should never have heard of its existence.

On many other occasions, Tacitus shows obvious sympathy with the nastiest suspicions and accusations against Tiberius. Yet the strangest feature of all his work is the frequent contrast between this hostile attitude and the known facts – facts which he himself openly records. These, often enough, are stated quite objectively, without any bias against the emperor. And so they continually clash with the unpleasant appended interpretations, which, even according to Tacitus' own version of events, they totally fail to justify. Exploiting his rhetorical training and talent, he behaves, perhaps unconsciously, like a lawyer conducting a case against a man who has all the evidence in his favour. These discrepancies are particularly noteworthy in his story of Tiberius' treason trials. The facts are not always particularly damaging to the emperor: but Tacitus manages to find an invidious explanation for them all. Yet he remains far too good a historian to falsify the facts, even when they undermine the very thesis and impression for which he himself is seeking acceptance.

And so Tacitus' version of Tiberius, with these ulterior preoccupations which conflict with his narrative, can hardly be described as a psychological study. But it is an indelible and unforgettable picture of one powerful personality seen through the eyes of another. The account seems to convict the historian of the hatred and partiality which he denies. But it is so enthralling that it carries conviction as a work of art – and very nearly carries conviction as history.

After Tiberius, his character-studies of Claudius and Nero can afford to be more direct. The latter, like Tiberius, deteriorated, or rather allowed his faults to take over,[13] under the impact of absolute power; and if we possessed the relevant portions of the story, we should probably be told the same about Claudius as well. Like their predecessor, they are revealed not in full-length portrayals, but by gradual build-ups, stressing the growth of their demoralisation (p. 286). The catalogue of Claudius' ludicrous personal defects and idiosyncrasies, savagely satirical like the stress on Vitellius' gluttony, scarcely does justice to the painstaking and bold administrative measures and reforms which modern research has attributed to his reign. Nor is credit given to Nero's sensible achievement in making peace with Parthia. It did not harmonise with the traditional Roman castigation of national enemies. This had become fashionable again in the historian's own day under Trajan (p. 276) – and we have learnt to be vigilant for such allusions to contemporary affairs.

But the evils of the courts of Claudius and Nero spring readily and convincingly to the eye in the pages of Tacitus. Chief among these scourges was the dominance of terrifying imperial woman. After the grim picture he had drawn of Livia (p. 286), we are told how, while Claudius was away, his nymphomaniac wife Messalina gave a party in the company of her lover Gaius Silius.

Messalina was indulging in unprecedented extravagances. It was full autumn; and she was performing in her grounds a mimic grape-harvest. Presses were working, vats overflowing, surrounded by women capering in skins like sacrificing or frenzied Maenads. She herself, hair streaming, brandished a Bacchic wand. Beside her stood Silius in ivory-wreath and buskins, rolling his head while the disreputable chorus yelled round him. Vettius Valens, the story goes, gaily climbed a great tree. Asked what he saw, his answer was: 'A fearful storm over Ostia.'[14]

For Claudius was at Ostia. But only for a short time: and when he returned Messalina was executed. His next wife, the even more formidable Agrippina the younger, had him poisoned.

An expert in such matters was selected – a woman called Locusta, recently sentenced for poisoning but with a long career of imperial service ahead of her. . . . Contemporary writers stated that the poison was sprinkled on a particularly succulent mushroom. But because Claudius was torpid – or drunk – its effect was not at first apparent; and an evacuation of his bowels seemed to have saved him. Agrippina was horrified. But when the ultimate stakes are so alarmingly large, immediate disrepute is brushed aside. She had already secured the complicity of the emperor's doctor Xenophon, and now she called him in. The story is that, while pretending to help Claudius to vomit, he put a feather dipped in quick poison down his throat. Xenophon knew that major crimes, though hazardous to undertake, are profitable to achieve.[15]

But when Agrippina's son Nero came to the throne, his mother's influence declined. Finally she lost her life, because the emperor, abandoning his pathetic wife Octavia to destruction,[16] fell in love with Poppaea who would not tolerate the queen mother. Or so says Tacitus.

Poppaea had every asset except goodness. From her mother, the loveliest woman of her day, she inherited distinction and beauty. Her wealth, too, was equal to her birth. She was clever and pleasant to talk to. She seemed respectable. But her life was depraved. Her public appearances were few; she would half-veil her face at them, to stimulate curiosity (or because it suited her). To her, married or bachelor bedfellows were alike. She was indifferent to her reputation – yet insensible to men's love, and herself unloving. Advantage dictated the bestowal of her favours.[17]

When Charles Merivale called Nero 'vulgar, timid and sanguinary', he was following Tacitus. And they were clearly right. But Tacitus' account of so outrageous a figure does not need to revive the techniques of damning suggestion lavished on Tiberius. Instead we can enjoy his extraordinary gift for pictorial description. We can read about the attempted murder of Agrippina on a collapsible ship, or about the Great Fire of Rome – those full-scale set pieces at which Tacitus excels – without worrying too much if he is playing fair, though the selective conventions of Roman historical writing mean that, on closer inspection, many problems remain unsolved.[18]

Or we can read of those bad, tragically bad, jokes of the régime which often attracted Tacitus' savage humour.[19] For instance, there was Nero's debut as a theatrical and musical performer.

First he recited a poem on the stage. Then . . . he made a second entree as a musician. Nero scrupulously observed harpists' etiquette. When tired, he remained standing. To wipe away perspiration, he used nothing but the robe he was wearing. He allowed moisture from his mouth and nose to be visible. And at the conclusion, he awaited the verdict of the judges in assumed trepidation, on bended knee, and with a gesture of deference to the public. And the public at least, used to applauding the poses even of professional actors, cheered in measured, rhythmical cadences.

They sounded delighted. Indeed, since the national disgrace meant nothing to them, they probably were. But people from remote country-towns of austere, old-fashioned Italy, or visitors from distant provinces on official or private business, had no experience of outrageous behaviour: and they found the spectacle intolerable. Their unpractised hands tired easily and proved unequal to the degrading task, thus disorganising the expert applauders and earning many cuffs from the guardsmen who, to prevent any momentary disharmony or silence, were stationed along the benches.[20]

Many other figures beside the rulers crowd on the stage. 'We know them', says Macaulay, 'as if we had lived with them.' And yet there are few ordinary men to be seen, but many freaks of varying degrees of grotesqueness. They are pilloried with a few acid words, the product of a sharp distorting eye.[21] Tacitus believes human character shapes events, not the reverse. And so an array of leading figures are isolated from the anonymous mass and accorded a vivid, garish illumination.

Usually this is done by brief, passing, parenthetical observations. That, for example, is the method by which we are told of the generals who emerged amid the turbulence of the Civil War, Caecina and Valens and Primus, light-fingered and open-handed, fishing skilfully in troubled water.[22] But this piece-by-piece method of presentation is occasionally varied by a longer descriptive note. Such treatment was merited by Sejanus, the evil genius of Tiberius' middle years. The great drama which brought him down is lost, and we do not clearly know who his allies and enemies were. But when he first appears on the scene we are told something about his personality.

After increasing his income – it was alleged – by a liaison with a rich debauchee, the boy Sejanus joined, while still young, the suite of Gaius, the grandson of Augustus. Next by various devices he obtained a complete ascendancy over Tiberius. To Sejanus alone the otherwise cryptic emperor spoke freely and unguardedly. Of audacious character and untiring physique, secretive about himself and ever ready to incriminate others, a blend of arrogance and servility, he [Sejanus] concealed behind a carefully modest exterior an unbounded lust for power. Sometimes this impelled him to lavish excesses, but more often to incessant work. And that is as damaging as excess when the throne is its aim.[23]

When his end came, we do not know if Sejanus was given an obituary by Tacitus; for the relevant passage has not survived. But that was the method preferred for dealing with some of the other bizarre luminaries of the epoch. The *Annals* contains obituaries of twenty men, mostly in pairs, but some treated singly. Many of these studies, though vivid enough, are little more than depictions of types. Yet, in the reign of Nero, the historian breaks off to offer a more unusual description of Petronius, who is believed by most critics to be the author of that remarkable novel the *Satyricon*.

Gaius Petronius deserves a brief obituary. He spent his days sleeping, his nights working and enjoying himself. Others achieve fame by energy, Petronius by laziness. Yet he was not, like others who waste their resources, regarded as dissipated or extravagant, but as a refined voluptuary. People liked the apparent freshness of his unconventional and unselfconscious sayings and doings. Nevertheless, as governor of Bithynia and later as consul, he had displayed capacity for business. Then, reverting to a vicious or ostensibly vicious way of life, he had been admitted into the small circle of Nero's intimates, as Arbiter of Taste. To the blasé emperor, smartness and elegance were restricted to what Petronius had approved.[24]

A device traditionally used by historians to delineate character is the speech. As an orator himself, Tacitus continued to show great interest in this medium (p. 276). The *Annals* includes so many references to its leading exponents that the work virtually amounts to a comprehensive historical sketch of eloquence during the early Empire. The orations introduced by Tacitus, as we can tell by comparing one with an authoritative version which has survived independently, follow an old convention by adapting and dramatising and rearranging their originals[25]–when an original existed at all, for such was not always the case.[26] The purpose of the speeches is to clarify obscure and debated issues, or to add reflections and soliloquies when a decision is about to be taken.[27] A speech gave an opportunity to expound a theme, or to show a personality in depth – for example, the personality of Tiberius, for whom the method is particularly appropriate, since he himself had been a speaker of considerable distinction.

Speeches also add variety. They help the historian to achieve a clever compromise between the chronological framework, inherited from his annalistic predecessors,[28] and the rival method of grouping events into elaborately worked-up series of episodes, diversified by digressions.[29] His linking of one episode or theme with another is very complex and subtle, persuasive rather than logical, dexterous in its avoidance of monotony, replete with illuminating associations and juxtapositions.[30]

This is a development of the episodic organisation of Livy. Tacitus' actual wording, too, owes quite a lot to Livy's colourful, eloquent phraseology.[31] The praise of Augustan historians in the preface of the *Annals* is intended as a compliment to him. Yet Tacitus' whole manner and rhythm display the sharpest contrast to Livy's rich, creamy flow, since his austere style, as it reached its climax in the *Histories* and the even more idiosyncratic *Annals*,[32] is full of trenchant, ominous words,[33] abrupt and apocalyptic sentences, staccato and enigmatic turns of phrase, biting and agonised epigrams,[34] garish flashes of metaphor out of the surrounding gloom. These effects were intended, in the first instance, to be heard, not read. For history was still recited,[35] and Tacitus, as a leading orator, was familiar with the contemporary rhetorical studies of Quintilian and the younger Pliny, who reiterated and elaborated the old comparisons of the historical art with oratory and poetry.[36] The vivid vocabulary of Tacitus is often archaic and Virgilian,[37] and his syntax contorts itself into a forcible, concentrated asymmetry far removed from the blandness of Cicero.

There are deep and varied debts to Sallust, in style as in episodic structure and astringent theme and approach, and he is referred to by name, in complimentary terms.[38] Linguistic echoes of writers of the first century AD can also be detected; if a greater part of the literary production of that epoch had survived, we should surely be able to point to many such transmissions (p. 294). Yet Tacitus, while absorbing the pointed rhetoric of the post-Augustan Silver Age, has somehow contrived to raise it to a brilliance without precedent. With the exception of the scintillating Seneca the younger (d. AD 65), whose career he treats sympathetically and whose dramatic, tragic effects are sometimes very close to his own (p. 285),[39] this was the only time in the first two centuries AD when Latin prose was really well written. In the hands of Tacitus, it became transcendently first-rate -- but impossible to copy, and he left no disciples behind him.

The problems he had to face when he was collecting material were considerable, since the periods covered by the *Annals* and by the earlier part of the *Histories* already lay far back in the past when he started upon his task of reconstruction. Hearsay evidence was of dubious value for such bygone events; and it was further invalidated by the controversial character of so much that had happened.[40] Take, for example, the death of Germanicus (AD 19), followed by the suicide of Cnaeus Piso who was suspected of murdering him: 'So the avenging of Germanicus ended. Contradictory rumours have raged around it among contemporaries and later generations alike. Important events are obscure. Some believe all manner of hearsay evidence. Others twist truth into fiction. And time magnifies both perversions.'[41]

For later times, Tacitus made great use of hearsay and of eyewitnesses.[42] However, for the earlier period at least, it was inevitable that he should depend very largely, either at first or second hand, on written material: on historians who had composed more or less contemporary accounts of the Julio-Claudian times.

Except for a minor adulatory figure Velleius,[43] and Quintus Curtius Rufus who in about the mid-first century carried on the tradition of writing about Alexander the Great, the historical writers of that epoch have not survived.[44] Often, therefore, we have no external check on what Tacitus says, and cannot identify the sources he is using. He himself does not usually do much to enlighten us. He does, however, mention certain of the authors in question. One of them was Pliny the elder (AD 23/4–79), whose numerous works included a thirty-one-book history of his own times[45] and a twenty-book narrative of Rome's German wars. Tacitus criticises Pliny both explicitly and implicitly:[46] though he may also have praised him in some passage now lost, since he managed to find a word of courteous praise for most other historical authors.

Tacitus cites authorities more often than any other known Roman historian, though just as unsystematically as his predecessors. He views his sources with marked suspicion, for the reasons already given by Josephus. For one thing, that is to say, although an occasional figure such as Cremutius Cordus might achieve a praiseworthy detachment and independence (p. 305), writers under an imperial régime tend to be excessively malevolent about their rulers. In times of civil war, they become mere partisans of one side or another.[47] Often, too, they are mere propagandists for a ruler[48] – indeed sometimes they are imperial personages themselves,[49] or their official mouthpieces.[50] Each of the two sides, those who hated the emperors and those who flattered them, were liars. And Tacitus is vigilantly concerned to denounce both kinds of partisanship alike.

So long as Republican history was their theme, men wrote with equal eloquence of style and independence of outlook. But when the battle of Actium had been fought and the interests of peace demanded the concentration of power in the hands of one man, this great line of classical historians came to an end. Truth, too, suffered in more ways than one. To an understandable ignorance of policy, which now lay outside public control, was in due course added a passion for flattery, or else a hatred of autocrats.

Thus neither school bothered about posterity, for the one was bitterly alienated and the other deeply committed. But whereas the reader can easily discount the bias of the time-serving historian, detraction and spite find a ready audience. Adulation bears the ugly taint of subservience. But malice gives the false impression of being independent.[51]

Yet this same question of whether, on principle, to approve of the emperors or dislike them created a dilemma from which Tacitus himself was quite unable to escape. On the one hand, he came of a line of historians who admired the traditional virtues of Rome and its antique Republic. And he himself shared their admiration almost to the point of obsession, echoing Sallust's adoration of a bygone Golden Age,[52] revering the early nobles[53] and praising the Republican tradition of free speech (p. 305). He is a staunch senator, whose strong sense of caste makes him an old-fashioned snob, with a supreme contempt for the lower classes and freedmen and people who (like himself) came from one of the municipalities.[54] When speaking of the Republic, he shows a marked dislike of its popular politicians.[55] In fact, he was devoted to the traditional, oligarchic view of society.

And yet at the same time he knew that the old Republic was a thing of the past. Emperors could say what they liked about their ostensible revivals of its institutions (p. 281). Gossip might even whisper that Drusus the elder and Germanicus had it in mind to restore the old regime in earnest.[56] But it was gone. It could never be revived.

Tacitus' heart, therefore, was with the Republic, but his head was on the side of the imperial present. He was perfectly well aware that the Republic, in its final degraded form and condition, had not been worth keeping any longer. The peoples of the Empire did not want it back, and he understood why: 'The new order was popular in the provinces. There, the government by Senate and people was looked upon sceptically as a matter of sparring dignitaries and extortionate officials. The legal system had provided no remedy against these, since it was wholly incapacitated by violence, favouritism and – most of all – bribery.'[57] If that was the best the late Republican oligarchy had been able to achieve, Tacitus places even less reliance on the Senate of imperial times. For he knew, firstly, that it was incapable of preserving law and order without having an emperor as its boss, and, secondly, that it was equally incapable of standing up against him. The business the Senate could still conduct was uninspiring. When, for example, it investigated the rights of asylum claimed by Asian cities, there is bitter nostalgic irony in the assertion that this activity was a source of profound satisfaction.

Tiberius, while he tightened his control . . . allowed the senate a shadow of its ancient power by inviting it to discuss provincial petitions.

It was a splendid sight, that day, to see the Senate investigating privileges conferred by its ancestors, treaties with allies, edicts of kings who had reigned before Rome was a power, even divine cults. It was free, as of old, to confirm or amend.[58]

On the contrary: the Senate's engagement in this trivial activity only showed up its essential humiliating helplessness.[59] Because of this, Tacitus was entirely pessimistic about the possibility of any real senatorial independence.

Accordingly, while expressing admiration for the characters of intransigent Stoic–Republican martyrs, Thrasea Paetus and Barea Soranus and then (under Vespasian) Helvidius Priscus, he offers a substantial hint that he regarded them as unpractical men at the mercy of bad advice.[60] Like Cicero, only more emphatically, he feels that the translation of philosophical enthusiasm from theory into practice is unbecoming. This realism means that political opposition to the autocrats, if it goes beyond passive resigned dis-approval, seems to him theatrical and immoderate. For Rome has declined so far that there is no longer any room for traditional valour: *any autocrat is better than civil war* (p. 300). Passivity, then, has become the only honourable course. Accordingly, what Tacitus approves of now is the decorous, cautious navigation of men like Marcus Lepidus under Tiberius,[61] or Memmius Regulus, or Seneca the younger,[62] or Lucius Verginius Rufus who twice refused the throne and received his funeral oration from Tacitus himself in 97 (p. 278). But the shining example of this quiet, inoffensive conduct was his own father-in-law Agricola.

The world, whose custom it is to judge great men by their parade, after seeing and watching Agricola missed his distinction and few deciphered it. . . . Let those whose way it is to admire only things forbidden learn from him that great men can live even under bad rulers; and that submission and moderation, if animation and energy go with them, reach the same pinnacle of fame, whither more often men have climbed – with no profit to the State – by the steep path of a pretentious death.[63]

Such were the men who sought to serve their country, however oppressive its government, rather than resist or stand aside: even under Domitian, theirs was the better course. The adoption of this line was a comforting self-justification for Tacitus himself, who had accepted high office under the same evil emperor. What is more, it was a justification of Nerva and Trajan, too, for both of them had served Domitian as consuls (90, 91).

And so one should endeavour to make the best of one's own times, whatever they might be like: 'As things are, since it is impossible for anybody to enjoy at one and the same time great renown and great repose, let everyone make the most of the blessings his own times afford without disparaging any other age.'[64] The people who habitually adjusted themselves to the imperial system in this way were usually 'new men', or at least men who lacked a glorious aristocratic lineage, and Tacitus repeatedly admires the old-fashioned thrift and morality of this class. His contempt for his fellow-municipals (p. 295) vanished when they achieved success, and pursued useful, careful, unresisting careers.

This same somewhat jaundiced compromise between cursing and blessing the imperial régime appears in his brief, introductory assessment of the reign of Augustus. When post-Augustan tyrants were in question, he almost seemed to be looking back on Augustus' principate as a golden age. And it is certainly high praise – perhaps even higher than he appreciated – to say that the first emperor attracted everybody's goodwill by the enjoyable conferment of peace. Yet Tacitus, who finds it hard to believe that an autocrat *can* be good, fails to appreciate the immensity of Augustus' achievement. If he had understood it better, the intention, which he once formed, of writing at greater length about his reign would surely not have been abandoned.[65] Meanwhile, the short sketch which he provides soon turns, for all its praises, into another masterpiece of innuendo. Augustus' methods of stamping out opposition are dwelt upon, and indeed the whole brief survey, while usefully counteracting the versions blaring forth from the imperial chancery, errs on the other side, for it is one long series of sneers. Many of them are placed, for artistic purposes, on the lips of contemporaries. We are shown an Augustus mirrored in the judgments of men. The approach is that of the dramatist who displays a situation by bringing together two people, or groups of people, of opposite views.

The ambivalence becomes graver still when we reach emperors whom it would be mistaken, or impracticable, not to recognise as good. These necessarily included the first Flavian emperors

Vespasian and his elder son Titus, who had ruled in praiseworthy fashion – apart from cruelty to Jews – and had also launched Tacitus on his public life.[66] Since the accounts of their reigns in the *Histories* are lost, we cannot fully judge how he chose to tackle this problem. But certain things are clear. He did not spare historians who were too complimentary about Flavian partisans in the Civil Wars (p. 294),[67] and he likewise did not spare the inadequacies or excesses of Flavian generals (p. 302). He was also prepared to admire the character (if not the good sense) of the Stoic-minded Helvidius Priscus who opposed the regime (p. 296).[68] Yet there is praise for Vespasian in the *Annals*, and there was no doubt a great deal more in the *Histories*. It would have been interesting to see how the historian modified his usual picture of a disgracefully subservient Senate when he was dealing with an emperor who had to be presented in favourable terms.

One surviving remark gives us additional guidance about his handling of the Flavian epoch: 'The varied complexion of the new dynasty was to signify both happiness and misery for the State, and personal success or disaster for its rulers.'[69] That is to say, Tacitus dealt with this whole Flavian house, which began so well with Vespasian and Titus and ended so catastrophically with Domitian, by the same formula as he had applied to the individual reigns of Tiberius, Claudius and Nero. He treated it, that is to say, as a single unit, comprising a process of deterioration.

Since Domitian's death, Nerva and Trajan had introduced a more beneficent régime – and Tacitus was living under it. He could hardly avoid speaking of this new order in eulogistic terms. To do so was in keeping with his conviction that one must make the best of one's own times and, besides, he no doubt felt great and genuine relief because Domitian was dead. He does not, however, let himself go. Echoing Livy, he retains the reservation that bodies are slow to grow but quick to decay, and cure operates more slowly than disease. All the same, things were better: 'Now, at last, heart is coming back to us. From the first, from the very outset of this happy age, Nerva has united things long incompatible, empire and liberty. Trajan is increasing daily the happiness of the times.'[70] And later he emphasises the same point, with reference to the freedom of speech he cherished so much (p. 305): 'Modern times are indeed happy as few others have been, for we can think as we please, and speak as we think.'[71]

Pessimism creeps in again when Tacitus feels obliged to point out that the Empire has surely passed its zenith.[72] Nevertheless, 'Earlier times were not better than ours in every way – our own epoch too has produced moral and intellectual achievements for our descendants to copy. And such honourable rivalry with the past is a fine thing.'[73] Indeed, Tacitus states that it was his intention to complete his historical work by writing an account of this new and happier age which had now begun: 'If I live, I propose to deal with the reign of the deified Nerva and the imperial career of Trajan. This is a more fruitful and less thorny field, and I have reserved it for my declining years.'[74] However, just as he had never fulfilled his promise to write about Augustus, so he never carried out this promise of a contemporary history either. Instead, his last years were devoted to the bygone days which are the subject of the *Annals*. There may have been various reasons for dropping the project of a history of his own times. For one thing, the work would have had to contain much praise, for reasons both of accuracy and tact. But the historian was less at home praising virtue than castigating vice. His taste for the former, such as it was, had been sated in dealing with the reign of Vespasian. Furthermore, a man of Tacitus' temperament probably did not, in fact, find Trajan's reign as wholly satisfactory as he suggests. He is likely to have been bored by the sedateness of political life. He may also have been hurt because a second consulship, which went to others,[75] never came his way. Besides, although Trajan's government was enlightened enough according to the spirit of the times, its efficient bureaucracy ensured that despotism continued its remorseless advance. Tacitus could scarcely say so. But he could refrain from saying the opposite, and, apart from a few courtesies, he did.

18

Anarchy and Humanity in Tacitus

A special reason why Trajan's regime seemed to Tacitus to fall below perfection was provided by the disagreeable circumstances in which that emperor had taken over. The short principate of Nerva (96–8), following the tyranny of Domitian, seemed to be crumbling into an anarchic situation all too painfully reminiscent of the chaos of the terrible year of the Four Emperors which began when Galba (68–9) briefly succeeded Nero. As consul in 97, Tacitus saw this alarming course of events from the inside.

The Year of the Four Emperors, which could not fail to come to mind at such a tense moment, was the theme Tacitus was working on during the years immediately following the death of Nerva, when he composed the early books of the *Histories*. These books, which comprise the surviving portion of the work, demonstrate the disasters that could occur when the succession to the throne was disputed. Weakness at the centre was what had caused the appalling Civil Wars of AD 69, and Tacitus felt convinced that civil strife was even worse than tyranny (p. 296). This was partly because internal dissensions were bound to weaken the Empire's power of resistance to potential German and Parthian invaders. But the main reason for the supreme undesirability of civil war was because it placed power in military hands. The secret of empire had been revealed when the lesson was learnt that the army, any part of the army, can create an emperor.[1] And so the hallowed formula 'the Senate and the Roman people' is unofficially and caustically changed by Tacitus to 'the Senate, the soldiery and the people'.[2]

The grim Thucydidean doctrine is enunciated that 'man has an instinctive love of power; with the growth of our Empire, the instinct has become a dominant and uncontrollable force'.[3] And this trend achieved a particularly horrifying significance when huge bodies of soldiers roamed at large in the Civil War of 69. Once the armies of Otho and Vitellius were locked in strife, reconciliation was out of the question: 'Roman legions did not shrink from civil war at Pharsalus or Philippi, and there is even less likelihood that the armies of Otho and Vitellius should have made peace voluntarily.'[3] A situation of this kind, when armies dominated events and Roman was fighting against Roman, bred gross outrages and excesses. They could begin all too easily, and soon got out of hand. The visit of Vitellius to the macabre battlefield of Bedriacum, where his generals had defeated Otho, displayed all the forces of evil inherent in this unrestrained, internecine militarism.

It was a dreadful and revolting sight. Less than forty days had elapsed since the engagement, and mutilated corpses, severed limbs and the decaying carcasses of men and horses lay everywhere. The ground was bloodstained and the flattened trees and crops bore witness to the frightful devastation. . . . There were indeed some few observers who were deeply affected by the diverse influences exerted by an inscrutable destiny. They were moved to tears and pity.

But not Vitellius. His gaze was unaverted, and he felt no horror at the multitude of fellow Romans lying there unburied. Blatantly exulting, and little knowing how near the judgment was, he proceeded to offer a sacrifice to the gods of the place.[4]

Finally, Rome itself was subjected to the horrors of military domination and licence.

The whole city presented a frightful caricature of its normal self: fighting and casualties at one point, baths and restaurants at another, here the spilling of blood and the litter of dead bodies, close by prostitutes and their like – all the vice associated with a life of idleness and pleasure, all the dreadful deeds typical of a pitiless sack. . . .

The execution of Vitellius marked the end of hostilities rather than the beginning of peace. The victors roamed through the city sword in hand, hunting the vanquished down with relentless hate. The streets were choked with bodies, the squares and temples stained with blood. The Flavians slaughtered their victims wherever they happened to come across them.

Soon discipline went to pieces. . . . While feeling still ran high, their brutality glutted itself with blood. They left no lurking place untouched, no door unopened: the excuse was that supporters of Vitellius might be hidden there. This was a signal for breaking into private mansions or, if resistance was offered, an excuse for murder. . . . Rome was filled with wailing and lamentation, and suffered the plight of a captured city. . . . The Flavian generals had been keen enough to start the civil war, but they were incapable of exercising control in the day of victory.[5]

Tacitus is interested in the behaviour and emotional attitudes not only of individuals but of masses,[6] and the most significant of all masses was the army. Consequently, the greater part of *Histories* is concerned with its psychology. The soldiers were the source of every emperor's strength and weakness. Again they are brought strongly to the fore at the beginning of the *Annals*, when mutinies on the German frontier threatened to open a yawning chasm in the imperial edifice.

As Drusus approached, the soldiers met him. Ostensibly this was a mark of respect. But there were none of the customary demonstrations of pleasure and glittering full-dress decorations. The men were disgustingly dirty, and their expressions, intended merely to display dejection, looked virtually treasonable. As soon as Drusus had passed inside the outworks, they picketed the gates, and set armed detachments at key points of the camp. Everyone else crowded round the dais in a gigantic mob. Drusus mounted it with a gesture calling for silence. The mutineers, looking round at the great crowd, set up a truculent roar. But the next instant, as they caught sight of the Caesar, their nerve faltered. Violent yells alternated with confused mutterings, and then silence. They were terrifying and terrified in turn, as their feelings shifted.

The night looked like ending in a disastrous criminal outbreak. But this was averted by a stroke of luck. Suddenly, in a clear sky, the light of the moon was seen to decline. The soldiers did not know why this was, and detected an omen of their own situation. . . . The light seemed stronger, and they were happy. Then it looked dimmer, and they were mournful. Finally clouds hid it from view altogether. Men's minds, once unbalanced, are ready to believe anything; and now they howled that heaven was sickened by their crimes, and endless hardships were in store for them.[7]

Here Tacitus is dealing with ignorant soldiers who were misguided enough to think an eclipse was a sign from heaven. He speaks with contemptuous detachment. Yet the possible intervention of heaven is not something he is prepared to reject out of hand. He is as inconsistent as most other ancient historians: or as most people are today. There were moments when everything seemed to be at the mercy of blind fate. At other times the course of events seems just an ironic mockery.[8] Surely Rome's unparalleled sufferings in the Civil War provided ample proof that the gods are indifferent to our welfare. And yet they are eager enough that we should be punished:[9] at times they seem positively malignant. Vitellius' indecent joy at the scene of his victory, followed so soon afterwards by his downfall, was no doubt a device of dramatic irony. But the sequence of events supplied more than a hint of Nemesis as well (p. 50). Mankind seems doomed. We can see why subsequent generations preferred to turn to the other-worldliness of mystics, Christians and monks.

And yet Tacitus, like so many of this predecessors, usually finds it wisest to see natural and supernatural causes in operation at the same time. Divine wrath and human madness acted in combination.[10] His attitude to prodigies shows the same traditional and equivocal ambiguity. Their inclusion is part of the annalistic tradition, and Tacitus, who held a state priesthood, was interested in antique religious institutions. The question whether he believed in such omens is a more difficult one. When describing a conventional portent associated with the infant Nero, he allows his sardonic humour to emerge: 'A further story, that in his infancy serpents had watched over him, was a fable adapted from foreign miracle-tales. Nero himself – who was not over-modest – used to say that just one snake had been seen in his bedroom.'[11] But when omens were seen on the very day of the first battle of Bedriacum, and again on the day when Otho committed suicide, Tacitus is not so sure: 'Though I feel that a wilful search for old wives' tales and the use of fiction to divert the reader is quite inappropriate in a serious work of this type, I hesitate all the same to be sceptical about events widely believed and handed down.'[12] This goes beyond the attitude that such reports deserve to count as history because they influenced events.

He reverts to the same point on another occasion: 'Most men find it natural to believe that the science of prophecy is verified by remarkable testimonials, ancient and modern; and that unfulfilled predictions are due merely to ignorant impostors who discredit it.' This is part of a digression in which the historian pauses to give a fairly extended account of the varying and contradictory strands of Stoicism and astrology and Roman tradition which contributed to his own attitude of non-commitment to any firm philosophical position. He is writing about the astrologer Thrasyllus, who established an ascendancy over Tiberius by correctly prophesying future events.

When I hear this and similar stories, I feel uncertain whether human affairs are directed by Fate's unalterable necessity – or by chance. On this question the wisest ancient thinkers and their disciples differ. Many insist that heaven is unconcerned, in fact, with human beings – so that the good often suffer, and the wicked prosper. Others disagree, maintaining that although things happen according to fate, this depends not on astral movements but on the principles and logic of natural causality. That school leaves us free to choose our lives. But once the choice is made, they warn that the future sequence of events is immutable. . . . Most men find it natural to believe that lives are predestined from birth.[13]

This version of the Tacitean ambivalence goes back as far as Herodotus. When something happens, either Fate or Chance may be at work. All the same, whichever it is, a part is also played by the principles and logic of natural causality. Events have detectable underlying causes.[14] What happens is produced by men, whose characters, therefore, are in the last resort what gives history its shape.

For all his gloom, Tacitus is far from sceptical about these potentialities of the human spirit. Whatever the oppressions of civil war and tyrannical government, he can point to actions of extraordinary virtue, courage and perseverance. Often humble people set an example to the great. When Nero broke the conspiracy of Gaius Piso (AD 65), the poet Lucan could not hold out against interrogation, and perhaps denounced his own mother and two of his closest friends. Epicharis on the other hand was a mere ex-slavewoman, and yet the most horrible tortures could not persuade her to talk. She managed to kill herself before she had incriminated anyone. 'And so, shielding in direst agony men unconnected with her, men who were almost strangers, this woman, who was a former slave, set an example which particularly shone when free citizens, Roman knights, and senators were betraying their nearest and dearest before anyone had laid a hand on them.'[15]

Even in the most terrible years of Domitian the same heroism persisted: and it was as edifying and glorious as anything that had ever been seen before.

Mothers accompanied their children in flight, wives followed their husbands into exile. There were resolute kinsmen, sons-in-law who showed steadfast fidelity, and slaves whose loyalty scorned the rack. Distinguished men faced the last agony with unflinching courage, and there were deaths no less noble than those held up to our admiration in the history of early Rome.[16]

For Tacitus is a humanist. His contribution to our Western tradition has been immense and inspiring. As Syme observed, 'he knew the worst, discovered few reasons for ease or hope or confidence, yet believed in human dignity and freedom of speech'. Undeterred by harrowing experiences and a pessimistic historical tradition, he nourishes his humanistic belief by the conviction that the most ruthless tyranny cannot, in the end, suppress free utterance. And such freedom is something that has effects beyond the grave. For even if the human soul does not itself survive death,[17] it outlives our bodies when a man has spoken or written imperishable words.[18] Before the imperial régime really got into its stride, Livy had not been prevented from speaking in praise of Brutus and Cassius (p. 230). But when the historian Cremutius Cordus did the same thing under Tiberius (AD 25) he was brought to trial. The emperor's formidable expression showed there was no hope for him.[19] Yet Cremutius spoke up and asserted his right to say whatever he wanted to – if not about the living, at least about men of the past. Then he walked out of the Senate, and starved himself to death. But that was not the end of him or his work.

The Senate ordered the books of Cremutius to be burnt by the aediles. But they survived, first hidden and later republished.

This makes one deride the stupidity of people who believe that today's authority can destroy tomorrow's memories. On the contrary, repressions of genius increase its prestige. All that tyrannical conquerors, and imitators of their brutalities, achieve is their own disrepute and their victims' renown.[20]

7

Greek and Latin Biographers

19

Plutarch

A few years older than Tacitus, Plutarch of Chaeronea in Boeotia (AD 45/50–120/7) wrote biographies of soldiers and statesmen in Greek. Most of the essays were grouped in pairs, a Greek with a Roman, linked by a comparison between the two. Twenty-three pairs are extant.

The Greek series in these Parallel Lives begins with ten Athenians, three Spartans, a Syracusan and a Theban. Next comes Alexander the Great, and the gallery goes on down to the Spartan reforming kings Agis IV (244–241 BC) and Cleomenes III (235–219). There is also a place for Philopoemen of Megalopolis, leader of the Achaean League (p. 155). The Roman Lives include the first two legendary kings Romulus and Numa, then three heroes of the early Republic, two of the Punic Wars, five personalities of the second century BC – including the Gracchi who figure in a double pair with the royal Spartan reformers – and eleven men from the first century BC, including finally Antony.[1] Four separate biographies, not included in the parallel series, are also extant: they are the Lives of Artaxerxes II Memnon of Persia, Aratus who built the fortunes of the Achaean League, and the Roman emperors of AD 68–9, Galba and Otho.

The Life of their rival Vitellius is lost, and so are studies of the five rulers of Augustus' dynasty. Missing, also, are the biographies of the younger Scipio, six Greek poets and statesmen,[2] and the heroic or divine figure Heracles. Unfortunately, the first pair of Parallel Lives that Plutarch composed has also failed to survive. Its subjects were Epaminondas the Theban and Scipio Africanus the elder.

At the time when Nero paid a famous visit to Greece in AD 66, Plutarch was at Athens, studying physics, natural science and rhetoric; though his favourite subject was ethics.[3] Not long afterwards he went to Rome on a political mission, making friends with a famous rhetorician Favorinus of Arelate (Arles) and forming a special connection with an eminent Roman statesman Quintus Sosius Senecio (consul in 99 and 107). The Lives are addressed to Senecio, and one of Plutarch's numerous and voluminous *Moral Studies*, a treatise known as the *Table Talks* (*Quaestiones Convivales*), is dedicated to him. The Latin names adopted by the writer, Lucius Mestrius,[4] indicate that he received Roman citizenship through Lucius Mestrius Florus (consul in 72), in whose company he visited the civil-war battlefield of Bedriacum.[5]

Although Plutarch never completely mastered Latin (p. 326), he lectured in Greek at Rome on various philosophical and rhetorical subjects, and again went to stay at the capital in the early nineties when his reputation was large enough to attract large audiences. He also visited Sardis and Alexandria, and travelled to various parts of Greece,[5] including Athens which granted him its citizenship. He held a life priesthood at Delphi (from the nineties), and was apparently given honorific positions in his native land by both Trajan and Hadrian.

He was a man who had many friends. The *Table Talks* record a hundred of them, of varied professions and places. No woman, however, took part in these dinner conversations. They had their meals with the men, but after the tables were cleared they withdrew.

Most of Plutarch's surviving works were written at his Chaeronean home during the years following the death of Domitian. While that emperor was alive he had perhaps agreed with Tacitus that it was better to be silent. His biographical writings mostly seem to belong to the years between 105 and 115, but some may be earlier or later.

Comparisons between one historical figure and another,[7] such as are attempted in these Parallel Lives, seem to us a barren and unreal exercise, since we do not believe that true parallels exist in such tidy forms. And Plutarch undertakes them with an ingenuity that is only superficial. However, such pairings were a commonplace of the Latin rhetorical schools.[8] The juxtaposition of a Greek with a Roman is also reminiscent of Latin poets, who were accustomed to compare themselves with Greek forerunners.[9] Nepos, perhaps copying Varro, had written a biographical work *On Illustrious Men* in which he compared Romans to eminent foreigners, though apparently the analogies were between groups rather than individuals(p. 331).[10]

Plutarch used a variety of methods to press his comparisons home, introducing contrasts as well as similarities. Instigated by persons unknown,[11] he started work on his Lives because of admiration for his fellow-Boeotian Epaminondas, whom he regarded as the greatest of all Greeks. It is therefore a curious mischance that this specially important biography is one of those which are lost. 'He also probably wished,' says A.J. Gossage, 'at least to begin with, to show that in the past Greece had produced men in every way equal to the great men of Rome. This can be seen from his procedure in selecting a famous Roman and then casting round for a Greek with whom to compare him.'

Plutarch's own life, like his work, epitomises the blending of Greek and Roman cultures, at a time when their association was at its closest. He is pretty impartial between Greeks and Romans – so much so that it is still being argued which of the two races he was chiefly trying to convince. But three-quarters of the material in his Lives and *Moral Studies* combined relates to Greece, and that is where his principal sympathies lay. Just as Delphi, where he served as priest, was the traditional focus of the Greek spirit, so Plutarch perfectly embodies the Greek attitudes of his time. He attached himself to its service from a mixture of patriotism, antiquarianism and theological interest (p. 324).

But he spent most of his life at his home-town of Chaeronea, where he belonged to a leading family and was appointed to the chief municipal offices. The motives behind his withdrawal to this tiny world are a little obscure. He wrote that Chaeronea 'was a small town, but if he moved away it would be still smaller'.[12] Plutarch enjoyed an intimate family life.[13] He liked being busy and had a distaste for leisure. But life moved at a slow pace, and he said his books were intended for readers who were not in a hurry.[14] Perhaps the principal reason for his retirement was his desire to write, although, in so remote a place, research presented problems (p. 326).

But he enjoyed his civil and religious duties, and was very loyal to his local attachments. Herodotus earned his castigation for alleged unfairness to Boeotia (p. 326), and tribute is paid to the admittedly imperfect Roman Republican general Lucullus because he had once helped Chaeronea in a legal case (p. 325).[15]

Except for university life at Athens, Greece had become a backwater. But Plutarch lived at a time of mild, very mild, revival. Trajan and the phil-Hellenic Hadrian spent a good deal of money on the country. True, as Plutarch said, Boeotia was still a land 'where in a whole day's journey you would scarcely find a single man looking after his flocks'. Yet at Lake Copais, near his home, Hadrian had completed the reclamation scheme begun by Caligula. Chaeronea possessed antique relics.[16] In the past, it had seen tremendous battles in 447 and 338 and 86 BC. The second of these engagements was commemorated, and still is, by a stone lion marking the graves of those who had fallen fighting against Philip II of Macedonia. This was the region which the war-god Ares had used as his dancing-floor, and Plutarch, faithful to this tradition, was always quick to admire military prowess. But in his day Chaeronea must have been a very quiet place indeed.

For Greece had lost its independence; and Plutarch's *Political Precepts* points out that it is no longer the slightest use trying to be a new Pericles.

When a man enters on any public office, he must not only keep in mind the considerations of which Pericles reminded himself when he assumed the general's cloak – 'Be careful, Pericles; you are ruling free men, you are ruling Greeks, Athenian citizens' – but he must also say to himself: 'Although you are ruling you are a subject, and the city you rule is under the control of proconsuls, and of the procurators of Caesar.'[17]

The boots of the Roman soldiers, he goes on to remark, are just above your head, and he quoted a Greek tragedian who had written of 'the dread chastiser, the axe that cleaves the neck'.[18]

This uncharacteristically grim reminder of the basic facts of power is aimed at any of his countrymen who might be discontented with the *status quo*. Most ancient historical writers were conservatives, and Plutarch is no exception. Various passages, especially in his *Pericles*, reveal sympathy for the right-wing elements in history. These were the sort of people who now supported the Romans, for

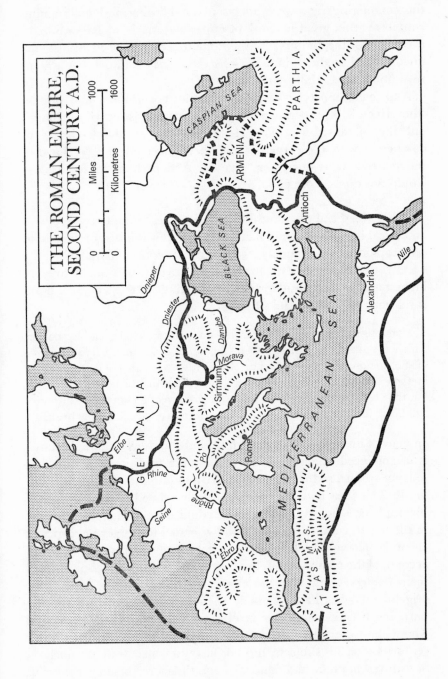

THE ROMAN EMPIRE, SECOND CENTURY A.D.

the conquering race were adepts at establishing and maintaining contacts with a great network of upper-class native collaborators in every city of the Empire. By the same token, Plutarch's distaste for uncontrolled soldiery in the *Galba* and *Otho* shows his alarm at revolution or instability at Rome itself.

And so he urges loyalty to the Roman government and throne, 'the principle of imperial power which maintains security through-out the inhabited world'.[19] He appeals to his fellow-Greeks to co-operate with the emperors and their government. 'We have as much freedom as our rulers give us. And perhaps more freedom would not do us more good.'[20]

This has an ethical ring, and Plutarch attaches himself very firmly to an ethical interpretation of life. In his case this is based on a definite philosophical idea, namely the Stoic conception, popularised by Cicero, that there exists a moral imperative, which ought to rank highest among the considerations of mankind (p. 154): and the point is relevant to the imperial situation.

Men long for immortality, to which no flesh can attain, and for power, which remains for the most part in the hands of fortune, while they give virtue, the only divine excellence of which we are capable, the last place in their scheme of values. But here they show themselves fools, since a life that is spent in the midst of power and great fortune and authority still needs justice to make it divine, for injustice renders it merely brutish.[21]

In view of his preoccupation with this ethical aspect of life, Plutarch is a convinced adherent of that venerable tradition that the past must be studied so that we may derive moral uplift from contemplating it. This idea had always been closely related to the practice of biographers, who, ever since the gradual development of their art in the fourth century BC, had usually tended to produce eulogies or encomia (p. 133). Such essays were not merely concerned to give an account of the man to whom they were dedicated. They also exhorted their readers to imitate his moral conduct and excellence. The original eulogists had to divide their attention between the two purposes, because they were dealing with recently deceased persons whose life-stories had to be described. But Plutarch, who lived many centuries after his subjects, did not have to concentrate so much on narrating what they had done, and was therefore able to dedicate his efforts more than ever to providing moral instruction, and presenting models for emulation.

This aim he erected into a carefully formulated philosophical purpose, for which the biographical genre was peculiarly well adapted.

A colour is well suited to the eye if its bright and agreeable tones stimulate and refresh the vision, and in the same way we ought to apply our intellectual vision to those models which can inspire it to attain its own proper virtue through the sense of delight they arouse. We find these examples in the actions of good men, which implant an eager rivalry and a keen desire to imitate them in the minds of those who have sought them out.

Virtue in action immediately takes such a hold of a man that he no sooner admires a deed than he sets out to follow in the steps of the doer. . . . Moral good, in a word, has a power to attract towards itself. It is no sooner seen than it rouses the spectator to action. And yet it does not form his character by mere imitation, but by promoting the understanding of virtuous deeds it provides him with a dominating purpose.[22]

Plutarch entered into this moralising tradition with all the more ease because he belonged to an age in which educated men were deeply concerned with moral endeavour and practical goodness. But times had, of course, changed. As he said, by reading about Pericles people were not intended to be inspired to become new Pericleses, which would have been an unpractical and inconvenient ideal under Roman rule (p. 314). Instead the idea was that they should be inspired to apply his moral example to their own walk of life, whatever it may be. 'Using history as a mirror,' says Plutarch, 'I try in one way or another to order my own life and to fashion it in accordance with the virtues of these lives'[23] – and he proposes that his readers should do the same.[24] Of his ability to guide them to do so he has no doubts, for when he is writing about an ancient lawgiver such as Numa or Lycurgus he believes that he too, in a literary way, can become a moral legislator in their footsteps.

He also intends to offer useful deterrents. For part of the process, he says, is to include a few *bad* examples, and so 'perhaps I may as well introduce one or two pairs of personages of a worse type into my Lives'.[25] This is the principal role of the biographies of the Macedonian Demetrius I the Besieger (d 283 BC) and Mark Antony.

They are both seen as despots, bearing witness to Plato's warnings about that class of man. Yet their characters contain good in addition to bad, so that they reveal how 'great natures produce great vices as well as great virtues'.[26] In his study of Alcibiades, too, it is clear that Plutarch felt very critical of the man he was describing. Yet he explained the weaknesses he manifested as offshoots of his fine qualities such as charm, brilliance and military talent. The biographer is very careful to point out that even many of his 'good' characters possess a flaw, though usually only one.[27] It may well be a shortcoming inherent in their virtue.[28]

For virtue is what most of his personages display, even when there is an accompanying defect. He is, indeed, excessively willing to see good where it does not always exist. Sometimes the detection and presentation of this excellent quality involves doing a great deal of violence to the tradition, though this does not matter when the personage is legendary like Lycurgus. Just as *one* flaw is often recognisable, there is also a strong tendency to make each good character representative of one particular virtue. Aristides, for instance, is the embodiment of justice.[29]

The consistent description of his heroes in terms of a leading concept of this kind makes Plutarch into a moralist rather than a biographer in any modern sense of the term. So does his deliberate selection of material that will illustrate moral character, and the consequent diminution of emphasis on the actual features of a man's career. This sort of procedure emphasises and explains the ancient idea that 'biography' was not the same thing as history (p. 134). Thus, in writing of the Athenian general Nicias, he deliberately disclaims any rivalry with Thucydides. And it was wise of him to do so.

His most explicit definition of what he is aiming at can be found in the introduction to *Alexander the Great*, who is, obviously, to be compared with Caesar.

In view of the great number of deeds forming the subject matter, I shall say no more by way of introduction than to beg my readers not to raise trivial complaints if I epitomise for the most part, instead of relating all the famous actions of these men and dealing exhaustively with separate actions in detail. I am not writing history but biography. And there is not always a complete proof of virtue or vice even in the most illustrious deeds. In fact, a small matter such as a saying or a jest often reveals a character more clearly than battles in which thousands of men are killed, or the greatest assemblies of troops, or sieges of cities.

Therefore, just as painters reproduce likenesses from the face and the expressions of the eyes, in which the character is revealed, and do not concentrate so much on the other parts, so must I be allowed to dwell on the signs of a man's soul and by their means to present a life in its true characterisation, leaving to others the description of great battles.[30]

Plutarch's view that seemingly little peculiarities show the man was taken over and given a theoretical basis by Sigmund Freud. But one of the differences between them is that Freud was interested in any and every individual, whereas Plutarch concentrates on those who directed events. He is a hero-worshipper, who looks at great men as a race apart. Sometimes this tendency results in superficial judgments and brings him perilously close to wholly unhistorical writers such as Theophrastus, who did not deal with individuals at all in his *Characters*, but listed and described different types (p. 431, n. 45). Yet Plutarch remains fascinated by actual people, and warmly concerned with their fortunes. More often than not, therefore, the tendency to provide mere specimens or patterns of character is successfully avoided. And he is at his best and most original when he sets out to analyse the characteristics and mental states of some actual person – and momentarily forgets the type and quality he is professing to illustrate.

However, like other ancient writers, Plutarch has no idea of dynamic biography. As the methods of Tacitus were revealing, the ancients were still mostly convinced that a man's character is fixed; at any point in his life he is what he always was and always will be (p. 286). Plutarch's *Marius*, for example, shows how he likes to set down his conclusions on the subject's personality at an early stage; and then he goes on to show why they are right. So Plutarch's heroes are generally there, all in one piece, from the very beginning.

And yet there are certain occasions on which their characters do seem to have changed, for better or worse. History, he points out, shows that men can actually, at times, *alter* their natures, and especially men of marked personality.[31] But the matter is a little more complicated than it might seem. On further inspection, Plutarch is not really prepared to envisage a change of basic character (*physis*) after all. Instead he is following an Aristotelian tradition by which people may change their acquired characteristics (*ethos*) – features they can pick up, and can therefore also discard, as they go along (p. 431, n. 46). On other occasions he falls back on the theory adopted by Tacitus that apparent changes are merely due to false appearances or dissimulation. Pericles, for example, *seemed* to change his character. 'As a young man he was inclined to shrink from facing the people. . . . He now entered upon a new mode of life. He was never to be seen walking in any street except the one which led to the market-place and the Council-chamber.'[32] But Plutarch goes on to observe that this was not a *real* change of character. It was merely play-acting, Pericles adopted his new line because he wanted to seem democratic, though this hail-fellow-well-met attitude 'was quite contrary to his own temperament, which was thoroughly aristocratic'.

That was the sort of thing that Tacitus, at about the same time, was suggesting about Tiberius, except that there the process worked the other way round: the play-acting had come first, and autocratic power revealed the real, underlying, hideous features. Whether Tacitus and Plutarch knew anything about each other's work it is impossible to say. But they had the same traditions to draw upon; and Plutarch thinks of applying to Sulla the same conclusions as Tacitus applied to Tiberius. For Sulla, too, seemed to deteriorate once the autocratic power was in his hands: 'It was natural that his behaviour should cast a certain suspicion on the very idea of high office and should make people think that these great powers bring about a change in the previous characters of their holders – a change in the direction of over-excitability, pomposity, and inhumanity.'[33] But was this a real deterioration of character, or only an apparent one? Plutarch refuses to commit himself. 'I should have to write another essay altogether to determine the point whether this is a real change and revolution in a man's nature, brought about by fortune, or whether it is rather the case that when a man is in power the evil which has been latent in him reveals itself openly.'

To him, as to Aristotle, life is activity. A man's nature is revealed by his actions, which, for this purpose, included his sayings. These actions and sayings form the evidence from which his character must be deduced – its intrinsic and acquired portions alike. And the range of human actions which Plutarch is prepared to consider is wide.

Indeed, it is limited by nothing except the selectivity imposed by his moral purpose. Rejecting the method of classifying his subject's features theme by theme, he mostly prefers to follow the basically chronological arrangement which the more scholarly biographers of Alexandria had tended to adopt, and had transmitted to their Roman imitator Nepos (p. 331). Even, therefore, if there is no development of character, there is at least a development of characterisation. But no hard-and-fast plan emerges. Plutarch's chronological narrative is suspended from time to time in order to permit the illustration of character by a variety of different means. However, he is also willing enough, if he feels like it, to introduce points quite out of their right order, usually without calling attention to the fact that he is doing so.[34] No doubt he assumed that readers would have histories on their shelves. If they wanted to, they could get the dates from them.[35]

One of his greatest attractions is this readiness to vary the pattern. The scheme is flexible, and each Life forms a unity of a different kind. The same applies to the forewords which introduce the biographies: brilliant use is made of a diversified array of clever 'leads'.[36] Perorations are generally factual and quiet, according to the classical tradition. But they, too, can possess a nostalgic effectiveness, like the epilogue to *Themistocles*, which refers to his supposed tomb and the honours that were still being paid to it six hundred years after his death.[37]

Digressions abound, because Plutarch, a man with time at his disposal, was writing for leisurely people (p. 311). 'He digressed', says R.H. Barrow, 'out of the sheer exuberance of his interest and the richness of his knowledge.' But he is aware that the practice must not be allowed to get out of hand, because 'such digressions are less likely to meet with condemnation from impatient critics if they are kept within bounds'.[38] Nevertheless, these deviations include an extraordinarily wide range of themes: Greek and Roman religious festivals and rites, philological enquiries and attempted etymologies of Greek and Latin words, meteors and shooting stars, the causes of a disease called *boulimia* involving ravenous hunger, the names of Greek and Roman months, Roman divorce, underground water-channels, the Atlantic islands, the volume and power of the human voice, the temple of Jupiter Capitolinus, ghosts and miracles and portents, Archimedes and the history of mechanics, the introduction of wine among the Greeks.*

When dealing with more specifically biographical material, Plutarch is no less varied. His unique talent, which even Boswell did not excel, lies in the selection of significant anecdotes. They never lack a point, and they always illuminate their subject, however bizarre or trivial the incident may be. Plutarch is an expert in all the techniques of catching and holding the reader's interest.

When the Athenians were voting to select one of their politicians for banishment [ostracism], the story goes that, while the votes were being written down, an illiterate and uncouth rustic handed his piece of earthenware to Aristides and asked him to write the name Aristides on it. The latter was astonished and asked the man what harm Aristides had ever done him. 'None whatever,' was the reply, 'I do not even know the fellow, but I am sick of hearing him called The Just everywhere!'[39]

Alcibiades owned an exceptionally large and handsome dog, which he had bought for seventy minae, and it possessed an extremely fine tail, which he had cut off. His friends scolded him and told him that everyone was angry for the dog's sake. Alcibiades only laughed and retorted, 'That is exactly what I wanted. I am quite content for the whole of Athens to chatter about this; it will stop them saying anything worse about me!'[40]

Crassus was in his later years accused of having had an affair with Licinia, one of the Vestal Virgins, and Licinia was actually prosecuted by a man called Plotius. She was the owner of a very attractive house in the suburbs which Crassus wanted to get hold of at a low price, and it was for this reason that he was always hovering about Licinia and paying his attentions to her, thus provoking a scandal. And, in a sense, it was his avarice which cleared him of the charge of having corrupted the lady. He was acquitted by the court. But he still did not let Licinia alone until he had acquired the property.[41]

When Valerius Leo was entertaining Caesar to dinner at Mediolanum [Milan], he served up asparagus dressed with myrrh instead of olive oil. Caesar ate this quite calmly himself and reprimanded his friends when they objected to the dish. 'If you didn't like it,' he said, 'there was no need to have eaten it. But if one reflects on one's host's lack of breeding it merely shows that one is ill-bred oneself.'[42]

When Antony and Dolabella were accused to him of plotting a revolution, Caesar said, 'I am not much afraid of these fat, long-haired

* This list is owed to A. J. Gossage.

people. It's the other type I'm more frightened of, the pale thin ones' – by which he meant Brutus and Cassius.[43]

Yet Plutarch's brilliant tapestry is not made up only of colourful minor threads. It contains exalted and sombre scenes as well. The drama of men caught up in mighty circumstances always finds a response from his heart. When the Peloponnesian War ended with the downfall of Athens, the tragedy is recaptured forever.

> Some people say that a proposal was actually laid before the congress of the allies to sell the whole Athenian people into slavery, and that on this occasion Erianthus the Theban went so far as to move that Athens should be razed to the ground and the country round it made a pasture for sheep. But later, so the story goes, when the principal delegates met for a banquet, a man from Phocis sang the opening chorus from Euripides' *Electra*. . . . At this the whole company was moved to pity and felt that it would be an outrage to destroy so glorious a city which had produced such great men.
>
> After the Athenians had finally given way to all Lysander's demands, he sent for a great company of flute girls from the city and collected all those who were in his camp. Then, to the sound of their music, he pulled down the walls and burnt the ships, while the allies garlanded themselves with flowers, rejoiced together, and hailed that day as the beginning of freedom for Greece.[44]

It is in terms of tragedy, of a play acted in an enormous theatre, that Plutarch sees life, and the lives of the people he is writing about. As he passes on from Demetrius the Besieger to Antony, he remarks: 'after the Macedonian drama, watch the Roman drama as it is brought next upon the stage'. His own treatment of a grand scene is beyond reproach. One of his most successful set-pieces is the description of Marius in flight from his all-powerful enemies. He has taken a boat to the little port of Minturnae, but the sailors who landed him have fled hastily from the scene, leaving the once terrible general deserted and alone.

> Making his way through deep marshes and ditches full of mud and water, he came upon the hut of an old man who worked in the fens. . . . The old man told him that, if he wanted to rest, then his cottage would be the best place; but if he were trying to escape from pursuers, he would hide him somewhere more out of the way. Marius begged him to do so and the old man took him into the marsh and told him to crouch down

in a hollow by the river bank. He put on top of him a lot of reeds and sticks, enough to cover him and not too heavy to hurt him.

Before long, however, he heard from the hut the noise of some sort of disturbance. What had happened was that Geminius had sent out from Tarracina a number of men to search for him, and some of these, coming by chance to the hut, were now terrifying the old man and shouting at him for having harboured and hidden a public enemy. So Marius got out of his hiding place, took off his clothes and plunged into the thick muddy water of the marsh. Yet even here he could not escape his pursuers. He was dragged out all covered in mud, taken naked to Minturnae and handed over to the local magistrates.

Like their counterparts all over Italy, they had received instructions that Marius should be caught and put to death. While steeling themselves to take the dread decision, they confined him in a house.

Marius lay down to rest, ordering the door of his room to be closed. No citizen of the town would take on the job of executioner. So a cavalryman, either a Gaul or a Cimbrian (both versions of the story are current), took a sword and went to Marius's room. There was not much light in the part of the room where Marius happened to be lying. In fact, it was almost dark, and we are told that it seemed to the soldier that the eyes of Marius were darting flames at him, and out of the darkness came a great voice: 'My man, do you dare to make an end of Gaius Marius?'

At this the foreigner threw down his sword and rushed straight out of the room. He ran out of doors crying out simply: 'I cannot kill Gaius Marius!'[45]

This caused a change of heart among the people of Minturnae. And so Marius was sent on his way, and another dramatic reversal of fortune soon made him consul of Rome yet again.

The principal enemy of Marius was Sulla, of whom we are given a striking picture: 'The terribly sharp and dominating glare of his blue eyes was made still more dreadful by the complexion of his face in which the pale skin was covered with angry blotches of red . . . "a mulberry with oatmeal scattered on it".'[46] Such passages remind us that Plutarch was an older contemporary of the most influential of all ancient experts of physiognomy, Antonius Polemo of Laodicea in Phrygia (*c.* AD 88–144).[47] The popularity of Polemo shows how keen the interest in this Hellenistic pseudo-science had become (p. 334). Plutarch prefaces his remarks about Sulla's appearance by a reference to the portrait statues of the dictator. He is eager to quote analogies between his own techniques and those of the visual arts, and compares his selective choice of material, aimed at characterisation, with the procedure of painters who concentrate on faces and the expression of the eyes, 'by which character is revealed' (p. 317). For the inner meaning is what one has to try to find. 'A portrait which reveals a man's character and inner qualities possesses a far greater beauty than one which merely reproduces his face and physical appearance.'[48]

For Plutarch wants us to enter into the hearts and emotions of his characters. He possesses great skill in giving us the illusion that we are doing so. This is partly because he provides hardly any historical background, so that the personages are isolated and brought nearer to ourselves. On the other hand, this method also carried grave disadvantages, because the separation of his heroes from most of their attendant circumstances means that we are only rarely allowed to see them as manifestations of their own times and conditions. Indeed, Plutarch himself, very much a product of his own age, possessed little real understanding of the past. The classical epoch of his own country had finished more than five centuries previously, and his judgment of those days is all at sea.[49] He does not know how to assess the sources that describe them. Events are interpreted in terms of his own attitudes and times, and anachronisms abound. Reading his Lives, one would think that there had scarcely been any social changes during the past thousand years.

That does not, however, mean that he is over-topical, in the sense of referring the past too explicitly to contemporary events. On the contrary the present is not described any more than the past. Such descriptions were for historians, not biographers (p. 316). Besides, it undoubtedly seemed to Plutarch, as to all the other millions who lived in the prolonged, almost unbroken calm of the Pax Romana, that the existing conditions would last unchangingly and timelessly for ever. There was therefore no point in noting or analysing them for posterity.

Plutarch was a much more religious man than most ancient historical writers. Extremely knowledgeable about cults, he excelled Herodotus in devotion to the Delphic oracle, of which he was a priest (p. 310). As late as the time when he himself was a boy, he recorded, the Pythian priestess could still have been seen and heard experiencing authentic trances,[50] though the oracle had declined as the population of the area grew less and less. Like most of his contemporaries, he was superstitious, abstaining for example from the consumption of eggs because of a dream.[51] But he deplored the beatnik asceticism which was coming into fashion and would eventually lead to the mass withdrawals of Christian monks.[52] Plutarch is sure, as others had been before him, that the rise and grandeur of Rome were due to divine intervention.[53] Yet his interpretation of 'Fortune' also vacillated in the usual way between Providence and Chance. Marius, whose alarming adventures he described in so much detail (p. 322), seems to him a classic instance of a man whose luck was bad, in contrast to Sulla, who was famous for good fortune (p. 175).

Plutarch is very keen to reconcile ancient beliefs with up-to-date theory by the application of a rationalising procedure. According to a tradition which went right back to the beginnings of historical writing, this attitude stops short of striking at the heart of the ancient values. Mythical or legendary antiquity are subjected to a familiar sort of partial rationalisation. Like Livy, Plutarch shies off the problem by justifying his method on the grounds of a traditionalist reverence for this venerable material: 'Let us hope, then, that I shall succeed in purifying fable, and make her submit to reason and take on the appearance of history. But when she obstinately defies probability and refuses to admit any element of the credible, I shall throw myself on the indulgence of my readers and of those who can listen with forbearance to the tales of antiquity.'[54]

And yet Plutarch is often seduced away from this usual woolly attitude to the revered past by a genuine scientific curiosity. He speculates a lot about true causes,[55] taking care, however, to accompany these flights by an explanation that such enquiries are thoroughly sound: far from being irreligious they are actually conducive to the best sort of religion.

Pericles seems to have learned from the teaching of Anaxagoras to rise above that superstitious terror which springs from an ignorant wonder at the common phenomena of the heavens. It affects those who know nothing of the causes of such things, who fear the gods to the point of madness and are easily confused through their lack of experience. A knowledge of natural causes, on the other hand, banishes these fears and replaces morbid superstition with a piety which rests on a sure foundation supported by rational hopes.[56]

Yet, although Plutarch was, in this sort of way, a thoughtful man, he was by no means an intellectual. Enquiries are not followed to their logical extremes. He took life with a cheerful ease which avoided disquieting solutions.

But he was a kindly person, who fully shared the moderation and gentle humanitarian philanthropy of the serene times in which he lived. In one way, however, he was not a typical contemporary figure. He did not share the taste for rhetorical fireworks which has earned that epoch the name of the second sophistic age, harking back to the sophists of over five hundred years earlier. Although very fond of words, Plutarch disliked the clever show-off lectures that had become more fashionable than ever before. Admittedly he himself was not above an occasional exploitation of the arts of rhetoric, even at times to excess. But more often, he employed such devices with a mild discretion which fell far short of the popular fireworks of the day.

Plutarch's factual accuracy is as variable as his relaxed mental attitude would lead one to suppose. His methods of selection were bound to lead to distortion. But at least he knows it is not always easy to discover what is true and what is not.

We find that even Stesimbrotus of Thasos [p. 428, n. 32] has dared to give currency to the shocking and completely unfounded charge that Pericles' seduced his son's wife. This only goes to show how thickly the truth is hedged around with obstacles, and how hard it is to track things down by historical research. Writers who live after the events they describe find that their view of them is obscured by the lapse of time, while those who investigate the deeds and lives of their contemporaries are equally apt to corrupt and distort the truth, in some cases because of envy or private hatred, in others through the desire to flatter or show favour.[57]

Realising the existence of these difficulties, Plutarch is sometimes unwilling to decide which version to support.[58] On other occasions, he makes a deliberate effort to be fair. With regard to Lucullus (d. 56 BC), for example, he suggests that although he had spoken up for Chaeronea in a case before the governor of Macedonia, and therefore deserves to be praised by Plutarch who came from that town, the general himself 'would not have regarded a false or fictitious account of his life as a fitting recompense for the truthful testimony which he gave'.[59]

In his essay *Concerning the Malignity of Herodotus*, he sets out in greater detail his disapproval of any distortion of the facts. The attack has little or no bearing on Herodotus, whom Plutarch the Boeotian really disliked on the grounds that the Father of History had failed to do justice to Boeotia's conduct in the Persian War. But the pamphlet does enumerate skilfully enough the various ways of creating prejudice which a historical writer ought to detect and shun.[60] These sentiments are well-expressed renderings of a conventional enough theme. Unfortunately, Plutarch himself lives up to them even less consistently than most other ancient writers about the past. Some of his biographies, however, are much more reliable than others. Independent sources have shown that the Life of Solon contains quite a lot of good material. *Cimon* is much better at chronology than some of the others. *Nicias* is basically sound, because it is founded on Thucydides. The biography of *Phocion*, a prudent and respected Athenian leader (d. 318 BC), is engrossing, but highly unreliable. Nearly all the Lives contain any number of historical mistakes.

And yet Plutarch's reading was enormous. He himself observed that a writer about the past must study widely, and must take pains to get hold of works unavailable in his own country.[61] This was a standard which he really did live up to. He was particularly well read in history, and best of all in the more emotional historians of the third and second centuries BC.[62] The Life of Romulus, mythical though its subject is, demonstrates his immense erudition and the great range of sources upon which he drew. Altogether, his works include quotations from as many as 250 Greek authors – of whom no less than eighty are only known through these citations. He picked up Latin as he went along.[63] Yet he had read a great many of the principal relevant writers in the language, and indeed there seem to have been few that escaped him.[64] Except where he advises us to the contrary, he himself seems to have read most of the writers he quotes. Some, no doubt, were only known to him at second hand. Yet Plutarch was not usually a mere copyist. Sometimes he may have use of collections of sayings, quotations and anecdotes. Other writers did the same. But he cannot be dismissed as a mere compiler from commonplace books of that kind.[65]

Nor would he have been content to base each biography on a single literary authority.[66] Different Lives, being differently designed, called for various approaches to the evidence. But in general he was rarely satisfied with a single source when others were available. Yet he has no understanding of the differences between one writer and another in quality or reliability or weight. It could be a sign of good judgment when he refuses to say which account he prefers. But the comforting ancient criterion of probability all too often leads to slovenly conclusions. The same old theory is brought out again in the *Theseus*, and the attempt to put it into practice makes the biography a strange display of entirely arbitrary decisions between conflicting accounts. Admittedly, the whole story was legend in any case. But when we come down to historical times, these aberrations do not disappear. Indeed, there are occasions when several quite contradictory versions are incorporated in adjacent biographies. For example, we are given no less than three contradictory and irreconcilable versions of the Conference of Luca (56 BC).[67] And elsewhere appears the fatal admission of a preference for the 'authors who are least contradicted'.[68]

Although Plutarch was accounted a fine scholar in his own day, the tribute is misplaced. The age of learning and research was over. Its methods were beyond him; he was not capable of applying critical methods. For example, he quotes thirty times from the letters of Alexander the Great: but the documents he cites are largely forgeries. They have been fabricated round one or two letters that may have been authentic.

On the credit side is his familiarity with an extraordinary number of local chronicles, and the personal inspection of a vast quantity of public monuments, tombs, statues and battle sites. The care with which he collected oral traditions was likewise exemplary: 'to hear rightly', he said, 'is the beginning of living rightly'. And his taking of notes was equally meticulous. These came in useful for the *Moral Studies* as well as the Lives. When a friend named Paccius asked him for an essay to provide him with comfort and consolation, Plutarch was able to turn to his notebooks in search of quotations and thoughts. The result was a consolatory essay. The covering letter with which he dispatched it gives a good illustration of Plutarch's curious blend of rather uninspired bookishness and kindly human sympathy.

Your letter in which you asked that something on comfort should be written for you was late. And now our friend Eros has to hurry back to

Rome after receiving a letter telling him to hurry. And so I have not the time to give to the matter which I should have liked; yet I cannot let him leave with empty hands. Accordingly I have gathered together some thoughts on comfort from the notes which I have in fact made for myself. I take it that you do not want a bit of fine writing to please your ears but something for practical use in your daily life.[69]

20

Suetonius

THE second outstanding biographer of the age, Suetonius, wrote a number of works in Greek, but his main literary productions, including those which are extant today, are Latin. Gaius Suetonius Tranquillus was born in about AD 70 and died some time after 130. His family, which was of knightly rank, probably came from Hippo Regius, near Bône in Algeria.[1] The most famous of his many writings is his collection of *Lives of the Caesars* – the 'Twelve Caesars', comprising Julius and the first eleven emperors, going down to Domitian (AD 81–96). The *Caesars* has survived complete, except for the first few chapters of the Life of Julius. These twelve biographies are grouped in eight books. One each is devoted to Julius and the five emperors of Augustus' house, one covers all three of the brief contestants of AD 69, and one comprises the three Flavians who followed.

Earlier, Suetonius had written another Latin series, the *Lives of Illustrious Men*. Following a Greek tradition, these were biographies of Roman literary personalities – poets, orators, historians, philosophers, grammarians (literature teachers) and rhetoricians. Only a few portions of this work have survived. Of the poets, we have Terence, Virgil, Horace, and part of Lucan. Brief Lives of Tibullus and Persius, who lived under Augustus and Nero respectively, may belong to the same collection, though perhaps these essays have been edited and abridged by other hands. The six studies of the historians have vanished except for a fragmentary account of Pliny the elder. Of the biographies of fifteen orators nothing is left except a brief abstract of a Life of Passienus the elder, a notable speaker of Augustan times (d. 8 BC). The section describing teachers of literature has survived almost complete.

Perhaps Suetonius himself held such a job for a time. It is also possible that he practised law. He may have served on the staff of a fellow-writer, Pliny the younger, when the latter was governor of Bithynia in north-western Asia Minor (110–12).[2] Otherwise he took no part in political life. In due course, however, he passed into the imperial service. A fragmentary inscription found at Hippo Regius, which has made it possible to infer that this was his place of origin, also enables us to reconstruct the succession of posts that he occupied at the imperial court. First he was 'secretary of studies', whatever this may mean. Then he became director of the imperial libraries, and finally he was promoted to take charge of the emperor's correspondence. Probably he served in the first two of these capacities in the reign of Trajan. The last appointment, which ranked high in the civil service, he held under Hadrian.

The *Lives of the Caesars,* or at least the first two of them, were dedicated to Hadrian's commander of the imperial guard Gaius Septicius Clarus, who took office in AD 119. A Life of Hadrian, forming part of the *Historia Augusta* (p. 345), states that Suetonius and Septicius alike were dismissed in 122 for disrespectful behaviour towards the empress Sabina.[3] Unreliable though the *Historia* is, we may at least accept the report that they lost their posts at this time. It seems likely that by then Suetonius had published the Lives of Julius and Augustus and collected some of the material for the three emperors who followed. His first publications in this field, therefore, occurred a decade or two after the Greek biographies of Plutarch.

A reference in Suetonius' Life of Titus suggests that he was still at work on these later Caesars after AD 130.[4] Perhaps the last two books (Civil Wars and Flavians) formed a supplement, published later than the rest. As the Lives proceeded, there is an increasing number of oblique references which could be construed as showing a lack of tact or loyalty towards Hadrian.[5] If, however, as some suppose, one of his many lost works, *On Public Offices,* was written last of all, this choice of subject, made at a time when Hadrian was reforming the administration, suggests that in the end he enjoyed at least a partial return to imperial favour.

Biographers of a sort had been in existence for more than a half millennium, though Plutarch was the first of the Greeks whose work has survived. The Latin biographers before Suetonius are likewise all missing, with the single exception of Cornelius Nepos. Nepos (d. *c.* 24 BC) was an inferior author, and he understandably suffered from something of an inferiority complex. 'I am well aware, Atticus,' he said, 'that a great many people will look upon this kind of writing as trivial and unworthy of the roles played in life by men of eminence.'⁶ This was not merely personal modesty, for it rested on the traditional conviction that biography is essentially a study different from history, and less ambitious in scope. 'I am uncertain', says Nepos about the Theban leader Pelopidas (d. 364 BC), 'how to expound his merits; I am afraid that I may appear to be writing history rather than giving an account of his life if I embark upon a systematic account of his achievements.'⁷ That is to say, Latin biographers, like their Greek predecessors, felt it desirable and necessary to get away from the wide canvas of the historians. It was up to them instead to find methods better calculated for their own purpose, which was to bring to life the individuals they had selected as their themes.

Plutarch had stressed this contrast with the historians (p. 316). Suetonius shows no detectable interest in anything Plutarch had said, but he, too, was equally conscious that he must strike out in a different direction from the writers of histories. Indeed, for him this was even more necessary since, in his language, there was the overpowering contemporary work of Tacitus to compete with. He therefore very wisely decided not to compete with it at all. In order to avoid doing so, he moved a further step away from history. Plutarch had, on the whole, favoured a chronological method (p. 319). But Suetonius adopted a different and more unhistorical line of approach, in which the straightforward narrative is interrupted by material classified according to topics, and dealing successively with different characteristics of his subjects. The same method had already been followed to some extent by early representatives of this type of literature such as Xenophon and Isocrates. Occasionally, too, it had been attempted by Nepos, for example in his *Epaminondas*. Inscriptional epitaphs, which played a part in the development of Latin biography (p. 173), suggested the same sort of subdivision. It may well be that writers whose works are lost played some part in developing the method to the sophisticated stage it reached with Suetonius. But it was he, as far as we can tell, who brought the practice to a fine art.

Following the practice of the Greek encomium, a form of literature which had subsequently been adapted to their own uses by Roman orators as well as historians,[8] Suetonius occasionally indicates the sort of way in which he is proposing to operate this sort of arrangement. After writing, for example, of Julius Caesar's family and birth,* and then of his career and activities as dictator, he breaks off to say: 'All these enterprises and plans were cut short by his death. But before I speak of that, it will not be amiss to describe briefly his personal appearance, his dress, his mode of life, and his character, as well as his conduct in civil and military affairs.'[9] Then and only then, after these themes have been handled without any regard for chronology, the biographer carries out his announced intention of describing Caesar's death. It may be possible to detect the expert on grammar and grammarians at work in this sort of classification (p. 338).

The Life of Augustus, too, is punctuated by a similar programmatic statement. 'Now that I have shown how he conducted himself in civil and military positions, and in ruling the State in all parts of the world in peace and in war, I shall next give an account of his private and domestic life, describing his character and his fortune at home and in his household from his youth until his last days.'[10] The scheme varies for each biography, but the pattern remains approximately the same. That is to say, the general procedure is to divide the narrative into two parts separated by an extensive parenthesis – amounting sometimes to the main section of the biography – in which the subject's characteristics and idiosyncrasies are analysed one after another.[11]

Suetonius' main contribution, however, lies in what may roughly be defined as objectivity. With him, we have left the traditional encomium altogether, and have entered a much more astringent atmosphere. It is difficult to judge whether he was a pioneer in this respect. Possible forerunners have been suggested among the Greeks.[12] Their extension of biographical literature to philosophers, poets and the like had encouraged a measure of detachment or even criticism, since such studies were concerned with the evolution of

* These sections are now lost.

this or that art at least as much as with personal eulogies of the practitioners themselves. Indeed, active debunking of these literary figures and artists had been quite an early development (p. 431, n. 45).

Moreover, this detached or critical sort of approach had soon been applied to people in public life as well, first perhaps by Greek biographers and then by Romans. If we still had the biographical studies written by Varro in the first century BC, we might already find in them something of this kind, especially as Suetonius himself chose to hail him as the founder of Greek-inspired Latin biography.[13] Certainly, the Romans had a strong eulogistic tradition. But at some point or other they also introduced, presumably from Greece, the practice of looking at personages with a more cool and disenchanted eye – the art at which Suetonius excelled.

The novelty of his attitude lies in his selection of Roman emperors as the targets of this exercise. He has collected information for and against them, and freely inserts either sort of material, usually without adding any personal judgment on one side or the other. And, above all, he does not introduce the moral constructions which had always so strongly influenced Greco-Roman biography and history alike, and were continuing to do so in his own day through the agencies of Plutarch and Tacitus respectively. It had become customary to protest, like Tacitus, that the available evidence was for the most part either too favourable or too unfavourable to the emperors. But Suetonius does not feel this to be an embarrassment, because he sees no need to choose between the two types of evidence at all. He is quite happy to quote either or both of them, with a cool absence of partisanship. Just occasionally conflicting statements are considered with care,[14] and very rarely the author's own sentiments are allowed to intrude.[15] But in general the presentation is drily indiscriminate, in some cases to such an extent that two contradictory versions of the same event may well find a place together.[16]

The outcome, it must be admitted, is not quite so balanced and objective as Suetonius evidently hoped. This is because he loved good stories, and in the nature of things good stories about people are more often sharp than kind. As a result, the emperors sometimes emerge in an even more deplorable light than they deserved.[17] Yet in spite of this, or because of it, the result is a unique, startling and thoroughly entertaining picture-gallery of the strange men who successively occupied the throne of the Caesars.

Perhaps the fullest and most bizarre opportunities for Suetonius' method are provided by the deranged Caligula (AD 37–41): 'His hair was thin and entirely gone on the top of his head, though his body was hairy. Because of this, to look upon him from a higher place as he passed by, or for any reason whatever to mention a goat, was treated as a capital offence. . . .'[18] These remarkable vignettes of personal appearance are the products of a growing interest in such details of physical and facial appearance. Disdained by historians, this sort of thing was now at the height of its fashion under the physiognomical expert Antonius Polemo (p. 322).

But Suetonius' eagle eye for the grotesque and macabre extended beyond the physiques of these appalling personages.

Whenever Caligula kissed the neck of his wife or sweetheart, he would say: 'Off comes this beautiful head whenever I give the word.' He even used to threaten now and then that he would resort to torture if necessary, to find out from his dear Caesonia why he loved her so passionately. . . .[19]

At Lugdunum in Gaul he gave a contest in Greek and Latin oratory, in which, they say, those who were least successful were ordered to erase their writings with a sponge or with their tongue, unless they elected rather to be beaten with rods or thrown into the neighbouring river.[20]

These pictures of Caligula, for all their anecdotal and perhaps legendary qualities, are valuable because Tacitus' version is missing. So is his account of Domitian, whom he particularly hated. But we have many curious details of that exceedingly disagreeable emperor from Suetonius.

At the beginning of his reign he used to spend hours in seclusion every day, doing nothing but catch flies and stab them with a keenly sharpened stylus. . . .

During the whole of every gladiatorial show there always stood at his feet a small boy clad in scarlet, with an abnormally small head, with whom he used to talk a great deal, and sometimes seriously. At any rate, he was overheard to ask him if he knew why he had decided at the last appointment-day to make Mettius Rufus prefect of Egypt. . . .

He was excessively lustful. His constant sexual intercourse he called bed-wrestling, as if it were a kind of exercise. It was reported that he depilated his concubines with his own hand, and went swimming with common prostitutes.[21]

Some details are a lot more obscene that that – for example the de-

scriptions of Tiberius' alleged sexual perversions. Vice and brutality
abound in the pages of Suetonius. He is too quick to accept scandalous
stories: though they are not presented pruriently, but as part of the
varied phenomena of a man's personality.

And yet, when all this strange material has been put together,
Suetonius seems to make little effort to reach a decision about the
true natures of the personalities that emerge. He shows no sign of trying to build up his data into a consistent or coherent account. The
characters cannot be expected to develop, since biographical tradition
envisaged that a man was born with the qualities he subsequently
displayed (p. 317). But the personages in Suetonius are not only static
but oddly speckled. There is little possibility of apprehending them as
a single unit or entity. It is difficult, for example, to see just why
Augustus was able to change the world. However, this dead-pan technique does enable Suetonius to bring out the point that people's
characters sometimes possess strangely discordant features which do
not form a harmonious whole and cannot therefore, without distortion, be shown as doing so. And it is a novelty (perhaps even a relief)
to be presented with these inharmonious pictures without their first
having been firmly designed, or redesigned, according to the powerful
preconceptions of a Tacitus. Instead, the materials are provided, and
we are expected to construct the picture ourselves. That is what a
later historian, though a dim one, meant when he praised Suetonius
for writing 'not so much eloquently as accurately'.[22] This may perhaps
be too high commendation (p. 333), but he is certainly accurate in the
sense that he does not believe in falsification by editing.

The highest praise of all, however, is deserved by Suetonius' rapid,
dramatic and often moving narratives. Take, for example, that decisive moment in history when Caesar, hearing that the tribunes
favourable to his cause had been expelled from Rome, crossed the
Rubicon and began the Civil War which brought him the mastery of
the world.

When news reached him that the veto by the tribunes who were his
friends had been disallowed, and that they had fled the city, he at once
sent a few battalions ahead with all secrecy, and disarmed suspicion by
himself attending a theatrical performance, inspecting the plans of a
school for gladiators which he proposed to build, and dining as usual
among a crowd of guests. But at dusk he borrowed a pair of mules from a
bakery near headquarters, harnessed them to a gig, and set off quietly

335

with a few of his staff. His lights went out, he lost his way, and the party wandered about aimlessly for some hours. But at dawn they found a guide who led them on foot along narrow lanes, until they came to the right road. Caesar overtook his advanced guard at the River Rubicon, which formed the frontier between Gaul and Italy. Well aware how critical a decision confronted him, he turned to his staff, remarking: 'We may still draw back. But, once across that little bridge, we shall have to fight it out!'[23]

Then, declaring 'the die is cast' – one of the many imperishable sayings preserved by Suetonius – Caesar crosses the Rubicon: though not before a superhuman portent has been introduced. Five years later, the account of his murder is again laced with omens and warnings. But once they have supplied their quota of dramatic embellishment the story goes on. The details of Caesar's death vary between authors. As often, the tale is more artistically told by Plutarch, but in Suetonius it proceeds on rigorously factual lines.

As soon as Caesar took his seat the conspirators crowded round him as if to pay their respects. Tillius Cimber, who had taken the lead, came up close, pretending to ask a question. Caesar made a gesture of postponement, but Cimber caught hold of his shoulder. 'This is violence', Caesar cried, and at that moment one of the Casca brothers slipped behind and with a sweep of his dagger stabbed him just below the throat. Caesar grasped Casca's arm and ran it through with his stylus; he was leaping away when another dagger caught him in the breast. Confronted by a ring of drawn daggers, he drew the top of his gown over his face, and at the same time ungirded the lower part, letting it fall to his feet so he that would die with both legs decently covered. Twenty-three dagger-thrusts went home as he stood there. Caesar did not utter a sound after Casca's blow had drawn a groan from him; though some say that when he saw Marcus Brutus about to deliver the second blow, he reproached him in Greek with; 'You, too, my son?'[124]

From high tragedy we descend to low comedy eighty-five years later, when the murder of Caligula brought Claudius to the throne.

He became emperor in his fiftieth year by a remarkable freak of fortune. When the assassins of Caligula shut out the crowd under pretence that the emperor wished to be alone, Claudius was ousted with the rest and withdrew to an apartment called the Hermaeum; and a little later, in great terror at the news of the murder, he stole away to a balcony hard by and hid among the curtains which hung before the door. As he cowered there, a common soldier, who was prowling about at random, saw his feet, and, intending to ask who he was, pulled him out and recognised him; and when Claudius fell at his feet in terror, he hailed him as emperor.[25]

Changes of reign almost invariably produced drama of one kind or another. One of the most brilliant stories in the *Caesars* describes the last hours of Nero, when the man who had been ruler of the world had scarcely a supporter left.

He was roused about midnight, and when he learnt that the troops on guard-duty had vanished, he leapt out of bed and sent round to his friends; and because he received no reply from any of them, he visited their lodgings in turn, with a few attendants. But all their doors were closed and no one answered. He returned to his room, to find his body-guards had also fled, having plundered his bedclothes and removed his box of poison as well. At once he asked for Spiculus the gladiator, or someone else who would kill him. When he could find no one, he said 'Have I neither a friend nor an enemy?' and rushed out, as if to throw himself into the Tiber.

But, recovering his spirit, he wanted some more secret hiding-place to collect his thoughts; and when his freedman Phaon offered him his surburban residence between the Salarian and Nomentan roads, about four miles out, just as he was, with one foot bare and wearing a tunic, he threw on a cloak of faded colour and mounted a horse, holding a handkerchief in front of his face, with only four companions, including Sporus. At once he was thrown into panic by an earthquake and a flash of lightning, and heard from the camp nearby the shouts of the soldiers, promising trouble to him and success to Galba. He also heard a traveller who met them saying 'These fellows are after Nero', and another asking 'Anything new about Nero in the city?' Moreover, his horse reared at the smell of a corpse lying by the road, so that his face was uncovered and he was recognised and saluted by a retired guardsman.

When they reached the side turning, he sent the horses away and made his way with difficulty among the bushes and brambles along a path in the reeds, having a coat thrown down for him to walk on, until he reached the rear of the house. There, when Phaon urged him to withdraw for the moment into a cave where sand had been dug, he said he was not going to be buried alive. He waited a little while, until a concealed entrance to the house should be made; and, wishing to drink some water from a pool close at hand, he took some in the hollow of his hand and said 'So this is the water Nero drinks!' Then, tearing his cloak on the brambles, he pushed himself through into a cellar which had been dug and lay down in the adjoining store-room on a bed fitted with a moderate mattress and an old robe laid on it.[26]

And so the tearful emperor, horrified by the news of the dreadful execution the Senate had in store for him, managed, with the help of his secretary, to put an end to himself, just as a cavalry officer rushed in to arrest him. 'What a loss', moaned Nero, 'I shall be to the arts!'[27]

Suetonius sometimes adopts an almost statistical, scissors-and-paste technique. But he is certainly not doing so here. The clue to his method in this passage, as G. B. Townend points out, is that every detail is given from Nero's own point of view. Sights, sounds, smells, taste and feelings are all employed to convey the fugitive's reactions. Suetonius is too good an artist to adopt the 'Nero must have been thinking . . .' method. But the account remains full of unsolved problems and unexplained suggestions, and it is, to say the least, uncertain whether a melodramatic masterpiece of this kind improves on the planned, preconceived structures of Tacitus in faithfulness to the ascertainable facts.

All that the styles of the two writers have in common is a preference for brevity. Suetonius is generally clear and straightforward, and he uses a well-chosen, effective vocabulary. But his diction is disjointed and staccato, and sometimes lapses into the obscure or verbose. In theory, he admired Cicero; but the controversy of more recent years – since no one attempted the grim sublimities of Tacitus – was between the moderate 'Attic' plainness advocated by the literary critic Quintilian and the pointed epigrams of Seneca the younger. As a writer about teachers of literature, and a man who had perhaps taught the subject himself, Suetonius was qualified to hold a view on such matters, and he evidently felt closer to the less pretentious method of Quintilian.

A remarkable feature is his readiness to quote verbatim from his sources. These quotations include Greek, which was normally never quoted by Latin writers for more than one or two words at a time. He offers literal citations of fascinating imperial letters and records, public and private alike. As far as we can tell, this feature was unprecedented in reputable writers of formal Greek or Latin prose. They had always preferred to doctor such archive material into conformity with their own styles.

Curiously enough, however, Suetonius' employment of this documentary evidence is almost entirely limited to Augustus. A few instances can also be found in the Lives which immediately follow; but it is to Augustus again that these quotations relate. It seems very likely that he copied such documents from the archives while he was holding secretarial appointments at court (p. 330), and that he had only got as far as the biography of Augustus when he was dismissed. The result is that the first Lives are the most interesting and valuable. The later ones prove much more sketchy.

They also show a new tendency to generalisation and vagueness.[28] Usually ancient historians become more detailed as they approach their own times, but Suetonius follows the reverse procedure. Evidently he felt most at ease when he was compiling from written sources; and he was proud of his ability in this field. When he emphasises his first-hand familiarity with *recherché* source-material and his ability to interpret it, he is overcoming the inferiority complex which biographers so often felt when they compared themselves to historians. For he appears to want to tell us that, in this respect, he has the better of them.

That Augustus was surnamed Thurinus I may assert on very trustworthy evidence, since I once obtained a bronze statuette, representing him as a boy and inscribed with that name in letters of iron almost illegible from age. . . .[29]

I myself find in the gazette [*acta diurna*] that Caligula first saw the light at Antium. . . .[30]

There have come into my hands note-books and papers with some well-known verses of Nero's, written with his own hand and in such wise that it was perfectly evident that they were not copies or taken down from dictation, but worked out exactly as one writes when thinking and creating; so many instances were there of words erased or struck through and written above the lines.[31]

Suetonius is justified in claiming that this sort of documentary exactitude could scarcely have been found in any of the historians. Their exalted interpretation of their literary task would have ruled out any such degree of precision.

And yet, unfortunately for us, he bears all too close a resemblance to other writers about the past in another respect: namely his reluctance to cite authorities by name. He is evidently acquainted, for example, with the speeches and letters of Cicero and Caesar. But we are not allowed to discover how extensively he made use of such material. He twice quotes Pollio, but does not mention Sallust or Livy. As for later historians, he must have used many of their works, but the only one of these writers he mentions is Cremutius Cordus (p. 305). He echoes the *Acts* of Augustus (p. 445, n. 40) at least four times, and was probably influenced by an autobiography written by the emperor Claudius (p. 453, n. 49).

His relation to Tacitus was more complicated. The infinitely more imposing nature of Tacitus' work made it out of the question to think in terms of any sort of competition (p. 331). The *Annals* may have been published only a very short time before Suetonius' *Caesars*. Indeed, according to another view, they may have followed the first of these biographies, since Suetonius did not necessarily wait for Tacitus' publication before offering the initial instalment of his own very different and more modest contribution (p. 330). But in any case, whatever the exact chronological relation, the biographer is unlikely to have drawn on Tacitus very extensively, since their genres were regarded as so different. Similarities or apparent echoes may indicate a common source.[32] Possibly the reference to Nero's poetry may be an implied correction of Tacitus' version,[33] and there seem to be certain other implicit criticisms as well.[34] It would not be surprising if the vast shadow of Tacitus' work exercised rather a damping effect on Suetonius, and it may well be that the diminished quality of his later Lives reflects a certain hesitancy, or lack of enthusiasm, about advancing to this subsequent period which was being so formidably illuminated by Tacitus.

8

Christian and Pagan

21

Eusebius

THE placid age in which Plutarch and Suetonius had composed their biographies continued under Antoninus Pius (AD 138–61). But the reign of Marcus Aurelius (161–80) already saw the first signs of the torments of later Rome. The defence first of the northern and then of the eastern frontier started to raise unprecedentedly formidable problems, which caused such a drain on the national resources that taxation finally almost wiped out of existence the middle class which had been the backbone of Greco-Roman society. In order to raise the sums needed to meet these threats, an emperor of formidable gifts, Septimius Severus (193–211) from north Africa, started the conversion of the Empire into a totalitarian state, and successive emperors of his dynasty accelerated the process.

In AD 235 began a terrible period of fifty years in which the central authority intensified oppression. At the same time, it was paralysed by continual revolts led by Roman generals who, at brief intervals, superseded one another on the imperial throne. The process was only arrested by Aurelian (270–5) and other emperors of Danubian origin who achieved the apparently impossible task of simultaneously mastering their internal enemies and repelling foreign foes.

Then started a new phase of stability under Diocletian (284–305), who shared the throne with a colleague and two subordinate emperors. A full-scale oriental authoritarianism was introduced. After his abdication, anarchy returned, but Constantine the Great emerged as ruler first of the west (312) and then of the whole Roman world (324–37). He took two decisive steps. During the previous half-century, Rome had ceased to be an adequate centre either for the economic or the military needs of the Empire, and Constantine moved the capital to Byzantium, now renamed Constantinople. Secondly, Christianity, hitherto the religion of a persecuted minority, was made the official religion of all territories governed by Rome.

This century and a half between Septimius Severus and Constantine was a time of many superlative cultural achievements, notably in the spheres of philosophy and sculpture and architecture. But poetry, in both languages, was dumb or insignificant; and history was undistinguished. A great many people had always liked reading the historians less than the fictitious material from which their art had originated (p. 15). In the last centuries BC, historical novels and various other sorts of fanciful literature had brought the purely romantic novel into existence, and this began to reach the climax of its popularity in the second century AD, with history suffering accordingly.

Nevertheless, historical writers were not altogether lacking during this century. There was a useful Greek chronicler, Appian of Alexandria, who wrote on the Roman conquests.[1] Arrian of Nicomedia (Izmit) in Bithynia soberly retold the story of Alexander the Great, with ambitions to become a new Xenophon.[2] There was even a theorist, the prolific and versatile Lucian of Samosata, whose treatise is our only surviving classical essay on historiography.[3] A good deal of what he said was derived from Thucydides,[4] but in another work he added, on his own account, an amusing parody of the traditional traveller's tales which had again become fashionable.[5]

Then, during the third century AD, it was not very safe to write about facts, and people in even larger numbers turned away from the grim circumstances of their lives to the vicarious thrills of romance. One of the few historians, again writing in Greek, was Dio Cassius of Nicaea (Iznik) in Bithynia (c. 155–235). His Roman history went down to AD 229 – the year in which he became consul for the second time. The portions of his work between 68 and 10 BC are fully preserved, and other sections survive in fragments or summaries. Although no master of style or narrative or judgment, Dio assumes importance as a historical authority owing to the gaps in our knowledge that he fills. Although ignorant of Republican institutions, he

344

possessed some historical sense and appreciated the danger of tainted sources. But his belief that detail is incompatible with the dignity of history means that a lot we should like to know is left out. The period 180–238 was also dealt with, very superficially, by a further writer in Greek, Herodian, a Syrian who was a minor Roman official. Later, an Athenian statesman and man of action, Dexippus, wrote a universal history down to 269–70. He also composed a history of the successors of Alexander, and an account of the Gothic Wars from 238 until Aurelian. Speeches which have survived from this work show that he was something of a stylist, employing Thucydides as his model.

But these writers are not enough, and darkness has fallen upon most of the events of the third century. It is only fitfully broken by the biographies of emperors between 117 and 284 that are collected in the so-called *Historia Augusta*. The authorship and date of this wretched Latin compilation are disputed. But it was not published earlier than the second half of the fourth century. The original title of the work is unknown. But in any case it is fraudulent fiction and must be called pastiche rather than history.

More remarkable, from the point of view of historiography, was an innovation which had taken place as early as the reign of Constantine. That was the creation of ecclesiastical history:* the description of the most astonishing and enigmatic phenomenon of the age, the rise of Christianity. This was the subject of a Greek work by Eusebius of Caesarea, an important harbour-city (near Zikhron Jaakov in Israel) and the capital of the Roman province which had formerly been called Judaea and was now Syria Palaestina.

Eusebius' life extended from *c.* 260 to *c.* 340, covering the whole of the most critical epoch of Christian expansion.

His *History of the Church*, divided into ten books, gives a consecutive story of Christianity from its beginnings until the early fourth century AD. The work begins with an analysis of its projected plan. Eusebius' intention is to describe the apostolic succession, the principal events recorded in the story of the Church, the outstanding Christian leaders, the most prominent heretics, the calamities that befell the Jews after their crucifixion of Jesus, and the deaths of the holy martyrs. The first four books tell of Jesus Christ and his contemporaries (I), the work of the Apostles to the deaths of St Paul and St Peter (II), enemies within the Church and early persecutions (III), and subsequent events

* For a mild fourth-century revival of secular history, see p. 463, n. 106.

down to the martyrdoms of Polycarp and Justin under Marcus Aurelius (161–80). The fifth book deals with the oppressions of Christians in Gaul during his reign, and the deviant movements (heresies) of Marcion and Montanus. The main subjects of Book VI are the persecutions of Septimius Severus (193–211) and Trajanus Decius (249–51) and the careers and writings of the Alexandrian theologians Clement (c. 150–211/216) and Origen (c. 185/6–254/5). Book VII describes how the persecution was intensified under Valerian (253–259/260), whose victims included Cyprian of Carthage. Valerian's son Gallienus, however, initiated a more lenient policy. Next, an account is given of the further crop of heresies that characterised the period.

The climax of Christian martyrdoms is reached in Book VIII (303–10), which describes the Great Persecution launched by Diocletian and his subordinate emperor Galerius. The latter recanted on his deathbed (311) but, as the ninth book describes, Maximinus II Daia continued to pursue anti-Christian measures until he also died two years later. Meanwhile in 312 Constantine the Great had overthrown the pagan Maxentius at the battle of the Milvian Bridge outside Rome. The last book celebrates the Peace of the Church. In unison with his eastern colleague Licinius, Constantine published the 'Edict of Milan' (313) establishing the tolerance which soon made Christianity the official religion of the State. Later, Licinius began to adopt an unfriendly attitude towards the faith. But Constantine suppressed him in 324 and became the sole ruler of the Empire.

Eusebius was credited with forty-six works, some of them very long. Fifteen have survived, as well as incomplete versions of four others, and translations in Syriac and Armenian and Latin. Before his *History of the Church* he had written a *Preparation for the Gospel* and *Proof of the Gospel*, in fifteen and twenty books respectively.[6] These works demonstrated how all previous history, and particularly Hebrew experience and thought, had led up to the Christian revelation. Far from being upstarts without respectable antecedents, the Christians possessed a glorious past.[7] Eusebius was justifying Christianity in the terms that Josephus had applied to Judaism.

He also compiled *Chronological Tables* (*Chronica*). This work, based on the *Chronography* of a Christian philosopher, Julius Africanus of Jerusalem,[8] epitomised the principal events among what seemed to him the most significant nations of the world.[9] Arranged side by side, these items brought the happenings of the pagan and Jewish past into a clearer time-relation, and provided a framework for the subsequent *History of the Church*. They contribute to our knowledge of Greek and Roman dates.

Eusebius' work *Against Hierocles* sought to refute a man who was one of the bitterest enemies of Christianity and, as governor of Bithynia and Egypt, played a leading part in the Great Persecution. Another early work was a biography of the author's own patron and friend the learned Pamphilus, who had been executed during the purge (310). Other historical or quasi-historical portions of Eusebius' voluminous output included an account of the *Martyrs of Palestine*, whose sufferings he himself had witnessed. Finally, he wrote a *Life of Constantine* after that emperor's death (337).

The first half of the *History of the Church* had probably been drafted by 309, at a time when Christianity was unrecognised and persecution still continued. Alternatively, the first eight books may represent the original edition, the remaining two having been added separately at intervals. The last book records the downfall of the eastern emperor Licinius in 324. Constantine's eldest son Crispus, however, is still in favour. He was executed in 326, so the publication of the work must have been completed during the year or two immediately preceding that date.

As a young man Eusebius worked at Caesarea in the school of Christian studies organised by Pamphilus. This institution possessed the library of the outstanding, though unorthodox, theologian Origen.[10] During the Great Persecution Palestinian Christians suffered severely, and it was at Caesarea that most of the trials took place. When Pamphilus was arrested and executed, Eusebius was briefly detained but escaped martyrdom, a circumstance which earned him subsequent criticism. Nevertheless, he became bishop of Caesarea (311). Shortly afterwards he formed close personal contact with Constantine and remained in his favour for the rest of the emperor's life.

During the previous decade the newly established church had continued to be rent by controversy. The principal quarrels now centred round the doctrines of the Alexandrian theologian Arius, whose Hellenising emphasis on the humanity of Jesus was held to involve depreciation of his divinity. As can be inferred from his own words, Eusebius was at first quite sympathetic to the Arians.[11] When the eastern bishops were summoned to the Council of Nicaea in order to settle the problem (325), he seems to have attempted to compromise; but he was compelled to give way to the anti-Arian views of the majority.[12] Declining promotion to the patriarchate of Antioch (331), Eusebius outlived his imperial patron by two or three years.

The rise of Christianity had stirred up profound curiosity about the causes and circumstances of this unprecedented and sensational development. And in his *History of the Church* Eusebius set himself the pioneer task of satisfying the demand.

> I am the first to venture on such a project and to set out on what is indeed a lonely and untrodden path. But I pray that I may have God to guide me and the power of the Lord to assist me. As for men, I have failed to find any clear footprints of those who have gone this way before me: only faint traces, by which in differing fashions they have left us partial accounts of their own lifetimes. Raising their voices like warning lights far ahead and calling out as from a distant watch tower perched on some hill, they make clear to me by what path I must walk and guide the course of my book if I am to reach my goal in safety. . . .[13]

The task was momentously worth while. 'Without this work,' says G. A. Williamson, 'what should we know of the progress of the early Church, its rapid extension, its glorious enthusiasm, energy and vitality, its tribulations, persecutions and martyrdoms, its sad divisions and astonishing heresies?'

Eusebius links Christ so closely with Old Testament events and prophecies that he even regards it as possible and necessary to describe Abraham, Moses and the rest as though they were Christians,[14] a rather disconcerting line of thought which had also been made use of by St Paul.[15] Nevertheless, the main story had to begin with the birth and life of Jesus, the event which divided the whole stream of human history into two parts, marking the completion of the first phase of the divine purpose and the beginning of the second. In other words, this account bears no relation to secular history. It reduces history to the fore-ordained movement of supernatural forces. Historical inevitability, which was to recur in Augustine and ever afterwards, was receiving its first classic expression.

In accordance with his chronological researches, Eusebius, following an indication in the Gospel according to St Luke, is at pains to link the career of Jesus with events in the pagan world. Not for him the completely distinct and even opposed Two Cities of Augustine, one human and the other divine. Noting that the renovation and expansion of the Roman world under Augustus had coincided with the coming of the Messiah, Eusebius interpreted the Empire's growth as part of the divine plan revealed in God's promise to Abraham. His own prosperous church at Caesarea reminded him of the good order and stability of the Pax Romana, without which the missionary church could never have expanded. Accordingly he claimed – in anticipation of a widespread medieval theory – that the communications and common language of the Empire had been willed by God so as to facilitate the dissemination of the Gospel. He also repeats a legend already reported by the north African apologist, Tertullian, to the effect that the emperor Tiberius, in whose reign Jesus was crucified, had expressed his support of Christian doctrine.[16]

And so the long story moves on its strange and fateful way, a mixture of invaluable detailed fact and devout fiction.

To a modern reader one of the most remarkable features of the work is the enormous and continuing list of 'heretics' – deviationists within, or almost within, the Christian Church. Eusebius' fierce denials and refutations of all these schools of thought bring us to the realisation that one of the decisive achievements of the Church was its successful establishment of the Canon which rejected unauthorised writings as spurious. Eusebius lists them at length, declaring each one in turn to be heretical fabrications, impious and beyond the pale.[17]

Heretics especially proliferated in Asia Minor, which was the training-ground not only of Christianity but also of every sort of aberration from its doctrines. Their tenets covered a vast range of divergent beliefs, including a variety of flirtations with secret esoteric (Gnostic) faiths and with the Manichaean dualism of good and evil which Gnostic sects often enshrined.[18] Eusebius breaks off his account of the second-century Church to describe this situation in terms which, incidentally, show how unconscious he was that his own tolerant attitude to Arianism might be regarded as heretical in a comparable sense (p. 348).

Like dazzling lights the churches were now shining all over the world, and to the limits of the human race faith in our Saviour and Lord Jesus Christ was at its peak, when the demon who hates the good, sworn enemy of truth and inveterate foe of man's salvation . . . employed new tactics contriving by every possible means that imposters and cheats, by cloaking themselves with the same name as our religion, should at one and the same time bring to the abyss of destruction every believer they could entrap, and by their own actions and endeavours turn those ignorant of the Faith away from the path that leads to the message of salvation.[19]

These condemned cults often contained a puritanical, fundamentalist, ecstatic streak. This was particularly prominent in the career and teaching of Montanus, whose influence gradually extended from Asia Minor to great numbers of men and women in the almost equally rich provinces of north Africa. Eusebius quotes an account of the founder of this huge movement.

There is, it appears, a village near the Phrygian border of Mysia called Ardabau. There it is said that a recent convert named Montanus . . . suddenly fell into a kind of trance and unnatural ecstasy. He raved, and began to chatter and talk nonsense. . . . Then he secretly stirred up and inflamed minds closed to the true Faith, raising up in this way two others – women whom he filled with the true spirit, so that they chattered crazily, inopportunely and wildly, like Montanus himself.[20]

The bishops, we are told, failed to silence one of the Montanist prophetesses, Maximilla, because they could make no headway against a plot in favour of her 'lying spirit which was leading the people astray'. As regards her male collaborators, Eusebius cites a right-minded writer, Apollonius: 'Tell me, does a prophet dye his hair? Does a prophet paint his eyelids? Does a prophet love ornaments? Does a prophet visit the gaming tables and play dice? Does a prophet do business as a moneylender? Let them say plainly whether these things are permissible or not, and I will prove that they have been going on in their circles.'[21] The government of Rome, in its pagan days, did not always successfully distinguish these extreme manifestations from the central stream of Christianity itself. What became clear, however, was that no sort of Christian could enjoy any measure of favour. Moreover, the populations throughout the Empire, even more than the government itself, saw Christians as a self-contained unit refusing patriotic duties and possessing secret customs that seemed to warrant the most sinister interpretations.

At intervals emperors indulged these popular suspicions, and sought to arrest the extension of Christianity. Hence the periodical recurrence of all the restrictions and persecutions which, in the end, so signally failed to achieve their purpose. The pages of Eusebius do not provide a balanced account of the varying motives and methods which were displayed by the imperial authorities and provincial governors in each successive purge. His account also gives an exaggerated idea of the scope of the repressions. Nevertheless, even if they are regarded with a more precise eye than his, it is clear that they were both miscalculated and bestial. And, as time went on, they became worse, especially in the eastern provinces. Eusebius describes the ordeals of 146 'witnesses' (martyrs) who died for this cause. Polycarp, bishop of Smyrna (Izmir) under Marcus Aurelius, seemed to him the greatest of them all. In Palestine, where Eusebius himself saw what was going on, he declared that his own patron Pamphilus was the noblest of the sufferers. He also saw some of the executions in Egypt.

We are spared none of the horrors; and his account of the willingness of determined Christians to offer themselves to a painful death is evidently true.

All the time I observed a most wonderful eagerness and a truly divine power and enthusiasm in those who had put their trust in the Christ of God. No sooner had the first batch been sentenced, than others from every side would jump on to the platform in front of the judge and proclaim themselves Christians.

They paid no heed to torture in all its terrifying forms, but undaunted spoke boldly of their devotion to the God of the universe and with joy, laughter and gaiety received the final sentence.[22]

This striving for redemption at a cost of suffering and death, as Reinhold Niebuhr remarks, cannot be explained to a non-Christian, because such ordeals could not have been borne without the faith which was Christianity's indispensable feature.

Another aspect of the rise of the Church is the strong vein of asceticism, a feature of pagan cults which became accentuated when it was combined with Christian beliefs. Origen for example (who castrated himself to avoid temptation):

Sometimes trained himself by periods of fastings, sometimes by restricting the hours of sleep, which he insisted on taking, never in bed, always on the floor. Above all, he felt that he must keep the Gospel sayings of the Saviour urging us not to carry two coats or wear shoes and never to be worried by anxiety about the future. He displayed an enthusiasm beyond his years, and patiently enduring cold and nakedness went to the furthest limit of poverty to the utter amazement of his pupils and the distress of his countless friends, who begged him to share their possessions in recognition of the labours that they saw him bestow on his religious teachings.[23]

Animated by this spirit, and anxious as well to flee from desperate material conditions and extortionate imperial agents, thousands of men and women became monks and nuns, first in the deserts of Egypt, and then in Palestine and elsewhere. These people who took to the monastic life placed themselves beyond the arm of the Church, which at first regarded them as little better than heretics.

And the Church, even when it was still underground, was already powerful and efficient. Eusebius explains how the Christian authorities strengthened their system until it had become a state within a state. One of their principal methods was the effective humanitarian organisation of charity to the poor and oppressed. Philanthropy had been stressed as a religious duty in ancient Israel and Egypt; and Greece and Rome, too, from varying motives, went farther in this direction than has often been thought. But it was the Christians who made this activity into a vital element of their policy. A letter from Dionysius bishop of Corinth to the Romans (*c.* 168) is quoted to illustrate the point.

> From the start it has been your custom to treat all Christians with unfailing kindness, and to send contributions to many churches in every city, sometimes alleviating the distress of those in need, sometimes providing for your brothers in the mines by the contributions you have sent from the start. Thus you Romans have observed the ancestral Roman custom, which your revered Bishop Soter has not only maintained but enlarged, by generously providing the abundant supplies distributed among God's people.[24]

Eusebius gradually records the stages by which such efficiency and devotion, combined with other causes which are still partially obscure, led to those extraordinary developments of the early fourth century AD when Galerius, about to die, called a halt to the persecution (311). And then Constantine, victor at the Milvian Bridge, joined with his colleague Licinius to publish the 'Edict of Milan' introducing the universal religious tolerance which assured the free development and early triumph of Christianity (p. 346). The 'Edict' is quoted by Eusebius in the form transmitted by the emperors to one of their provincial governors.

This therefore is the decision that we reached by sound and careful reasoning: no one whatever was to be denied the right to follow and choose the Christian observance or form of worship. . . . Every individual still desirous of observing the Christian form of worship should without any interference be allowed to do so. . . . We have given the said Christians free and absolute permission to practise their own worship. . . . All property [taken from them] is to be handed over to the Christian body immediately, by energetic action on your part, without any delay. . . . In all these matters you must put all the energy you possess at the service of the aforesaid Christian body.[25]

Christianity had not, indeed, become a world faith. It did not even become dominant in all areas where there were large Christian communities. The Persian Empire, for example, contained a great many Christians: but the Government never fell under their control – because there never was a Persian ruler who felt like Constantine. Yet within the huge Roman dominions, during the rest of his reign, Christianity gradually but rapidly became the official religion. Finally Constantine was baptised (by another Eusebius), after postponing this, as many people did, until his deathbed, when he could sin no more (337).

Previously, he had been an adherent of the worship of the sun, which was the most powerful manifestation of paganism during this period. Constantine's determined but rather confused transition to Christianity, raising it from a far from irresistible minority to be the official faith of the Roman State, is a tantalisingly complex story of which we can learn all too little from Eusebius. Instead, we read much praise of Constantine; and in his Life, which was Eusebius' last work, the praise swells into full-scale encomium. There is no mention here of the pathologically violent suspicion and cruelty which led the emperor to put his wife and eldest son to death – the sort of happenings which later caused Augustine to feel understandable reservations about him, in spite of all he had done for the Church.

To his friend Eusebius, on the other hand, Constantine appears as a man of superhuman qualities who witnessed a sign from God, and acted upon his vision. While marching in Gaul, sometime before his conquest of Italy, he declared that he had seen a cross of light above the sun, inscribed with the words *Conquer with this*. And the army saw it too.[26] That all the soldiers, as well as Constantine, witnessed the vision is obviously unlikely, but at all events he himself, at least in later life, claimed he had received this heavenly visitation. 'It would have been hard to believe,' said Eusebius, 'if anyone else had spoken of it. But a long time later the triumphant emperor himself described it to the writer of this work. This was when I had the honour of knowing him and of being in his company. When he told me the story, he swore to its truth.'

Trances and visions and hallucinations were a feature of the age. Perhaps Constantine had seen a rare cross-like natural phenomenon, produced by the sun. At any rate, whatever the explanation, Constantine was able to convince himself that he had been granted a supernatural experience. According to another writer, Lactantius, the emperor was warned in a dream, before the Battle of the Milvian Bridge, to inscribe a monogram signifying 'Christos' upon his soldiers' shields.[27]

What then followed, according to Eusebius, was a reign fully in keeping with this divine protection. As he rightly says, the emperor's portraits on coins, like his statues, show him looking up to heaven.[28] Adapting old pagan philosophies of kingship to Constantine, Eusebius praised his autocracy as the earthly mirror of God's rule, the bulwark against chaos and anarchy.[29] But above all, though later Christian writers did not always agree that this was a good thing, Constantine had united Church and State and made each indispensable to the other: among all Roman emperors he was outstanding for his services to God and the Church.[30]

The emperor displayed the new power of the Church in immense, original buildings. It is useful that Eusebius describes their splendour because they have vanished. So great was the veneration they attracted that later rulers were eager to replace them by structures of their own. If Constantine's shrines had survived, we should surely see Roman architecture in a new perspective, with these daring creations as its climax. At his new capital, for example, he began the Church of the Holy Apostles, at which he himself was worshipped as the Thirteenth Disciple: and Eusebius describes its dazzling brilliance with great feeling.[31]

In these great buildings were enacted the rites and prayers that could alone ward off the menacing encroachments of evil. Eusebius and his contemporaries saw evil as a desperately real and palpable

354

thing, embodied in savage spirits, the *daimones* whose name translators once rendered as 'demons'.

The envy that hates good, the demon that loves evil, bursting with rage, lined up all his lethal forces against us. At first he was like a mad dog that closes his jaws on the stones thrown at him and vents on the inanimate missiles his fury against those who are trying to keep him away. He directed his ferocious madness against the stones of the places of worship and the inanimate timbers of the buildings, bringing, as he himself imagined, ruin on the churches. Then he uttered terrible hissings and his own serpentlike sounds, at one time in the threats of godless tyrants, at another in the blasphemous decrees of impious rulers. Again, he vomited forth his own deadly venom and by his noxious, soul-destroying poisons paralysed the souls enslaved to him, almost annihilating them by his death-bringing sacrifices to dead idols and letting loose against us every beast in human shape and every kind of savagery.

But once again the Angel of great counsel, God's great Commander-in-Chief, appeared suddenly. . . .

With extreme optimism, undamped by the ferocity of Constantine and the oppressions of bureaucrats, Eusebius sees the spectacular new order as the climax of human happiness. He quotes at length his own festival speech on the Building of the Churches, addressed to Paulinus, bishop of Tyre.

So now as never before the most exalted emperors of all, aware of the honour they have been privileged to receive from Him, spit in the face of dead idols, trample on the lawless rites of demons, and laugh at the old lies handed down by their father.

Day after day men kept dazzling festival; light was everywhere, smiling faces and shining eyes. They danced and sang in city and country alike, giving honour first of all to God our Sovereign Lord, as they had been instructed, and then to the pious emperor with his sons, so dear to God.[32]

The most important thing, Eusebius hopefully asserted, was that unity had been created – not only unity between Church and State, but unity *within* the Church. He himself had taken an active part in the attempts to create that unity, in the face of every obstacle (p. 348). The debates assumed a passionate and frenzied character, because it was widely believed that disharmony in the Church was a direct invitation to divine chastisement. Just as Josephus had called the destruction of Jerusalem a visitation by God upon the wicked, so Eusebius considered that the persecutions of Diocletian were due to the fault of the Church: because of the disastrous internal strife that had prevailed in its midst.

Increasing freedom transformed our character to arrogance and sloth. We began envying and abusing each other, cutting our own throats, as occasion offered, with weapons of sharp-edged words; rulers of the Church hurled themselves against rulers, and laymen waged party fights against laymen, and unspeakable hypocrisy and dissimulation were carried to the limit of wickedness. . . . Those of us who were supposed to be pastors cast off the restraining influence of the fear of God and quarrelled heatedly with each other, engaged solely in swelling the disputes, threats, envy and mutual hostility and hate, frantically demanding the despotic power they coveted.[33]

Now that the Church had been freed and exalted by Constantine, those days were over – or ought to be over. The recollection of that horrible time made it all the more important that the Church should now, at last, be undivided, since nothing angers God more than its division, which is the cutting up of the body of Christ.

The urgency of these warnings was topical enough. For all Constantine's efforts were in vain, and he did not succeed in unifying Christianity. The foundation of Constantinople involuntarily accelerated the division between Catholic and Orthodox. That lay in the future, but there was also an immediate schism. For the entire concept of Church and State was challenged, with the utmost determination, by the Donatists, the puritanical and extremist heirs of Montanus in northern Africa (p. 350). Eventually, Constantine lost his patience and employed force against the recalcitrants. By so doing he set the pattern for century after century of persecution of Christian by Christian.

In his *History of the Church* Eusebius appended imperial letters which showed how disgusted and horrified the emperor felt because of these divisions he was unable to prevent – divisions rising to a ferocity which shocked even pagans like Julian the Apostate (d. 363).[34] As Constantine wrote to Chrestus, bishop of Syracuse,

When on an earlier occasion base and perverted motives led certain persons to begin creating divisions regarding the worship of the holy and heavenly power and the universal religion, I determined to cut short such quarrels among them. . . . It has come about that the very persons who ought to display brotherly unity and concord are estranged from each other in a way that is disgraceful if not positively sickening.[35]

One of the most remarkable and valuable aspects of Eusebius' work is his inclusion of nearly two hundred and fifty of these verbatim quotations, including many official documents of historical importance. Here is an unusual feature which, paradoxically enough, he shares only with that utterly different writer Suetonius (p. 338). Not for them the stylistic adjustments which earlier historians had employed when they wanted to quote such documentary evidence. The authenticity of the imperial pronouncements cited by Eusebius has been corroborated by inscriptional evidence proving that his version of an edict of the emperor Maximinus II is correct and exact.[36]

A man of wide learning, Eusebius quotes or summarises letters or decrees from forty-nine authors and more than a hundred books. In marshalling this carefully collected material, he sounds, from time to time, a note of judicial caution. 'Eusebius,' says Guy Schofield, 'the dependable, the scholarly, was by far the most important and reliable historian of the ancient church.' And yet to call him also, as the same writer does, 'the shrewd discarder of the dubious' is excessive, or rather irrelevant, praise to apply to someone whose whole subject encourages departures from cold secular truth, and invites a deliberate neglect of plausible worldly causes and connexions. Such, for example, was the spirit which enabled him to include a translation from the Syriac of a long fictitious correspondence between Jesus and King Abgar v the Black of Edessa in Osrhoene (Urfa in south-east Turkey).[37]

Moreover, Eusebius' style was depressing. Never before had there been such a total departure from the ancient classical tradition, now over seven hundred years old, requiring that history should be well written. Eusebius employs a cumbersome, obscure and slovenly Greek. His narrative is shallow and uninspired, and follows a dull, muddled and haphazard plan. Even the most sensational events manage to trail along with tedious monotony. Josephus, writing of the Jews, was said to have had greatness thrust upon him. Eusebius' survey of the Christians was more original, because of an almost total lack of forerunners: but his ability as a historian was much smaller. The many gifts and achievements which had characterised Greek and Roman historians of the past were mostly beyond his grasp. Yet his subject was an overwhelmingly significant one; and he performed a vital task by devoting his ardent passion and tireless industry to the mastery and demonstration of its grandeur.

357

22

Ammianus

THE death of Constantine the Great (337) was followed by struggles between his three sons. Constantius II emerged as the sole survivor (350). Defeating a western usurper who had killed one of his brothers,[1] he appointed his nephew Gallus as Caesar (viceroy or subordinate emperor) in the east.

That is the point at which the surviving writings of Ammianus Marcellinus begin. They formed part of a Latin history of thirty-one books covering the period between the accession of Nerva in AD 96 to the death of the eastern emperor Valens in 378. The work was probably called *Books of Deeds* (*Rerum Gestarum Libri*), perhaps with the addition of the words 'From the Principate of Nerva'. The first thirteen books, covering more than nine-tenths of the epoch, are lost. But the last eighteen survive. Much more detailed, they deal with a period of only twenty-five years during his own lifetime.[2] Thus Ammianus experienced the opposite fate to Livy, whose contemporary sections were among the part of his work that disappeared. In view of the greater opportunities for originality available to a man writing about his own times, the achievement of Ammianus is the easier of the two to assess.

The extant portion of his history begins in the sixteenth year of Constantius II (353). Like other parts of the work, this fourteenth book, which is the first we possess, contains a wide variety of subjects. But particular attention is focused upon Ammianus' own commanding officer Ursicinus, commander-in-chief of the armies in the east. The beginning and end of the book, however, are concerned with the deputy emperor Gallus: it starts with his cruelties at Antioch, and concludes with his execution for misgovernment (354).

Book xv opens with a preface promising even greater accuracy than hitherto, now that the contemporary period has been reached. There follows a description of the bloody aftermath of Gallus' downfall. Meanwhile a *coup d'état* was staged by the Frankish general Silvanus at Colonia Agrippina (Cologne), but it was soon crushed by Ursicinus. Then came the promotion of Gallus' half-brother Julian to the Gallic command, with the same rank of Caesar as Gallus had possessed. Constantius himself was residing at Mediolanum (Milan), and Book xvi reports the only visit he ever made to Rome. The historian then recounts Julian's campaigns against the German coalition of the Alemanni, and his victory at Argentorate (Strasbourg) in 357. The next book describes his incursions into enemy country, followed by campaigns against the Sarmatians and Quadi on the Danube.

Books xviii and xix are concerned with the Persians, whose supersession of Parthia in the previous century had added greatly and permanently to the difficulties of the Roman Empire. Constantius, now engaged in a war against the Persian king Sapor (Shapur) ii of Persia (310–79), lost the fortress of Amida (Diyarbakir) on the Tigris after a grim siege (359). The twentieth book tells how Ursicinus was unfairly dismissed by Constantius. Suspicious of Julian as of everyone else, Constantius now ordered that the Gallic army should be transferred to his own command. But instead the troops hailed Julian as emperor at Lutetia (Paris) in 360. Constantius, marching against him in the following year, died on the way, leaving him as sole ruler.

The next four books deal with the reign of Julian, called 'the Apostate' because he abandoned the Christianity of his predecessors in favour of a philosophical, sun-worshipping paganism. He revived the religious toleration which had been the professed intention of the Edict of Milan (p. 346); but subsequently measures were introduced against the Christians. The twenty-second book describes the entry of Julian to his capital at Constantinople. He also began to purge the administration of the numerous abuses introduced during the previous reign. Then he spent the winter at Antioch where, as the following book indicates, he prepared for a new war against the Persians. Book xxiv describes his invasion of their empire as far as the Tigris, and xxv his death from a wound at Ctesiphon (363). His successor Jovian, an Illyrian Christian, made an unsatisfactory peace with Persia but died early in the following year. Thereupon the army gave the throne to another Christian of Danubian origin, Valentinian I.

Ammianus begins the twenty-sixth book with a new preface indicating that he had originally decided to stop at this point, and that what follows is supplementary. He tells of the accession of Valentinian I and the promotion of his brother Valens to be co-emperor in the east. The Empire was divided in a more formal fashion than hitherto, with the two emperors ruling at Augusta Treverorum (Trier) and Constantinople respectively. At the eastern capital Procopius revolted and was suppressed. Books XXVII and XXVIII record fighting in various theatres of war, including Britain, where a competent Spanish general, Theodosius the elder, fought successful campaigns. Meanwhile Valentinian's original attitude of friendship towards the Senate changed into an attitude of savage hostility against the aristocratic and educated classes. His elder son Gratian, aged eight, was promoted to be an additional co-emperor (367). The twenty-ninth book reports the trial of the lawyer Theodorus, whom Valens put to death at Antioch for high treason and magic (371–2), crimes for which many others were convicted as well. We are then told of the rebellion of Firmus in north Africa, and its suppression by Theodosius the elder. The next book describes Valentinian's campaign against the Quadi, and his sudden death in 375.[3] Finally, the long Book XXXI recounts the invasion of the Empire by the Visigoths. On the Balkan frontier these people, hard pressed by the Huns from the north, were allowed by Valens to settle inside the Empire in Thrace (376). But quarrels broke out, and although an attempt was made to expel the immigrants they returned, reinforced by other tribes, and overwhelmed Valens at Hadrianopolis (Edirne, Adrianople) in 378. His body was never found.

The Visigoths and their allies then made an unsuccessful attempt to reach Constantinople; and there the History of Ammianus comes to an end. But the events that followed must be briefly indicated here, because of the effect they exercised on what he wrote. Gratian now recognised Theodosius I as his colleague, a surprising choice since four years earlier the new emperor's father, Theodosius the elder had been executed – clearly on the orders either of Valentinian I or even of Gratian himself (or his regents). While Gratian ruled at

Augusta Treverorum and then Mediolanum, Theodosius I made his capital at Constantinople. In 379–82 both emperors introduced a series of measures persecuting pagans. Then, in 383, educated foreigners were expelled from Rome.

In the same year Gratian was murdered by a usurper, and Theodosius I gradually established himself as sole emperor.[4] Subsequently, he began to show rather more favour to the powerful pagan revival movement at Rome. But this phase came to an end when the aristocratic society embodying these tendencies supported the *coup d'état* of Eugenius (392), a professor of lukewarm Christian beliefs who was placed on the throne by a Frankish general. Theodosius I suppressed Eugenius (394), but died almost immediately afterwards, and the Empire was divided between his sons.[5]

Ammianus himself died either shortly before or shortly after the death of Theodosius I, probably at about the age of sixty. As his separate prefaces to Books XV and XXVI suggest, he published different parts of his work at different times. The history up to his second preface, at the death of Jovian in 364 (p. 360), had been published by about 392.[6] Ammianus gives various reasons for his original decision to go no further than 364, which he records at that point.

Having narrated the course of events with the strictest care up to the bounds of the present epoch, I had already determined to withdraw my foot from the more familiar tracks, partly to avoid the dangers which are often connected with the truth, and partly to escape unreasonable critics of the work which I am composing: who cry out as if wronged, if one has failed to mention what an emperor said at table, or left out the reason why the common soldiers were led before the standards for punishment, or because in an ample account of regions he ought not to have been silent about some insignificant forts. . . .[7]

The desire not to get caught up with contemporary trivialities was a valid point. But avoidance of 'the dangers which are connected with the truth' was a more urgently pressing consideration, since Ammianus was a pagan and the tendency for pagans to be frowned upon by the Christian imperial power, never altogether absent, was sharpened by the revolt of Eugenius in 392.

But then Ammianus had second thoughts, and decided to go on. What induced those second thoughts?[8] Did he find, or at least have reason to hope, that his misgivings about the official reaction were unjustified? Even if he did, he assures us that he still felt qualms about the evident explosiveness of such very recent history. The trials and executions of 366 enable him to remind us of this, and at the same time to declare that things were better now: 'Although, after long consideration of various circumstances, well-grounded dread restrained me from giving a minute account of this series of bloody deeds, yet I shall, relying on the better morals of the present day, set forth briefly such of them as are worthy of notice.'[9] However, he still had to be very careful, and his last books, which were published some time during these difficult years (or possibly just after the death of Theodosius I in 395), bear marks of this caution (p. 367).[10]

Ammianus was born between 325 and 330. He came of a prosperous semi-noble family at Antioch, a magnificent city of which he speaks with great pride, not unmixed with criticism.[11] As a young man he enrolled in a smart army regiment, the *protectores domestici*. In 353, or perhaps a few years earlier, he joined the staff of Ursicinus at the key frontier-station of Nisibis in Mesopotamia, now Nüsaybin in south-eastern Turkey. He accompanied Ursicinus on a journey from there to Gaul in order to put down the revolt of Silvanus, and stayed in Gaul long enough to join Julian's first German campaign (356). In the following year he was recalled to the eastern frontier, where he took part in the campaigns of Constantius II against the Persians. Ammianus was one of the besieged in the fortress of Amida (359). Then he apparently held a post in connection with army food supplies; and his next service was on the Mesopotamian expedition of Julian (p. 359).

Whether he left the army soon after Julian's death, or stayed on for a time, is unknown. In due course, perhaps soon after 378, he settled in Rome. It is conceivable that he was one of the educated aliens whose expulsion from the city in 383 (p. 361) he describes with indignation,[12] but he may have been exempted owing to his former military rank. We do not know where he spent the last period of his life, during which his history was written. He recited parts of his work at Rome,[13] but probably lived a good deal of the time at Antioch. He also travelled widely in the eastern parts of the Empire.[14]

Ammianus, said Harold Mattingly, is 'an astonishing apparition, an original mind in history after centuries of dry rot'. Indeed, it is by no means fantastic to compare his merits with those of Tacitus himself, whose Histories he deliberately set himself to continue (p. 383).

He stresses his firm determination to tell the truth. It was, of course, conventional to assert devotion to this ideal, but Ammianus does so with an insistence which is almost obsessive, and which, moreover, carries a large measure of justification.[15] 'The reliability of Ammianus' narrative,' says E. A. Thompson, 'even in matters of small detail, is not shown only by that narrative's internal consistency and its agreement with the very sparse notices of other Greek and Roman historians. It is also confirmed by an Armenian translation of a Syriac history of Armenia which is wholly independent but strongly corroborates Ammianus' version of eastern events.'[16]

Gibbon was so greatly impressed by the reliability of Ammianus that he saw him as a writer 'without the prejudices and passions which usually affect the mind of a contemporary'. That was, however, something of an overstatement, and indeed on one occasion Gibbon qualified it himself (p. 409). Anyone who has experienced the workings of a police state will appreciate that such an ideal was scarcely realisable in the Roman Empire of the time. It would indeed have been hard for a historian and public servant living in such a perilous age to have achieved complete objectivity about everybody, and Ammianus does not do so. For one thing, he paints an unmitigatedly black picture of Constantius' nephew and deputy Gallus, who was struck down (p. 359). Probably Gallus was cruel, perhaps monstrously so. But a more balanced picture would also have indicated his talents as a military commander, his popularity with the troops and proletariat, and the likelihood that, when he suppressed conspirators, at least some of them were guilty of the charges brought against them.

On the other hand Ammianus seems to have been too kind to the memory of his own general Ursicinus, whom Constantius dismissed in 360. Admittedly Ursicinus had served the emperor well, carrying out on his behalf a shabby and treacherous operation, the removal of the usurper Silvanus. But an emperor as dangerous as Constantius, though perhaps unjustified in suspecting Ursicinus of treason and embezzlement,[17] could hardly have been expected to welcome receiving this message from him: 'Let the emperor know, as if from the words of a seer, that so long as he grieves over what he has learned on no good authority to have happened at Amida, and so long as he is swayed by the will of eunuchs, not even he in person with all the flower of his army will be able next spring to prevent the dismemberment of Mesopotamia.'[18]

An even more conspicuous paragon than Ursicinus, however, is Julian, who served brilliantly in the north and then, as emperor, was Ammianus' commanding officer against Persia. Julian is made to embody the ideals of justice, self-control and military talent. Ammianus compares him with the legendary heroes of the early Republic, and, offering a salutary correction to our ideas of classical and post-classical periods, describes Julian's wars as the greatest Rome had ever fought.[19]

Yet his admiration is mixed with criticism, and the result is a balanced estimate. For we find, in particular, a less than whole-hearted support for some of Julian's actions and policies after he had been elevated to the imperial throne. When Ammianus' hero has finally become emperor and has thus obtained full scope to express his greatness, one would have expected the eulogistic note to be intensified. But the opposite is the case. Writing under a strongly Christian régime, Ammianus evidently felt free enough to speak warmly of Julian's behaviour when he was merely general and viceroy. But when the time came to speak of a pagan, apostate occupant of the throne, high praise would have been too likely to attract censure.[20] Furthermore, Ammianus genuinely believed that his own class had not received fair treatment from Julian (p. 376). He also felt that, after coming to the throne, he had behaved with less personal dignity than was incumbent upon an emperor – in an age when emperors were very grand indeed (p. 369). The historian also regarded his religious attitude as occasionally oppressive and unduly superstitious. For Julian, as Montaigne said, 'was besotted with the art of divination',[21] and Ammianus regarded this preoccupation with omens and mysticisms as excessive.

Above all, Julian seemed to have gone too far in his measures against the Christians. This was particularly apparent at Ammianus' home-town Antioch, a patriarchal see where he closed down Constantine's palace church and exhumed the remains of a local Christian martyr.[22] In these and other cases his usual fairmindness deserted him.

His own saying might be regarded as sound, namely that the ancient goddess of Justice, whom Aratus of Soli raised to heaven because of her impatience with men's sins, returned to earth again during his rule – were it not that sometimes he acted arbitrarily, and now and then seemed unlike himself.

For the laws which he enacted were not oppressive, but stated exactly what was to be done or left undone, with a few exceptions. For example, it was a harsh law that forbade Christian rhetoricians and grammarians to teach unless they consented to worship the pagan deities.[23]

Ammianus himself, who deplored this severity towards the Christians, was a moderate pagan. His own religious views show very much the same inconsistencies and indecisions that had characterised the beliefs of earlier writers. He speaks of Fortune and Fate and Nemesis, and mixes them up with one another and with Providence.[24] He is a determinist, but not a rigid one, and not a passive fatalist – a man who like earlier historians is able to believe, at one and the same time, that history's motive forces are human but that there is nevertheless some measure of truth in astrology, auguries, the interpretation of entrails, and premonitory voices and dreams.[25] Why, then, does he accuse Julian of too great a preoccupation with precisely the same kinds of divination? Because what Ammianus likes best in men is that they should be sober: they ought to exercise moderation. He is therefore hostile to all excesses in the propitiation of the unseen powers. This closely follows the old Roman tradition, which approved of religion in its proper place but did not want it to be overdone. And he cannot refrain from pointing out that Julian himself refused to pay any attention to signs when they happened to conflict what he himself wanted to do.[26]

Ammianus' own paganism is of the generalised sort characteristic of the day. He believes in a divine power which can, if you like, be regarded as made manifest through the various deities of polytheism, even if these are only names or aspects of divinity rather than actual separate gods and goddesses. He does not subscribe to the sharp dichotomy between pagan and Christian beliefs which had taken shape in Julian's mind owing to unpleasant childhood experiences. Quite on the contrary, Ammianus was a singularly broadminded man, who spoke up for religious toleration in the loudest and clearest tones possible at such an epoch. What he liked about Valentinian I was that

His reign was distinguished by toleration, in that he remained neutral in religious differences, neither troubling anyone on that ground nor ordering him to reverence this or that. He did not bend the necks of his subjects to his own belief by threatening edicts, but left such matters undisturbed as he found them.[27]

Ammianus did not share the Christian beliefs of Valentinian; but he had no prejudice against them. He admired the martyrs.[28] He also expressed admiration for 'some of the provincial bishops, whose moderation in food and drink, plain apparel also, and gaze fixed upon the earth, commend them to the Eternal Deity and to his true servants as pure and reverent men'.[29] Other bishops, however, seemed to him to waste far too much public money as they 'hastened hither and thither on the public post-horses to the various synods, as they call them'.[30] Worse still, some of the political churchmen in the cities were terrifyingly ambitious, not to say bloodthirsty.[31] Julian, though we know that he appreciated the efficiency of Christian charitable organisations, had expressed the same point in even stronger terms, declaring from his own experience 'that no wild beasts are such enemies to mankind as are most of the Christians in their deadly hatred to one another'.[32]

Ammianus did not hesitate to censure the brands of Christianity professed by earlier emperors. Constantius II, for example, comes under attack: 'The plain and simple religion of the Christians he obscured by a dotard's superstition; and by subtle and involved discussions about dogma, rather than by seriously trying to make them agree, he aroused many controversies. And as these spread more and more, he fed them with contentious words.'[33] But Constantius, like Valens, had favoured the Arian heresy (p. 347), and there was no danger in criticising Arianism under Theodosius I who disapproved of it. But Theodosius disapproved of pagans as well, at least during his final years (p. 361). Consequently, amid the general uncertainty of this epoch, the discussions of religion which had been quite freely present up to Book xxv of Ammianus' work are omitted from the last six books. The plural term 'gods' is no longer used, and eulogies of pagan philosophers are absent. Even his approval of Valentinian's policy of toleration must at that time have sounded significantly emphatic – perhaps perilously so.

Another noteworthy feature is Ammianus' treatment of Theodosius the elder, the father of Theodosius I. Most of the personages described in the last six books receive critical attention, but that is far from the case with Theodosius the elder. And indeed, although he seems in fact to have been a brutal man, it was only to be expected that the emperor's father should be praised, though some have detected a perfunctory note in Ammianus' fulsome analogies with Republican and imperial heroes. A more awkward problem lay in the fact that in 375 or 376 the elder Theodosius had been put to death by Valentinian I or Gratian or his representatives (p. 360). We do not know who was responsible or even why it happened. But clearly, when the victim's son had come to the throne, this was a most delicate subject. That is probably why Ammianus, who carries the story of the eastern empire down to 378, omits most western events from 375 onwards – and thus manages to avoid referring to the death of Theodosius the elder at all. Perhaps he had been executed for high treason; and he may have deserved it. We know that he was killed by the Prefect of Gaul, Maximinus,[34] who met his own end shortly afterwards. Ammianus, who writes very harshly of Maximinus, says he is going to describe his death in due course.[35] But he never fulfils his promise. The whole topic was too hazardous.

Those are the few men who, for pressing reasons, receive an assessment from Ammianus which is somewhat less than objective. But they are isolated cases which must not be emphasised, because his psychological studies are, in general, admirably balanced. He possessed a peculiar gift for the depiction of character, and these delineations yield nothing to Tacitus in their knowledge of the human heart. Many a personage stands out from his pages and comes alive – men such as the Christian convert Sextus Petronius Probus, the vastly wealthy commander of Valentinian I's guard, generous and loyal, but a jealous schemer and ruthless enemy, whose anxieties meant that his health was always below par.

But most remarkable of all is the manner in which Ammianus gradually brings out the characters of successive emperors. Their obituaries, described by him as 'brief epilogues',[36] are the best short characterisations in the whole of ancient history. Each ruler in turn receives this treatment. The last is Valens who ruled the eastern empire for fourteen years before meeting his end in the catastrophe of Adrianople (378).

He was a firm and faithful friend, severe in punishing ambitious designs, strict in maintaining discipline in the army and in civil life, always watchful and anxious lest anyone should elevate himself on the

13—TAH * *

ground of kinship with him. He was excessively slow towards conferring or taking away official positions, very just in his rule of the provinces, each of which he protected from injury as he would his own house, lightening the burden of tributes with a kind of special care, allowing no increase in taxes, not extortionate in estimating the indebtedness from arrears, a harsh and bitter enemy of thievish officials and of those detected in peculation. Under no other emperor does the Orient recall meeting better treatment in matters of this kind. . . .

He was immoderately desirous of great wealth, and impatient of toil, rather affecting awesome austerity than possessing it, and somewhat inclined to cruelty. He had rather an uncultivated mind, and was trained neither in the art of war nor in liberal studies. He was ready to gain advantage and profit at the expense of others' suffering, and more intolerable when he attributed offences that were committed to contempt of, or injury to, the imperial dignity. Then he vented his rage in blood-shed, and on the ruin of the rich. . . . He was in other ways unjust, hot tempered, and ready to listen to informers without distinguishing truth from falsity – a shameful fault, which is very greatly to be dreaded even in these our private affairs of everyday occurrence.

He was a procrastinator and irresolute. His complexion was dark, the pupil of one of his eyes was dimmed, but in such a way as not to be noticed at a distance. His body was well-knit, his height neither above nor below the average. He was knock-kneed, and somewhat pot-bellied.[37]

Whatever faults emperors might possess, Ammianus felt a profound consciousness of the necessity to serve them loyally. The imperial régime seemed to him a wholly legitimate system, ultimately deriving its power (though the process had become scarcely even a formality) from the people of Rome: 'The venerable city, after humbling the proud necks of savage nations, and making laws (the everlasting foundations and moorings of liberty) like a thrifty parent, wise and wealthy, has entrusted the management of her inheritance to the Caesars, as to her children.'[38] But even if the Roman people was, in this rhetorical sense, the ultimate fount of power, Ammianus made no bones about the fact – which Tacitus had so greatly resented – that the emperor was not only a soldier himself but the army's nominee. 'Behold, my dear Gratian,' says Valentinian to his son, 'you now wear, as we have all hoped, the imperial robes, bestowed upon you under favourable auspices by my will and that of our fellow-soldiers.'[39]

This supremacy which was the emperor's due had to be defended and upheld by every one of his subjects. 'The safety of a lawful prince, the protector and defender of good men, on whom depends the safety of others, ought to be safeguarded by the united diligence of every-one.'[40] Ammianus therefore echoed Tacitus' feeling that civil strife was the ultimate evil. Armed rebellion was flagrant disobedience to the ruler who had every right to exact loyalty; to act in such a way is to break a mutual obligation. When a man of imperial rank, Gallus Caesar, was put to death by his own emperor, it was a moral dilemma. Gallus was a hateful man, yet violence to a Caesar, even by orders of his superior, still constituted an affront to divine justice.[41]

So exalted were the rulers that Ammianus felt it was essential for them to behave impressively. In this, he felt, his talkative hero Julian failed. It was a point in favour of Constantius II, on the other hand, that he had 'always maintained the dignity of imperial majesty'.[42] The emperors of the time, surrounded by this atmosphere of rever-ence, kept up a remote oriental state. Their persons were exalted to a grandiose elevation half-way towards God who had made them his regents upon earth. Literature and sculpture tell the same story, and so does Ammianus' account of the deportment of Constantius II on the single occasion when he ever appeared in Rome (357).

Being saluted as Augustus with favouring shouts, while hills and shores thundered out the roar, he never stirred, but showed himself as calm and imperturbable as he was commonly seen in his provinces. For he both stooped when passing through lofty gates (although he was very short), and as if his neck were in a vice, he kept the gaze of his eyes straight ahead, and turned his face neither to right nor to left, but (as if he were a lay figure) neither did he nod when the wheel jolted nor was he ever seen to spit, or to wipe or rub his face or nose, or move his hands about. . . . Furthermore, during the entire period of his reign, he neither took up anyone to sit beside him in his carriage, nor admitted any private person to be his colleague in the insignia of the consulship, as other annointed princes did.[43]

This entry of Constantius to Rome was a solemn and symbolic occasion because Ammianus felt a profound, heartfelt belief in the glory of the eternal city. The magnificent Republican and imperial past seemed to him perpetually present and relevant. This was the very same State which had once conquered Hannibal. It was true that Rome had lost its supremacy, and was not even a political capital any more. Yet it was still a very powerful place, and had recently, with the emperor far away, actually increased its power, or rather its noble families had (p. 374).

In any case Rome remained the everlastingly glorious spiritual centre of the world. 'So then Constantius entered this city, the home of empire and every virtue, and when he had come to the Rostra, the most renowned Forum of ancient dominion, he stood amazed: and every side on which his eyes rested he was dazzled by the array of marvellous sights.'[44] For this was the place, declares Ammianus, which Virtue and Fortune, so often at variance, had united to make the greatest upon earth.

With hindsight, we look upon the late fourth century as a time when the Roman world was about to collapse, shattered into the fragments from which the modern nation-states then proceeded to emerge. And yet the Empire of Ammianus' day was still as vast and powerful as ever. Diocletian and Constantine had completed the reorganisation of every institution, clamping down an iron grip which ensured the upkeep of the huge imperial army and civil service. One result was that the comparative freedom of the individual, which had characterised the earlier Empire, was no more. All but the very rich suffered from far-reaching controls and oppressions. Hardship and misery abounded.

Ammianus knew this. Yet, like his predecessor Polybius, half a millennium earlier, he adopted an equivocal attitude towards the question of Decline and Fall. In many respects, the picture of deterioration was self-evident. He explains the phenomenon by comparing the Empire to a man who has reached advanced years. But this is a peaceful time of life, he says. 'Declining into old age, and often owing victory to its name alone, Rome has come to a quieter period of its existence.'[45] In fact, he knew that its best days lay far in the past. However, since it is eternal, he shies from following the metaphor up. He does not, cannot, envisage an impending end or transformation. His pagan literary contemporaries showed just the same surprising confidence. He and they would have utterly failed to comprehend Spengler's view that at some time 'the history of Western European mankind will be definitely closed'. The possibility of radical changes, such as were even now beginning to take place, was left unconsidered, because it appeared inconceivable.

There were troubles, certainly. They indicated that a decline from antique traditions had occurred. But Ammianus, like all ancient historians, believed that any such deterioration was directly due to the personal moral failings of bad and incompetent men. Once these faults were repaired, all would be well as in the past.[46] The system itself was not at fault. And it was the same with foreign affairs. There was no denying that the situation on the frontiers was terribly threatening. But was it really so abnormal or apocalyptic? Ammianus, looking at the past, feels it was not. This desire to place events in historical perspective, this unwillingness to be stampeded, was laudable – but in the present case misplaced, since the situation which had arisen was, in fact, about to sweep much of the ancient order away. Yet, pursuing his argument that one must maintain a sense of proportion, Ammianus refuses to take the view that there is anything exceptionally grave even about the obliteration of Valens by the Visigoths at Adrianople.

> Those who are unacquainted with ancient records say that the State was never before overspread by such a dark cloud of misfortune, but they are deceived by the horror of the recent ills which have overwhelmed them. For if they study earlier times or those which have recently passed, these will show that such dire disturbances have often happened.[47]

A study of the actual events and situations narrated by Ammianus as year succeeded year cannot fail to belie his words. He himself shows the emperor constantly engaged in checking break-throughs at one point after another on the frontiers. These breaches bear abundant testimony to the imminent collapse of Roman control in many provinces. But Ammianus only draws the stout-hearted deduction that the border must be defended against barbarian invasions with redoubled determination. Julian's advisers try to deter him from attempting aggressive war, which they rightly believe that the Empire is incapable of waging. But even they must concede that 'in the case of attack by an enemy the one fixed rule is to defend the safety of the State by every possible means and with unremitting effort'.[48]

The greatest problem of the day was presented by the influx into Rome's provinces of vast quantities of 'barbarians', immigrants to whom the disaster at Adrianople had given an unimpeded path. Ammianus does not seem to recognise that these men fulfilled a real need, since the Roman army needed them as recruits and indeed could no longer have existed without them. Nor does he see how these displacements of population were altering the face of Europe. Instead, following his traditional, ethical approach to the ills of the State, he repeats the old conventional view that it was wicked to 'buy off' or subsidise under-developed neighbours. This was a conclusion of questionable validity in his own times, when it was hard to find other ways of recruiting them for the army and keeping them at peace. But Ammianus felt that Julian was acting more wisely when he refused to pay such subsidies. 'From endless resources', he declares to his troops, 'the Roman empire has sunk to extremest want through those men who, to enrich themselves, have taught princes to buy peace from the barbarians with gold. The treasury has been pillaged, cities depopulated, provinces laid waste.'[49] And so Julian cut off payments to the Saracens, informing them that a war-like and watchful emperor disposed of steel and not gold.[50] This was noble unrealism, like the attitude of Ammianus who approved of it.

But in spite of Ammianus' belief that the imperial power could pull through, he duly records, and indeed stresses at great length, the reigns of terror instituted by successive emperors and by the deplorable crew of secret police, spies and informers who surrounded them. Such was the court of Constantius II:

Sometimes it happened that if the head of a household, in the seclusion of his private apartments, with no confidential servant present, had whispered something in the ear of his wife, the ruler learnt it on the following day . . . and so even the walls, the only sharers of secrets, were feared. . . . No one easily recalls the acquittal of anyone in the time of Constantius when an accusation against him had even been whispered.[51]

The guiding spirits of the emperor's secret service were Mercurius, a Persian who had formerly served as an imperial steward, and the Dacian notary Paulus.

Mercurius was called 'Count of Dreams', because like a slinking, biting cur, savage within but peacefully wagging its tail, he would often worm his way into banquets and meetings, and if anyone had told a friend that he had seen anything in his sleep, when nature roams more freely, Mercurius would give it a worse colour by his venomous skill and pour it into the open ears of the emperor. And on such grounds a man, as though really chargeable with inexpiable guilt, would be beaten down by a heavy burden of accusation.[52]

Paulus, on the other hand, was nicknamed the Chain.

This was because he was invincible in weaving coils of calumny, exerting himself in a wonderful variety of schemes, just as some expert wrestlers are in the habit of showing skill in their contests. . . .

Off went Paulus (as he was ordered) in panting haste and teeming with deadly fury, and since free rein was given to general calumny, men were brought in from almost the whole world, noble and obscure alike. . . . On his nod (I might almost say) depended the life of all who walk the earth.

For if anyone wore on his neck an amulet against the quartan ague or any other complaint, or was accused by the testimony of the evil-disposed of passing by a grave in the evening, on the ground that he was a dealer in poisons, or a gatherer of the horrors of tombs and the vain illusions of the ghosts that walk there, he was condemned to capital punishment and so perished.[53]

Valens, too, showed an equally lethal superstition, which was the cause of many executions.[54] So was the savagery of his brother Valentinian I.[55] It was at least fortunate that he was unconcerned with religion (p. 365), but his hot temper was exacerbated by a streak of bloodthirsty cruelty. What actually happened at the treason trials arranged by these emperors is not easy to reconstruct, for Ammianus' accounts contain as many omissions and obscurities as those of Tacitus. But the spirit of the times is clearly revealed.

Valentinian kept two savage, man-eating she-bears, one called Goldflake and the other Innocence, and looked after them with such extreme care that he placed their cages near his own bedroom, and appointed trustworthy keepers, who were to take particular care that the beasts' lamentable savageness should not by any chance be destroyed. Finally, after he had seen the burial of many corpses of those whom Innocence had torn to pieces, he allowed her to return to the forest unhurt, a good and faithful servant, in the hope that she would have cubs like herself.[56]

It would seem, in this atmosphere, that the Roman Senate, already reduced to impotence under a far less rigorous autocracy, could scarcely be thought of as playing any part at all. And yet Ammianus, full of his vision of antique, eternal Rome, still speaks of the institution with bated breath. The dignity of the Senate is what comes to his mind when Constantius paid his only visit to Rome.

When he was nearing the city, as he beheld with calm countenance the dutiful attendance of the Senate and the august likenesses of the patrician stock, he thought, not like Cineas (the famous envoy of Pyrrhus) that a throng of kings was assembled together, but that the sanctuary of the whole world was present before him.[57]

Nor, indeed, was the Senate by any means a cipher. Certainly, the deliberations at its meetings were of little importance, except on rare occasions. Yet the individual senators possessed enormous wealth and carried great weight, which was not diminished, indeed was perhaps increased, by the emperor's absence, so that these noblemen, on occasion, played a leading part in events (p. 361). They were often pagans, and to Ammianus, who was likewise a pagan, the Senate seemed a compendium of the glory of eternal Rome.

Nevertheless his admiration for an ideal Senate was by no means extended to its individual members. Their most distinguished representative, the orator and literary man Symmachus (d. *c.* 402), is duly complimented by flattering references to his father.[58] But Ammianus saw all too many of Symmachus' colleagues and fellow-aristocrats, including Petronius Probus' great family of the Anicii,[59] as possessing the faults which were directly responsible for the current decline (p. 371).[60]

These echoes of Sallust's moralising trenchancy are given added force by the consideration that Ammianus himself came from outside the charmed social circle. Could it be, perhaps, that the leading houses had failed to intervene when educated foreigners were expelled from the city – and Ammianus was among them? If so, this would be explicable; he is on record as deploring the incident, though perhaps in the end he himself escaped (p. 362). But in any case he may well have had enemies among the conservative pagan aristocracy because of what he wrote. For example, his treatment of Julian is unlikely to have pleased them. Ammianus praises him, but the praise is mixed with words of blame (p. 364); and Julian was their hero.

In due course, it appears that the historian made good at Rome. But at first he may well have received some social snubs. There seems to be personal feeling behind his comments on the frustration and tedium a 'stranger of good position' will have to endure in paying court to the great.[61] For the pretentiousness of some of these dignitaries was intolerable.

Taking great pride in coaches higher than common and in ostentatious finery of apparel, they sweat under heavy cloaks, which they fasten about their necks and bind around their very throats, while the air blows through them because of the excessive lightness of the material.[62] And they lift up their cloaks and wave them with many gestures, especially with their left hands, in order that the over-long fringes and the tunics embroidered in party-coloured threads with multiform figures of animals may be conspicuous.[63]

And the arrogance with which these lofty personages submit to other people's greetings is beyond endurance: 'Some of these men, when one begins to salute them breast to breast, like menacing bulls turn to one side their heads, where they should be kissed, and offer their flatterers their knees to kiss or their hands, thinking that quite enough to ensure them a happy life.'[64] Petronius Probus receives censure because of his enormous ambition (p. 367). But Ammianus reserves his sharpest remarks for the utter frivolity which other members of the aristocracy displayed.

When such characters, each attended by fifty servants, have entered the vaulted rooms of a bath, they shout in threatening tones: 'Where on earth are our attendants?' If they have learned that an unknown courtesan has suddenly appeared, some woman who has been a common prostitute of the crowd of our city, some old strumpet, they all strive to be the first to reach her, and, caressing the newcomer, extol her with such disgraceful flattery as the Parthians do Semiramis, the Egyptians their Cleopatras. . . .[65]

What Ammianus dislikes most of all in these noblemen is their lack of culture. They hate learning like poison. They never read anything except the satires of Juvenal and some dubious third-century bio-graphies by Marius Maximus.[66] They spend the whole time building water-organs and other musical instruments of ludicrous size, and meanwhile their libraries are kept locked up for ever like tombs.[67] This is a keynote of Ammianus' attitude. One of the principal criteria he uses in judging people is whether they are interested in the liberal arts. When educated aliens were expelled, he comments that thousands of dancing-girls received permission to stay. The emperor Valens was deficient in culture (p. 368), and so was his guard Commander Modestus, a man 'of a boorish nature refined by no reading of the ancient writers'.[68]

Modestus is also described as wholly under the influence of the court eunuchs, who at this time, in oriental fashion, exercised great power in the imperial circle. Ammianus shares the aristocracy's hatred for this powerful class, and thinks it necessary to apologise when he praises the only virtuous eunuch he knew. This was Julian's Armenian chamberlain Eutherius.[69] 'Among brambles, roses spring up, and among savage beasts some are tamed.'

Another branch of the imperial bureaucracy which he disliked intensely consisted of the huge mass of lawyers who played a dominant part in the ubiquitous oppressions of the régime. Judges and advocates alike he describes as utterly fraudulent – apparently with full justification.[70] And, as for the deplorable illiteracy of the nobles, lawyers are no better: 'Among them are some who are so ignorant that they cannot remember they ever possessed a law-book. And if in a circle of learned men the name of an ancient writer happens to be mentioned, they think it is a foreign word for some fish or other edible.'[71] Ammianus himself speaks for a category of the population which regarded itself as above the lawyers, but was below the aristocracy. This was the 'curial' class, well-to-do and half-noble. His rank gives him an unusual approach because most other surviving Roman historians, even if they criticise the governing group, still speak from that group's social point of view. Ammianus does not. His tributes to the ancient tradition, and his lamentations about its unworthy inheritors, are typical of 'new men' like himself, who did not belong to the inmost circle and viewed its corruption with provincial suspicion. Moreover, Ammianus goes out of his way to defend his own class. A criticism of his hero Julian is his alleged harshness towards these people. Julian is naturally given no credit for his efforts to restrain the economic exploitation of Antioch – which was conducted by Ammianus' curials.[72]

But if we suppose that this historian, being detached from the closed ranks of the inner aristocracy, is going to give us, for once, sympathetic insight into the depressed bulk of the population, we shall be disappointed. Their demonstrations in Rome seem to Ammianus wholly deplorable. Nor has he any sympathy with their motive – which was a scarcity of wine. 'It is by their eagerness for an unrestrained use of this commodity that the population is incited to frequent and violent disturbances.'[73]

Indeed, Ammianus wishes he was not obliged to refer to the lower classes at all. He feels constrained to apologise for the excessive length at which he has to describe 'nothing except riots and taverns and other similar vulgarities', themes he evidently regards as below the elevated level appropriate to history. The fact is that he feels the strongest distaste for the enormous unprivileged sections of society. He implies that they did not rally round the State as they should have after the Adrianople disaster.[74] And their coarse behaviour disgusts him:

Of the multitude of lowest condition and greatest poverty some spend the entire night in wineshops, some lurk in the shade of the awnings of the theatres. . . . Or they quarrel with one another in their games at dice, making a disgusting sound by drawing back the breath into their resounding nostrils. Or, which is the favourite among all amusements, from sunrise until evening, in sunshine and in rain, they stand open-mouthed, examining minutely the good points or the defects of charioteers and their horses. . . . These and similar things prevent anything memorable or serious from being done in Rome.[75]

The city is glorious and eternal. But its current manifestations, seen in high and low society alike, are vile, and call imperatively for the moral recovery which will save the Empire.

Yet Ammianus, for all his preoccupation with Rome, is very much less centred upon its affairs than Tacitus had been at a time when the city played a larger role. In keeping with the changed times, and with his own origins and experiences, Ammianus paints on a far wider canvas.

Yet he shows less artistry than Tacitus in the excessive amount of licence and space he allows himself for geographical, ethnological and scientific digressions, by no means all markedly relevant.[76] As in the days of Herodotus when this literary custom was initiated, Egypt supplies every necessary ingredient of the picturesque.[77] But the width of Ammianus' interests even carries him as far afield as the Chinese, then regarded as remarkable for their peace-loving character.

Beyond the lands of both Scythias, towards the east, the summits of lofty walls form a circle and enclose the Seres, remarkable for the richness and extent of their country. On the west they are bounded by the Scythians, and on the north and east they extend to a snowclad waste; on the south they reach India and the Ganges. . . . The Seres themselves live a peaceful life, for ever unacquainted with arms and warfare; and since to gentle and quiet folk ease is pleasurable, they are troublesome to none of their neighbours. . . . The Seres themselves are frugal beyond all others, live a quiet life, and avoid intercourse with the rest of mortals. And when strangers, in order to buy threads or anything else, cross the river, their wares are laid out and with no exchange or words their value is estimated by the eye alone. And they are so abstemious that they hand over their own products without themselves getting any foreign ware in return.[78]

When Ammianus turns to Europe, he offers a short description of the Gauls.[79] He also provides an arresting sketch of the Huns, whose direct menace to the Empire lay in the future, though they had already made their presence felt by pushing the Goths in front of them and thus indirectly causing the battle of Adrianople.

But little known from ancient records, they exceed every degree of savagery. . . . Since the cheeks of the children are deeply furrowed with the steel from their very birth, in order that the growth of hair, when it appears at the proper time, may be checked by the wrinkled scars, they grow old without beards and without any beauty, like eunuchs. They all have compact, strong limbs and thick necks, and are so monstrously ugly and misshapen that one might take them for two-legged beasts or for the stumps, rough-hewn into images, that are used in putting sides to bridges. . . .

They dress in linen cloth or in the skins of field-mice sewn together, and they wear the same clothing inside and out. But when they have once put their necks into a faded tunic, it is not taken off or changed until by long wear and tear it has been reduced to rags and fallen from them bit by bit. They cover their heads with round caps and protect their hairy legs with goatskins. Their shoes are formed upon no lasts, and so prevent their walking with free step. For this reason they are not at all adapted to battles on foot, but they are almost glued to their horses, which are hardy, it is true, but ugly, and sometimes they sit them woman-fashion and thus perform their daily functions.[80]

This description, though no doubt very largely true, is given with particular gusto because it harmonises with Ammianus' belief that most barbarians are no better than wild beasts – and should be treated as such, even to the extent of slaughtering them without provocation. For when the Romans annihilated a Saxon horde after agreeing to a truce, 'although some just judge will condemn this act as treacherous and hateful, yet on careful consideration of the matter he will not think it improper that a destructive band of brigands was destroyed when the opportunity at last offered'.[81]

Besides, the Saxons were German, and Ammianus had a prejudice against Germans, whether they were Goths or belonged to other tribes. He was prepared, it is true, to speak of individual members of the race with favour, including some men in the imperial service.[82] Moreover, he was severely critical of the bad treatment of the Goths by the Romans, which had contributed to the Adrianople catastrophe. And yet he refuses to face the dilemma of his age: Rome must have a strong army, and yet this was quite impossible unless the northerners were incorporated in its ranks (p. 371). Nor does Ammianus seem to discuss the phenomenon of the Germans as thoroughly as their current importance in Roman history deserved. This may, of course, have been rectified in a lost book or books, but in the surviving text they are not given the extended and systematic treatment that is called for. Possibly Ammianus may have felt that the *Germania* of Tacitus had done enough in this field, and that it was better to avoid too direct imitation or rivalry (p. 383).

Very different, and unusual, is his extended, handsome and relatively unbiased treatment of Rome's outstanding eastern enemies, the Persians. He is well aware, from personal knowledge, that they were not just a rebellious tribe delivering pinpricks on a distant frontier. Rome and Persia, said a Persian ambassador, were 'like two lighthouses illuminating the world'; and, in spite of the continual recurrence of hostilities, Constantius II and the Persian emperor Sapor II address one another as brothers.[83] Accordingly the Persians receive not only an ample share of Ammianus' narrative but a long digression as well. This includes an elaborate sketch of their national features. Summings up of the characters of whole nations usually fail, but the attempt of Ammianus is interesting because it comes from a man who had fought against them. It was typical, however, of an ancient writer that, even with this direct experience behind him, he must insert literary echoes of Herodotus, who had written eight centuries earlier.[84]

The Persians are almost all slender, somewhat dark, or of a leaden pallor, with eyes grim as goats', eyebrows joined and curved in the form of a half-circle, not uncomely beards, and long shaggy hair. . . . Most of them are extravagantly given to love-making, and are hardly contented with a multitude of concubines. They are free from immoral relations with boys. Each man according to his means contracts many or few marriages, whence their affection, divided as it is among various subjects, gets cold. . . . One seldom sees a Persian stop to pass water or step aside in response to a call of nature; so scrupulously do they avoid these and other unseemly actions.

On the other hand they are so free and easy, and stroll about with such a loose and unsteady gait, that one might think them effeminate. But in fact they are most gallant warriors, though crafty rather than courageous, and to be feared only at long range. They are given to empty words, and talk madly and extravagantly. They are boastful, harsh and offensive, threatening in adversity and prosperity alike, crafty, haughty, cruel, claiming the power of life and death over slaves and commons. They flay men alive, either bit by bit or all at once. No servant who waits upon them, or stands at table, is allowed to open his mouth, either to speak or spit.[85]

Even if this description owes as much to literary forerunners as to direct observation or report, nothing in all ancient history is so vivid as Ammianus' description of the wars against the Persians in which he himself took part. Like many historians of this later Roman Empire, in contrast to their famous predecessors, Ammianus welcomes the opportunity to include autobiographical information. He had seen more of the world than any previous historical writer except Herodotus, and he is glad to write of the part he had played in events.

In 359 the force in which he was serving on the eastern frontier suffered a cavalry defeat at the hands of the Persians, and was scattered far and wide. He and his commander Ursicinus, by separate routes, succeeded in reaching the fortress of Amida.

I myself, having taken a direction apart from that of my comrades, was looking around to see what to do, when Verennianus, one of the guard, came up with an arrow in his thigh; and while at the earnest request of my colleague I was trying to pull it out, finding myself surrounded on all sides by the foremost Persians I moved ahead at breathless speed and aimed for the city, which from the point where we were attacked lay high up and could be approached only by a very narrow ascent.

Here, mingled with the Persians who were rushing to the higher ground, we remained motionless until sunrise of the next day, so crowded together that in front of me a soldier with his head cut in two, and split into equal halves by a powerful sword-stroke, was so pressed on all sides that he stood erect like a stump.[86]

Ammianus managed to make his way into Amida. Three days later, the Persian monarch and his army arrived outside the walls, and the historian saw them come.

When the first gleam of dawn appeared, everything so far as the eye could reach shone with glittering arms, and mail-clad cavalry filled hill and dale. The King himself, mounted upon a charger and overtopping the others, rode before the whole army, wearing in place of a diadem a golden image of a ram's head set with precious stones. . . .[87]

Ammianus was particularly impressed by a contingent of elephants: 'To the western gate were opposed the Segestani, the bravest warriors of all. With them, making a lofty show, slowly marched the lines of elephants, frightful with their wrinkled bodies and loaded with armed men, a hideous spectacle, dreadful beyond every form of horror, as I have often declared.'[88]

Finally, after a seventy-two-day siege, the Persians broke into the town. Amid the confused fighting, Ammianus decided it was time to escape. On a dark night, he went into hiding and then got out through an unguarded postern gate. He moved away as rapidly as he could, but was glad to rest after ten miles because 'I was already unequal to the excessive walking, to which as a gentleman I was unused.'[89] Another frank touch reveals that at the time when he had decided to leave Amida the rest of the garrison was still desperately keeping up the fight. Like Josephus, he reckoned his readers would understand that self-preservation, even if inglorious, must come first (p. 251). However, Ammianus was prepared to express himself strongly about the cowardly behaviour of the Roman cavalry, whose defeat had originally forced him and his comrades to take refuge in the fortress.[90]

He was also critical of a deterioration in army discipline, which Julian later found it necessary to correct.[91] Indeed, some have detected in Ammianus' writing a certain contempt for the soldiery. But, although unsympathetic with the lower orders in general, he cannot really be accused of a bias against the rank and file of the army. Indeed, in matters of discipline he blames Valentinian for handling common soldiers more severely than he treated senior officers.[92] And Ammianus' opinion is worth hearing, because when his subject is military, he does know what he is talking about. It is useful, for a change, to have a Roman historian who is professionally competent in military matters – and this makes him our outstanding source for the army of his time. It is true that his battle-pieces and topographical background often have that all-too-familiar air of conventional vagueness.[93] Yet we do owe Ammianus certain expert contributions, for example a technical description of siege artillery.[94]

In the intervals between such digressions his narrative continues to move forward with speed, force and variety. Julian's expedition on the eastern frontier, in which Ammianus again participated, provides a further occasion for powerful first-hand pictures. But he is also able to infuse great vividness into events in which he did not take part, such as the death of Gallus, the battle of Adrianople, the agitated sessions of the council which discussed the rebellion of Silvanus, a drunken dinner-party in Illyricum, or the treacherous murder of the Armenian king Papa by Valens.[95]

Ammianus' attitude to details, however, is somewhat equivocal. He speaks sternly about foolish readers who call for them (p. 361), and in accordance with this conviction of the dignity of history he deliberately rejects, for example, minor skirmishes in Gaul, or exact statements of casualty figures,[96] or the sexual affairs of insignificant persons.[97] None the less, he himself retains a picturesque taste for what is curious and trivial. And so we are told of the geese which make no sound when they are crossing the Taurus so as not to attract eagles. We learn of the Mesopotamian lions which are only prevented from overrunning the entire east because they are continually persecuted by gnats; and the strange fact is noted that Constantius never ate fruit as long as he lived.[98] Ammianus also devotes much space to numerous minor stories of secondary happenings which build up atmosphere and reveal the thick texture of events. Speeches fulfil the same purpose; but only in a specific field. Far fewer than in earlier historians – only a dozen orations occur in surviving parts of the work – they consist of harangues by emperors to their troops. Their aim is to illustrate the ultimate dependence of rulers upon the army, and in general to define their relation to the State.

The excellence of Ammianus' descriptive powers is not equalled by the quality of his Latin diction. At its best, this displays the heady exuberance and intoxicating vigour which Stephen Usher sees as its principal characteristics, but sometimes the splendid stories are dimmed, the strong dramatic and pictorial effects blurred, by a turgid diffuseness of clumsiness, an unnatural word-order, a tendency to metaphorical obscurity and bombastic exaggeration. A copious use of historical examples from Rome's past seems to us to mar some of his best effects. He himself, however, was clearly proud of them. In general, however, he is modest about his achievement and the calibre of his writing, and one feels that the modesty is not merely conventional. The comparison with Tacitus kept on imposing itself upon his mind.

One of the reasons, perhaps, why he chose Latin rather than his native Greek was in order to try to live up to Tacitus whose *Histories* had ended where his own deliberately began. Nevertheless, his final disclaimer shows that he was fully aware that his Latin was nothing like up to the Tacitean standard: 'The rest may be written by abler men, who are in the prime of life and learning. But if they choose to undertake such a task, I advise them to forge their tongues to the loftier style.'[99] Just before that he had written: 'These events, from the principate of the emperor Nerva to the death of Valens, I, a former soldier and a Greek, have set forth to the measure of my ability, without ever (I believe) consciously venturing to debase through silence or through falsehood a work whose aim was the truth.' To be a Roman soldier and a Greek seemed almost a contradiction in terms; though Julian, too, was a soldier, and a Greek at least by education, which made him the target of many sneers. Ammianus' employment of Greek words and his use of moralising examples – a Greek custom, even if the source was often Roman history (p. 384)[100] – did not mean that his knowledge of Latin was defective. Nor do the peculiarities of his style. They are paralleled in some of his rhetorical Latin contemporaries, and no doubt seemed appropriate for a historian who was going to give recitations. Ammianus had reversed the situation of his predecessors, for he was not a Hellenised Roman, but a Hellene who had absorbed much of the Latin tradition of his day. He notes the names of two other men, a commander of the guard and a renegade, who had likewise performed the increasingly unusual achievement of attaining mastery in both languages.[101] Nevertheless, Ammianus remains very Greek, and consciously so. Phrases like 'as we Greeks say' recur half a dozen times. His vast curiosity and voluminous reading were also Greek, and so was the significance he attached to education (p. 375). At one point he produces, in passing, the remark that *diligentia*, painstaking thoroughness, is a Greek characteristic.[102]

The link with Tacitus is consciously maintained. He is echoed, for example, in Ammianus' description of the Isaurian mountaineers of Asia Minor.[103] The same passage likewise contains reminiscences of Sallust; who at another point is mentioned by name.[104] Ammianus' Latin reading was wide. There is a considerable infusion of Cicero, and numerous references to his works. Livy, too, is sometimes called upon, and so are the Greeks, going back to Herodotus (p. 379).[105] The question of Ammianus' sources belonging to his own time is, as usual, more problematical. In keeping with custom, he does not mention them. Yet there were certain contemporary historians whose writings he is likely to have utilised. Their works, representing a revival after the convulsions of the third and later fourth centuries, are timid and somewhat rudimentary. Yet they help to make the period an unusually well-documented one.[106] We can even, some-times, check one source against another – a process from which Ammianus emerges with credit (p. 363). In addition, he uses public archives and governors' reports.[107] But a remarkable amount also came from his own observations. He must have composed the most completely recent portions of his work from memory, with practically no written sources at all.

Here, as Syme has said, was 'an honest man in an age of fraud and fanaticism'. Ernst Stein saw no one to equal him between Tacitus and Dante. And indeed even Tacitus had to cede him certain important points. For Ammianus, though not to be compared with him in style, surpassed his great model in practical acquaintance with the problems of defence, in broad and balanced insight into human character, and even perhaps in adherence (so far as the attainment of this was humanly possible) to historical truthfulness and impartiality.

Epilogue

Epilogue

The Survival of the
Ancient Historians

HERODOTUS

CTESIAS of Cnidus, at the beginning of the fourth century BC, questioned the qualifications of Herodotus as a historian both of Greece and of the east. Aristotle went out of his way to criticise him as an inaccurate story-teller.[1] The Egyptian priest Manetho of Sebennytus (*c.* 280) wrote a pamphlet censuring his inaccuracies about Egypt. Yet Herodotus remained the standard authority on that country, and on Babylonia as well. His example showed Greek writers how to deal with the problems raised by the conquests of Alexander the Great. The discovery of a fragment of a commentary on his history by Aristarchus of Samothrace,[2] initiator of serious scholarship at Alexandria (*c.* 217–145 BC), shows that Herodotus was one of the very few prose writers honoured by the Alexandrians in this way. Probably Aristarchus also issued an edition of the text.

In the later first century BC Diodorus Siculus of Agyrium disbelieved his tales.[3] But Diodorus' contemporary Dionysius, of Herodotus' home-town Halicarnassus, regarded them as marvels of story-telling – 'we are filled with admiration till the last syllable and always seek for more'. From that time until the second century AD Herodotus was in special favour as a model of style, and a fashion for archaism operated in his favour. But then Plutarch and many others attacked his 'thefts' and 'lies' (p. 326).[4] Lucian, too, while admiring him for many good qualities, was another who called him a liar. Herodotus' breadth of mind irritated local chauvinistic feelings and it seemed that his breadth of knowledge must mean either plagiarism or untruthfulness. For this was an age which undertook very little direct historical or geographical research, thus missing the great opportunities offered by the Roman Empire. The collection of material was left to 'mere' antiquarians, and the methods of Herodotus went out of fashion.

One of the many achievements of Petrarch (1304–74) was to object to the implied contradiction between calling Herodotus the father of history and regarding him as the father of lies. In the final century of Byzantine Constantinople, interest in him revived owing to the conflict between Greeks and Turks, and he was studied and imitated by 'the last Athenian historian' Laonicus Chalcocondyles – the brother or cousin of Demetrius Chalcocondyles, who taught Italian humanists. Meanwhile, in Italy, Herodotus was redis-covered with joy by Guarino (*c.* 1416). A manuscript of his history appears on the list of those owned by Aurispa in Rome (1421), and five texts are traceable before the middle of the century. Under Pope Nicolas v, who commissioned many translations, a Latin version was undertaken by Lorenzo Valla in *c.* 1452 and printed in 1474. Herodotus was praised in *c.* 1460 in an unpublished work by Mattia Palmieri Pisano. At about the same time, however, other scholars were turning against him because the recent fall of Constantinople had discredited the Greeks.

However, his methods triumphed in the sixteenth century, when his comparative studies of varied traditions attracted an age inter-ested in travel and ethnography. Erasmus recommended Herodotus but not Thucydides for school reading, and the Reformation found him a useful supplement to the Bible. He was translated into Italian (M.M.Boiardo, 1533) and then into other modern languages, in-cluding English in which a version of Books i and ii appeared in 1584. The French scholar Henri Estienne (Stephanus) had published an 'Apologia' for Herodotus in 1566.

'The stupendous developments', says Arnaldo Momigliano, 'of the study of Greek and Oriental history in the last three centuries would never have happened without Herodotus. . . . The modern accounts of explorers, anthropologists and sociologists about primitive populations are ultimately an independent development of Herodotus' *historie*.' The eighteenth century was a great time for his cosmopolitan *histoire des moeurs*, which suited the pioneering spirits of Montesquieu (1689–1755) and Gibbon (1737–94). Besides, it was only then that Herodotus' willingness to tackle a mass of antiquarian and other detail and make it into history became fashionable again. Until then all such attempts had retained the inferior status to which they had been relegated (p. 388). To Francis Bacon, antiquities were still merely 'history defaced or some remnants of history which have casually escaped the shipwreck of time'. Voltaire felt the same. But the Göttingen Historical Institute (1766) was largely devoted to such auxiliary, antiquarian studies, and Gibbon, too, greatly advanced the assimilation of history with scientific antiquarianism. 'By rescuing the details from that *malheur* to which Voltaire had doomed them,' argues Momigliano, 'Gibbon made it possible both to preserve and to render more trustworthy what was after all the most endearing quality of classical historiography: the art of detailed narrative. . . . He is far more amusing than any other historian except Herodotus.'

However, before and after 1900, the wheel began to turn back again, for Herodotus came in for much criticism. At that time the ancient historians were regarded largely as sources of information, whereas now, says Syme, 'we ask what could they tell us and what did they want to'. From such enquiries, he continues, Herodotus emerges with enormous distinction, because he has such industry, and such a subject, and, according to his lights, keeps the whole vast theme under his control. His original, brilliant and endearing personality is appreciated once again.

THUCYDIDES

Thucydides cannot have been read with favour after the end of the Peloponnesian War. His tone was too sharp; there was something in his work to give offence to almost any section of the community. Besides, his Old Attic style must have sounded a distinctly archaic note to fourth-century Athenians. It is uncertain if work was done on him at Alexandria, but his 'scientific' ideals, though not unattractive to that city's scholars and antiquarians, did not appeal to the dramatically minded historians of the day. However Polybius, who reacted against such influences, was profoundly affected by Thucydides' approach (whether he had read his whole work or not), and approved of his rigorous insistence on politics and war.

Interest on a wider scale revived in the first century BC, when Caesar and Sallust stood for Thucydidean austerity against Cicero's preference for more romantic and rhetorical methods (p. 184). In Augustan Rome, Dionysius of Halicarnassus attacked Thucydides for writing about an unpleasant, parochial subject redolent of the Greek decline, and for being too kind towards Sparta.[5] He also objected to his style and his relatively sparing use of digressions, apparently believing, very obtusely, that the few he did insert were merely pleasant pauses to break the monotony.

Tacitus may not have owed large direct debts to Thucydides, because Sallust in his own language had come in between, and had spoken for a similar attitude of biting disillusionment. In later times, certain Greek historians, notably Dexippus (third century) and the outstanding Byzantine Procopius (sixth century) were more directly influenced by Thucydides. He was again imitated as late as the fifteenth century, with some skill, in Critobulus' eulogistic account of the Turkish Sultan Mahomet II the Conqueror.

Two generations earlier, a manuscript of Thucydides had been given by the Byzantine humanist Manuel Chrysoloras to his Italian pupil Pier Paolo Vergerio. Eight manuscripts (at least one of them complete) are traceable before 1450, and Valla's Latin rendering (1452) provided a basis for translation into modern languages. Machiavelli, who was attracted by Thucydides' ruthlessly observant analyses of reasons of state, had read this Latin version, and C. de Seyssel translated it into French for King François I (1527). It also formed the basis of T. Nichols' English translation (1550). Thucydides was the only historian lectured on by the Protestant theologian Melanchthon (d. 1560).

Greek studies declined thereafter, but in the sixteenth century the value of Thucydides was greatly appreciated by Hobbes. Neglected by the French Enlightenment, he gained the admiration of Thomas Jefferson, who wrote to John Adams in 1812 that Thucydides (like Tacitus) was better than the newspapers. Later in the same century much attention was focused on his methods, which seemed to foreshadow the 'scientific' attitude of Ranke and his followers (p. xvi).

No other historian, people felt, had contributed more than Thucydides to history as it was now understood.

Some said that the Peloponnesian War itself was insignificant, and would have attracted and deserved no attention had it not been for Thucydides. But in our own century not only the subject he chose, but his way of handling it, possess a further and poignant significance, because of two world wars. 'The actions', as Syme points out, 'took a Thucydidean course, one war following another after an interval of fraudulent peace; but, on a rational estimate, a single war with the "truest explanation" valid. And the same pleas or motives recurring, fear and honour, security or aggression.'

XENOPHON

Although Xenophon was widely respected after his death, he received little recognition in Hellenistic times. Scipio Africanus always kept a copy of the *Education of Cyrus*, the narratives in Cato's *Origins* and Catulus' memoirs were modelled on his narrative style, and Caesar and Antony both admired the *Anabasis*. Cicero, in his *Cato the Elder on Old Age*, turned parts of the epilogue of the *Cyrus* into Latin. In his youth he had also translated the work *On Estate Management*. Under the Roman Empire interest in Xenophon continued to rise, owing to the revival of an 'Attic' approach which favoured his simple, intelligible prose. Lucian even classed him with Herodotus and Thucydides,[6] and seven fictitious *Letters of Xenophon* were in circulation.

In the twelfth century he influenced the Byzantine contemporary historian Nicephorus Bryennius, who preferred this plain style to the artificial diction of his own wife, the learned Anna Comnena. Then in Italy Leonardo Bruni deposited a manuscript of Xenophon with Niccolò Niccoli (1405), and altogether twelve codices are known from the first half of the fifteenth century and twenty-six from the second half. There were Latin translations of the *Hiero* (1403), the *Hellenica* and *Apologia of Socrates* (both by Bruni before 1440), *Estate Management* (before 1447), *Agesilaus* and the *Spartan Constitution* (before 1460) and the *Education of Cyrus* (in 1471, after it had been paraphrased by Poggio Bracciolini thirty-four years earlier). The *Hiero* was translated into German in 1502, various other works of

Xenophon into Italian from 1521, the *Anabasis* into French in 1529 (by de Seyssel), *Estate Management* into English in 1532 (by G. Hervet). A comprehensive series of Spanish versions followed two decades later. Xenophon formed part of a French senior school curriculum in 1545–7; apart from Herodian and Plutarch, he was the only historical writer to appear in the list. Johann Lenklau produced an important edition of his works in 1569. The Elizabethan educationalist Roger Ascham praised the *Education of Cyrus*, but James Usher (1581–1656) regarded it as unduly romantic. In the eighteenth century Xenophon was one of the writers whom Winckelmann studied in order to prepare himself for the visual arts, and Goethe went on from Homer to Plato and Xenophon's *Memoirs of Socrates*. Nowadays, the *Anabasis* plays a useful but somewhat inglorious role in the elementary curricula of such schools as still teach Greek.

POLYBIUS

Polybius did not enjoy favour among the Roman historians of the later Republic, because they preferred the romantic historians whom he attacked. But he is an early and striking example of a writer whose thought has exercised a wide, enduring influence quite disproportionate to the limited reading-public of his voluminous and not-too-well-written works. Cicero took up his theory of the mixed constitution (p. 152), and Polybius provided a very great deal of material to Livy. In the second century AD Appian's treatment of the Third Punic War is an abbreviated version of his account, whether borrowed direct or through an intermediate source.

In the middle ages Polybius' *History* was already disappearing, the process being aided by the compilation of epitomes. The preservation of many excerpts is owed to the Byzantine emperor Constantine VII Porphyrogenitus (913–59). Polybius was again studied and imitated by Byzantine writers of the twelfth and thirteenth centuries. Bruni, writing on the First Punic War, offered a Latin paraphrase of surviving portions of his work (1421), and Latin translations of Books I to V were composed by Bishop Niccolò Perotto (1455) and incorporated in his first printed edition seventeen years later. The mixed constitution became the accepted creed of Machiavelli (d. 1527) and a notable group of Florentine political theorists, and it also affected Calvin's thought. The first Greek edition, at Hagenau, was printed in 1530, and translations followed in French (parts in 1545–6, complete 1568), Italian (1546), and English Book (1, 1568).

Polybius was the hero of the *Historical Art* of Gerhard Vossius (Voss) of Heidelberg, professor at Leiden (1623); and his popularisation of the cyclical theory influenced Giambattista Vico (1668–74).

In eighteenth-century England, the Whig ascendancy, with its long period of stability, was compared to the Polybian equilibrium. But John Locke (1632–1704) modified the mixed constitution into a balance between executive, legislative and judicial powers. Montesquieu, too, while expressing admiration of Polybius' 'profound sense', likewise saw the system as one of mutual controls and balances rather than as a union of different types of political organisation. Through him, Polybius passed into the main bloodstream of eighteenth-century thought, and inspired political and constitutional attitudes in the new United States of America. It is largely thanks to these influences that the American constitution is today the example *par excellence* of separated powers held in an equipoise of checks and counterchecks. Polybius' Book VI on constitutional affairs was constantly quoted by John Adams, especially in his *Defence of the Constitutions of Government* (1787). The *Federalist* essays of 1787–8 (Hamilton, Madison, Jay) discuss the Achaean League which was in Polybius' mind when he was dealing with the matter (p. 151).

Schelling regarded Polybius' pragmatic (utilitarian) history as inferior to the authentic syntheses of real and ideal achieved by Herodotus and Thucydides (1802). But Barthold Niebuhr (1776–1831), whose *Roman History* founded the modern critical tradition of historiography, owed Polybius his introduction to the subject, and was impressed by his criticism of cloistered pedantry and his insistence on personal experience of events. Soon afterwards, Polybius' theory of historical decline became implicit in Marxist history, and in our own century it has again found expression in Spengler and Toynbee. Few people, however, take the trouble of actually reading him: even the relatively small proportion of his work that has survived is of considerable length, his style and didacticism are forbidding, and translations are scarce. Yet his concept of universal history is close to modern preoccupations, and attuned to the problems of our own world.

CAESAR

Caesar's pellucid style was neither rhetorical nor archaic enough to find many admirers under the Roman Empire. Nor was he very popular in the middle ages. In the twelfth century William of Malmesbury made some use of the Commentaries. But it was not until the Renaissance that they really came into vogue, especially amid the rising nationalist feeling of the French which gave them an interest in Caesar's Gallic campaigns. His *Gallic War* was translated into French in *c.* 1488. Before the end of the century there were also Italian and Spanish versions of his works. The first printed edition of the original had been published at Rome in 1469. Then came German and English renderings of the *Gallic War* in 1507 and 1530 respectively. This English edition, which comprised only part of the work, was followed in 1565 by a translation by Arthur Golding. In *The Schoolmaster* (1570) Ascham urged that Caesar should 'be read with all curiosity, wherein specially, without all exception to be made either by friend or foe, is seen the unspotted propriety of the Latin tongue'.

Meanwhile, as the art of war came to be more systematically studied, his accounts of his own campaigns were regarded as a compendium of military science. Experts such as Marshal Henri Turenne (1611–75) and Marshal Maurice de Saxe (1696–1752) cited the work as an essential manual, and Napoleon I proclaimed that every general ought to read Caesar's account of how he commanded armies. Under protest from Trollope, Napoleon III frankly admired his autocracy and aggression, interpreting them as anticipations of imperial France. Theodor Mommsen, on the other hand, saw the *Civil War* as a desirable anti-oligarchic tract, foreshadowing the German Empire which was keeping the Junkers in their place. Desiré Nisard (1806–88), surveying Latin literature, allocated Caesar as much space as Sallust, Livy and Tacitus together; while W.H.D. Rouse (1898) somewhat strangely advocated him as suitable reading for girls' schools. Since then, the events of the twentieth century have created a more sophisticated insight into the arts of propaganda, and it is from this point of view that Caesar has been most extensively studied in recent years.

SALLUST

Sallust almost seemed classifiable as an orator rather than a historian (p. 211), and in any case his acidulated disillusionment was unlikely to appeal to official Augustan taste. Yet he was widely regarded as the writer who, for the first time, had written Latin history with the distinction that it deserved. Seneca the younger (d. AD 65) showed that his style had become an established fashion,[7] and towards the end of the same century Martial declared him to be 'the foremost among Roman historians, as the feeling of men of learning bears witness'.[8] Tacitus, expressing a manifest admiration, awarded him a rare superlative epithet – *florentissimus*.[9] Sallust had become a classic and a model. Subsequently, although his subjects might have seemed subversive, they were regarded (unlike those of Tacitus) as remote enough in time to be politically safe, and under Antoninus Pius and Marcus Aurelius he received further approval, notably from Fronto (d. *c.* 166), who was reintroducing archaisms into the literary language.

In late antiquity, again, Sallust was revered more than any other Latin writer with the sole exceptions of Cicero and Virgil, with whom he was grouped together in a 'four-horse chariot' (*quadriga*), the fourth member of the select group being the comic dramatist Terence. Ammianus carried on this tradition, and so did Jerome, who called Sallust *certissimus*. Another who praised, indeed over-praised, his accuracy and veracity was Augustine.[10] During the middle ages, the admiration persisted. At Christ Church, Canterbury, a catalogue of *c.* 1170 contained eight copies of Sallust. At that time his works, and the *Catiline* in particular, were more often drawn upon for ideas or turns of phrase than the writings of any other pagan author. *Les Faits des Romains*, written before 1250 and translated into Italian in 1313, treated him as a principal source for the life of Caesar, and throughout this period he continued to provide a major source of ethics as well as of history. The early humanists who started working under King Charles v of France translated him into French (*c.* 1380), and a German version dates back to about the same time. The first printed edition was published at Venice in 1470. In Spain, which paid great attention to Roman history, he was translated by Francisco Vidal de Noya (1493). The *Jugurtha* was rendered into English by Alexander Barclay (1520–3), and a version of the *Catiline* followed in 1541. Erasmus had recommended Sallust, rather than Livy or Tacitus, for school reading (1511). Milton, too, took him at his word as a high moralist.

In the following century the French revolutionaries, passing over his disillusion with Roman Republic of his own time, praised the attacks he had delivered on Catiline in the interests of an ideal Republic. Nowadays, in the school curricula of communist countries, he is given more emphasis than other Roman historians because of the lurid light he casts upon the decadence of the traditional governing class.

LIVY

In spite of sneers from Pollio and then the emperor Caligula (p. 237), Livy enjoyed immediate and almost universal success. His character-studies earned him enthusiastic recognition from the rhetorician Seneca the elder (d. AD 37/41), who called him 'by nature the fairest judge of all men of great parts'. Quintilian also admired Livy, and Tacitus, although so much more astringent, paid him an implied compliment and took over certain vivid turns of phrase (p. 292).[11] The younger Pliny missed seeing the eruption of Vesuvius because the perusal of a book of Livy kept him at Misenum. He was so much read in schools that Hannibal became a stock theme of debate.[12]

In surviving eleventh-century library catalogues Livy begins to make frequent appearances. Jean de Meung, in *The Romance of the Rose* (*c.* 1270), borrowed his story of Verginia. In *c.* 1318 the Oxford polymath Nicholas Trevet wrote a commentary on his *History* at the request of the Church. Just as the early Fathers had strangely chosen reliability as the special feature of Sallust, Dante spoke of Livy who 'does not make mistakes' – remembering his vivid description of the gold rings taken from the dead after Cannae,[13] in

> . . . that long war
> whose spoil was heaped so high with rings of gold,
> As Livy tells, who errs not.[14]

Petrarch put together his manuscript of Livy, now in the British Museum, while he was in his early twenties, copying parts of it in his own hand. It finally included twenty-nine books; although he had always hoped to find more, the five others which we possess were not discovered until the sixteenth century. The Roman heroes appear in his sonnets, and his Latin epic *Africa* was based on the Livian picture of the elder Scipio Africanus. Boccaccio was said to have made an Italian rendering of Livy, and he is also suspected of having played a part in the removal of the Monte Cassino manuscript to Florence. Petrarch's friend Bersuire translated parts of the *History* into a French version (1352), which was not superseded for more than two hundred years. Lopez de Ayala produced a Spanish translation (1407). The humanists of the High Renaissance, seeking for heroes, ranked Livy as the greatest of Roman historians. Petrarch's copy passed into the hands of Valla, who wrote comments in the margin, and produced his own scathingly controversial emendations of Books xxi–xxvi (1446–7). Italian translations date back to the same period, and the original was printed at Rome in 1469.

Erasmus omitted him from his reading-list for schools – perhaps because the cult of heroes was now being frowned upon. But Montaigne (d. 1529) knew him, and this was also an epoch of translations into German (1505) and Italian (1535). Livy's account of the marriage and death of Sophonisba (d. 203 BC),[15] wife of the Numidian Syphax, was the subject for one of the earliest Renaissance tragedies (Trissino, 1515). Machiavelli (d. 1527) wrote *Discourses on the First Decade of Livy*, but in the following century a committee of Venetian senators pointed out that Livy was less to blame than Tacitus for Machiavelli's undesirable political views. An English version of the Hannibal and Scipio passages appeared in 1544, and Philemon Holland published a translation in 1600. In Shakespeare's *Rape of Lucrece* (1594), the story of Lucretia, who was violated by Tarquin's son Sextus, is derived from the first book of Livy, as well as from Ovid.

The first complete edition of all the books now extant was published at Rome in 1616. Livy became a model for modern national histories, and his early books inspired Montesquieu to write against the tyranny of princes (1734). 'A young man', said the Corsican patriot General Paoli to Boswell, 'who would form his mind to glory must not read modern memoirs, but Plutarch and Titus Livius.' His account of the youthful Republic was a favourite source-book of the French Revolution, and a selection of his speeches translated by Rousseau served as models for the orators of the day.

Barthold Niebuhr rejected his early books as history. But

Macaulay, believing Livy to have used ballad sources that have subsequently been lost, attempted to reconstruct them in his *Lays of Ancient Rome* (1842), which enshrine the classic, legendary heroes, such as Horatius who held the bridge against the Etruscans (p. 239).

> Alone stood brave Horatius,
>   But constant still in mind;
> Thrice thirty thousand foes before,
>   And the broad flood behind.
> 'Down with him!' cried false Sextus,
>   With a smile on his pale face.
> 'Now yield thee,' cried Lars Porsena,
>   'Now yield thee to our grace.' . . .
>
> Round turned he, as not deigning
>   Those craven ranks to see;
> Nought spake he to Lars Porsena,
>   To Sextus nought spake he;
> But he saw on Palatinus
>   The white porch of his home;
> And he spake to the noble river
>   That rolls by the towers of Rome.
>
> 'Oh, Tiber! father Tiber!
>   To whom the Roman pray,
> A Roman's life, a Roman's arms,
>   Take thou in charge this day!'
> So he spake, and speaking sheathed
>   The good sword by his side,
> And with his harness on his back,
>   Plunged headlong in the tide.[16]

The lesson which Macaulay derived from Livy was that 'a truly great historian would reclaim the materials which the novelist has appropriated'.

Livy was Europe's principal textbook of Roman history, and exercised a decisive influence on the choice of periods studied in schools – where many boys and girls have consequently gained some familiarity with his account of the Second Punic War. His ideals seemed particularly well suited to the nineteenth-century public-school reformers of England. They were as interested in patriotism, public spirit, dignity and self-control as he was. Besides, as trainers of an *élite*, they liked the Livian, Carlylean cult of heroes.

Critics in Victorian times were not unduly disturbed by Livy's lack of practical experience of public affairs, since theirs was an age when very few historians took much part in them or ever witnessed a scene of violence. In our own century, however, a more critical attitude has emerged, in pursuance of the feeling, expressed by G.M.Trevelyan, that 'the historian needs better boots rather than better books'. Two other considerations have added to the factors operating against Livy. In the first place, Hitler and Stalin have sent the cult of Great Men out of fashion. Secondly, there has been a clearer appreciation of the perils created by nationalistic historians who can, if they are not very careful, make history into what Paul Valéry called 'the most dangerous product distilled in the laboratory of the human mind'. Livy's extraordinary literary talent, however, has continued to be recognised and admired, and modern archaeology has vindicated many features of his description of early Rome (p. 240).

JOSEPHUS

'When after the fall of Jerusalem', said E.R.Bevan, 'Judaism all the world over became Hebrew and Rabbinic, Hellenistic Judaism, as such, withered away. The Synagogue cast its works upon the scrap-heap, and there would be no human memory of them now, had not the Christian church, which succeeded to the great task of combining Hebrew religion with Greek culture, picked some of them up for its own guidance and preserved them for the Christians and Jews of today.'

The Jews rejected Josephus even more decisively than they cast off other Hellenisers, because he had deserted and betrayed their political cause. Yet to the Christians he seemed none the less fascinating for that. They cherished his descriptions of Palestine during the lifetime of Jesus, his accounts of Herod the Great and Pontius Pilate, and his brief references to Christianity itself – though nowadays we do not feel sure of the original form in which they were written (p. 263). Besides, the destruction of Jerusalem and the Temple, of which Josephus gave so detailed and terrible an account, was interpreted as a fulfilment of New Testament prophecies. In consequence, he was widely used as an authority by Christian writers. The enemies of Christianity, too, quoted his works – notably Porphyry (d. *c.* 305) who refers to his discussion of the puritanical Essene sect. Jerome, intending to be complimentary, called Josephus the Greek Livy.

Between the fourth and sixth centuries AD there appeared at least three Latin translations, one of which was edited by Cassiodorus (d. 583) and consisted of versions made by his friends. Certain of these renderings included extraneous and Christian material. Expanded and altered versions of the passages relating to Christianity are preserved in an Old Slavonic text which survives in some seventeen different manuscripts. It seems to be a twelfth- or thirteenth-century translation of a Greek paraphrase which dated back to the earliest Middle Ages and added new pro-Christian and anti-Roman elements (p. 449, n. 56). An early Syriac translation of the sixth book of the *Jewish War* became part of the Peshitta, the Syriac Bible.

At Byzantium, Photius (820–91) praised Josephus warmly for his stylistic and emotive qualities, and in the following century a Greek epitome of his works was in use. The Jews, too, were now appreciating his description of the Temple and his story of the final stages of their semi-independent kingdom. A south Italian writer of the tenth century, using a Latin manuscript, produced a free Hebrew paraphrase known as *Yosippon*. This composition, which passed as the work of Josephus himself but omitted Christian passages or interpolations and inserted pro-Roman additions, achieved great popularity throughout the Middle Ages. In the eleventh century *Yosippon* was translated into Arabic, and from that language later into Ethiopic. Moreover, half a millennium after its compilation, parts of this Hebrew version were rendered into English and French.

The earliest Latin manuscript of Josephus dates from the sixth century, and the earliest Greek text from the tenth. From before 1500 there survive six or seven good copies of the *Antiquities* and the *War*, five of the *Life* and one of the greater part of the *Apion* (the rest of it has to be deduced from Latin versions). The first printed Latin text was published at Augsburg in 1470 and the first edition of the Greek original at Basel in 1533. Meanwhile there had been various translations, starting with de Seyssel's French version of the *War* (1492). Fernandez de Palencia translated the *War* and *Apion* into Spanish at the same time, publishing the former forty-four years later.

According to J.J.Scaliger (1540–1609), Josephus deserves more credit than all other Greek and Latin writers together. In Britain, after Thomas Lodge had made an initial translation from the Greek text (1640), a loquacious version by the Cambridge Unitarian William Whiston, published at Dublin, enjoyed enormous success. Josephus' statements about Homer[17] inspired the *Prolegomena* of F.A.Wolf (1795) which originated modern Homeric scholarship. Schiller's play *Die Räuber* includes the line 'Josephus – that's what you ought to read.' In Kipling's *Captains Courageous* a seaman recites from him on Sundays. The German novelist Lion Feuchtwanger wrote a trilogy on his career (1932–42).

Josephus has moulded our subconscious. It is only from him, for example, that we learn that the daughter of Herodias who danced before Herod Antipas (one of the sons of Herod the Great) and asked for John the Baptist's head was called Salome.[18]

TACITUS

The conviction of the younger Pliny that the fame of his friend Tacitus would be immortal did not at first seem likely to be fulfilled. Tacitus was too individual and demanding a writer to leave a school of followers or attract much interest. We are told, on poor authority, that the emperor Tacitus (Marcus Claudius Tacitus, AD 275–6) had his works placed in all the libraries, claiming him as a relative.[19] A century later, Ammianus was attentive to his memory and began his history where Tacitus had left off (p. 383). He was also known to writers of the incipient Middle Ages.[20]

But when Cassiodorus, in the sixth century, quotes Tacitus (on the subject of amber), he cannot do better than cite 'a certain Cornelius' as the author.[21] Three hundred years later, the works of Robert of Fulda show that he had access to the *Germania* and the earlier books of the *Annals*. But for the most part the medieval epoch remains silent. For Books I–VI of the *Annals* we are dependent upon one manuscript, copied at Corvey in Saxony during the ninth century, but not studied until after it had been filched from there and taken to Rome (1508). The other half of what survives from the *Annals* (Books XI–XVI), together with the extant parts of the *Histories*, has likewise come down to us in a single codex, written at Monte

Cassino in the eleventh century. Both these 'Mediceans' are now at the Laurentian Library in Florence. The Monte Cassino manuscript may perhaps be identifiable with a text which was in Boccaccio's possession. It was printed at Venice by John of Speyer, with the *Germania*, in about 1470. The *Agricola* followed in 1482, and a complete edition of the surviving works, based on both Mediceans, was published at Rome by Beroaldus in 1515. Sir Thomas More's *History of Richard III*, written at about the same time and printed in 1543, shows Tacitean influence.

The first sixteenth-century translator was a Spaniard (Alamos de Barrientos in 1513), and then Italians, French and English got to work (*Agricola* and *Histories* by Sir Henry Savile 1591, *Germania* and *Annals* by R. Greenway 1598). A great scholarly edition was published at Antwerp in 1574 by Justus Lipsius, the central figure of the Tacitean revival. 'This is an age of disasters', said Lipsius. 'But these histories, I think, do much to make it tolerable, by furnishing comfort, advice and examples to follow.' And he offered to repeat any passage with a dagger at his chest, to be plunged into his body if his memory failed. A political commentary by Charles Pascal followed in 1581.

During the early Renaissance, people like the despot Sigismondo Malatesta of Rimini (d. 1468), who preferred Tacitus to Livy, were unusual. But his impact on the sixteenth century was widespread and enormous. In 1532, Erasmus' friend and biographer Beatus Rhenanus proclaimed him to be superior to Livy. Pope Paul III Farnese (d. 1549) and Cosimo de' Medici, the first grand duke of Tuscany (d. 1574), admired him more than any other secular author. 'Tacitismo' percolated through the political thought of the entire period. It inspired extensive new explorations of human dignity and passion; and it aroused Jesuit opposition. Machiavelli's devotion to Tacitus came second to his taste for Livy – perhaps partly because he did not know Books I–VI of the *Annals*. Yet he dwelt on Tacitus sufficiently to enable his own views to be discussed obliquely, under the cloak of Tacitus, when Machiavelli himself, relegated to the Papal Index of forbidden works, had become too dangerous a subject for direct debate. Nevertheless, the Venetians regarded even Tacitus, for all his distance in time, as a subversive figure, and prevented the publication of a commentary on his work by Traiano Boccalini (d. 1613). Tacitus was blamed for Machiavelli 'and other evil authors', and the publication of the commentary had to wait until 1678. Tacitus' style, too, was persistently criticised, notably by Cardinal du Perron, who declared that it made him the worst historian of all time.

Ben Jonson in *Sejanus His Fall*, acted in 1603 and published two years later, was indebted to Tacitus, as well as to Suetonius and Dio Cassius. Francis Bacon regarded him as the enemy of despots, and Milton denounced the suggestion of the Calvinist Salmasius (Claude Saumaise) that his work provided arguments in favour of Stuart absolutism (1651). Study of Tacitus is apparent in Corneille's *Othon* (1665) and Racine's *Britannicus* (1669). Towards the end of the seventeenth century there was a temporary decline in Tacitus' influence, since neither religious nor rationalistic thinkers found him sympathetic. After 1700, however, he found new followers. Prosper-Jolyot de Crébillon drew on him for his *Rhadamiste et Zénobie* (1711), describing a queen of Armenia in Claudius' reign who survived her husband's attempt to kill her so that she should not fall into the hands of their enemies. The vogue for Tacitus was particularly strong in England, where he was still seen as the enemy of autocrats; and he earned the profound admiration of Gibbon. Then, in Italy, Alfieri adapted him in his *Ottavia* (1780).

Voltaire disbelieved his accounts of the elderly Tiberius' secret vices, and declared concerning Nero's murder of his mother that 'the interests of humanity demand that such horrors *must* be exaggerated: they reflect too much shame on human nature.' However, Tacitus was translated by Rousseau and Mirabeau; although not the favourite of the revolutionaries, he formed a useful source of anti-monarchical propaganda. There was a *Tibère* by Chénier (1762–94), who declared that the utterance of Tacitus' name makes tyrants turn pale. Madame Roland read him in prison before her execution, and Tacitean echoes in *Le Vieux Cordelier*, the journal of Camille Desmoulins, caused Robespierre to have the paper burnt. Napoleon declared: 'Tacitus! Do not speak to me of that pamphleteer! He has abused emperors!' But, as Chateaubriand observed, 'it is in vain that Nero prospers: Tacitus is already born in the empire'. Meanwhile he had become the favourite historian of John Adams and Jefferson – though the Founding Fathers of the American Constitution were disturbed by his contemptuous warning against the Polybian mixed constitution, which they hoped to put into practice in America (p. 393).[22]

By 1837 the total number of English versions was at least thirty-five; the total in all languages had reached 393. A very large quantity of historical novels had been based on the *Annals,* and Tacitus' methods have also contributed to the development of modern studies on introspection and dissimulation. But the most intense interest, in recent as in previous years, has been focused upon his highly individual analysis of absolute power. This material was mobilised once again by Victor Hugo, as a weapon against Napoleon III; and it has lost none of its impact since then.

PLUTARCH

Plutarch was recognised and imitated in second-century Rome by the encyclopedic writer Aulus Gellius (*c.* 123–65),[23] but was scarcely heard of again in the West for a thousand years. In the east he was known to Eusebius (who mysteriously said 'he was appointed in 119 to be in charge of Greece') and other Greek fathers.[24] He was made great use of by St Basil, and was the subject of Greek epigrams of the sixth and eleventh centuries AD.[25] Then at last, in western Europe, John of Salisbury (d. 1180) quotes at length a work alleged to have been by Plutarch, the *Institutio Trajani,* though much of it cannot be authentic.

In about 1400 a manuscript of Plutarch was given by Manuel Chrysoloras to Vergerio, and there are records of seven others during the next quarter of a century. The Lives were made available in Latin before 1450 by Leonardo Bruni and Guarino and a number of other translators,[26] and a complete version was made by G. Campano in *c.* 1470. The first printed edition, comprising a Latin rendering by Niccolò Perrotto, was published at Rome in 1472 or 1473. Twenty-six Lives were translated into Italian by B. Jaconello da Rieti in 1482, and a Spanish version followed in 1491.

Several French renderings were followed in 1559 by the complete translation of Jacques Amyot of Melun, Professor at Bourges and Bishop of Auxerre. This work, which caught the spirit of Plutarch because the translator shared his interest in human personality, created a fashion for collective and comparative biography, and held its literary place in France for hundreds of years. Montaigne, whose intermediary was Amyot, described Plutarch, along with Seneca the younger, as the chief influence on his thinking. 'I cannot easily do without Plutarch,' he said. 'He is so universal and so full that, on every occasion, however extraordinary your subject, he is at hand to your need.'

In 1579 Thomas North translated Amyot's version in a form which exercised a profound influence on English literature and style. It was very extensively drawn upon by Shakespeare. *Coriolanus, Julius Caesar* and *Antony and Cleopatra* derive much material, through North, from Plutarch's *Coriolanus, Brutus, Julius Caesar* and *Antony*, and a host of other detailed derivations can be traced.[27] Plutarch was a modest historical writer, and North an inaccurate translator, and yet this was the material which Shakespeare, adapting in carefree fashion, transfigured and endowed with immortal new life.

In 1616, Ben Jonson's play *The Devil is an Ass* includes the following passage.

> *Meercraft.* . . . Who's this, thy son?
> A pretty youth! what is his name?
> *Plutarchus.* Plutarchus, sir.
> *Meercraft.* Plutarchus! how came that about?
> *Gilthead.* That year, sir,
> That I begot him, I bought Plutarch's lives,
> And fell so in love with the book, as I call'd my son
> By his name, in hope he should be like him,
> And write the lives of our great men.
>
> (Act III, sc. i)

The English Commonwealth greatly appreciated a 1636 translation of the *Moral Studies*. But the classical French dramatists preferred the Lives, deriving their material from the heroic characters and situations presented by Plutarch. What Homer had been to the Greek tragedians, said Ferdinand Brunetière, Plutarch was to those of France. John Dryden's tragic play *Cleomenes the Spartan Hero* owes much to Plutarch's Life of Cleomenes III, and in 1683–6 he sponsored a new translation of the Lives, to which he himself contributed a preface and a biography of the author. Dryden noted that Amyot was criticised for many mistakes, and he himself censured North for a variety of faults. But later the versions of Dryden's collaborators were in their turn subject to extensive revisions by their publishers in 1727 and 1758.

Plutarch himself, A. W. Gomme remarked, might be said to have belonged to the eighteenth century of ancient Greece. The real eighteenth century, with its urge towards enlightenment and cultural assimilation, found him peculiarly congenial. Pope praised his ethical qualities and 'good nature', and Goldsmith too, who published abridged translations of the Lives, grouped Plutarch with Nepos as an author whose readers 'will sensibly imbibe, and learn to compare ideas of great importance. He will become enamoured of virtue and patriotism, and acquire a detestation for vice, cruelty and corruption'. Boswell frequently echoes the Lives, and it was in the 1760s and 1770s that they reached the height of their popularity in England. Parallel biographies were much favoured; for example, Lord Chesterfield was compared to Samuel Johnson in Plutarchian style.

Alfieri, too, read Plutarch's Lives right through four or five times; they were the first work to provide subjects that kindled his imagination. Rousseau read Amyot's versions from the age of six and knew them by heart at eight. He wanted to emulate Plutarch as a moral influence and legislator, and the Lives of Numa and Lycurgus strengthened his belief that the inborn goodness of man could be developed by the institutions of a simple, disciplined Republic.[28] And so Plutarch became one of the forces inspiring the French Revolution. After reading one of his biographies, Jacques Brissot, editor of *Le Patriote Français*, 'burned to be like Phocion'. Charlotte Corday was brought up on the Lives. Madame Roland called them the pasturage of great souls, and wept because she had not been born a Spartan or a Roman. S.Just formed a disastrous plan to give France Spartan discipline (and cuisine). In 1793 the Hall of the Convention in the Tuileries was redecorated with laurelled statues of Plutarch's heroes Lycurgus, Solon, Camillus and Cincinnatus. Ten years earlier, the officers of the American Revolutionary Army, about to be disbanded, had called themselves the Society of the Cincinnati, and in 1790 Cincinnati in Ohio was given their name.

Beethoven, who greatly admired the ancients, liked Plutarch (together with the *Odyssey*) best of all. But an opposite trend was now setting in. On the basis of a new interest in more profound research, Conyers Middleton (d. 1750) had already questioned the biographer's reliability. In the 1780s Herder broke with the assumption that human thought and behaviour conform to a uniform pattern throughout different epochs. Instead, empathy, the art of feeling oneself into a period, became fashionable, and by this standard the Greek historian William Mitford (d. 1827), and Macaulay who so greatly admired Livy, saw many shortcomings in Plutarch. But Wordsworth's *Dion*, composed in 1816 and published in 1820, owed much to his Life of that Sicilian leader, and Ralph Waldo Emerson (1803–82), introducing a translation of the *Moral Studies*, declared that 'Plutarch's popularity will return in rapid cycles.... His sterling values will presently recall the eye and thought of the best minds ... And thus Plutarch will be perpetually rediscovered from time to time as long as books last.' That has been his destiny for eighteen hundred years. It is possible that the long cycle has now been broken; but time alone will show.

SUETONIUS

Suetonius' *Caesars* was continued a century later by Marius Maximus, whose work, now lost, was said to be verbose. Attempts to imitate Suetonius' method of arranging his material were also made by fourth-century compilers (p. 463, n. 106) and by the authors of the semi-fictitious *Historia Augusta* (p. 345). His Lives of literary personalities also influenced Jerome's series *On Illustrious Men*.

All our existing manuscripts are directly or indirectly based on a single copy of the *Caesars*, which found its way into the monastery of Fulda in Germany. There it was studied by the Frankish scholar Einhard, whose ninth-century *Life of Charlemagne* follows it closely but displays greater discrimination. William of Malmesbury's biographical description of William Rufus, in his *History of the English Kings* (1127–8), shows the influence of Suetonius as well as Sallust.

Petrarch's Latin *Lives of the Illustrious Romans*, on the other hand, use Suetonius as a source rather than a model. The vogue for translations in late fourteenth-century France produced a version of the *Caesars* (c. 1381), followed by an Italian rendering of the Life of Julius by Pier Candido Decembrio in 1438. At Rome, in 1470, there were two printings of the whole collection, in the original Latin. Montaigne quoted Suetonius more than forty times, and in 1576 Gerolamo Cardano, doctor and scientist, wrote a Latin autobiography based upon his methods. After a series of sixteenth-century versions in German, Italian, French and Spanish, Suetonius found a famous though wordy English translator in Philemon Holland (1600).

Richard Bentley (d. 1742) planned an edition which was never finished, though his material is preserved in the British Museum.

By 1820 there had been more than forty such editions of the *Caesars*, but now useful commentaries are far too rare. However, Suetonius has provided a rich quarry for historical novels, notably *I Claudius* and *Claudius the God* by Robert Graves.

EUSEBIUS

The *Chronicle* of Eusebius was translated by St Jerome into Latin, and by others into oriental languages. Part of it has come down to us in Armenian alone. For more than a thousand years this work was the principal source-book used throughout the Christian world. His *History of the Church*, too, was for all its faults a 'monumental work'. as F.J.Bacchus said, 'for which it would be difficult to overestimate the obligation which posterity is under to Eusebius'. As early as the fourth century, it was widely known in the West through the Latin version of Rufinus, an industrious translator who was unfortunate enough to incur the displeasure of Jerome. The latter, for his short history of Christian literature, borrowed seventy-eight of his 135 chapters from Eusebius, inserting a number of additional mistakes of his own.

The seven primary copies of the *History of the Church* which we possess date from the tenth to the twelfth centuries AD. There is also a Syriac version. The first edition by Robert Estienne (Stephanus), printer to the French king François I, was published at Paris in 1544. The earliest English translation was by Hanmer (1577). The Swiss Jakob Burckhardt (1818–97) voiced a feeling of distrust for Eusebius as a writer of factual truth, but his pioneer position as an ecclesiastical historian and panegyrist has remained unassailable.

AMMIANUS

Ammianus was imitated in his own time by the traditionalist poet Claudian (d. 404),[29] probably a pagan like himself. He was also apparently drawn upon by Jerome,[30] and there are further echoes in the *Historia Augusta*.[31] Soon afterwards, however, he seems to have fallen into a deep and long-lived neglect, because both his style and the epoch in which he lived were regarded as unclassical. The only relatively early citation occurs in the works of the Mauretanian grammarian Priscian, who taught at Constantinople after 500.[32] Later in the same century, however, Cassiodorus was said to have written out the entire *History*; and he imitated its style.

Out of seventeen surviving manuscripts, the two earliest, both of ninth-century date, are a Vatican codex from Fulda and a fragment from Hersfeld which is now at Kassel. It has been conjectured that both go back to a manuscript in capitals of *c.* 500–600.

Poggio Bracciolini located the Fulda and Hersfeld texts (1417) and took the former back to Italy, where Niccolò Niccoli thought it worth copying in his own hand. The *editio princeps* (Books xiv–xxvi) was published by Angelus Sabinus at Rome (1474) – less than six years after the first printed editions of Livy and Sallust and more than a generation before Tacitus' *Annals*. But the edition was almost valueless, because it was based on an inferior manuscript. A subsequent Bologna publication (1517), pirated by Erasmus in a reprint at Basel in the following year, used the Rome text as a model, but was disfigured still further by bad emendations. However, two further attempts in 1533, by Mariangelus Accursius at Augsburg and Sigismond Gelenius at Basel, produced improvements. Outstanding among subsequent editions was that of Henricus Valesius (Henri de Valois) (Paris, 1636), whose annotations and textual improvements formed the basis of subsequent scholarship.

In the following century, Ammianus' attacks on the aristocracy were brilliantly conflated by Gibbon.[33] Although, generally speaking, a strong believer in Ammianus' objectivity (p. 363), he concludes that the reader 'will perhaps detect the latent prejudices and personal resentments which soured the temper of Ammianus himself. But he will surely observe, with philosophic curiosity, the interesting and original picture of the manners of Rome.' It is fitting to conclude by recalling the generous words with which the one great historian bids farewell to the other: 'it is not without the most sincere regret that I must now take leave of an accurate and faithful guide'.

Chronological Table*

BC

c. 3200	Deeds of Egyptian kings sculptured on reliefs
26th century	Libraries of kings Cheops and Chephren
25th century	Preservation of ancient Egyptian annuals and king-lists
c. 2300	Description of military events by private Egyptian (Mery-re)
c. 2000	Narratives of Lagash (Sumeria)
20th century	Travel story of Sinuhe (Egypt)
c. 1700	Chronicle of Sargon (Akkad)
c. 1600	Akkadian Testament of Hattusilis I (Hittite)
c. 1500	Decree of Telepinus
15th century	Accounts of campaigns of Thothmes III (Egypt)
c. 1400	Historical reports in Hittite treaties
14th century	Epics of Ugarit (Phoenicia)
c. 1300	Annals of Mursilis II (Hittite)
13th century	Life-story of Hattusilis III
11th century	Sanchuniathon of Byblos
c. 1000	Journey of Wen-Amon to Byblos
10th century	David and Solomon
?8th–7th century	Deuteronomy
?8th century	*Iliad, Odyssey* (Homer): *Theogony, Works and Days* (Hesiod)
668–631	Archives of Ashurbanipal at Nineveh (Assyria)
c. 648	Archilochus: social criticism
?c. 600	Stesichorus: scepticism
559–525	Archives and pronouncements of Cyrus I (Persia)
c. 546	Anaximander: geography
c. 500	Hecataeus: *Journey round the World, Genealogies*
490, 480–479	Persian Wars

* For writers, the dates are those of their lives; for kings and emperors, their reigns.

411

Mid-5th century	Ion: memoirs
c. 444	Nehemiah at Jerusalem
c. 490/480–429/5	Herodotus
431–404	Peloponnesian War
d. 429	Pericles
c. 460/455–?c. 399/8	Thucydides
469–399	Socrates
424–405	Babylon archives of Darius II
c. 430–after 355	Xenophon
401–399	Xenophon's march to Babylonia (Anabasis) and back
436–338	Isocrates
359–336	Philip II of Macedonia
336–323	Alexander the Great
Soon after 400	Ephorus
384–322	Aristotle
c. 378–305	Theopompus
c. 356–260	Timaeus
c. 340–c. 270	Duris
?c. 300	Permanent Roman pontifical annals
Early 3rd century	Clitarchus
264–241, 218–201, 149–146	Punic Wars
?c. 250	Hieronymus
Later 3rd century	Phylarchus
271–213	Aratus of Sicyon
c. 270–201	Naevius
?end 3rd century	Fabius Pictor
239–169	Ennius
234–149	Cato the elder (Censor)
c. 230–118	Polybius
c. 130	Annales Maximi
111–106	War against Jugurtha
d. 87	Catulus
d. after 78	Rutilius Rufus
91–89	Social (Marsian) War: Italian revolt
81–79	Dictatorship of Sulla
d. 67	Macer
c. 135–50	Posidonius
106–48	Pompey
106–43	Cicero
63	Conspiracy of Catiline

60	First Triumvirate
100–44	Caesar (58–51 Gallic War; 49–48 Civil War with Pompey; 48–47 Egypt; 47–45 Civil War with sons of Pompey)
86–c. 34	Sallust
43	Second Triumvirate
31	Battle of Actium
31 BC–AD 14	Reign of Augustus
64/59 BC–AD 12/17	Livy
c. 19 BC–after AD 31	Velleius Paterculus
AD 14–37	Tiberius
37–41	Caligula (Gaius)
41–54	Claudius
54–68	Nero
23/4–79	Pliny the elder
66–73	Jewish rebellion
37/8–after 94/5	Josephus
69	Year of the Four Emperors (Galba, Otho, Vitellius, Vespasian)
69–79	Vespasian
79–81	Titus
81–96	Domitian
96–8	Nerva
98–117	Trajan
c. 45/50–120/7	Plutarch
c. 56/7–?after 117	Tacitus
117–38	Hadrian
c. 70–after 130	Suetonius
138–61	Antoninus Pius
c. 160	Appian
161–80	Marcus Aurelius
c. 95–175	Arrian
c. 120–after 180	Lucian
193–211	Septimius Severus
c. 155–235	Dio Cassius
c. 175–after 238	Herodian
284–305	Diocletian (d. 313)
303–10	The Great Persecution
306–37	Constantine the Great (312 battle of the Milvian Bridge, 313 Edict of Milan)
c. 260–c. 340	Eusebius
337–61	Constantius II

413

361–3	Julian the Apostate
364–75	Valentinian I
364–78	Valens (378 Battle of Adrianople)
379–95	Theodosius I
c. 330/5–c. 393/6	Ammianus
?end 4th century	*Historia Augusta*

Notes

FOREWORD

1. e.g. Cassiodorus (*Gothic History, c.* AD 535, now lost, and *Chronica*), Jordanes (*Origins and Deeds of the Goths*, 551–5), Einhard (p. 407), Bede, William of Poitiers, William of Malmesbury.
2. e.g. Leo Diaconus, late tenth century (perhaps the best written); Michael Psellus, mid-eleventh (cultured, cynical and amusing); the brothers Nicetas (the most fair-minded) and Michael Acominatus (a passionate admirer of classical Athens), twelfth and early thirteenth; Anna Comnena (the greatest of woman historians) and her husband Nicephorus Bryennius (p. 391); Laonicus Chalcocondyles (the only Athenian in Byzantine literature) (p. 388) and Critobulus (pro-Turkish), fifteenth century (p. 390).

INTRODUCTION

(a) The Near Eastern Background

1. Herodotus, II 77.
2. Mace-head of Scorpion king, palette of Narmer.
3. The site of Akhnaton's (fourteenth century BC) is known. The most famous is that of Rameses II (thirteenth century).
4. A much more sophisticated version dates from Senusert III (nineteenth century).
5. A. Erman, *The Literature of the Ancient Egyptians*, pp. 14 ff.
6. e.g. battle of Kadesh, and repulse of invaders by Merenptah (twelfth century).
7. J. H. Breasted, *Ancient Records of Egypt*, (Chicago, 1906–7), II 461–2.
8. Tabi-utul-Bel.
9. S. N. Kramer, *History Begins at Sumer* (New York, 1959), p. 41.
10. *Textes Réligieux Sumériens du Louvre*, II 73; and Nippur tablet.

11. The Anitta text. Later, however, Assyrian annals may have copied the Hittites.

12. The view that the whole document is later than Hattusilis I need not be accepted.

13. S. Moscati, *The Face of the Ancient Orient* (New York, 1962), p. 167.

14. Josephus, *Against Apion (Contra Apionem)*, II 6.

15. II Samuel, IX 20. No authorship for these books was named until *c.* AD 500 (?). The original biographies (I Chronicles, XXIX 29) are missing, but portions are no doubt preserved in I Samuel, XVI–I Kings, II 10. The account in I Chronicles, XI–XXIX, though it contains much additional material, is later and inferior, and idealises.

16. II Samuel, VI 15 f., 20.

17. Deuteronomy, XXVI 7–8.

18. Amos, V 18–20.

19. I Kings, XVI 16–17, 23–8

20. In spite of, or because of, material disasters, the Covenant of Jehovah was interpreted, at least during post-exilic times, in optimistic terms, envisaging the ultimate victory of good. A similar note is apparent in the Zend-Avesta of the Parsees, though in general it provides no historical, forward-moving pattern of interpreting events.

21. Nehemiah, II 12, 13, 16.

22. Ezra, IV 15.

23. Ezra, VI 1.

(b) The Greek Beginnings

1. Homer, *Iliad*, XVIII 501, XXIII 486.

2. Ibid. IX 443.

3. Ibid. IX 189.

4. Hesiod, *Works and Days (Erga)*, 109–78.

5. Semonides of Samos (the name 'Archaeology', ancient history, was later given to one of his works), Asius of Samos (?seventh–sixth centuries), Eumelus of Corinth (?eighth century or later).

6. Beguiling of Zeus, Punishment of Ares and Aphrodite.

7. Homer, *Odyssey*, VIII 44, etc.

8. Heraclitus (*c.* 500 BC) developed the idea that the world is a mass of conflicting tensions. The Erinyes, ministers of Justice, prevent the Sun from overstepping his measures. His ideas of eternal, simultaneous creation and decay were later given cyclical form. The Pythagoreans also believed in periodical recurrences; Eudemus in Simplicius on Aristotle's *Physics*, p. 732.

9. e.g. clay tablet from S. Babylonia (*c.* 600 BC, BM); cf. plans of fields and cities (Nippur).

10. Dionysius of Halicarnassus, *De Thucydide*, 5.

11. This *Periegesis, Periodos Ges* guided Alexander the Great on his campaigns in India.

12. Cadmus of Miletus, regarded by some ancient writers as the 'first historian', was probably a late forger. Earlier, Aristeas of Proconnesus was reputed to have written a geographical verse-epic, perhaps a travel fantasy.

13. Still with circumambient ocean (probably criticised for oversimplicity by Herodotus, IV 36). The *Periplus* attributed to Scylax of Caryanda, who travelled on behalf of Darius I (*c.* 500 BC) and may have drawn up a map for the Persians, is apparently of the fourth century (p. 431, n. 47).

14. e.g. Hecataeus, fragments 19 J, 26, 27.

15. The genealogies of Acusilaus of Argos (*c.* 500) and Pherecydes of Athens (*c.* 460) served a similar justificatory purpose. Acusilaus paraphrased Hesiod's genealogical poems in prose (in the Ionic dialect; a large fragment survives), drawing subjects from the Greek east, and Pherecydes started the line which led to the huge compendium of Apollodorus of Athens (second century BC).

16. Herodotus, II 43.

17. Xenophanes, fragment 18.

18. Xenophanes innovated by writing a poem on a contemporary event: the settlement of Ionians at Elea (Velia). He also wrote a *Foundation of Colophon*.

19. e.g. by Dionysius of Miletus.

20. e.g. Xanthus of Sardis, a Lydian writing in Greek.

21. *Epidemiae, Synecdemeticus* (meanings disputed).

22. Heraclitus, fragment 119. A generation earlier, the poet Theognis had taken the more fatalistic view.

23. A biography of Heraclides of Mylasa (early fifth century) was attributed by Suidas to Scylax of Caryanda (see n. 13).

PART I HERODOTUS

Chapter 1. The Life and Work of Herodotus

1. The division is at Herodotus, V 27. Some have seen a tripartite division.

2. The books were later named after the 9 Muses; Lucian, *Herodotus*, 1. The division into chapters only goes back to 1608.

3. Herodotus, i, beginning (trans. A.de Selincourt). *Barbaros*='non-Greek-speaking'.

4. Ibid. v 3 ff., 22, etc.

5. Ibid. VII 171, IV 82.

6. Ibid. IV 30 (trans. A.de Selincourt).

7. 'Longinus', *On the Sublime* (*De Sublimitate*), XIII 4.

8. The structure of Herodotus has suggestively been compared to the pediments of contemporary temples. Yet he does not offer visual descriptions of buildings (or scenery).

9. In fact, however, there had been earlier encroachments, and so, after beginning with Croesus, the first book goes far back in time.

10. Aristophanes, *Frogs* (*Ranae*), 52-3.

11. Plutarch, *Brutus*, 5.

12. cf. Winston Churchill, who dictated his historical works and liked to have an appreciative friend present while he was doing so.

13. e.g. Herodotus, VI 48 f., I 5, VI 102, 107.

14. Ibid. I 184; cf. I 106, VII 213 (other unfulfilled promises).

15. From the Argolid (Troezen and perhaps Argos).

16. Dittenberger, *Sylloge Inscriptionum Graecarum* (3rd ed.), p. 45.

17. Herodotus, VII 87 f. Her ship rammed a Calyndian vessel belonging to her own side, but Xerxes did not notice.

18. It appears on the earliest preserved tribute list, of that year.

19. Gellius, *Attic Nights* (*Noctes Atticae*), XV 23.

20. cf. Aristotle, *Rhetoric*, III 9, 1490*a* (29).

21. In the Peloponnesian War it no longer counted as an Athenian ally, and after briefly favouring the Athenian expedition to Sicily it became openly hostile.

22. Herodotus, VI 91, VII 137, 233, IX 73. The absence of systematic references to recent times would not have worried him, since it accorded with epic and tragic precedents.

23. Ibid. IV 99 seems to be based on material collected for a western public.

24. Aristophanes, *Acharnians*, 525 ff.

25. e.g. Pseudo-Hippocrates, *On Airs, Waters and Places* (*De Aeribus*), 3 ff.

26. Herodotus, I 95; cf. VII 8, in which Xerxes speaks of Persian acquisitiveness.

Chapter 2. *The Background and Beliefs of Herodotus*

1. The rhetorician Hermogenes of Tarsus (second century AD) called him a more careful writer than Heraclitus.

2. Herodotus, III 60.

3. Ibid. IV 142, V 124.

4. Ibid. v 36.

5. Ibid. IV 36, 45; cf. II 21. Sometimes, however, Herodotus' target may be not Hecataeus but people Hecataeus, too, had criticised.

6. Ibid. IV 36. The geometry of rectangular land-measurement was still more familiar than geography.

7. Ibid. VI 98, v 97; cf. also Pseudo-Hesiod, *The Shield (Aspis)*, 237–69, etc.

8. Herodotus, VI 86.

9. Ibid. III 80–2; cf. VI 43.

10. Dionysius of Halicarnassus, *De Imitatione*, 2; Quintilian, x 1 (54).

11. Pindar, *Nemeans* VII 12–16 (trans. C.M.Bowra).

12. Herodotus, VI 112 (trans. A.de Selincourt).

13. Ibid. IX 27 (trans. A.de Selincourt).

14. Ibid. VII 139; cf. 168, and VIII 73.

15. Ibid. VIII 144 (trans. A.de Selincourt).

16. Ibid. II 177; cf. I 29.

17. By Corax and his pupil Tisias.

18. Herodotus, VII 8 ff., 157 ff., VIII 140 ff., III 80 ff.

19. Ibid. VI 121 ff., VIII 68.

20. Ibid. VII 144, VIII 179.

21. Ibid. VI 123 f.; cf. v 71.

22. Ibid. VI 121, VII 162.

23. Ibid. VII 104.

24. Aristotle, *Politics*, II 8, 5, 1, 1267*b*.

25. Herodotus, v 97.

26. Pindar, *Pythians* VIII 15–18 (trans. C.M.Bowra).

27. Herodotus, VII 104.

28. Ibid. I 65 f.

29. Aeschylus, *Agamemnon*, 374, 380 (trans. L.McNeice).

30. Herodotus, VII 10 (trans. A.de Selincourt).

31. Ibid. I 207 (trans. A.de Selincourt).

32. Ibid. III 108, 126, VI 84, I 207, etc.

33. Ibid. I 8, II 61, v 33, IX 24.

34. Homer, *Iliad*, XXIV 28–30.

35. Solon, fragment 1 Diehl, 17–22 (trans. R.Lattimore). He is urging responsibility in public and political life.

36. Euripides, *Trojan Women*, 95–7 (trans. R.Lattimore).

37. Heraclitus, fragment 93.

38. Aeschylus, *Agamemnon*, 374–7.

39. Herodotus, VIII 110.

40. Aeschylus, *Agamemnon*, 749–51.

41. Herodotus, VII 35, 54; cf. Aeschylus, *Persians*, 94 ff., 827.

42. Ibid. IX 112 (Masistes).
43. Ibid. VII 137, VIII 13, 129.
44. Ibid. V 56, II 120, IX 65.
45. Accompanied sometimes by expiation, as also in Herodotus, VI 86 (Glaucus).
46. Diehl, *Anthologia Lyrica Graeca*, I 79. Herodotus, III 119, is echoed in Sophocles, *Antigone*, 905 ff.
47. Herodotus, I 60.
48. *Papyri from Oxyrhynchus*, 23 (1956), no. 2382.
49. e.g. Herodotus, VII 189, II 181.
50. Ibid. I 182.
51. Ibid. VII 129 (trans. A.de Selincourt).
52. Ibid. II 65 (trans. A.de Selincourt).
53. Ibid. II 45 (trans. A.de Selincourt).
54. Ibid. IX 100, IV 152, VI 84.
55. Ibid. II 51; cf. 47.
56. Ibid. VIII 36–9.
57. Ibid. I 91, VI 75, 86; cf. V 90.
58. Ibid. VI 27, VII 57, 12 ff. (but the dream might be a deception).
59. Ibid. VIII 77 (trans. A.de Selincourt).
60. Ibid. IX 43.
61. Ibid. II 3.
62. Ibid. I 8, IX 109, etc.
63. Ibid. I 8, VI 135.
64. Sophocles, *Oedipus Tyrannus*, 977, 1080. Bupalus of Chios had portrayed it in sculpture; Pausanias, IV 30 (6).

Chapter 3. The Methods of Herodotus

1. Herodotus, VI 86; cf. Democritus, B. 62, 68.
2. e.g. Herodotus, VIII 26.
3. Ibid. VIII 144.
4. Ibid. I 135, III 180, IX 107 ff., 122.
5. Ibid. I 137.
6. Ibid. I 30, IV 76.
7. Ibid. VI 129 (trans. A.de Selincourt).
8. Plutarch, *On the Malignity of Herodotus* (*De Malignitate Herodoti*), 856.
9. e.g. Athenians at Marathon, fight between Onesilaus and Artybius, story of Masistes.
10. e.g. Gyges in Candaules' bedroom, Arion, Cleobis and Biton, Adrastus, Alcmaeon.
11. Herodotus, VII 120 (trans. A.de Selincourt).

12. Ibid. I 197 (trans. A.de Selincourt).
13. Ibid. III 112 (trans. A.de Selincourt).
14. Ibid. VI 184 (trans. A.de Selincourt).
15. Ibid. I 94 (trans. A.de Selincourt).
16. Ibid. II 44 (trans. A.de Selincourt).
17. Ibid. IV 23.
18. Ibid. I 93.
19. Ibid. I 57, III 38, VII 181.
20. Ibid. IV 42–3.
21. Ibid. II 99 (trans. A.de Selincourt).
22. e.g. Democedes (doctor at Persian court) ? Zopyrus, Artabazus, renegade Greeks, sources on Thermopylae.
23. Herodotus, II 106, 125, VII 61 ff., VIII 82 etc.
24. At least for the previous 100–50 years Herodotus has a sense of the length of time (II 11, v 9), but he cannot give an over-all picture of the later part of the sixth century or use fixed points that readers would understand. Archon-lists were only recorded on stone in *c.* 425. But transitions are effected by synchronism (III 39).
25. e.g. fourth-dynasty Egyptian kings placed after eighteenth and nineteenth.
26. e.g. Herodotus, VI 134, IX 76.
27. Ibid. VI 137.
28. Ibid. v 86, VIII 8.
29. Ibid. III 115 (trans. A.de Selincourt).
30. Ibid. I 95 (trans. A.de Selincourt).
31. e.g. four versions of the Greek appeal to Gelon, tyrant of Syracuse; information on Plataea from three sources.
32. Herodotus, VII 152 (trans. A.de Selincourt).
33. e.g. on goat-footed men or the phoenix, IV 25, II 73.

PART 2. THUCYDIDES

Chapter 4. Thucydides and the Peloponnesian War

1. Thucydides, II 48.
2. Ibid. v 18.
3. Ibid. v 26.
4. Ibid. II 100.
5. The tradition that his death was violent may be true or may be an attempt to explain the fact that his work was left incomplete.
6. Thucydides, I 1.
7. Ibid. I 2–19 and 89–117.
8. Ibid. I 17.

9. Ibid. I 97.

10. Hermogenes, *On Style* (*Peri Ideon*), II 12; Cicero, *On the Orator* (*De Oratore*), II 12, 53.

11. Thucydides, I 23 (trans. R.Warner).

12. Ibid. I 97.

13. e.g. ibid. I 20.

14. Ibid. I 18, VI 59.

15. Ibid. I 21.

16. Ibid. I 22 (trans. F.E.Adcock).

17. e.g. (?) Hippocrates, *On the Sacred Disease* (*De Morbo Sacro*).

18. Anaxagoras, fragment 21 A.

19. Thucydides, I 23 (trans. R.Warner; but last sentence based on R.Sealey). An alternative interpretation, less easily derived from the Greek, tones down 'compel'—the Spartans felt they must attack Athens because its power was increasing so seriously.

20. Though elsewhere he uses these terms interchangeably or in varying senses.

21. Or who (less frequently) had disregarded benefits received from their opponents.

22. Thucydides has been accused of failing to explain just why Athens backed Corcyra (I 44), and the role of Pericles in the negotiations. Pericles may well have declared more than once, in 432 and before, that Sparta had long plotted war against Athens. The historian has also been accused of minimising the role of Athens' embargo against Megara (I 139), which some have regarded as contributing largely to the war. But its precise motives, and above all its date, are uncertain. It is often attributed to 433/2 but may be earlier.

23. e.g. Thucydides, I 118.

24. Ibid. II 65, v 26.

25. Ibid. v 25–6.

26. Eupolis, fragment 304 K; Plato, *Apology*, 26.

27. Plato, *Ion*, 535*c*.

28. Dionysius of Halicarnassus, *De Thucydide*, 15.

29. e.g. Thucydides, v 91: 'Sparta is not cruel to its vanquished enemies'; it was not vindictive after 404.

30. Ibid. I 34–46.

31. Ibid. II 60–4.

32. Ibid. II 65.

33. e.g. ibid. VIII 24 clashes with IV 120.

34. As in v, which has also been regarded as unfinished since its latter part likewise lacks speeches and includes verbatim documents; cf. p. 118.

35. Dionysius of Halicarnassus (*De Thucydide*, 16) says Cratippus reported that Thucydides abandoned speeches because they were hard for readers and slowed down the story.

Chapter 5. Speeches and Personalities in Thucydides

1. Two-thirds are in the first three books.
2. Homer, *Iliad*, IX 443.
3. Thucydides, III 42.
4. Ibid. III 60 (trans. R. Warner).
5. It is disputed whether the rhetorician and the sophist of this name are the same person or not.
6. Marcellinus, 22. But this may only have been said because of correspondences in their thinking.
7. Thucydides, I 22 (trans. R. Warner).
8. Perhaps there are traces in III 36, VI 18, VII 77.
9. Thucydides, II 89.
10. Speeches before battles, an ancient convention, sometimes reflect an original (the unrhetorical Spartans do not need them; ibid. v 69).
11. Ibid. I 120 ff., 140 ff. Some speeches do not lead to action, e.g. VI 76–87.
12. Plato, *Phaedrus*, 276A.
13. One of Protagoras' works was called *Antilogia*, a word used by Thucydides, I 31.
14. Thucydides, IV 59–65.
15. Ibid. I 122, V 103. For a list of Euripidean references, see J. H. Finley, *Three Essays on Thucydides*, pp. 181 ff.
16. Gorgias, *Encomium of Helen*, 8 f.
17. He was also influenced by Democritus and Antiphon.
18. Quintilian, X 1 (73); cf. Dionysius of Halicarnassus, *De Thucydide*, 24.
19. Cicero, *Orator*, 67.
20. e.g. Thucydides, II: delays of the Spartan king Archidamus while he hoped Athens might call the war off.
21. Thucydides, VII 84 (trans. R. Warner).
22. Ibid. VI 20, VII 55, VIII 96.
23. Democritus, B. 118.
24. Plato, *Euthydemus*, 274 A.
25. Protagoras, fragment 1 D–K.
26. Democritus, B. 242.
27. Thucydides, I 138.
28. Democritus, B. 169–217, 35–115.
29. He politely disregards his relative Cimon, who had opposed Pericles.

30. Cratinus had satirised Pericles as responsible for the war in his play *Dionysalexandros* (*Papyri from Oxyrhynchus*, 163p).
31. Thucydides, II 65 (trans. R.Warner); cf. II 82.
32. Ibid. II 65.
33. He had begun to attack Pericles in 431.
34. Thucydides, v 15 (trans. R.Warner).
35. Notably, bloody reprisals against Scione (Chalcidice) in 423.
36. Thucydides, VIII 73. This reference occurs at the time of Hyperbolus' murder (411).
37. Ibid. VII 86 (trans. R.Warner).
38. Ibid. v 15.
39. Yet it is not part of Thucydides' plan to blame him for the Melos massacre (Plutarch, *Alcibiades*, 16): that sort of point had already been made against Cleon.
40. Thucydides, VIII 86.
41. After a subordinate's defeat he took refuge with the Persian Pharnabazus, and in 404 the Thirty at Athens arranged for him to be murdered.
42. Thucydides, I 138.
43. Ibid. VII 71.

Chapter 6. Powers and Politics in Thucydides

1. Thucydides, IV 20.
2. Ibid. I 126.
3. Democritus, B.166 D–K.
4. Diogenes Laertius, IX 54.
5. Pseudo-Hippocrates, *On Airs, Waters and Places*, 22.
6. e.g. Thucydides, II 54.
7. Ibid. I 17.
8. Ibid. v 26.
9. Ibid. I 32, 124, II 63, III 40, 82, VI 87–92.
10. Democritus, B.2.
11. Ibid. B.19: cf. Anaximenes, Epicurus.
12. Thucydides, I 140.
13. Ibid. VII 28.
14. Ibid. v 16, VI 23.
15. Ibid. VIII 24 (5).
16. Ibid. I 71: new inventions always triumph.
17. e.g. Xenophanes, fragment 18 – against Hesiod, etc.
18. Sophocles, *Oedipus Coloneus*, 1224 f.
19. Thucydides, v 104.
20. Ibid. I 140.

21. Ibid. I 78 (trans. R.Warner).
22. Ibid. III 82 (trans. R.Warner).
23. Ibid. II 41 (trans. R.Warner).
24. Ibid. II 64, cf. 43.
25. Ibid. I 76, III 37, V 105, 109, etc.
26. Ibid. I 76. The Corinthians helped Epidamnus because they thought it right – but also from enmity with Corcyra (ibid. I 25).
27. Ibid. I 75 (trans. R.Warner).
28. Ibid. I 70 (trans. R.Warner).
29. Sophocles, *Antigone*, 332, 362 ff. (trans. E.Wyckhoff).
30. Democritus, B.3.
31. Thucydides, II 8, IV 108, VIII 2; though the masses may be loyal to Athens (III 47, VIII 48).
32. Nicias had unavailingly attacked them (426) and assessed them for tribute (424).
33. cf. Thucydides, I 118; and Spartan suggestions at Pylos.
34. Ibid. V 105 (trans. R.Warner).
35. e.g. Thrasymachus and Callicles, according to Plato, *Republic*, I, and Plato, *Gorgias*.
36. cf. Athenagoras and Hermocrates (whom Thucydides preferred) at Syracuse.
37. Thucydides, II 65 (imperfect tense).
38. III 80–2 (Darius). Probably written with Pericles in mind. Thucydides also deliberately introduces a digression on the Pisistratid 'tyrants' to evaluate their services more accurately and scoff at new fears of tyranny (VI 54–9). 'It seemeth that as he was of Regal descent, so he best approved of the Regal Government' (Hobbes).
39. Thucydides, II 37, III 82, VI 39, VII 55, VIII 96.
40. Ibid. I 70 (trans. R.Warner).
41. Ibid. II 65, IV 28, VIII 1.
42. Ibid. I 18.
43. Ibid. VIII 48 (trans. R.Warner).
44. Ibid. VIII 89.
45. Ibid. VIII 97 (trans. R. Warner).
46. Ibid. II 88 f.

Chapter 7. *The Methods of Thucydides*

1. e.g. the ostracism of Hyperbolus is only mentioned when he dies (p. 424, n. 36). Nicias' struggles with Cleon and Alcibiades are omitted. Little is said of relations between Athens and Persia. Cultural history is only implied, in the Funeral Speech.
2. Archilochus, fragment 103 Diehl.

3. Thucydides, II 97–9.
4. Pheidias was at work on the Parthenon *c.* 447–432 BC.
5. Thucydides, v 26.
6. Ibid. II 53, III 83, VII 29.
7. Ibid. I 22, II 65, III 83, more in VIII; III 36, 95, IV 34, v 16, VII 30.
8. Ibid. II 2; cf. v 25.
9. e.g. ibid. II 25.
10. Ibid. v 20.
11. Ibid. v 26.
12. Ibid. I 22 (trans. R. Warner).
13. Ibid. II 91, III 98 (?), IV 40; and Syracuse.
14. Ibid. I 22.
15. Ibid. v 26.
16. e.g. parts of Xerxes–Pausanias correspondence.
17. Thucydides, v 47, cf. 23, 39.
18. But cf. ibid. II 5; and three versions of Spartan–Persian agreement of 411.
19. Euripides, fragment 910 N.
20. Thucydides, II 47 ff.: ? typhus or measles or bubonic plague.
21. Herodicus of Selymbria (writer on dietetics).
22. e.g. Thucydides, II; cf. IV 73.
23. e.g. ibid. II 83.
24. Is Plataea so greatly stressed because it was a model Greek siege? Mantinea (418) is emphasised because almost all Greek cities were involved.
25. Thucydides, VII 44 (trans. R. Warner).
26. Ibid. I 20 (trans. R. Warner).
27. Ibid. I 22.
28. Ibid. I 10; cf. II 29, and Pausanias.
29. Ibid. I 8.
30. Plato, *Protagoras*, 337c.
31. e.g. Antiphon, *On Truth* (*De Veritate*), B4, fragment B, column 2: all men are equal.
32. Thucydides, II 96–7.
33. Ibid. II 100: *pace* Plato.

PART 3. THE LATER GREEKS

Chapter 8. Xenophon

1. Xenophon, *Anabasis*, VI 6, 9, seems to imply the withdrawal of the Spartan garrison in 379 from the Theban citadel which it had seized.

2. Ibid. IV 7 (trans. R.Warner).
3. Ibid. IV 3 (trans. R.Warner).
4. Themistogenes of Syracuse; Xenophon, *Greek History (Hellenica)*, III
1 (2); Plutarch, *On the Glory of the Athenians (De Gloria Atheniensium)*,
345*e*.
5. Xenophon, *Anabasis*, I 8.
6. Ctesias also wrote the first separate work on India. Another Persian
history had been written by Charon of Lampsacus: probably *c.* 400
rather than *c.* 465.
7. e.g. Ctesias, fragment 8*b* (*Papyri from Oxyrhynchus*, 2330).
8. Xenophon, *Anabasis*, IV 5 (trans. R.Warner).
9. Ibid. V 1 (trans. R.Warner).
10. Xenophon, *On Hunting (Cynegeticus)*, was perhaps an early work, not
necessarily spurious.
11. Xenophon, *Anabasis*, I 5 (trans. R.Warner).
12. Clearchus, Proxenus, Menon.
13. He may first have served under Thibron's successor Dercylidas.
14. Probably not, as was suggested, for joining Cyrus' expedition.
15. Xenophon, *Greek History*, IV 5 (37).
16. Cratippus of Athens, singled out by Plutarch (*On the Glory of the
Athenians*, 1), probably wrote down to 394. But it has been suggested
that he may have been of Hellenistic date. He has also, however,
sometimes been identified with the 'Oxyrhynchus Historian' – named
after a papyrus relating to 396–7 BC (*Papyri from Oxyrhynchus*, 842) –
whose history was written after 387 and before 346 (probably before
356). He is lucid and simple, though flat and dull, and covers a
wide range. The work remained largely unread, probably because
it was superseded by Ephorus. But the closest to Thucydides of all
Greek historians may have been Philistus of Syracuse (430–356/5),
who wrote a lucid History of Sicily defending the tyrant Dionysius I
of Syracuse. He said he found 'little or nothing' in Thucydides VI
or VII which needed addition or modification.
17. Though Xenophon, in *Ways and Means (De Vectigalibus)*, *c.* 355–354,
supports a defensible policy comparable to that of the statesman
Eubulus.
18. Notably Aeneas Tacticus (? mid-fourth century).
19. Critias' speech may be more or less authentic though condensed,
while Theramenes' seems to combine the memories of an eyewitness
with knowledge of Theramenes' general views.
20. Xenophon, *Greek History*, II 2 (3) (trans. R.Warner).
21. Xenophon, *Anabasis*, IV 6.
22. Xenophon, *Greek History*, V 4 (1).

23. Xenophon, *Constitution of the Spartans (Lakedaimonion Politeia)*, 14.

24. Xenophon, *Greek History*, i (25) (trans. R.Warner).

25. Xenophon, *Agesilaus*, x 3.

26. Xenophon, *Hiero*, is a talk between Hiero and the poet Simonides of Ceos, discussing the position of a peace-time leader.

27. Xenophon, *Education of Cyrus (Cyropaedia)*, vi 5, viii 3: romantic touches. The description of Panthea introduces and anticipates lofty concepts of love.

28. Ibid. viii 8 is a contradictory supplement which may not be authentic.

29. e.g. Xenophon, *Anabasis*, iii 1, 5.

30. e.g. by Polycrates. Xenophon, *On Hunting*, includes an outburst against sophists.

31. e.g. the wife of Ischomachus in the *Estate Management (Oeconomicus)*, featuring Socrates: perhaps inspired by Xenophon's wife Philesia.

32. e.g. Ion of Chios and Stesimbrotus of Thasos, *On Themistocles and Thucydides* (i.e. the son of Melesias) *and Pericles*.

Chapter 9. The Dramatic Historians

1. e.g. Isocrates, *Exchange of Property (Antidosis)*, iv 76, *Evagoras*, ix 76 f. History has always revealed an inexorable moral law, and will always do so. Unlike Socrates, who sought to justify virtue, Isocrates found it already justified and vice condemned, through the divine guardianship of human identity.

2. Isocrates, *Evagoras*, ix 7; cf. *Nicocles*, ii 48. 'Philosophy' aims at civic excellence, and the role of history as future guidance is sharpened. Isocrates, *Nicocles*, ii 35, stresses his own services to the community.

3. 'It is characteristic of language that one can represent the same subject in many different ways'; Isocrates, *Panegyricus*, iv 7–8 (cf. distortions of Alcibiades in *On Chariots (De Bigis)*, xvi 37; cf. *Busiris*, iii 108).

4. e.g. *Panathenaicus* (342–339). One product of this tendency, and of works such as the Attic History of Hellanicus, was a prolonged series of 'Atthidographers', historians of Attica who shed glamour on its past (in contrast to its present decline) and rationalised the myths. Phanodemus (d. after 330) gave his work the name 'Archaeology'. The *Attis* of Androtion (to 346) was the most famous local history of its time on the mainland, subsequently eclipsed by Philochorus (to 260), who was responsible for distinguishing history from antiquities. Philochorus collected documents, and Craterus the Macedonian (? *c.* 321–255) had collected and commented on Athenian decrees.

5. e.g., for the sake of the form, the assassination of Evagoras, king of Salamis, in Cyprus is not mentioned, and he is given a happy ending. (Biographies of contemporaries had a tendency to concentrate on characters rather than careers.) Isocrates passed from the legendary Busiris (391) and Encomium of Helen (370: a subject tackled by Gorgias) to this eulogistic Life of Evagoras, which he exaggeratedly claimed to be the first prose encomium of a living person: but cf. on Xenophon, p. 133. Isocrates' *Exchange of Property* is about his own life, and has been described as the first real autobiography.

6. Strabo, VII 3 (9). Much of it is embedded in Diodorus Siculus, XV–XVI; cf. Ephorus, fragment 191. Ephorus' history, in thirty books, went down to 341, Book XXX being added by his son. Each book was a unity, with its own preface.

7. He failed in source-criticism, showed little judgment or imagination and a feeble pro-Athenian bias and, although purposely excluding the mythical period, admitted the fabulous and inaccurate (Strabo, IX 3, 11 f.). Possibly one of his sources was the Oxyrhynchus Historian (p. 427, n. 16).

8. F. Jacoby, *Die Fragmente der griechischen Historiker*, 70.

9. Polybius, IV 20 5, cf. 6 ff., XXI 10–11.

10. Ibid. XII 25 f.

11. Ibid. XII 28a. Ephorus deplored speeches based on no genuine information.

12. Down to 356; it may have been intended to go as far as 334.

13. e.g. Isocrates, *Exchange of Property*, IV 77; *Panathenaicus*, XII 13: cf. Gorgias, *Olympicus*.

14. Though he made a serious attempt to arrange his material according to topics.

15. Theopompus, fragments 20, 22.

16. Ibid. fragment 24.

17. The theoretical basis for this attitude was derived from the austere moralist Antisthenes of Athens (*c.* 455–360), Socrates' pupil (regarded as founder of the Cynics), who revered Heracles for virtue and exertion. At the time of Theopompus Spartan hegemony had been destroyed by Thebes.

18. Theopompus, fragment 153 (148).

19. It contained fifty-eight books and went down to Philip's death. Probably it was written before Alexander's Persian War became a decisive historical factor.

20. Theopompus, who had thrice been exiled from Chios as an oligarchic leader, moved from aristocratic ideals to a belief in patriarchal

monarchy as their protector. He was very critical of Philip's enemy Demosthenes; Plutarch, *Demosthenes*, 13.

21. Theopompus was restored to Chios by Alexander in order to resist the pro-Persian oligarchy, but on his death fled to Egypt.

22. Polybius, II 8 (10).

23. Ibid. VIII 11 (3–4).

24. Ibid. VIII 9–11.

25. Dionysius of Halicarnassus, *Epistula ad Pompeium Geminum*, VI 7. Criticisms of this violence are mentioned in Lucian, *On Writing History* (*De Historia Conscribenda*), 59. Theopompus was particularly severe on Plato.

26. Strabo, I 2 (35).

27. Cicero, *Brutus*, XVII 66. For all his closeness to oratory, cf. Quintilian, X 1 (74). But he did not go all the way to the 'seductiveness' of Gorgias.

28. Dionysius of Halicarnassus, loc.cit., stresses his versatility: he aimed both at instruction and entertainment.

29. It is sometimes said that much of his work is preserved in Diodorus Siculus, but this is uncertain.

30. The original work had gone down to 320, but it was extended to include the Syracusan ruler Agathocles (who was responsible for his banishment) and finally Pyrrhus (or was this a separate work?).

31. He is also very censorious of Agathocles. But his views on most great men and events are unknown.

32. Polybius, XII 4a and 4c and 7 and 25 (trans. M. Chambers).

33. Ibid. XII 24 (5).

34. Ibid. XII 25e (4), 27a (3).

35. Especially wilful ignorance and falsification, e.g. of speeches (ibid. XII 25a, b), in spite of professions of their accuracy (XII 11a). He is accused of choosing a sluggish parochial hero in Timoleon of Syracuse (XII 23 (6)).

36. Ibid. XII 25e, 25th. The latter passage twists Timaeus' allusion to his long exile into an admission of this weakness.

37. Ibid. I 5 (1).

38. Cicero, *Orator*, II 14, 15. It foreshadowed the artificial verbal effects of Hegesias of Magnesia (*c.* 250).

39. Cicero, *On the Nature of the Gods* (*De Natura Deorum*), II 69.

40. Timaeus also introduced the reckoning by Olympiads into Greek history, presumably his work, though loosely constructed, provided a continuous narrative in chronological order.

41. The only surviving one of his 158 Greek constitutions (and some

non-Greek). Many leading fourth-century thinkers were more interested in such speculations on the State than in history.

42. Aristotle's original requirement of a very limited *polis* was modified later, by his experience of much larger states.

43. Aristotle, *Poetics*, IX 3, 1451*b*, 5–7. He denies that metre had anything to do with it – since tragic drama often dealt with supposedly real people.

45. e.g. as shown in the Lives of leading thinkers, especially the founders of philosophical schools; and the practice was widely extended, e.g. by the Peripatetics (pupils of Aristotle, n. 46) Dicaearchus of Messene and Phaenias of Eresus (who wrote about Sicilian tyrants as well as men of letters, not limiting himself to panegyric), the Academic Heraclides Ponticus (390–310), and Aristoxenus of Taras (b. 375/360), who wrote debunking biographies, e.g. of Socrates. He did this to score off Theophrastus of Lesbos (*c.* 372/69–288/5), whose study of types (*Characters*) developed the techniques that others used for biographies. After Alexander (n. 47), Alexandrian biographies were most accurate and better on character (because they were interested in chronology) but less well written, with the exception of Antigonus of Carystus (*c.* 240) – who was also an accurate writer. In *c.* 200 the Peripatetic Satyrus of Callatis wrote (uncritically) not only about literary figures (his *Euripides* has survived) but also about men of action.

46. cf. the theory of *proairesis;* Aristotle, *Nicomachean Ethics*, II 4 (3): 'he must "will" his action and will it for its own sake. The act must proceed from a fixed and unchangeable disposition' (trans. J.A.K. Thomson); cf. *Nicomachean Ethics*, II 6 (15); *On the Soul* (*De Anima*), 434*a* (31) (everything in nature exists for a purpose). By the time a man is grown up, his pattern of conduct is normally well enough established for predictions to be made about how he will behave in most circumstances. And so in these 'one-piece' Lives there is little desire to study development of character (though a chronological approach in Alexandria (n. 45) improved the situation). However, the Aristotelian tradition did provide that a man could change his acquired characteristics (*ethos*), if not his basic character (*physis*).

47. Modern historians have now become increasingly sceptical of the 'official' tradition. Early Lives of Alexander, now lost, range from those by Aristobulus of Cassandrea (who only started writing at the age of eighty-four) and Ptolemy I of Egypt (d. 283–282) – based on his own recollection and on official records – to Clitarchus of Colophon (after 280), whose work was attractive but largely

fictional. Nearchus of Crete, who commanded Alexander's fleet sailing from the Indus to the Tigris, wrote a memoir of the journey (and an account of India) before 312. Another geographical work of importance to historians was a late fourth-century *Periplus* which bore the name of Scylax of Caryanda who had conducted eastern explorations for Darius I. Agatharchides of Cnidus later continued the Herodotean tradition with a vivid account of the Red Sea (? *c.* 116), in which he sympathised with the sufferings of mine-workers. Polemo of Ilium (Troy) (*c.* 190) had used geography for archaeological purposes, e.g. the copying of inscriptions (he was called *stelokopas*, the 'stone-rapper').

48. He had accompanied Alexander's expedition as a historian. His execution turned the Aristotelian (Peripatetic) school against Alexander. Polybius probably used Callisthenes for some of his digressions on fourth-century history.

49. Trustworthy historian for period 323–272 or 263 BC: soldier and statesman, pro-monarchic, used official dispatches, disdained rhetoric. He may have written as a counterblast to the exuberance of Duris.

50. *c.* 340–260 BC. Ruled Samos as tyrant, ardent nationalist leader, wrote twenty-two-book history from 370 to *c.* 260. Polymath, may have been influenced by Peripatetics, applied theory of *mimesis* (imitation of reality and nature, much extending Plato, *Republic*, x 595–602) and tragic *catharsis* (Cicero, *Letters to Friends* (*Ad Familiares*), v 12 (4 f.)): carried picturesque methods of Herodotus to extremes: wrote books on tragedy and history of art. Did not invent 'tragic history' but developed features already found in Ctesias of Cnidus and Philistus of Syracuse and Timonides of Leucas: cf. Tolstoy, who said that what the public would like best would be his scenes of social and personal life – intrigues, chats and idiosyncrasies.

51. C. Müller, *Fragmenta Historicorum Graecorum*, 70 T.22 (76 F.I).

52. Polybius, II 56 (10), XII 25*b* (4).

53. Ibid. II 56 (63). Elsewhere he attacks the 'barber's shop and street gossip' of historians writing about Hannibal (Chaereas and Sosylus); III 20 (5).

54. Plutarch, *Themistocles*, 31.

55. He had anti-monarchist views, perhaps inherited from the passionate Demochares (*c.* 360–275), the nephew of Demosthenes and a historian of Athens.

56. The date of the battle of Sellasia in which King Antigonus III Doson of Macedonia finally defeated Cleomenes III of Sparta,

though at the same time the Achaean League was reduced to a position of virtual dependency.

57. Polybius, II 40.
58. Ibid. II 47 (10); cf. VIII 8 (8–9).
59. Ibid. III 9, I 14 (3). Another Roman, Aulus Postumius Albinus (consul 151), who had aims resembling those of Polybius (and was later praised by Cicero) is recognised but called loquacious and vainglorious (XXXIX 1). But he had shown hostility to the Achaean exiles (XXX 1 (5), etc.)! Albinus modestly deprecated his own Greek, but Cato said no one had forced him to write in it (Gellius, *Attic Nights*, II 8 (2)). Attacked for phil-Hellenism, Albinus was really a pro-Roman senatorial historian (Livy, XXXV 14 (5)).

Chapter 10. Polybius

1. Of Books XVII, XIX, XXXVIII and XL nothing survives. Polybius' own contents lists appended to Books I–VI (Polybius, XI 1*a* (5)) have disappeared.
2. Polybius, XV 9 (2); cf. Scipio in XV 10 (2).
3. Ibid. XXI 16 (8), XXIII 4.
4. The description of their friendship in XXXII, 9 f., echoes the Socratic circle. Polybius was first befriended by his elder brother Quintus Fabius Maximus Aemilianus.
5. He visited Locri Epizephyrii several times, and was honoured by it (Polybius, XII 5 (1–13)).
6. Ibid. XXXVIII 21 (2).
7. Callicrates (*c.* 149/8). He had originally opposed Polybius' father Lycortas.
8. Polybius, XXXIX 5.
9. Ibid. III 48 (12).
10. Since he wrote a work (now lost) on Scipio's victory over Numantia (133 BC) (Cicero, *Letters to Friends*, V 12 (2)), it is possible that he was with him during the war.
11. Pausanias, VIII 30 (8).
12. He lived long enough to refer to the Via Domitia in Gaul, *c.* 120 BC.
13. e.g. Polybius, II 37–70.
14. e.g. ibid. III 21 (9 ff.), IV 31 (3 ff.), IV 73 (6 ff.).
15. Ibid. III 4.
16. Ibid. XXXIX 5.
17. Ibid. I 1 (trans. M. Chambers).
18. Ibid. I 3 f.
19. Ibid. V 33.

20. Ibid. I 4 (trans. M.Chambers).
21. Ibid. II 37 (trans. M.Chambers).
22. Ibid. I 4, III 32 (trans. M.Chambers.)
23. Ibid. VII 7 (6).
24. Ibid. IX I (4).
25. Ibid. I 63 (trans. M.Chambers).
26. Ibid. III 4 (trans. M.Chambers).
27. Ibid. VI 10 (13 f.).
28. Ibid. XXXI 30, XXXV 3 (4) and 4 (3), XXXVI 8 (6). They shared a taste for riding and hunting, XXXI 14 (3); cf. XXIX 8.
29. Ibid. XVIII 35.
30. Ibid. VI 10 (12–14).
31. Cicero, *On the State (De Republica)*, VI 1, laid more stress on men and customs than on the constitution.
32. Polybius, VI 11 (trans. M.Chambers).
33. Ibid. VI 43–56, cf. 10. He felt that Rome was more successful than Sparta because it was better adapted to become a conqueror. Carthage was past its prime at the time of the Second Punic War. Athens and Thebes are excluded because their brilliant periods did not last.
34. e.g. Dicaearchus of Messene (Peripatetic) in his *Tripoliticus, c.* 300. The Stoics also approved of the mixed constitution.
35. Polybius, VI 5, VI 57. However, Polybius was prepared to detect progress in matters such as the advance of historiography.
36. Ibid. VI 5 (1), quoting 'Plato and other philosophers' (the Pythagoreans believed in periodical recurrences and similar theories could be deduced from Heraclitus; p. 416, n. 8). Cf. Plato, *Timaeus,* 39, on the cyclical Great Year, applied in *Republic,* VIII 544 ff., 557 ff., to the evolution of Greek cities. But Plato failed to close the circle with the change back from the worst (tyranny) to the best state. Aristotle, (*Physics,* IV 14, 223b; cf. *Rhetoric,* 1393a) saw a continuous biological cycle. Polybius, XXXVIII 21 f., accepts the idea in two forms, biological and 'fickle Fortune'.
37. Polybius, VI 11 (*c.* 450 BC).
38. Ibid. VI 3.
39. In this lost portion he evidently 'proved' his statement (IV 13) that Rome was the only clear case of a normal cyclical evolution.
40. Polybius, VI 9; cf. 57, I 64 (1–2). It is not necessary to claim that, while writing, Polybius changed his mind (for the worse) about Rome, or formed a guilty conscience.
41. Ibid. XXX 32 (10).
42. Ibid. XI 19, in contrast, e.g., to Livy. Polybius made use of an

anti-Roman source, Silenus of Calacte, for the Second Punic Wars, just as he used another, Philinus of Acragas, for the First War (ibid. I 15, III 26).

43. Ibid. I 14 (trans. M.Chambers).
44. Ibid. fragment 58 (fighting is a matter of the will); and VIII 7 (7) (Archimedes), X 47.
45. e.g. ibid. XXXI 26 (9); cf. IX 10 (8).
46. Ibid. III 4 (7), VIII 17, XV 5 (15, 17), XXIII 12 (4).
47. Ibid. XVI 4.
48. Ibid. VI 3. He also dislikes mongrel Alexandria, XV 27–30.
49. The arrangement is sometimes adjusted to suit campaigns.
50. Ibid. IV 20–1.
51. Ibid. XXXIX 4 (Diaeus).
52. Ibid. VIII 8 (5–9).
53. He also had political reasons for disliking Athens and Boeotia, XVIII 14, XX 5 (7).
54. Ibid. III 31 (trans. M.Chambers).
55. Ibid. IX 2 (5).
56. Ibid. I 35.
57. Ibid. II 7.
58. Ibid. III 4.
59. Ibid. IV 32 (74).
60. Created by Ssu-ma Ch'ien, c. 100 BC.
61. He became Demetrius I Soter.
62. Polybius, III 4.
63. Ibid. III 32.
64. Ibid. III 6 (5); cf. III 31, VI 2 (28).
65. Ibid. IX 2 (5).
66. Ibid. XII 25b, XXXVI 1.
67. Ibid. III 7 (6 f.); cf. IX 12–20, IV 40–3, XII 25e (pointing out that both history and medicine have their quacks).
68. Sometimes the verbal form (*to tuchon*) is used merely to mean 'what happened'; ibid. XV 6–8.
69. Ibid. XV 20, XX 7 (2).
70. Ibid. XXIII 12.
71. Ibid. I 86 (7), II 4 (3), IV 2, XXXVI 13 (2).
72. Ibid. I 35, XXIII 10–12, XXIX 21 – sometimes contradicting the doctrine of cyclical declines.
73. Ibid. I 63 (9), X 9 (2).
74. Ibid. I 35 (6).
75. Ibid. X 5 (8), XV 21 (3), II 71–3.
76. Ibid. II 35, XI 5 (8), XXIX 19 (2).

77. Ibid. xxxvi 17 (1–4).
78. Ibid. 1 4 (5). Chance may be the unforeseeable, or the unforeseen by man but foreseen (intended) by Providence.
79. Ibid. ix 1 (4); cf. vii 8 (7).
80. Ibid. xvi 12 (3–11).
81. Ibid. vi 56; cf. xi 12 (9), x 2 (10).
82. Ibid. iii 6 (Xenophon's expedition); cf. iv 3–12.
83. Ibid. 1 35, ii 7.
84. Ibid. 1 2 (8); cf. xii 2 (3), ii 37 (3), ix 1 (2).
85. Ibid. 1 14 (6).
86. Ibid. xii 25*e*.
87. Ibid. xii 7, xvi 20.
88. Ibid. ii 56 (10), xxxvi 1; cf. xii 25*b* (1).
89. F. Jacoby, *Die Fragmente der griechischen Historiker*, 124 F.44.
90. Polybius, xxix 12 (10).
91. e.g. ibid. ix 28–39 (Sparta).
92. Ibid. xii 4*c*.
93. Ibid. xii 25*e* (7).
94. Ibid. iv 2 (2).
95. Ibid. xii 27.
96. Ibid. xii 25*g*.
97. e.g. Raphia (217), at which Ptolemy IV Philopator of Egypt repelled Antiochus III (Book v).
98. More than one-third of Book vi.
99. e.g. we do not know where the light-armed troops were encamped.
100. Polybius, x 45.
101. Ibid. xii 25*e*.
102. Ibid. iii 59 (3 ff.).
103. Geminus of Rhodes, xvi 12.
104. Polybius, xxxiv 5 ff.; cf. xii 28 (1), iii 59 (7).
105. Strabo has preserved a number of them.
106. He is less sceptical about rationalised Homeric myths than about Eratosthenes; cf. xxxiv 2 (9–10).
107. Polybius, 1 5–6.
108. Ibid. v 21, iii 36.
109. Ibid. iii 22 ff., treaties with Carthage.
110. Probably Achaea. Not Aetolia or Macedonia. Probably not Rhodes, in spite of xvi 15.
111. e.g. the death of Cleomenes: sources evidently complex but unidentifiable. Books i and ii are naturally the most derivative.
112. Polybius, iii 59 (2) (trans. F.W.Walbank); cf. ix 2 (5).
113. Ibid. ii 56 (11), iii 6 (3), vii 7 (1).

114. Though his critical remarks about fabulous monographs (p. 149) seem directed against Hecataeus, Hellanicus, etc.
115. Polybius, VI 45, III 6.
116. Ibid. XVI 147 f. (20–8) (Zeno of Rhodes).

PART 4. LATIN WRITERS OF THE REPUBLIC

Chapter 11. Cato the Censor and after

1. Cicero, *De Oratore*, II 53 (M. Antonius Orator) (trans. E. W. Sutton).
2. Cato, fragment 77.
3. Ennius, fragments 194 ff.
4. Jacoby, *Die Fragmente der griechischen Historiker*, 680 (Berossus), 609 (Manetho, *c.* 300 BC).
5. The Latin annals, and a book on priestly law, attributed to him are likely to be the work of other writers – perhaps other Fabii.
6. e.g. Fabius Pictor, fragment 18 (on an early Fabius). He may also have hoped for Carthaginian readers, who would appreciate his blaming the Second Punic War on the Barcid family.
7. His story of the cradle of Romulus and Remus uses a 'recognition' theme that goes back to Sophocles, *Tyro*.
8. cf. Cincius Alimentus, a senator captured by Hannibal, who wrote another Roman history in Greek which helped to establish the senatorial tradition. C. Acilius wrote another history in Greek (at least to 184) in *c.* 142, with some apocryphal anecdotes.
9. cf. Quintilian, XII 11 (23).
10. Probably the title was only applied to the whole work after his death.
11. Cato, fragment 3.
12. Cato, fragment 45; cf. 31.
13. Cicero, *Tusculan Disputations*, IV 3; cf. *Brutus*, 75.
14. Cicero, *Brutus*, 66, 68, praises it but calls it uncouth; cf. *Laws* (*De Legibus*), I 6. Cicero, *De Oratore*, II 53, sees brevity as its only virtue. But fragments 57, 63, 83 show its variety; cf. next note.
15. e.g. Cato, fragments 86 (Maharbal), 95*a* (speech on Rhodians).
16. Cicero, *Brutus*, 294. He published them separately.
17. But he drew the line at Ser. Sulpicius Galba (consul 144) parading a child before the public to play on their emotions.
18. Even including the Transpadane area, which did not become formally part of Italy for another two hundred years.
19. The Basilica Porcia. The accounts of him by Cicero (*On Old Age* (*De Senectute*)), Nepos and Plutarch seem to be mere caricatures.
20. Known as the 'old' annalists. L. Cassius Hemina wrote history

showing Cato's influence, i.e. not published before at least the first part of Cato's history. Fragment 39 refers to 146 BC, indicating an extension of the work. L. Calpurnius Piso Frugi (consul 133) wrote a history to 146, factual but including rationalised legends and digressions, and showing signs of a feeling of inevitable decline (cf. Polybius, p. 152).

21. Livy, II 5, knows of records which may go back to extensive entries for fourth-fifth centuries BC in the Annales Maximi. Livy, XXXVI 2, 3–5, seems to elaborate on such items.

22. Cn. Gellius (attacked by Cato in court) wrote a history down to at least 146, fuller than previous annals and utilising Hellenistic methods. He started work before the publication of the Annales Maximi, but clearly had access to them.

23. e.g. C. Fannius (consul 122): the first contemporary historian of the conservatives.

24. Dionysius of Halicarnassus, V 17.

25. Cicero, *On Old Age*, 12.

26. e.g. *Corpus Inscriptionum Latinarum*, VI 2 (10230).

27. Coelius Antipater, fragment 2.

28. Next, Sempronius Asellio wrote a contemporary history down to 91 at least, in which he set himself the ethical aims of Isocrates and the methodology of Polybius.

29. Plutarch calls them *Hypomnemata* (Memoirs), Latin writers *Res Gestae*. Xenophon had used the term *Apomnemoneumata*.

30. The earliest Sulla (P. Sulla; *c.* 250 BC) was reached in Book II.

31. Battle losses grossly minimised on his own side and exaggerated on the other; fragment 19. Many divine warnings.

32. Plutarch, *Sulla*, 6 (trans. R. Warner).

33. Gellius, *Attic Nights*, I 12, 16.

34. Sallust, *Jugurtha* (*Bellum Jugurthinum*), 95.

35. Cicero, *Laws* (*De Legibus*), I 7.

36. Valerius Antias is the most notorious. He wrote a history of Rome in at least seventy-five books, in a vigorous, rhetorical style. Livy uses him but is very critical (XXVI 49, XXXIX 43, etc.). The twenty-three books of Claudius Quadrigarius were again crammed with poignant anecdote, and his style was praised for its devices. He wrote up to at least 82 BC. He innovated by starting not with the foundation of Rome but with its sack by the Gauls.

37. Livy, IV 7, 12, etc.

38. cf. Tubero, fragment 6.

39. Livy, VII 9 (5).

40. Cicero, *Laws*, I 6, criticising his speeches and elevated passages. He

himself favours the Polybian 'mixed' constitution; Cicero, *On the State*, II 59.

41. Cicero, *Letters to Atticus (Ad Atticum)*, II 6 (2). Not published until 42 (after he was dead) 'owing to fear of criticism for omitting details' (Ammianus, XVI 1, 2) – or fear of political reprisals.
42. Nepos, fragment 30.
43. Cicero, *De Oratore*, II 62 (M.Antonius Orator) (trans. E.W.Sutton).
44. Ibid. II 46; cf. *On Invention (De Inventione)*, I 27, *On the State*, II 10, 18–19.
45. Cicero, *Brutus*, 62 (trans. G.L.Hendrickson).
46. Cicero, *Letters to Friends (Ad Familiares)*, V 12 (trans. L.P.Wilkinson).
47. Cicero, *Letters to Atticus*, I 19 (10).
48. His Greek history, in fifty-two books or more, continued where Polybius left off (144) and continued to 85 or 82 BC: the last dateable fragments refer to 86.
49. Cicero, *De Oratore*, II 63.
50. In August 45 BC Cicero was prodded into praising Caesar's *Anticato* as insincerely as Caesar had praised his *Cato*.
51. Cicero, *Laws*, I 7; cf. *Brutus*, 259.
52. Cicero, *De Oratore*, II 58 (Timaeus), 94 (Ephorus, Theopompus).
53. Cicero, *Brutus*, 42.
54. Cicero, *De Oratore*, II 62.
55. Ibid. II 36 (M. Antonius Orator) (trans. E.W.Sutton).
56. Ibid. II 54.
57. Ibid. II 64.
58. This appears to be the meaning of Cicero, *Laws*, I 5 ('unum hoc oratorium maxime'). Or does he mean (as most have believed) 'history is the branch of study which is predominantly the concern of the orator'?
59. Cicero, *De Oratore*, II 64, 66. Callisthenes is blamed as over-rhetorical.
60. Ibid. *Orator*, 37.

Chapter 12. Caesar
BG=Gallic War (Bellum Gallicum); BC=Civil War (Bellum Civile)

1. Caesar, *De Analogia*, preface. This two-book work (now lost), dedicated to Cicero, was written on a journey from north Italy across the Alps to the theatre of war.
2. Knowledge of Polybius can be assumed: Cicero and Brutus knew his work.
3. Cicero, *Brutus*, 262 (trans. G.L.Hendrickson).
4. About the concluding campaigns of the war in 51 BC. Written to link *BG* and *BC*. Closer than *BG*, I–VII, to office records.

Notes

5. Hirtius (continuer of Caesar), *BG*, VIII, beginning.
6. Posidonius had launched a new interest in 'primitive' races, contrasted with the decadent old civilisations.
7. Caesar, *BG*, V 14 (trans. S.A.Handford).
8. Motives are discussed to explain subsequent actions: e.g. venality of Convictolitavis, greed of L.Fabius, motives of Commius.
9. e.g. I 21 (2) (Helvetii).
10. Cicero, Marcus' brother, gets both, in moderation (Caesar, *BG*, V 52, VI 36 ff.). Caesar refers to the good reputation of Publius Considius, and the Treveran cavalry, in order to emphasise their subsequent futures. Information about subordinate commanders, even his chief lieutenant Labienus (who turned against him in the Civil War) is generally sparse.
11. e.g. *BG*, I 53 (7), IV 12, 25 (3), V 35 (44).
12. He was also a well-known orator, poet and patron of letters. The work started from 60 BC and extended to some point after the battle of Philippi (42), perhaps his consulship of 40.
13. As a partisan of Antony and enemy of exuberance, he greatly disliked Cicero, as well as his follower Livy. But he also criticised Sallust.
14. Suetonius, *Julius*, 56 (4) (trans. J.C.Rolfe).
15. Caesar, *BG*, III, beginning, compared with Cicero, *Letters to Friends*, X 30, shows that this was sometimes so. Possibly, however, Pollio is referring mainly to the *Civil War*.
16. Caesar, *BG*, I 44 (trans. S.A.Handford).
17. Including important offices both at Rome and at Gallic headquarters. As consul in 59 he had shown a keen eye for the same point by starting the publication of senatorial and public proceedings, calculated to ensure that hostile acts by his enemies were published – and so noted by the friendly populace.
18. Caesar, *BG*, II 1.
19. Ibid. IV 14. f. (trans. S.A.Handford).
20. Hirtius, *BG*, VIII 44 (trans. S.A.Handford).
21. Caesar, *BG*, I 10 (trans. S.A.Handford).
22. e.g. German 'threat' of 58 is built up by magnifying the Germans and inventing a clear Gallo-German ethnic frontier on the Rhine. Caesar learnt from Posidonius, who had been the first to regard the Germans as a recognisable separate people.
23. e.g., ostensibly, by Labienus (who took a great dislike to him), *BG*, VI 8 (4), VII 62 (2).
24. Ibid. II 25 (trans. S.A.Handford).
25. e.g. Nervii, Octodurus, Ambiorix; cf. VI 59.

26. Ibid. VII 52 (trans. S.A.Handford).
27. Caesar, *BG*, also disguises the fact that in 58 he was very nearly defeated by the Helvetii.
28. *Bellum Alexandrinum* (probably by Hirtius; silence about Cleopatra shown loyalty to Caesar), *Bellum Africanum* (good military history by officer not in highest councils), *Bellum Hispaniense* (naive and poor, text badly preserved). Why did Caesar not write about these campaigns? Perhaps because he felt that the death of Pompey was the climax.
29. Caesar, *BC*, I 4 (trans. J.F.Mitchell).
30. Ibid. I 22 (trans. J.F.Mitchell).
31. Ibid. I 9 (trans. J.F.Mitchell).
32. Ibid. III 73.
33. Ibid. III 26 (trans. J.F.Mitchell); cf. I 21, 52.
34. Ibid. III 68 (trans. J.F.Mitchell).
35. According to his own lieutenant Curio (April 49), it was a bid for popularity, though he was 'not by nature averse to cruelty'.

Chapter 13. Sallust

BJ=Jugurtha (Bellum Jugurthinum); BC=Catiline (Bellum Catilinae)

1. Amiternum may have sided with Marius against Sulla (the Marian Sertorius came from Nursia). It is not certain that Sallust was *born* at Amiternum, *pace* Jerome.
2. Asconius, *Commentary on Cicero, In Defence of Milo (Pro Milone)*, 33.
3. Gellius, *Attic Nights*, XVII 8. He was also accused of sacrilege.
4. Dio Cassius, XLIII 9 (2). He was said to have bribed Caesar to suppress the case. He also possessed a villa at Tibur (Tivoli) which had belonged to Caesar.
5. Two *Letters to Caesar in his Old Age about the State* are included in manuscripts of Sallust. Their authorship and date are highly controversial, but it is extremely unlikely that they were written by Sallust. They seem like student exercises, perhaps several generations later.
6. He was venomous about Antony's father (*Histories*, IV 2 f.) and Lepidus' father (an abortive revolutionary in 78 BC), and praised Cato. The unpleasant young Pompey was surely meant to look like the young Octavian. Yet in 38 Sallust delivered the oration at the Triumph of Antony's supporter Ventidius.
7. Sallust, *BJ*, 3 (trans. I.Scott-Kilvert).
8. Sallust, *BC*, 4 (trans. I.Scott-Kilvert).
9. cf. Pliny the younger, *Letters (Epistulae)*, VII 335 B, 336 B, 340 f.
10. Sallust, *BJ*, 4 (trans. I.Scott-Kilvert).

11. Sallust, *BC*, 8 (trans. I.Scott-Kilvert).
12. Ibid. 5.
13. Sallust, *BJ*, 5 (trans. I.Scott-Kilvert).
14. Sallust, *BC*, 9 (trans. I.Scott-Kilvert).
15. Sallust, *BJ*, 41 (trans. I.Scott-Kilvert).
16. Sallust, *Histories*, I 7.
17. Sallust, *BJ*, 41 (trans. I.Scott-Kilvert).
18. Sallust, *BC*, 38 (trans. I.Scott-Kilvert).
19. Sallust, *BJ*, 3.
20. Sallust, *BC*, 3.
21. Ibid. 53 (trans. I.Scott-Kilvert).
22. Sallust, *BJ*, 13 (trans. I.Scott-Kilvert).
23. Ibid. 35 (trans. I.Scott-Kilvert).
24. e.g. threats of German invasion. It is disputed whether Sallust ought to have given greater prominence to the view of the knights.
25. Sallust, *Histories*, IV 69 (22, 20).
26. Sallust, *BC*, 40.
27. Perhaps this is an implied attack on the ideal picture of the elder Cato displayed by Cicero in his essay *On Old Age* (44 BC).
28. Sallust, *Histories*, III 48 (1) (trans. J.C.Rolfe).
29. Sallust, *BC*, 20 (trans. I.Scott-Kilvert).
30. The work ends on this note, not with the death of Jugurtha as might have been expected.
31. Sallust, *BJ*, 4 (trans. I.Scott-Kilvert).
32. e.g. Tanusius Geminus and Actorius Naso. Q.Aelius Tubero, who fought against Caesar but then led an attack on another anti-Caesarian Q.Ligarius, found it safer to write about the early Republic.
33. Sallust, *BC*, 53 (trans. I.Scott-Kilvert).
34. Pompey, on the other hand, seems to have been the principal villain of the *Histories*.
35. Sallust, *BC*, 31 (trans. I.Scott-Kilvert).
36. Ibid. 50.
37. Mutual invectives attributed to Sallust and Cicero and included in some Sallustian manuscripts are not authentic.
38. Sallust, *BC*, 8.
39. Ibid. 2.
40. Ibid. 1 (2) (trans. I.Scott-Kilvert).
41. Oppius, a member of a banking family who with Balbus was Caesar's principal agent, was interested in biography and wrote an account of his chief.
42. He was quoted as the founder of Latin biography; Suetonius in

Jerome in Migne, *Patrologia Latina*, XXIII 821. He also wrote a study of Pompey, various autobiographical reminiscences, and a book called *Sisenna on History*, all now lost. Works of his which exercised an influence on historians were his fifty-book antiquarian project *Human and Divine Antiquities* (*c.* 47 BC) and a sort of social history of Rome, *On the Life of the Roman People* (*c.* 43). Out of his seventy-four works, in 620 books, we retain only an agricultural work and about one-fifth of a linguistic study.

43. Nepos was born in Cisalpine Gaul but moved to Rome.
44. Of his sixteen books *On Illustrious Men* we have twenty-two short biographies of foreign leaders, and lives of Cato and Atticus (part of a collection *On Latin Historians*). He also wrote a *Chronica* (Universal History) in three books (now lost, but praised by Catullus) and a work on geography.
45. Nepos, a knight of the rising non-political class, praised Atticus' avoidance of public life.
46. Nepos, *Atticus*, preface, *Pelopidas*, XVI 1.
47. Sallust, *BJ*, 95.
48. Sallust, *BC*, 61 (trans. I.Scott-Kilvert).
49. Ibid. 25 (trans. I.Scott-Kilvert).
50. Sallust, *BJ*, 51.
51. Granius Licinianus, 36. Poor public speaker: Cassius Severus in Seneca the elder, *Controversiae*, III, preface, 8.
52. Sallust, *BC*, 3.
53. e.g. Taurus, Pontus and Black Sea (much imitated) – perhaps on the staff of Pompey or Lucullus or Marcius Rex.
54. Quintilian, X 1 (102).
55. Suetonius, *On Grammarians* (*De Grammaticis*), 10.
56. Seneca the younger, *Letters* (*Epistulae*), 114 (17); cf. Quintilian, X 3 (8).
57. The choice of this subject may have been influenced by the recent posthumous publication of Cicero, *On His Policies* (*De Consiliis Suis*).
58. Sallust, *Histories*, I 4.
59. Sallust also includes expressions emanating from Ennius; the early historians are intermediaries.
60. cf. Cicero, *In Defence of Plancius* (*Pro Plancio*), 66.
61. Velleius Paterculus, II 36 (2).
62. Quintilian, X 1 (101).

PART 5. THE TWO FACES OF EMPIRE

Chapter 14. Livy

1. Martial, *Epigrams*, XIV 190.
2. Livy, XXXI, preface.
3. *Corpus Inscriptionum Latinarum*, V 2975 (Dessau 2914) from Patavium is a tomb inscription of a T.Livius believed to be of Augustan date.
4. Suetonius, *Claudius*, 4.
5. Pliny the younger, *Letters*, II 3 (8): a man of Gades (Cadiz) came to Rome to see him.
6. Livy, I preface (trans. M.Grant).
7. Ibid. XXII 61 (trans. A.de Selincourt).
8. Ibid. XXI 28 (trans. A.de Selincourt).
9. Ibid. XXI 33 (trans. A.de Selincourt).
10. Seneca the elder, *Controversiae*, IX 1 (13).
11. Quintilian, II 5 (19).
12. Ibid. X 1 (32).
13. Ibid. X 1 (39).
14. Ibid. I 5 (56); cf. VIII 1 (3). Probably Pollio was also referring to peculiarities of grammar, syntax and style which cannot now be identified.
15. Ibid. X 1 (101 f.).
16. Polybius, VIII 4.
17. Livy, XXIV 33 ff.
18. Ibid. XXV 26 (7 ff.) (trans. P.G.Walsh).
19. Seneca the elder, *Suasoriae*, VI 21.
20. Quintilian, X 1 (101).
21. e.g. Livy, I 26 (10).
22. Ibid. XXX 30 (trans. A.de Selincourt).
23. Ibid. XXI 4 (trans. A.de Selincourt).
24. Ibid. I preface: e.g. Hannibal's failure was due to his army living soft in Capua, XXII 18 (45); the defeat by the Gauls in 390 was due to moral failings.
25. Ibid. V 27 (trans. A.de Selincourt).
26. Ibid. XXII 13 (11).
27. e.g. Pompeius Trogus of the Vocontii (Gaul), son of Caesar's secretary, who wrote Latin *Philippic Histories* in forty-four books – a sort of Greek-centred companion history to Livy, going down to 20 BC but saying little of early Italy (according to Justin XLIII 1 (2), whose epitome is all that has survived). Trogus may have been influenced by Timagenes of Alexandria, a friend of Pollio who wrote a Greek *History of Kings* (Ammianus, XV 9 (2)). Another

Greek *Universal History* was that of Diodorus Siculus of Agyrium, who wrote between *c.* 60 and *c.* 36. He stated the value of universal history impressively, and based his assertion on a broad vision of the world, but the execution of his project is derivative, undistinguished and confused. A further universal historian of the time was Nicolaus of Damascus, who was the tutor of the children of Antony and Cleopatra and then lived at the court of Herod of Judaea.

28. e.g. on peace-terms after Zama (202).
29. Livy, VIII 40 (4). But Livy ignores the family alliances which have been stressed by modern authorities.
30. Ibid. XXI 63 (trans. A.de Selincourt) (Flaminius, consul 223 and 217); cf. Minucius Rufus (consul 221; magister equitum 217), Varro (consul 216).
31. Ibid. XXXIX 6, *Periochae* (epitome), LX.
32. Livy, *Periochae* (epitome), LX.
33. He praised the military gifts of the Marian Sertorius but stressed his deterioration.
34. Tacitus, *Annals*, IV 34.
35. Seneca the younger, *Naturales Quaestiones*, V 18 (4).
36. Jerome, *Commentary on Hosea*, II, preface.
37. Tacitus, *Annals*, IV 34.
38. Livy, CXX, in Seneca the elder, *Suasoriae*, VI 22.
39. After Actium there was talk of the ruler as the new Romulus, and Numa appeared on his coinage.
40. Augustus also wrote two eulogies of Drusus senior (d. 9 BC), one in prose and the other in verse. On his death he left five documents, including his extant *Res Gestae* (for the title see p. 438, n. 29) and a political testament.
41. It has been conjectured that Augustus' programme may have been encouraged by Livy's writings.
42. Livy, I preface.
43. Ibid.
44. Horace, *Odes*, III 6 (46–8); cf. Aratus, *Phaenemena*, 123.
45. Livy, IX 19 (17).
46. Ibid. I preface (trans. M.Grant).
47. Macrobius, *Saturnalia*, I 11 (2); Cicero, *Twelfth Philippic*, 10.
48. Livy, I 1, IV 6 (12), X 2.
49. Ibid. XXVII 50.
50. Ibid. XXII 5 (trans. A.de Selincourt).
51. cf. also confusion between Hippo Regius and Hippo Diarrhytus, etc.

52. e.g. Livy, XXIII 9 (1–8), xxv 6 (5), XXXVI 29 (1–11); cf. Polybius, XX 10.

53. Cicero, *Letters to Atticus*, XIII 33 (3), is insufficient evidence for supposing that Livy could consult published books of senatorial decrees.

54. Livy, VIII 11. He prefers to cite Fabius Pictor's version.

55. Ibid. IV 20 (7).

56. e.g. ibid. IV 29 (6), VII 9 f.

57. Ibid. IV 22–3 (trans. A.de Selincourt); cf. also XLV 44 (19 f.). He may also have used Valerius Antias and Claudius Quadrigarius for the legendary period.

58. Quintilian, II 4 (19).

59. Livy, XLV 44 (19 f.).

60. In XXX 45 (4), Livy rightly prefers an annalist's version to Polybius.

61. Coelius Antipater may well have been his main source in the early part of the third decade, and may have handed on touches of Ennius (unless these came through the rhetoricians). In the fourth and fifth decades (as in the first) Valerius Antias and Claudius Quadrigarius were followed. Cato is once queried, XXXIV 15 (9). Probably Livy consulted Posidonius for the period after 146.

62. Suetonius, *Gaius* 34.

63. Quintilian, X 1 (32).

64. The most notable was the *Roman Antiquities*, in twenty books, written in Greek by the rhetor and historian Dionysius of Halicarnassus (30–8 BC), who was the guiding spirit of a literary circle at Rome. He is sometimes more aware of the significance of an event than Livy (e.g. Livy, VI 26 (8)), but ten times more prolix and less effective.

65. Livy, XLIII 13 (2), (trans. A.C.Schlesinger).

66. Ibid. V 21 (9) (trans. A.de Selincourt).

67. Ibid. I preface (trans. M.Grant).

68. Ibid. II 10 (trans. A.de Selincourt).

69. Dionysius of Halicarnassus (*Roman Antiquities* (*Antiquitates Romanae*), I 89) exploited the Greek character of these myths and other early stories in order to claim for Greece the credit of founding Rome.

70. But the two Tarquins, good and bad, are a rhetorical doublet. We cannot tell how many Etruscan kings there were.

71. Livy, I 8 (trans. A.de Selincourt).

72. e.g. ibid. I 24–6.

73. e.g. ibid. I 13 (5); cf. VII 6 (3).

74. e.g. ibid. IX 30 (5), XXVII 8 (5).

75. Ibid. XXVIII 11 (trans. A.de Selincourt).

76. Ibid. xxiv 10 (6).
77. Ibid. xxvii 23 (4).
78. Ibid. iii 8 (trans. A.de Selincourt).
79. Twenty-eight times; only nine in third decade, thereafter only three times in surviving portions.
80. Elsewhere Fortuna is sometimes merely a literary motif, with debts to the Hellenistic Tyche, a patron-goddess of cities.

Chapter 15. Josephus

AJ=Jewish Antiquities (Antiquitates Judaicae); BJ=Jewish War (Bellum Judaicum); Vita=Life (autobiography); *C. Ap.=Against Apion (Contra Apionem)*

1. In AD 50 he was given Chalcis, in 53 the tetrarchy of Philip (Gaulanitis, Trachonitis, Batanea and Panias). Nero added four regions of Galilee and Peraea. He ceased to reign before 93 and died in *c.* 100.
2. Josephus, *AJ*, I 2 (trans. H.St J.Thackeray).
3. Josephus, *Vita*, 2.
4. Ibid. 9.
5. For a time he joined the ascetic Banus (probably an Essene); ibid. 11 f.
6. Josephus, *BJ*, ii 118, etc.
7. Ibid. v 9 (3–4).
8. Ibid. iv 6 (4); cf. Numbers, xxiii 4 (Balaam).
9. Josephus, *BJ*, ii 22 (1) (trans. G.Williamson).
10. Josephus, *Vita*, 6 (trans. N.N.G.Glatzer).
11. Josephus, *BJ*, ii 17 (9) (execution of Menahem).
12. Ibid. ii 42 (4 f.).
13. Josephus, *Vita*, 29.
14. Josephus, *BJ*, iii 9 (3).
15. Ibid. iii 14 (15) (trans. G.A.Williamson).
16. Ibid. iii 26 (6 f.) (trans. G.A.Williamson).
17. According to Tacitus (*Histories*, v 13), the number of the besieged was 600, 000 (the extant portion breaks off with Titus' preparations.
18. Josephus, *BJ*, vi 45 f. (trans. G.A.Williamson).
19. Josephus, *Vita*, 75.
20. Josephus' reference to Caecina as a traitor must date after Caecina's arrest and execution in June 79 since before that he was a 'patriot' who had deserted Vitellius for Vespasian.
21. Perhaps the account of the capture of Jerusalem was written first, and then added to.
22. Josephus, *AJ*, xx 11 (2).
23. Josephus, *C. Ap.*, I 9 (trans. H.St J.Thackeray).

24. Josephus, *BJ*, III 108. References to Roman greed and perfidy in the Slavonic version were inserted in a later age (p. 400).
25. Ibid. v 9 (4).
26. Suetonius, *Vespasian*, 5.
27. Josephus, *BJ*, VI 5 (4); cf. Tacitus, *Histories*, I 10.
28. *Talmud*, Gittin 56. He was allowed to establish a school at Jamnia (Yibna), which saved Judaism.
29. Josephus, *Vita*, 65; *C. Ap.*, I 56.
30. e.g. the burning of the Capitol is blamed on the Vitellians, whereas Tacitus tends to blame the Flavians; cf. on Caecina, p. 447, n. 20.
31. Josephus, *BJ*, 4 (3), *pace* Sulpicius Severus, *Chronica*, II 30, based on a lost passage of Tacitus.
32. Josephus, *BJ*, 8 (1) (trans. G.A.Williamson).
33. Ibid. 10 (10).
34. Josephus, *Vita*, 65 (trans. H.St J.Thackeray).
35. Josephus, *C. Ap.*, I 9.
36. Josephus, *BJ*, II 429.
37. Josephus, *Vita*, 65 (trans. H.St J.Thackeray).
38. Josephus, *C. Ap.*, I 9.
39. Josephus, *BJ*, I, preface (trans. G.A.Williamson).
40. Josephus, *C. Ap.*, I 9 (trans. H.St J.Thackeray).
41. cf. Josephus, *AJ*, I, preface.
42. Berossus, Manetho: both sources for Josephus, *AJ*. So, especially, were Strabo, Dionysius of Halicarnassus (the decision of Josephus to write the same number of books may have been deliberate) and Polybius.
43. The first had apparently been Demetrius, *On the Kings in Judaea* (end of third century BC). Philo the elder (*c.* 200 BC) and Theodotus wrote verse histories. Eupolemus (*c.* 150 BC) was the author of a popular history of the Jews in rhetorical style.
44. Josephus, *AJ*, XVI 7 (trans. N.N.G.Glatzer).
45. Josephus, *BJ*, I, preface.
46. Josephus, *AJ*, XX 4.
47. Ibid. XVI 11 (8) (trans. N.N.G.Glatzer).
48. Ibid. XV 10 (4); cf. *BJ*, V 2. He had planned a further work on Jewish beliefs and laws; *AJ*, XX 11 (3). His views most closely coincided with those of the Pharisees at Jamnia (above, n. 28), where the Old Testament canon was beginning to be fixed.
49. Josephus, *BJ*, VII 44.
50. Josephus, *AJ*, I, preface.
51. Ibid. XI 8.
52. In ibid. XII–XIII I Maccabees was extensively used.

53. In 144 books, from the earliest times to the death of Herod (4 BC). The work had also been utilised for *BJ*. Nicolaus insisted that Herod (of Idumaean convert stock) was a true Jew.

54. Josephus, *AJ*, XIV 16 (4). The high priest Ananus, dismissed by Agrippa II, is deplored in *AJ*, but had been praised in *BJ* for his opposition to the zealots.

55. There are two 'endings', at *AJ*, XX 9 (7) and 11 (2).

56. Josephus, *AJ*, XVIII 3 (3), XVIII 5 (2), XX 9 (1). Origen did not know the passage about Jesus, and the longer passages on Jesus and John in the Slavonic version likewise do not go back to Josephus.

57. Perhaps Cluvius Rufus.

58. Josephus, *AJ*, XX 7 (3).

59. According to Photius it was 'extremely concise', and made no mention of Jesus.

60. Josephus, *AJ*, XX 11 (2).

61. Josephus, *Vita*, 65 (trans. H.St J.Thackeray).

62. Ibid. 19 f., 43 ff.

63. If the Epaphroditus to whom *C. Ap.* and *AJ*, are dedicated is the same man, *C. Ap.* is likely to have appeared before the death of Domitian (96), who condemned the grammarian of that name.

64. Josephus, *C. Ap.*, II 143. The name 'C. Ap.' probably arose from references by Eusebius, in *History of the Church* (*Ecclesiae Historia*), II 5, III 9.

65. The addition 'to the Greeks' (Porphyry, *On Abstinence* (*De Abstinentia*), IV 11) is unlikely to be original.

66. e.g. Manetho, Josephus, *C. Ap.*, I 228 ff., 251–87.

67. Ibid. II 40 and 17.

68. Ibid. I 3 (5) (trans. H.St J.Thackeray).

PART 6. TACITUS

Chapter 16. Tacitus and the Empire

Hist.=*Histories; Ann.*=*Annals; Germ.*=*Germania; Agr.*=*Agricola; Dial.*=*Dialogue on the Orator (Dialogus de Oratore)*

1. Dessau, *Inscriptiones Latinae Selectae*, 4841, is a dedication by Tacitus at this capital of the Vocontii.

2. Pliny the elder, *Natural History* (*Historia Naturalis*), VII 76.

3. Tacitus, *Hist.*, I 1.

4. Pliny the younger, *Letters*, VII 33, VI 20.

5. Tacitus, *Hist.*, I and II may have been published together at an early date, followed (? soon afterwards) by III.

6. Tacitus, *Ann.*, II 61; 'the red sea' need not be held to refer to the

Persian Gulf or Trajan's advance to it, but to the Red Sea, reached by Octavian in 30 BC.

7. It has been argued that the succession of Tiberius, his bad relations with the Senate, his removal of Agrippa Postumus and other possible rivals, and Nero's phil-Hellenism all imply critical allusions to Hadrian: cf. *Ann.*, IV 4 (3), 32 (2), XII 20 (1). But this interpretation is disputed.

8. Pliny the younger, *Letters*, VII 20 (6). Pliny addressed eleven letters to him.

9. The work was probably attributed to him on the Hersfeld archetype manuscript.

10. Tacitus, *Germ.*, 37 (2), mentions the second consulship of Trajan in that year.

11. Ibid. 19 (3).

12. Ibid. 33 (2).

13. Tacitus, *Agr.*, 3 (1), seems to imply that Nerva (d. 98) is still alive – probably it was not corrected when Trajan succeeded him (succession implied by ibid. 44 (5)).

14. In honour of L. Verginius Rufus, also celebrated by his pupil the younger Pliny (*Letters*, II 1).

15. Tacitus, *Agr.*, 46 (2 f.).

16. Jerome omitted the work from the category of biography, perhaps because his source Suetonius regarded it as history.

17. Tacitus, *Agr.*, 3.

18. Tacitus, *Ann.*, IV 32 (1).

19. Tacitus, *Ann.*, IV 33.

20. Ibid. III 65.

21. Ibid. IV 32.

22. Tacitus, *Hist.*, V 3–8 (Jews), *Ann.*, XV 44 (3) (Christians). This relates to their alleged responsibility for the Great Fire (now regarded as unlikely), about which Tacitus suspends judgment in somewhat contradictory fashion (38 (8) and 39 (2) against 39 (1–2)).

23. e.g. in relation to the rising which heralded the end of Nero's reign. There is particularly little information on provinces governed by imperial legates such as Nearer Spain (Hispania Tarraconensis) or Judaea. But a historian scarcely thought of provinces as units; the units were towns (or tribes).

24. Tacitus, *Agr.*, 10 (trans. M. Hutton).

25. Tacitus, *Ann.*, II 88; cf. *Germ.*, 33 (2).

26. Tacitus, *Hist.*, IV 14 (trans. K. Wellesley); cf. V 10, on Judaea.

27. Ibid. IV 74 (trans. K. Wellesley).

28. Tacitus, *Ann.*, I 2 (trans. M. Grant).

29. Ibid. I 81 (trans. M.Grant).
30. Tacitus, *Dial.*, 41 (trans. W.Peterson).
31. Tacitus, *Hist.*, IV 8 (Eprius Marcellus).
32. Tacitus, *Ann.*, VI 48 (L.Arruntius).
33. That is his justification for the special emphasis. But it was the longest of the post-Augustan reigns and filled with events; though Tiberius himself was not in the centre of the military scene.

Chapter 17. Tacitus and the Emperors
(For abbreviations, see notes to Chapter 16)

1. Tacitus, *Hist.*, I 1.
2. Tacitus, *Ann.*, I 1.
3. Characterisation in the *Annals* is generally more indirect than in the *Histories*. But Jerome called the *Annals* 'Lives of the Caesars'.
4. Tacitus, *Hist.*, I 2 (trans. K.Wellesley).
5. Tacitus, *Agr.*, 2 (trans. M.Hutton).
6. e.g. in 83 (if there was a plot) and 87. The final plot was particularly humiliating because the liberators were freedmen and a woman (the emperor's wife).
7. Tacitus, *Ann.*, I 11 (trans. M.Grant).
8. Ibid. I 10.
9. Ibid. IV 57 (trans. M.Grant).
10. Ibid. VI 51 (trans. M.Grant).
11. Ibid. IV 38 (trans. M.Grant).
12. Ibid. I 76 (trans. M.Grant).
13. The break is less sharp than for Tiberius: 59 and 62 and 65 are significant years. His visit to Greece (missing) was no doubt savagely described.
14. Tacitus, *Ann.*, XI 31 (trans. M.Grant).
15. Ibid. XV 66 f. (trans. M.Grant).
16. Octavia and the younger Seneca's wife Pompeia Paulina are among the tragic women whom Tacitus treats with compassion.
17. Tacitus, *Ann.*, XIII 45 (trans. M.Grant).
18. cf. those of the *Histories*; e.g. who sacked Cremona, and destroyed the amphitheatre at Placentia (Piacenza) and the Capitol at Rome? On military affairs Tacitus is arbitrary and misleading. The description of the great British rebellion of Boudicca (*Ann.*, XIV 29–39) includes the names of only eight persons, four places and two tribes. Vitellius apparently made three attempts to resign; Tacitus compresses them into a single dramatic episode.
19. Tacitus is sarcastic on Tiberius, funny on Claudius' public

451

pronouncements, and makes a good joke of his choice of wife (*Ann.*, xii f., parodying a cabinet council).

20. Tacitus, *Ann.*, xvi 4 f. (trans. M.Grant).

21. e.g. ibid. iv 18 (3), iv 33 (6).

22. cf. Tacitus, *Hist.*, ii 86. To Tacitus, Primus has every vice, to Martial every virtue.

23. Tacitus, *Ann.*, iv 1 (trans. M.Grant).

24. Ibid. xvi 18 (trans. M.Grant).

25. Ibid. xi 24 (Claudius on Gauls): cf. Dessau, *Inscriptiones Latinae, Selectae*, 212; *Ann.*, ii 63 (4): he knows of a surviving speech (Tiberius on Maroboduus) but does not quote it.

26. Tacitus, *Ann.*, xiv 53 ff., gives invented antiphonal speeches, cf. iv 34 f. (and letter, iv 39 f.). Ibid. xiv 1, and 53–6, must also be inventions.

27. Tacitus, *Hist.*, i 21, ii 74 f.

28. He deviates when the subject demands it, *Ann.*, iv 71, ii 4.

29. In *Ann.*, geographical and ethnographical excursuses are supplemented by digressions on Roman antiquities.

30. e.g. Tacitus, *Ann.*, xvi 1: the comic hoax of Dido's buried treasure after the horrors of Piso's conspiracy.

31. There are also specific echoes, e.g. Tacitus, *Hist.*, iv 62 (cf. Livy, ix 5 (11 ff.).

32. The *Agricola* is on the way to this maturity, the *Germania* more uniform in style. The *Annals* are stronger and tighter, more archaic and majestic and Sallustian, less eloquent and fluent, than the *Histories*. The style of the *Annals* seems to become rather more straightforward from Book xii onwards (Nero being the first emperor of his own lifetime).

33. Vulgar words, and the usages of common speech, are avoided, e.g. *Hist.*, ii 93 (brothels), *Ann.*, i 65 (spade).

34. Already in *Agr.*, x 42; 'it is a principle of human nature to hate those whom you have injured'; cf. *Germ.*, 19.

35. Pliny the younger, *Letters*, vii 17 (3).

36. Quintilian, x 1 (31), ii 7 (2); Pliny the younger, *Letters*, v 8 (9), v 4, etc.

37. e.g. Tacitus, *Ann.*, ii 61 (1) (cf. Virgil, *Aeneid*, vi 198 ff.), ii 29 (2). His hexadic structure is repeated from the *Aeneid*, and from Ennius. But apparently poetical words in Tacitus may have prose forebears now lost.

38. Tacitus, *Ann.*, iii 3.

39. Seneca the younger also wrote monographs on India and Egypt (now lost) which may have influenced the genre of the *Germania*

(Servius, commentary on Virgil's *Aeneid*, VI 154, IX 30; Pliny the elder, *Natural History*, VI 60).

40. Tacitus is very sceptical of popular rumour, but he quotes traditional anecdotes, if only to refute them (*Ann.*, IV 10 (1)).

41. Ibid. III 19 (trans. M. Grant).

42. e.g. ibid. IV 81 (3).

43. Velleius (*c.* 19 BC–AD 31), was an officer of Tiberius who wrote a history of Rome to AD 30. The date of Curtius is disputed. He is dramatic and rhetorical; he despises non-Romans; his ten books are written in a modernised Livian style.

44. e.g. Cremutius Cordus, *Civil Wars* and on to at least 18 BC; Seneca the elder (*c.* 55 BC–AD 37/41), from outbreak of Civil War to his death, perhaps the source of many Taciteanisms; Aufidius Bassus, *History of German Wars* (probably under Tiberius) and general history from 44 BC to *c.* AD 41 or 50 or 54; Cluvius Rufus, orator, consul and governor (AD 68), histories perhaps from Gaius to Otho – slanderous according to Tacitus. Cf. Servilius Nonianus, consul (35) and reciter; another falsifier was Fabius Rusticus 'the new Livy' (who favoured the younger Seneca), cf. Josephus, *Jewish Antiquities*, XX 154. An unidentifiable lost author (writing after 79) is the main source of Tacitus, *Hist.* and Plutarch, *Galba* and *Otho*. The epic of Lucan (AD 39–65) on the Civil War (the 'Pharsalia') is quasi-historical, and Tacitus' causes of Roman decadence are very close to Lucan's.

45. Continuation of Aufidius Bassus. From *c.* 41 to *c.* 71 (?). Dedicated to Titus; composed 70–6. Cf. Tacitus, *Ann.*, IV 53 (3), XIII 20 (3). Tacitus, *Hist.*, utilised and superseded his later books, perhaps cutting out the younger Pliny who may have hoped to do the same. When Tacitus twice mentions Locusta (*Ann.*, XII 66 (4), XIII 15 (4)), this means he is drawing on the elder Pliny and another source.

46. Tacitus, *Ann.*, XV 53 (3 f.), XIII 13 (1), XV 6 (1), XIV 15 (1).

47. Tacitus, *Hist.*, II 101.

48. Tacitus, *Ann.*, XV 16 (3), is even sceptical about the truthfulness of Nero's great general Corbulo, whose memoirs he used (at least indirectly).

49. e.g. forty-one-book History by Claudius, and autobiographical memoirs by emperors (including Tiberius, Claudius, Vespasian and Trajan) and empresses (Agrippina jun.). Tacitus refers to Tiberius' reports with approval or criticism (*Ann.*, III 47, IV 74 (1)).

50. e.g. Tacitus or his informant consulted the Acta Diurna and Acta Senatus (e.g. *Ann.*, II 32, III 20 (65), VI 7, XIV 64 (3)). For the unreliability of official calendars, *Hist.*, IV 40: e.g. *Fasti Ostienses*.

51. Tacitus, *Hist.*, I 1 (trans. K.Wellesley).
52. Tacitus, *Ann.*, III 26 (1), cf. 27 (1), *Hist..* II 38 (2). But there is a sharp word against Polybius' mixed constitution, *Ann.*, IV 33.
53. Tacitus, *Ann.*, II 37, III 23.
54. Sejanus is a 'small-town adulterer' (ibid. IV 3 (4).
55. e.g. ibid. V 27 (3) (Gracchi).
56. Ibid. I 33 (4), II 82 (3).
57. Ibid. I 2 (trans. M.Grant).
58. Ibid. III 60 (trans. M.Grant).
59. This must have shown up most clearly in the missing passages relating to the accession of Claudius and the death of Domitian.
60. Ibid. XVI 32.
61. Ibid. IV 20.
62. Ibid. XIV 47.
63. Tacitus, *Agr.*, 40 (42) (trans. M.Hutton).
64. Tacitus, *Dial.*, 41 (trans. W.Peterson).
65. Tacitus, *Ann.*, III 24 (4).
66. Tacitus, *Hist.*, I 1.
67. Ibid. II 101. And his account of Vespasian's planned *coup* conflicts with the official version of the irresistible initiative of the legions.
68. Ibid. IV 5.
69. Ibid. II 1 (trans. K.Wellesley).
70. Tacitus, *Agr.*, 3 (trans. M.Hutton).
71. Tacitus, *Hist.*, I 1 (trans. K.Wellesley).
72. Tacitus, *Germ.*, 33.
73. Tacitus, *Ann.*, III 55 (5).
74. Tacitus, *Hist.*, I 1 (trans. K.Wellesley).
75. e.g. Q.Glitius Agricola, Q.Sosius Senecio (consul for the second time in 103 and 107 respectively).

Chapter 18. Anarchy and Humanity in Tacitus
(For abbreviations, see notes to Chapter 16)

1. Tacitus, *Hist.*, II 76.
2. Tacitus, *Ann.*, I 7 (2), XI 30 (2), etc.
3. Tacitus, *Hist.*, II 38 (trans. K.Wellesley).
4. Ibid. II 70 (trans. K.Wellesley).
5. Ibid. III 83, IV 1 (trans. K.Wellesley).
6. cf. the people of the city of Rome in the Great Fire (AD 64); helpless, panic-stricken, a prey to rumours.
7. Tacitus, *Ann.*, I 24 f., (28) (trans. M.Grant).
8. Ibid. III 18.
9. Tacitus, *Hist.*, I 3.

10. Ibid. II 38.
11. Tacitus, *Ann.*, XI 11 (trans. M.Grant).
12. Tacitus, *Hist.*, II 50 (trans. K.Wellesley).
13. Tacitus, *Ann.*, VI 22 (trans. M.Grant). But he also sometimes confuses fortune and fate, both being used as literary rather than theological concepts, with fate meaning some inexplicable cause, or what would happen in the natural course of events if human beings do not manage to divert it. Fate and didactic purpose are hard to reconcile. Tacitus is also tempted by cyclical conceptions, ibid. III 55 (6).
14. cf. Tacitus, *Hist.*, I 4.
15. Tacitus, *Ann.*, XV 57 (trans. M.Grant).
16. Tacitus, *Hist.*, I 3 (from K.Wellesley).
17. cf. doubts in Tacitus, *Agr.*, 46.
18. Tacitus perhaps echoes the emphasis on free speech by Demochares (p. 432, n. 55).
19. He wrote on the Civil Wars, carrying his history to at least 18 BC, Suetonius, *Augustus*, 35 (2).
20. Tacitus, *Ann.*, IV 35 (trans. M.Grant).

PART 7. GREEK AND LATIN BIOGRAPHERS

Chapter 19. Plutarch

1. The complete series of double lives, in its present order, is as follows: Theseus-Romulus; Solon-Publicola; Themistocles-Camillus; Aristides-Cato the elder; Alcibiades-Coriolanus; Demosthenes-Cicero; Phocion-Cato the younger; Dion-Brutus; Timoleon-Lucius Aemilius Paullus Macedonicus; Eumenes-Sertorius; Philopoemen-Flaminius; Pelopidas-Marcus Claudius Marcellus sen.; Alexander-Caesar; Demetrius-Antony; Pyrrhus-Marius; Agis and Cleomenes-Tiberius and Gaius Gracchus; Lycurgus-Numa; Lysander-Sulla; Agesilaus-Pompey.
2. Hesiod, Pindar, Crates, Daiphantes, Aristomenes, Aratus of Soli (poet).
3. Plutarch, *On the E at Delphi* (*De E apud Delphos*), 385*b*. His teacher was Ammonius, head of the Academy.
4. Dittenberger, *Sylloge Inscriptionum Graecarum* (3rd ed.,), p. 829.
5. Plutarch, *Otho*, 14. Another patron was Minicius Fundanus (consul, 107). Plutarch knew members of the younger Pliny's household.
6. e.g. Sparta, Corinth, Patrae.
7. e.g. contest of Aeschylus and Euripides in Aristophanes' *Frogs*, 758 ff.
8. Quintilian, II 4 (21).

9. e.g. Horace (Alcaeus, etc.), Propertius (Callimachus, Philetas, etc.).
10. cf. Nepos, *Hannibal*, 13 (4).
11. Plutarch, *Aemilius Paullus*, 1.
12. Plutarch, *Demetrius*, 1.
13. Plutarch, *Table Talks* (*Quaestiones Conviviales*), etc.
14. Plutarch, *Timoleon*, 15.
15. Plutarch, *Cimon*, 2.
16. Pausanias, ix 40: divine honours were paid to the sceptre of Agamemnon.
17. Plutarch, *Precepts for Ruling the State* (*Praecepta Reipublicae Gerendae*), 813 D–E (trans. A.J.Gossage).
18. A.Nauck, *Tragicorum Graecorum Fragmenta*, p. 918, no. 412.
19. Plutarch, *On Exile* (*De Exilio*), 602 E, *On the Oracles of the Puthia* (*De Pythiae Oraculis*), 408 E.
20. Plutarch, *Precepts for Ruling the State*, 824 C.
21. Plutarch, *Aristides*, 6 (trans. I.Scott-Kilvert).
22. Plutarch, *Pericles*, 1 f. (trans. I.Scott-Kilvert).
23. Plutarch, *Aemilius Paullus*, 1.
24. Plutarch, *Aratus*, 1.
25. Plutarch, *Demetrius*, 1.
26. Ibid.
27. e.g. Pericles, Dion, Philpoemen, Pelopidas, Marcellus.
28. Plutarch, *Cimon*, 2; cf. perhaps Coriolanus.
29. In contrast to Themistocles (ambition). Ambition is also presented as the keynote of Caesar – whose love affairs are therefore treated as irrelevant.
30. Plutarch, *Alexander*, 1 (trans. A.J.Gossage); cf. *Galba*, 2.
31. Plutarch, *On the Late Vengeance of the Divinity* (*De Sera Numinis Vindicta*), 552 D.
32. Plutarch, *Pericles*, 7.
33. Plutarch, *Sulla*, 30 (trans. R.Warner); cf. the apparent decline in the character of Sertorius.
34. e.g. ibid. 18; *Alcibiades*, 15.
35. Plutarch, *Fabius Maximus*, 16.
36. e.g. Sertorius, Pericles, Flamininus, Pelopidas, Timoleon.
37. Plutarch, *Themistocles*, 32.
38. Plutarch, *Alexander*, 35.
39. Plutarch, *Aristides*, 7 (trans. I.Scott-Kilvert).
40. Plutarch, *Alcibiades*, 9 (trans. I.Scott-Kilvert).
41. Plutarch, *Crassus*, 1 (trans. R.Warner).
42. Plutarch, *Caesar*, 17 (trans. R.Warner).
43. Ibid. 62 (trans. R.Warner).

44. Plutarch, *Lysander*, 15 (trans. I.Scott-Kilvert).
45. Plutarch, *Marius*, 37–9 (trans. R.Warner).
46. Plutarch, *Sulla*, 2 (trans. R.Warner).
47. Known to us through an Arabic translation and the paraphrase of the physician Adamantius.
48. Plutarch, *Cimon*, 2.
49. e.g. Plutarch, *Pericles*, 13, 15 f., 24–5, 30–1.
50. *On the Failure of the Oracles* (*De Defectu Oraculorum*), 438 B. Plutarch rejected the theory that she was intoxicated by vapours.
51. Plutarch, *Table Talks* (*Quaestiones Convivales*), 635 E.
52. Plutarch, *On Superstition* (*De Superstitione*), 168o.
53. Plutarch, *Camillus*, 6, etc.
54. Plutarch, *Theseus*, 1 (trans. I.Scott-Kilvert).
55. Plutarch, *Flamininus*, 9; *Aemilius Paullus*, 14.
56. Plutarch, *Pericles*, 6 (trans. I.Scott-Kilvert).
57. Ibid. 13 (trans. I.Scott-Kilvert).
58. Plutarch, *Demetrius*, 15.
59. Plutarch, *Cimon*, 2.
60. Plutarch, *On the Malignity of Herodotus*, 855 f.
61. Plutarch, *Demetrius*, 2.
62. But he knows little drama or poetry. There are two quotations from Horace.
63. Plutarch, *Demetrius*, 2.
64. e.g. Nepos, Cicero, Caesar. In approaching his own day (e.g. *Galba*, *Otho*) sources are rarely mentioned because they, and the facts, were easier to obtain.
65. It has been suggested that the twenty-four writers quoted in the *Alexander* were only known to Plutarch from a variorum biography. This is conjectural, but possible. For his own notebooks, see below n. 69).
66. e.g. *Coriolanus* is a transposition of Dionysius of Halicarnassus, v–viii, but wide additional antiquarian reading is added. Timaeus is a main source for the *Timoleon*, and the *Lysander* is based mainly on Xenophon (who is favourably commented on in the *Nicias*) and Theopompus and Ephorus.
67. In other respects, however, the Lives of Pompey, Crassus and Caesar show a common source, perhaps partially dependent on Pollio.
68. Plutarch, *Lycurgus*, 1.
69. Plutarch, *On Peace of Mind* (*De Tranquillitate Animi*), 464 F. (trans. R.H.Barrow). Probably the notebooks were his own, not a commonplace book.

Chapter 20. Suetonius

1. *L'Année épigraphique* (1953), no. 73. His father may have settled at Hippo.
2. Pliny the younger, *Letters*, III 8 (1), shows Suetonius asking a favour.
3. *Scriptores Historiae Augustae, Hadrian*, 11 (3).
4. Suetonius, *Titus*, 10 (2).
5. e.g. death of Tiberius (cf. Trajan); early repressions by Titus (cf. Hadrian); *Claudius*, 44 (2), *Nero*, 18 (foreign policy). In contrast to tact in *Augustus*, 98 (5), *Tiberius*, 21 (1).
6. Nepos, *Atticus*, preface.
7. Nepos, *Pelopidas*, xvi 1 (1).
8. Cicero, *Brutus*, 302, etc. (Q. Hortensius was said to be the originator).
9. Suetonius, *Julius*, 44 (4) (trans. J.C. Rolfe). Possibly the lost beginning of the Life explained the procedure he was going to follow.
10. Suetonius, *Augustus*, 61.
11. and ibid. has a long, mainly chronological account of the Civil Wars; *Tiberius* tells at length of his exile on Rhodes; *Gaius* includes a short biography of Germanicus.
12. e.g. Phaenias of Eresus (p. 431, n. 45).
13. Jerome in Migne, *Patrologia Latina*, xxiii 82 f.
14. Suetonius, *Gaius*, 8.
15. Suetonius, *Tiberius*, 21 (3); *Titus*, 1.
16. Suetonius, *Claudius*, 44 (2); *Nero*, 33 (1); cf. 39 (2). Sometimes there are attempts at conflation.
17. Suetonius, *Tiberius*, 42 (1) and 49 (1), *Nero*, 37 (1), *Galba*, 22.
18. Suetonius, *Gaius*, 50 (trans. J.C. Rolfe).
19. Ibid. 33 (trans. J.C. Rolfe).
20. Ibid. 20 (trans. J.C. Rolfe).
21. Suetonius, *Domitian*, 1, 3, 22 (trans. J.C. Rolfe).
22. *Scriptores Historiae Augustae, Probus*, 2, 7.
23. Suetonius, *Julius*, 31 (trans. R. Graves).
24. Ibid. 82 (trans. R. Graves).
25. Suetonius, *Claudius*, 10 (trans. J.C. Rolfe).
26. Suetonius, *Nero*, 47–8 (trans. G.B. Townend).
27. *Qualis artifex pereo* – 'what an artist perishes in me'.
28. e.g. Suetonius, *Tiberius*, 61 (5), *Nero*, 11 (1), *Otho*, 7 (1).
29. Suetonius, *Augustus*, 7 (1) (trans. J.C. Rolfe).
30. Suetonius, *Gaius*, 8 (2) (trans. J.C. Rolfe).
31. Suetonius, *Nero*, 52.
32. e.g. Suetonius, *Vitelluis*, 16 f.; cf. Tacitus, *Histories*, III 84 (but there are discrepancies).

33. Tacitus, *Annals*, XIV 16 (1).
34. e.g. Suetonius, *Tiberius*, 21 (2), *Gaius*, 8.

PART 8. CHRISTIAN AND PAGAN

Chapter 21. Eusebius

EH=*History of the Church* (*Ecclesiae Historia*); VC=*Life of Constantine* (*Vita Constantini*)

1. Appian was born at latest under Trajan and wrote a history of Rome in twenty-four books (*c.* AD 160), of which the preface and eleven complete books, as well as parts of others, have survived. His work was ethnographically arranged, but he was principally interested in wars (of special value for 133–70 BC). But he was unperceptive about Republican institutions and enthusiastic about the Imperial Peace. He is over-dramatic and telescopes events. His sources are varied but disputed.
2. Arrian governed Cappadocia and repelled an Alan invasion (134). His chief work was the *Anabasis*, a history of Alexander, which survives. It avoids rhetoric and makes a serious attempt to go back to the best sources. His Histories of Alexander's successors, and of Parthia, are lost.
3. *On the Writing of History*, written as a letter, attacking historiography as practised at the time.
4. Though Lucian speaks of the historian as a sculptor who has to fashion materials supplied by others. Perhaps he was influenced by Isocrates and Theophrastus.
5. *True Stories* (*Verae Historiae*) (two books).
6. Only the first ten books (and fragments of the fifteenth) of the *Proof* are extant.
7. Cf. Tertullian, *Apologeticus*, 19 f. – older than any other faith because it stems from the Jews. Celsus had attacked Christianity for its novelty and upheavals of ancestral practices.
8. Five books. Africanus went on an embassy to the emperor Elagabalus in *c.* 220.
9. Assyrians, Hebrews, Egyptians, Greeks, Romans.
10. Pamphilus, who had come from Berytus via Alexandria, employed in the library a group of students engaged in collecting and transmitting manuscripts.
11. Eusebius, *EH*, I 2.
12. His role in the preparation of the Creed is much disputed.
13. Eusebius, *EH*, I 1 (trans. G.A.Williamson).
14. Ibid. I 4; cf. *Preparation of the Gospel* (*Praeparatio Evangelii*).

15. Hebrews, XI 13 ff., I Corinthians, x 4.
16. Eusebius, *EH*, I 2; cf. Tertullian, *Apologeticus*, 5.
17. Ibid. III 25. But the position of Revelation was still not finally established; *EH*, III 24 (15).
18. cf. ibid. VII 31. Like his predecessor Irenaeus, Eusebius saw that the weakness of Gnosticism was its lack of a canon.
19. Ibid. II 7 (trans. G.A.Williamson).
20. Ibid. v 16 (letter to Abircius Marcellus) (trans. G.A.Williamson).
21. Ibid. v 18 (trans. G.A.Williamson).
22. Ibid. VIII 9 (trans. G.A.Williamson).
23. Ibid. VI 3 (trans. G.A.Williamson); cf. II Corinthians, XI 27.
24. Dionysius of Corinth in Eusebius, *EH*, IV 23 (trans. G.A.Williamson).
25. Constantine and Licinius in Eusebius, *EH*, x 5.
26. Eusebius, *VC*, I 28.
27. Lactantius, *On the Death of the Persecutors* (*De Morte Persecutorum*), 44 (5).
28. Eusebius, *VC*, 15.
29. Ibid. 14.
30. Ibid. IV 75.
31. Ibid. IV 58; cf. earlier, the Basilica at Tyre; *EH*, x 4 (34 ff.). These buildings were subsequently reconstructed.
32. Eusebius, *EH*, x 4 and 9 (trans. G.A.Williamson).
33. Ibid. VIII 1 (6 ff.) (trans. G.A.Williamson).
34. Ammianus, XXII 5 (4).
35. Constantine in Eusebius, *EH*, x 5 (trans. G.A.Williamson).
36. Ibid. IX 7; cf. *Corpus Inscriptionum Latinarum*, III 12132, 13625*b* (Arycanda).
37. Eusebius, *EH*, I 13.

Chapter 22. Ammianus

1. Magnentius, who had slain Constans near Augustodunum (Autun) (350). Constans had defeated and killed his eldest brother, Constantine II, at Aquileia (340).
2. Some have believed there were two separate works, with the break at 337 (when treatment became fuller).
3. Gratian was now obliged to recognise his half-brother Valentinian II, aged four, as ruler in Illyricum.
4. The usurper Magnus Maximus, who killed Gratian, was captured and executed by Theodosius I at Aquileia (388). Valentinian II, whose sister had married Theodosius I, was found hanged in 392.
5. Arcadius and Honorius, named Augustus since 383 and 393 respectively.

Notes

6. Ammianus, XXII 16 (12) must have been written before the destruction of the Serapeum at Alexandria in summer 391.

7. Ibid. XXVI 1 (1) (trans. J.C.Rolfe).

8. The death of Valentinian II may have influenced his change of mind.

9. Ibid. XXVIII 1 (2) (trans. J.C.Rolfe).

10. For echoes in Claudian and Jerome, see p. 408, nn. 29, 30. Ammianus, XXIX 6 (15) was perhaps not written before 392. Libanius, *Letters (Epistulae)*, 983 Wolf = 1063 Forester (AD 392), refers to the history down to XXV and no further.

11. Ammianus, XIX 8 (12), XXII 9 (14), etc.

12. Ibid. XIV 6 (9). Three thousand dancing girls were allowed to stay.

13. Libanius, *Letters*, loc. cit.

14. e.g. Greece (Methone, after tidal wave of 366), Egypt, Thrace (site of a battle preceding Adrianople, XXXI 6 (16)).

15. Ammianus, XXXI 16 (9); cf. XV 1, XXVII 4 (2), XXIX 1 (24).

16. Faustus of Buzanta in Cilicia.

17. Ammianus, XIV 11 (2), XV 5 (36).

18. Ibid. XX 2 (4).

19. Ibid. XXIII 5 (19), XVII 1 (14).

20. Yet Eunapius (p. 463, n. 106) was for some reason less afraid of praising Julian's reign.

21. Ammianus, XXV 4 (16–19), XXII 1 (1), XXIII 3 (3).

22. St Babylas. The church was closed after the burning of the Temple of Apollo (Daphne). Lampoons against Julian were countered by his *Misopogon* (Beard-Hater).

23. Ammianus, XXV 4 (19) (trans. J.C.Rolfe).

24. Ibid. XIV 11 (25).

25. Ibid. XXI 1 (9–12).

26. Ibid. XXV 2 (8).

27. Ibid. XXX 9 (5) (trans. J.C.Rolfe).

28. Ibid. XXII 11 (10).

29. Ibid. XXVII 3 (15).

30. Ibid. XXI 16 (18). Christian technical terms are usually avoided not from ignorance but as a standard stylistic device.

31. Ibid. XXVII 3 (13).

32. Ibid. XXII 5 (4) (trans. J.C.Rolfe).

33. Ibid. XXI 16 (18) (trans. J.C.Rolfe).

34. Jerome (T.Mommsen, *Chronica Minora*, I 631).

35. Ammianus, XXVIII 1 (57).

36. Ibid. 7 (1).

37. Ibid. XXXI 14 (2–7) (trans. J.C.Rolfe).
38. Ibid. XIV 6 (3) (trans. J.C.Rolfe).
39. Ibid. XXVII 6 (12) (trans. J.C.Rolfe).
40. Ibid. XIX 12 (17) (trans. J.C.Rolfe).
41. Ibid. XIV 11 (24).
42. Ibid. XXI 16 (1).
43. Ibid. XVI 10 (9) (trans. J.C.Rolfe).
44. Ibid. XVI 10 (13) (trans. J.C.Rolfe).
45. Ibid. XIV 6 (4).
46. Ibid. XXXI 5 (14); cf. XIV 6 (10).
47. Ibid. XXXI 5 (10) (trans. J.C.Rolfe).
48. Ibid. XXIII 1 (7) (trans. J.C.Rolfe).
49. Ibid. XXIV 3 (4) (trans. J.C.Rolfe).
50. Ibid. XXV 6 (10).
51. Ibid. XIV 1 (7) and 5 (9) (trans. J.C.Rolfe).
52. Ibid. XV 3 (5) (trans. J.C.Rolfe).
53. Ibid. XV 3 (4), XIX 12 (7) and 13–12 (trans. J.C.Rolfe).
54. Ibid. XXIX 2–10.
55. Ibid. XXVII 7 (4); cf. XXVI 10 (13), XXVIII 1.
56. Ibid. XXIX 3 (9) (trans. J.C.Rolfe).
57. Ibid. XVI 10 (5) (trans. J.C.Rolfe).
58. Ibid. XXVII 3; cf. XXI 24.
59. Ibid. XVI 8 (13).
60. Ibid. XXVIII 4 (5), etc.
61. Ibid. XIV 6 (12).
62. Indignation seems to have introduced a contradiction here.
63. Ibid. XIV 6 (9) (trans. J.C.Rolfe).
64. Ibid. XXVIII 4 (10) (trans. J.C.Rolfe).
65. Ibid. XXVIII 4 (6) (trans. J.C.Rolfe).
66. Ibid. XXVIII 4 (14). For Marius Maximus, a prefect of the city who 'continued' Suetonius down to Elagabalus (218–22) in a Latin work now lost, cf. *Scriptores Historiae Augustae, Firmus*, etc. (*Quadriga Tyrannorum*), 1 2, Dio Cassius, LXXIX 14 (3). Possibly there are echoes of Juvenal in Ammianus' tirade.
67. Ammianus, XIV 6 (18).
68. Ibid. XXX 4 (2).
69. Ibid. XVI 7 (4).
70. Ibid. XXX 4 (2–22).
71. Ibid. XXX 4 (16–17) (trans. J.C.Rolfe).
72. Julian introduced various financial remedies to try to arrest the rising costs of foodstuffs.
73. Ibid. XIV 6 (1).

74. Ibid. xxxi 5 (14).
75. Ibid. xiv 6 (25) (trans. J.C.Rolfe).
76. e.g. earthquakes, eclipses, rainbows, prophecy, pearls, the calendar.
77. Ibid. xxii 15 (1–16 and 24).
78. Ibid. xxiii 6 (64 and 67) (trans. J.C.Rolfe).
79. Ibid. xv 12 (1).
80. Ibid. xxxi 2 (1–2 and 5–6) (trans. J.C.Rolfe).
81. Ibid. xxviii 5 (7).
82. Ibid. xv 5 (32–3) (Silvanus, Bonitus).
83. Ibid. xvii 5 (3 and 10).
84. Herodotus, i 133–5.
85. Ibid. xxiii 6 (75–80) (trans. J.C.Rolfe).
86. Ibid. xviii 8 (11–12) (trans. J.C.Rolfe).
87. Ibid. xix 1 (3) (trans. J.C.Rolfe).
88. Ibid. xix 2 (3) (trans. J.C.Rolfe).
89. Ibid. xix 6 (6).
90. Ibid. xviii 8 (2).
91. Ibid. xxii 6 (6–8).
92. Ibid. xxx 8 (1).
93. e.g. in Mesopotamia. Egyptian totography is also confused, ibid. xxii 15 (2).
94. Ibid. xxiii 4.
95. Ibid. xxx 1 (18–23).
96. Ibid. xxxi 5 (10).
97. Ibid. xxviii 1 (15).
98. Ibid. xviii 3 (9) and 7 (5), xxi 16 (7).
99. Ibid. xxxi 16 (9) (trans. J.C.Rolfe).
100. e.g. the cruelty of Simplicius explicitly echoes the classic cases of Busiris, Antaeus, Phalaris, ibid. xxviii 1 (46).
101. Ibid. xv 13 (1) (Musonianus), xviii 5 (1) (Antoninus).
102. Ibid. xv 9 (2). This refers to the historian Timagenes (p. 444, n. 27).
103. Ibid. xiv 2 (1–20).
104. Ibid. xv 12 (6) (on Gaul).
105. e.g. Dio Cassius, Herodian, Dexippus.
106. e.g. Eutropius (ibid. xiv 11, xv 5 (8)) who took part in Julian's Persian campaign and wrote in 369 an unpretentious, succinct Latin survey (*Breviarium*) of Roman history to 364 (still used as a school text in the twentieth century); Rufius Festus, who like him was one of the chief secretaries of Valens and write another Latin summary; and Eunapius of Sardis who wrote Greek praises of Julian and Lives of the Sophists (*c.* 400). Eutropius shares a common source with Aurelius Victor (city prefect 388/9) who had terminated his

Caesars in 360. It has been suggested that, for Constantius and Julian, Ammianus uses two sources, one annalistic (by consular years) and the other seasonal. The *Historia Augusta* may also have been written in the later fourth century (p. 348), and St Jerome published his *Chronicle* in 380–1 and his biographies of *Illustrious Men* (lives of 135 Christian writers) in 392.

107. Ammianus, XVI 12 (70), XXVIII 1 (15), XVI 12 (69), XXVIII 3 (7).

Epilogue. The Survival of the Ancient Historians

1. Aristotle, *On the Generation of Animals (De Generatione Animalium)*, III 75*b* (5); cf. *Rhetoric*, III 9 (2 ff.).
2. Papyrus 357 P.
3. Diodorus Siculus, I 69 (7).
4. e.g. lost works by Valerius Pollio, Aelius Harpocration and Libanius.
5. Dionysius of Halicarnassus, *Ad Pompeium Geminum*, 3; cf. *De Thucydide*, 24.
6. Lucian. *On the Writing of History*, 4.
7. Seneca the younger, *Letters*, CXIV 17.
8. Martial, *Epigrams*, XIV 191.
9. Tacitus, *Annals*, III 30 (1).
10. Augustine, *City of God (Civitas Dei)*, VIII 3.
11. Tacitus, *Annals*, IV 34 (3), *Agricola*, 1.
12. Juvenal, *Satires*, X 417 ff.
13. Livy, XXIII 12.
14. Dante, *Inferno*, XXVIII 10.
15. Livy, XXX.
16. Macaulay, *Lays of Ancient Rome*, LVII–LIX.
17. Josephus, *Against Apion*, I 12.
18. Josephus, *Jewish Antiquities*, XVIII 5 (4); cf. Matthew, XIV 6–11.
19. *Scriptores Historiae Augustae, Tacitus*, 10 (3).
20. Sulpicius Severus, Orosius (historian and pupil of Augustine), Sidonius Apollinaris.
21. Cassiodorus, V 2.
22. Tacitus, *Annals*, XIV 33 (1).
23. Gellius, *Attic Nights*, XII 5, I 26.
24. e.g. Clement of Alexandria, John Chrysostom, Theodoret.
25. Agathias, John Metropolitan of Euchaita.
26. Aurispa, d'Angeli, Filelfo, L. Giustiniani, F. Barbaro, L. da Castiglionchio.
27. e.g. *Timon of Athens* is based on Plutarch's *Antony*, 70. *Henry V*, Act IV, sc. 7, gives a burlesque of a Plutarchian comparison.
28. But he altered Plutarch's Prometheus myth to make civilisation a

nuisance and corruption. Plutarch's Fabricius appealed to him as a virtuous simple hero.

29. Claudian, *Against Rufinus* (*In Rufinum*), II 357 ff. (cf. Ammianus, XVI 10 (8)), 365 f. (cf. Ammianus, XVI 10 (7)).

30. Jerome, *Commentary on Isaiah*, VII 21 (cf. Ammianus, XXXI 2 (2)), *Letters* (*Epistulae*), LXXVII 8 (cf. Ammianus, XXXI 2 (11)), LX 17 (cf. Ammianus, XXXI 2 (6)) on the Huns.

31. *Scriptores Historiae Augustae, Firmus*, etc. (*Quadriga Tyrannorum*), 8, 10 (cf. Ammianus, XV 3 (7–11)), 4 (cf. Ammianus, XV 5 (15 f.), 12 and 14 (cf. Ammianus, XV 12 (1)).

32. H. Keil, *Grammatici Latini*, II 487.

33. Edward Gibbon, *Decline and Fall of the Roman Empire*, ch. XXXI.

Some Books on the Ancient Historians

BEFORE THE GREEKS

The Idea of History in the Ancient Near East, ed. R.C.Denton (New Haven, Conn., 1966); A. Erman, *Literature of the Ancient Egyptians* (1927); O.R.Gurney, *The Hittites* (Penguin, 1952); T.B.Jones, *Paths to the Ancient Past* (New York, 1967); C.F.North, *The Old Testament Interpretation of History* (1946); A.T.Olmstead, *Assyrian Historiography* (Columbia, Mo., (1916); G. Östborn, *Yahweh's Words and Deeds* (Uppsala-Wiesbaden, 1958); H.W.F.Saggs, *The Greatness of Babylon* (1962).

GREEK AND ROMAN HISTORIANS: GENERAL

H.E.Barnes, *A History of Historical Writing* (2nd ed., New York, 1963); R.R.Bolgar, *The Classical Heritage* (1954); J.A.Garraty, *The Nature of Biography* (New York, 1957); G.A.Highet, *The Classical Tradition* (1967); H.-I.Marrou, *The Meaning of History* (New York, 1966); G.Misch, *A History of Autobiography in Antiquity* (1950); A.Momigliano, *Contributo alla storia degli studi classici* (Rome, 1955); also two further volumes in the same series: *Secondo* (Rome, 1960), *Terzo* (Rome, 1966); *Studies in Historiography* (1966); H.Strasburger, *Die Wesenbestimmung der Geschichte* (Wiesbaden, 1966); D.R.Stuart, *Epochs in Greek and Roman Biography* (New York, 1928); S.Usher, *The Historians of Greece and Rome* (1969).

GREEK HISTORIANS: GENERAL

N.Austin, *The Greek Historians* (1968); J.B.Bury, *The Ancient Greek Historians* (New York, 1958); M.I.Finley, *The Greek Historians* (1959); K.vonFritz, *Die Griechische Geschichtsschreibung*, vol. 1 (Berlin, 1967); C.G. Starr, *The Awakening of the Greek Historical Spirit* (New York, 1968).

HERODOTUS

H.F.Burnitz, *Herodotstudien* (Berlin, 1968); T.R.Glover, *Herodotus* (1924);

C.Hignett, *Xerxes' Invasion of Greece* (1963); H.R.Immerwahr, *Form and Thought in Herodotus* (Cleveland, Ohio, 1967); J.L.Myres, *Herodotus: The Father of History* (1953); L.Pearson, *Early Ionian Historians* (1939); J.E. Powell, *The History of Herodotus* (Amsterdam, 1967); A.de Selincourt, *The World of Herodotus* (1962); J.Wikarjak, *L'Histoire Générale d'Hérodote* (Poznan, 1961).

THUCYDIDES

F.E.Adcock, *Thucydides and his History* (1963); C.N.Cochrane, *Thucydides and the Science of History* (New York, 1965); F.M.Cornford, *Thucydides Mythistoricus* (1965); J.H.Finley, *Thucydides* (Cambridge, Mass., 1942), *Three Essays on Thucydides* (Cambridge, Mass., 1967); P.J.Fliess, *Thucydides and the Politics of Bipolarity* (Baton Rouge, 1966); A.W.Gomme, *Historical Commentary on Thucydides*, vols I (1945), II and III (1956); G.B.Grundy, *Thucydides and the History of his Age* (Oxford, 1948); J.de Romilly, *Histoire et Raison chez Thucydide* (Paris, 1956); *Thucydides and Athenian Imperialism* (Oxford, 1963); H.-P.Stahl, *Thucydides: Die Stellung des Menschen im geschichtlichen Prozess* (Munich, 1966); R.Syme, *Thucydides* (British Academy Lecture, 1963); R.Weil, *Thucydide: La Guerre du Péloponnèse* (Paris, 1965); H.D.Westlake, *Individuals in Thucydides* (1968).

XENOPHON

F.Delebecque, *Essai sur la Vie de Xénophon* (Paris, 1957); J.Luccioni, *Les Idées Politiques et Sociales de Xénophon* (Paris, 1957); G.R.Nussbaum, *The Ten Thousand* (Leiden, 1967).

OTHER HISTORIANS
OF THE FOURTH AND THIRD CENTURIES BC

T.S.Brown, *Timaeus of Tauromenium* (Berkeley, 1958); I.A.F.Bruce, *An Historical Commentary on the Hellenica Oxyrhynchia* (1967); R.van Campernolle, *Étude de Chronologie et d'Historiographie Siceliotes* (Brussells, 1960); W.R. Connor, *Theopompus and Fifth Century Athens* (Cambridge, Mass., 1968); K.von Fritz, *Aristotle's Contribution to the Practice and Theory of Historiography* (Berkeley, 1958); L.Pearson, *The Lost Histories of Alexander the Great* (New York, 1960); R.Pfeiffer, *History of Classical Scholarship from the Beginning to the End of the Hellenistic Age* (1968); R.Weil, *Aristotle et l'Histoire* (Paris, 1960).

POLYBIUS

G.J.D.Aalders, *Die Theorie der gemischten Verfassung in Altertum* (Amsterdam,

1968); V.la Bua, *Filino-Polbio: Sileno-Diodoro* (Palermo, 1966); K.F.Eisen, *Polybiosinterpretationen* (Heidelberg, 1966); K.von Fritz, *The Theory of the Mixed Constitution in Antiquity* (1954); G.A.Lehmann, *Untersuchungen zur Historischen Glaubwürdigkeit des Polybios* (Munster, 1967); P.Pédech, *La Méthode Historique de Polybe* (Paris, 1962); F.W.Walbank, *Historical Commentary on Polybius*, vols I (1957), II (1967).

ROMAN HISTORIANS: GENERAL AND BEGINNINGS

Latin Biography, ed. T.A.Dorey (1967); T.A.Dorey, *Latin Historians* (1966); M.Grant, *Roman Literature* (Penguin, 1964); M.L.W.Laistner, *The Greater Roman Historians* (Berkeley, 1963); E.Löfstedt, *Roman Literary Portraits* (1958).

F.della Corte, *Catone Censore* (Turin, 1949), *Varrone: Il terzo gran lume Romano* (Genoa, 1954); D.Kienast, *Cato der Zensor* (Heidelberg, 1954).

CAESAR

F.E.Adcock, *Caesar as Man of Letters* (1956); J.P.V.D.Balsdon, *Julius Caesar and Rome* (1967); M.Borda et al., *Gaio Giulio Cesare* (Rome, 1957); M.Gelzer, *Caesar als Historiker*, Kleine Schriften II (Wiesbaden, 1963), *Caesar: Politician and Statesman* (Oxford, 1968); M.Grant, *Julius Caesar* (1969); *Julius Caesar* (Greece and Rome, IV i (O.U.P., 1957); M.Rambaud *L'Art de la Déformation Historique dans les 'Commentaires' de César* (Paris, 1953); *Caesar*, ed. D.Rasmussen (Darmstadt, 1967); O.Seel, *Caesar-Studien* (Stuttgart, 1967).

SALLUST

E.Bolaffi, *Sallustio e la sua fortuna nei secoli* (1949); K. Büchner, *Sallust* (Heidelberg, 1960); D.C.Earl, *The Political Thought of Sallust* (1961); A.La Penna, *Sallustio a la Rivoluzione Romana* (1968); L.O.Sangiacomo, *Sallustio* (1954); W.Steidle, *Sallusts Historische Monographien*, Historia, Einzelschr. III (Wiesbaden, 1958); R.Syme, *Sallust* (1964).

LIVY

R.Bloch, *Tite-Live et les Premiers Siècles de Rome* (Paris, 1965); *Wege zu Livius*, ed. E.Burck (Darmstadt, 1967); *Les Origines de la République Romaine*, Entretiens Hardt, XIII (Geneva, 1967); I.Kajanto, *God and Fate in Livy* (Turku, 1957); K.Lindemann, *Beobachtungen zur Livianischen Periodenkunst* (Marburg, 1964); M.Mazza, *Storia e Ideologia in Tito Livio*

(Catania, 1966); R.M.Ogilvie, *A Commentary on Livy*, vol. 1 (1965); P.G.Walsh, *Livy: His Historical Aims and Methods* (1961).

On Augustus: *Res Gestae Divi Augusti*, ed. P.A.Brunt and J.M.Moore (1967).

JOSEPHUS

L.Feldman, *Scholarship on Philo and Josephus, 1937–1962* (New York, 1963); F.J.Foakes Jackson, *Josephus and the Jews* (1930); R.J.H.Shutt, *Studies in Josephus* (1961); H.St J.Thackeray, *Josephus: The Man and the Historian* (New York, 1929); G.A.Williamson, *The World of Josephus* (1964); Y.Yadin, *Masada* (1966).

TACITUS

D.R.Dudley, *The World of Tacitus* (1968); E.-L.Etter, *Tacitus in der Geistesgeschichte des 16 und 17 Jahrhunderts* (Basel, 1966); R.Häussler, *Tacitus und das historische Bewusstsein* (Heidelberg, 1965); C.W.Mendell, *Tacitus: The Man and his Work* (New Haven, Conn., 1958); *Cornelii Taciti Vita Agricolae*, ed. R.M.Ogilvie and I.A.Richmond (1967); R.Paratore, *Tacito* (2nd ed., Rome, 1962); D.M.Pippidi, *Autour de Tibére* (Bucharest, 1944); R.T.Scott, *Religion and Philosophy in the Histories of Tacitus*, American Academy, Rome, XXII (1968); R.Syme, *Tacitus* (1958); J.Tresch, *Die Nerobücher in den Annalen des Tacitus* (Heidelberg, 1965); B.Walker, *The Annals of Tacitus* (2nd ed., Manchester, 1961).

PLUTARCH AND SUETONIUS

R.H.Barrow, *Plutarch and his Times* (1967); *Plutarch: Alexander*, ed. J.R.Hamilton (1968); M.A.Levi, *Plutarco e il V secolo* (Milan, 1955); C.A.Robinson, *Plutarch: Eight Great Lives* (New York, 1960); P.A.Stadter, *Plutarch's Historical Methods: An Analysis of the 'Mulierum Virtutes'* (Cambridge, Mass., 1965).

F.della Corte, *Svetonio: eques Romanus* (2nd ed., Florence, 1967), *Svetonio: Grammatici e Retori* (Turin, 1968); M.A.Levi, *Suetoni Divus Augustus* (Florence, 1951); W.Steidle, *Sueton und die Antike Biographie* (Munich, 1951).

See also books on biography listed above under Greek and Roman Historians, Greek Historians, Roman Historians.

OTHER WRITERS
OF THE SECOND AND THIRD CENTURIES AD

G.Avenarius, *Lukians Schrift zur Geschichtsschreibung* (Meisenheim, 1956);
E.Gabba, *Appiano e la storia delle guerre civili* (Florence, 1956).
H.Homeyer, *Lukian: Wie man Geschichte schreiben soll* (Munich, 1963).
F.G.B.Miller, *A Study of Cassius Dio* (1964).

EUSEBIUS

A.Alföldi, *The Conversion of Constantine and Pagan Europe* (1948); G.Bardy, *Eusèbe de Césarée: Histoire Ecclésiastique*, Sources Chrétiennes, LXXIII (Paris, 1960); H.Butterfield, *Christianity and History* (1949); K.Löwith, *Meaning in History* (Chicago, 1949); R.L.Milburn, *Early Christian Interpretations of History* (1954); D.S.Wallace-Hadrill, *Eusebius of Caesarea* (1960).

AMMIANUS

P.M.Camus, *Ammien Marcellin* (Paris, 1967); A.Denandt, *Zeitkritik und Geschichtsbild im Werk Ammianus* (Bonn, 1965); *The Conflict between Paganism and Christianity in the Fourth Century*, ed. A.D.Momigliano (1963); H.T. Rowell, *Ammianus Marcellinus: Soldier–Historian of the Late Roman Empire*, Semple Lectures, 1st series (1968); R.Syme, *Ammianus and the Historia Augusta* (1968); E.A.Thompson, *The Historical Work of Ammianus Marcellinus* (1947); J.Vogt, *Ammianus Marcellinus als Erzählender Geschichtsschreiber der Spätzeit* (Mainz, 1963).

For the *Historia Augusta*, see the bibliography in R.Syme's book mentioned in the last paragraph.

Index

Abdera, 34, 60, 92 f.
Abgar *v.* the Black, 357
Abraham, 348 f.
Absalom, 11
Accursius, Mariangelus, 409
Achaea, 34, 136, 140, 142, 146 f., 151, 153 ff., 163, 309, 393
Actium, 217, 221, 294
Acton, Lord, xv, 282
Adams, John, 390, 393, 403
Adiabene, *see* Assyria
Adrianople, *see* Hadrianopolis
Aedui, 182
Aegospotami, 129, 132
Aelius, *see* Sejanus, Tubero
Aemilius, *see* Lepidus, Paullus, Scaurus
Aeschylus, 20, 45–8, 50 f., 90, 118
Aetolia, 136, 155
Afranius, L. 191
Africa (North), xiv, 18, 24, 27, 145, 147, 191, 199, 209, 211 f., 397
Africa Nova, *see* Numidia
Africanus, Julius, 346
Africanus, *see* Scipio
Agesilaus, 129 f., 133, 391
Agis IV, 309
Agricola, Cn. Julius, 272, 276, 278, 280, 296, 402
Agrippa I (Herod Agrippa), 244 f.
Agrippa II, 244, 257 f., 263, 265
Agrippina, Colonia, *see* Colonia
Agrippina the younger, 275, 289 f.
Agyrium, 387
Ahenobarbus, L. Domitius, 191, 193 f.
Akkad, 4 f., 7
Albius, *see* Tibullus
Alcibiades, 72, 99 f., 102 f., 316, 320

Alcmaeonidae, 24, 44
Alemanni, *see* Germans
Aleppo, 7
Alesia, 182
Alexander the Great, 129, 136, 141 f., 159, 220, 243, 263, 294, 309, 316, 326, 344 f., 387
Alexandria, 25, 147, 161, 176, 191, 244, 251, 253, 259, 262, 267, 310, 344, 347, 387, 389
Alfieri, Vittorio, 403, 406
Alityrus, 246
Alps, 145, 147, 223, 273
Ambiorix, 182
Amida, 359, 362 f., 381
Amiternum, 198
Ammianus Marcellinus, xiii, 358–84, 395, 401, 408 f.
Amos, 13
Amphipolis, 72, 74, 98, 116
Amyot, Jacques, 404 ff.
Anatolia, *see* Asia Minor
Anaxagoras, 53, 79, 83, 104
Anaximander, 16 f., 19, 39, 55
Anicii, 374
Anna Comnena, 391
Annaeus, Seneca, *see* Seneca
Annales Maximi, 172, 236
Annius, *see* Milo
Antalcidas, 130
Antigonus I, Antigonids, 136
Antioch, xiv, 274, 348, 359 f., 362, 364, 376
Antiochus III the Great, 145, 159, 220
Antiochus IV Epiphanes, 243
Antiochus of Syracuse, 120, 140
Antipas, Herod, 245, 401
Antipater, Coelius, 173

473

Antipater of Idumaea, 244, 261
Antiphon of Rhamnus (rhetorician), 89, 100, 111 f.
Antiphon (sophist), 91
Antium, 241, 339
Antoninus Pius, 343, 395
Antonius, M. (Mark Antony, triumvir), 177, 191, 193, 195, 199, 217, 221, 230, 233, 244, 309, 315, 320 f., 405
Antonius Creticus, M., 198
Antonius Orator, M., 177
Antonius Polemo, *see* Polemo
Antwerp, 402
Apamea (Syria), 154
Apion, 267, 400
Apollonius, 350
Appian, 344, 392
Appuleius, *see* Saturnius
Aquitani, 182
Arabia, 28, 61, 253
Arabic, 400
Aratus of Sicyon, 143, 146, 155, 163, 174, 309
Aratus of Soli, 232, 364
Arcadia, 34, 72, 138 f., 144, 146, 154, 163
Archelaus, 74, 121
Archilochus, 16
Archimedes, 320
Ardabau, 350
Arelate (Arles), 310
Argentorate (Strasbourg), 359
Argippaei, 62
Argos, 117, 130
Ariovistus, 182, 187
Aristagoras, 39
Aristarchus of Samothrace, 387
Aristides, 316, 320
Aristophanes, 36, 45 f., 96, 98 f.
Aristotle, 95, 112, 141, 160, 317 f., 387
Arius, 347 ff., 366
Armenia, 126, 128, 346, 363, 403, 408
Arretium, 196
Arrian, 344
Artabanus, 47
Artaphernes, 24
Artaxerxes I, 13 f.
Artaxerxes II Memnon, 125, 127, 309
Artemisia, 33
Artemisium, 25

Arverni, 182
Ascham, Roger, 392, 394
Ashurbanipal, 7
Asia Minor, 7, 9, 15, 18, 23 f., 33, 71, 125 f., 129 f., 136, 174, 191, 272, 280, 291, 295, 322, 330, 344, 347, 349 f., 384; *see also* Armenia, Lydia, Pontus
Asidates, 126
Asinius, Pollio, *see* Pollio
Assinarus, R., 94
Assyria, 7, 9, 13, 16 f., 30, 253, 261, 263
Atarantes, 61
Athens, Attica, 24 f., 27 ff., 31, 33–8, 43–7, 50–4, 59, 69, 71 f., 74, 77, 80–5, 88, 90–112, 114–19, 121, 125, 129–32, 139–42, 158, 200, 225, 310, 312, 321, 345, 389
Atticus, T. Pomponius, 179, 208, 331
Atys, 51
Augsburg, 400, 409
Augusta Treverorum, 360 f.
Augustine, St, 348 f., 353, 395
Augustus (Octavian), 195, 199, 217, 221, 224, 227, 230–3, 236, 244, 274, 278, 281, 285 ff., 291, 297, 299, 309, 329 f., 332, 335, 338 ff., 349, 390, 395
Aurelian, 343, 345
Aurelius, Marcus, 343, 346, 351, 395
Aurelius, *see also* Symmachus
Aurispa, Giovanni, 388
Auxerre, 404
Ayala, Lopez de, 397

Babylon, 4 f., 7, 9, 13 f., 17, 24, 53, 60, 125, 169, 253, 261, 387
Bacis, 54
Bacon, Francis, 389, 403
Barclay, Alexander, 395
Barea Soranus, 275, 296
Barrientos, Alamos de, 402
Basel, 400, 409
Basil, St, 404
Batavi, *see* Germans
Beatus Rhenanus, 402
Bedriacum, 273, 301, 303, 310
Beethoven, 406
Belgae, 182
Bentley, Richard, 408
Berenice, 257
Beroaldus, 402

Bersuire, 397
Berytus (Beirut), 10
Beth-Horon, 245, 248
Bithynia, *see* Asia Minor
Black Sea, 126, 129
Boccaccio, Giovanni, 397, 402
Boccalini, Traiano, 402
Bocchus I, 197
Bogotia, 42, 46, 71, 105, 130, 309, 312, 326
Bogazkoy, *see* Hattusas
Boiardo, M. M., 388
Bolingbroke, Henry St John, 230
Bologna, 409
Borodino R., 64
Bosphorus, Thracian, 126
Boswell, James, 397, 406
Boudicca (Boadicea), 272, 275
Bourges, 404
Bracciolini, *see* Poggio
Brasidas, 71 f., 74, 98, 116
Brissot, Jacques, 407
Britain, 182, 185, 272, 275, 280, 360
Britannicus, 275, 403
Brunetière, Ferdinand, 405
Bruni, Leonardo, 391 f., 404
Brutus, 179, 195, 230 f., 233, 305, 321, 336, 405
Bryennius, Nicephorus, 391
Burckhardt, Jakob, 408
Bury, J. B., 225
Byblos, 4, 9 f.
Byzantium (Constantinople), xiv, 126, 145, 265, 344, 354 f., 359 ff., 388, 390, 392, 400, 409

Caecilius, *see* Metellus, Pliny
Caecina Alienus, A., 291
Caere, 241
Caesar, Gaius Julius, 116, 175, 177, 181–96, 198–201, 205, 207, 212, 220 f., 229 f., 233, 244, 261, 272, 316, 320, 329 f., 332, 335 f., 339, 390, 394 f., 405, 407
Caesarea Maritima (Stratonis Turris), 253, 256, 345, 347, 349
Caesonia, 334
Calabria, 168
Caledonia, 272
Caligula (Gaius), 237, 244, 262 f., 267, 275, 334, 336, 339, 396

Callias, 121
Callisthenes, 142, 160
Calpurnius, *see* Piso
Calvin, John, 393, 403
Cambridge, 401
Cambyses, 23 f., 57
Camillus, M. Furius, 218, 228, 230, 406
Campania, 198, 227
Campano, G., 404
Cannae, 145, 222, 396
Canterbury, 395
Cantii (Kent), 185
Capreae, 275, 285
Cardano, Gerolamo, 407
Cardia, 142
Caria, *see* Asia Minor
Carlyle, Thomas, 11, 58, 399
Carthage, 137, 140 f., 143–8, 151, 153, 156, 158, 169 f., 173, 197, 201, 209, 220, 223, 227 ff., 242, 309, 346, 392, 398
Casca Longus, P. Servilius, 336
Cassel, *see* Kassel
Cassino, M., 397, 401 f.
Cassiodorus, 400 f., 409
Cassius Dio, *see* Dio
Cassius Longinus, Q., 195, 230 f., 233, 305, 321
Catilina, L. Sergius, 177 f., 181, 195 f., 200, 203, 205 f., 209, 211, 248, 395 f.
Cato the elder (Censor), 151, 155, 169–73, 212, 235, 391
Cato the younger, 178, 187, 192, 196, 203, 205 f., 212, 230
Catulus, Q. Lutatius (senior), 174, 391
Caudine Forks, 220
Celtiberians, 147
Celts, *see* Gaul
Ceos, 91
Cerialis, Q. Petillius, 273, 280
Cestius Gallus, *see* Gallus
Chaeronea, 261, 309–12, 325
Chalcidice, 130, 141
Chalcocondyles, *see* Demetrius, Laonicus
Chaldaeans, 52
Charlemagne, 407
Charles V of France, 395
Chateaubriand, Francois-René de, 403
Cheirisophus, 125 f.
Chenièr, André, 403

Cheops, 3

Chephren, 3

Chesterfield, Lord, 406

China, 136, 156, 377

Chios, 20, 105, 109, 138

Chrestus, 356

Christianity, Christ, 246, 263, 275, 279, 303, 324, 344–57, 359 ff., 364–7, 399 f., 408

Chrysoloras, Manuel, 390, 404

Churchill, Sir Winston, xv

Cicero, M. Tullius, 167, 176–81, 184, 195 f., 198, 208, 212 f., 222, 224, 228, 230 f., 241, 276, 293, 296, 314, 338 f., 384, 390, 392, 395

Cimber, L. Tillius, 336

Cimbri, *see* Germans

Cimon, 71, 74, 326

Cincinnati, 406

Cincinnatus, T. Quinctius, 218, 406

Cineas, 374

Citium, 154

Civilis, C. Julius, 273, 280

Clarus, C. Septicius, 330

Claudian, 408

Claudii, 229, 232, 285

Claudius (emperor), 222, 244, 263, 272, 275, 288 f., 298, 336 f., 340, 403, 408

Claudius, Ap. (decemvir), 218

Claudius Caecus, Ap., 220

Claudius Marcellus, *see* Marcellus

Claudius Tacitus M., *see* Tacitus (emperor)

Cleisthenes (Athens), 45

Cleisthenes (Sicyon), 59 f.

Clement of Alexandria, St, 346

Cleomenes I, 24, 53

Cleomenes III, 155, 309, 405

Cleon, 72, 88, 96 ff., 103, 111, 116 f.

Cleopatra VII, 191, 217, 221, 230, 375, 405

Clitarchus, 176

Clitus, 256

Clodius Pulcher, P., 198

Clodius Thrasea, Paetus, P., *see* Thrasea

Cloelia, 218

Cnidus, 127, 387

Cobden, Richard, 117

Colaeus, 53

Comnena, Anna, *see* Anna

Constantine I the Great, 343–8, 352–6, 358, 364, 370

Constantine VII Porphyrogenitus, 392

Constantinople, *see* Byzantium

Constantius II, 358 f., 362 f., 366, 369 f., 372 f., 379, 382

Constantius Gallus, *see* Gallus

Copais, L., 312

Corbulo, Cn. Domitius, 275

Corcyra, XVI, 69, 80, 92, 106 f., 116

Corday, Charlotte, 406

Corfinium, 191

Corinth, 43, 69, 71, 81, 108, 114, 130 f., 146 ff., 352

Coriolanus, Cn. Marcius, 218, 239, 405

Corneille, Pierre, 403

Cornelius, *see* Fronto, Lentulus, Nepos, Scipio, Sisenna, Sulla, Tacitus

Coronea, 130

Corsica, 397

Corvey, 401

Cos, 36, 119

Cosimo de' Medici, *see* Medici

Crassus, M. Licinius, 181, 190, 201 f., 320

Crassus, P. Licinius, 182, 221

Crathis, R. 33

Crebillon, Prosper-Jolyot de, 403

Cremera, R. 218

Cremona, 273

Crete, 151, 253

Crispus Caesar, 347

Crispus, Sallustius, *see* Sallust

Critias, 132

Critobulus, 390

Croesus, 23, 29, 48, 50 f., 55

Croton, 33

Ctesias, 127, 387

Ctesiphon, 360

Cunaxa, 125, 127

Curio, L. Scribonius, 191

Cursor, L. Papirius, 220

Curtius, Mettius, 218

Curtius, Rufus, Q., *see* Rufus.

Cyme, 132

Cynoscephalae, 42

Cyprian, St, 346

Cyprus, 154

Cyrene, Cyrenaica, 24, 264

Cyrus I, 14, 23, 25, 36 f., 48, 57, 65, 133, 261, 391 f.

Cyrus (prince), 125, 127 ff.

Dahlmann, Friedrich, 112
Damascus, 263
Daniel, 262
Dante, 396
Danube, R., 24, 273, 343, 359
Dardanelles, *see* Hellespont
Darius I, 24 f., 51, 58
Darius II, 14, 125
Datis, 24
David, 11 f.
Dead Sea, 255
Decapolis, *see* Syria
Decembrio, Pier Candido, 407
Decius, Trajanus, 346
Decius, Mus, P., *see* Mus
Delium, 71
Delos, 71, 115, 121
Delphi, 54, 310 f., 323 f.
Demaratus, 46
Demetrius I Soter, 156
Demetrius I the Besieger, 215, 321
Demetrius Chalcocondyles, 388
Democritus, 58, 93–6, 104 f., 109
Descartes, René, 117
Desmoulins, Camille, 403
Deuteronomy, 12
Dexippus, 345, 390
Dio Cassius, 344 f., 403
Diocletian, 343, 346, 355, 370
Diodorus Siculus, 387
Diodotus, 88
Dion, 407
Dionysius (bishop), 352
Dionysius of Halicarnassus, 387, 390
Dodona, 62
Dolabella, P. Cornelius, 320
Domitian, 256, 264, 271 ff., 278, 283 f.,
  296 ff., 300, 305, 310, 329, 334
Domitius, *see* Ahenobarbus, Corbulo
Donatus, Donatists, 356
Dorians, 33, 38, 46
Dostoievsky, Fyodor, 48
Drusus the elder, 221, 295
Drusus the younger, 287, 302
Dryden, John, 405
Dryo, 31
Dublin, 401
Duris, 142
Dyrrhachium, *see* Epidamnus

Eburones, 182
Edessa (Urfa), 357
Edom, *see* Idumaea
Egypt, 3 f., 7, 12, 14 ff., 19, 23, 27 f., 30 f.,
  39, 53 ff., 58 f., 61 f., 71, 136, 169, 191,
  243, 261, 267, 334, 347, 351 f., 377,
  387
Einhard, 407
Eleazar ben Yair, 252 f.
Elephantine, 63
Eleusis, 54
Elis, 28, 34, 120, 130
Emerson, Ralph Waldo, 407
Ennius, 168–71
Entemena, 5
Epaminondas, 130, 132, 146, 310 f.,
  331
Epaphroditus, M. Mettius, 261
Ephesus, 33
Ephorus, 138, 141, 149
Epicharis, 304
Epidamnus (Dyrrhachium), 69, 191
Epirus, 137, 168, 220
Erasmus, 388, 396 f., 403, 409
Eretria, 24
Erianthus, 321
Eros, 327 f.
Estienne, Henri, 388
Estienne, Robert (Stephanus), 408
Ethiopic, 400
Etruria, 196, 218, 239 f., 398
Euboea, 24, 71 f.
Eugenius, 361
Euphrates, R., 5
Eupolis, 83
Euripides, 92, 103, 106, 134, 321
Eurymedon, R. 71
Eusebius of Caesarea, XIV, 343–57, 404,
  408
Eusebius of Nicomedia, 353
Eutherius, 376
Ezra, 14

Fabius Justus, L., *see* Justus
Fabius Pictor, Q., *see* Pictor
Faesulae, 196
Favorinus, 310
Feuchtwanger, Lion, 401
Fidenae, 218
Firmus, 360
Flamininus, T. Quinctius, 145, 227, 237

Flaminius, C. 229
Florence, 392, 397, 402
Florus, L. Mestrius, 310
Forum Julii, 271
Francois I, 390, 408
Franks, *see* Germans,
Fregellae, 241
Freud, Sigmund, xvii, 116, 317
Fronto, M. Cornelius, 395
Fulda, 401, 407, 409
Furius Camillus, M., *see* Camillus

Gaius (emperor), *see* Caligula
Gaius (grandson of Augustus), 291
Galatia, 229
Galba, 271, 273, 275, 300, 309, 314, 337
Galerius, 346, 352
Galilee, 245, 248, 259, 264 ff.
Gallienus, 346
Gallus, C. Cestius, 244, 247 f.
Gallus, Constantius, 358 f., 363, 369, 382
Ganges, R. 377
Gauls, 147, 167, 181 f., 184 f., 188, 190 f., 193 f., 196, 218, 223, 225 f., 242, 274, 322, 334, 336, 346, 353, 359, 362, 378, 382, 394
Gelenius, Sigismond, 409
Gellius, A., 404,
Geminius, 322
Gergovia, 182, 189
Germanicus, 274, 286, 293, 295
Germans (Alemanni, Batavi, Cimbri, Franks, Goths, Saxons, Suebi, Teutones, Visigoths), 174, 182, 185, 197, 204, 273 f., 276, 294, 300, 322, 345, 359 f., 362, 371 f., 378 f., 401 f., 407
Gibbon, Edward, xvi, 59, 363, 389, 403, 409
Gibraltar, 53
Gilgamesh, 5
Gischala, 248, 251, 266
Goethe, J. W. von, 392
Göttingen, xvi, 389
Golding, Arthur, 394
Goldsmith, Oliver, 406
Gorgias, 43, 84, 91–4, 137
Goths, *see* Germans
Gracchus, C. Sempronius, 173, 201, 204, 229, 309

Gracchus, Ti. Sempronius, 173, 201, 204, 220, 229, 309
Graetz, Heinrich, 251
Granius Licinianus, *see* Licinianus
Gratian, 360 f., 367 f.
Graupius, M., 272
Graves, R., 408
Greenway, R., 402
Guarino Veronese, 388, 404
Gyges, 50 f.

Hadrian, 272, 274, 281, 310, 312, 330
Hadrianopolis (Edirne, Adrianople), 360, 367, 371, 377 ff., 382
Hagenau, 393
Halicarnassus (Bodrum), 23, 33, 35, 38, 42, 46, 64, 387, 390
Hamilcar, 144
Hamilton, Alexander, 393
Hanmer, Meredith, 408
Hannibal, 144 f., 151, 153, 158, 160, 162, 173, 220, 222–5, 227 f., 236 f., 242, 369, 396 f.
Hanno, 223
Hasdrubal (brother of Hannibal), 235
Hasdrubal (brother-in-law of Hannibal), 144
Hasmon, Hasmonaeans (Maccabees), 243, 246, 257, 263
Hattushash, 7
Hattusilis I, 7, 9
Hattusilis III, 9
Hebrews, *see* Jews
Hebron, 251
Hecataeus, 18 ff., 30 f., 38 ff., 52, 62, 77
Hellanicus, 76 f., 117, 121
Hellespont (Dardanelles), 24 f., 50, 129
Helvetii, 182, 187 f.
Helvidius, *see* Priscus
Heraclitus, 20, 38, 48 f.
Herder, Johann von, 406
Herennius Philo, *see* Philo of Byblos
Hermocrates, 92, 108
Herod the Great, 244 f., 257, 261, 263, 399, 401
Herod, *see* Agrippa, Antipas
Herodes, 89
Herodian, 344, 392
Herodias, 401
Herodium, 252

Herodotus, XIII, 3, 11, 19, 23–66, 76, 78, 84, 88 ff., 93, 95 f., 99 f., 102 ff., 110, 115–18, 120 f., 127, 137, 139, 161, 304, 323, 326, 377, 379, 384, 387 ff., 391, 393
Hersfeld, 409
Hervet, G. 392
Hesiod, 15
Hiero I, 133, 391
Hierocles, 347
Hieronymus, of Stridon, *see* Jerome
Hippias (sophist), 91, 120
Hippias (tyrant), 44
Hippo Regius, 329 f.
Hippocleides, 59 f., 64
Hippocrates, 36, 39, 79, 104 f., 119
Hippodamus, 34, 44
Hirtius, A. 185, 188
Historia Augusta, 345, 407 f.
Hittites, 7, 9, 14
Hobbes, Thomas, 390
Holland, Philemon, 397, 407
Homer, 15 f., 28, 40 f., 43, 48 f., 55, 58, 60, 88, 105, 120, 161, 171, 392, 401, 405 f.
Horace, 218, 231 f., 329
Horatius, Cocles, 218, 239, 398
Hugo, Victor, 404
Hume, David, 121
Huns, 360, 378
Hyperbolus, 98
Hyrcanus II, John, *see* John Hyrcanus

Idumaea, 244, 257
Ilerda, 191
Iliad, see Homer
Illyricum, 181, 198, 360
India, 377
Inni, 4
Ion, 20, 34
Ionia, 15–18, 23 ff., 27, 33, 38 f., 42, 47 f., 55, 72, 79, 92, 95, 104,
Isaurians, *see* Asia Minor
Isocrates, 134 f., 137–41, 179, 184, 331
Israel, *see* Jews, Judaea

Jaconello da Rieti, B., 404
James, brother of Jesus, 263
Jason of Pherae, 130

Jay, John, 393
Jefferson, Thomas, 390, 403
Jerome, St, 395, 400, 407 f.
Jerusalem, 13 f., 244–8, 251, 253, 255, 258 f., 261, 265 f., 346, 355, 399
Jesus, *see* Christianity
Jews, XIV, 10–15, 48, 52, 57, 78, 242–68, 273, 275, 279, 298, 345 ff., 352, 357, 399 ff.
Johanan ben Zakkai, 255
John Hyrcanus II, 244
John of Gischala, 248, 251, 266
John of Salisbury, 404
John of Speyer, 402
John the Baptist, 263, 401
Johnson, Dr Samuel, 406
Jonathan of Cyrene, 264
Jonson, Ben, 403, 405
Josephus, XIV, 10, 243–68, 271 f., 275 f., 294, 355, 381, 399 ff.
Jotapata, 248, 253, 266
Jovian, 360 f.
Judaea, *see* Jews
Judah, 12 f.
Judas Maccabaeus, 243, 245, 261
Jugurtha, 174, 196 f., 200–4, 211 f., 395
Julia, 190
Julian the Apostate, 356, 359 f., 362, 364 ff., 372, 374, 376, 381, 383
Julius, *see* Africanus, Agricola, Caesar, Civilis, Vindex
Junius, *see* Brutus
Justin Martyr, St, 346
Justus, L. Fabius, 276
Justus of Tiberias, 265 f., 276
Juvenal, 375

Kassel, 409
Kent, *see* Cantii
Khafre, *see* Chepren
Khufu, *see* Cheops
Kipling, Rudyard, 401
Kish, 5
Kuban, R. 62
Kurdistan, 126

Labarnas, 7
Lacinium, Cape, 162
Laconia, 60
Lactantius, 354
Lade, 24

Lagash, 5
Lampon, 34
Laodicea (Phrygia), 322
Laonicus Chalcocondyles, 388
Larissa, 119
Lars Porsen(n)a, *see* Porsenna
Latins, 218, 220
Lenklau, Johann, 392
Lentulus Sura, Q. Cornelius, 192
Leo, Valerius, 320
Leonidas, 25, 41
Leontini, 43, 84
Leotychidas, 25
Lepidus, M. Aemilius (consul 78 BC), 197 f.
Lepidus, M. Aemilius (Triumvir), 195, 199, 217
Lepidus, M. Aemilius (consul AD 6), 296
Lesbos, 71, 76
Leuctra, 130 f.
Levites, 11
Libri lintei, *see* Linen Books
Licinia, 320
Licinianus, Granius, 211
Licinius I, 346 f., 352
Licinius, *see* Crassus, Lucullus, Macer
Linen Books, 176, 236
Lipsius, Justus, 402
Livia, 274, 285 f.
Livy, XIV, 142, 176, 179, 217–42, 254, 260, 278 f., 288, 292, 298, 305, 311, 340, 358, 384, 394, 396, 400, 402, 407, 409
Locke, John, 393
Locusta, 289
Lodge, Thomas, 401
Luca, 190, 327
Lucan, 304, 329
Lucceius, L. 178
Lucian, 344, 388, 391
Lucretia, 397
Lucullus, L. Licinius, 198, 312, 325
Lugdunum, 334
Luke St, 348
Lutetia, 359; *see also* Paris
Lycurgus, 133, 315 f., 406
Lycus, 126
Lydia, 17, 20, 23, 27, 29, 48, 51, 61
Lygdamis, 33
Lysander, 129, 321
Lyxes, 31, 33

Macaulay, T. B. 94, 290, 398, 407
Maccabees, *see* Hasmon
Macedonia, 24, 27, 60, 69, 74, 98, 115, 121, 136, 139, 142, 145 f., 148, 170, 195, 220, 312, 315, 321, 325
Macer, C. Licinius, 176 f., 203, 236
Machaerus, 252
Machiavelli, Niccolò, 100, 390, 392, 397, 402
Madison, James, 393
Maecenas, C., 218
Maelius, Sp., 218
Magnesia ad Sipylum, 145
Mahomet II, 390
Malatesta, Sigismondo, 402
Malmesbury, *see* William of Malmesbury
Manetho, 387
Mantinea, 72, 83, 130 f.
Manuel Chrysoloras, *see* Chrysoloras
Marathon, 23 ff., 27, 42, 50, 74, 77, 118
Marcellinus, 72
Marcellinus, *see* Ammianus Marcellinus
Marcellus, M. Claudius, 227
Marcion, 346
Marcius, *see* Barea, Coriolanus
Mardonius, 25, 46
Marius, C., 174, 197 f., 220, 229, 317, 321 f., 324
Marius, Maximus, *see* Maximus
Marsi, Marsian War, 174, 220, 235
Martial (M. Valerius Martialis), 221, 395
Marx, Karl, 116, 204, 393
Masada, 246, 252 f., 258
Massilia (Massalia), 191
Mataurus, 16
Matthias, 245
Mauretania, 409
Maxentius, 346
Maximilla, 350
Maximinus II Daia, 346, 357
Maximinus (prefect), 367
Maximus, Marius, 375, 407
Medes, 23
Medici, Cosimo de', 403
Mediolanum (Milan), 233, 320, 346, 352, 359, 361
Megabyzus, 24
Megacreon, 60
Megalopolis, 144, 146, 155, 309

Melanchthon, 390
Melesias, 34, 74
Melos, 72, 83, 92, 103 f., 109 f.
Melun, 404
Memmius, C. 204
Memmius Regulus, P., *see* Regulus
Menorah, 152
Mercurius, 372
Merivale, C., 290
Mery-Re, 3
Mesopotamia, 5, 7, 9, 14, 64, 125 f., 190
   243, 253, 261, 364, 382
Messalina, 275, 288
Mestrius, *see* Florus, Plutarchus
Metaurus, R., 235
Metellus Numidicus, Q. Caecilius, 174,
   197, 204
Mettellus, Scipio, Q. Caecilius, 192
Mettius, *see* Epaphroditus, Rufus
Meung, Jean de, 396
Meyer, Edward, 149
Michal, 11 f.
Michelet, Jules, 40
Middleton, Conyers, 406
Milan, *see* Mediolanum
Miletus, 16, 18 f., 24, 33 f., 39 f., 44, 51
Mill, John Stuart, 27
Milo, T. Annius, 198
Miltiades, 24, 72
Milton, John, 396, 403
Milvian Bridge, 346, 352, 354
Minturnae, 321 f.
Minucius, *see* Rufus
Mirabeau, Honoré de, 403
Misenum, 396
Mitford, William, 407
Mithridates VI, 174, 181, 198, 220
Modestus, 375 f.
Mohammed, *see* Mahomet
Mommsen, Theodor, 164, 184, 394
Monobazus, 263
Montaigne, Michel de, 397, 404, 407
Montanus, 346, 350, 356
Monte Cassino, *see* Cassino
Montesquieu, Charles-Louis de, 389,
   393, 397
More, Sir Thomas, 402
Moses, 265, 345
Mucius, Scaevola, P., *see* Scaevala
Mursilis II, 9
Mus, P. Decius, 218, 230

Mutina (Modena), 195
Mycale, 23, 25, 43
Mycalessus, 105
Mysia, *see* Asia Minor
Mytilene, 71, 88, 90, 97, 107

Naevius, Cn., 168
Napoleon I, 394, 403
Napoleon III, 404
Naramsin, 5
Naupactus, 71
Naxos, 71
Nebuchadnezzar, 262
Nehemiah, 13 f.
Nepos, Cornelius, 177, 208, 311, 319,
   331, 406
Nero, 244 ff., 264, 273 ff., 288-92, 298,
   300, 303, 310, 329, 337, 340, 403
Nerva, 272, 297-300, 358, 383
Nervii, 182
Nicaea, 344, 348
Niccoli, Niccolò, 391, 409
Nicephorus Bryennius, *see* Bryennius
Nichols, T., 390
Nicias, 72, 74, 82, 92, 94, 99 f., 104, 118,
   316, 326
Nicolas V, 388
Nicolaus of Damascus, 263
Nicomedia (Izmit), 344
Niebuhr, Barthold, G., 393, 397
Niebuhr, Reinhold, 351
Nietzsche, Friedrich, 58
Niger, R., 62
Nile, R., 62 f.
Nineveh, 7
Nippur, 5
Nisard, Désiré, 394
Nisibis, 362
North, Thomas, 405
Noya, Vidal de, *see* Vidal
Numa Pompilius, 309, 315, 406
Numantia, 147
Numidia, 147, 174, 196 f., 199, 202, 209,
   226
Nymphidius Sabinus, C., *see* Sabinus

Octavia, 275, 289, 403
Octavian, *see* Augustus
Odyssey, see Homer
'Old Oligarch', The, 44, 112
Olorus, 72, 74

Olympia, 28, 130, 145, 154, 169, 243
Olynthus, 130, 142
Omri, 13
Origen, 267, 346 f., 351
Osrhoene, 357
Ostia, 289
Otho, 271, 273, 301, 303, 309, 314, 403
Ovid, 397

Paccius, 327
Paetus, P. Clodius Thrasea, *see* Thrasea
Palaestina, *see* Jews
Palencia, Fernandez de, 400
Palmieri Pisano, Mattia, 388
Pamphilus, 347
Panaetius, 154
Panyassis, 33, 42, 54
Paoli, Gen. Pasquale, 397
Papa, 382
Papirius, Cursor, L., *see* Cursor
Paris, 408 f., *see also* Lutetia
Paros, 16, 24
Parthia, 190, 194, 221, 244, 253, 276,
    288, 300, 359
Pascal, C., 402
Passienus, 330
Patavium, 218, 222, 224, 233 f.
Paul, St, 246, 345, 348
Paul III Farnese, 403
Paulinus, 355
Paullus Macedonicus, L. Aemilius, 146,
    220
Paulus the Chain, 372 f.
Pausanias, 25
Pelopidas, 331
Peneus, R., 53
Pepe I, 3
Pergamum, 126, 136
Pericles, 34 f., 44 f., 71 74, 81, 85, 89,
    91, 96 ff., 102 f., 105, 107 f., 110 ff.,
    312, 315, 318, 325
Perotto, Niccolò, 392, 404
Perron, Cardinal du, 403
Perseus, 145, 220
Persia, 13 f., 17 f., 20, 23 ff., 27–30, 33,
    35 f., 38 f,. 41–8, 50, 54, 58 f., 61 f.,
    64 f., 69, 71, 76 f., 95, 108, 115, 120 f.,
    125–30, 133 f., 136, 149, 159, 243,
    246, 309, 326, 353, 359 f., 364, 372,
    379 ff.,
Persius, 329

Peshitta, 400
Peter, St, 246, 345
Petillius Cerialis, Q., *see* Cerialis
Petrarch, 388, 396 f., 407
Petreius, M. 191
Petronius (novelist:? T. Petronius
    Niger), 291 f.
Petronius Probus, Sex., *see* Probus
Phaon, 337
Pharisees, 246 f., 262
Pharnabazus, 129, 133
Pharsalus, 191, 221, 301
Pherae, 130
Philip II, 136, 139, 142, 312
Philip V, 145, 220
Philippi, 195, 301
Philo Judaeus, 262
Philo, Herennius, of Byblos, 10
Philopoemen, 146, 155, 173, 309
Phocion, 326, 406
Phocis, 321
Phoenicia, 4, 9 f., 15 f., 62, 137, 244
Phormio, 71, 90
Photius, 265, 400
Phrygia, *see* Asia Minor
Phrynichus, 51
Phylarchus, 142 f., 164
Pictor, Q. Fabius, 143, 169 f., 228 f.
Pilatus, Pontius, 244, 399
Pindar, 42, 46
Piraeus, 82, 115, 132
Pisano, Mattia Palmieri, *see* Palmieri
Pisistratus, 44
Piso, C. Calpurnius, 275, 304
Piso, Cn. Calpurnius, 274, 293
Pistoria (pistora), 196
Placentia, 193
Plataea, 23 ff., 43, 54, 71, 104, 107, 118
Plato, 48, 83, 89, 96, 134, 199, 316, 392
Pliny the elder (C. Plinius Secundus),
    294, 330
Pliny the younger (C. Plinius Caecilius
    Secundus), 276, 293, 330, 396, 401
Plotius, 320
Plutarch (L. Mestrius Plutarchus)
    XIV, 59 f., 170, 175, 309–28, 330 f.,
    333, 343, 388, 392, 397, 404–7
Poggio Bracciolini, 391, 409
Polemo, Antonius, 322, 334
Pollio, C. Asinius, 186, 224, 233, 339,
    396

Polybius, XIII, 138 ff., 142–64, 169 f., 173, 184, 222, 225, 227, 233, 237, 240, 255, 259, 370, 390, 392 ff., 403
Polycarp, St, 346, 351
Polycrates, 24, 48
Pompeius, Cn. jun., 199
Pompey (Cn. Pompeius, Magnus), 177 f., 181, 190 ff., 198, 201 f., 221, 230, 244, 255, 261
Pompilius, Numa, *see* Numa
Pomponius Atticus, T., *see* Atticus
Pontifical Chronicles, *see* Priests' Chronicles
Pontius Pilatus, *see* Pilatus
Pontus, 174, 181, 198, 220
Pope, Alexander, 406
Poppaea, 246, 275, 289 f.
Porcius, Cato M., *see* Cato
Porphyry, 400
Porsen(n)a, Lars, 398
Portugal, 147
Posidonius, 154, 178, 241
Potidaea, 69, 80
Priests' Chronicles, 167 f.
Primus, 273, 291
Priscian, 409
Priscus, C. Helvidius, 296, 298
Probus, Sex. Petronius, 367, 374 f.
Procopius (historian), XIV, 390
Procopius (usurper), 360
Prodicus, 91
Propertius, 218
Protagoras, 34, 39, 91 ff., 95, 104, 110
Proust, Marcel, 115
Ptolemy I, Ptolemies, 136, 243
Ptolemy XIII, 191
Punic Wars, *see* Carthage
Pydna, 145, 220
Pylos, 71, 96, 98, 103, 106, 118
Pyrrhus, 137, 168 f., 220, 374
Pytheas, 161

Quadi, *see* Germans
Quinctius, *see* Cincinnatus, Flamininus
Quintilian, 213, 237, 293, 338

Racine, Jean, 403
Ranke, L. von, XVI, 390
Ras Shamra, *see* Ugarit
Reate (Rieti), 207; *see also* Jaconello
Regulus, P. Memmius, 296

Rhadamistus, 403
Rhamnus, 89
Rhine, R., 182, 187, 273, 276
Rhodes, 136, 154
Rhône, R., 223, 225
Richard III, 402
Rimini, 402
Robert of Fulda, 401
Robespierre, Maximilien, 403
Roland, Madame, Manon, 403, 406
Romulus, 230, 239, 309, 326
Rousseau, Jean Jacques, 397, 403, 406
Rubicon, R., 191, 335 f.
Rudiae, 168
Rufinus, 408
Rufus, Q. Curtius, 278, 294
Rufus, M. Mettius, 334
Rufus, M. Minucius, 229
Rufus, M. Rutilius, 174
Rufus, L. Verginius, 296

Sabina, 330
Sabines, 171, 198
Sabinus, Angelus, 409
Sabinus, C. Nymphidius, 275
Sadducees, 246 f.
Saguntum, 228 f.
Sahara, 62
S. Just, Antoine, 406
Salamis, 23, 25, 33, 43, 47, 50, 52, 54
Salisbury, John of, *see* John
Sallust (C. Sallustius Crispus), XV, 176, 195–213, 223 f., 226, 228, 230, 233, 235, 248, 254, 279, 282, 285, 293, 295, 339, 394 ff., 407, 409
Salmasius, *see* Saumaise
Salome, 401
Samaria, 263
Samnites, 218, 220
Samos, 24, 33, 38, 48, 53, 71 f., 100, 118, 142
Samosata, 344
Samothrace, 54, 387
Samuel, 11
Sanchuniathon, 10
Sapor II, 359, 379
Saracens, 372
Sardinia, 198
Sardis, 17, 24, 51, 125, 147, 310
Sargon, 5, 7
Sarmati, 359

Satricum (Conca), 241
Saturninus, L. Appuleius, 174
Saul, 11
Saumaise (Salmasins), Claude, 403
Savile, Sir Henry, 402
Saxe, Marshal Maurice de, 394
Saxons, *see* Germans
Scaevola, P. Mucius, 167, 172
Scaliger, J. J., 401
Scapte Hyle, 74
Scaurus, M. Aemilius, 174, 197, 204
Schelling, Friedrich von, 393
Schiller, Johann von, 401
Scillus, 130
Scipio, P. Cornelius, 160, 242
Scipio, P. Cornelius Africanus the elder (Scipio), 145, 220, 227, 230, 237, 242, 310, 391, 397
Scipio, P. Cornelius Africanus the younger (Aemilianus), 145 ff., 150, 154, 170, 309
Scotland, *see* Caledonia
Scott, Sir Walter, 238
Scribonius, *see* Curio
Scythia, 24 f., 27, 38, 51, 61 f., 377
Sebennytus, 387
Secundus, *see* Pliny
Seeley, John, 113
Segestani, 381
Sejanus, L. Aelius, 274, 285 f., 291, 403
Seleucus, I, Seleucids, 136, 243
Semiramis, 375
Sempronia, 196, 208 f.
Sempronius, *see* Gracchus
Seneca, L. Annaeus the elder, 396
Seneca, L. Annaeus the younger, 285, 293, 296, 338, 395, 404
Senecio, Q. Sosius, 310
Senusert, I, 4
Septicius, *see* Clarus
Septimius, *see* Severus
Sequani, 182
Seres, 377 f.
Sergius, Catilina, L., *see* Catilina
Sertorius, Q., 198
Seuthes, 126
Severus, Septimius, 343, 346
Sextus Tarquinius, *see* Tarquinius
Seyssel, C. de, 390, 392, 400
Shakespeare, William, 405

Sicily, 43, 72, 83 f., 92, 99, 101 f., 108, 120, 133, 137, 140, 407
Sicyon, 59, 143
Sidon, 9
Sigismondo Malatesta, *see* Malatesta
Silius, C., 289
Silvanus, 359, 363, 382
Simon bar Gioura, 251 f.
Sinute, 4
Sisenna, L. Cornelius, 176, 179
Slavonic, 400
Smyrna, 351,
Socrates, 83, 96, 107, 134, 391 f.
Soli, 232, 364
Solomon, 11 f.
Solon, 43, 49, 326, 406
Sophaenetus, 127
Sophocles, 20, 45, 50 f., 55, 90, 105, 109, 118, 254
Sophonisba, 397
Soranus, Barea, *see* Barea
Sosius, Senecio Q., *see* Senecio
Soter, 352; *see also* Demetrius
Spain, 147, 161, 191, 198, 280, 360
Sparta, 19, 24 f., 27 f., 34 f., 46 f., 52 f., 69, 71 f., 74, 80–3, 91, 96 f., 102, 106–9, 111, 114, 117 f., 125 f., 129 f., 132 ff., 139, 146, 151, 158, 309, 390 f., 405
Spartacus, 198
Spengler, O. 107, 370, 393
Speyer, John of, *see* John
Sphacteria, 98
Spiculus, 337
Sporus, 337
Stagirus, 141
Stephanus, *see* Estienne
Stesichorus, 16
Stesimbrotus, 325
Stuarts, 403
Stymphalus, 127
Suebi, *see* Germans
Suetonius (C. Suetonius Tranquillus), XIV, 379–40, 343, 357, 403, 407 f.
Suidas, 31
Sulla, L. Cornelius, 174 ff., 184, 189, 193, 197 f., 200, 208, 220, 230, 318, 322, 324
Sumerians, 4 f.
Surus, 172
Sybaris, 33
Symmachus, Q. Aurelius, 374

Syphax, 397

Syracuse, 72, 92, 94, 99, 101, 108, 120, 133, 140, 225, 309, 356,

Syria, 9, 136, 156, 178, 243 f., 247 f., 265, 344, 346, 363, 400, 408; *see also* Phoenicia

Syria Palaestina, *see* Jews

Tabor M. 258

tabulae partificum, *see* Priests' Chronicles

Tacitus, M. Claudius (emperor), 401

Tacitus, Cornelius (historian), XIII ff., 263 f., 271–305, 309, 318, 331, 333, 335, 338, 340, 363, 368 f., 373, 377, 379, 383 f., 394–7, 401–4

Tanaquil, 240

Taras (Tarentum), 33, 35

Tarquinius II Superbus, 397

Tarquinius, Sextus, 397 f.

Tarquins, 240

Tarracina, 241, 322

Tauromenium, 140

Taurus, Mts., 382

Telepinus, 7

Tencteri, 182

Terence, 329, 395

Terentius Varro, *see* Varro

Tertullian, 349

Teutones, *see* Germans

Thasos, 62, 74, 325

Thebes (Egypt), 19

Thebes (Greece), 71, 130 ff., 146, 309, 321, 331

Themistocles, 44, 49, 57, 95, 100, 319

Theodorus, 360

Theodosius I the Great, 360 f., 366 f.

Theodosius the elder, 360, 366 f.

Theogony, see Hesiod

Theophrastus, 317

Theopompus, 138, 141 f.

Theramenes, 72, 112, 132

Thermopylae, 25, 41

Thessaly, 53, 130, 191

Thibron, 126

Thothmes III, 4

Thrace 24, 27, 60, 71, 74, 92 f., 104 f., 115, 119, 121, 126, 130, 360,

Thrasea Paetus, P. Clodius, 275, 296

Thrasylius, 304

Thrasymachus, 91

Thucydides (son of Melesias, politician), 34, 74

Thucydides (son of Olorus, historian), XIII, XV, 69, 71–121, 137, 139, 154, 156–61, 163 f., 184, 186, 212 f., 222, 225 f., 228, 254, 259, 301, 316, 344 f., 388–91, 393

Thurii (Thuria), 33, 35, 38 f., 50

Tiber, R., 239 f. 337, 398

Tiberias, 255 f., 265

Tiberius, 221, 232, 244, 263, 274 f., 281–8, 291 f., 296, 298, 304 f., 318, 334, 349, 403

Tibet, 62

Tibullus, Albius, 329

Ticinus, R., 145, 242

Tigris, R., 5, 359

Tillius, Cimber L., *see* Cimber

Timaeus, 140 f., 145, 154, 163 f.

Tisander, 60

Tissaphernes, 125 f.

Titus, 245 f., 251, 255 ff., 259, 264, 266, 271, 273, 298, 330

Tolstoy, Count Leo, 64, 120

Toynbee, Arnold, 393

Trachis, 51

Trajan, 272, 274, 276, 278, 280, 286, 288, 297–300, 310, 312, 330, 404

Trajanus Decius, *see* Decius

Tranquillus, C. Suetonius, *see* Suetonius

Trapezus (Trabzen, Trebizand), 126

Trasimene, L., 145

Trebia, R., 145

Trevelyan, G. M., 399

Treveri, *see* Augusta, Treverorum

Trevet, Nicholas, 396

Trissino, Giangiorgio, 397

Trollope, Antony, 394

Troy, 16, 106

Tubero, Q. Aelius, 236

Tullius, Man., 178

Tullius, Cicero M., *see* Cicero

Turenne, Marshal Henri, 394

Turks, 388, 390

Tusculum, 172

Tyre, 9, 62, 355

Ugarit, 9 f.

Umna, 5

Ursicinus, 359, 362 f.

Ush, 5

Usher, James, 392
Usipetes, 182
Uxellodunum, 188

Valens (emperor), 358, 360, 366 ff., 375, 383
Valens, Fabius, 291
Valens, Vettius, 289
Valentinian I, 360, 365–8, 373, 381
Valerian, 346
Valerius, *see* Leo, Martialis
Valèry, Paul, 399
Valesius, *see* Valois
Valla, Lorenzo, 388, 390, 397
Valois, Henri de, 409
Varro, C. Terentius, 229
Varro, M. Terentius, 207, 311, 333
Vasio, 271
Vatican, 409
Veii, 218, 238
Velleius Paterculus, 212, 278, 294
Venetia, Venice, 223, 395, 397, 402
Veneti (Brittany), 182
Vercingetorix, 182
Verennianus, 380
Vergerio, Pietro Paolo, senior, 390, 404
Vergil, *see* Virgil
Verginia, 218, 396
Verginius, Rufus, L., *see* Rufus
Vespasian, 245, 248, 251, 253, 255 f., 259, 264, 266, 271, 273, 298 f.
Vesuvius, Mt., 396
Vettius, Valens, *see* Valens
Vico, Giambattista, 393
Vidal de Noya, Francisco, 395

Vindex, C. Julius, 275
Virgil, 58, 218, 227, 230 f., 239, 254, 293, 329, 395
Virginia, *see* Verginia
Vitellius, 255, 271, 273, 288, 301 ff., 309
Volcae, 223
Volsci, 218
Voltaire, François, 389, 403
Voss (Vossius), Gerhard, 393

Wen-Amon, 4
Whiston, William, 401
William II Rufus, 407
William of Malmesbury, 394, 407
Winckelmann, Johann, 392
Wolf, F. A., 401
Wordsworth, William, 407

Xenophanes, 18 f.
Xenophon (historian), XIII, 125–38, 141, 159, 163, 170, 174, 186, 222, 391 f.,
Xenophen, C. Stertinius (physician), 289
Xerxes I, 24 f., 46 f., 50, 52, 58, 60, 64, 151, 259, 331, 344

Yair, Eleazar ben, *see* Eleazar
Yoseph, *Yosippon*, *see* Josephus

Zakkai, Johanan ben, *see* Johanan
Zama, 145, 220
Zealots, 247, 255
Zeno, 154
Zenobia (wife of Rhadamistus), 403